LOOK AT THE RECORD

LOOK AT THE RECORD

An Album of Toronto's Lyric Theatres 1825-1984

Compiled and Annotated by
JOAN PARKHILL BAILLIE

With an Introduction by
WILLIAM KILBOURN

OAKVILLE NEW YORK LONDON

CANADIAN CATALOGUING IN
PUBLICATION DATA

Baillie, Joan Parkhill, 1923-
  Look at the Record
  Include index.
ISBN 0-88962-236-1

1. Musical revue, comedy, etc. – Ontario – Toronto. 2. Opera – Ontario – Toronto – History and criticism. 3. Operetta – Ontario – Toronto – History and criticism. 4. Toronto (Ont.) – Theatres – History. I. Title.

ML1713.8.T67B34 1985 782.81'09713'541
C85-098371-1

No part of this book may be reproduced or transmitted in any form, by any means, electronic or mechanical, including photocopying and recording, information storage and retrieval systems, without permission in writing from the publisher, except by a reviewer who may quote brief passages in a review.

Published by Mosaic press, P.O. Box 1032, Oakville, Ontario, L6J 5E9, Canada. Offices and warehouse at 1252 Speers Road, Unit 10, Oakville, Ontario, L6L 5N9, Canada.

Published with the assistance of the Canada Council and the Ontario Arts Council.

Copyright © Introduction: William Kilbourn 1985

Copyright © Joan Parkhill Baillie 1985
Design by Doug Frank.
Typeset by Labelle Typesetting & Graphics
Printed and bounded in Hong Kong

MOSAIC PRESS:

In the United States: Flatiron Book Distributors, 175 Fifth Avenue, Suite 814, New York, N.Y., 10010, USA.
In the U.K.: John Calder (Publishers) Ltd., 18 Brewer Street, London, W1R 4AS, England.
In New Zealand: Pilgrims South Press, P.O. Box 5101, Dunedin, New Zealand.
In Australia: Bookwise International, 1 Jeanes Street, Beverley, South Australia 5007, Australia.

First Annual Ball of the Grand Opera House Company – From a sketch by F. M. Bell-Smith
Canadian Illustrated News. Vol. II Feb. 27, 1875.

CONTENTS

Foreword /7
Introduction by William Kilbourn /9
Acknowledgements /10
Setting the Scene /11
Epilogue
Charts

LYRIC THEATRES

1)	1825	Franks' Hotel/15		26)	1889	Academy of Music/129
2)	1839	Theatre Royal/19		27)	1894	Massey Hall/133
3)	1842	Old City Hall/23		28)	1896	Princess Theatre/151
4)	1842	Deering's Theatre/25		29)	1903	Shea's Theatre/159
5)	c.1845	Open Air/29		30)	1910	Royal Alexandra/163
6)	1846	New City Hall/33		31)	1912	Mutual Street Arena/173
7)	1848	Temperance Hall/35		32)	1922	Coliseum, CNE/179
8)	1848	Royal Lyceum/39		33)	1923	Hart House Theatre/183
9)	1849	Masonic Hall/45		34)	1928	Regent Theatre/191
10)	1851	St. Lawrence Hall/49		35)	1929	Royal York Hotel/197
11)	1860	Crystal Palace/55		36)	1931	Eaton Auditorium/201
12)	1861	Horticultural Gardens/59		37)	1936	Varsity Arena/213
13)	1861	Yorkville Town Hall/63		38)	1936	Maple Leaf Gardens/219
14)	1861	Music Hall (Mechanics' Institute)/67		39)	1938	Victoria Theatre/223
15)	1874	Grand Opera House/71		40)	1948	Art Gallery of Ontario/229
16)	1875	Royal Opera House/85		41)	1958	Heintzman Street Hall/233
17)	1875	Albert Hall/91		42)	1961	O'Keefe Centre/237
18)	1877	Shaftesbury Hall/93		43)	1964	St. Anne's Church/249
19)	1880	St. Andrew's Hall/97		44)	1964	MacMillan Theatre/251
20)	1883	Zoological Gardens/99		45)	1967	Central Technical School/259
21)	1883	Holman Opera House/103		46)	1970	Vaughan Road Collegiate Institute and Others/263
	1884	Semi-Centennial/107		47)	1973	St. Lawrence Centre/267
22)	1884	Theatre Royal/113		48)	1979	Ryerson Polytechnical Institute Theatre/275
23)	1884	Summer Pavilion/115		49)	1980	Harbourfront/279
24)	1884	Hanlan's Point/119		50)	1982	Roy Thomson Hall/283
25)	1886	Toronto Opera House/123				

FOREWORD

The problems arising from the scarcity of books dealing specifically with Canadian music and musicians are compounded by the fact that the general histories of Canada devote little space to the arts and, in most of them, music is seldom given so much as a footnote.

The Report of the Commission on Canadian Studies 1975

The history of operatic performances, in such form as was practicable or available, in York/Toronto is very nearly as long as the town/city's social history, of which it is a significant component. This fact comes as a considerable surprise to many Torontonians, native-born or adoptive. Almost before the ink was dry on the Treaty of Versailles 1783 touring companies from south of the border created by the treaty were crossing it to visit the established populous centres of Halifax and Montreal. When the garrison town of York, easily accessible by water, acquired the status of capitol of the new province of Upper Canada it became part of the itinerary.

The intent of the following pages is to present, graphically rather than textually, a sampling of the operatic fare over the past 160 years in Toronto, together with some of the personalities who took part, and some of the signs of the times and the varied locations in which it was presented.

The possibilities for the production of opera, which has always been the most complex and the most expensive of the performing arts, are controlled by countless factors such as the size of population, the state of the economy, the mores of the period, the availability, fame and cost of singers, and, above all, the locations in which it is possible to produce this 'exotic and irrational entertainment' in a manner that will appeal to a widely varied audience. From the very early days, while local and touring companies performed now-forgotten works in places such as the Assembly Rooms of Mr. Franks' Hotel, eminent operatic singers gave concerts in what passed for theatres, and even band concerts included familiar selections from the great contemporary operas. Before the days of the railroad 'Operatic Soirees' and 'Grand Concerts of Opera in Costume' were a standard form of theatrical entertainment and these evolved into performances of one fully-staged act of an opera. By the early 1850's full operas were being given by touring companies and in 1859 at least 37 complete operas were performed in Toronto. The evidence, unearthed by researchers in the field, of the remarkable number of performances which included opera in one form or another, frequently under extremely unlikely conditions, seems to indicate that Torontonians have always had a taste for this particular art form, wherever it was available.

ACKNOWLEDGEMENTS

In reviewing my indebtedness for assistance and support on this work, I begin to wonder if my efforts, gigantic as they seemed at times, had much to do with the completion of the project. I find it difficult to believe that anyone has ever received more enthusiastic support and encouragement in an undertaking. The first seeds were sown several years ago by two incidents: Bill Armstrong, designer for the Canadian Opera Company's Caravan Pavilion, requested a graphic historic display for the Pavilion; and Dorith Cooper came into the Canadian Opera Company Archives in search of information for her Ph.D. thesis.

The Ontario Arts Council has most generously provided the funds for the innumerable photographs and for the services of an outstanding Research Assistant – David Boyd-Thomas.

The most straightforward method of acknowledgement seems to be an expression of heartfelt thanks to the following:

RESOURCES

Archives of Ontario – Manuscript Division – William Cooper
                  Government Records Division – Richard Ramsay
Art Gallery of Ontario Archives – Margaret Machell
Arts and Letters Club Archives – Hunter Bishop
Canadian Children's Opera Chorus – Sue Bradshaw
Canadian National Exhibition Archives – Nancy Hurn
Canadian Opera Company Archives
City of Toronto Archives – Linda Price, Elizabeth Cuthbertson
City of Toronto – Department of Buildings and Inspections
Eaton's of Canada Limited Archives – Judith McErvel, Fay Wood
Metroplitan Toronto Library
    Baldwin Room (especially John Crosthwait and Alan Walker)
    Map Department
    Newspapers on Microfilm — (Norma Dainard)
    Picture Department (Patricia Rogal)
    Theatre Department (Heather McCallum)
    Photo Reproduction Department
National Library of Canada
    Music Division
    Newspaper Reference Division – Sandra Burrows
Opera Canada
Opera in Concert – Kathryn Brown
Public Archives of Canada – Photo Reproduction Department
Ryerson Polytechnical Institute Archives – Claude Doucet
St. Anne's Music and Drama Society – Diana Schatz
Toronto Opera Repertoire – Giuseppe Macina
Toronto Opera Society – Leo Evason
Toronto Symphony Archives – Richard Warren
University of Toronto Archives – Harold Averill
University of Toronto, Faculty of Music – Edith Binnie
University of Toronto Library and Thomas Fisher Rare Book Library
York Community Opera – Giuseppe Macina

TEXTS

Opera in Montreal and Toronto: A Study of Performance Traditions and Repertoire 1783-1980 – Dorith Cooper, Ph.D. thesis; University of Toronto 1984
Pre-Confederation Music Societies in Toronto – David John Sale, M.A. thesis University of Toronto 1968
Encyclopedia of Music in Canada – University of Toronto Press 1981
Dictionary of Canadian Biography – University of Toronto Press
Dictionary of Canadian Biography – University of Toronto Press
as well as any available histories of Toronto.

Individuals to whom I owe much are Carl Morey, Faculty of Music, University of Toronto; Harold Rosenthal, Editor of *Opera*; Pat Wardrop, National Library of Canada; Bill Cousintine, Winter Garden Theatre; John Lindsay, author of *Turn Out the Stars Before Leaving*; James B. McPherson of the Toronto Sun; Foster Hewitt; John Gibbon and Whitney Smith on the English Music Festivals; Keith MacMillan; Clarke Walker, formerly of Eaton Auditorium; the late Stan Obodiac of Maple Leaf Gardens; Wayne Gibson of The Terrace; David Argles of The Copy Shop; my son, Trevor Baillie, Statistician, and my husband Robert who aided, abetted and offered helpful criticism at every step; and Grace Brooks proof-reader beyond price.

About The Author

Joan Parkhill Baillie has been archivist of the Canadian Opera Company since 1974 and held a similar position with *Opera Canada* before that. After graduation from St. Clements School she spent nine years working in the Canadian Bank of Commerce Archives and Library prior to her marriage to Robert Baillie who besides sharing her commitment to opera is a past president of the C.O.C. The Baillies have three children and two grandchildren.

Mrs. Baillie's love of opera began with her attendance at the age of ten at a production of *La Traviata* by the San Carlo Company, and her enthusiasm and commitment have been maintained ever since.

She is a descendant of three United Empire Loyalist families and of Georgina Lodge-Wilcocks and Thomas Baines who moved about 1830 from Cobourg to Toronto, where descendants have lived ever since.

INTRODUCTION
William Kilbourn

Toronto is the home of a superb opera company, and the place where a number of the world's greatest singers have received their training: this much we more or less know. What we have forgotten is that lyric theatre has always been a central part of our culture, as Joan Baillie, archivist of the Canadian Opera Company, shows us in the hundreds of fascinating bits of evidence she has assembled in this album.

The tunes and lyrics of Verdi's *Il Trovatore* were popular in Toronto soon after the premiere of the opera in Rome. They were familiar enough that minstrel shows could parody them to the delight of their local audiences.

Our first resident opera company, named for its founder George Holman, goes back to the time of Confederation. So popular were Holman's comic operas that when their home, The Royal Lyceum, burnt down in 1873, construction on two new opera houses began immediately. The Royal Opera House was built on the Lyceum's King Street site between York and Bay where the Toronto Dominion Centre now stands. It opened in September of 1874. A week later the Grand Opera House began its first season – with a repertoire consisting of the works of Offenbach. Even if you do not stand on that site in downtown Toronto and try to conjure up the strains of, say, *La Belle Helene*, you may still walk a few paces west of Yonge Street along the south side of Adelaide and there observe a street sign: Grand Opera Lane. Think of Toronto's first *Carmen* being performed on that spot by the Grand Italian Opera Company of Max Strakosch, the impresario who had a love affair with the great diva, Adelina Patti.

Torontonians adored Patti too – from the time she sang in St. Lawrence Hall in 1853 at the delicate age of ten, to her farewell performance in Massey Hall fifty years later, at which with the aid of seats crammed on the stage and standing room only everywhere else, she sang for an ecstatic mob of 3000 people – far more than the fire marshals have ever let into the place since.

1879, the year in which Strakosch brought *Carmen* to Toronto, saw the first Gilbert and Sullivan production here. *Pinafore* and the rest outdid even the Offenbach operas, just as these in turn had surpassed Holman's performances of Rossini and Donizetti in popularity. Nor was Wagner neglected. The Toronto Opera House, converted from a roller skating rink in 1886, put on *The Flying Dutchman* in 1887. It was a substitute for *Lohengrin* (which was done the following year) because an indisposed tenor could not be replaced at the last moment.

A banner season in Toronto towards the end of the nineteenth century might see as many as one hundred different performances of at least two dozen different works, even though most of these were usually light opera.

The first visit of New York's young Metropolitan Opera Company took place in 1899 at the Grand. The soloists, chorus, ballet and orchestra of the Met presented *Faust*, *Carmen* and *The Barber of Seville*.

Toronto's most frequent visitor in the early twentieth century was the San Carlo Company run by the Italian-born New Yorker Fortune Gallo. He brought his troupe regularly to the Royal Alexandra and to Massey Hall from 1914 to the mid-1940s. Though its quality may have suffered because of Gallo's reliance solely on the box office to pay his way, he somehow managed to finance his tours until the San Carlo's last visit to Toronto, at the new Odeon Carlton Theatre, in 1950.

The Met took over as the great visiting attraction during the 1950s with its fullscale productions in Maple Leaf Gardens, though members of the company had appeared in a number of occasions before that. My own first experience of grand opera was in Massey Hall in 1944 and what seemed to me at seventeen the absolute magnificence of *Traviata* sung by Bidu Sayao and her colleagues.

Ernest MacMillan had opera productions at the Conservatory in the days before the Depression and the Second World War; but perhaps the most significant milestone for opera in Toronto was the Royal Conservatory Opera Company's season of Mozart, Verdi and Puccini at the Royal Alexandra in 1950. The annual productions which followed led directly to the emergence of the Canadian Opera Company in 1959. During the 1950s leadership in training and production was provided by Arnold Walter, Nicholas Goldschmidt, Boyd Neel, Herman Geiger-Torel, Ettore Mazzoleni and Ernesto Barbini. The great and varied achievements of Lotfi Mansouri and the Canadian Opera Company since 1976 have been built on solid foundations.

All in all the story of opera in Toronto is long, rich and diverse. This brief introduction must end, however, with what has been an all too familiar plea these past thirty years and more: When will we be experiencing opera, not in a building designed for something else, but in our own opera house?

William Kilbourn is a Toronto writer and history professor, past Chairman of the Toronto Arts Council and currently a member of the Canada Council.

SETTING THE SCENE

In order to create a suitable atmosphere, historically speaking, in which to approach the following record, let us imagine that my great-great-great-grandparents, John and Maria Lodge-Wilcocks, came from Cobourg to spend Christmas 1825 in Toronto. John, with his brothers Henry and William, had been a prisoner of war in France in 1795. Henry died while serving under Sir Arthur Wellesey in India and William and another brother Richard took part in the (by then) Duke of Wellington's Peninsular campaigns where William was killed. They may well have served under Generals Sir Peregrine Maitland (who caused a considerable stir in the social circles of England and Upper Canada when he married Lady Sarah Lennox, daughter of the Duke of Richmond) and Sir John Colborne, each of whom served as Lieutenant-Governor of Upper Canada. Among the festivities of the season were opera performances at Franks' Hotel. Perhaps Maria clipped some newspaper items which she pasted into a scrapbook, a practice which was continued by her descendants....

Sir Peregrine Maitland
Lieutenant Governor of Upper Canada – August 13, 1818 – August 23, 1828

MTLB JRR416

Sir John Colborne
Lieutenant Governor of Upper Canada – November 4, 1830 – November 1835. Founder of Upper Canada College

MTLB JRR417

To the memory
of
all those who contributed to the record of operatic performances in Toronto and, in particular, to three outstanding Canadians...

Photo: art associates ltd   UTFM

SIR ERNEST MacMILLAN

"... I should, however, very much like to see something permanent in the way of an operatic school established at the Conservatory with a thoroughly experienced director, and would therefore suggest that a subcommittee of the Conservatory Board discuss these matters with you and your associates with a view to future developments..."
Letter to Harrison Gilmour (Opera Guild of Toronto) October 31, 1938

DR. ETTORE MAZZOLENI

Principal, Toronto Conservatory of Music	1926-42
Dean, Faculty of Music, University of Toronto	1927-52
Musical Director, Conservatory Opera Company	1928-30

Principal, Royal Conservatory of Music	1945-68
Director, Royal Conservatory Opera School	1952-66
Artistic Director, Opera Festival Association of Toronto	1953-54
Managing Director, Opera Festival Association of Toronto	1954-56
General Director, Opera Festival Association of Toronto	1956-59

Photo: Robert C. Ragsdale   COCA

HERMAN GEIGER-TOREL, O.C., L.L.D.

Stage Director, Royal Conservatory Opera School	1948-76
Stage Director, Opera Festival Association of Toronto	1950-56
Artistic Director, Opera Festival Association of Toronto	1956-59
General Director, Canadian Opera Association	1959-76

... whose efforts proved beyond all possible doubt that, despite an overwhelming neighbour and a small population, indigenous opera was not only desirable but possible in Canada.

and to their living successors,
  Lotfi Mansouri
  Stuart Hamilton
  Giuseppe Macina
  Opera Division, Faculty
  of Music, U. of T.

LYRIC THEATRES

1825
FRANKS' HOTEL

Concert halls were non-existent during York's early days despite the fact that it was a garrison town and the British army was accustomed to civilized living. Lovers of music and theatre, however, united one way or another and the first operas were given in the Assembly Rooms of Mr. Franks' Hotel.

Water colour: Frederic V. Poole   MTLB JRR 849

FRANKS' HOTEL

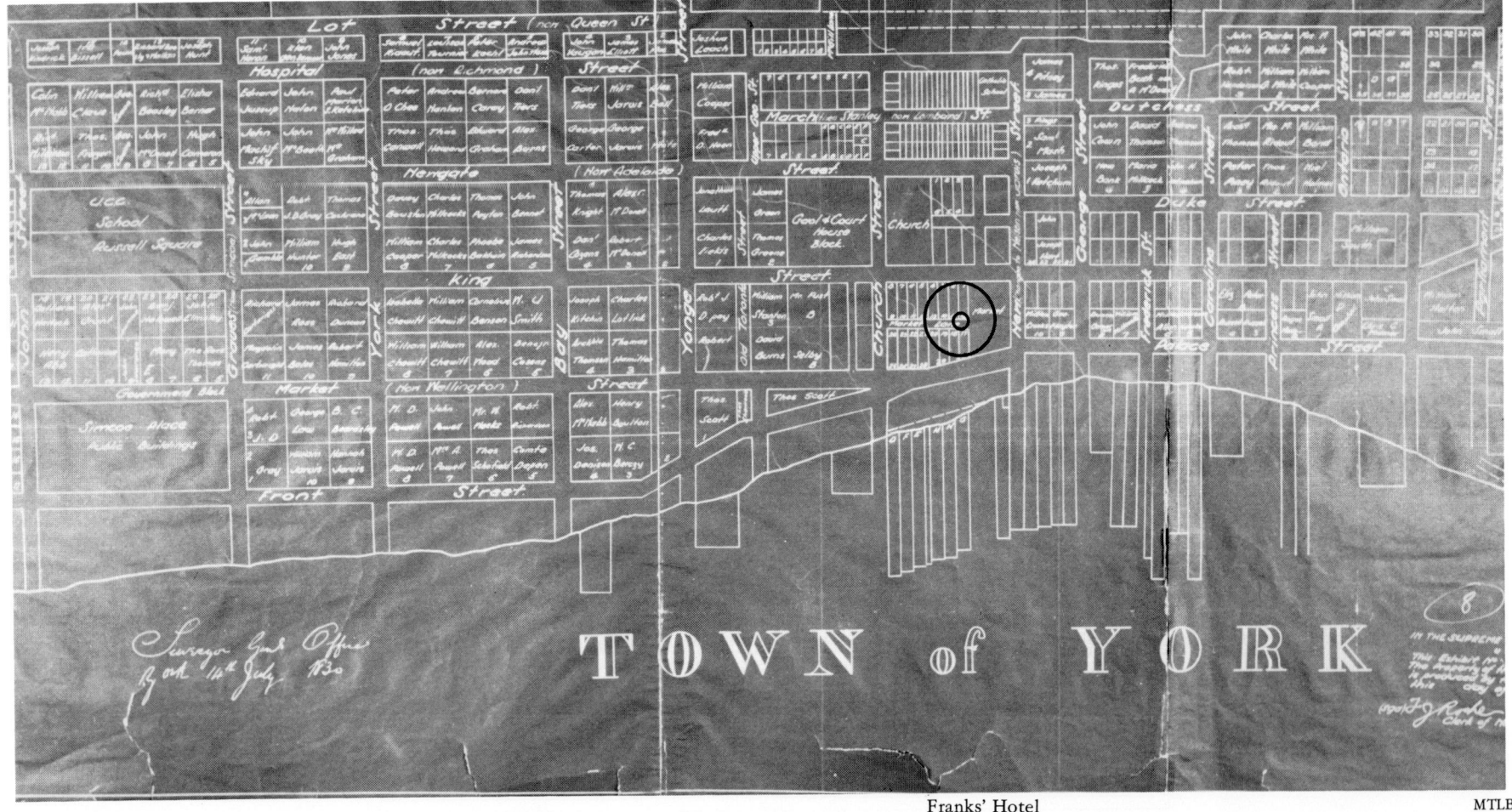

Franks' Hotel MTLB

FRANKS' HOTEL

In the 1820's and 30's Franks' Hotel, a two-storey white frame building, stood on the north side of the street at the eastern end of Market Lane (later Colborne Street) where it abutted the market square. The hotel, in an extremely convenient location, catered to the gentry. The town of York's earliest theatrical performances were given in the Assembly Rooms which were on the second floor in an extension at the back and to which access was gained, by audience and performers, via an outside staircase. In his *Toronto of Old* (1873) Henry Scadding, who was born in 1813, recalled with tolerant affection, performances which "to unsophisticated yet active imaginations, seemed charming". As a general rule, music was provided by Mr. Maxwell, the violinist, who wore a patch over one eye, and the supernumeraries were frequently soldiers from the garrison.

THEATRE.

YORK.

At Mr. Franks' Assembly Room, On Thursday Evening, Dec. 22, 1825, Will be presented,

Colman's Justly Admired Opera of the

MOUNTAINEERS,

Or, LOVE AND MADNESS.

Octavian,	Mr. DAVIS,
Bulcazin Muley,	" TROWBRIDGE,
Sadi,	" SMITH,
Lepe Tocho,	" GILBERT,
Kilmallock,	" ASHLEY,
Florentine,	Mrs. GILBERT,
Agnes,	" THOMPSON.

During the Opera, a number of Songs, Duetts, and Choruses.

(For particulars see Bills.)

After the Oopera, the following Songs, Comic Song, "The Yorkshireman's Visit, to London," Mr. GILBERT. Song, "The Carrier Pigeon," Mrs. THOMPSON,

The Evenings Entertainment to conclude with the laughable farce of

THE RENDEZVOUS,

Or, WE ARE ALL MET.

☞ For Characters see Bills.

Doors open at Six, and Performance to commence at Seven o'Clock precisely.— Box Tickets, 3s.9d. Pit, 2s.6d. Children, half price.—Two Tickets will admit two Ladies and one Gentleman.

Entrance to the Theatre from Market Lane, on the south side of the Ball-Room.

Colonial Advocate, Dec. 22, 1825   AO

THEATRE.

YORK.

On Friday Night, Dec. 30, 1825. Will be presented Cherry's fashionable, and admired Comedy in 5 Acts, of the

Soldiers' Daughter.

Governor Heartall,	Mr. Gilbert,
Frank Heartall,	" Davis,
Timothy Quaint,	" Smith.
Widow Cheerly,	Mrs. Gilbert.

After the Comedy, the following Songs, Duett, "Tho' you leave me now in sorrow," (from the celebrated Drama of Rob Roy,) Mr. & Mrs. Smith, Comic Song, "Hard times, or The year 1672," Mr. Gilbert,

The evening's entertainment to conclude with (for the first time in this place,) the Musical Opera of

NO SONG, NO SUPPER,

OR THE

LAWYER IN THE SACK.

(For particulars see Bills.)

Doors open at Six, and Performance to commence at Seven o'Clock precisely.— Box Tickets, 3s.9d. Pit, 2s.6d. Children, half price.—Two Tickets will admit two Ladies and one Gentleman.

Entrance to the Theatre from Market Lane, on the south side of the Ball-Room.

Colonial Advocate, Dec. 29, 1825   AO

SIR HENRY ROWLEY BISHOP.
1786 — 1855.
The Musical Composer.
Presented, February 1869, by Mrs C.H. SMITH.

NPGL

Best known today for "Home Sweet Home" and "Lo, hear the gentle lark"

THE THEATRE.

[This article only appeared in the second edition of last week's paper.]

Last Friday evening, we freed ourself from the toils and vexations of a provincial newspaper, and, for the first time in America, essayed to drive dull care away in a Theatre, this too in despite of the praiseworthy writings of our respected brother journalist, Mr. Andrew Heron against the Drama, in despite of Dr. Wotherspoon—nay—(worse and worse;) contrary even to our own consistent declaration against players in general as expressed in last year's Advocate.

We think we hear our friend Mr. Andrew, in his satirical dry way, exclaim—"Consistency and the Colonial Advocate have no great affinity," which is a postulate that we would willingly contend against if we had room or time.

To the play-house we went, and, as in the elegant theatre in the gude town where we were born, "VELUTI IN SPECULUM," in fair letters, painted over the vaulted dome, served to remind us that there our follies would be reflected as thro' a mirror, so here the mottoless device above the green curtain, and the confined space in which the votaries of Thespis, the son of Erechtheus were likely to be compelled to occupy, convinced us that the follies of the town" creep slowly among us, for, as we have no stage in this country, they cannot, as in Hardcastle's neighbourhood, approach us "in the basket."

The house was truly a thin one, consisting of a few barristers' clerks, attorneys' apprentices, shopkeepers, with an editor or two; even the pit (which answers to the one shilling gallery, occupied by the gods, in Old Drury,) was well nigh desolate. Mr. Heron would have given a silver dollar to have seen the triumph obtained by puritanism over "jollity, mirth and frivolity," in the pious town of York.

On monday night we found the scene had changed in more respects than one, the house was literally crammed: Gentlemen and Ladies of rank and fashion, peers, parliament men, placemen, cabinet ministers, *and other ministers*: all had agreed to save the reputation of the capital from the stigma, of s ding a meritorious company of comedians " empty away."

Among the gentlemen present we observed the Hon. Mr. Allan, the Hon. Mr. Macaulay, Colonels Adamson and Ingersol, Major Heward, Messrs. Matthews, Hamilton, Clark, Fothergill, Lefferty, Gordon, Morris, D. Jones and Wilkinson, M. P.'s—also Messrs. Campbell, Richardson, Washburn, Boulton, G. Monro, Gamble and Rogers.

We had written from our notes a critical dissertation on the merits and demerits of the respective actors, but our foreman tells us (11 P. M. Wednesday) that it is too late for this week.

Yesternight they had a full house to see the Miller and his Men; and, as His Excellency's eldest son was there, we think they ought to assume the title "Theatre Royal." Messrs. C. Jones, Proudfoot, Lee, J. Jones, Lyons, and others of our fashionable people this night honoured the play with their presence.

We have often seen Kean in his favorite character of Richard,—and, if it is considered that Drury Lane affords to a player many peculiar advantages; that the reverberation of its lofty arched roof marvellously aids the actor's voice; that its internal splendour and magnificence, added to the power given the player of choosing his distance, heightens the effect produced on the spectators by his acting, we would say that Davis was at home in the humpbacked Gloster. At times, 'tis true, his voice was *loud* where Kean's is deep, and any approaches to rant in playing such a character should be carefully guarded against; but Davis's person and voice had a resemblance to Kean's, the height of the two is about the same—and in the scene where the usurper tells Lady Anne how cordially he hates her, his acting was really beyond our praise. Upon the whole, we were highly gratified with the performance.

Mr. Gilbert's person, his voice, and his lofty bearing, well fits him for the part of a noble, generous character, and Mr. Smith is quite at home in the droll parts of low comedy. The comic powers of this latter actor would command approbation even in a more fastidious audience; and whether as the Lord Mayor, Sancho, or Sharp, his performing was honoured by the boxes and pit with loud and continued peals of laughter.

As to the ladies, we must postpone our criticism, but cannot help remarking, that if the manager would choose his loving maidens from among the smokes beyond eight years of age, and give Mrs. Gilbert the hint to bestow on her pretty face certain appropriate streaks, and on her hair a little hair-powder, when she condescends to appear as the representative of wintry three-score, it would, we think, be well enough. The chief beauty of an opera is its close resemblance to scenes in real life; and the strength of a company is shewn to great disadvantage when young women wont grow old, and babies play the parts usually allotted to their mothers.

Colonial Advocate, Jan. 5, 1826   AO

York 19th December 1827

My Dear Sir,

.....I was very apprehensive some few weeks ago, that there would be a breach between the two
(Willis)
Titled Ladies - Lady Mary imagined that it was
(Maitland)
the place of Lady Sarah to call first upon her - which it seems the other never dreamt of doing - The consequence was, - the two ladies remained in York for some time utter strangers, frequently passing each other in the Street without recognition - However after some negotiation in which Colonel Givens acted a conspicuous part and what had always been the Established Etiquette in the Colony fully explained, Lady Mary call'd upon Lady Sarah, and has since been frequently invited to dinner and evening parties - Judging by Lady Marys Manner at these parties, I doubt whether there exists that degree of Cordiality, which could be desired - I should not be surprised, if the feeling was revived when the Willis' take possession of the House they have engaged - (they are still living at Franks) - Her Ladyship may perhaps return Lady Sarah's civility by inviting her to Dinner - If the invitation is accepted, it will be productive of other embarrassment - If she refuses, it is not impossible
    Lady Mary
for she seems to inherit all the pride of her family - she may chuse to drop the acquaintance. Should the in vitation be accepted, I fear His Honor the Chief Justice
(William Campbell)
would feel his highland blood rise - and Mrs. C. will of course have her back up, - for I hear she already claims the rank of Lady Mary as being the Wife of the Chief Justice - Thus you see the old Feudal feeling of rank, for which York has been celebrated I believe from the earliest periods of her history is again about to be revived - ...

The Hon'ble W.D. Powell   S.P. Jarvis

Manuscript Collection L16 vol. B82   MTLB

"There (Franks') was given the famous masked ball of Byron's friend, Mr. Galt and the too-sprightly Lady Mary Willis, whose misadventures during her residence in Toronto gave rise to the *cause celebre* of Willis v. Bernard."

C.P. Mulvany – *Toronto Past and Present until 1882*

APPEARANCES		
1825	*The Mountaineers*	
	Soldier's Daughter	
	No Song, No Supper	Colman
1826	*The Miller and His Men*	Bishop
	The Devil's Bridge	Bishop
	No Song, No Supper	

1839
THEATRE ROYAL

*The second location in which opera
(Sir Henry Bishop's* Maid of Cashmere
in 1839) had at least the characteristics of a theatre.

Water colour: Frederic V. Poole MTLB JRR 853

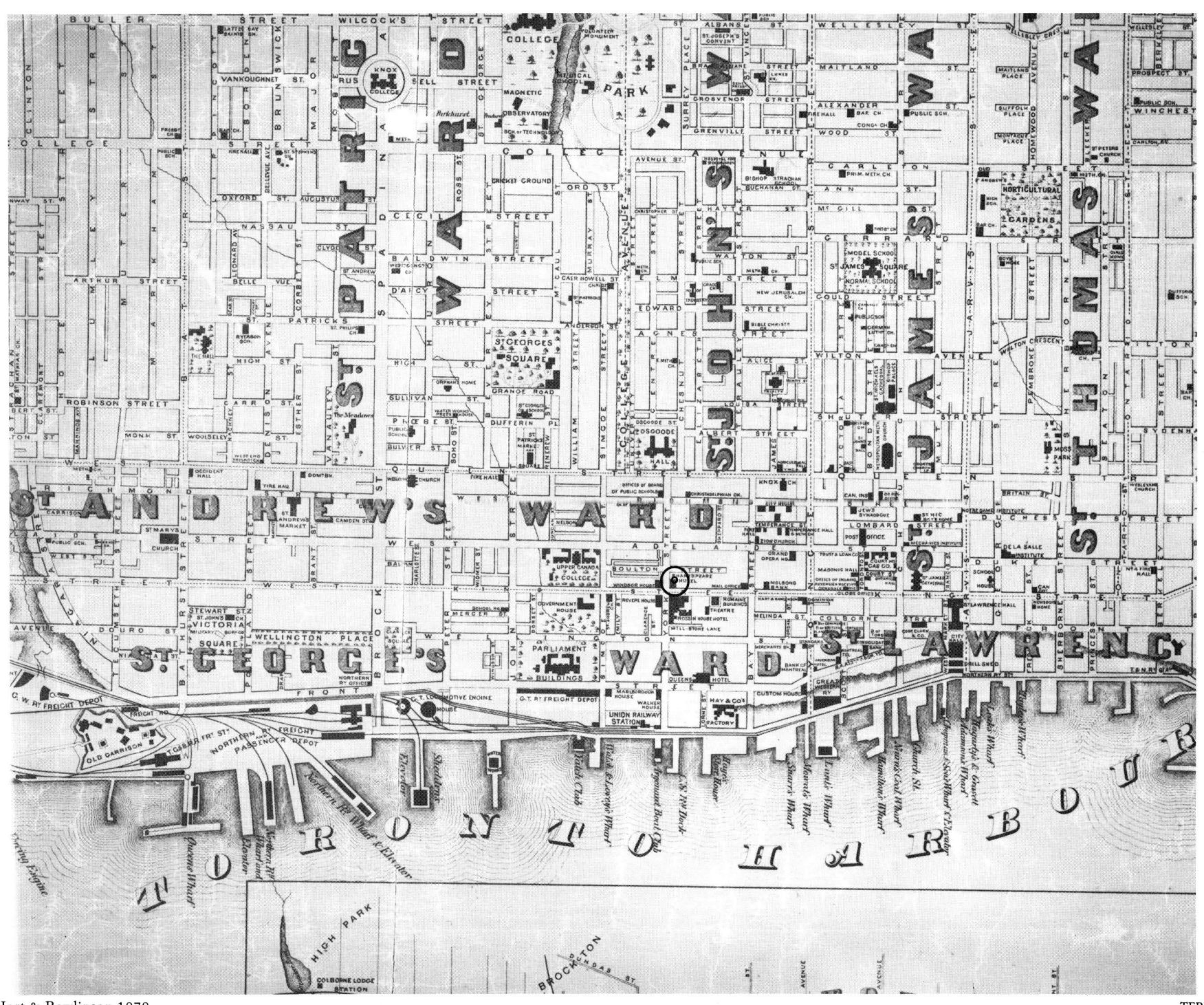

Hart & Rawlinson 1878

THEATRE ROYAL

The Theatre Royal had been converted from an old carpentry shop. It was set back from the street on the north side of King and was reached by an alley between the Shakespeare (on the northeast corner of York) and Merfield Hotels. A stage door opened onto Boulton (now Pearl) Street which ran eastwards as far as the racquet court. The building had 30 feet of frontage and 60 feet in depth and boasted tiered seating, a considerable improvement over previous theatres. Within a few years this theatre was destroyed by fire.

Water colour: Frederic V. Poole   MTLB JRR 524

SHAKESPEARE HOTEL

NPGL

Near to the corner of York Street and King Street, in this city, there stands a small tenement, which has been dignified by the name of the "*Theatre Royal*," and, in confirmation of this title, the place has been recently taken possession of by a party of strolling players from *Yankee land*. Any of our readers who are curious to see the place, or if they choose the play, can be at no difficulty to find it out, as every evening the name is displayed in large letters over the door, through the transparency of a huge lantern,—"THEATRE ROYAL."

It so happened, that on Saturday evening last, when passing along with a friend, we were induced to enter,—the evening's entertainment, being, as we were informed, for the benefit of Miss E. Ince. A benefit night at a Theatre, is generally expected to produce something more than common, both in the shape of entertainment by the performers, and larger receipts of dollars and cents from the public who honor them with their company. If any extra effort were made to please, on this occasion, the ordinary performance of these strollers, must be very ordinary indeed; —and, for the taste of Toronto, we trust, that a somewhat more than ordinary attendance took place on Saturday,—as pit, boxes, and gallery, seemed to be well filled.

The performance commenced with what was styled on the bills, "*The much-admired farce* of Nature and Philosophy, or the Youth who never saw a woman." This farce may be admired across the lines,—but neither in the sentiment, nor in the manner in which it was acted, was there any thing to excite admiration here, -both the farce and the actors of it are altogether too contemptible for criticism.

An attempt was made by one of the company to sing a Scotch song. It was noticed in the bills of the evening, "*Scotch Song by Mrs. Lennox*,"—and we would beg as a favor, of this songstress, that she may never attempt the like again in this place. Never before had it been our lot to listen to the beautiful song by the Ettrick Shepherd,—" *Cam ye by Athol*,"—so brutally murdered. This was followed by an attempt to act the opera of the "*Maid of Cashmere*," and it was but an attempt. Miss Ince danced tolerably well—and that is all that can be said in favour of the performance. By this time our patience was quite exhausted, we left, and immediately set to write this notice, lest by delay, we might so far forget what we had witnessed, as to do injustice afterwards to any of the company, by detracting from their just merits as players.

We will not take upon us to say, whether Toronto is capable of supporting for a season, an establishment that may be frequented by such of the respectable part of the community as relish these amusements; but whether or not, there is no reason why such a miserable catchpenny as that at present in operation should be tolerated. The municipal authorities should interfere and abate the nuisance.

British Colonist, Sept. 4, 1839   AO

PERFORMANCES

1839 *The Maid of Cashmere* Bishop

OLD CITY HALL

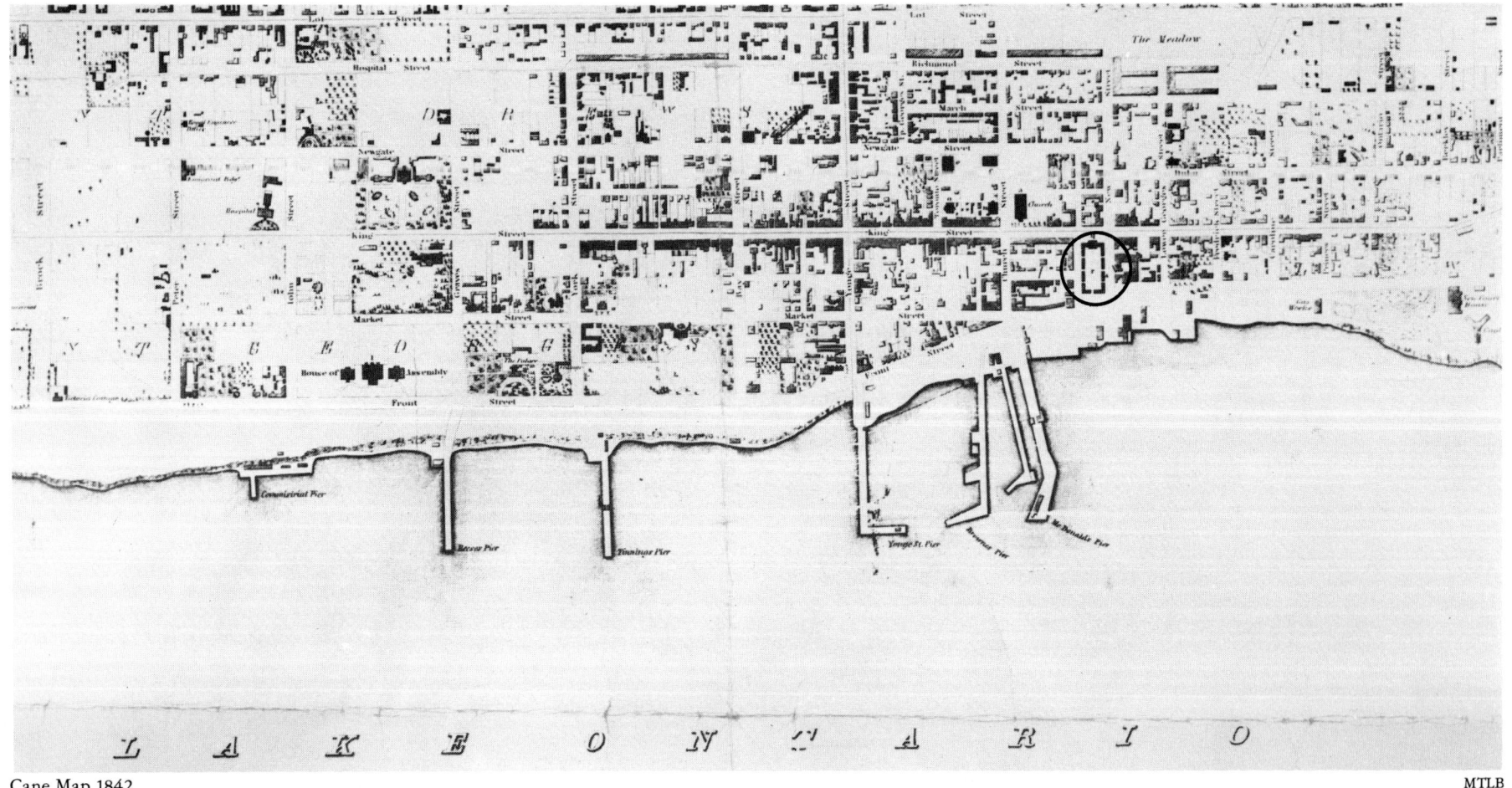

Cane Map 1842

MTLB

1842
OLD CITY HALL

Any place in which a fairly large number of people could be accommodated served the purpose for those with determination.

Toronto's 100 Years – Middleton   CTA

The first City Council of the newly incorporated City of Toronto met in 1834 on the second floor of the new market which had been built in 1831. The police station was beneath it. In the Council Chambers the popular operatic artists of the day, such as Anna Bishop and John Braham, performed. Following the destruction of the northern end of the quadrangle in the great fire of April 7, 1849, the entire building was demolished and the St. Lawrence Hall and Market built.

Mr. BRAHAM
has the honor to announce that he will give a
CONCERT,
AT THE CITY HALL,
(By permission of his Honor the Mayor,)
On Friday, Sept. 23rd,
ASSISTED BY HIS SON AND PUPIL,
Mr. Charles Braham.

MR. BRAHAM will sing "*The last words of Marmion;*" "*William Tell;*"— "*Woman;*" "*Scots wha hae;*" "*Blue Bonnets over the Border;*" "*The Miniature;*" "*Lover's Vow;*" Irish Love-song, "*Molly Bawn;*" and with Mr. C. BRAHAM, the Duet of "*All's Well;*" "*Gallop on gaily,*" and "*God save the Queen.*"

Mr. C. BRAHAM will sing '*My Sister dear,*' from *Masaniello;* "*My Boyhood's Home;*" "*There's a charm in Spring,*" by Boz; "*The Lads of the Village,*" by Dibden.

TICKETS, $1; Children half price.
Concert to commence at Eight o'clock.
Toronto, Sept. 23, 1842.   77

Mr. Braham.

This unrivalled Vocalist, still the acknowledged sovereign of English song on a throne of half a century's duration, is, we are happy to learn, again a visitor to Toronto.

His son, Mr. C. BRAHAM, of whose vocal powers we have heard such highly flattering accounts, is also with his father, and both will gratify our citizens at the CITY HALL this Evening.

A glance at the advertisement will convince our readers of the rich treat they may safely anticipate. Many of the songs of this prince of Vocalists were born with and will surely die with him.

Doctor Rolph.

We are happy to see our valued friend Dr. ROLPH once more back in our city.— He has but just arrived from England and will return in a few weeks. The arrival of between Forty and Fifty Thousand British Settlers in Canada this season at-

Toronto Patriot, Sept. 23, 1842   AO

Anna Bishop, 19th century English soprano, wife of Sir Henry Bishop, was a popular international artist and visited Toronto on several occasions.

John Braham, 18th-19th century tenor. Weber composed the role of Sir Huon in *Oberon* for him after hearing his portrayal of Max in *Der Freischutz*.

By Permission of the Presiding Aldermen.

SECOND AND LAST GRAND INSTRUMENTAL AND VOCAL
CONCERT

At the particular request of some of the Ladies and Gentlemen who were present at the former Concert—
SIGNORA DE GONI,
The Celebrated Guitar Player,
AND
MR. KNOOP,
The Unrivalled Violoncellist,

MOST respectfully inform the inhabitants of Toronto, that they will give a Second and Last
Grand Instrumental Concert,
On Friday Evening, September 30th, 1842,
AT THE CITY HALL.

☞Tickets—One Dollar each; to be had at MEAD's Music Store, and at the Door in the evening.

The Concert to commence at 8 o'clock precisely.
Sept. 28, 1842.   79

Toronto Patriot, Sept. 30, 1842   AO

MR. BRAHAM'S CONCERT.
ASSISTED BY HIS SON AND PUPIL
MR. CHARLES BRAHAM,
AT THE TOWN HALL,
On Wednesday Evening, Sept. 28

PART 1ST.
Song.—When I beheld the Anchor weighed. Balfe....................Mr. C. Braham.
Duet—The Minute Gun at Sea.............Mr Braham and Mr C. Braham
Song—Stand to your Guns........Mr Braham.
Hayn's Canzonet—My mother bids me bind my hair....................Mr Braham
Song—When the Trump of Fame.—Rossini. ....Mr C. Braham.
Song—Celebrated Ballad, Black Eyed Susan.— Poetry by Gay, Music by Levidge, the Bass Singer in the Reign of Queen Anne.......... ....Mr. Braham.
Duet—Rest Weary Traveller from the Devil's Bridge.—Braham. Mr Braham & Mr C. Braham.
Song—The Old English Gentleman. Mr. Braham.

PART II.
Song—Oh! no we never mention her......... ....Mr. C. Braham.
Grand Brigand scene from Fra Diavolo.—Auber. Describing Fra Diavolo's Robberies Exploits, &c. ....Mr. Braham.
Song—The Anchor's Weighed.—Braham....... ....Mr. C. Braham.
Song—Ally Croaker and Goosey Gander....... ....Mr. Braham.
Duet—In Infancy—Dr. Arne................. ....Mr. Braham and Mr. C. Braham.
Song—The Bay of Biscay.........Mr. Braham.
God save the Queen. Mr Braham & Mr.C. Braham.
Rule Britannia... Mr. Braham & Mr. C. Braham.

TICKETS—One Dollar each. Children half price.
Toronto, Sept. 26, 1842.   222

Examiner, Sept. 28, 1842   MTLB

In 1842 Toronto was also visited by Charles Dickens who was favourably impressed by the courtesy of its citizens.

APPEARANCES:
1842 John Braham, Charles Braham
1846 Toronto Philharmonic Society
1848 Anna Bishop

1842
DEERING'S THEATRE

Again a primitive theatre accommodated opera lovers with a performance of Guy Mannering *(probably Sir Henry Bishop's*

Watch colour. Frederic V. Poole   MTLB JRR 854

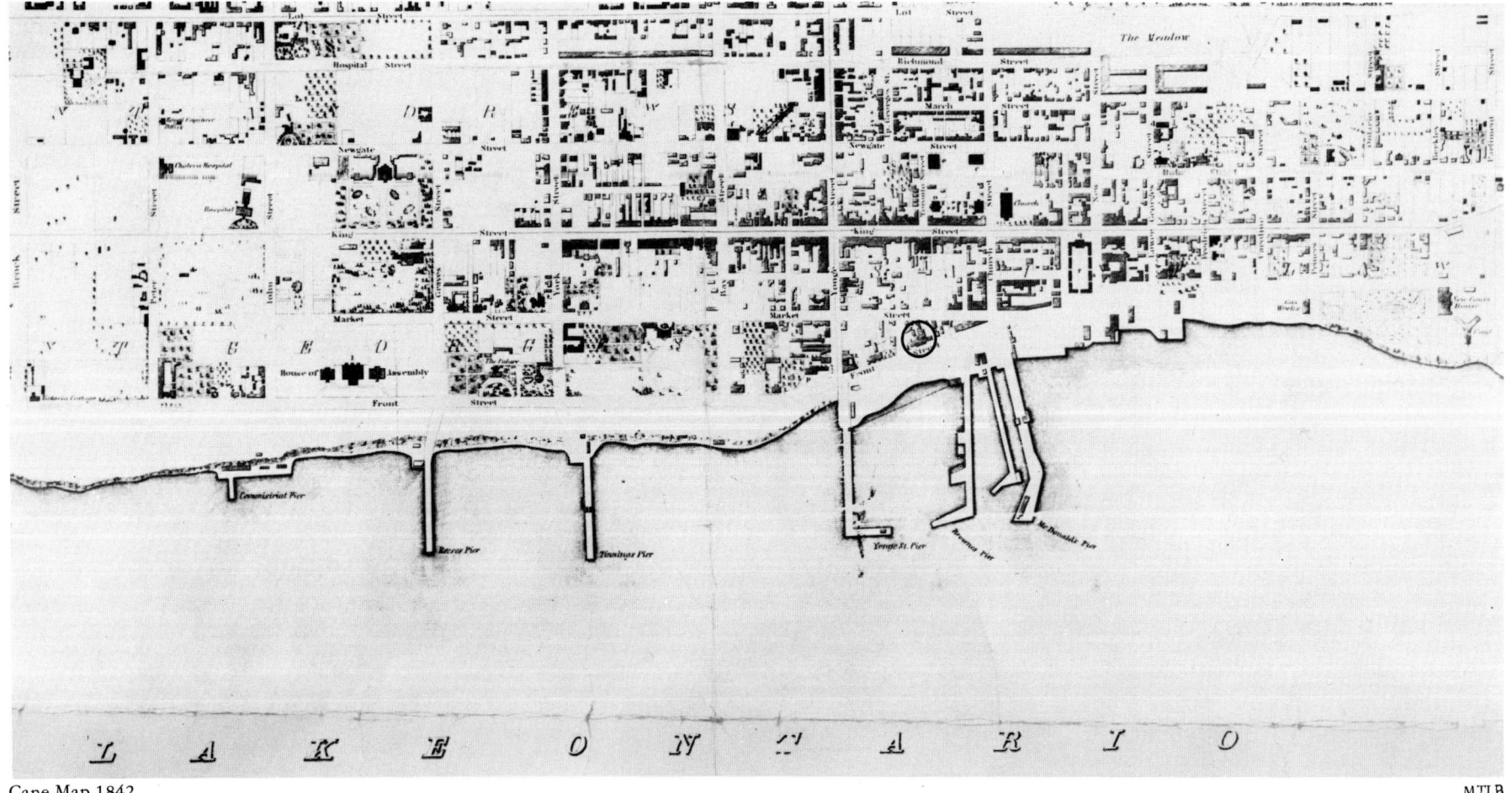

Cane Map 1842

DEERING'S THEATRE

Deering's Theatre, another barnlike structure, was on the northeast corner of Scott and Front Streets, west of the North American Hotel. Its career as a theatre was shortlived as a result of financial reverses and, after serving for a few years as an immigration office, it was replaced by the Niagara House, a restaurant kept by William Guest.

John Braham

NPGL

Landmarks of Toronto – Robertson

MTLB

GRAND
Dramatic Performance
POSITIVELY FOR ONE NIGHT ONLY.
On Saturday next, October 1st, 1842,
Messrs. DEAN and FORREST'S
COMPANY

WILL perform at *Deering's New Theatre* — adjoining the North American Hotel, the Celebrated Opera of
GUY MANNERING,
in which (by particular request), the part of Harry Bertram will be performed by the distinguished Vocalist
Mr. BRAHAM,
who, assisted by Mr. Charles Braham and others, will, in the course of the performance, introduce all the original DUETS, SONGS, and GLEES, in that well known and popular Entertainment.

☞ After the Opera, Mr. Braham and Mr. C. Braham will give a
Grand Vocal Concert.
in which most of the admired and favourite Melodies will be introduced.
For particulars see small Bills.
Toronto, Sept. 29, 1842. 79

Toronto Patriot, Sept. 30, 1842   AO

APPEARANCES
1842   Dean and Forrest's Company

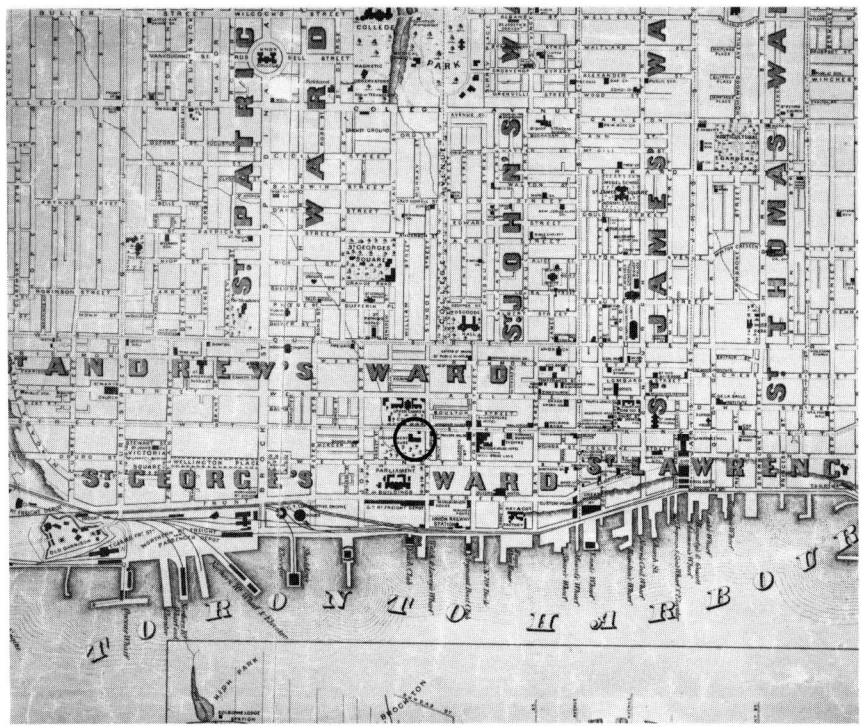

Hart & Rawlinson 1878 TFRB

Government House

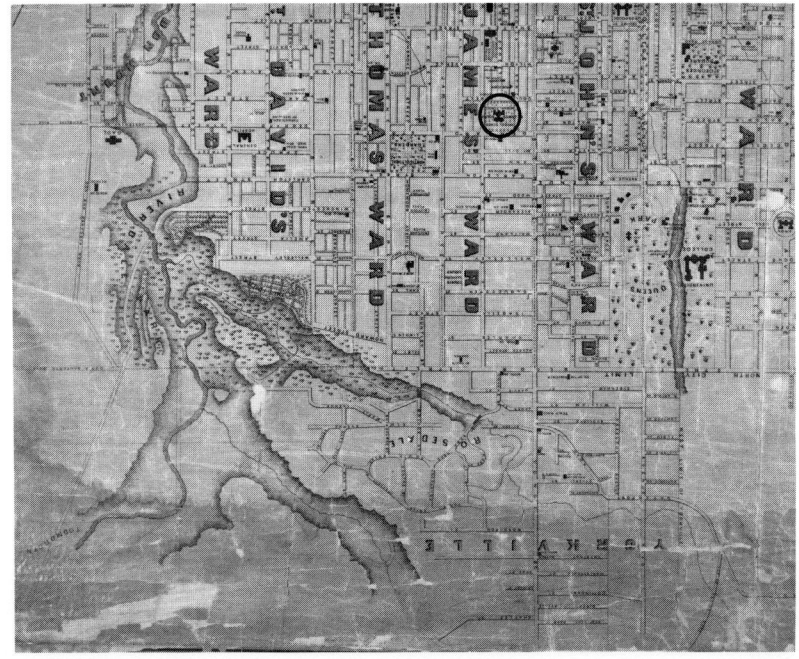

Hart & Rawlinson 1878 TFRB

Model School

CIRCA~1845
OPEN AIR

Al fresco concerts, which usually include operatic selections, have always appealed to Torontonians.

Litho: O'Brien, Ellis

GOVERNMENT HOUSE, Simcoe Street
The Queen's Birthday, 1854

MTLB JRR 296

OPEN AIR

For many years band concerts, especially *al fresco*, were a popular feature of Toronto life. For the most part they were given by military bands and almost invariably included numbers from the operas of the day. Sites for the concerts included the Grounds of Government House – today Roy Thomson Hall – Elmsley Villa, Old City Hall, the Normal School, the Barracks, Sleepy Hollow (residence of the mayor), Vauxhall Gardens, Summerhill Gardens, Rosedale Pleasure Grounds, the Horticultural Gardens, University Grounds, Queen's Park, the Crystal Palace, the Exhibition and the skating rinks. The entertainment was provided by the bands of the 16th, 17th, 30th, 47th, 81st and 82nd Regiments, the 10th Royals, 71st Highlanders, the Rifle Brigade, Royal Canadian Rifles, 13th Hussars (on one occasion, on horseback), the Queen's Own Rifles, Maul's Band and the City Brass Band. The works of such operatic composers as Adam, Auber, Balfe, Bellini, Boieldieu, Donizetti, Flotow, Herold, Mercadante, Meyerbeer, Pacini, Rossini, Verdi and Weber were standard selections.

On 1st July, 1867 a "Monster Concert" was given at the Horticultural Gardens by the combined bands of the 17th Regiment and 13th Hussars.

Photo
TADDLE RAVINE, McCAUL'S POND 1870
MTLB T13042

Lithotint
MTLB T13231

QUEEN'S OWN RIFLES
Presentation of silver mace by Mrs. Draper, wife of the Chief Justice, Normal School Grounds 25th May, 1863

COC at Ontario Place

OPERAS MOVE OUTDOORS

By KASPARS DZEGUZE

WHEN OPERA has its debut at Ontario Place on Sunday night at 7:30, Herman Geiger-Torel will be anxiously tending to worrisome details to make sure that the Canadian Opera Company's three offerings at The Forum will be staged in the grandest possible fashion.

"It won't be ideal – it can't be," cautions the COC's witty and genial general manager. "The difficulties we have been facing this rehearsal week have been fantastic. Audio is the enormous problem. We have been fiddling around on the set since Monday, but only with piano accompaniment. The first rehearsal with orchestra will tell. If the sound is catastrophic, we may revert to a concert version."

One suspects that the music will have to come across very badly indeed for Geiger-Torel to abandon the full-scale performances, with props and costumes, of La Boheme, Tosca, and Aida. One act from Boheme is to be staged at 8 p.m. tomorrow, Tuesday, Friday and next Saturday, and one from Tosca on Monday, Thursday and Saturdays at 5. The Triumphal scene from Aida will provide the spectacular tail-piece on each occasion.

Witnessing the great success of the Toronto Symphony concerts and performances by the National Ballet during Ontario Place's inaugural season last year, Geiger-Torel decided that The Forum was the ideal place to stage opera that would reach people who are rarely exposed to it, or who can't afford tickets for the COC's regular fall season at O'Keefe Centre, where top price is $10.

Still, it was "economics, not audience, that dictated the operas that would be performed. We couldn't possibly afford a completely new production. It was out of the question. But why not give tid-bits of the big season – hors d'oeuvre, antipasto, forspeise?" Hence, excerpts from three of the five operas that will be staged at O'Keefe were selected. Geiger-Torel grins: "It's by calculated chance that we will do things that are probably popular."

The proscenium staging of all three operas has been dropped, and new arrangements made to suit the Forum's theatre-in-the-round configuration. Alterations to Tosca and Boheme have been successful, the general manager reports, "but I haven't succeeded with Aida very well. There are so many extras. Sometimes 120 people sing at once, and they all must be able to glimpse the conductor out of the corner of their eye. I have turned people around this way or that, but there is a compromise with the proscenium style.

"In Tosca and Boheme, there aren't nearly so many performers, and these artists are all very musical and can sometimes sing with their back to the conductor. With the help of God they don't get lost in the music – until now they haven't, in rehearsal."

The volume of sound produced by the pit orchestra makes it absolutely necessary for singers to use microphones, and that creates another problem. "You cannot perform an opera nine inches away from a microphone," Geiger-Torel says. He agrees that broadcast microphones, which require no wires, might provide a solution, but they're not in use at the Forum.

Part of the staggering $91,200 cost of the week of rehearsal and week of performance can be attributed to such strange entries in the accounting books as leotards. "We have to forget about body make-up for Ontario Place because there are only two showers. Make-up on the face and hands, yes, but not on legs or arms – it's not human." Instead, the COC has suffered the "fantastic expense" of purchasing tights for the entire company. "First, so the singers don't freeze, since some of them are half-naked, and second, so that you don't have this disgusting white skin showing."

Globe & Mail Aug 19, 1972   MTLB

OPEN AIR

Globe & Mail Aug 19, 1972   MTLB

Stephanie Bogle (Mimi), Judith Lebane (Aida), Alderman David Rotenberg, R.L.T. Baillie (COA President), Herman Geiger-Torel (General Director, COA)

On behalf of the Mayor, Mr. Rotenberg proclaims *Opera Month* at ONTARIO PLACE

John Arab (Radames), Herman Rombouts (Ramfis), Nancy Greenwood (Amneris) *Aida* at the Forum

COCA

ONTARIO PLACE (foreground) 1976   MTCV

COC'S Peter Barcza, Stephanie Bogle, David Meek (front) Ed Matthiessen, Donald Oddie, Peter Milne (back)

Globe & Mail Aug. 19, 1972   MTLB

NEW CITY HALL

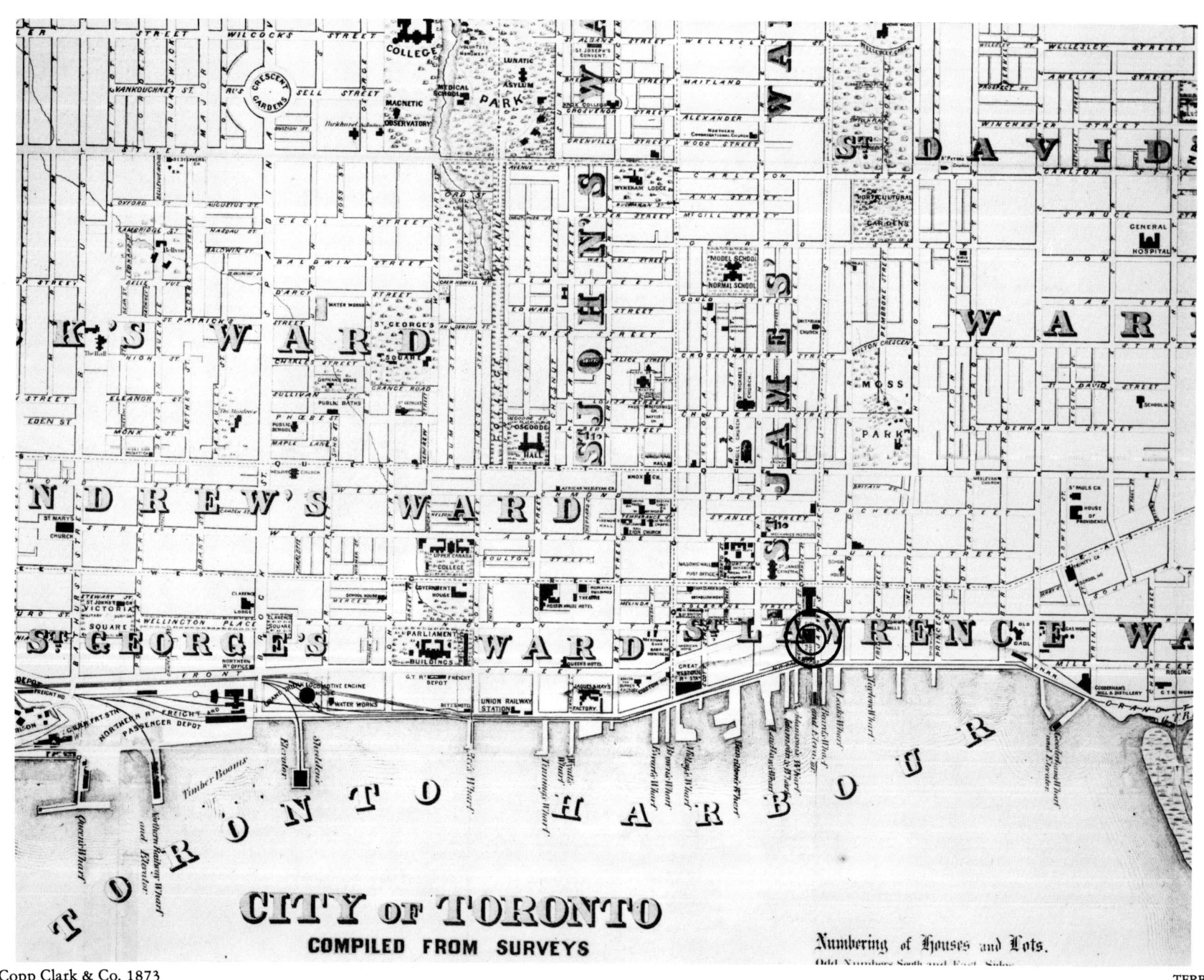

Copp Clark & Co. 1873

TFRB

1846
NEW CITY HALL

After the success of the Toronto Philharmonic Society's concerts international artists appeared at the newest building which could hold a gathering.

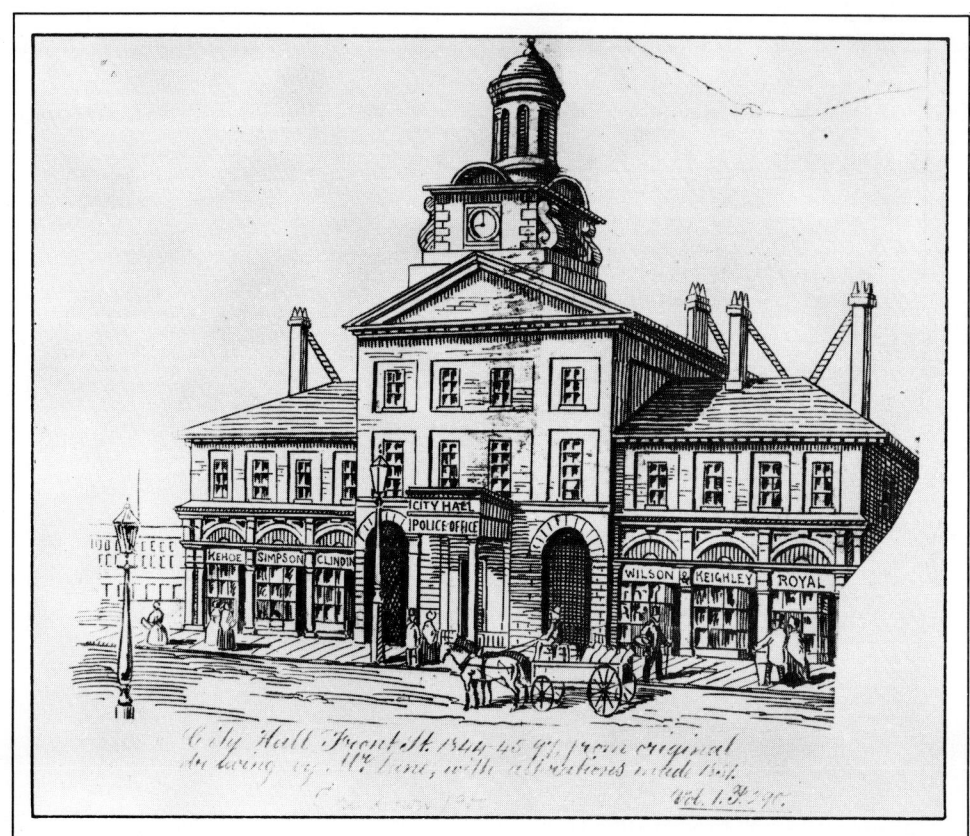

Drawing: C.W. Jefferys

MTLB T11785

NEW CITY HALL

Before the fire of 1849 destroyed the first market, a new City Hall had been erected at the corner of Front and New (later Nelson and still later Jarvis) Streets. The Architect was Henry Bower Lane and the cost of construction was $52,000. This Hall served from 1844 to 1899. The original structure is enclosed in the present south building of the St. Lawrence Market.

Illustrated London News, April 14, 1849   ILN

Italian soprano TERESA PARODI, who made her London debut as Norma at Her Majesty's Theatre in 1849, sang at the New City Hall in 1857.

Globe April 21, 1857   MTLB

NYPL

Mezzo soprano AMALIA PATTI-STRAKOSCH was a sister of Adelina Patti and the wife of Czech impresario Maurice Strakosch. She sang at the New City Hall in 1857.

APPEARANCES
1846	Toronto Philharmonic Society
1850	Toronto Philharmonic Society
1850	Eliza Valentini Concert
1857	Teresa Parodi and Amalia Patti-Strakosch – Vocal Concert

1848
TEMPERANCE HALL

Meeting places usually offered the best facilities for operatic concerts.

TEMPERANCE HALL Methodist News Connexion which was later a printers workshop.   Photo   MTLB T12799

TEMPERANCE HALL

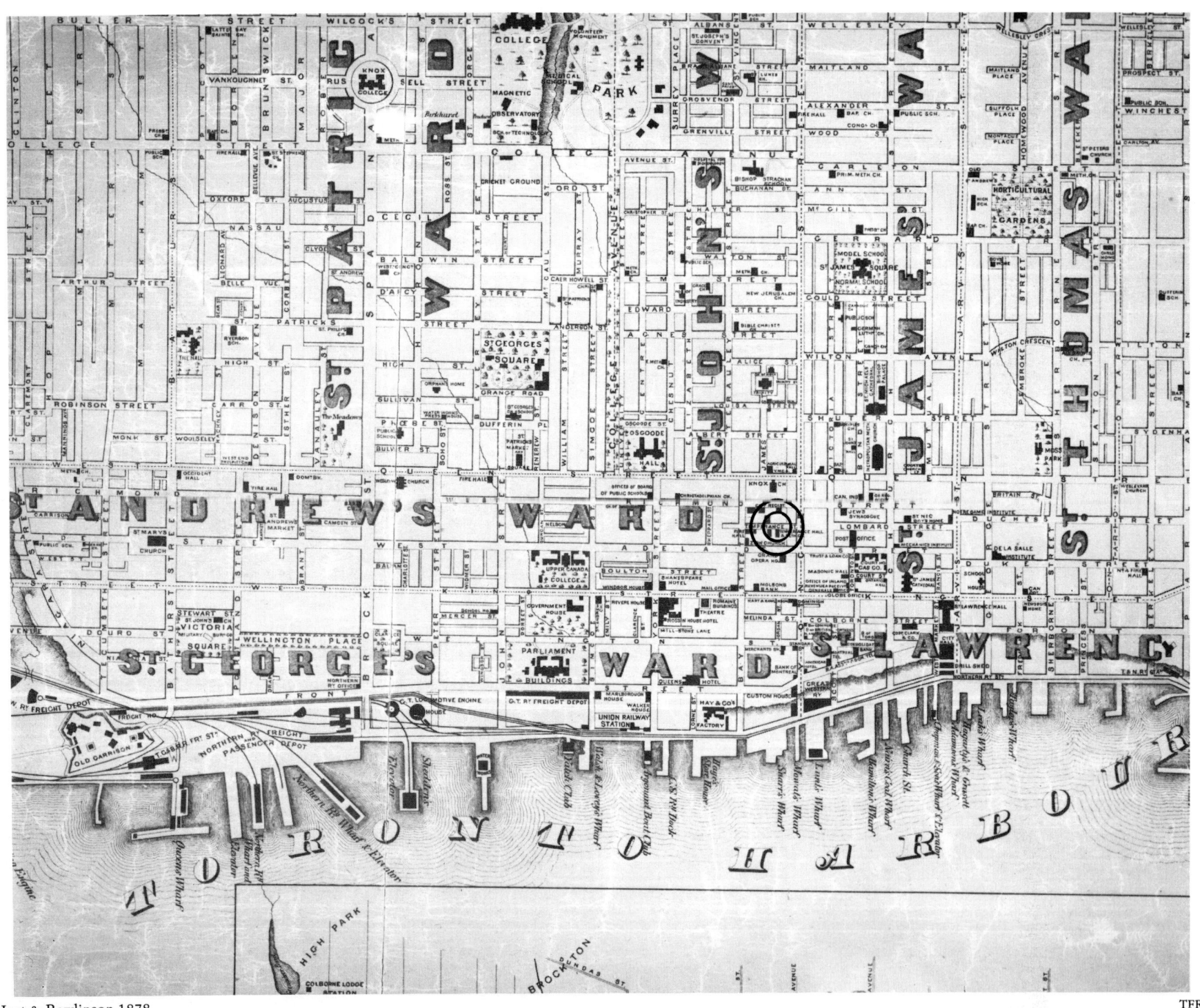

Hart & Rawlinson 1878

TEMPERANCE HALL

Jesse Ketchum, wealthy American-born tanner, politican and philanthropist, was Vice-President of the York Temperance Society which, in 1830, arose out of the excessive drinking habits of many of York's inhabitants. In 1848 he built Temperance Halls on Davenport Road near Yonge Street and on Alfred Street. Over the years a belief has persisted to the effect that Ketchum gave the latter to the city on the condition that liquor would never be sold on that street. Be that as it may, Alfred Street became Temperance Street in 1850 and has remained so. In 1899 the Empire Theatre replaced the Temperance Hall on this site.

ANNA BISHOP made her first Toronto appearance at Temperance Hall in 1848

Globe, August 6, 1850

Soprano ROSA DEVRIES sang at the Paris Grand Opera, Brussels, Le Havre and New Orleans. Her first of several appearances in Toronto was with the French Opera Troupe of New Orleans in 1850.

Globe, June 27, 1849

APPEARANCES
1848	Anna Bishop – Vocal Concert
1848	The Seguins Operatic Troupe in Concert
1850	French Opera Troupe of New Orleans
1852	Emma G. Bostwick – Vocal Concert
1861	Italian Opera Company, Academy of Music of New York
1861	Madame L. Gomez de Woloska, Girolamo di Fossati – Vocal Concert
1862	Carlotta Patti – Vocal Concert

ROYAL LYCEUM

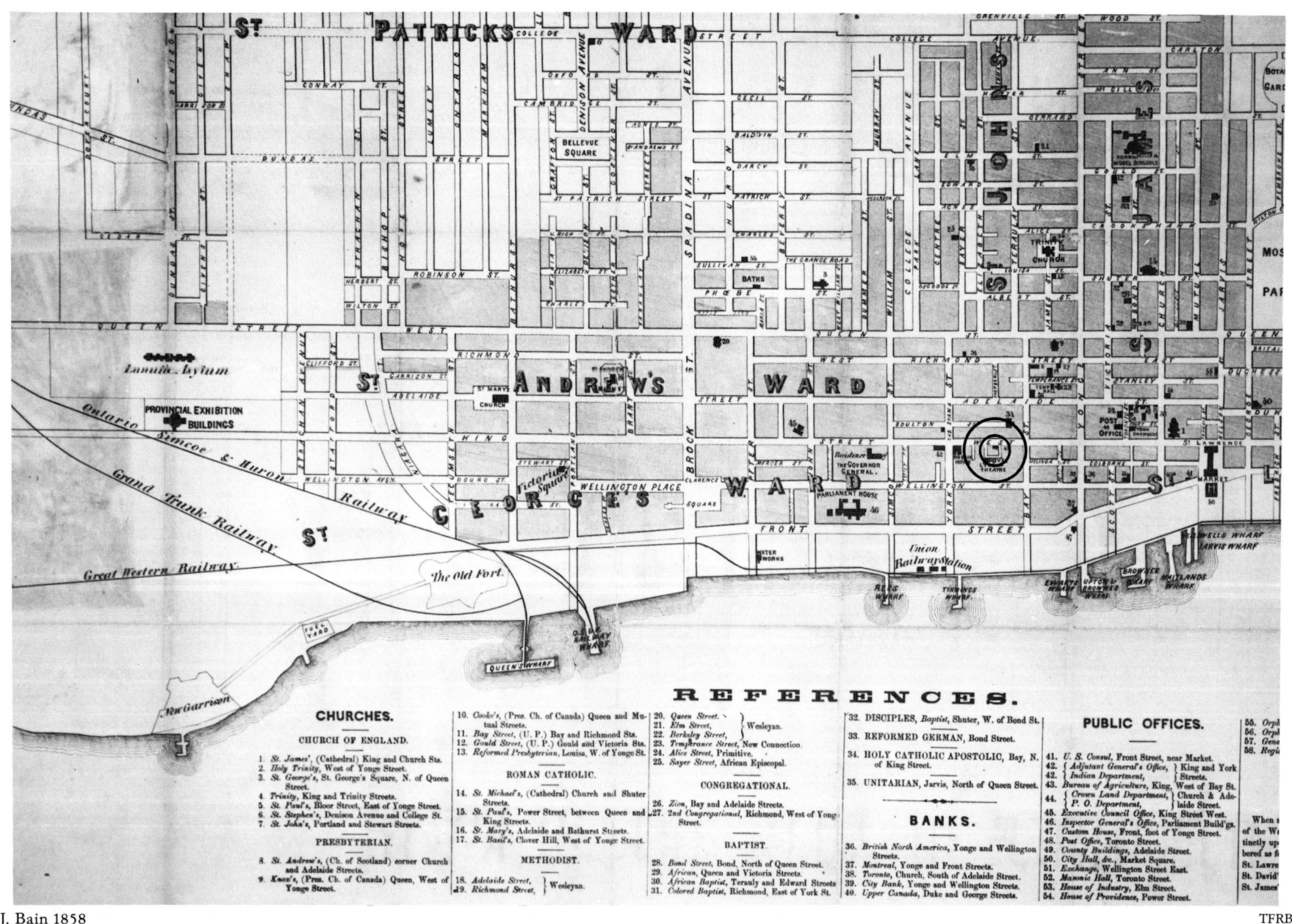

J. Bain 1858

1848
ROYAL LYCEUM

A more promising venue for the performances of drama – lyric or legitimate.

Water colour: John W. Cotton

MTLB JRR 857

ROYAL LYCEUM

In 1848, the year that Toronto suffered a cholera epidemic, John Ritchey built a theatre on the south side of King Street, between Bay and York. The opening performance, on December 28, was a concert, which included operatic selections, by the Toronto Philharmonic Society. Over the next 25 years it was leased by a succession of proprietors, including Mr. Nickinson whose daughter Charlotte (later Mrs. Morrison of the Grand Opera House) was a popular performer; Mr. Kero, who disappeared suddenly (an occupational hazard? see Grand Opera House and Ambrose Small); and George Holman who formed Toronto's first resident opera troupe. The Holman Troupe performed from 1867 to 1873 in the theatre. The building was redecorated several times and in 1872, after its latest renovation, was referred to as the New Royal Lyceum. During the visit of the Prince of Wales in 1860 it was called the Prince of Wales Theatre. On three occasions it suffered fires, the last of which, on January 30, 1874 was a total disaster. The site is listed in the City's Assessment Rolls from 1872-4 as the Royal Lyceum; in 1874 as 'burnt building'; in 1875 as the Royal Opera House; in 1883 as 'burnt opera house'; in 1885-6 as 'ruins of burnt opera house' and in 1887 as a lithographer's establishment.

INTERIOR – ROYAL LYCEUM

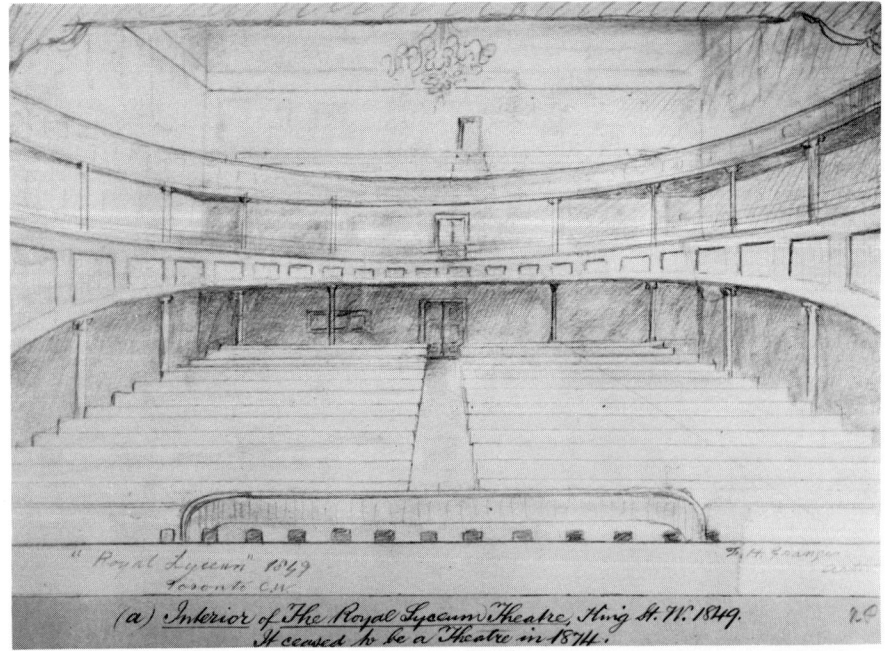

Pencil: F. H. Granger   MTLB T12935

HOUSE PLAN – ROYAL LYCEUM

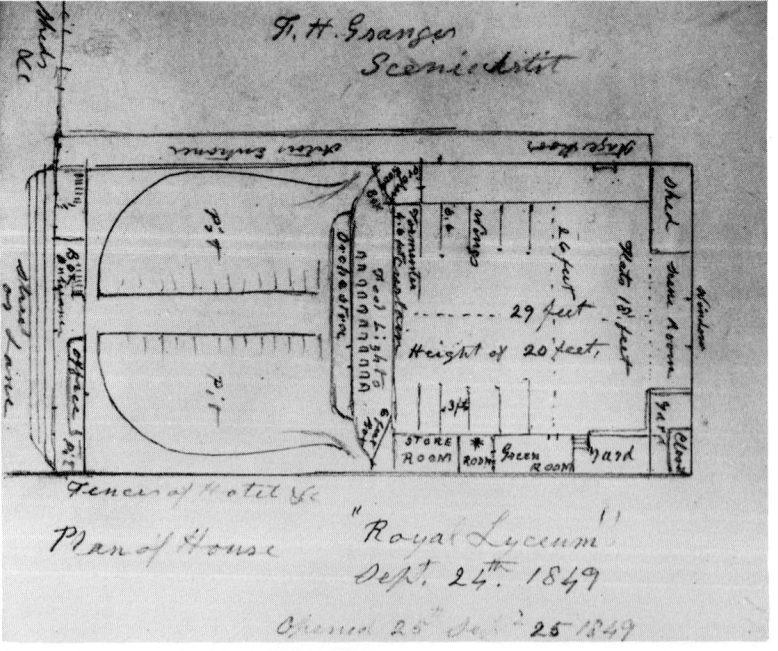

Pencil: F. H. Granger   MTLB T12936

Opening of the Royal Lyceum.—Philharmonic Society's First Concert.

The Philharmonic Society of this City, gave their first Subscription Concert last evening, in the Royal Lyceum, which has just been erected, at the Waterloo Buildings, King Street West,—the entrance being by the gate-way, of the premises lately known as Macdonald's Hotel, and the Lyceum itself, being in rear of these premises. This building has been erected by Mr. Ritchey, to whom it belongs. It is built in the most solid and substantial manner, and the interior is fitted up with very great neatness, comprising Stage, Pit, Boxes, and Gallery, and the usual appendages of Dressing Rooms, &c. It is arranged to accomodate from 600 to 700 people, comfortably; and on extraordinary occasions, from 800 to 900 might manage to occupy the different departments, without being very much discommoded for room. There are comfortable seatings in the Boxes, for upwards of 150 persons; in the Gallery, for upwards of 200; and in the Pit, for upwards of 300 but these may be additionally occupied, should occasion require. The interior of the Lyceum is neatly formed. The Gallery and Boxes, being in a horse-shoe form, and the ceiling coned and suitably painted and decorated. The Stage is very spacious, 42x32 feet; the front of the proscenium 20 feet in height, and surmounted by the Royal Arms. The scenery is entirely new, and does credit to Mr. Craig, by whom the decorations were supplied. The building is creditable to all concerned and it forms an important addition to the places of public assemblages in the city. It is lighted with gas. The opening Concert of the Philharmonic Society was an appropriate commencement of amusements in the new "Royal Lyceum," which is well adapted for concerts, as well as for other descriptions of public amusements usually held in such places, and we trust that the spirited proprietor, Mr. Ritchey, may find this a profitable investment of capital.

The Prospectus of the Philharmonic Society informs us that the Society is one of a private character, but established on such principles as to encourage the hope that no person will object to take part in the concerts, more particularly when it is known that the nobility, and even the Royal Family, join in the performances of the similar private Society in London. The object is to foster a taste for the pleasing and humanizing art of music. The Society consists of a limited number of performing and non-performing members and subscribers; the former having the entrée to rehearsals, and a vote in the affairs of the Society. Members are admissible by ballot; subscribers being nominated by any member or subscriber, parties being admitted in the order of their application. Tickets are not transferable: and any person violating this rule, subjects himself to expulsion. Single Tickets can be purchased by non-residents, but only through a member of the committee, whose name, together with the purchaser's must appear on the Tickets. The Society proposes to give four Concerts, during the winter, the first of which was that which took place last night, Herr Schallehn being the Instrumental Conductor, and Mr. J. D. Humphreys the Vocal Conductor. The ordinary season of the society commences in October, and ends 30th April. The foregoing explanation will convey to our readers, the objects of the Society, and the rules by which they are guided.

The performances last evening, comprized the following, as announced in the programme:

PART I.

Overture—Masaniello	AUBER.
Ballad—"In this old chair my Father sat." —Mr. Humphreys—accompanied by a Lady Amateur	BALFE.
Solo—Tema con variazioni—Violin—Mr. Schallehn, accompanied by a Gentleman Amateur	KALLIWODA.
German Glee—"The Swallows"—(Orchestral Accompaniments)	POHLENS.
Cavatina—"Ciel a miei lunghi spasimi"—A Lady Amateur—(Orchestral Accompaniments)	DONIZETTI.
Glee—"Crabbed age and youth"	STEVENS.
Chorus—"Vive le Roi"—(Orchestral Accompaniments	BALFE.
Overture—Cenerentola	ROSSINI.

PART II.

Overture—Don Juan	MOZART.
French Romance—"Le Lazzaroni"—Mr. Humphreys, accompanied by a Lady Amateur	COUNT D'ADH[illegible]
Duo Concertante—Piano-forte and Violin—Mr. Strathy and Mr. Schallehn	HERZ & L[illegible]
Song—"From the Alps the horn resounding" by a Lady Amateur—Sax horn obligato (Mr. Schallehn)	PROCH.
Song—"Bold Robin Hood"—Mr. Humphreys, accompanied by a Lady Amateur	BALFE.
Glee and Chorus—"Give me a cup of the grape's bright dew" (The Doom-kiss) with Orchestral Accompaniments	SIR H. R. B[illegible]
Overture—Semiramide	ROSSINI.
Finale—"God Save the [illegible]"	

The attendance last evening, was large and fashionable,—the boxes crowded, and the [illegible] gallery tolerably well occupied, showing that the Philharmonic Society, at its [illegible], on the new system that has been [illegible] supported, and contains a large number of performing and non-performing members [illegible]. The company was so large, that the [illegible] Hall (the place at which the Philharmonic Society formerly held their concerts) would have been too small for their accommodation. The [illegible] as they entered, took their places indiscriminately,—pit, boxes and gallery, being alike [illegible] by the members and subscribers of the Society only, and a few non resident visitors. The company appeared in full dress, and the "Royal Lyceum," at its opening, was [illegible] off to the best advantage. The performances were admirable, and the utmost gratification pervaded the entire company, with the character of the entertainment, the excellent arrangements, very pleasant and agreeable amusements, [illegible] success which attended the first performance in the new "Royal Lyceum;" so much so, that [illegible] look forward with much avidity for the [illegible] Concert of the "Philharmonic Society." The performances last evening, commenced at [illegible] o'clock, and closed shortly after eleven.

British Colonist Dec. 29, 1848 NLC

NYPL

ROSA DEVRIES who sang the title role in Toronto's first complete *Norma* in 1853

ROYAL LYCEUM.

OPERATIC SOIREES.

MR. MANVERS

HAS the honour to announce that by very general request, he has made arrangements with the proprietor of the above establishment, for a limited number of nights.

This Evening, Saturday, June 23,

will be given, selections from Donizetti's celebrated Comic Opera, of the

"*ELIXIR OF LOVE:*"

ADINA, (beloved by Nemorino and Belcore) - MISS BRIENTI.
NEMORINO, (in love with Adina) - - - - MR. MANVERS.
SERGEANT BELCORE, (suitor to Adina) - - MRS. CLARK.

Previous to which will be given a

ONE ACT CONCERT!

☞ Boxes 2s. 6d.; Pit 1s. 10½d.; Gallery 1s. 3d.
Doors open at half-past Seven; commence at Eight o'clock.
Toronto, June 22, 1849. 414-1t

Globe, June 23, 1849 MTLB

ROYAL LYCEUM.

LAST NIGHT!!

THIS EVENING, WEDNESDAY, June 27, 1849.—Selections from DONNIZETTI's Opera

"Lucia di Lammermoor."

Lucy Ashton, - - - - Miss Eliza Brienti.
Edgar of Ravenswood, - - Mr. Manvers.

To conclude with the Comic Opera of the

"Postillion of Lonjumeau."

Madelaine (Mistress of the Inn) Miss E. Brienti.
Chapelon (Postillion of Lonjumeau) - - - - - - Mr. Manvers.

☞ To-morrow evening Miss BRIENTI's *Benefit*, and positively the last night of the Operatic Soirees.
Toronto, June 27th, 1849. 415-1t

Globe, June 27, 1849 MTLB

Royal Lyceum!

The proprietor has the honor to announce that the above establishment will be opened on

Tuesday Evening, Sept. 25th, 1849.

Acting Manager.......MR. C. K. MASON.
Stage Manager.......MR. CHAS. HILL.
Scenic Artist.......MR. GRANGER.

The Theatre has undergone many improvements in the Stage Department, and some

SPLENDID NEW SCENERY

HAS BEEN SUPPLIED.

Special Constables will be in attendance to ensure the strictest order and propriety; and the patrons of the Toronto Theatre may rest assured that no pains will be spared to make the Drama what it claims and is acknowledged to be elsewhere, a source of instruction and rational entertainment.

Engagements have been made with

MR. CHARLES HILL!

MR. BARTON HILL,

MRS. CHARLES HILL,

MISS ROSALIE HILL,

MR. GLASSFORD, MR. MONFORD,
MR. MARSHALL, MR. VANCE,
MRS. MARSHALL, MISS SUSAN WALTERS,

And likewise with

MR. CHARLES K. MASON!

The Manager has the pleasure to announce that, for a limited number of nights, an arrangement has been made with the celebrated

ETHIOPIAN HARMONISTS,

Who were received on a former occasion with enthusiastic approbation.

TUESDAY EVENING, SEPT. 25, 1849,

The performance will commence with the laughable Comedy, (as arranged for stage representation in 3 acts), called the

HONEYMOON!

Duke Aranza, - - - - - - - Mr. C. K. Mason.
Rolando, - - - - - - - Mr. Chas. Hill.
Count Montalban.......Mr. Barton Hill. | Lopez.......Mr. Marshall.
Balthazar.......Mr. Munford. | Campillo.......Mr. Vance.
Jacques.......Mr. Glassford.
Juliana, - - - - - - Mrs. Chas. Hill.
Volante.......Mrs. Marshall. | Mrs. Lopez.......Miss S. Walters.

After which, the grotesque entertainment of

THE ETHIOPIAN HARMONISTS!

PART 1. AS DANDY NEGROES.

OVERTURE—La Polacca—FULL BAND.
INVITATION SONG—"Commence, ye Darkies all."—PARKER and CHORUS.
PLAINTIVE MELODY—"The Belle of Tennessee."—RICH and CHORUS.
LAMENT—"Old Pine Tree."—STANTON and CHORUS.
DESCRIPTIVE SONG—"The Belle of Baltimore."—EVANS and CHORUS.
LAMENT—"Ephraim! don't you cry!"—RICH and CHORUS.
OPERATIC BURLESQUE—"Stop dat Knocking."—PARKER and CHORUS.

PART 2.—Banjo Solo by the celebrated FRANK STANTON.

PART 3.—AS SOUTHERN PLANTATION DARKIES.

MEDLEY OVERTURE—The Bold Soldier Boy—FULL BAND.
PLANTATION SONG—"I Strut in my Long Tail Blue."—STANTON and CHORUS.
QUARTETTE—"My Rosy Lub."—EVANS and CHORUS.
SONG—"Gib me a Chaw of Tobacco."—RICH and CHORUS.

To be followed by the Popular Farce of

THE YOUNG WIDOW

Mandeville.......Mr. Barton Hill.
SPLASH (his Valet).......MR. CHARLES HILL.
Aurelia (the Young Widow).......Miss Rosalie Hill.
LUCY (her Maid).......MRS. CHARLES HILL.

The whole to conclude with the Operatic Burlesque of

LUCY LONG!

LUCY (as danced by him [illegible] nights at the Theatre Royal, Montreal) ... MR. G. H. RICH.
DANDY JIM ... MR. C. EVANS.

Prices of Admission—Boxes, 2s. 6d.; Pit, 1s. 10½d.; Gallery, 1s. 3d.

Doors open at half-past 7. Performance will commence at 8, precisely.

☞ NO SMOKING ALLOWED in any part of the Theatre. ☜

PRINTED AT THE BRITISH COLONIST OFFICE, TORONTO.

MTLB

Playbill, The Royal Lyceum Theatre 1849

MM

LUIGI ARDITI, who conducted the performance of *Norma* by the Artists' Association Italian Opera Company on July 8, 1853 at the Royal Lyceum. Also a composer, he is today chiefly remembered for *I'Bacio.*

ROYAL LYCEUM.

FOR ONE NIGHT ONLY.

(POSITIVELY.)

THE ARTISTS' ASSOCIATION ITALIAN OPERA COMPANY, comprising 40 Members, under the able direction of SIGNOR L. ARDITI, who will give the first and only representation of a full ITALIAN GRAND OPERA ever attempted in Canada West, complete with Scenery, Costumes, Full Chorus, male and female, and Grand Orchestra.

On FRIDAY EVENING, July 8, 1853, will be presented, complete in all its effects, &c., Bellini's "Chef d'ouvre"—the Grand Opera, in three acts, of

NORMA!

Norma .... Signora Rosa Devries.
Adalgisa .... Signora Eliza Sidenburg.
Oreveso .... Sig. Colletti.
Pollione .... Sig. Forti.
Flavio .... Sig. Barratini.
Clothilde .... Sig. Parozzi.

Chorus of Druids, Bards and Warriors.

Director—Sig. Arditi. Prompter—Sig. Lanza.

PRICES OF ADMISSION.—Secured Seats, Dress Circle 7s. 6d.; (obtainable at the Box Office of Royal Lyceum from Ten till Six o'clock on the day of Perfomance.) Dress Circle, Seats not secured 5s.; Upper Boxes, 3s 9d; Parquette, 2s 6d.

Tickets are sold at Messrs. Nordheimer's and Small & Paige's Music Stores, at the Royal Lyceum, and at the door on the night of performance.

Doors open at half-past 7, to commonce at 8

God save the Queen!

Toronto, July 8, 1853. 508-k

British Colonist July 8, 1853 NLC

ROYAL LYCEUM

Irish composer and singer MICHAEL BALFE whose *Bohemian Girl* was first performed in Toronto by the Cooper English Opera Troupe at the Royal Lyceum in 1858. It took the city by storm at the time that the Whiteoaks moved to Jalna.

Drawing: John Wood NGI

ROYAL LYCEUM: NORMA.

Thanks to Mr. Nickinson, Torontonians have been gratified with a sketch of an Italian Opera. A very good sketch it was, and one from which they could realise all the beauties of the composer.

The Theatre is so small that Devries voice was a little too loud, and the prompter was perhaps too audible, but these are minor imperfections. Coletti as Oroveso, both sang and acted remarkably well, and the chorusses were much better than those six years ago at the Astor Place Opera House. The Ochestra was very fair, but rather too loud, and it would be as well for them, if they return, to keep in mind the size of the house. We shall not attempt to criticise, that an Entire Opera has been performed in Toronto is a great fact, and one worthy of a corner in a note-book. We saw it mentioned a short time ago in a daily journal that twenty years since, the opera was for the first time introduced into Scotland. We remember the circumstance well, and we remember that the company was not as good as that which has just visited Toronto. Donzelli was a better tenor than Forté, but De Merie the prima donna, was not as finished a singer as Devries, and the Orchestra and Chorusses were certainly inferior.

The Italian Opera but a few years since, was unknown in New York. We again assert, then, that a prodigious stride has been made, and we would earnestly advise the Torontonians to fill up the subscription lists as speedily as possible, so as to induce the company to return. There are eighteen Operas on their list, which will afford a rich treat. A word now to the audience: Frequent applauding may evince much good nature, but at the same time it has the sure effect of making artists careless, as it must convince them that the applauders do not really know what or why they are applauding. Frequent interruptions are particularly inadmissible in an Opera, and we were as much amused at the first chorus girl being applauded, instead of Norma, as we were disgusted with the interruption in the midst of the "*Deh! con te.*" Nothing is admissable in Opera either as applause or encore except, at rare intervals, when some celebrated covatina or duet has been really well given, and when it will be a gratification to both artist and audience, to have an enthusiastic encore.

MTLB

Anglo American Magazine August, 1853

EXETER HALL.

Miss Greenfield (the Black Swan) gave a concert in the large room of the Hall on Wednesday evening, aided by several eminent *artistes*. From the great reputation heralded before her, much might have been anticipated; but after hearing the lady, all preconceived charm must have been wofully broken. Her first attempt, *The Cradle Song*, by Wallace, was marked throughout by an utter want of intonation, partly arising probably from nervousness; but the impression left on the audience was that her singing flat was for the most part a natural failure. In all her songs Miss Greenfield was equally unsuccessful, and *Home, Sweet Home* (which was not marked down in the programme) was never to our knowledge worse vocalized.

Anglo American Magazine MTLB
August, 1853

THE BLACK SWAN (Miss Greenfield), a coloured singer with a range of 31 notes, sang at the Royal Lyceum in 1852 and 1855 and on other occasions at the St. Lawrence Hall and the Music Hall.

TERESA PARODI'S Opera Company gave a concert of excerpts from *La Traviata*, *Lucrezia Borgia* and *Il Trovatore* at the Royal Lyceum in 1859.

ROYAL LYCEUM.

An Engagement has just been effected
WITH
H. C. COOPER'S
UNRIVALLED
English Opera Troupe!
FOR
FOUR NIGHTS ONLY.
COMMENCING MONDAY NEXT, NOV. 8th.

THE OPERAS for representation will be produced in the following order:

Nov. 8th, Monday........La Somnambula.
Nov. 9th, Tuesday......The Bohemian Girl.
Nov. 10th,........Lucia di Lammermoor.
Nov 11th,................Ill Trovatore

CONSEQUENTLY THERE WILL BE
A NEW OPERA EVERY NIGHT.

ANNIE MILNER...........Prima Donna.
MRS. HOLMAN...........Seconda Donna.
CHARLES GUILMITH.....Baritone.
D. MIRANDI.............Primo Tenore.
F. RUDOLPHSEN.........Basso.
GEORGE HOLMAN........Secondo Tenore.

Conductor and Director of the Music:
H. C. COOPER.
Operatic Stage Manager, GEORGE HOLMAN.

THE BOX PLAN
will be opened for the securing of seats at Nordheimer's Music Store this morning Saturday, and every succeeding day, from 10 to 12 a. m., and from 3 to 5 p. m

Prices:
Dress Circle and two front rows of Pit ONE DOLLAR. Remaining Seats in Pit and Second Boxes 25c as usual.

Toronto, November 6, 1858.   2673-6t

Globe, Nov. 6, 1858   NLC

ILN

ROYAL LYCEUM.

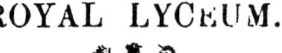

A FEW NIGHTS ONLY.

COOPER'S
English Opera Company!

FOURTEEN DISTINGUISHED ARTISTES.

ANNIE MILNER, PRIMA DONNA.

THIS EVENING,

WEDNESDAY, JUNE 15th. 1859, will be performed the Grand Opera, in three acts, entitled

"LUCIA DI LAMMERMOOR."

BOXES ONE DOLLAR!

Pit and Family Circle 25c as usual.
Seats secured at Messrs. Nordheimer's Music Store from 10 till 1. and from 3 to 5
Toronto, June 14, 1859.   2566-1t

Globe, June 14, 1859   NLC

ROYAL LYCEUM!

MR. & MRS. MARLOWE, have pleasure in announcing a RE-ENGAGEMENT with

Cooper's World Renowned Opera Troupe

This Evening, Tuesday, June 21, will be performed, the favourite Opera

"L'ELISIR D'AMORE,"

Boxes one dollar; Pit 25c; Family Circle, 37½c.
Toronto, June 21, 1859.   2571-1t

Globe, June 21, 1859   NLC

ROYAL LYCEUM

ANNA BISHOP gave a concert at the Royal Lyceum in 1861.

THE OPERA.

The "Love Spell" was performed at the Lyceum last evening to a delighted audience. All the company were in good order, and did their best to please, in which they succeeded. Mr. Cook, especially, brought down the house by his wonderfully grotesque delineation of the quack doctor, and as this gentleman is so evidently popular, doubtless, the house will be crowded to excess this evening on the occasion of his benefit, when "The Bohemian Girl" will be produced, and Mr. Cook appears in his celebrated character of, "Devilspoof, the chief of the Gipsies."

Globe, June 21, 1859

Tenor PASQUALE BRIGNOLI brought his Italian Opera Company to the Royal Lyceum in 1869.

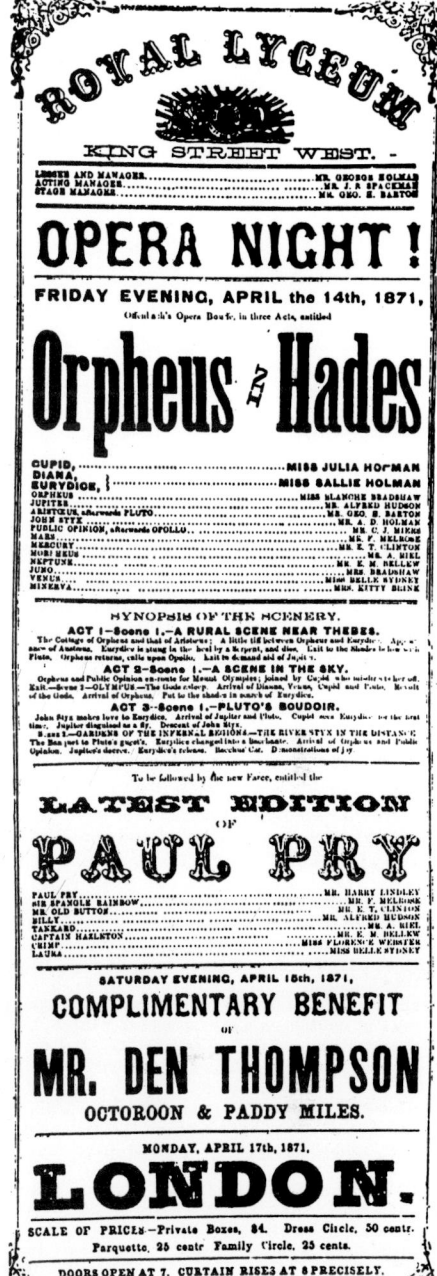

Playbill, The Royal Lyceum Theatre, 1871

Globe, Oct. 30, 1867

THE HOLMAN ENGLISH OPERA COMPANY PLAYED IN THE OLD ROYAL LYCEUM THEATRE?

More than fifty years ago this group of artists formed part of a stock company exceedingly popular in Toronto. They belonged to the Holman English Opera Company. That company had the Lyceum Theatre here from 1866 till 1872. They alternated operas with Shakespearian tragedies, with comedies, with farces and with dramas. George Holman, Sr., the manager, was the head of an unusually talented family. All acted and all sang. All were sometimes on the stage at once. The family consisted of Mr. Holman and his wife, Harriet; their sons, Alfred, George, Jr., and Allie and their daughters, Sallie and Julia. The sisters, Sallie and Julia Holman, were the principal artists of the company, along with Joe Banks, the noted comedian, who composed and used to sing the comic song, "Over the Don," referring to the jail on Gerrard street east.

The personnel of the group, with the exception of No. 19, who has not been identified in the picture, is:— 1, J. R. Spackman; 2, John L. Sophmore (manager); 3, Mr. Leonard (treasurer); 4, DeWitt Waugh (manager); 5, Mrs. Bradshaw; 6, Mrs. Tannehill; 7, Frank Tannehill; 8, Blanche Bradshaw; 9, Mr. Brandisi; 10. Mr. Cushing (leader of orchestra); 11, Alf. Hudson; 12, Belle Vernon; 13, Mrs. Hattie Sophmore; 14, Mrs. Vernon; 15, Posie Bellew; 16, Mr. Lyons (prompter); 17, Joe Banks; 18, Lottie Banks (Mr. Banks' first wife); 20, J. K. Vernon.

The picture is from Mr. W. K. Tinning's antique collection.

Telegram, July 10, 1926

In the photograph GEORGE HOLMAN is the unnumbered man between #2 and #12. Toronto's first resident Opera Company performed at the Royal Lyceum from 1867 to 1873 and continued to visit Toronto thereafter until 1884. Sallie's early death in June 1888 was followed four months later by that of her father George.

ROYAL LYCEUM

Tenor ERNEST NICOLINI, Adelina Patti's second husband, who sang with the Grand Italian Troupe of Associate Artists at the Royal Lyceum in 1872. He was London's first Lohengrin and Radames.

MM

Irish composer VINCENT WALLACE, composer of *Maritana* and *Lurline* and numerous other operas which were popular in the 19th century.

Artist: J. Hanshew   NGI

FIRE.
Destruction of the Royal Lyceum.

About a quarter to twelve last night P.C. Cranston while on his beat on King street west observed smoke curling from the roof of the Royal Lyceum Theatre. After satisfying himself that this was really the case, he hurried to the corner of York street and gave the alarm from box 16. The engines were soon on the spot, but by the time the hose was attached to the hydrants, the smoke from the roof had been succeeded by a small tongue of fire, which seemed to spring from the centre of the building, and which was seen to increase in volume with alarming rapidity. The engines were at once set to work, but the water so far from dimming the lustre of the flames, but increased their intensity, and in less than half an hour the whole of the roof from front to rear was one vast sheet of fire. A ladder had been procured previously to this, and placed against the north wall, with the view of sending in a stream of water through the window over the main entrance, but no apparent good was effected. Notwithstanding the praiseworthy efforts of the firemen, who worked with the thermometer at zero, and a stiff breeze blowing from the east, the fire communicated to the interior of the theatre, and by one o'clock this morning it was completely gutted, and little but the bare walls left standing. The flames had not been completely extinguished when we went to press.

The Theatre was insured in different offices to the extent of about $12,000, and was owned by Mr. French, by whom it had lately been leased to Mr. Tannehill. This is the third time the building has been attacked by fire, and it has at last succumbed to its assailant. The origin of the fire has not been ascertained, but it is supposed that it commenced in the carpenter's shop, which being stored with paint, wood, shavings and other inflammable material, caused it to spread with such unaccountable rapidity.

Mail & Empire Jan. 31, 1874   NCL

APPEARANCES

1849	*Daughter of the Regiment* – Selections	1857	Sanford's Opera Troupe
1849	*Elixir of Love* – selections	1858	H. C. Cooper's English Opera Troupe
1849	*Lucia di Lammermoor* – selections	1859	Italian Opera Company,
1849	*Postillion of Longjumeau*		Academy of Music of New York
1849	*Norma* – selections	1859	Cooper Opera Troupe
1849	*Sonnambula* – selections	1859	Parodi's Opera (Italian) Company
1849	*Child of the Regiment* – selections	1859	French Operatic Concert Troupe
1850	Grand Costume Concerts		**PRINCE OF WALES THEATRE**
	– *Lucia di Lammermoor* – scenes	1860	Cooper Opera Company
	– *Barber of Seville* – scenes		**ROYAL LYCEUM**
	– *Sonnambula* – scenes	1864	Italian Opera Company
	– *Elixir of Love* – scenes	1864	Holman's Opera Troupe
1850	*Lucia di Lammermoor* – excerpts	1867	Holman's Opera Troupe (7 weeks)
	Norma – scenes in full costume	1868	Holman's Opera Company (c 17 weeks)
	Elixir of Love – scenes in full costume	1869	Holman Opera Company (c 14 weeks)
	Barber of Seville – scenes in full costume	1869	Local amateurs
1850	*La Sonnambula* – selections	1869	Brignoli's Italian Opera Company
	Fra Diavolo – selections	1870	Holman Opera Company (c 5 months)
	Child of the Regiment – selections	1871	Holman Opera Company
1852	The Black Swan – (Miss Greenfield)	1872	Holman Opera Company (c 3 months)
1853	Artists' Association Italian Opera Company	1872	Grand Italian Troupe of Associate Artists
1854	Sanford's New Orleans World-Renowned Opera Troupe	1873	English Comic Opera
1855	The Black Swan (Miss Greenfield)		

1849
MASONIC HALL

Once more the dimensions of a hotel lent themselves to a musical occasion.

Water Colour: Frederic V. Poole   Russell's Hotel   MTLB JRR 703

MASONIC HALL

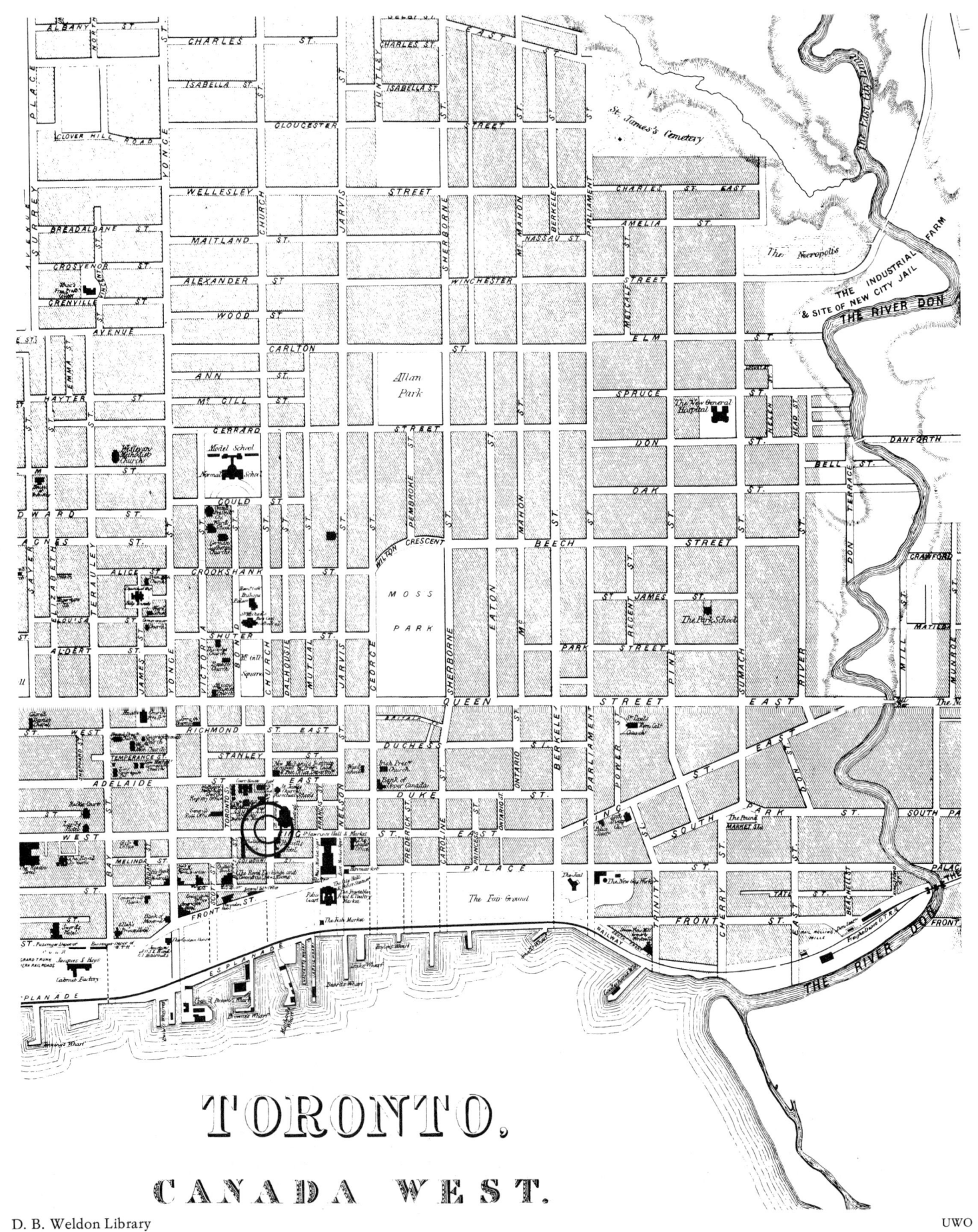

TORONTO, CANADA WEST.

MASONIC HALL

The Order of Freemasons, dating from 1793, was the first beneficent organization to be established in York. There were several lodges which met in various locations, including Market Lane School on Market Lane (Colborne Street) between Church and Market Streets. It housed the Masonic Hall on the 2nd floor and its chief claim to architectural distinction was its cupola, the first in York. In 1848 Snow's Inn, a frame building on the northeast corner of Church and Colborne Streets, was torn down and Joshua Beard put up a brick structure, which was managed by Snow for several years. About 10 years later Azro Russell acquired the hotel which was popular during the years the Parliament of Canada met in Toronto. A later lessee was John Montgomery who had gained fame in the rebellion of 1837. The upper floor was specially built for St. Andrew's Lodge of Freemasons and it was here that Mr. Manvers gave his Soirees. In 1857 a masonic Hall was built by architect William Kaufman on Toronto Street. Originally there were four shops on the ground floor. It became the Canada Permanent Building.

Pen & ink: Daniel S. Eastwood   MTLB T12232

MARKET LANE SCHOOL

CANADA PERMANENT BUILDING
on Toronto Street

OPERATIC SOIREE.

A very rich feast is in store for the lovers of the highest class of Operatic music, in the Entertainment announced by Miss Brienti and Mr. Manvers, for to-night, at the Masonic Rooms, Church-street; and we have no doubt but that the room will be crowded to hear these celebrated artistes. Of the lady, our cotemporaries speak in the highest praise. Educated in the school of Garcia, a school that produced Malibran and Jenny Lind, and also possessing natural talent of a high order, Miss Brienti is destined to rank with the best artistes in Europe. The Opera of to-night is considered more admirably adapted to her voice than any other. In New Orleans, where she played it last winter with great success, for several successive nights, the press were universal in their approbation, preferring her in some passages to Madame Bishop and others equally celebrated.

Since Mr. Manvers last appearance here he has been studying in Italy and singing with the greatest eclat at Covent Garden Theatre, the Philharmonic and Ancient Concerts, London. Altogether, we think our music-loving community cannot fail to be delighted with these artistes. This will, in all probability, be their only visit to Toronto as they contemplate returning to Europe next year; so we sincerely urge all our amateurs and others, who are able to appreciate really finished vocalization, to go and add their meed of praise to these singers. They are ably assisted by Mrs. Clark and Mr. George Brainard—particularly the latter—whose admirable accompaniment well seconds the efforts of the vocalists.

Globe, June 20, 1849   MTLB

RUSSELL'S HOTEL,
LATE BEARD'S,
Church Street,
TORONTO.
RUSSELL BROTHERS, PROPRIETORS.
Toronto, Oct. 11, 1852.   81-r

Leader, Dec. 28, 1853   AO

Masonic Hall, Church Street, over the Phœnix Hotel.

OPERATIC SOIREES
IN FULL COSTUME.

THE celebrated Vocalist, MISS ELIZA BRIENTI, Prima Donna, Pupil of the celebrated Mazzucato, of Milan, and late of the Astor Place Opera House, New York, and MR. MANVERS, Prima Tenore, from the Theatres Royal the Philharmonic and Ancient Concerts, London, assisted by MRS. CLARK and MR. GEORGE BRAINARD, from the St. Charles Theatre, New Orleans, whose unique and original entertainments have created such a furore, beg leave to announce their intention of giving their first Performance on WEDNESDAY EVENING, June 20, consisting of selections from Bellini's beautiful Opera of

LA SOMNAMBULA!

Amina (an Orphan), - - Miss Eliza Brienti.
Elvino (betrothed to Amina) Mr. Manvers.
Count Rodolpho, - - - - Mrs. Clark.
Previous to which will be given a
ONE ACT CONCERT.
☞ An intermission of fifteen minutes for Costuming.
Tickets 2s. 6d. each. Doors open at 7 o'clock, to commence at 8 o'clock, precisely.
Toronto, June 19, 1849.   413-1t

Globe, June 20, 1849   MTLB

APPEARANCES
1849   Operatic Soirees.
1863   The Black Swan (Miss Greenfield).

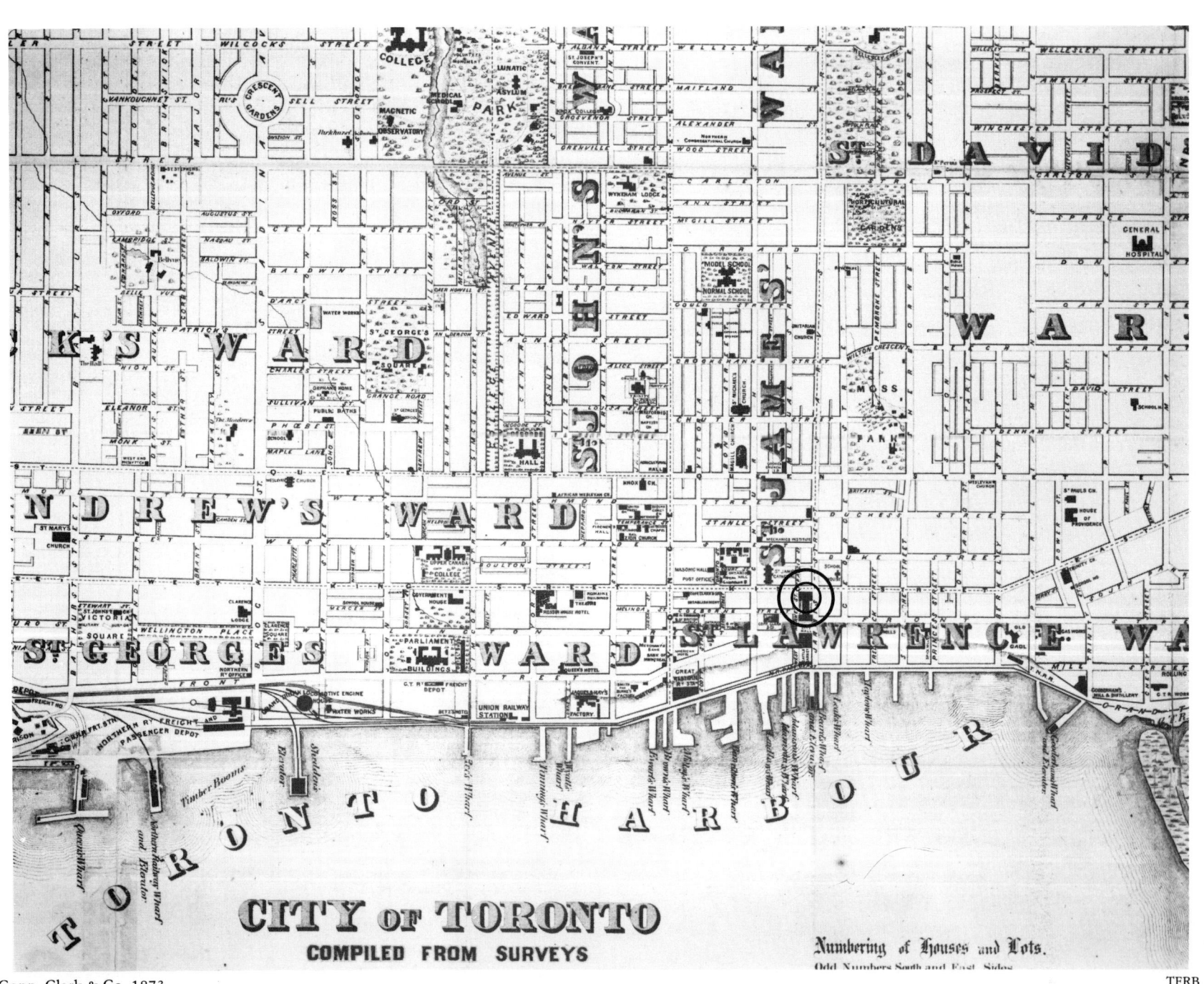

Copp, Clark & Co. 1873

TFRB

1851
ST. LAWRENCE HALL

Toronto's first distinctive concert hall.

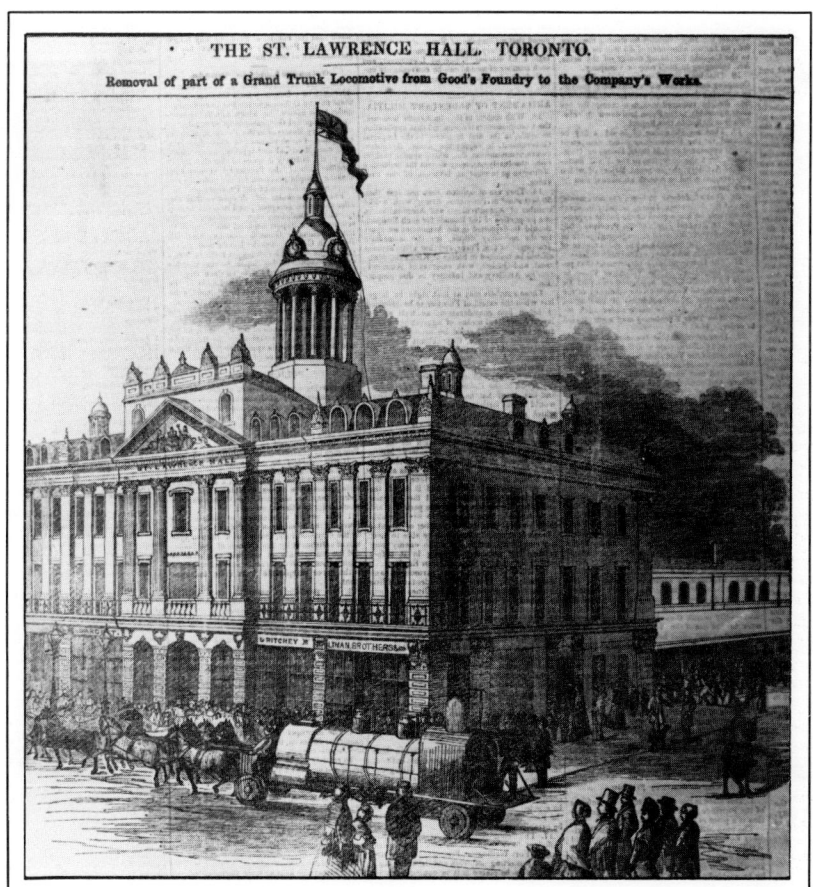

Wood engraving: Bryce Smith MTLB T30102

ST. LAWRENCE HALL

After the destruction, by the fire of 1849, of the old Town Hall and Market House, new buildings were erected by the Corporation of the City of Toronto and private individuals, at a cost of $7,000. The centre building was owned by the Corporation and the eastern and western wings were private property. The architect was William Thomas whose object was to provide a multi-purpose structure. The Hall, with its entrance on King Street, was on the second floor and could accommodate 1,000 people, while the Market entrance was on Front Street. The decoration of the Hall was in extremely beautiful Renaissance style. There is no record of a ceremonial opening – the first event, on 1st April, 1851, was a lecture on Slavery by an English M.P. Balls, concerts, meetings and lectures followed and the first operatic event was a concert by Parodi and Patti. The Hall enjoyed a heyday until, apparently, the building of the Grand Opera House west of Yonge Street, led to its decline.

Canadian Illustrated News
Nov 22, 1862 MTLB

CITIZENS' BALL –

ILN

TERESA PARODI sang at the St. Lawrence Hall in 1851, 1853 and 1861

Globe, July 12, 1851 AO

CPI

ANNA BISHOP deserted her husband and children for her accompanist Mr. Bochsa but continued to be known as Madame Bishop. She appeared in Toronto for 13 years after this 1851, advertisement; in the St. Lawrence Hall in 1851, 1853 and 1861.

Globe & Mail, Sept. 6, 1851 AO

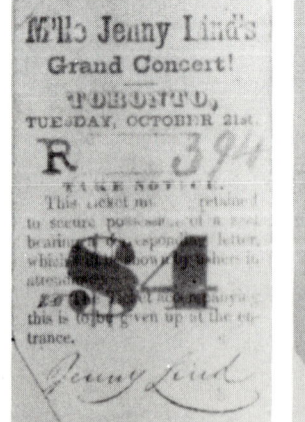
Ticket MTLB

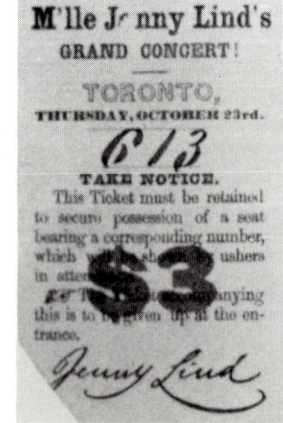
Ticket

ST. LAWRENCE HALL

19th CENTURY DIVAS

AMALIA PATTI sang in concerts at the St. Lawrence Hall in 1851, 1856, 1861 and 1864

JENNY LIND, the *Swedish Nightingale*, most famous of 19th century sopranos, first toured North America under the auspices of P. T. Barnum, legendary circus manager who presented her, not as a great artist, but as a remarkable natural phenomenon. She married the conductor Otto Goldschmidt. During the 1850's in Britain "Jenny Lind mania" captured the public fancy and products of all sorts and descriptions were named for the great diva. In Canada, Jenny Lind chocolates were rivals of Laura Secord for many years. She came to the St. Lawrence Hall in 1851.

CATHERINE HAYES, Irish soprano who sang in Italy, Austria and London. She gave a concert in the St. Lawrence Hall in 1852.

ADELINA PATTI, Italian-born soprano, much-admired internationally. She sang first in Toronto at the St. Lawrence Hall in 1853 when she was 10 years old and again in 1860 when she was 17.

Globe, Nov. 23, 1853

Playbill, Oct. 21, 1851

Playbill, Oct 23, 1851

ST. LAWRENCE HALL

German soprano HENRIETTA SONTAG gave a concert on January 2, 1854 at the St. Lawrence Hall. Six months later she died of cholera in Mexico.

NEW ADVERTISEMENTS
MADAME SONTAG
WILL GIVE ONE
GRAND CONCERT,
IN the St. LAWRENCE HALL, in this City, on MONDAY, JANUARY 2nd, on which occasion she will be assisted by
PAUL JULLIEN,
The wonderful Violinist;
ALFRED JAELL,
The celebrated Pianist and Composer, and
SIG. LUIGI ROCCO.
The famous Basso from the Italian Opera.
☞ Full particulars in future advertisement.
Toronto, Dec. 28th, 1853.   656-t

British Colonist, Dec. 30, 1853

French soprano ROSA DEVRIES sang at the St. Lawrence Hall on three occasions, in 1854, 1855 and 1856.

MARIETTA PICCOLOMINI, Italian soprano, sang Violetta in London's first English *La Traviata* at Her Majesty's Theatre in 1856 and the title role in London's first *Luisa Miller*. In Toronto she performed with Mlle. Ghioni, Sig. Lorini and Sig. Maggiorotti in 1859 at the St. Lawrence Hall.

Lyons, September 16th, 1864
My dearest Max:
I have received your charming letter, which gave me *indeed* a great deal of pleasure; – only dear Max there was one great disappointment in it, and that was to hear, that Mr. Bagier has the selfish intention of sending Brignoli to Madrid and of course you will have to go with him. Oh! Max *dear* can't you remain near me? do you wish to go? I can assure you, I cryed to Maurice about it and when he saw my

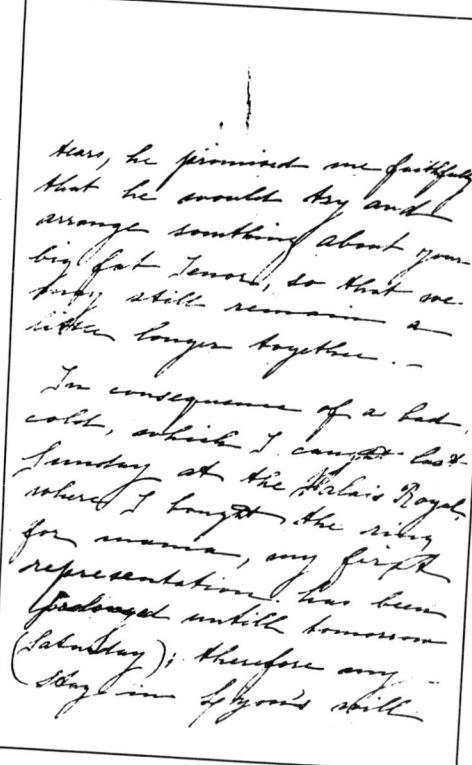

tears, he promised me faithfully that he would try and arrange something about your big fat tenor, so that we may still remain a little longer together – In consequence of a bad cold, which I caught last Sunday at the Palais Royal, where I bought the ring for mama, my first representation has been prolonged until tomorrow (Saturday); therefore my stay in Lyons will

Letter of Adelina Patti to Max Strakosch

ST. LAWRENCE HALL

PASQUALE BRIGNOLI, the "big fat tenor" who is referred to in Patti's letter and with whom she made her operatic debut as Lucia, New York, 1859.

MAX STRAKOSCH, was a brother of the noted pianist, teacher and impresario Maurice Strakosch who was born in Bohemia and came to the U.S. in 1848. Maurice married Amalia Patti, sister of Adelina. Maurice's company performed in New York, Chicago and Europe. He managed Adelina's concerts and when he returned to Europe Max took over his enterprises. Evidence of a love affair between Max and Adelina when she was 21 exists in letters of Adelina which are preserved in the Metropolitan Opera Archives. Max Strakosch brought the Italian Opera Company of the Academy of Music of N.Y. to the St. Lawrence Hall in 1856.

probably be lengthened for a few days, or even a week (another consolation). Now dearest Max I must conclude my letter, as I have a rehearsal with orchestra waiting for me. The most charming maiden Louise, sends to the most charming *old bachelor* Max her most charming compliments, and Maurice, papa send

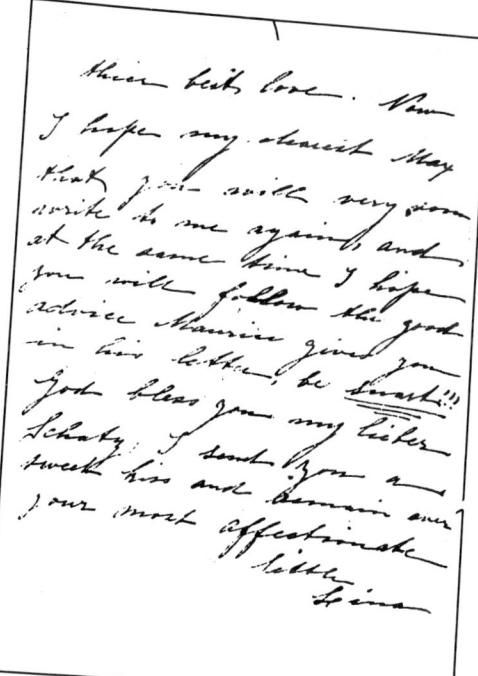

their best love. Now I hope my dearest Max that you will very soon write to me again, and at the same time I hope you will follow the good advice Maurice gives you in his letter, be *smart*!!! God bless you my lieber Schatz, I send you a sweet kiss and remain ever your most affectionate little
Lina.

ST. LAWRENCE HALL

RE-BIRTH AND SECOND CAREER

The circumstances which attended the renaissance of the St. Lawrence Hall quite possibly exceeded in dramatic quality those at the time of its inauguration in 1851. By 1951 it had become the home of the National Ballet for part of the year and a men's hostel for the remainder. However, in 1952 the Toronto Civic Historical Committee (later the Toronto Historical Board) recommended its restoration. In the years that followed other citizens' groups took up the cause and, after the passing of the National Centennial Act, City Council appointed Professor Eric Arthur Centennial advisor on civic building restorations. His credo was that "no project could be more in keeping with the spirit of the Centennial Act than a restoration of the St. Lawrence Hall". The Toronto Chapter of the Ontario Association of Architects was one of the most concerned groups and in 1966 W. E. Barnett, Chairman of the Chapter's Centennial Committee, enlisted the support of the Toronto Construction Association which was celebrating its own centennial and agreed to supply materials and labour. City Council's plans for Toronto's Centennial project had focussed, more or less, on an Arts Complex and the restoration of the St. Lawrence Hall. Economic realities and political priorities delayed constructive decisions and it was not until June 28, 1967 that the restoration became an official Centennial project. In the meantime problems with the reconstruction had not been lacking. On March 10, 1967, just as the evening rush hour traffic was starting, the whole northeast corner collapsed; in addition, strikes of the various construction unions caused a five-month delay. Despite setbacks, the enthusiasm and determination of everyone involved made possible the events of December 28, 1967. On that day Governor-General Roland Michener officially re-opened the St. Lawrence Hall with a symbolic lighting of the gas fire in the Great Hall; then Canadian soprano Elizabeth Benson Guy brought to the capacity crowd the songs that Jenny Lind sang in 1851 in the same hall.

'A miracle no one was killed'
Section of St. Lawrence Hall falls into busy intersection

Headline & Photo: Globe & Mail Mar 11, 1967   MTLB

CPD

ST. LAWRENCE HALL 1983

APPEARANCES	
1851	Grand Concert – Teresa Parodi, Amalia Patti, Maurice Strakosch, Miska Hauser. Excerpts from *Semiramide, Ernani, Maria Padilla,*
1851	Anna Bishop concert – excerpts from *La Cenerentola, Roberto Devreux, Lucia di Lammermoor*
1852	Jenny Lind in Concert
1852	The Black Swan (Miss Greenfield) in Concert
1852	Catherine Hayes in Concert
1853	First Grand Subscription Concert – operatic excerpts
1853	Ole Bull Concert with Adelina Patti
1854	Henrietta Sontag in Concert
1854	Rosa Devries in Concert
1855	Rosa Devries in Concert
1855	Grand Operatic Concert
1855	Pierce's Ethiopian Opera Troupe
1855	Curran's Ethiopian Opera Troupe
1856	Rosa Devries in Concert
1856	Operatic Concert – Teresa Parodi, Amalia Patti-Strakosch, Maurice Strakosch
1856	Anna de la Grange in Concert
1856	Pyne-Harrison English Opera Company
1856	Italian Opera Company, Academy of Music of New York
1856	Strakosch Grand Opera
1857	The Black Swan (Miss Greenfield) in Concert
1858	Holman's Juvenile Opera Troupe
1859	Italian Opera Company, Academy of Music of New York
1859	Concert – Piccolomini, Ghioni, Lorini, Maggiorotti
1859	Concert – Biscaccianti, Dennet
1859	French Operatic Concert Troupe
1860	Concert – Adelina Patti, Amalia Patti-Strakosch, Pasquale Brignoli, Sig. Ferri, Sig. Junca
1860	The Black Swan (Miss Greenfield) in Concert
1861	Italian Opera Company, Academy of Music of New York
1861	Holman Parlor Operas
1861	Concert – Carlotta Patti, Amalia Patti-Strakosch, Pasquale Brignoli, Ettore Barili (half-brother of the Pattis)
1861	John Carter with amateur musicians
1861	Italian Opera Company, Academy of Music of New York
1961	Anna Bishop in concert
1861	George Christy's Minstrels
1861	Craven's Minstrels and Burlesque Opera Troupe
1864	Amalia Patti-Strakosch in Concert
1864	Italian Opera Company, Academy of Music of New York

1860
CRYSTAL PALACE

To honour a Royal visitor – a concert by a popular English opera singer, in a building copied from London's Crystal Palace, built for the Great Exhibition in 1851.

Pencil drawing: Robert Newbery (1860?)   MTLB T10507

THE CRYSTAL PALACE, PROVINCIAL EXHIBITION BUILDINGS

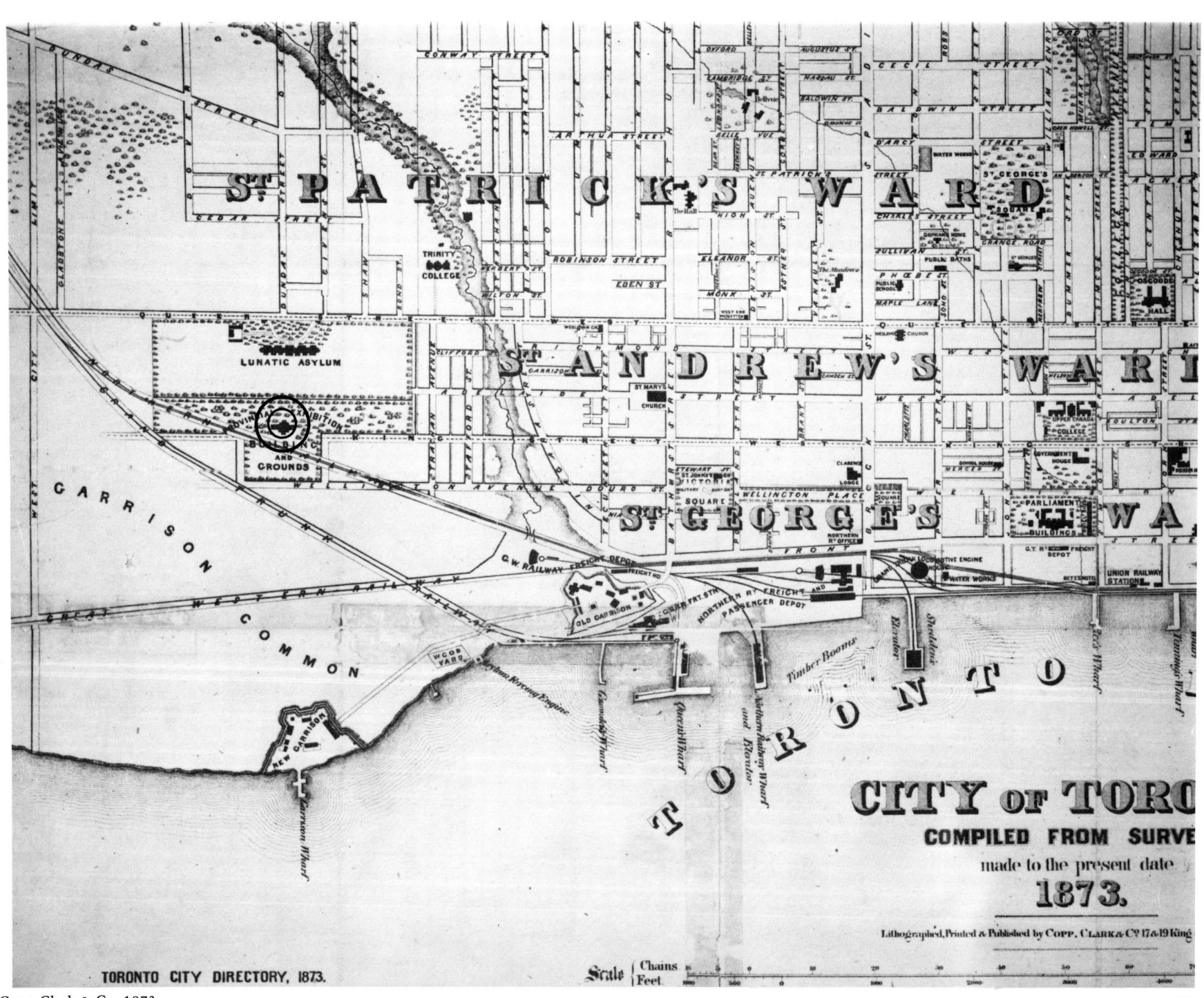

Copp Clark & Co. 1873

CRYSTAL PALACE

Toronto's first Agricultural Fair was held in 1846 on the grounds of Government House at King and Graves (Simcoe) Streets. In the years that followed Cobourg, Kingston, Niagara, Brockville, London and Ottawa vied for the benefits of playing host to this annual event. By 1858 a section of the Garrison Reserve in Toronto, immediately south of the lunatic asylum at 999 Queen Street, had been set aside and the Crystal Palace, inspired by London's for its Great Exhibition of 1851 and built of glass framed in iron, was erected. The architects were Sandford Fleming (inventor of Standard Time) and Collingwood Schreiber. In 1879 the building was moved to the present Canadian National Exhibition Grounds. It was destroyed by fire in 1906.

CRYSTAL PALACE!

FETE IN HONOUR OF

H.R.H. the Prince of Wales.

GRAND

PROMENADE CONCERT

ON

WEDNESDAY EVENING, SEPT. 12.

THE Citizens' Ball Committee take pleasure in announcing to the Citizens of Toronto and vicinity, that they have succeeded in effecting an engagement (for this occasion) with the world-renowned Cantatrice,

MADAME ANNA BISHOP,

ALSO,

MISS HATTIE BROWN,

THE YOUNG AMERICAN PRIMA DONNA, (LATE OF THE PARODI ITALIAN OPERA TROUPE)

F. RUDOLPHSEN,

THE EMINENT BARITONE.

T. A. HOGAN,

THE CELEBRATED PIANIST.

AND

FRED. MILLER,

Together with

POPPENBERG'S

GRAND ORCHESTRA OF TWENTY EMINENT PERFORMERS!

Single Tickets, including refreshments, 75c. Tickets admitting a lady and gentleman, $1. To be had at the Music Stores, Jewellery Stores, Book Stores, at the Hotels and at the door.

☞ The Refreshments will be provided by the well-known Caterer, Mr. Webb.

Doors open at 7½ o'clock. Concert will commence at Eight.

N.B.—Trains for the accommodation of the Concert will run from the Union Station every fifteen minutes, from 7½ o'clock until the close of the entertainment.

Toronto, Sept. 11, 1860. 3256-2t

Globe Sept 11, 1860   NLC

ANNA BISHOP sang at the Crystal Palace in 1860 and 1863

Promenade Concert

TO BE GIVEN

IN THE CRYSTAL PALACE,

ON

FRIDAY EVENING, JULY 20th.

BAND OF H. M. 17TH REGT.,

BY kind permission of Colonel McKinistry and Officers, will be present.

PROGRAMME:

PART 1.

1—OVERTURE. Masaniello. AUBER.
2—QUADRILLE. Mirella. COOTE.
3—SELECTION. Attila. VERDI.
4—VALSE. Claribel. GODFREY.
5—GALOP. Die Eng Flossel. GUNCH.

PART 2.

1—PAS REDOUBLE. La Postal. MARION.
2—POLKA. Selina. COOTE.
3—QUADRILLE. Glasgow. GUERNSEY.
4—SELECTION. Fra Diavolo.
5—VALSE. Fruhlings Grusse. GUNGT.
6—GALOP. Charlotten KIEHNIEO.

The Street Cars will run up to close of Concert. Tickets admitting a lady and gentleman, 25 cents. Refreshment table open all evening.

☞ Dancing to commence at eight o'clock.

GOD SAVE THE QUEEN.

Toronto, July 20. 5089-1t

Globe July 20, 1866   NLC

APPEARANCES	
1858	Inaugural Concert
1859	John Carter Concert
1860	Anna Bishop Concert
1863	Anna Bishop Concert
1866	Concert of operatic selections

HORTICULTURAL GARDENS

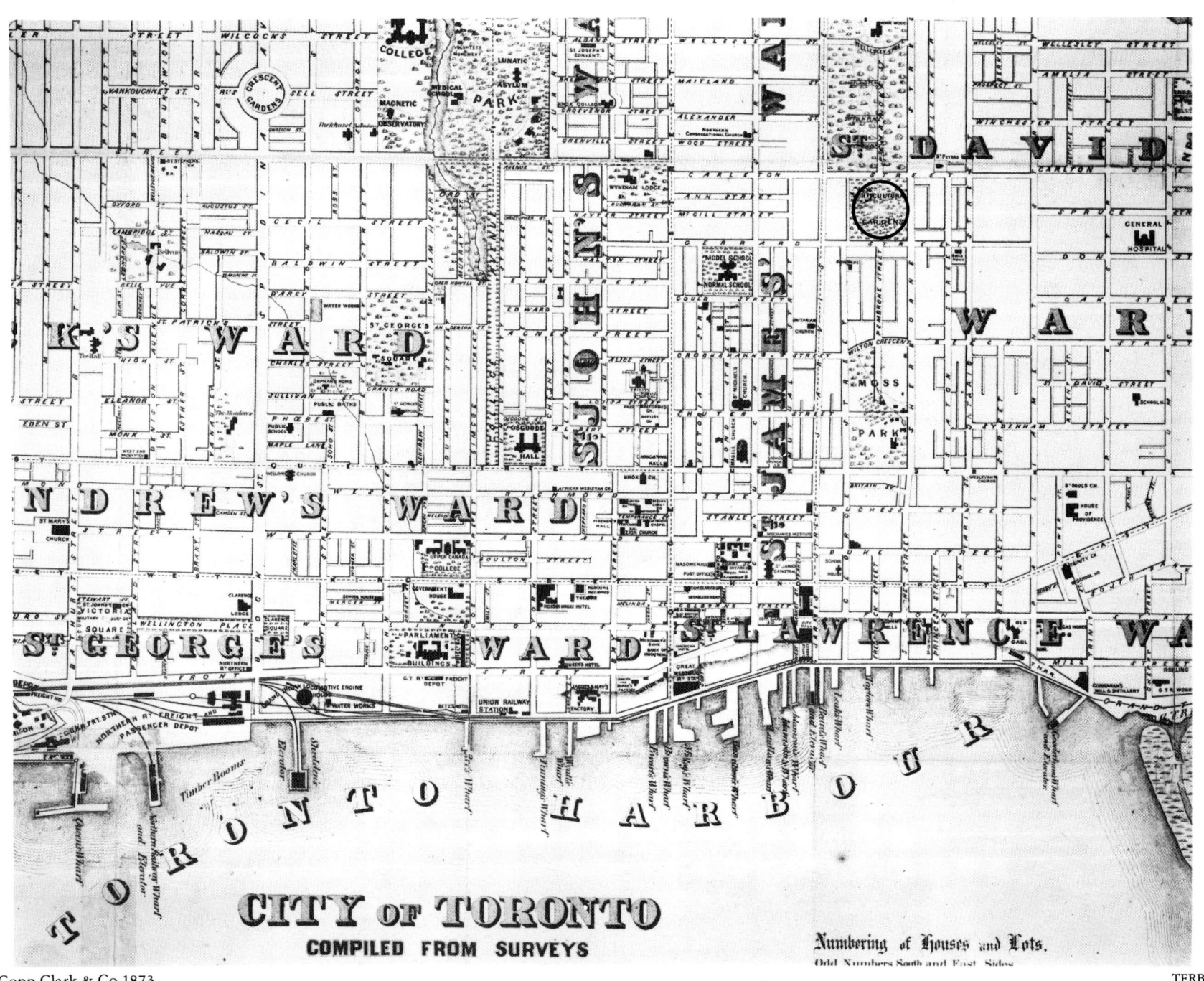

Copp Clark & Co 1873

TFRB

1861 HORTICULTURAL GARDENS

Both the Pavilion and the Gardens themselves were used for operatic concerts and performances.

Original Pavilion 1860-1878

HORTICULTURAL GARDENS

In 1860 an oval shaped parcel of land between Carlton, Gerrard, Sherbourne and Jarvis Streets, was opened as a Botanical Garden on the occasion of the visit of the Prince of Wales (later Edward VII). An oak tree planted by the Prince survived until 1938 and another, planted by Mrs. William Allan, wife of the owner of the lands, until 1957. In 1861 Mr. Allan gave the land to the Toronto Horticultural Society and in 1864 the city acquired from Mr. Allan additional land which it leased to the Society. The original pavilion became dangerously dilapidated and was replaced in 1878. Electricity replaced the gas lights in the Gardens in 1889 but not in the pavilion until 1896. On June 16, 1902 the second building was destroyed by fire. Numerous social events were held in what was considered the most complete hall in Toronto for large occasions.

Photo: Matthew Brady

Edward, Prince of Wales Oct. 13, 1860

1863, 1964

ANNA BISHOP

THE DIRECTORS BEG TO ANNOUNCE THEIR

SECOND GRAND CONCERT,

AT THE

HORTICUTURAL GARDENS,

ON

Monday Evening, July 17th.

JAS. C. KENNEY, MUSICAL DIRECTOR.

PART 1ST.

1.—Grand March—Strangers Yet..........Claribel.
   BAND OF THE QUEEN'S OWN.
2.—Duett—Il Trovatore....................Verdi.
   Miss TAYLOR and Mr. DREW.
3.—Solo—Let all obey.....................Leach.
   H. T. ALLEN.
4.—Cavatina—Il Trovatore................Verdi.
   Miss MARION TAYLOR.
5.—Song—Sweet Flowret..................Massini.
   C. H. DREW.
6.—Quartette—Dreaming of Angels......Blamphin.
   Messrs. DREW, ALLEN, KENNEY, and Miss TAYLOR.
7.—Musical Glasses,......................
   J. C. KENNEY.
8.—Adela Polka..........................Robinson.
   Cornet obligato with Band accompaniment.
   Mr. ROBINSON.

PART 2ND.

1.—Solo.................................
   H. T. ALLEN.
2. Song—Beats there a Heart, (by request)..Auber.
   C. H. DREW.
3.—Trio—Bohemian Girl—Thro' the World....Balfe.
   Messrs. DREW, ALLEN, and Miss TAYLOR.
4.—Galop—Helter Skelter.................Faust.
   BAND OF QUEEN'S OWN.

Gates open at 7 o'clock. Concert to commence at 8.
Admission, 20 Cents.

GOD SAVE THE QUEEN.

Globe, July 17, 1871 AO

HORTICULTURAL GARDENS !

GRAND OPERATIC CONCERT.

TUESDAY EVENING, JUNE 13.

ISABELLA McCULLOCH,

BRIGNOLI,

ROUCONI,

BOSCOVITZ.

Single admission, 30 cents. Lady and gentleman, 50 cents.

Tickets at A. & S. Nordheimer's; and at the gate on the evening of the performance.

Globe, June 12, 1871 AO

PASQUALE BRIGNOLI

The "big fat tenor" (see St. Lawrence Hall – Patti's letter to Strakosch) who sang with Adelina Patti at her debut.

Canadian Illustrated News July 26, 1879 MTLB

Second Pavilion 1878-1902

60

HORTICULTURAL GARDENS

MAURICE GRAU, Director of the Metropolitan Opera 1891-1903, Covent Garden 1896-1900, brought to the Horticultural Pavilion his own opera company in 1884 and Adelina Patti with Metropolitan Opera singers in 1892.

ADELINA PATTI

EMMA ALBANI, Canada's Queen of Song at the Pavilion in 1889.

HORTICULTURAL GARDENS.
ONE GRAND CONCERT,
SEPTEMBER 13.

Under the distinguished patronage of

His Excellency the Marquis of Lorne
AND
Her Royal Highness the Princess Louise.

ARTISTS:
SIG. P. BRIGNOLI, Tenor.
SIG. P. POGGI, Baritone.
SIG. ADAMOUSKI, Violinist.
SIG. DE NOVELLIS, Musical Director.
MME. THERESA CARREÑO, Pianist, and
MISS CARRIE E. MASON, Soprano.

Sale now open at Nordheimer's. Seats, $2, $1.50, and $1; admission 50c. The usual reduction made to ladies' schools. Orders by letter promptly executed.

GILMORE'S REGIMENTAL BAND, Sept. 19th and 23rd. Box office now open.

Globe, Sept 10, 1883 — NLC

HORTICULTURAL HALL
GREAT MUSICAL EVENT!
THE
NEVADA GRAND CONCERT.

Under the direction of Mr. C. A. CHIZZOLA,

Monday Evening Feb. 1st,
MME. EMMA NEVADA

Will be assisted by the following eminent artists:
Mons. Edmond Vergnet, Tenor.
Sig. Carlo Buti, Baritone.
Sig. Luigi Casati, Violinist.
Sig. Gustavo Lewita, Pianist.
Sig. Paolo Giorga, Musical Director. 4561

Prices—$1.50, $1 and 50c. No extra charge for reserved seats. Sale of seats will begin Thursday, Jan. 28th, at Nordheimer's Music Store.

Telegram Feb 1, 1886 — NLC

Amusements.

HORTICULTURAL GARDENS.
Under the Management of John Templeton.

A GRAND SPECTACULAR PRODUCTION.
MIKADO.
One Week, Commencing Monday, August 16. "Stage Enlarged," Increased Chorus and Orchestra. Special Scenery and Novel Effects.

ORIGINAL MIKADO COMPANY.

Special Matinee MONDAY (Civic Holiday) and SATURDAY.

Seats on sale at Nordheimer's Music Store this Morning at 10 o'clock.

Mail, August 19, 1866 — AO

ALBANI AT THE PAVILION.

A Crowded Audience Charmed by the Famous Singer.

The Pavilion has seen some large and brilliant audiences, but never any more so than that which occupied it last when the Canadian Queen of Song made her first appearance in Toronto after a lapse of six years. Every seat was taken and many campstools had to be placed in the passages and still there were many, both ladies and gentlemen, who were compelled to stand. The brilliancy of dress and flowers, usual to our audiences, was exhibited to a marked degree. The appearance of Mme. Albani was the signal for round after round of applause, which only subsided when the introduction to the "Ah Fors 'e Lui," from "Traviata," was heard. When Mme. Albani commenced to sing the recognition of the giant voice of the world was instantaneous and every other sound was hushed. The voice which has charmed most of the civilised world proved to have lost none of its charm. Its wonderfully clear and bright quality, resonant even to the lightest whisper, was the same as when first it won for its owner fame and renown. To this rare clearness and roundness, and with its absolute fidelity to pitch, a rare gift nowadays, is to be added the greatest flexibility and distinctness in the bravura work, and an extremely high compass. Mme. Albani's versatility was admirably shown in the "Traviata" aria and its contrast with the encore song,

"ANGELS EVER BRIGHT AND FAIR,"

which the most perfect sostenuto was combined with strong pathetic feeling. Another gem was the balcony scene from "Lohengrin," sung in German, but what is probably the most popular number was the beautiful "Bird Song" from Handel's "Il Penseroso," in which the brilliant roulades were admirably supported the efficient flute obligato played by Mr. Barrett. Encores were, of course, insisted on, and floral compliments were profuse; recalls eliciting the "Shadow Song" from "Dinorah," and "Home, Sweet Home," the latter touching the hearts of all present. Not the least charm of Mme. Albani's singing is her evident conscientiousness and desire to do her best to please her audience, to which must be added her personal grace and attractiveness. Mme. Albani's support is well worthy of so great an artist.

Globe, Feb. 12, 1889 — AO

HORTICULTURAL PAVILION PAVILION PAVILION

1 NIGHT ONLY, To-morrow Eve

Under the direction of Abbey, Schoeffel & Grau, one Grand Operatic Concert by

MME. ADELINA PATTI
MME. ADELINA PATTI

Assisted by Mme. Fabbri, M. Guille, Sig. Del Puente, Sig. Novara and Sig. Arditi, together with full orchestra.

A special sale of seats on lower floor at $4 each will begin this morning.

Globe, Jan. 25, 1892 — MTLB

Canadian Illustrated News, Feb. 24, 1877 — MTLB

PATTI AT THE PAVILION.

THE GREAT SINGER DRAWS AN IMMENSE AUDIENCE — A BRILLIANT PROGRAMME AND A SUCCESSFUL EVENING.

It may not seem gallant to say how many years the name of Adelina Patti has been one to charm thousands with, yet that same charm has lost none of its power, as the large audience that filled the pavilion abundantly proved. Every seat was filled when at the close of the first part the lesser lights who had bought admission tickets overflowed into the vacant seats. The audience was one typical of Toronto fashion and elegance, being brilliant in full-dress effects, and was by no means niggardly in its applause of the programme offered. The concert was given under the direction of Messrs. Abbey, Schoeffel and Grau, Mr. O. B. Sheppard being the local manager. The programme that was placed in the hands of the audience stated that "the entire Metropolitan Opera House chorus and orchestra" would take part, but the chorus did not materialise, while the orchestra, some twenty in number, were conducted by Sig. Arditi. The band was very good, but sadly lacking in strings, only two first violins being in the party, a combination which somewhat detracted from the artistic effect of the pieces which fell to their share. These were the "Oberon" and "Semiramide" overtures and Arditi's gavotte "L'Ingenue."

The programme was divided into two parts, the first comprising miscellaneous selections, while the second part was made up of selections from Rossini's "Semiramide." Madame Patti, of course, was the centre of attraction, though she was down for only two solos and a duet. Her first solo was the Rondo from "Lucia," which she sang exquisitely. Her voice showed less of the wear and tear of the fell destroyer, time, than was noticeable when she appeared here five years ago, and was full and resonant, and replete with the old-time purity and beauty, the smooth cantabile character of the selection serving to show her at her best. In the florid passages their ease and ready flow made no demands that she was not able to meet to the fullest extent, while the chromatic runs were sung with the most delightful delicacy and grace as well as with the most charming clearness and accuracy. Great enthusiasm was aroused by this number, which led to a double encore, "The Last Rose of Summer," and "Home, Sweet Home" rewarding the audience for their plaudits. Not so satisfactory was her rendering of the "Bel Raggio" from "Semiramide," in which greater effort was noticeable, with the effect of loss of ease and purity of tone. This defect, again, was more than counterbalanced by the delightful tone-quality shown in the duet from "Semiramide," with M'lle G. Fabbri, in which the two voices were blended most beautifully.

M'lle Fabbri has a contralto voice of great range and of most exquisite quality in her lower register, being rich, sympathetic and highly dramatic. She gave an excellent rendering of the Romanza from "La Gioconda," and showed the excellence of her training in the florid Cavatina from "Semiramide." All her runs and cadenzas were done most accurately and with perfect intonation. Signor Guille, already favorably known here, was the tenor of the party, and never sang better in Toronto. His rendering of "O Muto Asil" from "William Tell," and "Cielo e Mar" from "Gioconda" showed what can be done by an almost perfect voice and method, and he was most deservedly encored, responding with "La Donna e Mobile" and "Di Quella Pira," giving in all his selections a ringing high C. Signor Novara, the basso, has been here before and on this occasion won hearty applause by his careful and correct singing. The baritone, Signor del Puente, sang the well-known "Il Balen" and "Toreador," being encored for the former.

Globe, Jan. 27, 1892 — MTLB

HORTICULTURAL GARDENS

Baritone GIUSEPPE DEL PUENTE who took part in Patti's concert MM

LUIGI ARDITI, conductor for Adelina Patti and Met singers MM

Telegram, Oct. 23, 1924 MTLB
O.B. SHEPPARD, local manager for Patti's concert at the Pavilion.

Horticultural Pavilion

TO-NIGHT! TO-NIGHT! TO-NIGHT!

GRAND POPULAR CONCERT.

ANTON SEIDL

And his entire Metropolitan Orchestra.

EMMA JUCH

And 16 Eminent Soloists—85 Artists 85.
Popular prices. Popular Prices. Reserved seats, 50c, 75c and $1, at Nordheimers' to-day.

UNDER ROYAL PATRONAGE.

Globe, Apr. 22, 1893 MTLB

APPEARANCES

1861	Summer concerts by 30th Regiment – music of Weber, Rossini, Verdi, Flotow, Meyerbeer, Auber and Balfe
1863	Anna Bishop – Vocal Concert
1864	Anna Bishop – Vocal Concert
1871	Brignoli Opera & Concert Society Grand Concert
1874	Grand English Opera Combination
1874	Grand English & Italian Opera Combination
1875	Holman English Opera Troupe
1876	Holman English Opera Troupe
1877	Holman English Opera Troupe
1877	Brignoli Italian Opera Company
1879	Fifth Avenue Opera Company
1879	Amateur Operatic Society of Toronto
1880	Toronto Church Opera Company
1880	Amateur Juvenile Company (Toronto)
1880	D'Oyly Carte Opera Company
1880	Holman Opera Company
1881	Norcross Comic Opera Company of Boston
1882	Haverly Comic Opera Company
1883	Collier & Rice's Comic Opera Company
1883	Fay Templeton and Her Star Opera Company
1883	Standard Opera Company, New York
1883	Grand Concert – Brignoli and others
1884	Grau Opera Company
1886	Emma Nevada – Vocal Concert
1886	Fay Templeton's Opera Company
1889	Emma Albani – Vocal Concert
1892	Adelina Patti with singers of the Metropolitan Opera Company, New York
1893	Anton Seidl and Company

1861
YORKVILLE TOWN HALL

The site for opera production moves outside the old city core.

Neg: Salmon 147 CTA

YORKVILLE TOWN HALL,
West side of Yonge Street, 2 blocks north of Bloor Street.

YORKVILLE TOWN HALL

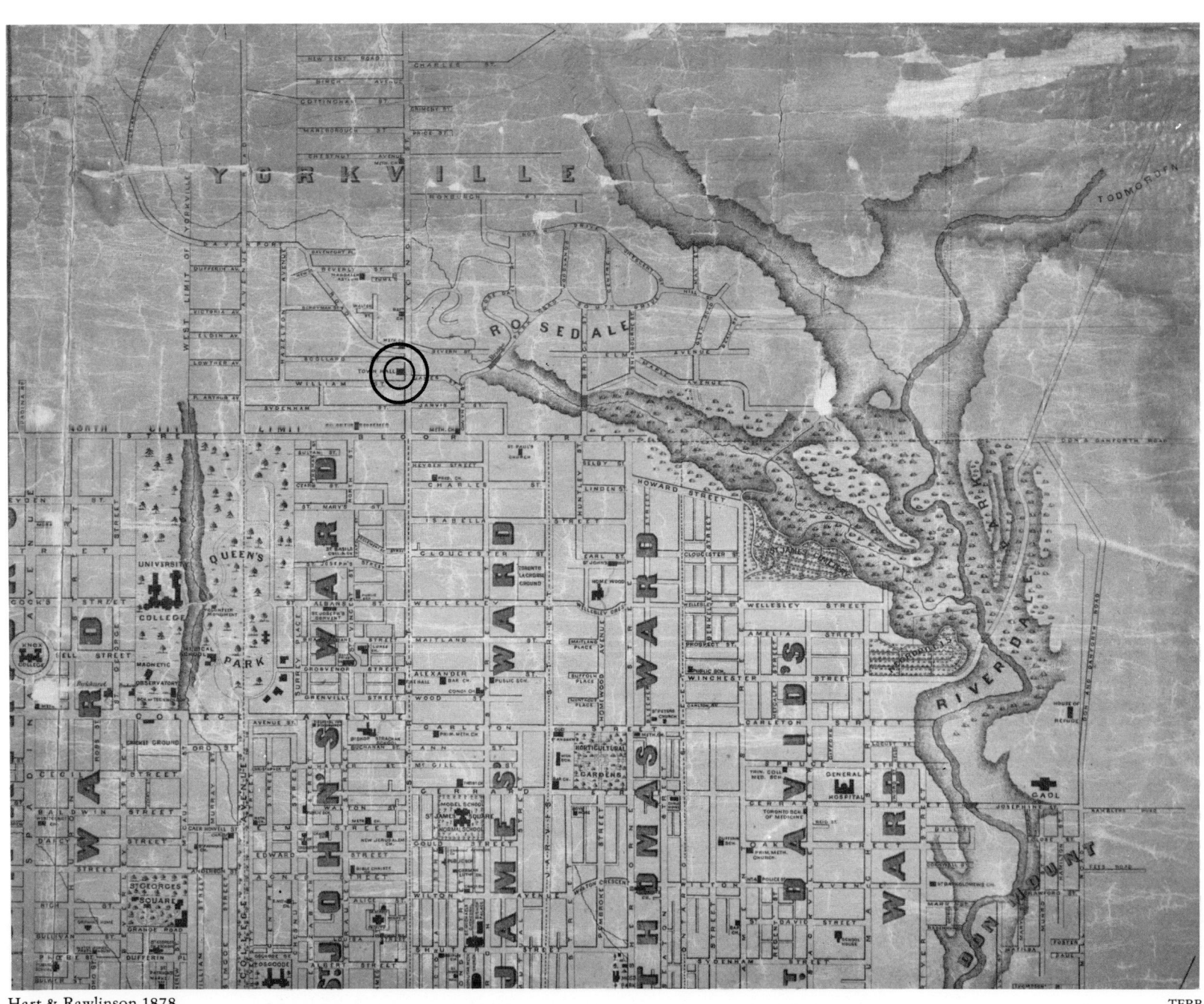

Hart & Rawlinson 1878

TFRB

YORKVILLE TOWN HALL

YORKVILLE TOWN HALL was built in 1859 by architect William Hay and was located on the west side of Yonge Street, opposite the present Collier Street. It was demolished in 1942. The Coat of Arms displayed symbols indicating the trades of the first four aldermen – a beer barrel with an S (Mr. John Severn), a brick mould with an A (Mr. Thomas Atkinson); an anvil with a W (Mr. James Wallis); a jack plane with a D (Mr. James Dobson), and centre, the animal's head being the mark of Mr. Peter Hutty, the butcher. In 1861 a Ball and Concert were given as part of the Toronto Street Railway Opening Festivities and June 1865 saw three concerts (in aid of the Organ Fund of Old St. Paul's Church, Yorkville) of excerpts from Handel's *Messiah* and *Creation*. When Yorkville was incorporated with Toronto in 1883, the Council Chamber was used as a public library, and continued in that capacity until a library was built on Yorkville Avenue in 1907. In its last days the Hall was the armouries of the Yorkville Company of the York Rangers.

Drawing: John Wood NGI

MICHAEL BALFE, composer of *THE BOHEMIAN GIRL*

GRAND CONCERT FOR THE BENEFIT OF THE POOR OF YORKVILLE.

Mrs. Carre's Lyceum Company will present BALFE'S "BOHEMIAN GIRL," with full chorus and orchestral accompaniment; and also the laughable farce, "The Young Amazon," Thursday Evening, January 20th, 1876. Admission 25c; reserved seats, &c. Doors open at 7; performance to commence at 8 o'clock.

Globe Jan. 19, 1876 NLC

STREET RAILWAY FESTIVAL!

ON THE OCCASION OF THE OPENING OF THE

Toronto Street Railway,

ON

TUESDAY NEXT, THE 10th INSTANT,

A

GRAND FESTIVAL!

WILL TAKE PLACE,

UNDER THE PATRONAGE OF

His Worship the Mayor,
The Hon. G. W. Allan,
Col. Mauleverer, C. B., 30th Regiment,
The Rev. Dr. McCaul,
J. B. Robinson, Esq., M.P.P.,
John Crawford, Esq., M.P.P.,
The Hon. George Brown,
Doctor Connor, M. P. P.,
Angus Morrison, Esq., M.P.P.
The Reeve of Yorkville,
The Hon. Chief Justice Draper, C. B.,
The Hon. John Ross,
The Hon. J. C. Morrison,
The Hon. J. H. Cameron,
The Recorder,
Lieut. Colonel Jarvis,
Lieut. Colonel Durie,
D. L. McPherson, Esq.
F. Widder, Esq.

PROGRAMME

OF

THE DAY'S PROCEEDINGS.

THE DEJEUNER!

AT TWO O'CLOCK in the afternoon a Grand *Dejeuner* will be held at

YORKVILLE.

TICKETS 50c. each, to be had of the Secretary, the members of the Committee, at the Terrapin and Fountain Restaurants, and at the Albion Hotel.

THE CONCERT!

In the Evening a Grand Concert of Vocal and Instrumental Music will be given

IN THE TOWN HALL, YORKVILLE.

Under the able direction of Mr. J. P. CLARKE, MUS. BAC., on which occasion

The Band of the 30th Regiment,

(By the kind permission of the Colonel and Officers) will be present.

Mr. John Carter,
Mr. Noverre,
Mr. Andrews,
Mr. Cooper,
Mrs. J. Beverly Robinson,
Miss Davis,
Mr. McCarrol,
Mr. Armstrong,
Mr. Elrick,

And several other distinguished Amateurs have consented to render their valuable assistance.

CONDUCTOR............Mr. J. P. CLARKE, MUS. BAC.
LEADER...............Mr. NOVERRE.

☞ Doors open at Seven ; Concert to commence at Eight o'clock precisely.

THE BALL!

The Quadrille Band will be in attendance

FOR THE BALL,

Which will immediately succeed the Concert, under the direction of the following

STEWARDS:

Major Dillon, 30th Regt.
Capt. McPherson, do.
Capt. Smith, do.
Capt. Clarkson, do.
William Armstrong, Esq.
Wm. B. Heward, Esq.
Lewis W. Ord, Esq.
A. M. Clark, Esq.
G. S. McKay, Esq.
Geo. Perkins, Esq.

Gentlemen's Ticket for Concert and Ball, $1 50 ; Ladies' do., $1 each ; to be had at the Music Store of Messrs. A. & S. Nordheimer, Toronto ; at the store of Mr. J. Macdonald, and at the Post-office, Yorkville.

THE RAILWAY

WILL BE OPENED by a Train leaving the Railway Depot at ONE O'CLOCK, P. M. The Cars will continue to run during the remainder of the day, and at intervals of ten minutes during the night.

N. B.—Members of the Royal Canadian Yacht Club and Officers of Militia will please appear in uniform.

G. S. McKAY,
Secretary of the Committee Street Railway Festival.

Toronto, Sept. 4, 1861.

Globe Sept. 4, 1861 MTLB

CONCERT AND TABLEAUX,

OLD ST. PAUL'S CHURCH,

TOWN HALL, YORKVILLE,

Friday, May 19th, 1871.

PROGRAMME.

PART I.

SONG.....................Mr. Baines
TABLEAU, King Lear - "Cordelia and the Doctor"
RECITATION, "The Bells,".......Mr. Jas. B. Kay
TABLEAU "Prince Charles Edward and Flora Macdonald."
SONG, "Love's Request," (Illustrated) Mrs. A. Jarvis
RECITATION, "Shakespeare"......Mr. Jas. B. Kay
SONG, Consider the Lilies.....Mrs. J. B. Robinson
TABLEAU, Irish Courtship
Intermission - 10 minutes—PART II.
SONG, Then You'll Remember Me.....Mr. Heron
TABLEAU, Hiawatha
QUARTETTE Hark ! I hear the Organ peal, Adelphi Club
RECITATION............Mr. Jas. B. Kay
TABLEAU, Kenilworth.
SONG The Lover and the Bird......Mrs. A. Jarvis
TABLEAU, Mary Stuart going forth to Execution
BALLAD, (Illustrated)........Mrs. J. G. Rhodes
SONG.................Mr. C Baines
TABLEAU, Nursery Rhymes

Doors open at 7 o'clock. Concert to commence at 8 precisely. Tickets 50 cents. God save the Queen

Globe May 19, 1871 NLC

APPEARANCES

1861   J. P. Clarke & Amateur Performers-Selections from *Il Trovatore*
1866   Grand Concert-Selections from *Il Trovatore, La Sonnambula*
1876   Mrs. Carre's Lyceum Company

MUSIC HALL (MECHANICS' INSTITUTE)

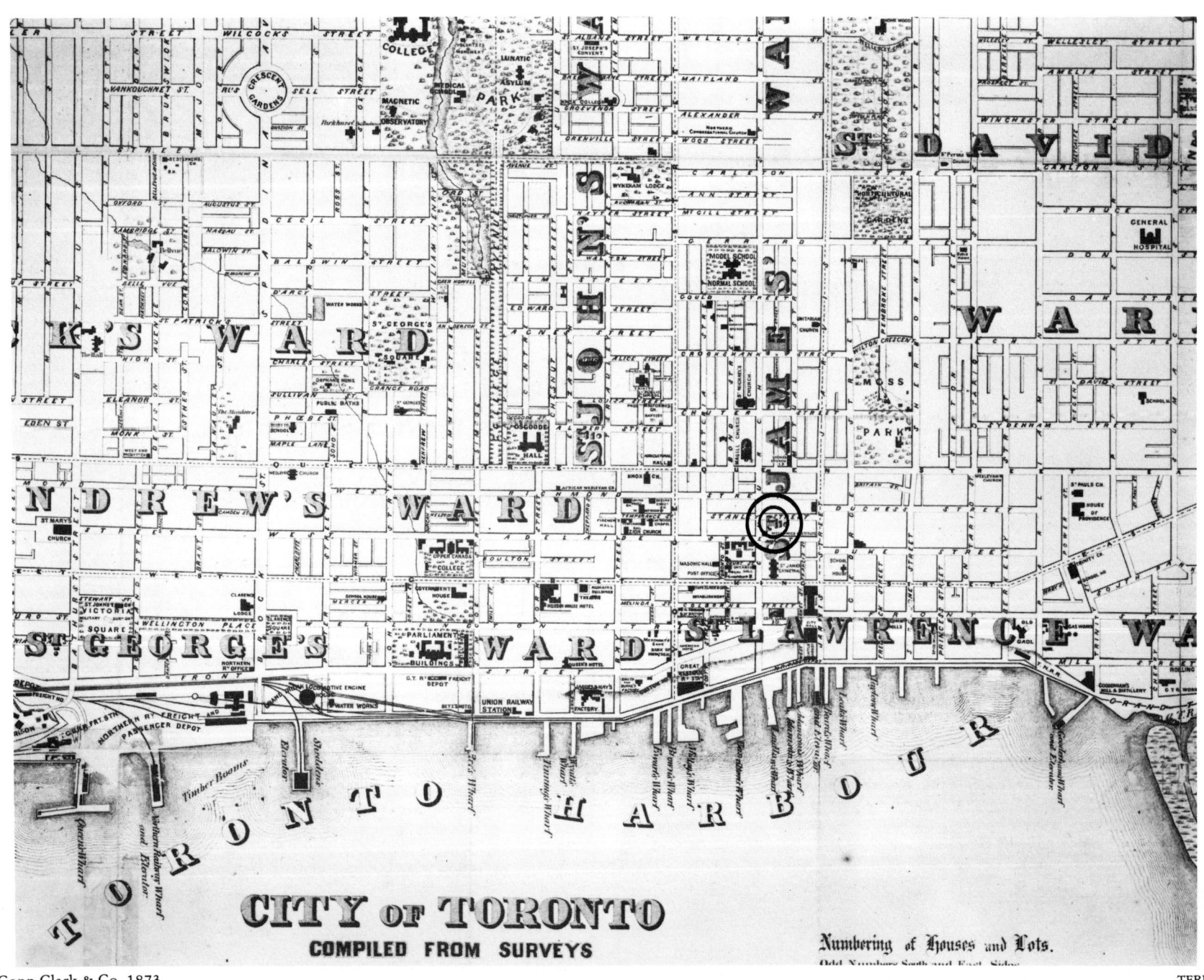

Copp Clark & Co. 1873

TFRB

1861
MUSIC HALL
(Mechanics' Institute)

An early instance of an educational organization's promotion of music

Armstrong, Beere & Hime

North-East corner of Church & Adelaide

MUSIC HALL (MECHANICS' INSTITUTE)

The Mechanics' Institute was organized in York in 1830 for the improvement of mechanics and others by means of a reference and circulating library. In 1858 the Institute moved into its last home at the north-east corner of Church and Adelaide Streets, and three years later the work of decorating a Music Hall in the building was completed. It was opened with a grand ball and a concert by Madame Wookey on October 1, 1861. In 1883 the Free Library By-Law was passed and the Institute became merged into the Public Library.

THE MUSIC HALL OF THE NEW MECHANICS' INSTITUTE.

The work of decorating the Hall of the New Mechanics' Institute is rapidly approaching completion, and when finished the room gives promise of being the finest in Toronto for Lectures, Concerts, Balls, &c. The Music Hall is situated on the first floor in the eastern portion of the building, and access is gained to it by a broad and handsome stairway leading from the Church-street entrance. It is seventy-six feet in length by fifty-three feet in breadth, and is lighted by three large windows at each end of the room. The ceiling, which springs from a handsome cornice, is thirty-six feet from the floor, and has a very large domical centre panel on which is painted a number of figures representing the Muses. The Hall will be lighted in the evenings by gasaliers projecting from the walls. On the eastern side of the room a large platform has been erected, but it has been suggested that a portion of it should be so constructed that it can be removed for balls, which would certainly be a great improvement. In rear of the platform are ante-rooms for performers, and also an arched recess, supported by Corinthian columns, in which it is intended to place the organ. On the western side of the hall a semi-circular platform projects from the wall, and is supported by neat iron columns. Mr. A. Todd, artist, is busily engaged decorating and frescoeing the walls, and the hall, when finished, will present a very handsome appearance as great taste has been displayed in the decorations. It has been arranged that the hall will be opened to the public on Tuesday the first proximo, on which occasion Madame Wookey will give a grand concert of vocal and instrumental music. It has been announced that on the occasion she will have the able assistance of Mr. J. P. Clarke, Mus. Bac., Mr. J. D. Humphreys, Mr. J. McCarroll, Miss Wookey, and other talented musicians. Madame Wookey since her arrival in Toronto has on numerous occasions volunteered her able services in behalf of the several charitable institutions, and it is confidently anticipated that on the occasion of this her first concert in this city she will be greeted by a large audience. There will be a grand ball after the concert. Full particulars will be published in a few days.

Globe, Sept. 18, 1861   AO

Contralto AMALIA PATTI-STRAKOSCH appeared at the Music Hall in 1867.

ANNA BISHOP, was at the Music Hall in 1861, 1863 and 1864.

INAUGURATION OF THE NEW MUSIC HALL!

GRAND PROMENADE

CONCERT & BALL!

TUESDAY, OCTOBER 1st.

MADAME WOOKEY

HAS THE HONOUR to announce that she has been permitted by the President and Directors of the Toronto Mechanics' Institute to formally OPEN THE NEW MUSIC HALL with a

GRAND CONCERT AND BALL,

WHICH WILL TAKE PLACE

On Tuesday, October the 1st.

MADAME WOOKEY will be assisted on the occasion by the principal Professional and Amateur Musicians of the City and neighbourhood who have kindly volunteered their services.

GENTLEMEN'S TICKETS $2 50; LADIES' TICKETS $1.

☞ An interesting and attractive programme, containing full particulars, will be issued in a few days.

GOD SAVE THE QUEEN!

Toronto, Sept. 24.   3575-34 STuS

Globe, Sept. 24, 1861   NLC

OPENING OF THE NEW MUSIC HALL.

The interior alterations and fitting up of the Mechanics' Institute may be said to be finished with the completion of the Music Hall, which is destined henceforth to become the local habitation of the Muses. Hitherto they have moved like shadows between the St. Lawrence and Temperance Halls—at one time banished from their temporary resting place by the noisy declamations of popular speakers, or, at other times by the still more noisy demonstrations of unruly mobs. At last they have found a fit abode, no more to be ruthlessly assailed or cast adrift by the unfeeling and prosaic world. The concert and ball last night was a fitting inauguration for such a building, and Madame Wookey deserves every praise from the public for her exertions in getting up the entertainment. The Hall, by gas-light, looked superb. The ornamentation is chaste, and does not display the needless and often vulgar decorations that deface many similar places. The colouring is light and cheerful, without being too glaring; and the allegorical figures on the roof are drawn with ease, while the attitudes are graceful and without that coarseness which distinguishes the "half nude angels"—to quote a remark of the defunct Old Countryman—which adorn the walls of the St. Lawrence Hall. The dome is especially fine, the colouring being so arranged that while it pleases the eye, it also gives variety and relief to the surrounding decorations. The pannelling on the side walls is not yet finished, and, with the exception of the east end wall, we think they would be better as they are. The gas brackets will interfere with the completeness of the figures, and, besides, there is no necessity for them. There is, however, a useless length of platform, and if any alterations are made, we would suggest that it terminate at the columns on either side of the arch. Between these points there is ample room for a platform large enough for all ordinary purposes. The programme of the concert was well selected, and embraced some fine pieces from the great composers. Without attempting anything in the way of criticism we may particularize the solo and chorus from "Stabat Mater" and the duet from Mozart's "M'abbraccio Argerio," sung by Madame Wookey and Mr. J. D. Humphreys. In the first the chorus was correct and well balanced, but the singers stood too far back under the arch and the notes were in consequence somewhat confused and indistinct. When the singer is at the front of the platform, however, every note is clear and well defined. The quartette, "God Save the Queen," with variations, by Messrs. Noverre, was well performed and was loudly applauded. Miss Wookey's "Swiss Echo Song" was tastefully rendered and received an encore. In the second part the duet and chorus from "Il Trovatore" was the principal feature, and it was rendered in every respect worthy of the music. Miss Monro, who possesses a fine voice, acquitted herself in a very creditable manner in the two pieces which she sung, and was loudly applauded. At the termination of the concert there was a grand ball. Maule's quadrille band furnished the music, and those present appeared to enjoy themselves in a very high degree, and dancing was kept up with great spirit till a late hour. Mr. Coleman, as caterer, supplied abundance of excellent refreshments, and the tables in the lecture room were well patronized during the evening. The concert and ball were very successful, but it is to be regretted that the entertainment was not more numerously attended.

Globe, Oct. 2, 1861   AO

MUSIC HALL (MECHANICS' INSTITUTE)

MAX STRAKOSCH
Brought his Opera Troupe to the Music Hall in June of 1865 and Christine Nilsson in 1871.

PASQUALE BRIGNOLI
Sang in concerts at the Music Hall in 1867, 1870 and 1871.

Swedish coloratura soprano CHRISTINE NILSSON created the role of Ophelia in Ambroise Thomas' *Hamlet* and sang Marguerite in the Metropolitan Opera's opening production, *Faust*, Oct. 22, 1883.

The Protestant Orphans' Home Ball held at the Mechanics' Institute Music Hall on April 19, 1870. The photograph of the gala event was made by the Toronto firm of Notman and Fraser, using a new technique developed early in 1870, the 'composite photo'. Photographing group scenes had always posed problems. A large negative required a lengthy exposure, and people in a crowd invariably moved, blurring the picture. In a 'composite photo', however, the figures were photographed individually or in small groups, then properly scaled, hand-tinted, fitted together into a composition, and a background painted in behind them.

Soprano EUPHROSYNE PAREPA-ROSA wife of impresario Carl Rosa, was at the Music Hall twice in 1867 – in May and October.

American contralto
ANNIE LOUISE CARY

MUSIC HALL.
NILSSON'S FAREWELL

MAX STRAKOSCH has the honour to announce to the public of Toronto and vicinity, that M'lle

CHRISTINA NILSSON.

Will give her FAREWELL CONCERT in this city, on WEDNESDAY EVENING, MAY 31st, at 8 o'clock

M'lle CHRISTINA NILSSON will be assisted by

Miss ANNIE LOUISE CARY, the eminent American Contralto;

Sig. BRIGNOLI, the popular Tenor;

Sig. RANDOLFI, the favourite Baritone;

Mr. HENRY VIEUXTEMPS, the world-renowned Violin-Virtuoso.

Musical Director and Conductor, Sig BOSONI.

General admission, $2. Reserved seats, $1 and $2 extra, according to location. Seats for sale, commencing Friday, May 26th, at 10 a.m., at Messrs A & S. Nordheimer's music store. Doors open at 7:15, commence at 8. The Steinway Piano is used at all Nilsson Concerts.

Globe, May 23, 1871

MUSIC HALL.
For Six Nights only, commencing MONDAY, June 12th,

CRANE, DREW AND DAVIDGE,

In an Operatic Combination, supported by 15 talented artists, of acknowledged ability.

ON MONDAY NIGHT

Will be presented Planche's operatic extravaganza, THE INVISIBLE PRINCE, to commence with the laughable farce, THE DEAD SHOT. Doors open at 7:30 p.m. Performance to commence at 8:15. Reserved seats 50c. Can be secured at Messrs. Nordheimer's without extra charge.

Globe, June 12, 1871

Notman and Fraser
THE MECHANICS' INSTITUTE

APPEARANCES		
1861	Inaugural Concert	
1863	The Black Swan (Miss Greenfield)	
1863	Anna Bishop	
1863	Carlotta Patti in Concert	
1864	Anna Bishop	
1864	*Lay of the Bell* – Romberg	
1865	L. M. Gottschalk and Troupe	
1865	Italian Opera Company	
1865	Max Strakosch and Troupe	
1865	Grand Concert – Marie Abbott, Mrs. F. L. Fiske, George Simpson	
1866	*Stabat Mater* – Rossini	
1866	*Il Trovatore* – Verdi	
1866	Holman Opera Troupe	
1867	Strakosch Opera Troupe	
1867	*La Sonnambula* – Bellini	
1867	Grand Concerts	
1867	Marietta Gazzaniga	
1868	H. L. Bateman's French Opera Bouffe	
1870	Brignoli's Opera Company	
1871	Christine Nilsson Farewell Concert	
1871	Crane, Drew and Davidge Operatic Combination	
1874	*The Black Crook*	

GRAND OPERA HOUSE

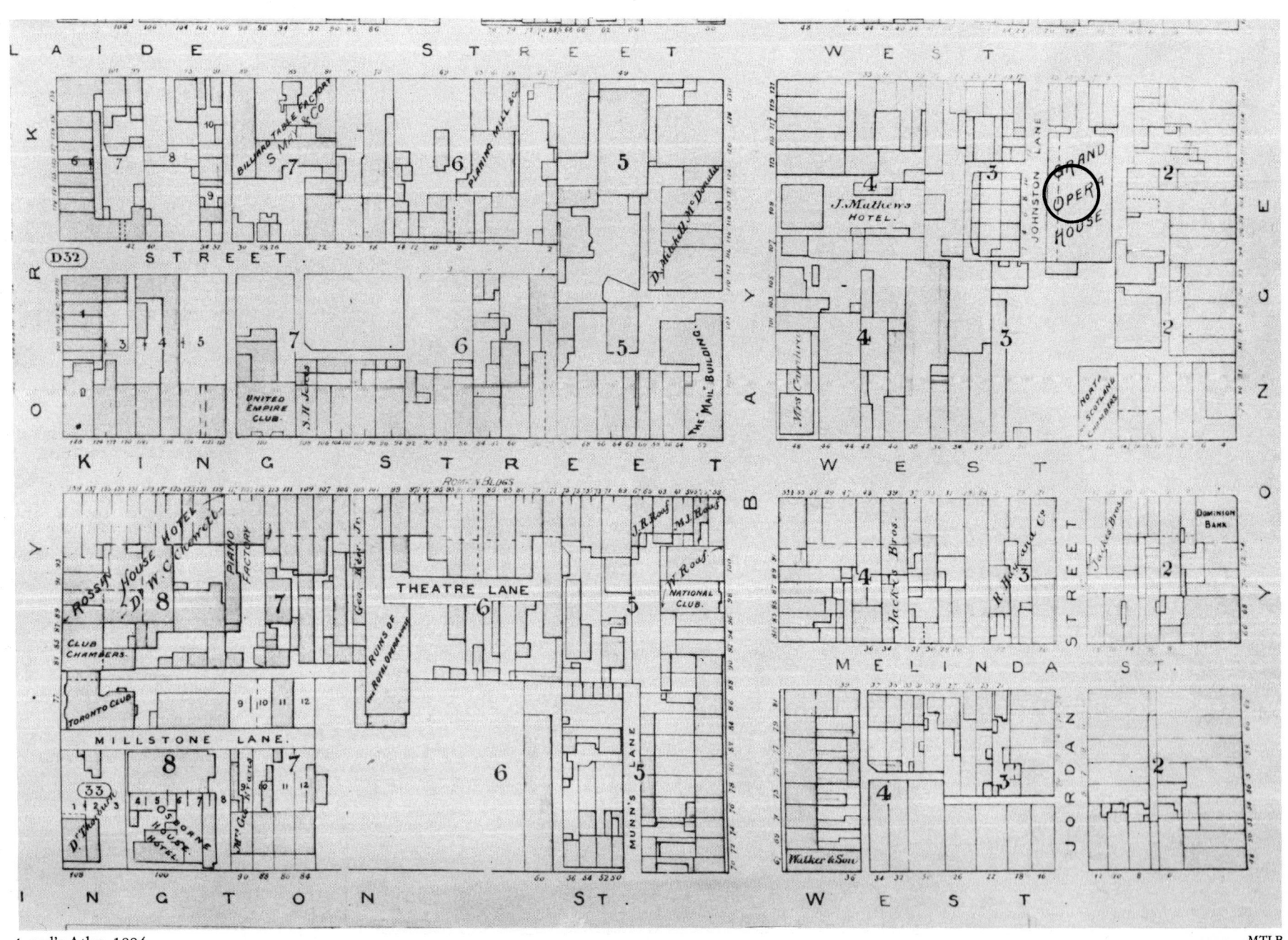

Goad's Atlas, 1884

1874
GRAND OPERA HOUSE

Within one week the opening of two Opera Houses!
Neither of which survived an opera alone.

Canadian Illustrated News Aug. 29, 1874   MTLB

THE GRAND OPERA HOUSE

GRAND OPERA HOUSE

The Grand Opera House, with a seating capacity of 1750, was opened by Mrs. Charlotte Morrison on September 21, 1874 on the south side of Adelaide Street, between Yonge and Bay Streets. It was destroyed by fire in 1879, rebuilt in 51 days and re-opened with *As You Like It* starring the great favourite Adelaide Neilson. Successors to Mrs. Morrison were Augustus Pitou, O.B. Sheppard and the man of mystery, Ambrose Small. Among the glittering non-operatic stars who appeared during its 52 years were Sarah Bernhardt, Sir Henry Irving, Ellen Terry, Dan Daly, Maurice Barrymore (father of John, Ethel and Lionel), John Drew, Sir Herbert Beerbohm Tree, Sir John Martin Harvey, Mme. Modjeska. George Rignold, who first appeared in 1876, was famous because of his horse which accompanied him everywhere. On one occasion the horse climbed the stairs of a photographer's studio at the corner of King and Yonge. The resulting portrait is reported to have had a beneficial effect on the box office. Newspaper advertisements during the 20th century indicate that the theatre became increasingly devoted to drama and vaudeville. After an illustrious and eventful career the house was finally demolished in 1927 when the days of grand opera houses were believed to be at an end.

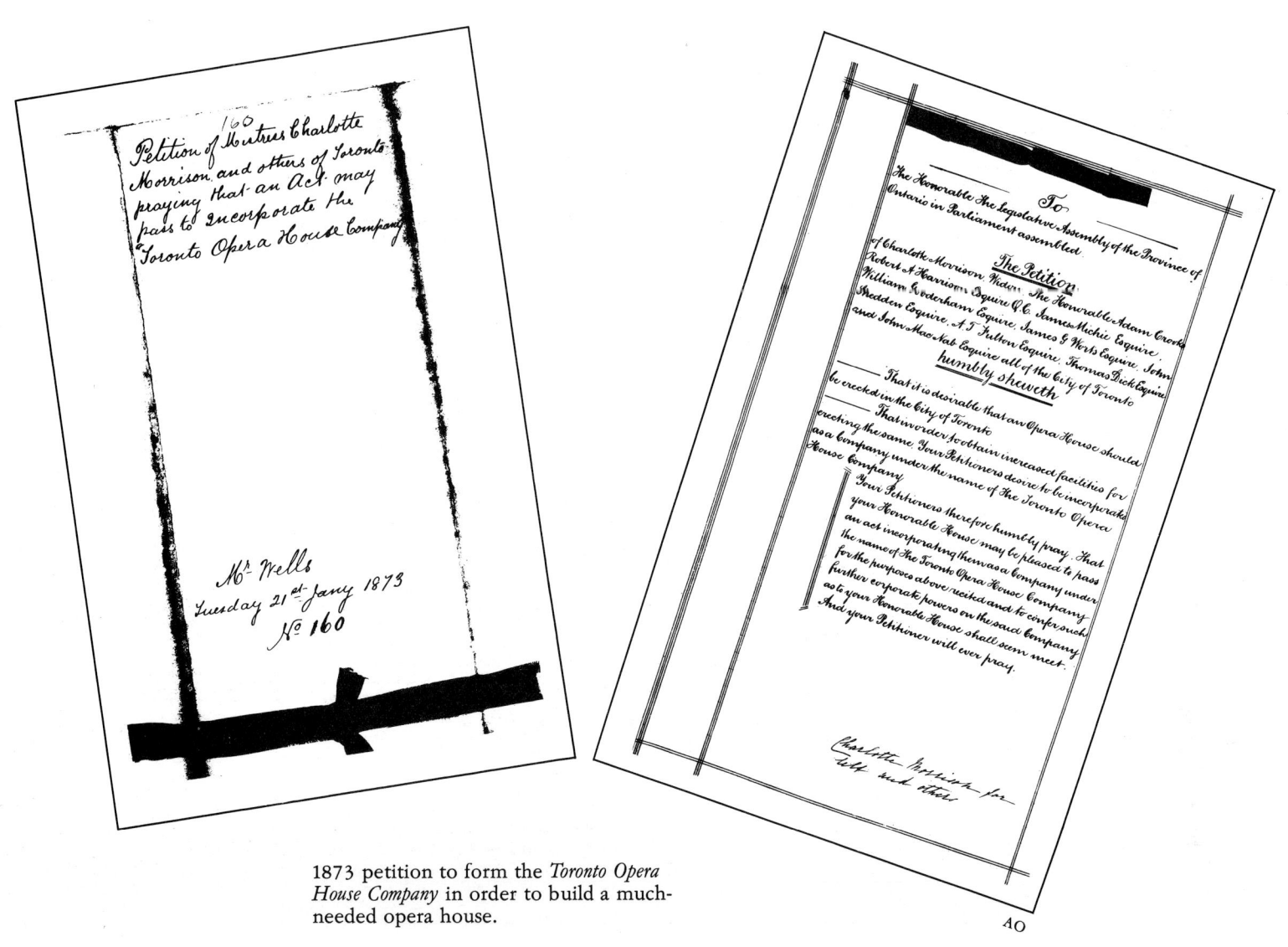

1873 petition to form the *Toronto Opera House Company* in order to build a much-needed opera house.

GRAND OPERA HOUSE

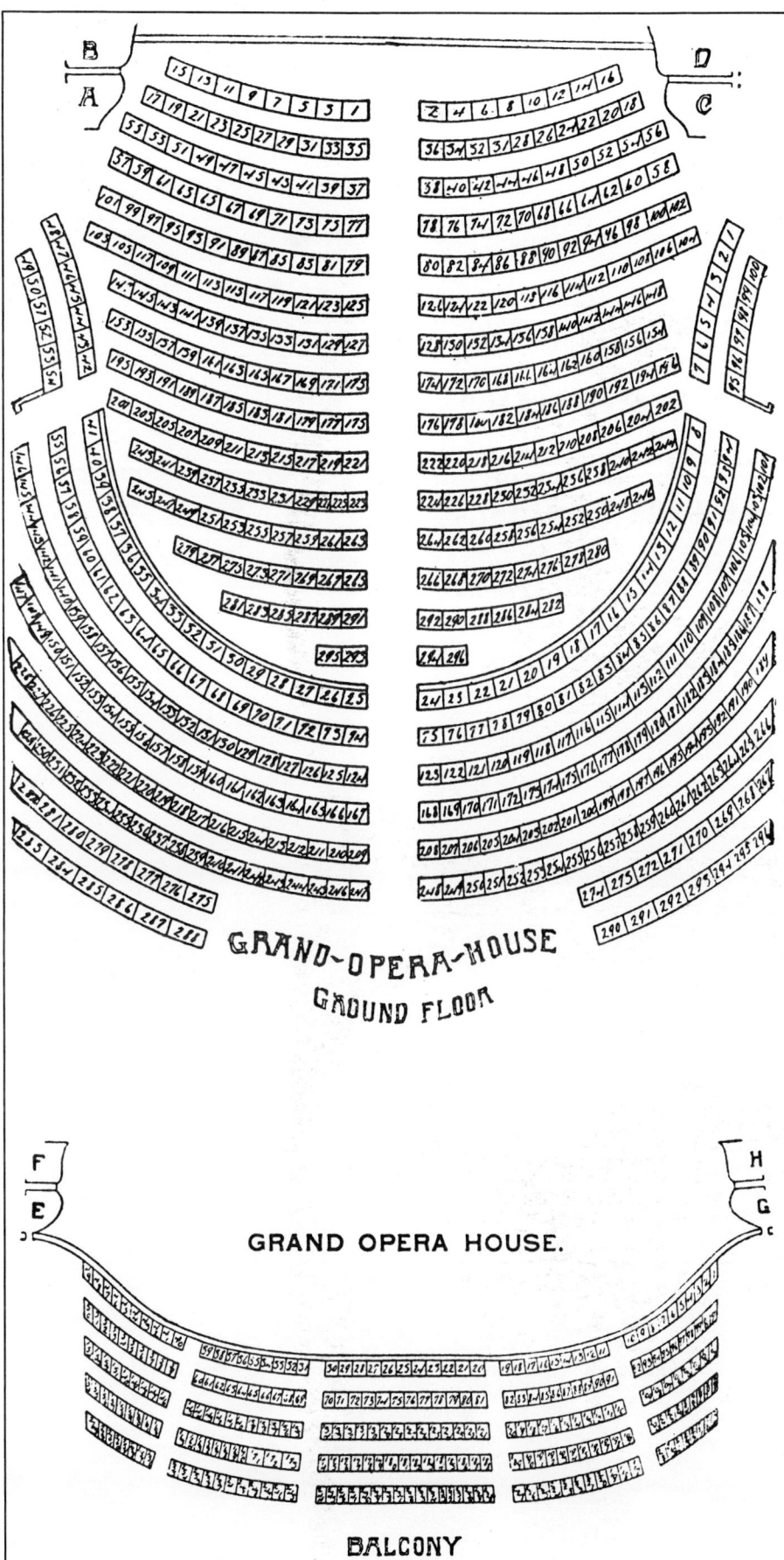

Foster's Toronto Blue Book 1900

MRS. MORRISON'S GRAND OPERA HOUSE.

The Opening.

The opening of Mrs. Charlotte Morrison's Grand Opera House took place last night. The published descriptions of the building, its size, magnificence, and completeness, and still more the return of Mrs. Morrison to the stage under circumstances so flattering to her professional fame and personal worth, had raised the public expectation to the highest pitch. Long before the time at which it was announced that the ceremonies proper to the occasion were to commence, the house was crowded in every part, and to excess. Among those present were great numbers of the most prominent and influential of our own residents, while large parties had come from London, Hamilton, Montreal, Ottawa, and other cities, to take their share in an event of so much interest and importance. His Excellency the Governor-General and the Countess of Dufferin, though not able to be in Toronto, had desired that the evening should be regarded that the evening imperial patronage. All the prestige, therefore, that rank, fashion and popularity could confer was attendant upon the inauguration of this dramatic reign, amid hosts of warm friends and sincere admirers. The aspect of the house was brilliant in the extreme. To the beauties of colour and shape, of which we have before attempted to give an idea, was added the indescribable brightness of a crowd of beauty and fashion, gay as fair parterre, while high over all glittered the great jewel of clustered dazzling light. And, later, the drop scene, whose radiance beamed a centre of coming far to see, which shows in exquisite tints and drawing, the "Dream of Byron," completed a spectacle so radiant, so lovely, and so perfect, that these few poor words of ours can only hint at.

THE OPENING ADDRESS.

After a considerable pause the green curtain suddenly rose, when Mrs. Morrison and the Prompter were discovered upon the stage.

Mrs. Morrison: Hold, for your lives!
You know not what ye do.

Why, Mr. Prompter, I'm surprised at you.

Prompter: Madam, your pardon; shall it fall or rise?

Mrs. Morrison: Your voices, lords, with you that question lies.
Yet stay, a word or two ere we begin—
Solicited by numerous friends within,
Beyond your suffrages to represent
The Drama in this House of Parliament.
I pledge myself to reasonable reform,
Not only "pledge" myself, but I'll perform.
The Ministry shall have my firm support,
If I have theirs! I'll give my vote in short
For all their Acts, so they oppose not mine;
They too are Managers in another line;
And if they would a sterling peace maintain,
They will not treat my measures with disdain.

Are men alone to hold the sovereign sway!
"No cat to mew — no dog to have his day!"
Why should not Women guide the Drama's course,
Since to "Old Women" States have had recourse?
Will you, because a nation will be more
Than they can manage, shut the door
On humbler efforts to deserve your praise,
Since men have failed in their attempts to raise
The sinking Drama from oblivion's bed?
While women have victoriously led,
Their Companies through scenes of many glories,
Aided by Whigs, Stage Properties and Tories.

Why, then, should I refuse to take the reins!
Great Alexander's history contains
No mighty feat achieved but I'll outvie,
In efforts, every pledge to ratify.
Now as to what I am as you all well know,
And what I am my gratitude shall show.
If 'tis your will my credit to sustain,
Let Comedy resume her throne again.
If Novelty can satisfy your wish,
New plays we'll serve you up a constant dish.
I' faith we'll serve you up new faces shall appear,
In this, our Grand New House, throughout the year;
And if our utmost efforts fail with you,
'Twill in Toronto be a thing quite new.
We shall succeed! oh, yes I will ne'er be said
The Drama's corner stone is here mislaid!
Oh, grant us then your voices in our cause,
And be our guarantee your kind applause,
Say then the word — with you depends it all;
Your hands must warm or chill the hearts of those
Whose fate is resting on your "Ayes and Noes."

This address was recited with excellent effect, and was greeted with much applause.

The curtain again rose, and the first scene in the "School for Scandal" appeared. Upon the stage were the full company, among whom were the actors in the play appropriately costumed. The orchestra gave the signal, and the whole house rising, the National Anthem was sung in solo and chorus, the last notes being followed by cheers from all parts.

There was some little delay after this, but at length the first representation in this new Temple of the Drama began. The following was the cast:—

Lady Teazle .... Mrs. Morrison.
Mrs. Candour .... Miss Mary Carr.
Maria .... Miss Lizzie Rich.
Lady Sneerwell .... Mrs. Bernard.
Sir Peter Teazle .... Mr. Ben Rogers.
Sir Oliver Surface .... Mr. J. B. Fuller.
Joseph Surface .... Mr. Jos. P. Clarke.
Charles Surface .... Mr. August Pitou.
Crabtree .... Mr. F. W. Melton.
Sir Benjamin Backbite ..... Mr. S. J. Davis.
Rowley .... Mr. J. Armstrong.
Moses .... Mr. G. Semblar.
Trip .... Mr. J. Gobey.
Snake .... Mr. J. Sambrook.
Careless (with song) ......

Mail, Sept. 22, 1874

Amusements.

MRS. MORRISON'S GRAND OPERA HOUSE, ADELAIDE-ST. WEST.

AIMEE,

(The Queen of Opera Bouffe,) and the NEW FRENCH OPERA BOUFFE COMPANY,

This (Wednesday) evening, Oct. 28, Offenbach's successful opera,

LA PERICHOLE.

Admission to ground floor, $1. Reserved seats in orchestra chairs, parquet balcony chairs or parquet sofa seats, 50 cents extra; dress circle balcony chairs, 75 cents; dress circle sofa seats, 50 cents; family circle, 25 cents; proscenium boxes, $10. Seats can now be secured at the box office of the Grand Opera House, and at A. & S. Nordheimer's music store. Thursday—La Fille de Madame Angot. Friday—La Princesse de Trebizonde. Saturday, matinee—Mme. Angot. Saturday evening—La Belle Helene, and positively last performance. Doors open at 7½. Commence at 8.

SATURDAY MATINEE

ONE DOLLAR all over the house. No extra charge for securing seats.

Mail, Oct. 28, 1874

The French Opera Bouffe.—Mrs. Morrison's Grand Opera House was crowded last night in every part. "La Fille de Madame Angot" being again represented. The performance was marked by the same excellence as on the first occasion, and with the same flattering applause. To-night Offenbach's "La Princesse de Trebizonde" will be given. It is one of his most popular operas, and always highly successful when adequately produced, as it will be to-night.

Mail, Oct. 30, 1874

MRS. MORRISON'S GRAND OPERA HOUSE.

FIRST ANNUAL BALL.

In consequence of the great success of Mr. FREDERIC ROBINSON, to allow of his re-engagement the Ball intended to be given on the 25th inst. has been postponed until MONDAY, the 8th of FEB. next. Those who have not received circulars will please apply to the Secretary or members of the Committee. The following is the Committee of Management:—

Mrs. Morrison. Lieut.-Col. Gzowski.
R. A. Harrison, Esq. J. Gordon Brown, Esq.
Hon. Frank Smith. Hon. J. B. Robinson.
Wm. Gooderham, Jr., Esq. Angus Morrison, Esq.
Geo. Gooderham, Esq. W. H. Howland, Esq.
A. T. Fulton, Esq. W. Davidson, Esq.
S. Nordheimer, Esq. J. J. Foy, Esq.
W. J. Baines, Esq. W. Francis, Esq.
Major Arthurs. James Michie, Esq.

Family Ticket, admitting one Gentleman and two Ladies, $5; Single Ticket, $2.

STEPHEN HEWARD, Chairman. A. R. BOSWELL, Secretary.

Mail, Jan. 9, 1875

GRAND OPERA HOUSE

One of the members of the Committee of the First Annual Ball, Lieut.-Col. Casimir Gzowski, had made a dramatic escape from Poland in 1830. He was knighted by Queen Victoria in recognition of his contribution to Canada's railway system.

Toronto Philharmonic Society.

"THE MESSIAH."

Mrs. MORRISON'S OPERA HOUSE.

JANUARY 11TH, 1875.

TICKETS:—RESERVED SEATS, $1; at Messrs. Nordheimer; Mason, Risch & Newcombe; the Opera House; and the Rossin House. FAMILY CIRCLE, 50 cents, at Messrs. Nordheimer's; and Mason, Risch & Newcombe's.

SUBSCRIBERS' TICKETS
Do Not Admit to this Concert.

Mail, Jan. 9, 1875

Impresario MAX STRAKOSCH brought Opera in Italian and English to the Grand in 1876, 1879, 1881 and 1882.

Canadian Illustrated News, Jan. 30, 1875

PERFORMANCE OF HANDEL'S *MESSIAH*

Canadian Illustrated News, Feb. 27, 1875

FIRST ANNUAL BALL OF THE GRAND OPERA HOUSE COMPANY

Photo: Mora, N.Y.   GOS

ANNIE LOUISE CARY, American mezzo-soprano who sang Amneris, Mignon and Azucena with the Strakosch company in 1876.

ALCA

Belford's Monthly Magazine
Vol. 1, #1,
December, 1876

Musical Notes.

The musical season, which may now be said to have commenced in Toronto, was inaugurated by the performance of Max Strakosch's Operatic Company at the Grand Opera House just a month ago. It is, perhaps, too late now to enter into any detailed criticism of the manner in which the three operas of "Faust," "Il Trovatore," and "Martha" were given; but we may be permitted to say that the general style of the performance was no great compliment to the critical or appreciative powers of a Toronto audience. The various soloists were, it is true, artists who are above the imputation of incapacity. This being the case, the imperfect acquaintance with their parts which some of them evinced, and which necessitated constant and audible prompting, was the more inexcusable. Again, the *mise en scène* was poor and inadequate. Although the practice of omitting a scene or a song, here and there is too general to be denied sanction, yet the indiscriminate elimination which was adopted in the performance of "Martha," for instance, is slovenly, and is greatly to be deprecated. The choruses were flat in both senses of the word. There is, however, much to be said *per contra*. Signor Brignoli's voice still retains much of its old sweetness. His acting was unusually spirited, and he never appeared to be more of a gentleman. Miss McCullough's vocalization was not only sweet but also conspicuously correct. Signor Gottschalk also deserves a word of praise, for, although evidently suffering from a bad cold, he nevertheless sang in very good form. The "Calf of Gold," in "Faust," was perhaps his best effort. The orchestra was fair. One feature in connection with these performances requires special notice. On each night no programmes were to be had till the opera was half over. The object of this manœuvre was to induce persons, in despair at not being able to ascertain the names of the various performers, to purchase libretti, which were being sold for a quarter of a dollar. Such a proceeding, entailing as it did much inconvenience to the audience, is greatly to be reprehended, and we trust will not be repeated.

CPI

CLARA LOUISE KELLOGG, American soprano, sang at the Grand with her own company in 1875 and 1889 and with the Strakosch company in 1879.

HISTORIC TYPO. Dates at the tops of these playbills are printer's errors and should read 1879.

MTLB

MTLB

MM

Italian tenor PASQUALE BRIGNOLI sang at the Grand with the Strakosch company in 1876 and Emma Abbott's company in 1881.

GRAND OPERA HOUSE

Telegram, Oct. 23, 1924   MTLB

O.B. Sheppard, for many years the manager of the Grand Opera House and later of the Princess.

EMMA ABBOTT, American soprano, formed her own company which performed at the Grand in 1881, 1882, 1883 and 1890.

CPI

ALEXANDER MANNING, a former Mayor of Toronto

Telegram, Oct. 23, 1924   MTLB

A DISASTROUS FIRE.

Destruction of the Grand Opera House.

THREE PERSONS BURNED TO DEATH

The Story of a Survivor—Scenes and Incidents of the Conflagration—Insurances, &c.

Shortly after three o'clock on Saturday morning a policeman on the Adelaide street beat discovered the Grand Opera House to be on fire, and immediately sounded an alarm. The firemen from the different stations in the centre of the city, with their apparatus, were quickly in attendance; but when the officers of the brigade saw that the fire was likely to prove a hot one, a general alarm was sounded, and the hose sections from outlying stations summoned. The flames first made their appearance in the King street or stage end of the building, and spread with great rapidity towards the front. While the firemen were busy laying the hose in the Opera House lane, they noticed a man stagger to one of the windows of the burning building, fifty feet from the ground. He climbed to the window-sill, but seemed afraid to jump. He turned around as if to go back into the room again, when the firemen called to him to

LEAP FOR HIS LIFE.

There was no ladder long enough to reach the window, and if there had been one, it would have been impossible to reach it, for the dressing rooms on this side are built out from the building, and to reach the apartment where the man was it would have been necessary to rear the ladder from the roof of the dressing room. The firemen ran a ladder up against the dressing-room, and several of them ascended to the roof, in order to catch the man when he jumped. The smoke was bursting in black clouds from the windows along the side of the building, and seeing there was no alternative but to jump, the man caught the window sill with his hands and dropped to the roof. He slipped on the wet shingles, but saved himself from falling to the ground by grasping a chimney. He was then helped down the ladder. He was black with smoke, and suffering from burns on the face and hands. As soon as he recovered sufficiently to speak, he said his name was Thomas Scott, and that Robert Wright, the stage carpenter and caretaker, and his wife, and little girl, Mamie, were in the room which he had just left. Scott was taken to Dr. Pollard's, Bay street, where his injuries were attended to. As soon as it became known that there were lives to save, Chief Ardagh instructed his men to burst open the door of the stairway leading from the lane to the upper part of the building. It was useless to think of searching for Wright and his family through the window. The door was battered down in an instant and the firemen swarmed up the stairs; but the smoke was so thick and the heat so intense that they were compelled to beat a hasty retreat. Shortly afterwards the floor fell in.

Mail, Nov. 30, 1879, excerpt only.   AO

GRAND OPERA HOUSE

A Brilliant Reopening of the New Theatre.

Miss Neilson's Enthusiastic Reception.

The new Grand Opera House was crowded to the doors last night with the wealth and fashion of the city, the events being the opening of the new house and the re-entrée of Miss Adelaide Neilson. An hour before the doors opened a crowd commenced to collect in the lobby of the theatre, and when seven o'clock arrived the throng reached to the street. When the portals were thrown open, there was a great rush, and, though a number of policemen stationed near the door attempted to stay the human torrent, their efforts were useless and they were thrust to the wall. The upper parts of the house were soon filled, and by degrees the seats in the parquette were occupied. Those who remembered the old house then lighted up, could at once see the great contrast between it and the new. All the wood and iron-work in the present house has been painted white, and the others are covered with a brighter coloured velvet, so that when the gas is lighted it presents a much brighter and more attractive appearance than the old house. The gasaliers have been bestowed with more judgment than formerly, and the great chandelier which hangs from the centre of the ceiling gives more light, and in juxtaposition with the sparkling lights, the rich surroundings, make up the bright and happy scene.

The college boys, who occupied their favourite position in the upper gallery, considerably enlivened proceedings before the rise of the curtain by singing a number of songs, though the chorus was somewhat boisterous at times.

About eight o'clock Mr. Pitou appeared before the curtain. He was received with applause. He said that, on behalf of Mr. Manning and on his own behalf, he welcomed the audience to the new house, which was a most beautiful structure. (Applause.) All that money could do had been done to make the theatre a pride to the city, and he was confident in saying that in point of design and finish it was not surpassed by any theatre on this continent. He had been in many theatres in the course of his professional career, but he knew of none which was so well provided with means of egress in case of accident. All the work had been done under the supervision of Mr. Manning, and his great prime could not be given to those positions for the engines he occupied while much of construction was going on. He (Mr. Pitou) had made many engagements for the future, and the audience might rest assured that he would always consult their taste in the management of the house. (Applause.)

Mr. Pitou then had the green curtain ran up, revealing the drop scene, a view of the Acropolis and the Temple of Jupiter, all of which, painted by Mr. Joseph Puggett. Loud calls were made for the gentleman, but he did not put in an appearance.

"As You Like It" is one of Shakespeare's most delightful and sweetly philosophical comedy. Other theatres have displayed their share of private and intellectual talent in Toronto boards, and have been more or less praised for their meritorious performances, but none of them has succeeded in awakening the enthusiastic admiration which Miss Neilson first aroused. Torontonians look upon her as the greatest actress that ever visited the city, and it is doubtful if any help to their estimation as the does to-day. Cautious enthusiasts are said to be temperately cold and slow to manifest appreciation, but Miss Neilson appears to be the master hand that stirs them to their very depths.

Mail, Feb. 19, 1880, excerpt only

Amusements.

GRAND OPERA HOUSE.
A. PITOU.....................Manager.

GRAND OPENING
Monday, Feb. 9th, 1880.

Engagement for ONE WEEK only of

Miss Adelaide Neilson

Supported by Mr. EDWARD COMPTON and her own Company.

Monday Ev'g.—As You Like It.

Tuesday—Romeo and Juliet. Wednesday—Twelfth Night. Thursday—As You Like It.

Scale of Prices.—Reserved seats in any part of the house, $1 50. Admission to lower floor and dress circle, $1. Admission to gallery, 50c. Lower boxes, $10. Upper boxes, $8. The plan for sale of reserved seats will be opened at the Box Office of the Opera House, Thursday, Feb. 5th, at 9 a.m.

Monday, Feb. 9.—Arabian Night Combination

Globe, Feb. 3, 1880   AO

Amusements.

GRAND OPERA HOUSE!
AUGUSTUS PITOU.....................Manager

TO-NIGHT. TO-NIGHT.
E. A. McDowell's Company

IN
H.M.S. PARLIAMENT,
Received nightly with

Shouts of Laughter and Applause!

NEW COSTUMES—MAGNIFICENT SCENERY.

PARLIAMENT BUILDINGS
(By Moonlight). Interior of the Parliament LIBRARY.

Grand Matinee Saturday.

Grand Opera House.
A. PITOU.....................Manager.

Positively two nights only, MONDAY and TUESDAY, MARCH 15 and 16,

THE STRAKOSCH
Grand Italian Opera.

GRAND CHORUS AND ORCHESTRA.

The Company comprises 100 Artists.

MONDAY EVENING, MARCH 15th,

First time here of Rossini's Masterwork,

WILLIAM TELL.—WILLIAM TELL.

With the following Great Star Casts:

Miss Maria Litta..........................Matilda
Miss Lancaster...........................Gemmy
M'lle Ricci (first appearance here).....Hedwiga
Sig. Petrovich (his first appearance here)....Arnoldo
Sig. Storti (his first appearance here)........Tell
Mons. Castelmary (first appearance here)..Gualtiero
Sig. Lafontaine.........................Sig. Barberis
Sig. Tagliapietra.......................Sig. Bocell

TUESDAY EVENING, MARCH 16th,
Bizet's Grand Romantic Opera,

CARMEN.—CARMEN.—CARMEN.

M'lle Valerga (first time here)............Carmen
Miss Lancaster..........................Michaela
M'lle Ricci...............................Mercedes
Miss Arcoue..............................Frasquita
Sig. Lazarini (his first appearance here)..Don Jose
Mr. L. G. Gottschalk (Toreador)..........Escamillo
Sig. Papini.............................Sig. Tagliapietra
Sig. Lafontaine.........................Sig. Barberis

Incidental Ballet by M'lles Canes and Leotilda, Musical Director..........S. Behrens

Admission to lower floor and Dress-circle, $1; reserved seats in Orchestra and Parquette, $2; reserved Dress-circle Chairs, $2; reserved Dress-circle Sofas, $1 50; Gallery, 50c. Sale of seats will commence at Box-office, Grand Opera House, Thursday, March 11, at 9 a.m. Parties residing out of town can secure seats by mail or telegraph.

Globe, Mar. 11, 1880   AO

MINNIE HAUK, first American soprano to sing the roles of Juliette, Carmen and Manon and London's first Carmen (Her Majesty's Theatre, June 22, 1878).

MM

TORONTO, MONDAY, NOVEMBER 27, 1882.

Grand Opera House,
TORONTO, ONT.

O. B. SHEPPARD, ... Manager.

RE-ENGAGEMENT FOR TWO NIGHTS OF

STRAKOSCH

English Opera Company.

AUBER'S CHARMING OPERA
— OF —

FRA DIAVOLO.

CAST OF CHARACTERS

LADY ALLCASH	ZELDA SEGUIN WALLACE
Zerlina	Miss Letitia Fritch
Fra Diavolo	Mr. G. W. Traverner
Lorenzo	Mr. Montegriffo

Mr. Montegriffo has kindly consented to sing the role of Lorenzo.

Lord Allcash	Mr. Vincent Hogan
Beppo	Mr. Wagner
Giacomo	Mr. J. Juergens
Mateo	Mr. Leone

Grand Chorus and Orchestra.

SIGNOR DE NOVELLIS .... MUSICAL DIRECTOR

TO-MORROW EVENING—Minnie Hauk as CARMEN.

WEDNESDAY EVENING—Prof. Richardson's Art Illustrations.

Remainder of Week—The Great Comedian, Chas. L. Davis, as "ALVIN JOSLIN."

MTLB

TORONTO, THURSDAY, NOVEMBER 23, 1882.

Grand Opera House,
TORONTO, ONT.

O. B. SHEPPARD, ... Manager.

Engagement for Three Nights and Grand Saturday Matinee of

STRAKOSCH

English Opera Company.

Thursday Evening, Nov. 20th, will be presented Balfe's Charming Opera,

THE BOHEMIAN GIRL.

CAST OF CHARACTERS

Arline	Miss Letitia Fritch
Thaddeus	Mr. Traverner
Count Arnheim	Mr. George Seaman
Devilshoof	Mr. Vincent Hogan
Buda	Miss Campbell
—AND—	
The Gypsy Queen	Zelda Seguin Wallace

Who will introduce Balfe's famous song, "Bliss forever Past," in the Second Act.

Grand Chorus and Orchestra.

SIGNOR DE NOVELLIS .... MUSICAL DIRECTOR

FRIDAY EVENING—First appearance of Minnie Hauk, in her unrivalled creation of "CARMEN."

SATURDAY MATINEE—"BOHEMIAN GIRL."

SATURDAY EVENING—Farewell appearance of Minnie Hauk, taking the part of ZERLINA, in Auber's Charming Opera "FRA DIAVOLO."

MTLB

Amusements.

GRAND OPERA HOUSE.
O. B. SHEPPARD, MANAGER.

THREE NIGHTS AND SATURDAY MATINEE.

BEGINNING THURSDAY, NOV. 23rd.

MINNIE HAUK

AND THE

Strakosch English Opera Company,

Comprising the following distinguished artists:— Zelda Seguin Wallace, Letitia L. Fritch, Carrie Hun King, Cora Miller, Messrs. G. W. Traverner, A. Montegriffo, George Sweet, Willet Seaman, Vincent Hogan.

GRAND CHORUS AND ORCHESTRA.
Musical Director .... Mr. De Novellis.
Thursday Evening, Nov. 23—

THE BOHEMIAN GIRL,
Letitia Fritch, Montegriffo, George Sweet, Hogan, and Zelda Seguin Wallace.

Friday evening, Nov. 24th, first appearance of MINNIE HAUK in her unrivalled creation of

CARMEN.

Saturday Matinee, "Bohemian Girl." Saturday Night—Farewell appearance of MINNIE HAUK as Zerlina in

FRA DIAVOLO.

Prices—Reserved seats, $1.50; admission, 50c, 75c. and $1. Matinee prices—Reserved seats, 75c. Admission, 25c and 50c. Box plan for Matinee opens this morning at 10 a.m.

Globe, Nov. 23, 1882   AO

GRAND OPERA HOUSE—THE FLORENCES.

The attractions for the Grand Opera house are now nearly completed, and the theatre will be one of the cosiest and most comfortable places of amusement on the continent. The heavy Brussels carpets which have been laid down in the aisles both in the balcony and ground floor will be much appreciated by the patrons of the Grand, as late arrivals will now be able to go to their seats without disturbing the audience. In the main entrances and foyer the plate glass panels to the doors and the designs in stained glass above present a very attractive appearance, and with the new and handsome chandeliers and dark-coloured wall papers have a very rich effect. The opera house lane has been block paved and a new sidewalk put down, and these improvements with the new entrance for holders of reserved seat tickets, prove that the manager has done everything that has been suggested which would conduce to the comfort of his patrons. The universal favourites, the Florences, will open the season on Monday in "Our Governor," and the mere announcement in a city where the name of the Florences is a household word with lovers of amusement should be sufficient to fill the house.

Mail, Aug. 28, 1886   AO

MR. AND MRS. FLORENCE AT THE GRAND OPERA HOUSE.

This evening the well known Toronto favorites, Mr. and Mrs. W. J. Florence will open the Grand Opera House for the season of 1886-7, in the popular comedy, "Our Governor." It is claimed that these famous artists will be supported by an exceptionally strong company this season, and a thoroughly good performance may be confidently looked for. The Grand Opera House has been thoroughly renovated and so far improved that its old patrons will scarcely recognize it. The main entrance on Adelaide-street has been newly painted, very richly papered, furnished with new and highly ornamental chandeliers and massive French plate glass doors, with tastefully ground patterns. The vestibule is also beautifully papered and painted, and fancifully ornamented with elegantly stained glass windows and fan-lights. The lobby and interior of the auditorium have also been greatly improved and richly carpeted, while the walls are ornamented with rare and costly oil paintings, while the lighting arrangements have been so improved that the interior of the house will be shown to much better advantage than heretofore. The dress circle has also been handsomely carpeted. That portion of the theatre which is not seen by the audience has also been greatly improved. The walls and wood have been freshly painted, new carpets have been laid, and the rooms re-furnished, so that the actors will find them as comfortable and convenient as those of the best theatres on this continent. Altogether the Grand was never anywhere nearly as fine a theatre as it is now, and the handsome appearance of its interior cannot fail to afford an agreeable surprise to both play-goers and actors.

Globe, Aug. 30, 1886   AO

GRAND OPERA HOUSE

MM

'COLONEL' J. H. MAPLESON, British operatic impresario, who managed Her Majesty's and Drury Lane Theatres in London and took his own opera company on a coast-to-coast tour of the United States, presenting such headliners as Adelina Patti, Emma Albani and Christine Nilsson.

HER MAJESTY'S OPERA.
Albani as "Lucia."

The Grand Opera House was literally packed from pit to dome last night on the occasion of the second appearance of Col. Mapleson's Opera Company. The parquette, balconies, and boxes were crowded with the *elite* of the city, the Lieutenant-Governor and Mrs. Robinson, with their party, occupying the gubernatorial box. The galleries were occupied to their fullest capacity, while all available standing room was filled. The occupants of the upper gallery followed their usual custom of entertaining the rest of the audience between the acts by the performance of the musical selections for which they have become famous, and which were duly appreciated by their hearers. The brilliant reputation which Mme. Albani has won in the English and Continental capitals promised us a rare treat, and the announcement that she would appear in Donizetti's "Lucia di Lammermoor" was received with unmixed satisfaction. The cast last evening was as follows:—

Egardo.............................Signor Ravelli
Enrico Aston.................Signor Ciampi-Cellaj
Raimondo.............................Signor Monti
Arturo............................Signor Rinaldini
Normando.........................Signor Bieletto
Alisa.................................M'lle Valerga
Lucia................................Mme. Albani

When Albani appeared she was received with vociferous cheers, and it was some moments before the enthusiasm subsided sufficiently for the music of the opera to proceed. The first notes of the recitative "Ancor non grimse" proved that the expectations of the audience, however great, were to be fully realized. It remained, however, for the aria, "Regnava nee Silenzio," to demonstrate how just had been the verdict of the European critics as to the rare beauty of her voice. It is a pure, full soprano, of great range, and of exquisite sympathetic quality. It has a surprising breadth and roundness, and is of unsurpassed evenness throughout all its registers. The hearer feels that the same voice is before him, whether used *pianissimo* or *fortissimo*, high or low. One need not look at Albani, nor need one know the words or subject, to ascertain whether it is joy or anguish that is being delineated. The superb voice tells the whole story.

MTLB

EMMA ALBANI, Canada's *Queen of Song*, who made her Canadian operatic debut as Lucia at the Grand, Feb. 13, 1883.

MM

LUIGI ARDITI, Conductor for the Mapleson Company.

MM

SOFIA SCHALCHI, Italian mezzo-soprano who toured with Mapleson and later played Siebel in the Metropolitan's first performance – *Faust*, Oct. 22, 1883.

With all its sonorousness and power it is deliciously smooth and flexible, rivalling in its extreme ease of vocalization the finest and lightest *leggiera* voices. Given these extraordinary vocal gifts, her appearance completes the charm. A sweet, honest, good face and a fine majestic figure please the eye as much as the voice charms the ear. Albani appeals to the senses, and conquers her audience by the essential womanishness of voice and person. In the aria just mentioned she overcame the difficulties of the florid music of the number with the greatest ease. Her phrasing was perfect, her colouring in the highest degree artistic, and her command of gesture and facial expression showed careful study and the strictest attention to proper rules of acting, while the sublime instinct of the true actress showed through and governed her whole performance. Act by act the impression made by her first aria increased until it culminated in the celebrated mad scene, in which her perfect control and great resources were fully displayed. It is now over forty years ago since this magnificent piece of florid writing was given to the world, and it is still the criterion by which the capabilities of a great singer are measured. Albani sang it with delightful ease, and sang a setting still more ornate than the original scoring. The applause at the end of this number was tremendous, as indeed it was after every effort of the great *cantatrice*. She responded by repeating the movement "Alfin son tuor," at the end of which she was the recipient of a beautiful floral trophy in the shape of a wreath of lilies and roses, presented by Mrs. Robinson.

In the duett "Soffriva nel Pianto" she was ably assisted by Sig. Ciampi-Cellaj as *Enrico*. This gentleman has a fine sympathetic baritone voice, somewhat marred by an excessive *vibrato*. It is, however, of a pleasing quality and well trained. Being of a smooth, flexible character, it was well suited to the more florid numbers of the part. The tenor, Sig. Ravelli, was suffering from severe indisposition, which prevented the audience from forming a fair estimate of his ability and resources. This illness culminated at the end of the third act, causing the final scene of the opera to be omitted, owing to his withdrawal. This was to be regretted, as Sig. Ravelli had sung and acted most acceptably during the evening in spite of evident physical disability. His voice is a fine *tenore di grazia*, and in good health would have prepared a great pleasure for the audience. Sig. Menti (*Raimondo*) has a fine sonorous bass voice of good compass, and sang his part in the earlier acts well. The sombre character of his role seemed to affect him, and his rendering of "Dalo Strazze" was disappointing. The famous Sestettino, in the second act, was splendidly rendered, surpassing any previous rendition in Toronto. The choruses were characterized by the same life and brilliancy of tone that made so favourable an impression on the previous evening, while the orchestra, under the command of Sig. Arditi, was nearly all that could be desired.

Globe, Feb. 14, 1883

AO

Stereo MTLB T12681

KING STREET West, opposite Jordan, at south end of Johnson Lane looking east (1894?).

MM

ANTONIO GALASSI, Italian baritone, a member of Mapleson's company at the Grand.

GRAND OPERA HOUSE

RICHARD D'OYLY CARTE whose productions of Gilbert and Sullivan's operas appeared regularly at the Grand from 1879 to 1888.

EMMA JUCH, American soprano who organized her own opera company in 1889 and brought it to the Grand Opera House in 1890.

COMIC OPERA.

Helen Lamont, who is the prima donna of the Rudolph Aronson Comic Opera Company, which will visit Toronto and play a week's engagement at the Grand Opera house Nov. 19, is described as an exceedingly handsome woman and a fine singer. She is supported by an admirable company of trained artists. The operas to be performed consist of "Nadjy" and "Erminie." No more thoroughly equipped organization of its kind travels to-day throughout the United States and Canada. Every city the company has visited thus far this season has awarded to it the warmest praise.

Mail, Nov. 6, 1889 — NLC

BOSTON IDEAL COMPANY.

The Boston Ideals engagement at the Grand Opera House for the last three nights of this week will commence on Thursday night with a performance of Donizetti's "Lucia di Lammermoor." In this opera the Ideals have made a great success throughout the country, with Pauline L'Allemand in the title role. The cast for this opera will include the following artists:—Pauline L'Allemand as Lucia, Jenny Corea as Alice, Frank Baxter as Lord Edgar, W. H. Mertens as Sir Henry Ashton, E. A. Torpi as Sir Arthur Bucklaw, and Sig. Miranda as Bide-the-Bent. On Friday night the Ideals will sing Verdi's "Rigoletto" for the first time here in English by any company. On Saturday afternoon "Bohemian Girl," and on Saturday night "Trovatore." The Ideals carry their own orchestra of thirty skilled musicians, and a well-trained chorus of forty voices.

Globe, Apr. 28, 1890 — NLC

TORONTO, THURSDAY, APRIL 19, 1883

Grand Opera House,
TORONTO, ONT.

O. B. SHEPPARD, ... Manager.

Engagement for Three Nights and Saturday Matinee of the

Boston Opera Company.

MR. H. G. SNOW .... PROPRIETOR AND MANAGER

Miss LOUISE BALDWIN .... Soprano
Miss MAUD HOTCHKISS .... Contralto
MR. HARRY G. SNOW .... Tenor
MR. PENSON .... Basso
MR. LEON KEACH .... Pianist

In Flotow's beautiful English Opera,

'MARTHA'
In Four Acts and Six Scenes.

Scene 1.—Lady Harriet's Apartments.
Scene 2. The Fair at Richmond.
Scene 3.—At the Farm House.
Scene 4.—Forest Scene
Scene 5. The Farm House
Scene 6. Fair Scene

CAST OF CHARACTERS.

Lady Harriet (Martha) .... Miss Baldwin
Nancy (Julia) .... Miss Hotchkiss
Lionel .... Mr. Snow
Plunkett .... Mr. Penson
Sir Tristan ....
Pianist .... Mr. Leon Keach

THE STORY.

Lady Harriet, a Maid of Honor to Queen Anna, is wearied by the monotony of court life. No novelty can amuse her. The songs of the peasants on their way to the fair at Richmond, incite her to accompany them in disguise, under the name of Martha. Her maid, Sir Tristan, and her maid, Nancy, are also induced to join. Arriving at the fair, the young farmers, Lionel and Plunkett, offer to hire Lady Harriet and Nancy as servants. They accept, and are legally bound to their masters for one year. The young men carry them off to their farm-house, and, finding them unacquainted with menial duties, begin to instruct them. Lionel falls in love with Lady Harriet, and, when alone makes an avowal of his passion. The lady laughs at his raptures. The farmers retire for the night, and Sir Tristan, who has traced the whereabouts of the ladies, enters and carries them off. Lionel's affection preys on his mind. In the forest he encounters Lady Harriet, who is out on a hunting party with the Queen, and pleads his passion with more warmth than before. The lady dismisses him rudely. His only solace is the friendship of Plunkett. Lionel is an orphan. His father, on his death-bed, bequeathed him to the care of Plunkett, and gave him a ring, with the charge that whenever Lionel was involved in distress, the ring should be given to the Queen. The ring is presented to the Queen, and Lionel proves to be the only son of the Earl of Derby, unjustly banished. The young Earl is duly reinstated in his rank and possessions, but his mind is distracted and he will take no comfort, even from the lips of Lady Harriet, who confesses her hand and heart. The lady, with the assistance of Plunkett, in alarm for the health of his foster-brother, is persuaded to take part in a scheme to bring about the reconciliation. The three then have the Fair scene enacted, and Lionel, meeting the Lady under the same circumstances as at first, awakes from his delirium and both couples are finally united and made happy.

MTLB

TORONTO, MONDAY FEBRUARY 1, 1886

Grand Opera House,
TORONTO, ONT.

O. B. SHEPPARD, ... Manager.
HERBERT SHEPPARD, ... Treasurer.

One Week Only, commencing Monday, Feb. 1, every Evening and Wednesday and Saturday Matinees.

Gilbert & Sullivan's Opera Season

with

D'OYLY CARTE'S OPERA COMPANY

Under the management of

MR. JOHN STETSON,

Only authorized performance of Mr. W. S. Gilbert and Sir Arthur Sullivan's

MIKADO!
OR, THE TOWN OF TITIPU.

Written by W. S. Gilbert and composed by Arthur Sullivan, interpreted by

50 —ARTISTS— 50

Selected from the Best Musical Talent in the Profession.
And a Grand Orchestra.

From the Author's Libretto and the Composer's Orchestration. The only Company authorized to present this Opera in New England and Canada.

CAST OF CHARACTERS

The Mikado of Japan .... Mr. S. S. Burnham
Nanki-Poo, his son, disguised as a wandering minstrel, and in love with Yum-Yum .... Mr. Roy Stanton
Ko Ko, Lord High Executioner of Titipu .... Mr. J. W. Herbert
Poo-Bah, Lord High Everything else .... Mr. Harry Allen
Pish-Tush, a noble lord .... Mr. Louis J. Monico
Yum Yum .... Miss Mary Beebe
Pitti-Sing } Three Sisters, ... Miss Agnes Stone
Peep-Boo } Wards to Ko-Ko, ... Miss Mamie Cerbi
Katisha, in love with Nanki-Poo .... Miss Alice Carle

Chorus of School Girls, Nobles, Guards and Coolies.

SYNOPSIS

ACT I. Court yard of Ko-Ko's official residence, by Jos. Clare
ACT II. Ko-Ko's garden, by H. L. Reid.

MR. STETSON'S STAFF

Musical Director .... Mr. F. W. Zeung
Stage Manager .... Mr. W. H. Rohde
Advance Representative .... Mr. Paul Nicholson
Business Manager .... Mr. P. O'Brien

The Dresses and Embroideries are imported from Japan by Messrs. Liberty & Co., and adapted by Madame Leon.

The Pianos used at the Grand Opera House are supplied by Messrs. A. & S. Nordheimer, 15 King Street East.

MTLB

WEEK ENDING SATURDAY, DECEMBER 14TH, 1889.

Grand Opera House,

O. B. SHEPPARD .... Manager
O. H. SHEPPARD .... Treasurer

THE BOSTONIANS
IN ENGLISH OPERA

TOM KARL, W. H. MacDONALD and H. C. BARNABEE
Proprietors and Managers

FRIDAY, DECEMBER 13

Ambrose Thomas' Romantic Opera

MIGNON
IN FOUR ACTS.

Wilhelm Meister .... Mr. Tom Karl
Lotario .... Mr. Eugene Cowles
Laretes .... Mr. Fred. Dixon
Giarno .... Mr. Geo. Frothingham
Mignon .... Juliette Corden
Frederic .... Josphine Bartlett
Filina .... Marie Stone

Ladies, Gypsies, etc.

F. F. Pond .... Business Manager
D. M. Dewey .... Agt. in Advance
S. L. Studley .... For the Bostonians { Musical Director
Fred. Dixon .... Stage Director

"KNABE" Piano used by the Bostonians

— NEXT WEEK —

DUNCAN B. HARRISON'S MILITARY COMEDY DRAMA

THE PAYMASTER

MTLB

GRAND OPERA HOUSE

Emma Albani

GIUSEPPE DEL PUENTE, Italian baritone, who sang Valentin in the Metropolitan's opening opera *Faust*, Oct. 22, 1883, was a member of Albani's company in 1890.

GRAND OPERA HOUSE.

ALBANI
Tuesday evening, April 29th.
LA TRAVIATA
Reserved seats now on sale at Box Office. Top gallery tickets $1, can be bought to-day.

GRAND OPERA HOUSE

MAY 1, 2 AND 3,
THE FAMOUS
BOSTON IDEALS.

Thursday, "Lucia" (with L'Allemand).
Friday, "Rigoletto" (with L'Allemand).
Saturday Matinee, "Bohemian Girl."
Saturday Night, "Trovatore."
PRICES—$1, 75c, 50c and 25c.
Sale of seats begins Tuesday morning.

Globe, Apr. 28, 1890

GRAND OPERA HOUSE.

GRAND OPERA by the company, including chorus ballet and orchestra, from the Metropolitan Opera House, New York. Under the direction of Mr. Maurice Grau.
TO-NIGHT, OCT. 20—BARBER OF SEVILLE.
Mmes. Sembrich, Bauermeister, MM. Ed de Roszke, Salignac, Campanari-Pini-Corsi, Vanni, Meux, Conductor, Signor Mancinelli.
SATURDAY AFTERNOON, OCT. 21—FAUST.
Mmes. Suzanne Adams, Olitzka, Bauermeister, MM. Sippel, Illy, Meux and Plancon. Conductor, Mr. Gustav Heinrichs.
SATURDAY EVENING, OCT. 21—CARMEN.
Mmes. Calve, Bauermeister Van Canteron, Clementine Devere, MM. Bonnard, Campanari, Devries, Bars, Dufriche, Queyla, Conductor, Signor Mancinelli.
Prices, $1.50, $2.00, $3.00, $4.00, $5.00.
The Weber Piano is used by this Company and its Artists.
Thursday, Oct. 26—FRANK DANIELS.

Evening News, Oct. 20, 1899

LUIGI RAVELLI, Italian tenor who sang with Mapleson's company in 1883 in Toronto and with Madame Albani's in 1890.

MUSIC AND THE DRAMA.

Improvements at the Grand Opera House—Some Needed Additions—Valuable Violins to be Sold—Permits For Theatre Alterations—Notes.

Mr. Alexander Manning, the proprietor of the Grand Opera house, has decided to make several improvements in the theatre which will tend to increase the comfort of the patrons of the house. The alterations, which were begun on Monday, will include the enlargement of the foyer, a rearrangement of the offices which will permit the setting apart of a room for smoking and another for the accommodation of bicycles, and the building of new toilette and cloak-rooms. The interior of the theatre will be repainted and redecorated, and the seating accommodation, it is understood, will be improved. Mr. Jennings has been engaged as leader of the orchestra in place of Mr. Faeder, who will be at the Academy. The season will be opened in September by Sol Smith Russell, and one of the early events will be the appearance of Sir Henry Irving and his company.

Mail & Empire, July 10, 1895

MARCELLA SEMBRICH

ALBANI.

Canada's Great Songstress in "Traviata."—A Brilliant Audience—Successful Performance of Grand Italian Opera—Splendid Supporting Talent.

Never has there been a finer tribute paid to a Queen of Song in the Grand Opera House than was tendered to Mme. Emma Albani-Gye last evening on the occasion of her appearance in the character of Violetta, in Verdi's "Traviata." The floor of the house, the first gallery and the first rows of the top gallery were occupied by the cream of fashionable society in all the brilliancy of full dress. When Mme. Albani made her first appearance she was received with rounds of applause that threatened to seriously retard the progress of the opera. She bowed her acknowledgments in the gracious manner that has made her a favorite here, and the business of the opera proceeded. She was recalled again and again after each act, and received some beautiful floral tributes.

At the close of the opera she was recalled until she finally came forward and sang "Home, Sweet Home," to the infinite delight of the audience, a performance that was cheered to the echo. The opera is one that is well known from its many gems, but it has never been performed in Toronto before, and in its entirety was quite new to the majority of the audience. It is based on Alexander Dumas' "La Dame aux Camellias," and follows the general plot of the great author's drama quite closely, though the date of action and the names of the characters have been changed. The opera is full of gems of arias, and has some fine concerted pieces, notably the ensemble at the close of the second act. Mme. Albani's "Violetta" was a fine piece of acting, being presented with a richness of detail that won the close attention of the audience. In her singing she was very successful, though evidently laboring under a cold. She gave a splendid rendering of the "Ah Fors 'e Lui," her voice coming out full and rich on the high notes, but the "Sempre Libera" was taken rather slowly for its brilliant character. A similar leisurely delivery characterised much of her other performance. She showed a thorough control of her voice throughout the work, which is not by any means sparing in its demands upon the vocalist. Her runs were clear and distinct, and her shading judiciously employed. Her singing, in the last act especially, was very dramatic in its effect. A fine rendering of the celebrated duet, "Parigi, O Cara," was given by Mme. Albani and Signor Ravelli. This gentleman, as Alfred, made his second appearance in Toronto, having supported Mme. Albani in "Lucia" some seven years ago. He has a fine lyric tenor voice and sang with ease and fluency, rising in brilliancy in the finale to the second act and at the close of the opera. He also was warmly applauded and made himself a favorite with the audience. Another Canadian was M'lle. Attalie Claire, a young lady who was born in Toronto, and who gave efficient support as Nannina and as Flora. Her parts were light in their demands upon her resources. She has a pleasing mezzo-soprano voice, which she uses judiciously, and is very much aided by her pretty appearance. Signor Del Puente had a splendid role in "George Germont," and sang at his best. He gave a beautiful rendering of "Di Provenza," and was warmly encored. In both acting and singing he gave a memorable representation. Signor Novara had a very small part as the Doctor, but his fine bass voice was a valuable factor in the ensembles. The chorus was very good, and a very efficient orchestra assisted under the direction of Signor Sapio.

Globe, Apr. 30, 1890

GRAND OPERA HOUSE

MAURICE GRAU, Director, Metropolitan Opera Company.

EDOUARD DE RESZKE

MATTHILDE BAUERMEISTER

EMMA CALVE

The Grand Opera House was packed to the doors last night, on the return of the Kirke La Shelle Company in Julian Edwards' opera, "The Princess Chic." The opera was, as usual, beautifully staged, and there was a large and handsomely costumed chorus. The star of the evening was really Mr. Joseph C. Miron, who reappeared in his original role of Brevêt, the soldier of fortune, and who, of course, made a tremendous hit in the famous "War" song. Miss Vera Michelena, the new impersonator of the Princess, was pleasing, and the other principal parts were well received. The opera is billed for the week.

Globe, Apr. 14, 1903

THE METROPOLITAN OPERA COMPANY of New York made its first appearance in Toronto at the GRAND OPERA HOUSE where, in 1899, it gave performances of *Il Barbiere di Siviglin* (Oct 20), *Faust* (Oct 21 mat) and *Carmen* (Oct 21 eve). Among the artists were French baritone Edouard de Reszke, soprano Emma Calve, mezzo-soprano Matthilde Bauermeister and soprano Marcella Sembrich.

MR. A. J. SMALL'S ABSENCE CAUSES GRAVE CONCERN

Well-Known Theatrical Magnate Has Not Been Seen for Five Weeks.

WHEN LAST SEEN IN BEST OF HEALTH

The whereabouts of Mr. Ambrose J. Small one of Canada's most prominent theatrical men, is causing gravest concern to his relatives and business associates. Mr. Small was last seen in Toronto on Dec. 2nd, after he had closed the sale of his vast theatrical holdings to the Trans-Canada Theatres, Ltd., and had received a very large check as initial payment.

The Star interviewed Mr. E. W. M. Flock, of London, Ontario, by long distance telephone this morning who said: "I left Mr. Small in his office, about 5.30 p.m. on Tuesday, December 2nd, and further than that I know nothing about him. He had closed up the sale of his Grand Opera circuit, six houses in all, on Monday to the Trans-Canada Theatres, Ltd. He closed with me, as his solicitor, on Tuesday. He received the initial payment, which was a large sum of money on Monday, and deposited it on Tuesday.

"I was with Mr. Small about twenty minutes at his office and he was never more pleasant or genial in his life and was full of pep and vim. I told him that I might be down to see him the following week. I have been down to Toronto two or three times since then, but have been told that he was not at the office. As in cases of this kind newspapers are invaluable in locating a man, I see no reason why I should not tell you what I have."

Police Making Inquiries.

Inspector Guthrie, of the Toronto Detective Department, when interviewed by The Star said: "We are making inquiries all around, but have found nothing yet."

Completed Big Deal.

On Saturday, November 29, Mr. Small got back to Toronto from Montreal, where he had closed the sale of all his theatrical interests, including the above-mentioned, to a syndicate incorporated as the Trans-Canada Theatres, Limited. On Monday he received a marked check for a million dollars on account of the transaction. On Tuesday he deposited this money in a savings banks account in one of the city banks he does business with. He was around the Grand Opera House. He met Mrs. Small downtown and after lunch went for a short distance with her and returned to his office in the Grand Opera House, where he met Mr. E. W. Flock, barrister, of London, who had been his legal adviser in the transaction closed the previous week in Montreal. He went out on the street about half past five. That is the last known so far of Mr. Small in Toronto. No trace of him of any kind since that date, five weeks ago, can be found.

For a few days Mrs. Small and his assistants at the Grand Opera House imagined that he had been called suddenly to one of the out-of-town theatres or to Montreal, and some days later on, when no word had come from him, that perhaps he had gone to New York on some pressing business. This suspense continued for two weeks, then a third and for a fourth week.

Search Was Made.

A quiet but diligent search of the city, including hospitals and hotels, stations, and the like, was made by the police, fearing that he might be ill.

It is remarkable that, as far as is known, Mr. Small had with him at the time of his disappearance no

(Continued on Page Two.)

MR. AMBROSE J. SMALL.

(Continued from Page One.)

luggage or clothes other than those he wore, and it is not believed that he had much money upon his person.

Mr. Small is a very wealthy man and as was said above has several bank accounts with large balances; but an examination of these show no withdrawals made or attempted by anyone.

A. J. SMALL'S ABSENCE IS CAUSE OF CONCERN

Mr. Small was naturally of a nervous temperament, and for several months he had been working long hours at the task of arranging the details of the many and varied phases of his business that had to be settled in order to bring about the theatrical amalgamation which he desired to effect. He was an exceedingly keen business man, and knew personally every detail of his affairs. Towards the end of the negotiations he worked far into the night, and had latterly complained of nervous exhaustion and loss of appetite.

Conferences have been held between members of his family, his business associates and his counsel, but nothing has transpired to throw a ray of light on the mystery. The last such gathering was held yesterday afternoon. Mr. Small retained a large block of stock in Trans-Canada Theatres, Ltd., and will be intimately concerned in its management.

Like most wealthy men, Mr. Small bore in some quarters the reputation of carrying money about with him, and in view of the epidemic of hold-ups much apprehension as to his safety is felt.

The hope is however, that the publicity started by this announcement will result in the discovery of Mr. Small's whereabouts. The photograph reproduced herewith is an old one. It is an excellent portrait of Mr. Small, but since it was taken he has worn his moustache shortly clipped. With the exception of that change it should greatly help in his identification.

Said He Would Take Rest.

Montreal, Que., Jan. 3.—George F. Driscoll, general manager of Trans-Canada Theatres, Ltd., this morning said that he had seen or heard nothing of Mr. Small after cleaning up the theatrical deal. He stated, however, that in the course of the last conversation he had with him at the meeting when the deal was put through, Mr. Small said that he would now go away for a rest. Mr. Driscoll said that Mr. Small never carried any money on him, drawing a check whenever he needed it.

Star, Jan. 3, 1920

Gas Lights And Radiant Stars In Old Grand Opera House

Glamor and Magic of the Great Old Days in Toronto, When Footlights Flickered While Real Brilliance Held the Stage

A THEATRICAL SERIES

Reminiscences of Thomas H. Scott, Sr., Who Was for Years Gas Engineer in the Old Grand Opera House and Illumined the Triumphs of Famous Actors and Actresses in Days Gone By

THE "GAS PLOT."

Even in those old days, much attention was given to proper stage lighting but, instead of electricity, we used illuminating gas and calcium. Very important was the crude but nevertheless efficient layout of my lighting equipment at that time.

The house illuminations were lighted by means of a long pole with a wax taper. Stage lighting was arranged and worked according to the "gas plot" or gas-cue sheet, which each company placed with the gas engineer. Following is a sample "gas plot":

Act I.
Scene 1. Full Up 5
Scene 2. Foots Up 1
Scene 3. Half Dark 5
Bunch lights back of drop to light up moon.
Green strip back of platform to light up water on drop. White calcium R.2, E. Flies.

Act II.
Scene 1. Full Up 5
Scene 2. Foots Up 1
Scene 3. 1st and 2nd borders up 3
3rd, 4th and 5th borders down, foots up.
White calcium R.3 E. flies.

Act III.
Scene 1. Full up 5
Scene 2. Foots 3-4 down 1
Scene 3. 1-2 dark 3
Foots up on picture at end of scene.
Green calcium R.3
Scene 4. 1-2 foots up at cue.1
Scene 5. Full up 5
Curtain.

DID YOU PAY THE GAS BILL?

The gas plot, as you may notice, was a document of much importance. Just here I would like to remark that, on more than one occasion, we had our gas plot but no gas. The gas company would probably drop a point in connection with sacred edifices but not so with the Grand Opera House. On several occasions when I was ready to light up the house, I found the task impossible, the gas company having cut off the flow. Mrs. Morrison then had to hustle someone down to the company, pay the bill or religiously promise to do so, and bring back the requisite official to turn on the gas again. This happened with people arriving to see the play: is there any house in Toronto working under such conditions to-day?

In 1878, Mr. Augustus Pitou became connected with the Grand Opera House as actor-manager, with Mr. O. B. Sheppard as treasurer. Mr. Sheppard continued for a great many years to guide the destinies of the Grand and latterly the Princess Theatre. Mr. Pitou always booked a season of refined and interesting attractions, creating in this city a demand for the best in theatrical art.

Telegram, Oct. 23, 1924, Excerpt   MTLB

Fade Out – and Curtain

If you should see an unusually large number of ghosts in downtown Toronto during these next few nights, you will know that they have all come back for a farewell performance. For that musty old storehouse of memories, the Grand, is going where all great theatres must finally go—which is into the hands of the dealers in second-hand lumber and bricks, into the junk yards and ash heaps.

The wreckers are in, stripping the dim interior of its last faded glories. The dusty and red drapes have been lowered out of the loft and ripped off their batons. They are relics, some of them, of days when choruses were judged by weight, when one-two-three-kick was an adequate education in dancing, when a leg was a limb and an ankle a sensation.

The battered wardrobe trunks, the property boxes pasted with labels, which lay in grimy off-stage corners for years, are gone. The carving is being torn off the boxes. The gilt chairs have disappeared. They are taking the brass rail off the orchestra pit. The paint-frame is empty. Not a stick is left in the carpenter-shop. The plush chairs are being pulled off the floor. On them, in other days, sat gentlemen of much refinement and elegance, surrounded by ladies in quantities of magnificent clothes and carrying considerable weight in jewels. With decorous applause they endorsed the art of the world's great stars and between acts whispered the latest gossip behind gloved hands.

By James A. Cowan

THE DESERTED DRESSING ROOM CORRIDOR

BENEATH THE TRAPDOORS OF THE STAGE.

WORLD-FAMOUS STARS HAVE USED THESE ANCIENT DRESSING ROOMS

THE GREAT HEIGHT OF THE OLD GRAND THEATRE BACKSTAGE MADE IT THE FINEST SCENE PAINTING STUDIO IN THE COUNTRY

Star Weekly, Dec. 10, 1927   MTLB

GRAND OPERA HOUSE

THE GRAND OPERA HOUSE near the end of its days.

GRAND OPERA LANE, Adelaide Street, west of Yonge, 1983.

APPEARANCES

1874	New French Opera Bouffe
1875	Kellogg English Opera Company
1875	Emily Soldene and Her Most Complete English Comique Opera Company
1875	Mohalbi Grand Italian Opera
1876	Strakosch Grand Italian Opera Company
1877	Alice Oates and her Superior English Opera Company
1879	Strakosch Grand Italian Opera Company
1879	Saville English Opera Company
1879	Haverly's Juvenile Pinafore Company
1879	Haverly's Church Opera Company
1879	Haverly's Church Choir Company
1880	Toronto Church Choir Opera Company
1880	E. A. McDowell's Company
1880	Strakosch Grand Italian Opera Company
1880	Juvenile Opera Company (Toronto)
1880	Boston Ideal Opera Company
1880	D'Oyly Carte Opera Company
1880	Soldene Opera Comique Company
1881	Emma Abbott Grand English Opera Company
1881	Toronto Opera Company
1881	Strakosch and Hess Grand Opera Company
1881	Ford Comic Opera Company
1881	Rice's Opera Comique Company
1881	Comley and Barton's Company
1882	Haverly's Opera Company
1882	Emma Abbott Grand English Opera Company
1882	Lilliputian Opera Company
1882	Strakosch English Opera Company
1882	Haverly's Opera Company
1883	Emma Abbott Grand English Opera Company
1883	Wilbur Opera Company
1883	Her Majesty's Opera Company
1883	Boston Opera Company
1883	Patterson's New York Opera Company
1883	Mrs. W. J. Obernier's Company
1885	Hamilton Amateur Opera Company
1885	Rentz-Santley Novelty and Burlesque Company
1885	Toronto Opera Company
1886	D'Oyly Carte Opera Company
1886	Toronto's Harmony Club
1886	Hamilton Musical Union
1887	D'Oyly Carte Opera Company
1888	J. C. Duff Comic Opera Company
1886	Rice and Dixey
1888	Stetson Opera Company
1889	Kellogg English Opera Company
1889	New American Opera Company
1889	Rudolph Arenson's Comic Opera Company
1889	Lyric Operatic Society (Toront)
1889	Carleton Comic Opera Company
1889	J. C. Duff English Opera Company
1889	Boston Ideal Opera Company
1890	Emma Abbott Grand English Opera Company
1890	Emma Juch English Opera Festival
1890	Emma Albani Opera Company
1890	Boston Ideal Opera Company
1893	The Harmony Club
1893	Anton Seidl & Co.,
1893	Grand English Opera Co.,
1893	Mapleson & Whitney.
1896	Metropolitan English Grand Opera Co.
1896	Emma Albani & Co.
1896	*Wang*
1898	Alice Nielsen Opera Company
1899	Metropolitan Opera Company
1901	*The Cadet Girl*
1903	Jules Grau Comic Opera Company
1903	Kirke La Shelle Company
1903	*The Fortune Teller*
1905	*The Fortune Teller*
1805	*The Show Girl*
1905	Haverly's Minstrels
1906	Mantelli Opera Company
1923	De Wolf Hopper and His Gilbert & Sullivan Comic Opera Co.

KING STREET, THE GREAT THROUGHFARE OF TORONTO.

Canadian Illustrated News
July 31, 1880

The third building from the left is Notman and Fraser, Photographers to the Queen, at 39 King Street East.

1875
ROYAL OPERA HOUSE

At long last – recognition of lyric drama and its requirements, even though the theatre's presentations were by no means exclusively operatic.

Stereo ca. 1875 King Street West, looking east on York Street.   MTLB

ROYAL OPERA HOUSE

King Street West, looking east on York Street. Immediately east of the Rossin House on the right (corner of King and York Sts) was Heintzman and Company – #'s 115-117. Farther east, between #'s 99 and 101 was the laneway to the Royal Opera House.

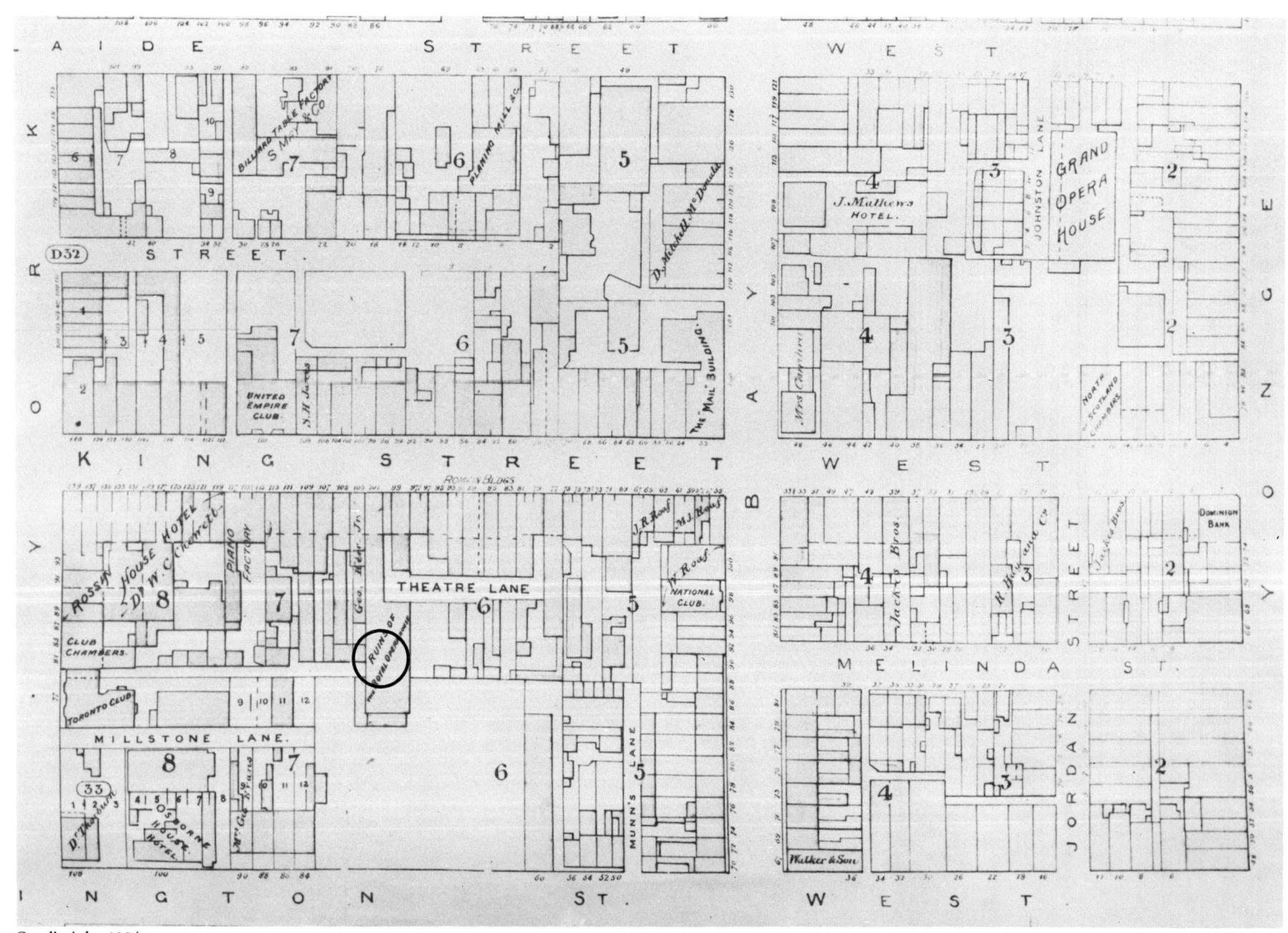

Goad's Atlas 1884

ROYAL OPERA HOUSE

On September 14, 1874, seven months after the destruction of the Royal Lyceum, the Royal Opera House, erected on the same site, opened its doors exactly one week before the Grand Opera House. For some years it maintained its predecessor's tradition of engaging opera companies, among them again the Holman company. However, on 9th February, 1883 it, too, was wiped out by fire.

Painting: Frank Hall — NPGL

W. S. GILBERT

Painting: Sir John Millais — NPGL

ARTHUR SULLIVAN

Globe, Sept. 14, 1874 — MTLB

Globe, Sept. 15, 1874 — NLC

Globe, Feb. 13, 1879 — NLC

Globe, Feb. 13, 1879 — NLC

In actual fact, *H.M.S. Pinafore* was presented a few days earlier in Montreal.

ROYAL OPERA HOUSE

Impresario RICHARD DOYLYCARTE brought (and kept) together the operatic phenomenon "Gilbert and Sullivan".

French tenor VICTOR CAPOUL was a member of Maurice Grau's Great French Opera Company in performances at the Royal Opera House in 1880.

Impresario MAURICE GRAU brought his Great French Opera Company to the Royal Opera House in 1880.

KERO'S CORPSE.

How the Body of the Theatrical Manager was Disposed Of.

THROWN OVER SUSPENSION BRIDGE.

It is three years ago, or over, since Mr. Kero, then manager of the Royal Opera house in this city, mysteriously disappeared. It will be remembered that at the time it was supposed that financial difficulties had compelled him to abscond, but it was subsequently learned that he was a wealthy man who was free from indebtedness as far as anyone in Toronto knew. Then followed the supposition that he had been murdered, but the entire absence of any clue to the disposal of the body, and the fact that the remains were never discovered, at length led to the belief among many that there had been no foul play in the case. There were some, however, who held to the opinion that Kero had been murdered, and more than one prophesied that at some distant day the body would be found buried beneath the Royal Opera house. However, when the theatre was recently reduced to ruins by fire there was no one to argue that an excellent opportunity was offered for search; or perhaps by that time Kero and his sudden disappearance had passed out of men's minds. The subject has been again revived in a startling manner. Mr. J. Gillespie, well known in this city, has just returned from an extended tour in the Old Country, and being well acquainted with Kero was naturally led to tell the following story upon revisiting his old home:—

He states that he was in Dublin about eighteen months ago, and while walking along Grafton street in that city accidentally met Frank Tannehill, jr., whose father was at one time manager of the Royal Opera house. After greetings the pair continued their walk, when they were met by a man who was acquainted with Tannehill. Gillespie was introduced to

SUNDAY CONCERTS.

Judgment Delivered in the Royal Opera House Case.

BOTH DEFENDANTS FINED.

The Police Magistrate delivered judgment yesterday morning in the case of M. Kero and Lucien Barnes, lessee and manager of the Royal Opera House respectively, for keeping a disorderly house, to wit, the Royal Opera House, by holding a concert there on Sunday, February 22nd. The following is the substance of the judgment:—

The defendants M. Kero and Lucien Barnes are charged before me that on Sunday, the 22nd February, they were unlawfully the keepers of a certain disorderly house known as the Royal Opera House, Toronto, which was then unlawfully used for public entertainment and amusement upon a part of the said Lord's Day, to which persons were then unlawfully admitted by the payment of money and by tickets sold for money. The charge is laid under 21 George III., chap. 49. Mr. Murphy, counsel for defendants, admits that the Royal Opera House was opened and used by defendants on 22nd February for a sacred concert, and that the programme produced was carried out; that secular songs were sung and also encores not on the programme; that admission was made by ticket on payment of money; that admission was open to all comers on the payment of 25 cents each; that there was an audience of several hundreds, and that the usual applause was given, and encores called for and responded to; that the doors opened at 7:30 p.m., and the concert commenced at 8 p.m.; that Mr. Kero is the lessee, and Mr. Barnes is the manager, and that Mr. Barnes is paid by a salary; that the Royal Opera House is an ordinary theatre on week days, and under the same management. The consideration of the question naturally resolves itself into two points. First, is the statute 21 George III., chap. 49, in force in this Province; and second, do the facts admitted constitute an offence under it.

Globe, Mar. 17, 1880

"LAST SCENE OF ALL."

The Royal Opera House Burned to the Ground.

WAS IT THE WORK OF AN INCENDIARY?

Total Loss, $80,000; Insurance, $15,000 — The Ravel Company in Great Distress — History of the Building, and Reminiscences of the Old Lyceum.

At an early hour yesterday morning the Royal Opera house was destroyed by fire, and nothing now remains of the building but a few yards of smoke-blackened brick wall. The theatre was already the prey of the flames before the alarm was given. About five o'clock in the morning Mary Burke, a servant in the employ of Messrs. Mitchell & Ryan, who had risen to do some work that required early attention, went to one of the back windows overlooking the theatre. She was dreadfully frightened on seeing tongues of fire and volumes of smoke coming from the building, while the roar of the conflagration in the interior could be plainly heard. She at once rushed to the front of the house, threw up a window, and screamed "fire" with all the strength she was capable of. Her cries were heard by Constable Cuddy, who was passing at the time, and he immediately gave the alarm. Almost simultaneously some other person sounded an alarm from the box at the Rossin house. The firemen from the Bay street and Court street halls were soon on the spot, being guided by the smoke and showers of burning cinders that proceeded from the theatre, but it was seen that it would be impossible to save the building. A pretty stiff breeze was blowing at the time, and it was feared that the burning cinders might set fire to the neighbouring houses. Fortunately there was a good deal of snow on the roofs of the adjacent buildings, and to this circumstance and to the efforts of the firemen must be attributed the fact that the fire did not become a conflagration. In less than ten minutes powerful streams of water were playing on the north, south, and east sides of the theatre, but apparently with little effect. Suddenly the roof fell in with

A TERRIFIC CRASH,

and a few seconds later the south wall collapsed. Previously to the advent of the firemen, a couple of loud reports were heard from the interior of the theatre, and it is believed that the noise was occasioned by the fall of the galleries. The firemen, finding it useless to attempt to save the theatre, directed their efforts towards saving the neighbouring houses, and in this they were entirely successful. The scene at the time of the fall of the roof was a grand and impressive one. A huge mass of flame shot up into the air, followed by myriads of sparks, and then dense clouds of black smoke. In a comparatively short space of time the theatre was a complete wreck, the upper portion of the wall facing King street being the last to topple over. The firemen had several narrow escapes from death. The men of the Portland street hall were within an inch of being crushed by the fall of the wall facing King street, and later in the day a number of the men who were working on the ruins near the western wall had a similar escape from being crushed by the fall of a portion of it at the northern end. Fortunately, Chief Ardagh had perceived the danger they were in, and called them away just in time to save their lives.

THE ORIGIN OF THE FIRE.

The fire is supposed to have started in the scene-room at the south end of the building. Mr. French considers it to have been the work of an incendiary, as the room had been locked for some days, and contained nothing that was capable of spontaneous combustion. There was no night watchman employed on the premises, but the janitor reports that everything appeared to be all right when he made his final tour of inspection on leaving the place for the night. Mr. French offers a reward of $1,000 for evidence that will lead to the discovery of the supposed incendiary. The performance on the previous evening was the Humpty Dumpty pantomime by the Ravel Company, but nothing was used of a more dangerous nature than a little red fire.

LOSSES OF THE RAVEL COMPANY.

The members of the Ravel Humpty Dumpty Company have been left in a truly deplorable condition by the fire. Nearly the whole of their wardrobes and properties were destroyed, and unless something is done for them they will be unable to fill the engagements which they had secured for the next five weeks in Canada. Mr. Comstock, the manager of the company, puts his loss down at $2,000. He says he fears he will be forced to cancel all the advance dates of the company. He received a telegram yesterday morning from the manager of the Royal Opera house, Montreal, inviting him to fill his engagement there and do the best he could, and offering to supply the company with whatever properties that could be obtained. Mr. Levantion has lost $500 in trapeze apparatus.

the stranger, and the latter proposed that the others should accompany him to his hotel. They did so, and in the course of conversation which followed between drinks Mr. Gillespie reverted to the time when the Royal Opera house was destroyed by fire just after the dissolution of partnership in the management between Messrs. Tannehill and Glenn. The stranger, who Mr. Gillespie remembers only by his title of "Captain," immediately became interested in the subject, although previously taking no part in the conversation about Toronto. He asked Mr. Gillespie if he had ever

HEARD ABOUT THE MURDER

of the proprietor of a theatre in Toronto. Mr. Gillespie replied in the negative, saying that he knew a Mr. Manning and a Mr French, but that both of these gentlemen were yet alive as far as he knew. Suddenly the incident relating to Kero flashed across his mind, and he asked the captain if Kero was the name of the man he had referred to.

"That's the name," exclaimed the other, slapping his knee.

"But Kero was only a manager," said Mr. Gillespie, enquiringly.

"Manager or proprietor, I am not sure, same man anyway." And then he related the following to two very interested listeners :—

"Several months ago," said he, "I was in New York, and a friend of mine, who was in trouble, sent to me a request that I should visit him at the Tombs. I did so, and while passing through a corridor I heard my name called by an occupant of one of the cells. Turning in response to the call I found another acquaintance of mine who was under sentence of fourteen years' imprisonment. He told me the circumstances in connection with his case, and said he wished me to try and procure a new trial for him. I spoke of the impossibility of making the effort without funds to commence with, and he told me that he had plenty of money. He then directed me to call upon a certain woman with whom he had been living, and that upon an order from him the money would be forthcoming. I followed his instructions, got the cash, the new trial was obtained, and the prisoner was discharged. Upon his release he took me into his confidence, and being an old friend, had no hesitation in telling me how he had become possessed of so much money, when I knew that a comparatively short time before he had been in needy circumstances. I was sufficiently well acquainted with him to believe what he told me. He said that while in Toronto, Canada, he heard that

A MAN NAMED KERO,

manager of a theatre in that city, was a rich man and in the habit of carrying a large sum of money around with him. He succeeded in getting acquainted with him, and followed him around for three months in the hope of a chance to rob him. At length he induced him to leave the city for Buffalo in the expectation of joining in a heavy poker game to be played in the latter place. He accompanied him, ostensibly for the purpose of joining in the poker game, but really in pursuance of another plan he had formed. They passed through Hamilton, and towards nightfall left St. Catharines, the man who contemplated murder having decided that the deed should be committed when the conductor of the train had made his last round for tickets before reaching the American side of the Suspension bridge. At some point between St. Catharines and the bridge Kero was called out by his companion to enjoy a smoke on the platform, and while standing there the latter dealt the unfortunate manager a murderous blow on the head. It is not probable that Kero was killed outright, but at all events he was knocked insensible. He was held on the platform by the other until the train was passing over the bridge, when he was flung over into the waters beneath. The murderers had previously rifled his pockets, securing a little over $1,000."

This was the story told to Mr. Gillespie in the hotel at Dublin, and he gives it just as he received it. The captain, he was afterwards informed, was a professional gambler, and, therefore, not unlikely to be well acquainted with a villain like the one who had confessed the murder of Kero. The story is in a measure borne out by the statement, published at the time of Kero's disappearance, that he had been last seen at the Hamilton railway station.

Globe, Mar. 28, 1884 NLC

King Street West, c. 1925. between #99 and #101

MTLB

MTLB

King Street West c. 1925. Entrance to old Royal Opera House left of second lamppost from right.

The marvels of Peru, Messrs. Samwells, Durand, and Evans, were sufferers to the extent of $400, and have saved nothing but the clothes in which they stand. Archie Daley, the contortionist, lost his wardrobe and high-kicking apparatus, and considers he is $500 out of pocket. Mr. and Mrs. Ravel had $2,000 worth of various kinds of stage goods destroyed, including their pantomime scenery, and wardrobe. The Ventuis lose probably $150. Altogether the personal losses of the company will reach very nearly $7,000. A loss which Mr. Ravel feels keenly is that of the educated pig, which was burnt in the flames. It was quite a pet, and would follow the members of the company about like a dog. The trained ponies being stabled away from the theatre escaped, but their harness was destroyed. Several members of the orchestra lost their band instruments; so that on the whole the company is completely stranded. It would be an act of professional kindness and a Christian deed if the Black Crook Company, now at the Grand Opera house, would devote one performance to the relief of their distressed brother artists. Mr. Sheppard, the manager of the Grand, when spoken to on the subject by a MAIL reporter, expressed his willingness to co-operate in any arrangement that might be made in this direction, and he has also decided to give the Ravel Company a benefit performance on Friday week. To add to the distress caused by the fire, the regular employes of the theatre, about thirty in number, are thrown out of employment, and something ought to be done to relieve them.

INCIDENTS.

James Forsyth, a fireman, was severely hurt by falling bricks.

The firemen, who were much exhausted by their exertions, were treated to a substantial breakfast by Mr. Coleman, of King street west.

When the alarm bell first sounded many of the guests at the Rossin house, on seeing the glare from the theatre, thought the hotel was on fire, and began to make preparations for a hasty exit. Their fears were, however, soon quieted when they were informed of the true state of affairs.

HISTORY OF THE THEATRE.

The original theatre, which stood on the site of the Royal Opera house, was the Royal Lyceum, which was built by the late Mr. John Ritchie, and was at first leased by Mr. T. P. Bernard. Subsequently Mr. John Nickinson assumed the lease, and under his management the theatre was opened March 28th, 1853, after having been redecorated, improved, and repaired. Mr. Nickinson held the theatre for six years, and his management was on the whole a very successful one. This period is of course associated with the artistic triumphs of Miss Charlotte Nickinson (Mrs. Morrison), who proved a great favourite with the theatre-going public, and whose attractive acting drew many a crowded house. After Mr Nickinson relinquished the management, the Royal Lyceum passed through the hands of Messrs. Marlowe, McFarlane, Harry Linden, Henry & Little, J. C. Myers, George Holman, Saphore & Waugh, Tannehill & Glen. In 1874 Mr. Tannehill alone became the lessee. His occupancy was abruptly terminated on Friday, January 30th, by a fire which broke out just before midnight in the carpenter's shop, spread to the stage, and did not cease to rage till nothing but the bare walls were left standing. The play performed on the night of the fire was "The Murder on the Hudson," on the occasion of the benefit of Mr. Dominick Murray. The theatre was the property of Mr. James French, who purchased it in 1866. Although he was insured to the amount of $15,000, his loss was considerable. Mr. French was, however, nothing daunted by the catastrophe, and

DETERMINED TO BUILD A NEW THEATRE,

which in point of beauty, comfort, and size should far eclipse the old Lyceum. His arrangements were so well made that by September the Royal Opera house stood on the old site, and was formally opened under Mr. C. L. Graves' management on Monday, September 14th, 1874, with the play of "The Hunchback." The architect was Mr. Wallace Hume, Chicago. It may be interesting to note en passant that the Grand Opera house was completed about the same time and was opened on September 21st, 1874. The cost of the Royal Opera house at its completion was $64,500. Since that time additional outlays have been made in improving the property. A new set of dressing rooms were added costing $6,000, and an extra scene room costing $2,000. The apparatus for the calcium light was recently purchased, and involved an additional expenditure of $400. Altogether the total cost of the building is put down by the manager, including the properties and improvements, at $80,000. As the insurance was only for $15,500, Mr. French's loss will be heavy. Mr. French states that he has not yet made up his mind whether he will rebuild, but if he should put up another theatre, he says it shall be a finer building than the old one. The insurance losses are distributed among the Royal, Royal Canadian, Queen's, and Imperial insurance companies.

Mail, Feb. 9, 1883 AO

APPEARANCES

1875	Holman English Opera Troupe
1876	Julia Matthews English Opera Bouffe and Burlesque Troupe
1876	Holman English Opera Company
1878	Holman English Opera Company
1879	Holman English Opera Company
1879	Mrs. Henry Drayton's Opera Company
1879	Rentz-Santley Novelty Company
1879	Haverly's Minstrels
1880	Alice Oates and Oates' English Comic Opera Company
1880	Maurice Grau's Great French Opera Company
1880	Holman Opera Company
1880	Tagliapietra's Grand Italian Opera Company
1880	Toronto Opera Company
1881	Leavitt's Grand English Opera Burlesque Company

ALBERT HALL

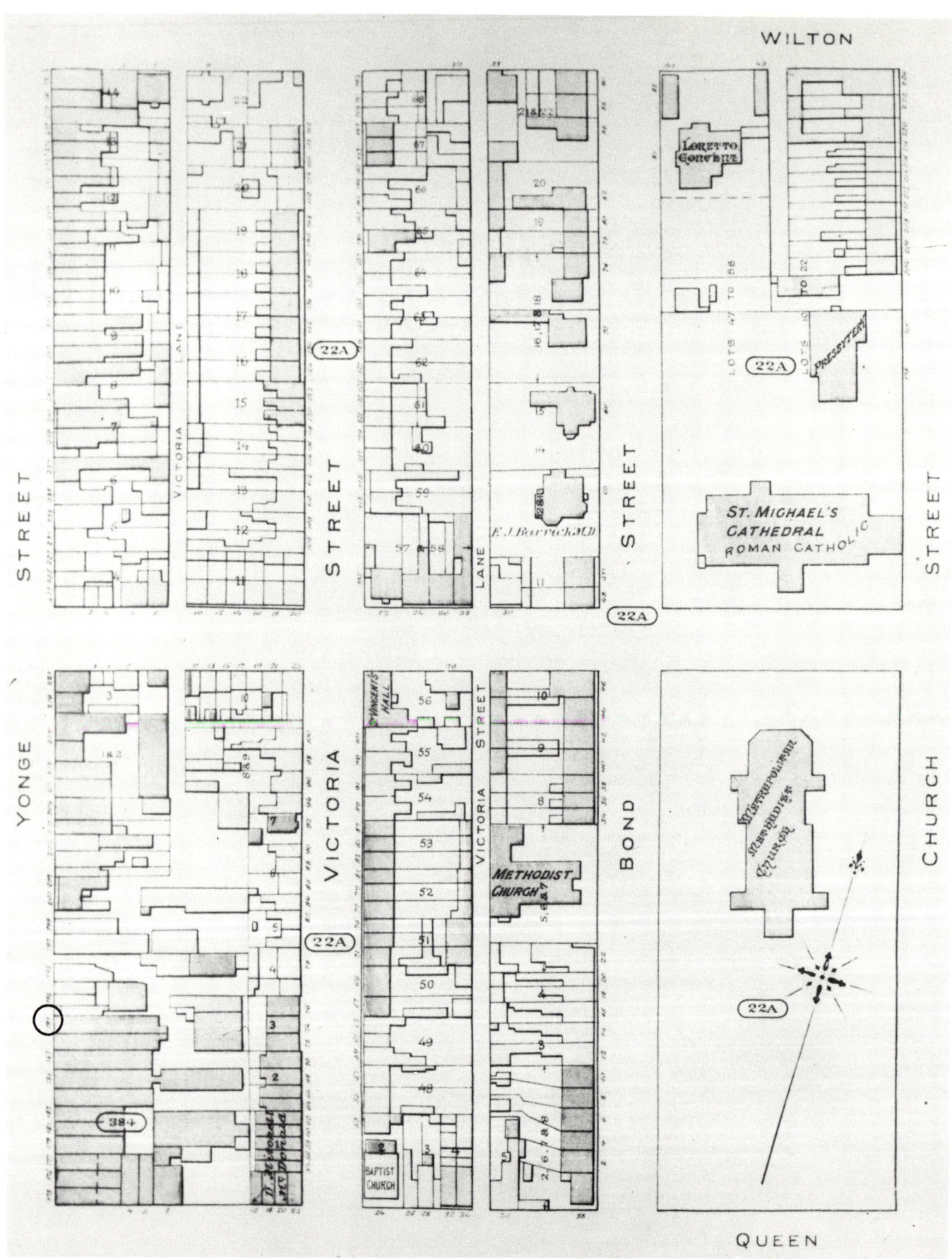

Goad's Atlas, 1884

1875
ALBERT HALL

What are Halls for? What else...

Illustrated Toronto: Past and Present – J. Temperlake   CTA

ALBERT HALL (c. 1877)

ALBERT HALL

Built in 1874, Albert Hall at 191 Yonge Street near Queen, was adapted for chamber and public concerts and balls. As was customary at the time, it was on the second floor, the first being occupied for many years by Neil McEachren, military tailor, and J. B. Cook, photographer. By 1890 the City Directory no longer listed Albert Hall. Since this was the very centre of the city, the hall was exceedingly popular in its time.

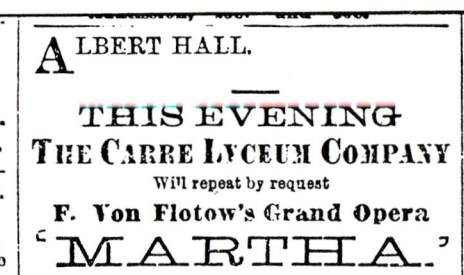

Globe, Nov. 10, 1875   NLC

Photo   MTLB T12891

YONGE STREET, east side between Shuter and Queen Streets 1903. The facade of the second floor of the building behind the telephone pole is unchanged.

PERFORMANCES
1875   Mrs. Carre's Lyceum Company
1878   Hamilton's English Opera Company

1877
SHAFTESBURY HALL

This hall promoted temperance but was also used for lectures and concerts.

Toronto Past and Present until 1882 – C. P. Mulvany

JPB

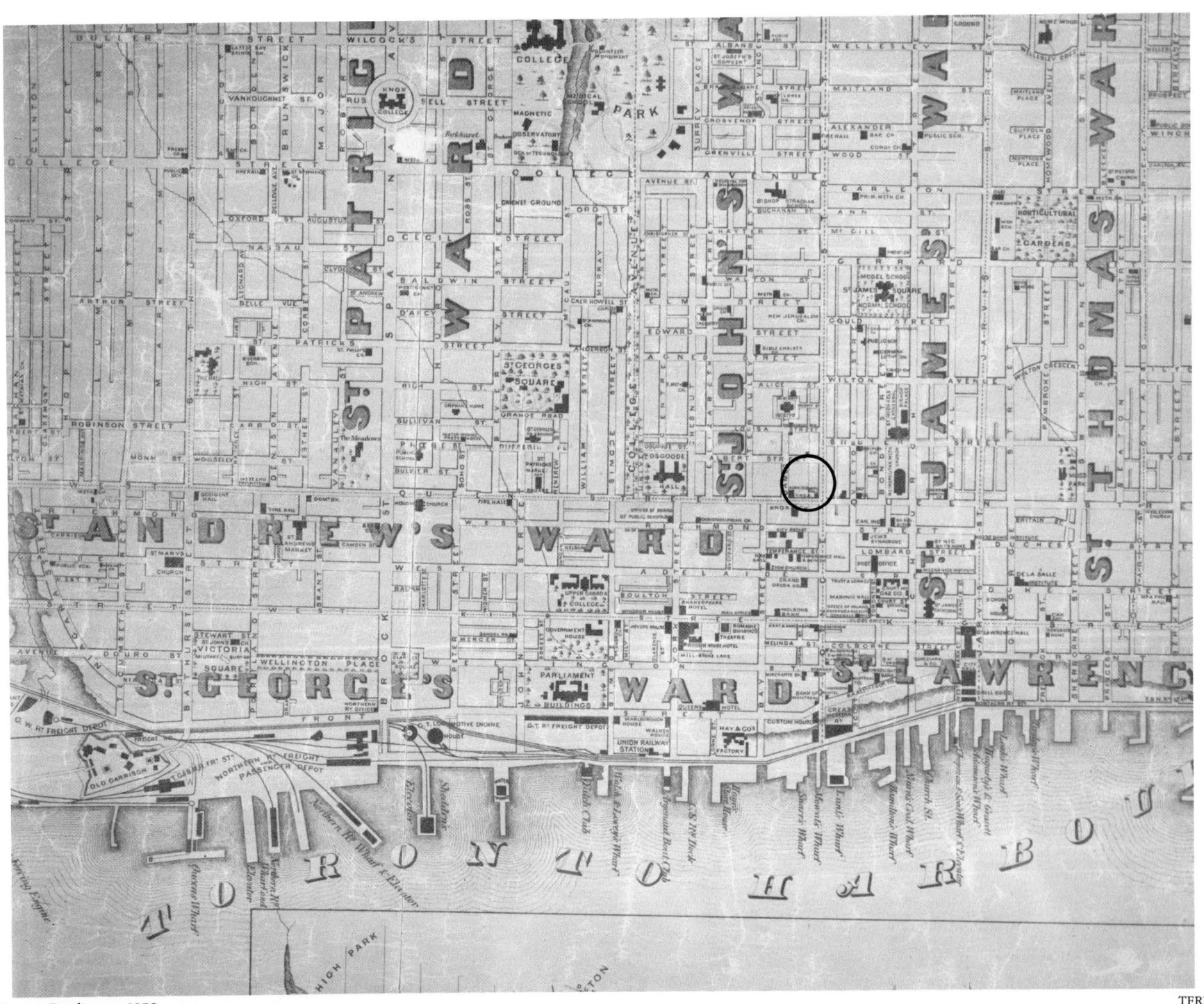

Hart & Rawlinson, 1878

SHAFTESBURY HALL

SHAFTESBURY HALL, 26-30 Queen Street West at the corner of James Street, was built about 1871-2 and was the premises of the YMCA. It contained a free reading room and bureau of enquiry available to newcomers to Toronto. The Hall itself, which seated 1,700, promoted temperance and was used for lectures and concerts. In addition to the Auditorium, the building accommodated, during the 1890's, the offices of several beneficent organizations and the New Bijou Theatre (presumably to distinguish it from the old Bijou Theatre at 91 Yonge Street [see Shea's Theatre], destroyed by fire in 1897). Later, after 1902, the building housed the Adams Furniture Company until 1905 by which time Eaton's Store, which had opened on Dec. 8, 1869, had expanded to cover the entire block between James and Yonge.

Artist: J. Hanshew — NGI

VINCENT WALLACE, composer of *Maritana*.

Globe, Dec. 4, 1877 — AO

Drawing: John Wood — NGI

MICHAEL BALFE, composer of *The Rose of Castile* and *The Bohemian Girl*.

Globe, Feb. 3, 1880 — AO

OPERATIC CONCERT

Last night an appreciative audience gathered in Shaftesbury Hall, drawn by the announcement that a programme of operatic *morceaux* would be performed by a company, which has been organized for that purpose by Mr. Wm. Hamilton.

Mr. Hamilton has been a resident of Toronto for some time, and recognizing the desirability of a thoroughly efficient company, which could render selections from the operas in a manner acceptable to our audiences, took steps to engage the artists, who made their first appearance in Toronto last night.

The programme was a varied one, comprising besides the usual solos, a number of concerted pieces, which were very well sung, and which met with great applause. Conspicuous among these were "The Magic Wove Scarf," from the *Mountain Sylph*, and Bishop's "Blow, Gentle Gales." These ladies and gentlemen sing well together, and display great taste and judgment, the piano passages especially being well done.

Madame Rieve Wilmot has a light, clear soprano voice, with considerable cultivation, and sang a song by Ricci with great success, and on the demand for an *encore* sang "Home, Sweet Home." Later Madame Wilmot sang the "Shadow Song," from *Dinorah*, and "Within a Mile of Edinboro' Town." Miss Louisa Phillips, a contralto of great sweetness and compass, besides taking part in the concerted music, sung "Alas! Those Chimes," from *Maritana*, which was warmly *encored*. Mr. A. Bowman, the tenor of this Company, sang "Ah! Love, how Blest," from *Trovatore*, and in response to a recall sang, "Then You'll Remember Me" in a very ornate manner. Mr. Hamilton sang two songs, in which his fine full baritone voice showed to excellent advantage:— "Tho' Fortune Darkly o'er Me Frowns," and "Alone in the Desert." Mr. Kerrison performed the arduous duties of accompanist with satisfaction to the performers, and credit to himself. The "Good Night" Quartette from *Martha* brought the programme to a close, the only drawback to the evening's enjoyment being that Mr. Bartleman was delayed at Buffalo and unable, in consequence, to appear as announced.

Globe, Dec. 3, 1877 — AO

MTLB T12751

Queen Street West, Yonge to Simcoe Streets 1888. SHAFTESBURY HALL is the farthest tall building from the right.

APPEARANCES
1875   William Hamilton's Opera Company

ST. ANDREW'S HALL

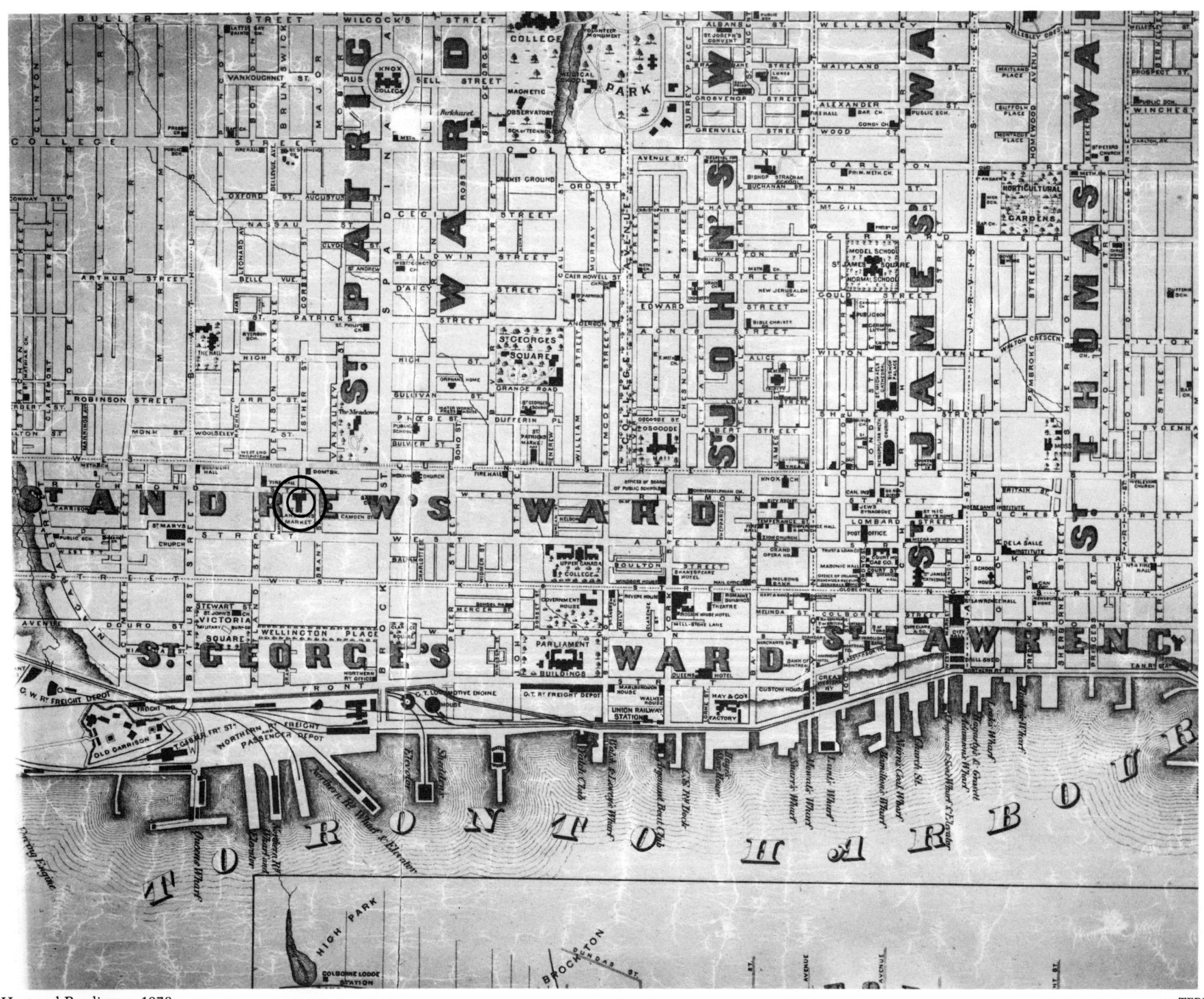

Hart and Rawlinson, 1878

1880
ST. ANDREW'S HALL

A Hall that hasn't been tried? Let's have a go.

OLD ST. ANDREWS MARKET,
Richmond Street West, 1921. The Hall is at the left.

ST. ANDREW'S HALL

On May 22, 1837, a grant of Crown Land (1 ¾ acres) bounded by Farley Avenue (after 1909 Richmond Street West), Maud, Brant and Adelaide, was made to the city for use exclusively as a market. Apparently this ruling was not strictly observed and after December 1911 was removed. In 1920 the Hall was listed at #511 Richmond Street West and the market at #507-523. It was demolished in January, 1932.

AMATEUR JUVENILE
Comic Opera Troupe,
Under the patronage of the LIEUTENANT-GOVERNOR OF ONTARIO and MISS MACDONALD.
Second performance of
H.M.S. PINAFORE
At St. Andrews' Hall, on Tuesday February 3rd, 1880.
Proceeds to be devoted to charitable purposes.
Tickets, 25c.; children, 15c. Can be had at Nordheimer's, Suckling's, and Harvard's Drug Store, No. 816 Queen-street West, and at the door. Reserved seats, 25c. extra. Only a limited number of tickets will be issued.
Ticket-holders for the last performance who were unable to obtain admission owing to the crowded state of the hall, are notified that their tickets are good for this occasion.

Globe, Feb. 3, 1880   AO

THE JUVENILE PINAFORE COMPANY repeated their performance of Gilbert and Sullivan's comic and pleasing opera at St. Andrew's Hall last night before a large and appreciative audience. The cast was the same as on last Friday night, and was well sustained throughout, notwithstanding the fact that two or three of the young performers were suffering from colds. The chorus was strong and kept good time, being a powerful addition to the individual efforts of the leading characters. The audience entered into the spirit of the piece as much as the little people on the stage, and went away thoroughly delighted with the evening's amusement they had provided. The rather difficult duties of accompanyist were well discharged by Mrs. Lawlor, and Mrs. Featherstonhaugh directed the stage business. The proceeds of the entertainment will be devoted to charitable purposes.

Globe, Feb. 4, 1880   AO

TORONTO MUSICAL FESTIVAL.
CHORUS ENROLMENT.
Students residing west of Simcoe and south of Queen's Park intending to join the Festival Chorus will meet for organization
THIS (MONDAY) EVENING, FEB. 1ST
at eight o'clock, at St. Andrew's Hall.
By order.   E. L. ROBERTS, Sec.

Telegram, Feb. 1, 1886   NLC

ST. ANDREWS HALL c.1932

APPEARANCES
1880   Juvenile Pinafore Company

1883
ZOOLOGICAL GARDENS

Even the Zoo offered possibilities.

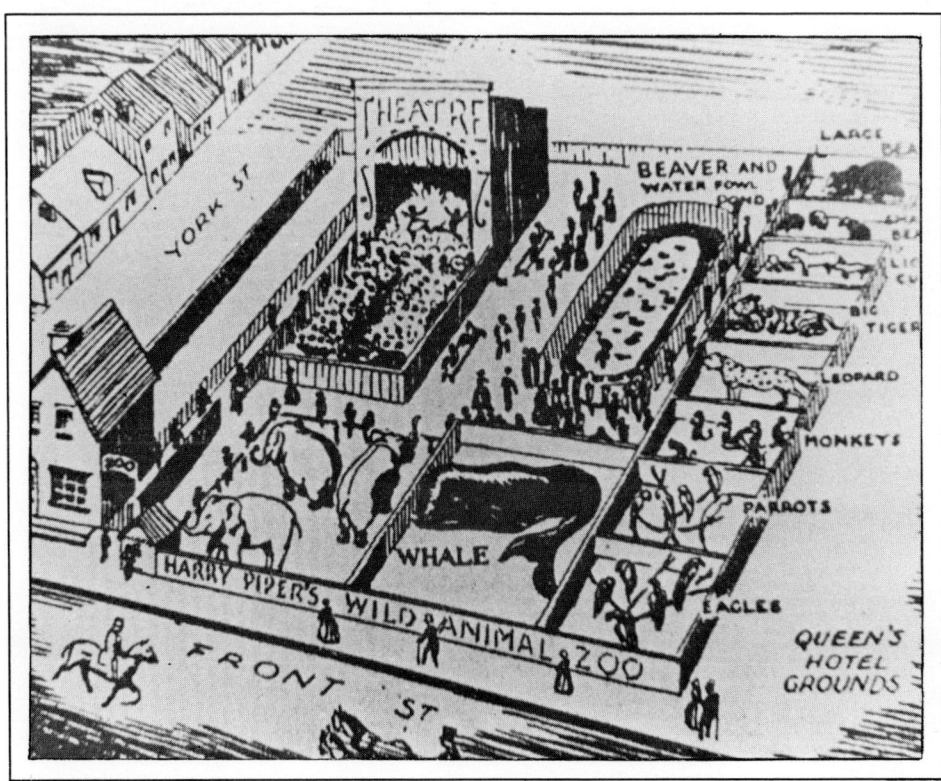

A Street Called Front
Marathon Realty Company Ltd. Toronto, 1983

ZOOLOGICAL GARDENS

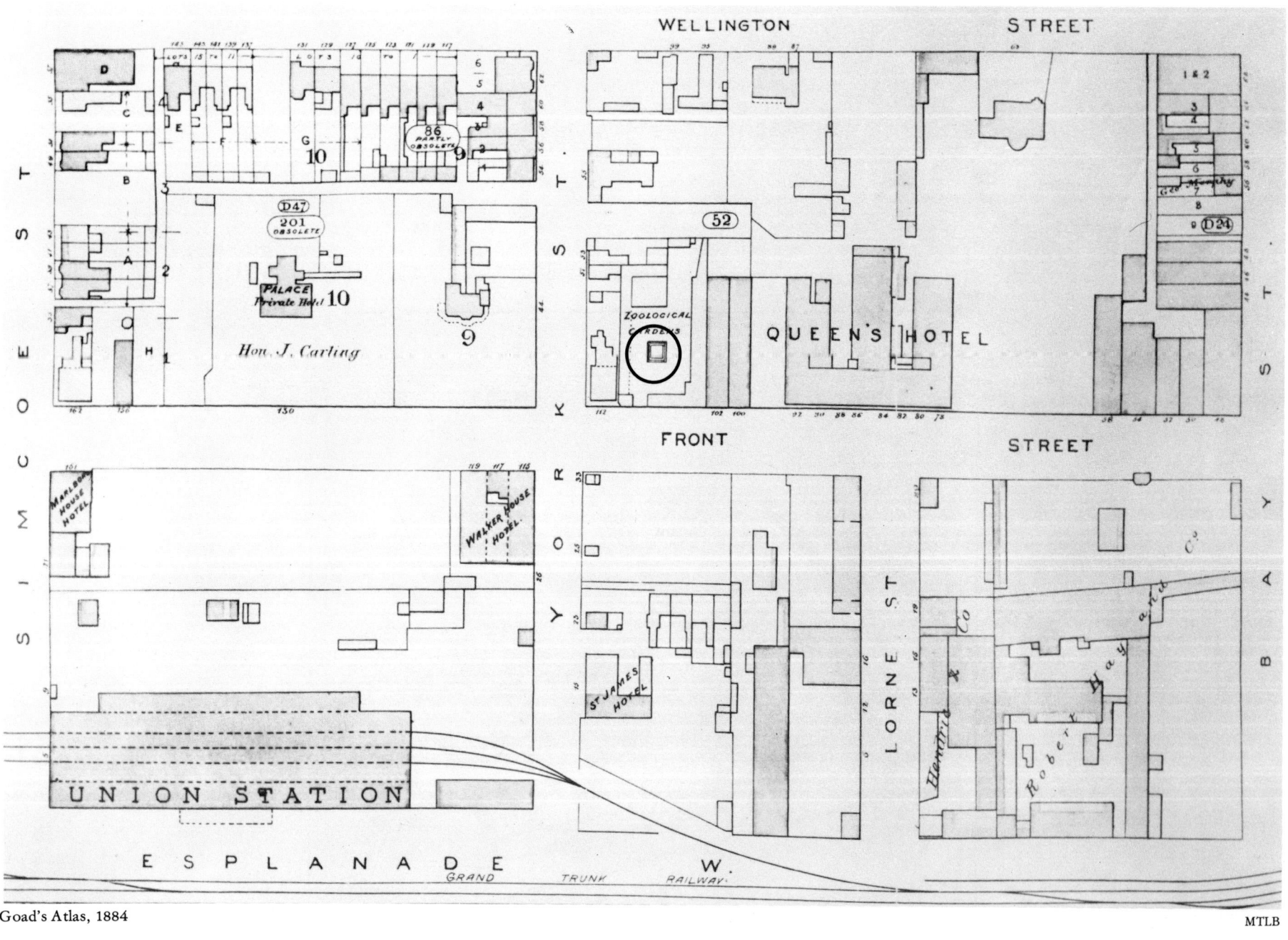

Goad's Atlas, 1884

ZOOLOGICAL GARDENS

In 1872, Mr. Harry Piper kept a collection of wild animals in an old iron yard at the rear of John Harrington's hardware store on King Street near Toronto Street. At a meeting of the Toronto Zoological and Acclimatization Society on July 22, 1881 in the grounds at the northeast corner of Front and York Streets, the Society, which had accepted responsibility for the animals, reached a decision to open the grounds on Civic Holiday, the Lieutenant-Governor to officiate. The Toronto Mail of July 31, 1884 reported that Mr. Piper had bought a pair of camels, a leopard, two sun bears, a yak, monkeys and coons in an auction of animals at Detroit. There were some notable animals – Peter the Great, a bear; Romeo and Juliet, lions; Sir John, an elephant; and in the early 80's a whale. Minstrelsy was also a feature of the gardens and during the summers of 1883 and 1884 operas were performed. On August 21, 1885, Lieutenant-Governor Robinson laid the cornerstone of the Zoological Gardens building at Exhibition Park. By September 10 that year the animals were housed and the Zoo officially opened, to the relief of the residents around Front and Yonge. In 1886 the newspapers were still reporting new acquisitions.

Canadian Illustrated News, Oct. 22, 1881

Globe, Sept. 10, 1883

Telegram July 10, 1926

GEORGE HOLMAN

MAURICE GRAU whose company performed at the Zoological Gardens for three days in July of Toronto's 50th Anniversary year.

Globe, June 30, 1884

APPEARANCES
1883   Holman Opera Company
1884   Grau Opera Company
1884   St. Quinten Opera Company

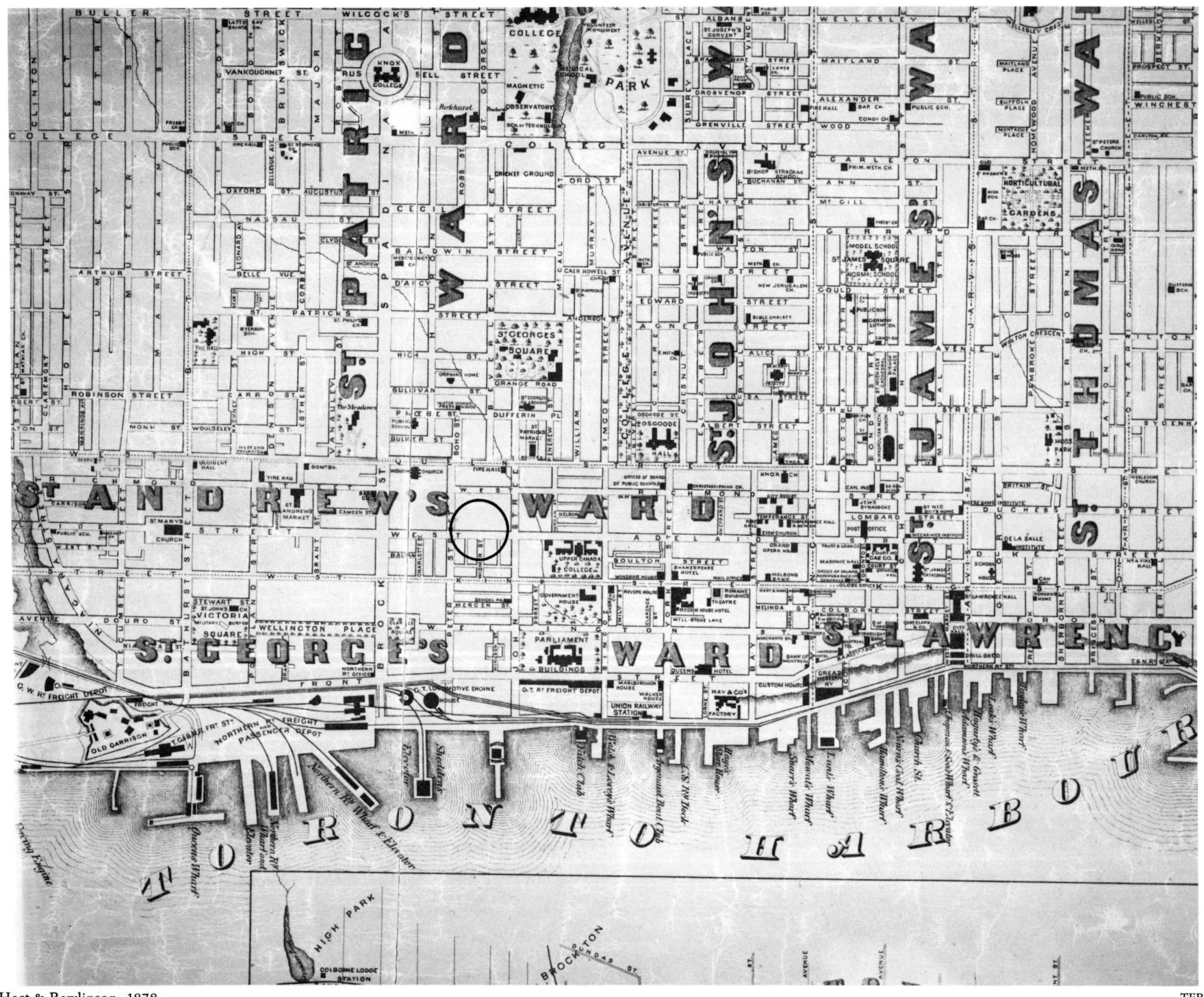

Hart & Rawlinson, 1878

1883
HOLMAN OPERA HOUSE

The first use of a skating arena.

Canadian Illustrated News, Mar. 17, 1877
w.c. F.M. Bell-Smith

HOLMAN OPERA HOUSE

Skating and curling rinks were numerous in Toronto during the 19th century and frequently served as public halls for large events such as carnivals, masquerades and concerts, particularly band concerts. In September 1883 George Holman's Opera Troupe performed in one which stood at the northwest corner of Adelaide and the present Widmer Streets. Holman had opened the Holman Opera House in London where the troupe had made their headquarters after the destruction of Toronto's Royal Lyceum. Possibly he hoped to establish a chain of houses. History does not record the reason for the single season in this building – it may be that Toronto had become too sophisticated for his company. The repertoire in 1883 consisted of *Olivette* (Audran), *Billie Taylor* (Solomon/Stephens), *The Lakes of Killarney, The Mascot* (Audran), *H.M.S. Pinafore* (Gilbert & Sullivan), *Kate Kearney* (a play) and *Patience* (Gilbert & Sullivan).

Telegram, July 10, 1926   MTLB

GEORGE HOLMAN

Canadian Illustrated News, Feb. 10, 1877   MTLB

Mail, Jan. 26, 1875   NLC

Globe, Feb. 13, 1879   NLC

ADELAIDE-ST. SKATING
RINK

The Band of the 10th Royals
will be in attendance

This Evening (Tuesday), February 3rd.
OPEN 7:30 P.M.

Wednesday, February 4th, 2:30 p.m.
Thursday, February 5th, 7:30 p.m.
Saturday, February 7th, 2:30 p.m.

Admission, 25 cents.
Season ticket-holders free.

Globe, Feb. 3, 1880 — AO

THE DIRECTORS
OF THE
ADELAIDE-ST. SKATING
RINK

Beg to announce that a Committee of Lady and Gentleman members of the Toronto Skating Rink has been formed to arrange for a

FANCY DRESS CARNIVAL,
on a grand scale, to take place on

Tuesday Ev'g., 20th inst.

Parties wishing to appear in Costume will require to send their names, addresses, and the style of Costume proposed to be worn to the Committee, not later than SATURDAY, the 17th, who will issue Special Costume Tickets to admit the applicants to the ice. None admitted otherwise. Only four clowns will be allowed, and no objectionable characters will be admitted.

The Management will spare no expense in their endeavour to make this the Grandest and most Select Carnival of the Season.

The Grand Trunk Railway Company have kindly consented to issue Return Tickets at single fare to Toronto from Port Hope, Hamilton, Guelph, and all intermediate stations.

Further particulars in future advertisements.

All communications to be addressed to the Secretary.

DAVID WALKER,
Secretary, Toronto Curling and Skating Club.

Globe, Feb. 12, 1883 — AO

Stereo by James Esson? MTLB T12125

TORONTO CURLING & SKATING RINK c.1880. During a Flower Show.

The Toronto Curling and Skating Club ceased to exist after 1884.

HOLMAN OPERA HOUSE.
(Late Adelaide-street Rink.)

J. C. CONNER................Manager.

GRAND OPENING NIGHT.

MONDAY EVENING, SEPT. 10th,

With Audran's Comic Opera,

"OLIVETTE."

Miss Sallie Holman as *Olivette*.

Small prices and large audiences is our motto.
Reserved seats only 35 cents, admission 25 cents.

Globe, Sept. 10, 1883 — NLC

APPEARANCES
1883 Holman Opera Troupe

1884
SEMI-CENTENNIAL

Photo: Picturesque Canada MTLB
TORONTO FROM THE KINGSTON ROAD circa 1884.

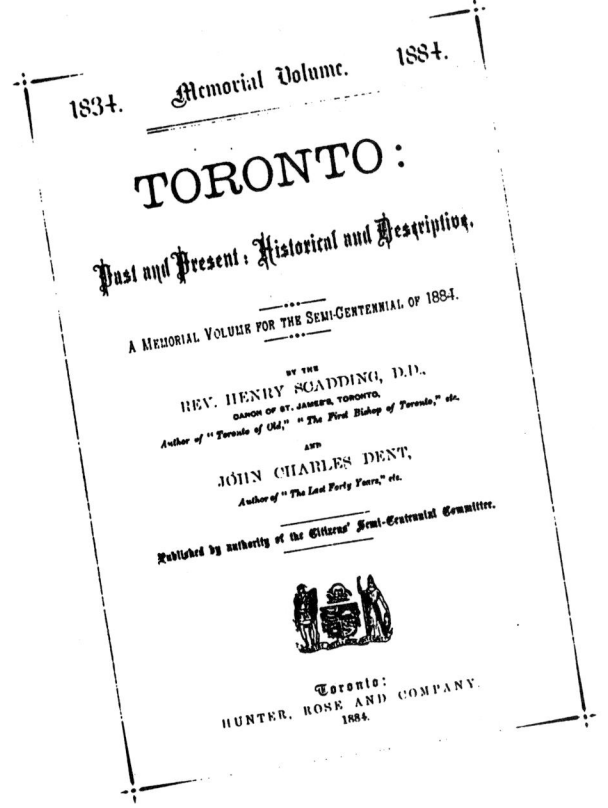

The Globe, Toronto, June 30, 1884   MTLB

The Globe, Toronto. July 1, 1884   MTLB

Semi-Centennial Celebration

TICKETS FOR THE

GRAND BALL

AT THE PAVILION

HORTICULTURAL GARDENS,

This (Monday) Evening,

MAY BE PROCURED AT

A. & S. NORDHEIMER'S, SUCKLING & SONS',
ROBINSON BROS., J. E. ELLIS & CO.,
QUEEN'S HOTEL, ROSSIN HOUSE,
WALKER HOUSE, AMERICAN HOTEL,
SEMI-CENTENNIAL ROOM, 34 Toronto-street,
and at the Office of PELLATT & PELLATT, 40
King-street East, where all information may be
obtained.

Ladies' Tickets, $2.   Gentlemen's Tickets, $3.

J. WEIR ANDERSON,
Hon. Sec. Ball Committee.

N.B.—Entrance to the Gardens from Gerrard-street only.

GRAND OPERA HOUSE,

O. B. SHEPPARD, Manager.

Great attractions for Semi-Centennial week only, commencing MONDAY EVENING, JUNE 30th. The greatest of spectacular melodramas,

THE WORLD,

With all its wealth of magnificent scenery, Direct from Colvile's 14th-st. Theatre, New York.
MATINEES TUESDAY AND SATURDAY.
N.B.—Volunteers in uniform admitted at half-price, except to top gallery.

TO-NIGHT
Granite Covered Rink.
LIBERATI

The Greatest Attraction of the Semi-Centennial Celebration. The
WORLD'S GREATEST CORNET-PLAYER
Supported by the Full Band of the Foot Guards of Ottawa. ARTHUR E. FISHER, Solo Pianist. Magnificent Programme. Tickets 50 cents. Doors open at 7:30. Concert begins at 8 o'clock.

Semi-Centennial Celebration

GRAND CONCERT

OF

600 CHILDREN

OF T...

Public and ...

E. W. SCH...

MR. W. WAUGH L...
MISS BERRY
MISS S...
MIS...
AND CLAXTON'S O...
MR. F. H. TORRINGTON, ...OMPANIST.
Horticultural Garden Pavilion, Saturday Evening, July 5th.

FIREWORKS!

THURSDAY NIGHT.

Str. "Southern Belle."
A limited Number of Tickets will be issued to see the
GRAND DISPLAY ON THE WATER,
leaving Milloy's Wharf at 11 o'clock p.m. Tickets, $1. Apply at 109 King-street West or on the steamer.

Semi-Centennial Celebration.

GRAND ORATORIO

'CREATION'

CHORAL SOCIETY,

E. FISHER . . CONDUCTOR.

Miss FANNY KELLOGG, Soprano;
Mr. WM. COURTNEY, Tenor;
Mr. IVAN J. MORAVSKI, Basso.

HORTICULTURAL GARDENS PAVILION,

Wednesday Evening, July 2nd.

A1 FIREWORKS

PROF. HAND & CO., the Champion Firework Makers of America, are engaged for the great Bombardment on Toronto Bay, July 3rd, during the Semi-Centennial week, and will be prepared to supply steamboats, row-boats, and all parties wishing to illuminate either their dwellings or boats either with Coloured Fires, Roman Candles, Rockets, or Chinese Lanterns, on the very lowest terms. Private or public displays sent out for the first of July with experienced men from $150; without man from $25. Send for price list. Address PROF. HAND & CO., King-street, Hamilton, Ont.

Semi-Centennial Celebration

GRAND ORATORIO
"REDEMPTION!"

PHILHARMONIC SOCIETY

F. H. TORRINGTON, Conductor.

MISS FANNY KELLOGG, Soprano.
MR. WM. COURTNEY, Tenor.
MR. IVAN E. MORAVSKI, Basso.

Horticultural Gardens Pavilion

THURSDAY, JULY 3rd.

SEMI-CENTENNIAL CELEBRATION.

CHILDREN'S CHORUS.

REHEARSALS.

SEPARATE SCHOOLS—9 a.m. Wednesday, at De LaSalle Institute.
COMBINED REHEARSAL WITH ORCHESTRA—8:45 a.m. Thursday, at St. James' Schoolhouse.
COMBINED DRESS REHEARSAL WITH ORCHESTRA—10 a.m. Friday, at the Pavilion.
☞ A full and prompt attendance is indispensable.
E. V. SCHUCH, Conductor.

MENDELSSOHN QUINTETTE CLUB.

HORTICULTURAL GARDENS,

FRIDAY, July 4.

Assisted by Miss FANNY KELLOGG, Prima Donna, Soprano,
IVAN E. MORAVSKI, Basso, and
W. WAUGH LAUDER, Solo Pianist.

Plan of Pavilion at Messrs. Suckling & Sons' Pianoforte Warerooms.

THEATRE ROYAL,

Cor. Bay and Adelaide streets, H. L. MONTFORD, Manager.

DURING CENTENNIAL WEEK THE
HOLMAN ENGLISH OPERA TROUPE

WILL GIVE

Two Grand Performances Daily

Every Afternoon at 2:30.
Every Evening at 8 o'clock.
Popular prices—Dress circle, 25c; orchestra, 35c; family circle, 15c.
Matinees—First floor, 20c; second floor, 10c.

PRIDE & SACKETT'S BIG TENTS,

York-street, opposite Rossin House.

The greatest show in the city. Lucia Zarate, the smallest being in the world; also P. T. Barnum's collection of strange people, and a first-class stage entertainment. Open during Centennial week from 10 a.m. to 10:30 p.m. Curiosities on exhibition all the time. Stage performance 2:30 and 8. Admission to all only 10 cents.

Semi-Centennial Celebration!

DON'T FORGET THE

FIREWORKS!

AT THE

HORTICULTURAL GARDENS

DOMINION DAY.

Usual charges.

H. PELLATT,
Hon. Sec.-Treas.

CENTENNIAL WEEK.

During the 50 years that followed Toronto's incorporation as a city the population increased from 10,000 to 105,211. By 1884 the city was vastly different from the garrison town of muddy York. It had all the characteristics of a solid Victorian metropolis, including countless churches and the head offices of several major banks. The manner in which the citizens celebrated the Golden Jubilee was traditionally English – a military parade consisting of four divisions of corps from Montreal, Niagara, Kingston, Hamilton, London and elsewhere as well as Toronto, followed by 12 historical tableaux; a review of the troops in Queen's Park; a grand costume ball at the Horticultural Pavilion; fireworks; with every place of entertainment exploiting the occasion.

In 1884, as in 1984, Toronto's Anniversary festivities included much operatic activity – at the Grand Opera House, the Theatre Royal, Hanlan's point (Mr. Mackie's Summer Pavilion) the Summer Pavilion (York Street), the Horticultural Gardens and the Zoological Gardens.

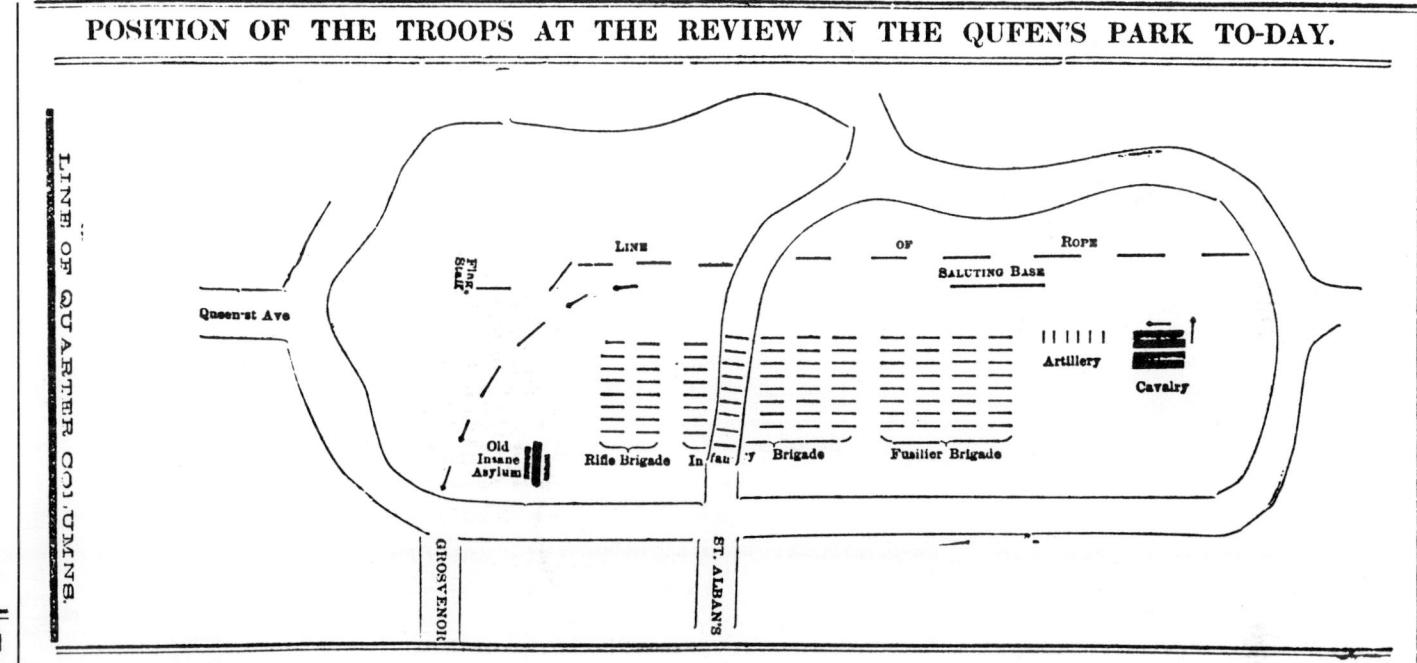

Extracts from The Globe, July 1, 1884, page 3.

THE TABLEAUX

MTLB TR 917 354 H388

Illustrations from Historical Tableaux in Honour of Toronto's Semi-Centennial.

TORONTO'S JUBILEE

The First Day an Unqualified Success.

ENTHUSIASM UNIVERSALLY DISPLAYED

An Imposing Procession and Elegant Tableaux.

GRAND FANCY DRESS BALL.

The Queen City Crowded With Visitors.

DECORATIONS AND ILLUMINATIONS

Programme for the Grand Military Review.

LIST OF CORPS TAKING PART.

LANDING OF GOVERNOR SIMCOE.

The idea of this tableau was conceived by a member of the Committee who had glanced over the designs or the photographs of the tableaux used on the occasion of the 150th anniversary of the city of Baltimore, and had observed a representation of the landing of Governor John Smith. One end of the car, which measured 30 feet by 9, showed a sandy shore running down to a sheet of water, on which was a boat pointed towards the shore, and containing Governor Simcoe and attendants. On the beach stood an Indian or two, and one or two other red men were in a canoe which was being shoved off from the shore, the object of the occupants evidently being to welcome the Governor and his party.

NAMING THE HARBOUR.

This tableau represented the naming of Toronto harbour, and measured 35 feet by 9. Half the car was taken up by a sand bank, surmounted by a stockade shown in profile; the whole affair was made of canvas, but painted to represent the different objects to be called to mind. The logs were pointed, and stood about six feet high. On the sand bank outside the palisades was left a narrow platform, along which, with measured steps and slow, guards were pacing. Inside the stockade was a small log house, constructed of canvas, and in front of the stockade, one on either side were a couple of cannon. From the sand bank there was a step descent into the other half of the car, which was covered with canvas painted to represent water. About the centre a boat was let in, as if sunk to the proper depth in water. Standing in the boat was an officer holding aloft the Union Jack, and giving to Toronto Harbour the name it has ever since so proudly borne.

FIRST MEETING OF PARLIAMENT.

This tableau measured 30 feet by 9, the area of the car being almost fully taken up with the representation of a stone edifice wherein were assembled the Governor and the half-dozen legislators who first met in York Legislative Chambers to administer the affairs of Upper Canada. The side walls of the edifice are left out and four handsome pillars on each side substituted, so that the interior of the Legislative Chamber was fully open to view. The structure stood about ten feet in height, measuring from the surface of the car. An embattled frieze ran around the top, and painted drapery hung from capital to capital, looped up midway between each. In the interior was a table covered with green cloth, and opposite the far end was the Governor's throne, with a canopy overhanging it. The six legislators were seated three on either side of the table, intent on business.

EDUCATIONAL TABLEAU.

This was one of the most interesting of the tableaux, and brought out clearly the immense progress, almost out of proportion with its still rapid strides in other respects, which Toronto has made in educational facilities and intellectual development. The car was 35 feet by 9 in dimensions, and was almost wholly taken up by the base of a large platform with several rises, on the highest of which was seated the goddess Minerva, whose presence was supposed to denote her approval of the many institutions dedicated to her and represented below. Over the goddess hung a canopy, resting on golden pillars. There were four slender tapering pillars painted in gold at the several corners of the car, with bannerets attached, and garlands of flowers running from each to the centre of the top of the canopy where they joined. The sides and base of the platform were painted to represent shelves of books; the artist divided them into panels, and in the centre was a panel bearing the inscription "Free Library." On the corners of the same rise, which was very wide, were various figures representing the working men and women who avail themselves of the privileges of the Free Library. They were shown comfortably ensconced by their fireside enjoying free of cost a class of literature which their slender means would never allow them to do more than dream of were it not for the invaluable institution in question. On the several rises of the platform were figures symbolical of the public schools, high schools, and the University of the city; and on each side of the car stood two female figures supporting large paintings, respectively, of the University, the Upper Canada College, the Collegiate Institute, and a public school.

TORONTO WELCOMES ALL.

This tableau came last in the procession. The title explained the idea set forth, which was that, irrespective of nationality, creed, or colour, Toronto welcomed all who came to add to its stores of wealth, or industry, or intelligence. A lady representing Toronto sat on a platform under a canopy supported by four painted poles and surmounted by a beaver. Around her stood an array of immigrants of every colour, creed, and clime. Here was Wah Hoo, a Chinaman, who intended to establish a laundry in the city; here a negro, who meant to become a "tonsorial artist"; here a young Englishman, who was "going to try farming"; and here were Irish, and Germans, and Scandinavians, and Icelanders, and Russians, and Italians, and many others, all seeking opportunities to make a successful start in a fresh life in the New World.

TORONTO WELCOMES ALL

THE FANCY BALL.

The citizen's ball at the Pavilion last evening was fairly successful in point of numbers while in other respects the event was highly satisfactory. The attendance was fairly representative of the citizenship of Toronto. The idea of a fancy dress ball was not strictly carried out, but although there was a large proportion of black coats, there were gay costumes enough to relieve the scene from the appearance of sombreness. The presence of a considerable volunteer force in the city was made apparent in the large number of military uniforms—the gay dress of the Fusiliers of Montreal and the Ottawa Foot Guards contrasting pleasantly with the dark green of the Queen's Own. A novel and very sensible costume was worn by one youth, who appeared in a cool suit of linen. "Sebastian," a character drawn from "Twelfth Night," attracted attention by his tall figure and his gay costume. The dress of the 17th Century appeared to be rather a favourite among the gentlemen. Of the ladies, many appeared in ordinary ball-dress, without any attempt at personation. Of those in costume, there were peasants, fishwives, and "twilights" and "mornings," while one young lady recorded one of the scientific features of the age by appearing as the Electric Light.

The following programme of dances was prepared:—1, Semi-Centennial Quadrille, in costume; 2, Valse; 3, Polka; 4, Lancers; 5, Valse; 6, Valse; 7, Lancers; 8, Polka; 9, Valse; 10, Lancers; 11, Valse; 12, Polka; 13, Valse; 14, Valse; 15, Lancers; 16, Valse; 17, Polka; 18, Valse; 19, Sir Roger de Coverley. The first dance on the programme was omitted. The music was furnished by Seager's String Band, and was of excellent quality, a large proportion of it being quite new. The conservatory to the south of the Hall was thrown open, and proved a cool and pleasant retreat for tired dancers. An excellent supper was furnished in the room adjoining the Hall on the north side. Dancing was kept up until an early hour this morning.

The following were among the ladies and gentlemen noticed on the floor:—

Among those present were:—Mr and Mr Frederick Moffat, Mrs Arkell, Mr, Mrs, and Misses Pellatt, Mr and Mrs W B McMurrich, Miss Vivian, Mr and Mrs Henry Moffat, His Worship the Mayor, Mr and Mrs E Boswell, Mr and Misses Spratt, Mr and Mrs Cosgrave, Mr and Mrs Wyld, Mr and Mrs Myles, Major and Mrs Hamilton, Misses McCutcheon, Capt and Mrs Anderson, the Misses Anderson, Mr and Miss Ince, Mr Ald, Mrs and Misses Walker, Mr and Mrs T B Smith, Mr and Mrs Bruce Harman, Sheriff Jarvis, Judge and Mrs Paterson, Judge and Miss Cameron; Major King and officers of Welland Field Battery; Lieut Beatty and Lieut Myles, of Toronto Field Battery; Lieut. Michie, 10th Royals; Capt Lightall, 6th Fusiliers; Capt Hodgins, G G F G; Dr Bell, G G F G; Mr Barry, Ottawa; Mr C A Hirschfelder, American Vice-Consul; Mr and Mrs E W Schuch; Mr A Boite; Miss Besford; Mrs Cope, San Francisco; Miss Crawford; Mr and Mrs J F Thomson.

THE FANCY COSTUMES.

The following are some of the principal costumes and characters:—

Mr Geo Michie, Sebastian, in Twelfth Night.
Mr C G D Roberts, Gentleman of 17th Century.
Mr J E Collins, Gentleman of 17th Century.
Mr Sykes, Ace of Diamonds.
Mr A B Canning, Jockey.
Mr J Kingvett (St Catharines), Gentleman of 17th Century.
Mrs L Cosgrave, white satin and silk, Spanish lace.
Mrs J G Beard, cream silk, Spanish lace over dress.
Mrs W Greaves, cream silk.
Miss Barry (Ottawa), Morning.
Miss Kate Barry (Ottawa), Starlight.
Miss Hirschfelder, Oriental lady.
Miss Maud Hirschfelder, Electric Light.
Miss Ince, Kate Greenaway.
Miss Brunell, green satin and gauze.
Miss Besford, pink satin and natural flowers.
Miss Cope (San Francisco), pink satin and brown embroidered satin.
Miss Grace Walker, white and gold muslin.
Mrs McMurrich, dove coloured silk and crimson velvet.
Miss Walker, terra cotta satin and white lace.
Mrs. John Cosgrave, Egyptian Princess, white brocaded satin with stars and crescents, gold veil and diamonds.
Mrs. L. H. Moffatt, mauve watered silk and white lace, powdered hair.
Mrs. F. C. Moffatt, white brocaded velvet and Brussels point lace.
Miss Maud McCutcheon, white silk trimmed with white satin.
Miss Vivian, white satin.
Miss Wall, "For goodness sake don't say that I to'd you."
Mrs. Arkell, black satin and black lace.
Mrs J F Thomson, Flower Girl, white tulle, red, pink, and white roses.
Mrs J Weir Anderson, Flower Girl.
Miss Ince, Red, White, and Blue.
Mrs Andrews, dress of 1834.
Miss Elliott (London), Sister of Mercy.
Miss Myers (Philadelphia), Japanese lady.
Mrs Warren (Niagara), Dresden China.
Miss Anderson, Bonnie Fishwife.
Miss Carrie Smith—Dress, cream satin merve, trimmed with Honiton lace; ornaments, natural flowers.
Miss Merrick, Mutual-street—Dress of white silk, trimmed with lace and flowers.

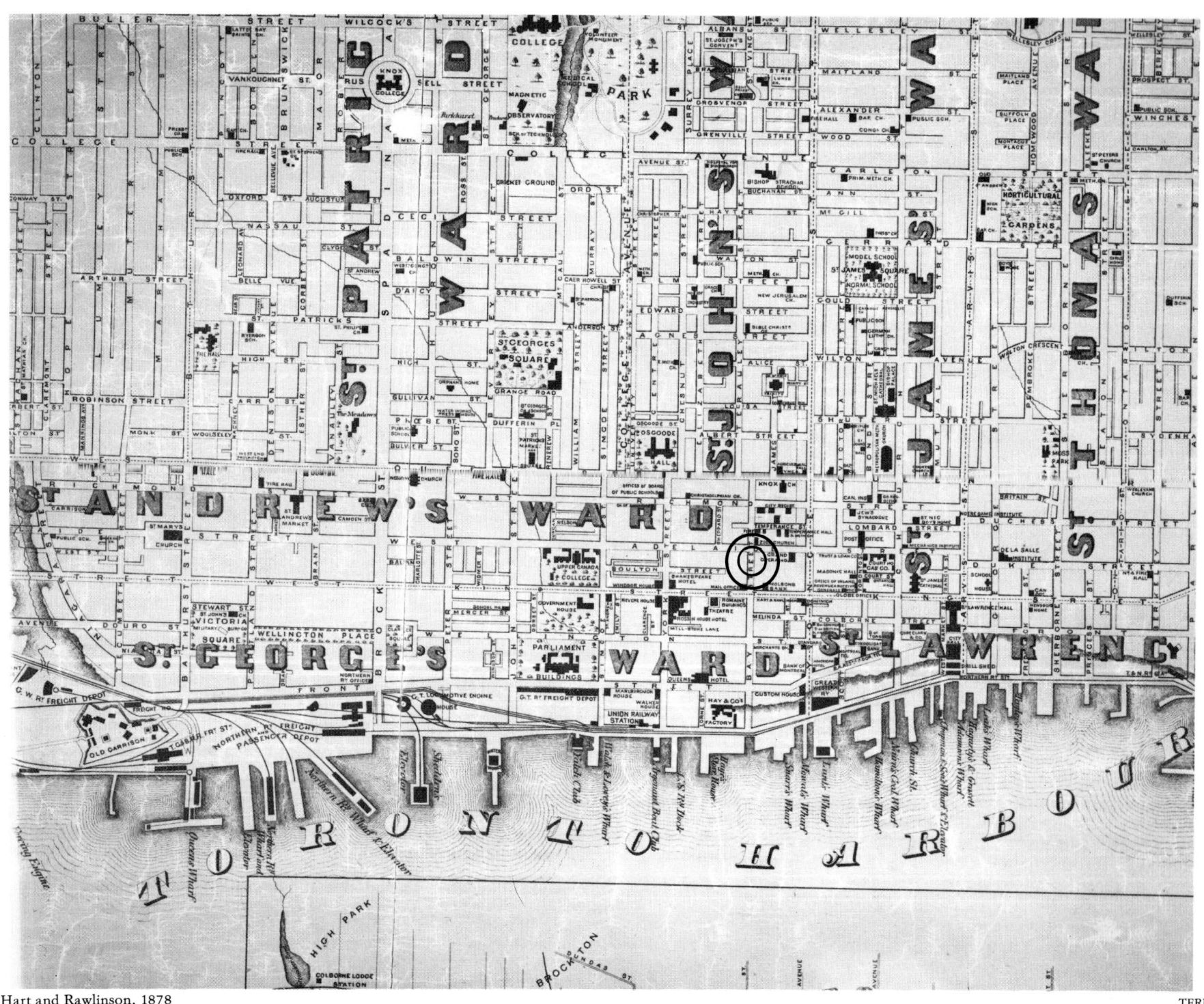

Hart and Rawlinson, 1878

1884
THEATRE ROYAL

During semi-centennial year an abandoned church provided ample seating.

Photo: Octavius Thompson   MTLB T10848
ZION CONGREGATIONAL CHURCH c.1867

THEATRE ROYAL

The ZION CHAPEL was first built in 1839 on the northeast corner of Bay and Adelaide Streets and was destroyed by fire in 1855. The second building was erected in 1856, serving until 1882 as a church and hall for social meetings and concerts. The latter included selections from Haydn's *Creation* and Handel's *Messiah*. During Semi-Centennial Week in 1884 George Holman named it THEATRE ROYAL and his English Opera Troupe gave two performances daily of *Bubbles,* which had been written by Joe H. Banks, a member of the Holman Company, for Sallie Holman. This was the company's last appearance in Toronto. At that time the building was described in the City Directory as "unoccupied church", thereafter as People's Theatre and in 1886 as "unfinished building" which may indicate that new construction was in process.

Telegram, July 10, 1926 — MTLB

GEORGE HOLMAN

Globe, June 30, 1884 — NLC

Globe, Aug. 5, 1884 — NLC

APPEARANCES
1884   Holman Opera Company

1884 SUMMER PAVILION

The first performances (of light opera) in a tent.

The four corners of King and York Streets showing York Street front of Rossin House 1890. Osgoode Hall is visible at the top of York Street.

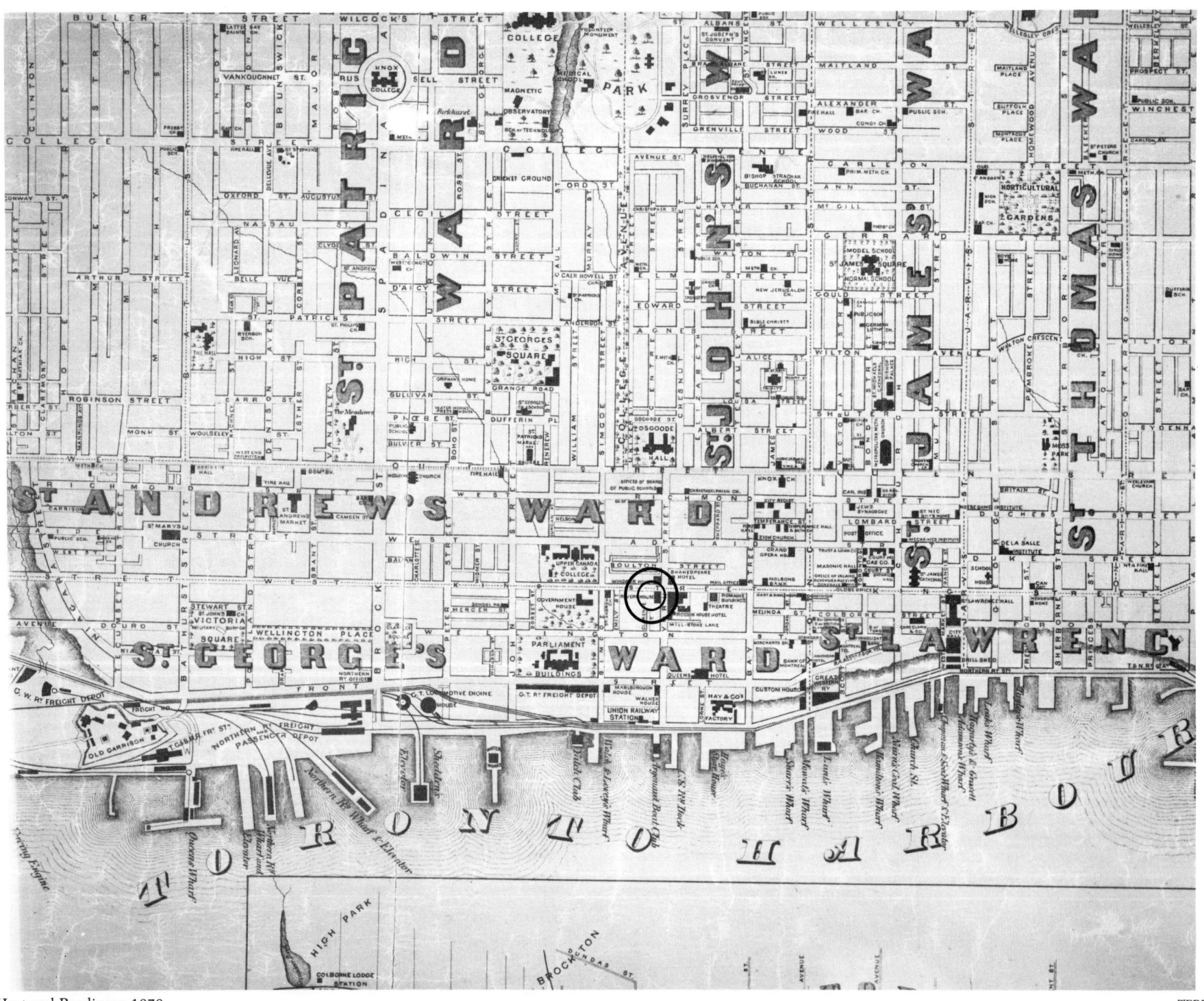

Hart and Rawlinson 1878

SUMMER PAVILION

The SUMMER PAVILION was situated across York Street from the Rossin House which had been built in the mid-19th century and was, by all accounts, a most reputable, commodious and convenient hotel. Miss St. Quinten and her opera company performed at the pavilion during most of August 1884. Their repertoire consisted of *Patience, H.M.S. Pinafore,* by Gilbert and Sullivan; *Olivette* by Audran, and *Bunthorne Abroad, or the Lass that Loved a Pirate* (featuring Miss St. Quinten as Ethel), a satire on a combination of *Patience, H.M.S. Pinafore* and *The Pirates of Penzance*. Satires and "burlesques" of the standard works were extremely common at the time and Gilbert and Sullivan, the greatest satirists of all, came in for their share. *Bunthorne Abroad* was the creation of J. W. Bengough, caricaturist and editor of Toronto's comic weekly *Grip*.

PRIDE & SACKETT'S BIG TENTS,
York-street, opposite Rossin House.
The greatest show in the city. Lucia Zarate, the smallest being in the world; also P. T. Barnum's collection of strange people, and a first-class stage entertainment. Open during Centennial week from 10 a.m. to 10:30 p.m. Curiosities on exhibition all the time. Stage performance 2:30 and 8. Admission to all only 10 cents.

Globe, July 1, 1884 MTLB

SUMMER PAVILION, YORK-STREET, OPPOSITE Rossin House. W. J. Dill, manager. Engagement for one week of the St. Quinten Opera Company, commencing To-night, MONDAY, AUG. 4th, with matinee Wednesday and Saturday afternoon at 2 o'clock. Monday, Tuesday, Wednesday evenings, Gilbert & Sullivan's Comic Opera, "PATIENCE." Admission, 10c. Reserve seats, 20c and 25c. Seats now on sale at Nordheimer's. Monday, Aug. 11th, "Bunthorne Abroad."

Globe, Aug. 4, 1884 MTLB

APPEARANCES
1884   St. Quinten Opera Company

HANLAN'S POINT

1884
HANLAN'S POINT

A summer opera house for semi-centennial year and fifty-two years later a baseball stadium.

Postcard
1880

MTLB T13899

HANLAN'S POINT

The first Hanlan's Hotel, at HANLAN'S POINT on the western end of the string of islands which guards Toronto's harbour, was built by the father of Ned Hanlan, Canada's world-renowned oarsman, winner of the Diamond Sculls. The second was built by Ned himself in 1880. When he went to Australia (where he was finally defeated) in 1884, Mr. Mackie of another hotel family, took over the hotel and erected a summer opera house or pavilion where Miss St. Quinten's opera company performed. The entire amusement area, including the hotel and stadium, was destroyed by fire in 1909. The second stadium, in which the Canadian Grand Opera Association gave its open air performances, was demolished to make room for the island airport in 1937.

Canadian Illustrated News, July 26, 1879   MTLB

EDWARD HANLAN, Champion Sculler of the World.

JEANNE PENGELLY who sang the title role in *Aida*

COCA

HANLAN'S POINT
FREE CONCERTS.

Grand attractions all this week. Monday and Tuesday afternoons the St. Quinten Opera Company—30 artists 30—will give selections from popular operas, ballads, duetts, etc., in front of Hotel Hanlan each afternoon commencing at 3:30. Fares as usual, 5c each way.

Globe June 30, 1884   NLC

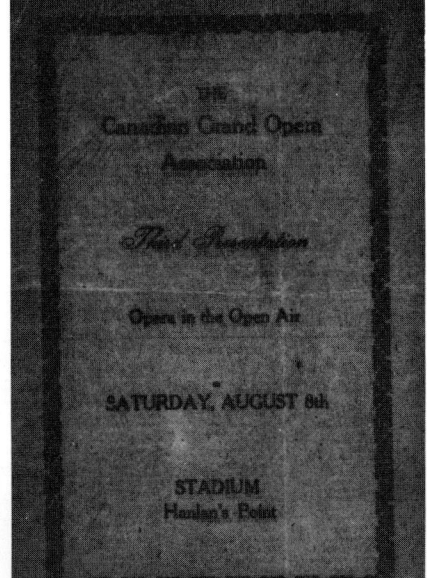

Programme 1936

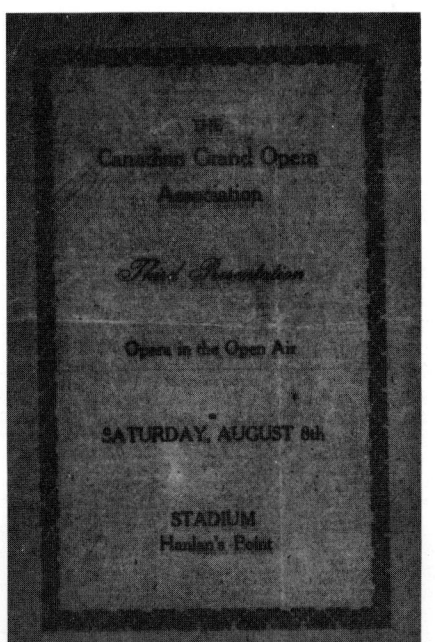

DBT

HANLAN'S POINT

Photo

HANLAN'S POINT BASEBALL
STADIUM 1904-1909

MTLB T11743

Photo

Hanlan's Hotel original Building as it stood in 1870

MTLB T11027

Postcard

SECOND STADIUM

MTLB T13942

APPEARANCES
Mackie's Summer Pavilion
1884   St. Quinten Opera Company

Stadium
1936   Canadian Grand Opera Association
1937   Canadian Grand Opera Association

TORONTO OPERA HOUSE

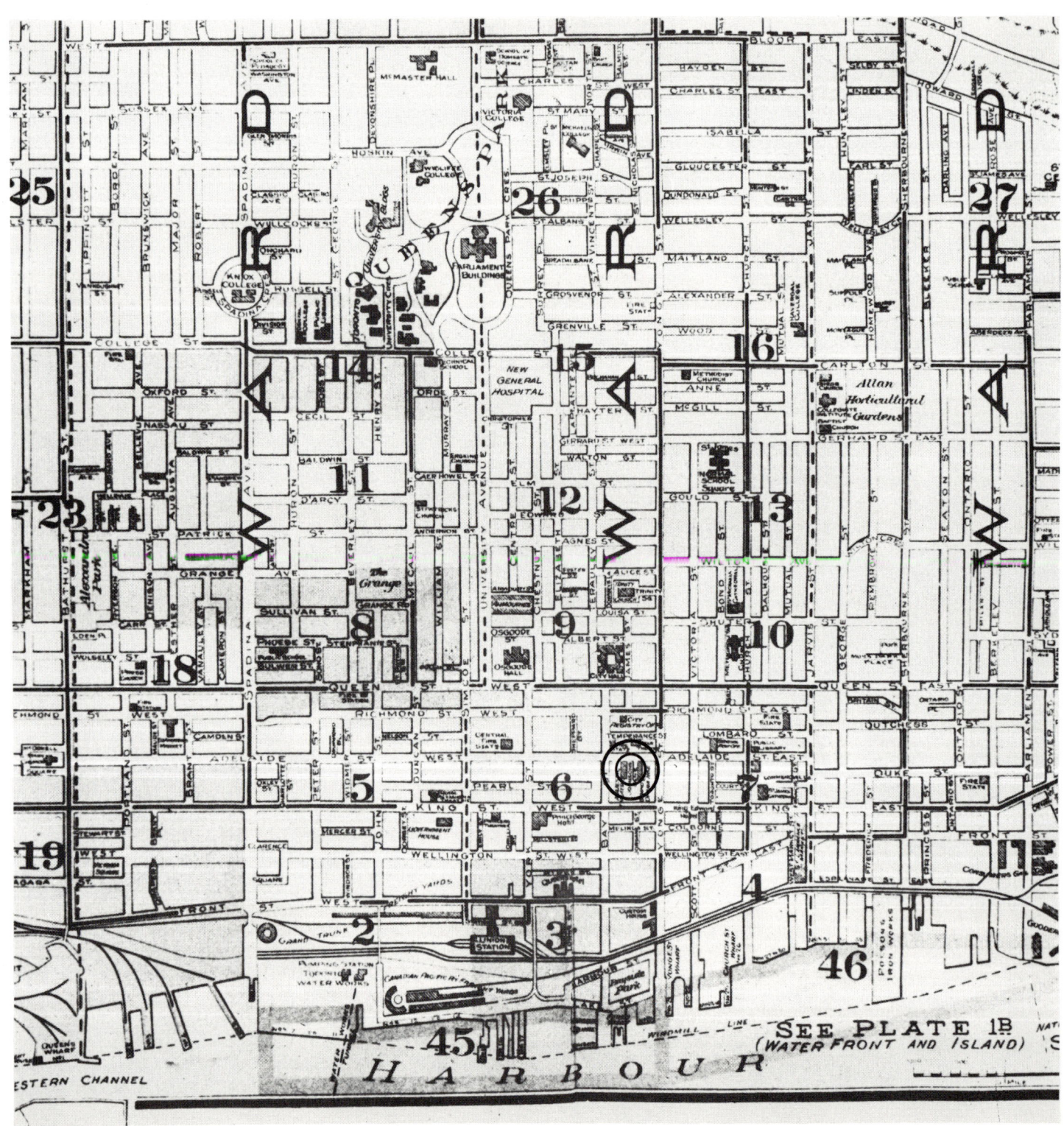

Goad's Atlas 1910

MTLB

1886
TORONTO OPERA HOUSE

For this theatre the original skating rink was completely converted.

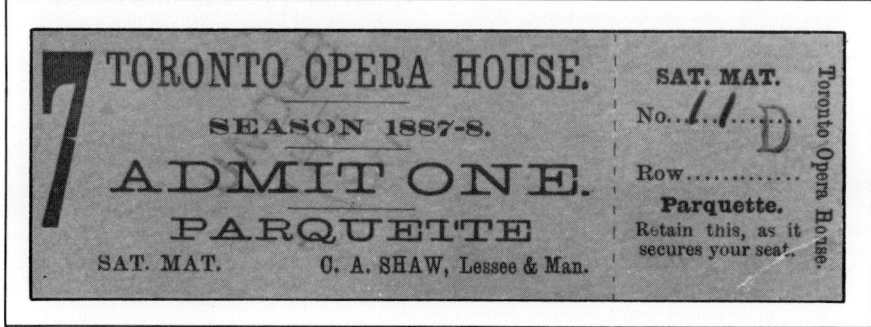

Photo: Gary Beechey

TICKET

JRG

TORONTO OPERA HOUSE

The TORONTO OPERA HOUSE, a few doors to the west of the Grand Opera House on Adelaide Street, opened on August 30, 1886 with a performance of Dellinger's *Don Caesar*. The house had been converted from a roller skating rink. The first complete performances of Wagner's *The Flying Dutchman* and *Lohengrin* and Goldmark's *Queen of Sheba* were given here. It was said to be an excellent house for operatic purposes (possibly because of a larger orchestra pit) which may account for the decline in the number of opera performances at the Grand after 1890. While it was under the management of Messrs. Jacob and Sparrow the Toronto Opera House was frequently referred to as Jacobs and Sparrow's Opera House.

The Toronto Opera House was destroyed by fire on March 25, 1903 and later that year the Majestic Theatre was built on the site. No illustrations of the House appear to have survived.

Photo: Gary Beechey TICKET JRG

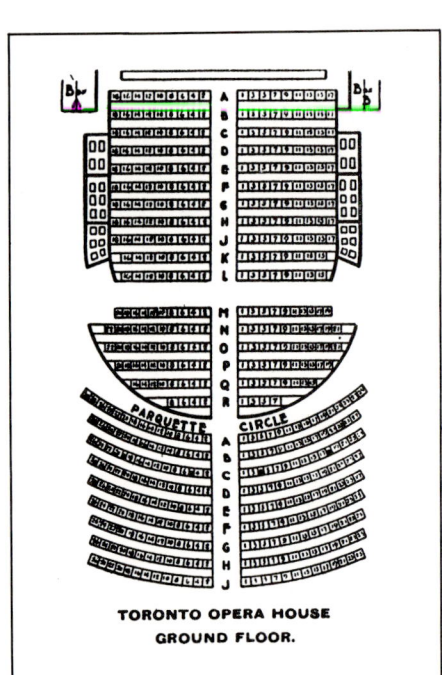

Foster's Blue Book of Toronto 1900 MTLB

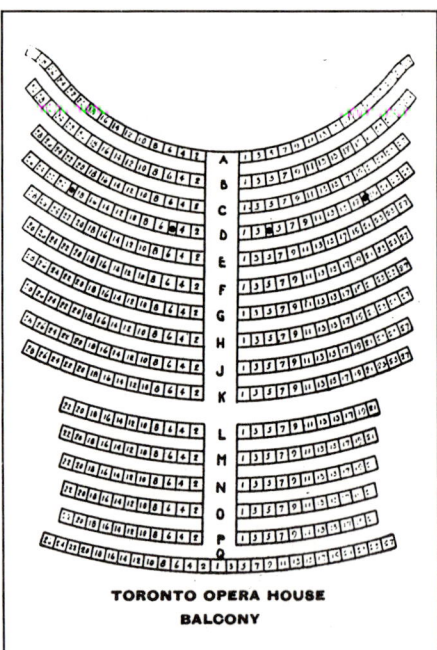

Foster's Blue Book of Toronto 1900 MTLB

THE NEW THEATRE.
Preparations for the Opening of the Toronto Opera House.

Although the work on the new theatre, to be known as the Toronto Opera house, was not commenced till June last, the preparations are now in such an advanced state that by the end of this month the building will be ready for occupation and the opening performance will be given on September 1st. The interior of the roller skating rink on Adelaide street has been completely remodelled, and now presents a very cosy and attractive appearance. The auditorium will be compact and comfortable, and the acoustic properties promise to be all that can be desired. The building has seven exits, so that in case of necessity it can be emptied in a very short time. There is a total width of fifty-four feet in exits. The main entrances are on Adelaide street. There is a large entrance and smaller ones on either side. The smaller ones will be used exclusively for the family circle, or top gallery. The larger entrance will admit to the balcony and pit. The family circle will accommodate six hundred persons. The seats are finely finished, and a good view of the stage can be had from any part of the gallery.

IN THE BALCONY, which will seat 500, and the pit, where 650 can be accommodated, there will be iron folding seats with veneered backs and bottoms. These, it is thought, will be cleaner and cooler than cushioned seats. There will also be 14 family boxes in a semi-circle around the pit, with brass railings between them and moveable seats. There will be one private box on each side of the stage. The width of the stage is 50 ft., the height 54 ft. and the depth 50 ft. The decorations of the interior of the theatre will be of terra cotta and old blue. At the entrance there will be a ladies' parlour and gents' parlour, from which there will be an entrance, hung with curtains, to the auditorium. Toilet rooms will also be provided. The total seating capacity of the building will be 1,700. The seats are being manufactured in Chicago. Scenery and a drop-curtain are being prepared at London. The building will be lighted by a London sun-burner chandelier of 70 lights. Altogether the Toronto Opera house promises to be a most comfortable and attractive resort.

Mail, Aug. 19, 1886 AO

Toronto Opera House — McCaull's Opera Company.

This new theatre will be opened on Monday evening by Mr. McCaull's Opera Co. with Herr Dellinger's opera comique, "Don Cæsar," which is now being presented in Vienna, where it has enjoyed a continuous run since last September, leaping at once into immediate and marked popularity. The libretto, founded on Hugo's novel, was made by Otto Walthers, of Leipzic, and the translation by William von Sachs, jr., of New York. A New York paper says:—"While the story has been used in 'Maritana,' yet in 'Don Cæsar' it presents a very marked contrast to the former opera, as in the present case the action is bright and rapid, with a strong comedy element, while the music is rich in local colour, with telling situations that furnish unusually good opportunities for introducing that element of picturesqueness which opera comique requires. The music adapts itself most gracefully to the various situations, adheres, particularly in the first act, very strongly to the national Spanish character, employs dance rythms with marked success, and gives a stamp of individuality to the many pretty melodies in which the score abounds. There is a delightful serenade, which is reproduced now and then with strikingly beautiful effect, and in fact the music throughout shows the handiwork of a skilful composer." The cast for this engagement will include Miss Bertha Ricci and Miss Lillie Post, soprani, who have been for the past four years *prime donne* in separate companies under Mr. McCaull's management; Miss Laura Joyce-Bell, contralto; Signor Perugini, tenor, who returns here after having achieved great success in England; Mr. Edwin Hoff, who made such a success last year in the "Black Hussar," and George Olmi, baritone. The comedian of the company is Mr. Digby Bell, of whom Sir Arthur Sullivan said that he gave the best interpretation of *Ko-Ko* he had seen. The chorus will number thirty-five, and the manager states that their voices are fresh, the material having been selected with great care. The opera "Don Cæsar" was first produced at Wallack's theatre, New York, and after running successfully for six weeks was succeeded by Audran's "Serment d'Amour," or the "Crowing Hen," as it is called in the English version, which also ran for six weeks. All the operas which Mr. McCaull has produced within the last five years have been operas which could only be obtained on payment of royalties. Mr. McCaull, having always been willing to pay these, has been able to produce a succession of the best European novelties.

Mail, Aug. 28, 1886 — AO

TORONTO OPERA HOUSE.

The McCaull Opera Company arrive this morning. They will open the Toronto Opera House this evening with the new opera, "Don Cæsar." Mr. Shaw, the proprietor and manager of the new house, has been indefatigable in his exertions to have it ready for this evening's performance, and promises his audience a surprise, both as to the beauty of the house and the excellence of the entertainment. The company and the opera which, as well as the new place of amusement, will be introduced to a Toronto audience this evening, come with the highest recommendations, and it is doubtful if the Toronto Opera House could be opened under better auspices.

Globe, Aug. 30, 1886 — AO

MUSICAL AND DRAMATIC.

THE "FLYING DUTCHMAN."

To say that the first performance of Wagner's opera in Toronto was a success is to give but small expression to the popular verdict returned last night at the Toronto Opera House, when the "Flying Dutchman" was performed. One of those brilliant and fashionable audiences for which Toronto has earned a continental reputation greeted the first efforts of the great National Opera Company and received with enthusiasm a well-timed applause that may well rank the finest operatic performance ever witnessed in Toronto. The first visible item of its large force of the company on the stage was the Orchestra, of which the first bars of the overture were at once commendable. The moment the coats had been removed, the programme that followed the overture was performed in the earnest of the excellent performance that followed.

"The Flying Dutchman" is not what the admirers of Wagner will classify with the ideals of its "musical dramas," and is typical of a lyric opera of earlier days. It was, in fact, the second of his great operas, following Rienzi, and was begun twenty years later. It was written in 1843. It was long considered a failure, but has steadily increased in favour and is now a standard opera in Italian, German, and English. Being constructed on an old legend, it has afforded great scope for Wagner's brilliant imagination and is well worked out in every detail, musically and dramatically. "The Flying Dutchman" is well proven a fairadom, even if he kept sailing around the Cape of Good Hope, only by the evil power to land the one until the day of judgment, being allowed to seek a maiden who shall love him faithfully until death. The overture, in twenty descriptive of a violent storm, being finished,

THE CURTAIN RISES

and gives him small encouragement. Daland and the Dutchman then appear and the latter stands transfixed gazing at Senta. A beautiful duet returns his fixed regard. A beautiful duet follows in which the Dutchman declares his love and with success. Daland gives his consent and the curtain falls.

In the **THIRD ACT** cheerers the two ships in the bay; that of Daland being brilliantly decorated and illuminated, while the Flying Dutchman is lying in ominous darkness. The sailors are joined by the maidens merry, a bright tandal and the scene is a horror-stricken one, and the latter is one of reproaches, between the phantom ship, and Senta, the Dutchman. The latter, thinking that Senta has become unfaithful to him, bids her farewell, and casts off from land past, and vows to sea. Senta, in despair, sings herself into the sea, that her noble death may save him.

THE ORCHESTRATION

was wonderfully rich and weird, and one performed as might be expected from such an orchestra, characteristics noticed by all those present, the perfect in-musical people in the audience, the strong contrast of force and countless admiration and applause elicited by Mr. Gustav Hinricks conducted the orchestra with marked ability. Mr. Theone, an important of Mr. Theone, has given to the full instrumental forces produced, however, at the expense of direction, enunciation, as very and always above the pictures, details to those who were but should above the instruments themselves heard above the instruments of the orchestra.

The chorus was large and excellently trained as well. The central figure was displayed in the cast, Mme. Fursch Madi, which heightens the great histrionic talent, and in the dignity of her lovely voice, and in the part she was delightful throughout, set was a gem. The duet by Mr. William Ludwig she was ably supported by the Dutchman. He has a charmingly sympathetic voice, which with a depth of admirable quality and phrasing are hearts and a pathetic quality seldom equalled to artistic excellence. Their singing of the duet was by far the balance, triplet nearly was isolated on Keith, showed a light of pleasing quality, but lacking in power of pleasing quality, and largeness. Mr. Myron reserve for heavy forces here, many times favorite here, was always a dignity, and shewed the general strength of Mary, added much Mathilde Phillipps, as but is had not a part adequate to her usual fine style. She was made the most of in her usual fine style. She was made the most of in the opera were one of the greatest features of the opera were the admirable.

SCENE AND STAGE EFFECTS

The two large ships sailing about, the playing of real lightning and the varied running of the Phantom lightning about the stage remembered here as in the best and truest stage setting in an opera as produced in Toronto, the evening's enjoyment was over of attributable to the crowding of some one hour before the opening of the door was the half hour before ultra-fashionable people to display the half hour before the opening of the door. If the management would exclude every late arrival until the first act is over, it would confer a boon on those who go to enjoy music, not to display bad taste in their arriving late.

There is sure to be another crowded and fashionable audience at the Toronto Opera tomorrow night, when Delibes' for the first time in "Lakmé" will be heard for the first time of popularity. This work has for the elements of beautiful music, a strong dramatic story, and one of the finest orchestral, choral, and light effects in the modern stage. Those who were fortunately brilliant by attend Pauline L'Allemand's interpretation of the delightful show time here as Lakmé, one of the greatest roles in America these days, where the greatest character and of which the two women played the best. Among the Alonzo Stoddard has seen the best, with William Castle, Amanda Fabris, Agnes Stortling, Mathilde Hamilton, Charles Bassett and Castle Bassett, Ritchie, In the evening the Mlle. Thoede, ballet of Bayadere, will Canciate in gorgeous ballroom and Mlle., Censale for the morning at the Toronto Opera House there will be a grand matinee tomorrow, at the close of which the Toronto Opera House will be opened.

On Saturday there will be a grand matinee, at the special prices, when Flotow's ever popular opera, "Martha," will be the attraction at 2 p.m. With a strong cast and two new resources of the opera in the way of orchestra and chorus, a splendid performance of rich and melody may be expected. Next week will be that of the American opera. New forces will include Pauline L'Allemand and Mathilde Hamilton, Mme. L'Allemand has made a great success as Lady Harriet, Stoddard and is expected to sing L'Allemand, and she may be expected with beautiful effect.

"The Last Rose of Summer" is a great ballad. Tomorrow evening will be a benefit for the three night, where "Coppélia" will be given for the first time here. This has been acknowledged to be by far the finest ballet ever given in America, and it will bring out the full strength of its American opera ballet of 60 dancers. In the ballet a simple story is clearly and intelligibly told with many fascinating effects, and, interspersed with many dances properly introduced. The ballet will be produced by the garden scene of "Faust," in which Misses Zach will appear as Rebel, Mathilde Phillipps as Marthe, Charles Bassett as Faust, with Amanda Fabris as Mephisto, and Alonso William Stoddard as Valentine.

Globe, June 17, 1887 — NLC

Amusements.

TORONTO OPERA HOUSE.

MONDAY, AUGUST 30th.

Matinees Wednesday and Saturday. Formal Opening and first appearance here of the

McCAULL OPERA COMIQUE CO.

JNO. A. McCAULL, Proprietor and Manager.

Monday, Tuesday, Wednesday and Wednesday Matinee,

DON CÆSAR,

From the German of Rudolph Dellinger.

Thursday, Friday, Saturday and Saturday Matinee,

THE CROWING HEN,

By Audran, composer of "Olivette" and "Mascotte."

Seats now on sale at Nordheimer's Music Store.

Mail, Sept. 1, 1886 — AO

CTA

TORONTO OPERA HOUSE.

THURSDAY and FRIDAY, } JUNE 16 and 17.

AMERICAN OPERA,

BY THE

National Opera Company.

THEODORE THOMAS....MUSICAL DIRECTOR.
CHARLES E. LOCKE......GENERAL MANAGER.

GRAND OPERA IN ENGLISH.

Thursday, June 16, at 8 p.m., } THE Flying Dutchman. { Wagner's Romantic Opera in Three Acts.

In the Cast:—Emma Juch, Mathilde Phillippe, Messrs. Bassett, Fessenden, Ludwig and Whitney.

Wonderful Scenic and Electrical Effects in the Storm Scene.

Friday, June 17, at 8 p.m. } LAKME In Three Acts { Delibes' Grand Opera Given Entire.

In the Cast:—Pauline L'Allemand, Jessie Bartlett Davis, Mathilde Phillippe, Amanda Fabris, Rose Ritchie, Charles Bassett, Alonzo E. Stoddard, William Fessenden and William H. Lee.

In Second Act—Grand Ballet of the Bayaderes.

Eminent Soloists.
60—The Unrivalled Thomas Orchestra—60.
100—The National Opera Chorus—100.
92—Grand Dancing Ballet—92.
Elaborate Scenery, Costumes, Mechanical and Electrical Effects.

Prices, according to location, $2, $2 50 and $3—Gallery, $1. Proscenium Boxes, admitting six, $25. Tickets now on sale at Box Office of Toronto Opera House. Address orders for tickets by mail to C. A. Shaw, Manager Toronto Opera House.
Week June 20, E. K. Crocker's Equirationals.

Globe, June 16, 1887 NLC

NATIONAL OPERA CO'Y.

A BRILLIANT AUDIENCE WITNESSES "LOHENGRIN."

A Brief Glance at the Features of the Play—"The Queen of Sheba" To-night—Career of Mme. Pierson.

The second performance of a Wagner opera in Toronto took place last evening at the Toronto Opera-house, when the National Opera Company performed "Lohengrin." The opera is the great composer's most popular work, at all events with those who are not stricken with the Wagner craze. It is full of noble melodic phrases and never fails in its continuous musical interest. The bold ideas as to harmony and instrumentation which became Wagner's distinctive characteristics are observable throughout, and the student finds in it ample matter to ponder over, while the mere seeker after musical pleasure still finds it free from pedantry and is charmed with its sensuous beauty. The dramatic interest is no less great. Elsa, the heroine, is accused by Telramund, who has usurped her dead father's throne, of abandoning her brother in order to gain the crown for herself. The King orders a trial by combat between Telramund and any knight Elsa might choose as her champion. Lohengrin appears, and before doing battle for her is betrothed to Elsa, and vanquishes Telramund, who is disgraced. Telramund and Ortrud plot against the honored couple, but cannot prevent their marriage, which is consummated with great pomp. Ortrud's malicious words urge Elsa to ask Lohengrin his name, breaking a condition he made, and causing him to leave her and return to his guardianship of the Holy Grail. Before leaving he disenchants the swan upon which he appears on the scene, and which turns out to be Gottfried, Elsa's brother, who had been bewitched by Ortrud. In the performance of this opera last night Toronto witnessed the grandest tableaux and most gorgeous pictures ever presented on the stage here. The space was filled with people wearing costumes of correct historical design and of the utmost brilliancy; nobles in armor, pages, ladies, heralds, acolytes, completed an ensemble never equalled here. Add to this the continual change in the orchestral accompaniments, scored as only Wagner can score, and the senses of both sight and hearing are in a state of constant delight. The orchestra played magnificently, and certainly was a triumph for Mr. Kinrichs, the conductor. Mr. Barton McGucken, as Lohengrin, displayed a fine large tenor voice and eminent histrionic ability. He has a fine presence and became a favorite at once. Mme. Bertha Pierson has a dramatic soprano voice, of great range and volume, and is a thorough actress. As Elsa she made a powerful impression. Miss Clara Poole, as Ortrud, had a part in which her decided dramatic talent and beautifully clear, resonant voice showed to great advantage. These ladies sing to-night in the "Queen of Sheba," and may be expected to renew their triumphs. Mr. Ludwig was exactly fitted with the part of Telramund, and sang it admirably. Mr. Frank Vetta, as the King, and Mr. William Merton, as the Herald, sang most artistically. Altogether it was a performance which has never been excelled in Toronto.

To-night Goldmark's great work, "The Queen of Sheba," will be performed with the following cast:—The Queen, Clara Poole; Sulamith, Bertha Pierson; Astaroth, Amanda Fabris; The King, Alonzo Stoddard; Assad, Charles Bassett; Baal-Hanan, William Merton; High Priest, George Broderick. Priests, levites, singers, harpists, body guards, women of the harem, bayaderes and people of the city, will people the stage, and a gorgeous procession will be made. In the fourth act there will be a grand ballet—the bee dance of the Almeex. The scenery will be of the perfect description which has signalised the past efforts of this company. Costumes and armor of the same sumptuousness as that seen last night will be displayed this evening.

MADAME PIERSON.

Mme. Bertha Pierson made her debut in this country last season with the National Opera Company, having for some years previously occupied leading operatic positions in Germany, France, Italy and Spain. Mme. Pierson was born on July 15th, 1861, at Vienna. Her early musical education was with a view to becoming a pianist, but her voice attracted so much attention in musical circles that at the advice of Mr. Goldmark, the famous composer of the "Queen of Sheba," in which opera Mme. Pierson will to-night appear in the character of Sulamith, it was decided to prepare her for the operatic stage, and she entered the Vienna Conservatory, studying under Prof. Laufer. She made a brilliant success in her debut in Dresden as Valentine in "The Huguenots, and after singing Donna Anna in "Don Giovanni" and "Aida," was engaged for one year at the Dresden Court Theatre. She appeared for three years under her maiden name of Bertha Brethol, and until her marriage with Mr. Henry Pierson, a member of a well-known Dresden publishing house. Under Pollini she played a brilliant engagement at the Hamburg Opera-house. Going to Italy, Mme. Pierson studied in Florence with Mme. Varesi and appeared at Parma as Elsa in the earliest Italian performances of "Lohengrin." In Brussels she studied for some time with Lamperti, son of the famous Milan teacher. Among the many important appearances of Mme. Pierson have been that in Venice as Gioconda in the first performance of that opera; in Berlin, Breslau, Turin and Livorno, and in Barcelona, where she sang in "The Flying Dutchman" with Maurel. Her latest success was as Elizabeth in the first Italian performances of "Tannhæuser" at the Apollo theatre, Rome, in the spring of 1886.

Globe, Jan. 4, 1888 NLC

TORONTO OPERA-HOUSE

SEASON OF GRAND OPERA.

Seats now on Sale at Box Office for

NATIONAL OPERA COMP'Y.

TO-NIGHT,
"FAUST."

TUESDAY, JAN. 3,
"LOHENGRIN."

WEDNESDAY, JAN. 4,
"QUEEN OF SHEBA."

Prices—$1, $2, $2 50, $3. Box seats $4.
Seats can be procured by letter, telephone or telegraph.

Globe, Jan. 2, 1888 MTLB

AMUSEMENTS

JACOB'S & SPARROW'S OPERA HOUSE
MAT. TUE. WED. SAT.

This week—The greatest of all Irish picturesque plays, TRUE IRISH HEARTS. Prices 15c, 20c, 30c and 50c. Week of November 25—Wages of Sin.

Globe, Nov. 20, 1889 MTLB

TORONTO OPERA HOUSE IN RUINS.

Fire Loss Estimated at $60,000, Insurance $25,000.

FAMILY'S NARROW ESCAPE

Got Out of the Burning Building by Skylight—Theatre to be Rebuilt.

Not often does the fire king leave a scene of devastation so complete as marked his sudden and sinister appearance in a one-night stand at the Toronto Opera House in the early hours of yesterday morning.

No advance agents heralded his approach—unless the warning smell of a burning electric light wire could be called such—no lurid posters presaged his production. Scorning all such aids, for the fire king never plays to the gallery—the unwelcome visitor demonstrated once more his ability to put on alone and unassisted a production which for brilliant and costly spectacular effect has never been witnessed in the auditorium of the opera house.

Disastrous as the fire was, and thrillingly dangerous as it proved to be for Janitor Geo. Champion, his wife, and three children, and Mr. Jas. Burton, a brother-in-law, who escaped in their night-clothes over the roof to the west, there are two reasons for congratulation when one contemplates what might have been. Fortunate indeed is it that the fire did not break out six or seven hours earlier, for then the story might have been very different, and there is reason for gratitude also that the firemen were able notwithstanding the high wind that prevailed and the difficulty they had in reaching the fire—to confine it practically to the limits of the theatre.

As early as midnight Mr. Champion detected a smell of smoke in the building, and with the aid of Night Watchman Bell and the policeman on the beat, broke open the bill-room door, whence the smell apparently proceeded. A thorough search here and through the entire building revealed nothing suspicious and the family retired. At five minutes to four Mrs. Champion first became aware that the building was on fire, and woke her husband, who speedily gave the alarm. Policeman Brown promptly turned in the alarm, and in a couple of minutes the Bay Street section of the fire brigade was on the scene.

RUINS OF THE OPERA HOUSE.

Meanwhile no time was lost by the family, who lived in the top storey at the front of the building. Realising at a glance that escape by the stairway was impossible, Mr. Champion and Mr. Burton hastily piled up the furniture in the room so as to enable them to reach the skylight, which was forced open. Burton was out on the roof in little more time than it takes to tell it. In less than a minute Champion had passed up his wife and three little children and soon stood beside them. Escape was made by jumping on to the roof to the west, six feet lower, and getting down through the skylight. The doorway to the street was forced, and soon the little group were safe on the sidewalk, clad only in their night robes and exposed to the penetrating March winds. Coats were forthcoming and the party were taken to the Bay Street fire hall and put to bed.

Work of the Firemen.

The battle with the fire was now at its height. Chief Thompson was early on the scene, followed by No. 7 hose. His experience with theatre fires soon showed him that there was desperate work ahead, and a general alarm was turned in at 4.14 a.m. The greatest difficulty was experienced by the brigade in getting at the scene of the trouble in the auditorium. Entrance from the front was seriously impeded by the vast network of wires, while the absence of windows or doors in the side or south walls added to the difficulties.

The origin of the fire is said to have been a defectively insulated wire under the gallery in the rear of the auditorium, but if this is the case the fire must have promptly transferred its operations to the orchestra chairs, stage, and scenery farther south, for these are entirely obliterated, so complete is the wreck, while the balconies and that portion of the auditorium where the fire is supposed to have started are fairly intact, though, of course, much damaged from water, smoke, and debris of falling roof and walls. About 5 o'clock the roof fell in with a terrific crash, burying everything in a dense cloud of flying dirt and dust, which obscured the scene for some minutes afterwards. This showed the galleries to be still standing, and afforded the firemen a better chance at their relentless foe from the lanes to the east and south.

The walls still stood, but remembering the tragic event of the McIntosh fire last summer, the chief withdrew his men from the ruins, where they had been playing on the blazing timbers. Not long after a large part of the east wall at the south end fell in, and this completed the wreck. Streams of water were thrown on the building till well on in the afternoon.

Loss $60,000, Insurance $25,000.

The losses are estimated as follows:—

Toronto Opera House	$30,000
Sullivan, Harris, and Woods' Dramatic Company	8,000
Max Brown, tailor	2,500
John Treddleck, cigar manufacturer	2,000
George Champion, janitor	500
James Ward, confectioner	400

The Toronto Opera House was insured in the following companies:—

British American	$ 5,000
Western	5,000
Royal	2,500
Mercantile	2,500
Manchester	2,500
Sun	2,500
National	2,500
Phoenix (Hartford)	2,500
Total	$25,000

John Trebilcock had $500 insurance in the Waterloo Mutual, but Brown and Ward carried no insurance on their property. Mr. Brown's chief loss was that of about 2,000 vests, which he was making up for different firms. He valued them at over $2,000, and said $500 would about cover the loss to his machines and fixtures.

Fire and water completely destroyed Trebilcock's stock of tobaccos, which was worth about $2,000.

A circumstance of interest in connection with the fire is the fact that only about a week ago Chief Thompson and Building Inspector Copping went through the building, and recommended, among other things, that automatic sprinklers be installed. This matter was under consideration at the time of the fire.

Will Build New Theatre.

Manager Small, who was in Detroit yesterday, telegraphed that the house will be rebuilt at once on a finer scale than ever, and be ready for the opening in September.

The members of the "King of Detectives" Company, which were billed to appear all week, suffered severely by the fire, their total loss being estimated at $8,000. This consisted largely of costumes, wardrobes, and scenery, and particularly a flying machine apparatus which cost much time and money in experimenting with. Mr. J. B. Isaac, the manager, stated that the property was uninsured. All immediate engagements must of course be cancelled, and the company, consisting of sixteen people, will return to New York.

History of the Theatre.

The Toronto Opera House was opened about seventeen years ago, with Dellinger's opera, "Don Caesar," presented by the McCaull Opera Company, with Bertha Ricci and Tillie Post as leading ladies, and Digby Bell as comedian. Among the biggest of the early attractions was the appearance of the National Opera Company, with Theodore Thomas' orchestra, about fourteen years ago. The ballet was composed of more than one hundred people. George McGuckin, Charles Basset, Franz Vetta, Amanda Faberj, and Emma Juch being the principal members of the cast. "The Queen of Sheba," "Lohengrin," "Faust," and "Tannhauser" were part of the repertoire.

Among the managers have been Chas. Shaw, whose father-in-law owns the house; Franks, Morris, Jacobs, Jacobs and Sparrow, Sparrow and Small, and now Small and Stair. The building was converted from a roller skating rink by Col. W—. L. of Detroit, who built the Russell Theatre in Ottawa. Two or three years ago the interior was redecorated in an elaborate manner by J. A. Rolf of [?]

Mail & Empire, Mar. 26, 1903   NLC

APPEARANCES

1886	McCaull Opera Comique Company
1887	National Opera Company
1888	National Opera Company
1888	Kimball Opera Company

ACADEMY OF MUSIC

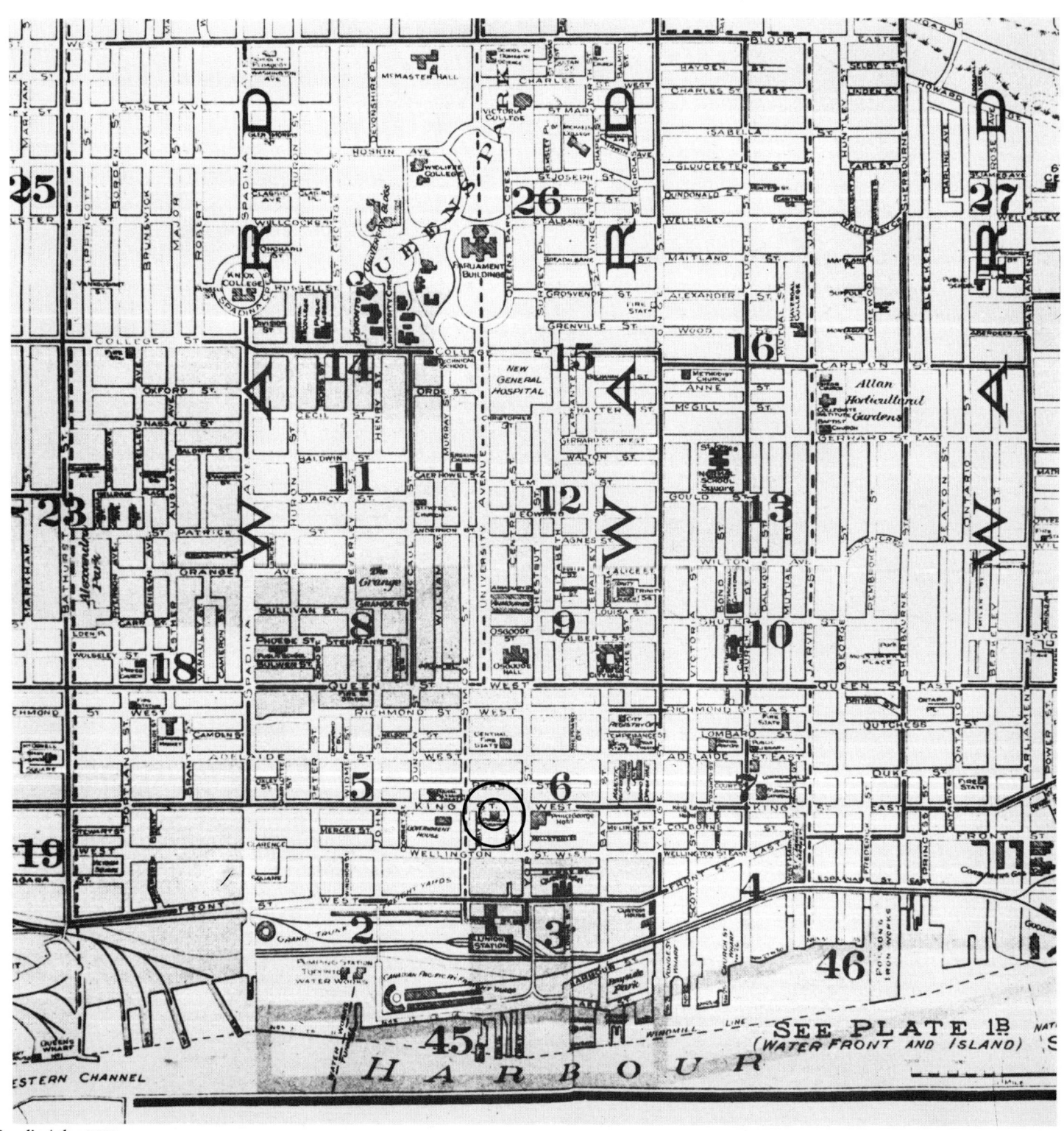

Goad's Atlas 1910

MTLB

1890
ACADEMY OF MUSIC

The need for a music hall was becoming increasingly apparent.

The Academy of Music after renovations

ACADEMY OF MUSIC

THE ACADEMY OF MUSIC was built in 1889 on the south side of King Street West between York and Simcoe in order to provide a needed music hall. It was the first public building to be lighted by electricity and the first theatre to open the drop curtain from the centre. The hall was renovated in 1895 and the name changed to the Princess Theatre.

Adolph Neuendorff, who conducted the Emma Juch Festival in 1890, was the conductor of the first productions of Wagner's *Lohengrin* (1871) and *Die Walkure* (1877) in America.

MUSIC AND THE DRAMA.

NEW ACADEMY OF MUSIC.

Amusement lovers are no doubt looking forward with curiosity to the time when the new Music hall, which is now being built on the south side of King street, between York and Simcoe streets, shall throw open its doors. From the number of strong attractions already secured by Manager Percival T. Greene, the natural inference is that the new house will prove a decided accession to our places of amusement. A more convenient assembly room, situated as the new hall is, in the midst of the leading hotels, all street cars passing the door, etc, it would be hard to find. In connection with the house proper, there will be a banqueting hall, an art gallery, and a drawing-room. The banqueting hall may be used separately for those who wish a small hall for "At Homes," or for private matinees, recitals, etc. The suite of reception rooms in connection with the building forms a special feature, and is the outcome of the existing social craze for large receptions, etc. These rooms are quite distinct from the large hall, and consist of dressing-room, supper-room, and ball-room. The whole suite will be handsomely decorated and furnished, and will easily accommodate two hundred couples.

Mail, Aug. 13, 1889   NLC

MUSIC AND THE DRAMA.

Coming Operatic Attractions—Concerts by Benevolent Societies—George W. Cable—New Academy of Music—Boston Symphony Orchestra—The Norah Clench Concert—At the Theatres.

ACADEMY OF MUSIC.

The first dramatic performances to be given in this house commence at the Thanksgiving matinee by Geo. M. Wood, Miss Marguerite St. John and Co. There will be three representations of "David Garrick" and "Man Proposes," Thursday afternoon and evening and Friday evening, and seats can be secured at once to prevent disappointment. Miss Marguerite St. John's modern costumes are by M. Felix and Madame Rodrigues, of Paris, and her old English comedy costumes by Nathan, of London and Paris. The Montreal *Gazette*, on the occasion of the company's second visit to the Academy of Music in May last, says:—"Miss Marguerite St. John, as May Denstone (David Garrick), acted the loving, true-hearted woman to the life. Miss St. John is no stranger here, and her work of yesterday will go to deepen the impression she has already created, and to increase the esteem and respect in which she is held. Her manner is naturally girlish and deliciously fresh, and her appearance and figure a most attractive personality." The plan is now open at Messrs. Nordheimer's.

NORAH CLENCH CONCERT.

The plan for this concert to-night at the Academy of Music shows that the young Canadian artist will be greeted by a large assemblage of our citizens, who will, it is certain, give her a reception deserving of her merit.

I. P. B. S. CONCERT.

Mr. Charles V. Slocum, of Buffalo, will sing at this concert on the 11th inst. He is a singer of repute, as witness the following from the Cleveland *Daily News*:—"An audience of over 4,600 people assembled last evening at the opening concert in the new Music hall, the programme consisting of the oratorio 'Samson,' by Handel, and miscellaneous numbers by Mme. Emma Nevada and her company. Mr. Slocum sang the numerous tenor solos and recitatives allotted to him with fire and vigour, his recitatives being especially broad and declamatory."

THE LEVY CONCERT.

At the concert to be given by the Heintzman band on Monday evening at the new Academy of Music, the great cornet player Jules Levy will appear. Of Miss Rosa Linde, the contralto with the company, the Lacrosse (Wis.) *Herald* says:—"Miss Rosa Linde has a heavy contralto of the Wagnerian measure, and appeared well as Siebel, deserving more applause for the garden song than she received."

Mail, Nov. 6, 1889   NLC

MUSICAL AND DRAMATIC.

Miss Juch's Brilliant Performance at the Academy—Rosina Vokes.

Last evening the second performance in Toronto of Wagner's "Lohengrin" was given at the Academy of Music before a large and brilliantly fashionable audience, nearly every available seat being occupied. Apart from the interest naturally evoked by the rare event of a Wagner night in Toronto, the great attraction was Miss Emma Juch, who has made herself a great favorite here by her artistic work in concerts, and more especially by the occasional appearances she has made in opera. Miss Juch is supported by an excellent company, comprising efficient principals, a very good chorus and a comprehensive orchestra, directed by Mr. Adolf Neuendorff. The cast of the opera was as follows:—

Henry I., King of Germany........Franz Vetta
Lohengrin, Knight of the Holy Grail....
    Chas. Hedmondt
Elsa of Brabant....................Emma Juch
Frederick Telramund, a Noble of Brabant
    Otto Rathjens
The King's herald.................E. N. Knight
Ortrud, wife of Telramund........
    Georgine Von Januschowsky
Duke Godfrey.....................Eva Walton
Chorus of Saxon and Brabantian nobles, ladies, pages, etc.

The part of Elsa is a sufficiently exacting one to prove a severe test of the resources of a singer, and its performance by Miss Juch fully met all demands. Her beautiful voice and her essentially Saxon appearance, which emphasises her graces of person, give her a most favorable natural equipment for the part, while her thorough artistic training, both musically and historically, add all that is required to make her rendition of the character an ideal one. She sang the difficult music with absolute fidelity to the text, and with delightful certainty and correctness. Her acting was strong and spontaneous, with great reserve power, winning hearty and repeated rounds of applause. Altogether her representation of Elsa will long be remembered in Toronto as one of the rare ideal performances given here. Mme. Georgine von Januschowsky has a strongly dramatic part as Ortrud, and she worthily supported Miss Juch in this difficult role. She has a brilliant dramatic soprano voice and is an actress of great power. Her by play during the first act and her singing, especially in the second act, were very effective. She has a gift of immediately securing the sympathy of her audience, and her strong personality specially fitted her for the part of Ortrud and her generally fine performance won her frequent applause. Ortrud, and she worthily supported Miss Juch in this difficult role. She has a brilliant dramatic soprano voice and is an actress of great power. Her by play during the first act and her singing, especially in the second act, were very effective. She has a gift of immediately securing the sympathy of her audience, and her strong personality specially fitted her for the part of Ortrud and her generally fine performance won her frequent applause. The title-role was sung by Mr. Charles Hedmondt, a young Montrealer, who has been very successful as an operatic tenor. The part is a heroic one, and Mr. Hedmondt's voice is lyric, rather than heroic, but he sang it very efficiently, rising to a grand climax in the last act, where he sang magnificently. Occasional faulty intonation somewhat marred the great duet with Elsa in the third act, but in the main Mr. Hedmondt's singing was more than satisfactory. The Telramund of Mr. Otto Rathjens was a very fine performance. He has a fine, vibrant baritone voice, and he sang and acted with great power and effect, the only fault in his work being a slight difficulty with the English language, making his diction a trifle indistinct. Mr. Franz Vetta is an old favorite here, and as the King had a role that hardly gave him the prominence his admirers would have wished. He sang it excellently, especially the fine prayer in the first act. The chorus was large and effective, especially in the male section, but was hardly as crisp and decided in its work as might have been wished. The costumes were very fine and the mounting generally was excellent and generous in its details. The orchestra is a very effective one, complete in the wind section and a trifle light in the strings. It was excellently conducted by Mr. Neuendorff, who bore a watchful supervision over all the musical details. Verdi's melodious opera "Rigolette, or the Fool's Revenge" is announced for this evening with Madame Januschowsky, Miss Macnichol, Mr. Payne Clarke, Mr. Otto Rathjens, Mr. Knight and Mr. Miron in the leading roles. "Faust" will be given at the matinee to-morrow, and "The Huguenots," with Miss Juch as Valentine, and Miss Maconda, Miss Macnichol, Mr. Hedmondt, Mr. Rathjens, Mr. Vetta, Mr. Miron and Mr. Stephens in the remaining principal roles will be given to-morrow night.

Globe, Oct. 21, 1890   MTLB

MANAGER GREENE'S BENEFIT.

Louis James, who has attained high rank as a tragedian, will open a week's engagement to-night at the Academy of Music. "Othello" will be given, and, as the evening is also a benefit for Manager Greene, there ought to be an overflow house. Mr. Greene has shown great enterprise in the musical and dramatic line, having brought in some of the best talent on this Continent. He deserves well at the hands of theatregoers.

Globe, Apr. 28, 1890   NLC

ACADEMY OF MUSIC.
TO-NIGHT

And every night this week, with Wednesday and Saturday Matinees, the eminent tragedian

LOUIS JAMES,

In Shakespeare's Grand Tragedies. To-night and Saturday night, "Othello"; Tuesday night and Saturday Matinee, "Virginius"; Wednesday Matinee and Friday evening, "Ingomar"; Wednesday evening, "Julius Cæsar"; Thursday evening, "Hamlet." To-night, Manager Greene's benefit. Prices—25c, 50c, 75c, $1. Plan now open.

Globe, Apr. 29, 1890   NLC

Academy of Music.

There has been a large demand for seats to witness the production of the new comic opera, "Fauvette," which will mark the opening of the Academy of Music by the Boston Ideals to-night. The company, numbering 60 persons, have arrived from New York, where rehearsals of the opera and the making of the new costumes have been in progress for several weeks. The new opera will doubtless be enthusiastically welcomed.

Globe, Sept. 8, 1890   NLC

ACADEMY OF MUSIC.
C. J. WHITNEY............Lessee.

GRAND OPENING TO-NIGHT
BY THE FAMOUS

BOSTON IDEAL OPERA CO.

In the great comic opera "FAUVETTE." Prices, evening, $1, 75c, 50c and 25c; matinees Wednesday and Friday, 50c and 25c. Plan open. Telephone 2,191. No Saturday performances. The curtain will rise at 8 o'clock sharp.

Globe, Sept. 8 1890   NLC

ACADEMY OF MUSIC — OPERATIC Festival — three nights and Saturday matinee, commencing October 15. The Emma Juch Grand English Opera Co.:—Thursday evening, "Cavalleria Rusticana," Mascagni (first complete production in Canada); Friday evening, "Lohengrin," Wagner; Saturday matinee, "Il Trovatore," Verdi; Saturday evening, "Tannhauser," Wagner (by request). Seats on sale at box office, Tuesday, October 13. Next attraction—Oolgar Selden in "Will o'-the-Wisp; three nights, commencing Monday, October 19.

Globe, Oct. 15, 1891 — NLC

JUCH'S FAREWELL PERFORMANCES.

The matinee performance of "Faust" by the Emma Juch Opera Company on Saturday was well attended and was very well received. Miss Amanda Fabris played the part of Marguerite and showed herself to be still suffering from a cold, in spite of which she gave an extremely satisfactory rendition of the role. Her singing of the Jewel Song was especially good. M. Guillo, as Faust, sang beautifully but was rather stiff in his acting. Mr. Franz Vetta, on the other hand, left nothing to be desired as Mephistopheles. His fine voice and his finished acting make this one of the best representations ever seen in Toronto. The Siebel of Miss Lizzie Macnichol was, as always, a pleasing performance. The orchestra and chorus, the latter especially in the Soldiers' Chorus, were excellent. In the evening Tannhaeuser received its first performance in Toronto, and was witnessed by an immense and extremely fashionable audience for whose benefit the block was lined with a double row of carriages. The opera was, of course, new to most of those present, but its many beauties called forth waves of applause that demonstrated the readiness of the audience to accept the new musical cult. Just how far this would apply to the later operas of Wagner can hardly be estimated, but "Tannhaeuser" has assuredly won its popularity in Toronto. And this in spite of the long monologues which abound. The opera was not performed in its completeness, the ballet and part of the last act being omitted. To those whose acquaintance with opera is derived from the lyric Italian operas and the comic operas of the day, the almost total absence of continuous melodies must have seemed strange, yet the rich phrases and richer orchestral movement continually going on provided a charm which amply repaid the cultured audience for the lack of conventionalism. Miss Emma Juch as Elizabeth showed her great versatility in the splendid rendition she gave of this role. She has developed in the few years she has been before the public into a magnificent actress, and her Elizabeth is one of her noblest roles. Her acting is finished in every detail and her singing is as careful and artistic as if she were on the concert platform. Her voice and singing on Saturday evening were absolutely flawless. Her singing of the prayer in the third act was exquisitely tender and beautiful in its femininity.

JUCH'S SUPPORT.

Mr. Montegriffo made an excellent Tannhaeuser, giving a very conscientious rendering of the part. Mr. Franz Vetta as the Landgrave frequently elicited the applause of the audience by his fine singing. To Mr. Mertens most of the honors of the evening fell, next to Miss Juch. His singing of the part of Wolfram von Eschenbach was finished and artistic. He sang two numbers, one being the well-known "Evening Star" aria, in German, by which his performance gained in musical value, though doubtless it confused some of his hearers. Miss Amanda Fabris had a small role as Venus, which well suited her handsome appearance. She sang excellently. The orchestra was again very good, although a little uncertain in the last act. The chorus was effective, but a little rough in both the Pilgrims' and Festal choruses. Taken altogether it was a very fine performance, reflecting great credit upon the company and upon Signor Bevignani, the conductor.

Globe, Oct. 19, 1891 — MTLB

GOS

EMMA JUCH, American soprano, who reorganized the National Opera Company after 1889 as the Juch Grand Opera Company.

MUSIC AND THE DRAMA

THE PROPOSED ALTERATIONS AT THE ACADEMY OF MUSIC.

Recitals at the College and Conservatory of Music — Remarkable Success of Old-fashioned Opera in London — The New "Macaire" — Mr. Watkin Mills' Farewell Recital — General Notes.

It now seems pretty certain that the proposed improvements at the Academy of Music theatre will be carried out this season, the Canada Life Assurance Company, which holds a mortgage of $25,000 on the building, having resolved to undertake the work of reconstruction. The intention is to transform the house into a first-class theatre, so as to play attractions which will equal those that have been presented to the public for so many years at the Grand Opera house. The reconstructed theatre will probably be known as the Princess. The alterations will include the building of a new gallery, new promenades, a smoking-room, a retiring room for ladies, the enlargement of the stage, and the improvement of the foyer. If everything goes well, the theatre will be ready for the opening of the season on September 2nd. Mr. Frank Darling, who prepared the plans of the improvements for Mr. J. E. Thompson, has been retained as architect.

It is easy to foresee that some difficulty will be experienced in obtaining a constant succession of first-class attractions for two theatres in this city. If the result should prove that both the Grand and the Princess can be profitably conducted as first-class theatres, then the public of this city will indeed be better catered to in the way of amusements than Buffalo and Cleveland, which are much more populous cities.

Mail & Empire, June 12, 1895 — NLC

THEATRE IMPROVEMENTS.

Permits have been granted to the Musee for alterations $1,200, and to the Academy of Music, alterations and additions, $8,000.

Mail & Empire July 10, 1895 — NLC

APPEARANCES	
1890	Boston Ideal Opera Company
1890	Emma Juch Grand English Opera Company
1891	Emma Juch Grand English Opera Company

Lights of a City Street
"Painted in 1894 by F.M. Bell-Smith, O.S.A., R.C.A., this fine painting that has been loaned to the Art Gallery many times and also hung in the Palm Room (Arcadian Court) shows the corner of King and Yonge Streets in Toronto looking east on King Street and the spire of St. James.

The policeman in the painting, Bill Radford, was later employed by Simpson's and the artist is depicted purchasing a paper. The gentleman raising his hat is Rev. F.M. Bell-Smith, son of the artist."

Photo: Everett-Roseborough Ltd.

SL NGC

1894
MASSEY HALL

A magnificent auditorium to honour a name which meant so much in Toronto's cultural life.

Photo: *Toronto, Canada's Queen City*　　　　　BC
MASSEY MUSIC HALL, circa 1912.

MASSEY HALL

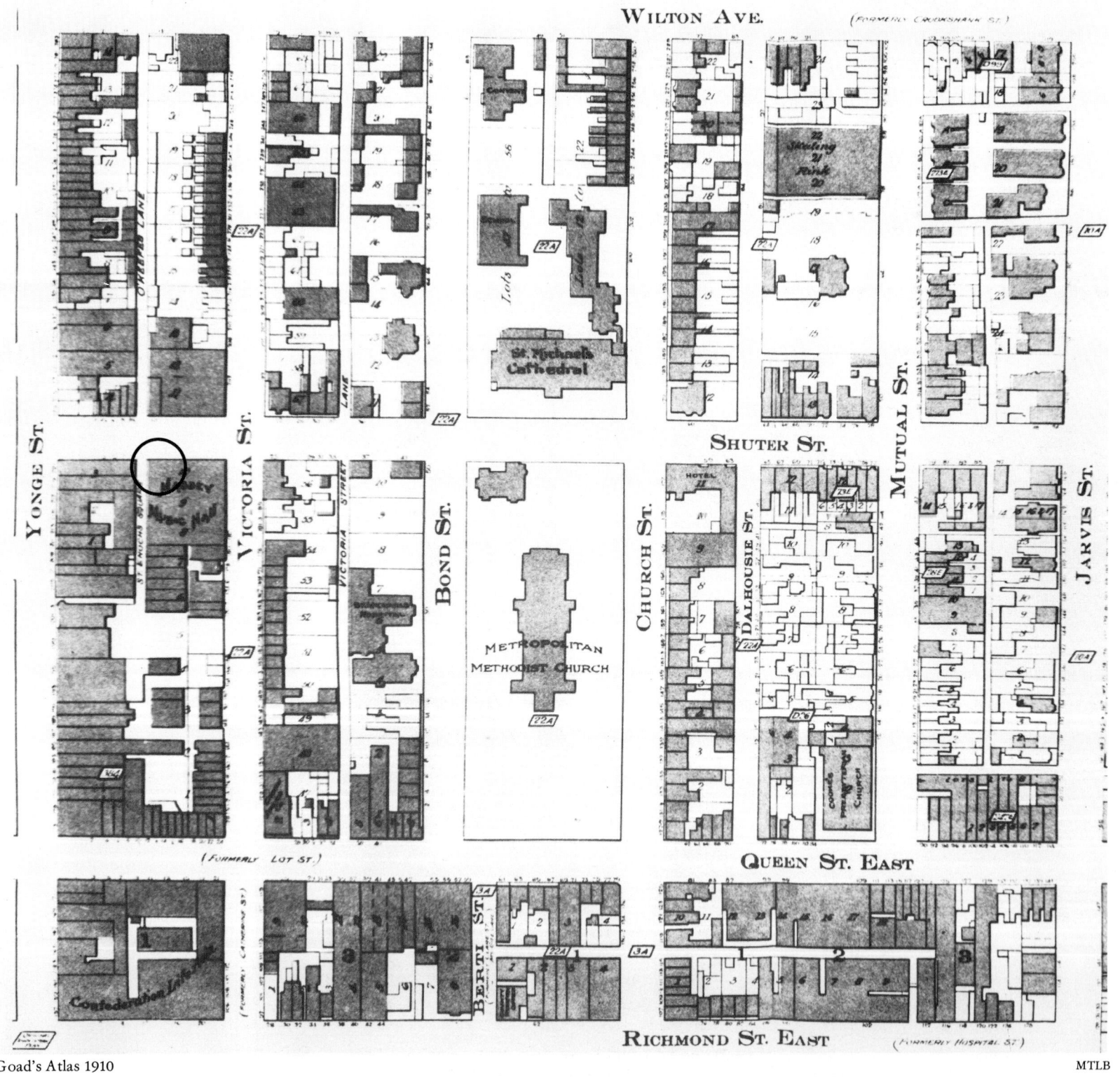

Goad's Atlas 1910

MASSEY HALL

Within a decade of the opening of the Academy of Music, Toronto was again in need of an adequate music hall. Hart Massey gave the city $100,000 to fill the need and on 20th September, 1893, in an informal ceremony, the cornerstone was laid by Charles Vincent Massey, grandson of the donor. On Thursday, 14th June, 1894, the Hall opened with a performance of Handel's *Messiah* – the first of three days of celebration. From the beginning, the excellence of the hall's acoustics was remarkable. Massey Hall was the home of the Toronto Mendelssohn Choir and the Toronto Conservatory Orchestra (which became the Toronto Symphony) with first performances on January 15, 1895 and October 2, 1907 respectively, until Roy Thomson Hall opened in 1982.

Headline, Globe, Dec. 16, 1893   MTLB   TS   Globe, June 14, 1894   NLC

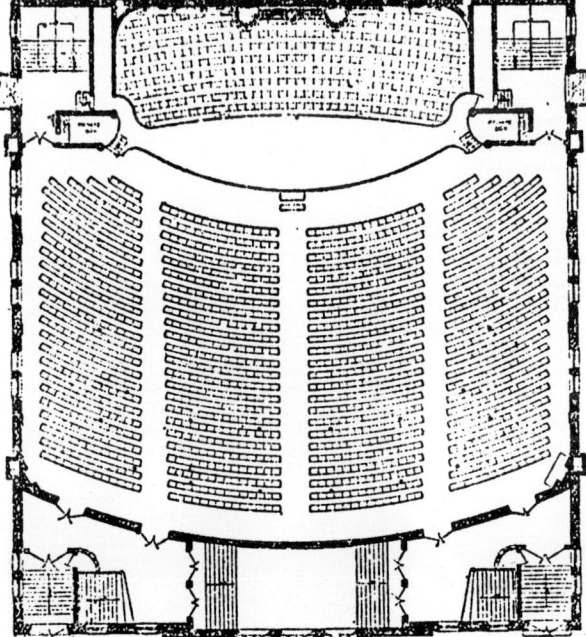

MAIN FLOOR, MASSEY MUSIC HALL.

Globe, Dec. 16, 1893   MTLB

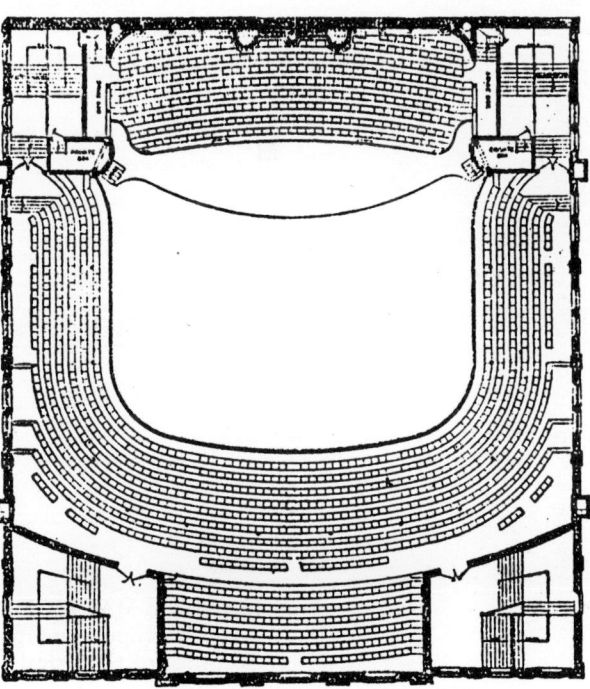

FIRST GALLERY, MASSEY MUSIC HALL.

Globe, Dec. 16, 1893   MTLB

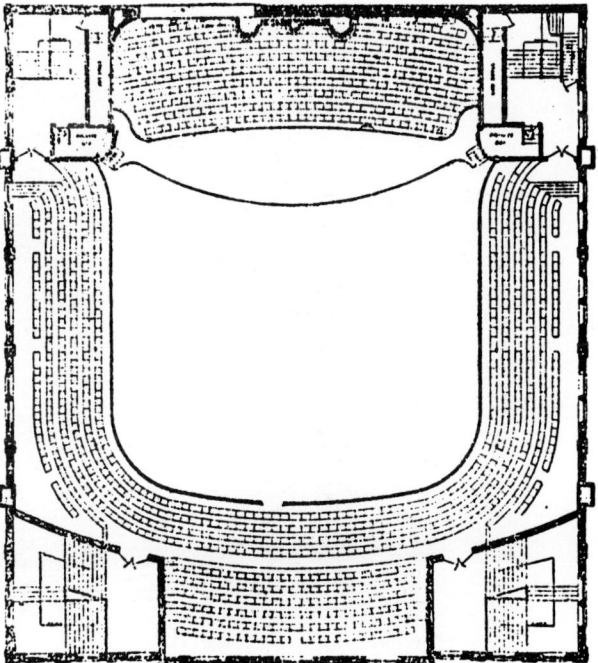

SECOND GALLERY, MASSEY MUSIC HALL.

Globe, Dec. 16, 1893   MTLB

MASSEY HALL

H.R.H. the Duke of Cornwall and York.

Visit of the future King George V and Queen Mary.

H.R.H. the Duchess of Cornwall and York.

Sir Wilfred Laurier, Premier of Canada.

His Excellence Lord Minto, Governor-General of Canada.

Sir Oliver Mowat, Lieutenant-Governor of Ontario.

Impresario MAURICE GRAU brought the Metropolitan Opera Company to Toronto for the Royal Musical Festival.

ROYAL CONCERT AT MASSEY HALL.

A Musical and Social Function Conceived on Magnificent Lines and Splendidly Carried Out.

IT WAS A GORGEOUS SPECTACLE.

Through streets filled with cheering people, who waved flags and handkerchiefs as they cheered, the regal and viceregal parties passed last night to the grand concert in Massey Hall, where a scene of splendor was presented which far surpassed anything ever before seen in Toronto.

The immense arch over the tiers of seats back of the platform had been filled in most effectively in the semblance of a beautiful proscenium arch, supported by marble columns. To the right and left of the columns the space was filled in with blue material, while the centre was one magnificent crimson curtain. At the sides of the arch great banks of palms had been built up, the whole being so well proportioned as to take away all sensation of barrenness from the great expanse of wall, and to make Massey Hall look better than it ever looked before. A new platform for the performers had been built in front of the old one, bringing the singers well toward the centre of the auditorium, and adding by its crimson carpet to the warmth of the tones of the building. The decoration of the galleries in red, set off with flowers, had the same effect, and the building presented throughout a color scheme that was simply magnificent.

But, added to all this carefully-planned scheme of decoration, was the great sea of color of hundreds of the smartest and most beautiful costumes ever seen in Toronto, rendered all the more dazzling by the sparkle of gems and the sheen of the scarlet cloth and gold lace of military costumes.

When the Duke and Duchess entered and the vast throng of handsome and beautifully-gowned women rose to greet the party of men in brilliant military and naval uniforms, and ladies in lace and jewels, a scene was presented such as Toronto has never known in all its previous history. It was a musical and social function conceived on magnificent lines and magnificently carried out.

In the Royal Loge.

In the Royal loge were their Royal Highnesses the Duke and Duchess of Cornwall and York, Lady Mary Lygon, Mrs. Derek Keppel, Lord Wenlock, Sir Arthur Bigge, Duke of Roxburghe, Hon. Derek Keppel, Major Denison, Sir Charles Cust, Commander Faussett, Major Bor, Sir Donald Wallace, Mr. Sydney Hale, Dr. Manby, Canon Dalton, Sir John Anderson.

In the viceregal loge were his Excellency the Governor-General and Lady Minto, Major Maude, C.M.G., Capt. Graham, Mr. Arthur Guise.

In the Lieutenant-Governor's loge were Miss Mowat, Mrs. Langton, Commander Law, and Lieut. Elmsley, A.D.C.

In the next loge were Sir Wilfrid and Lady Laurier, Hon. Senator and Mrs. Cox.

In the special loge, immediately behind the Royal loge, were Hon. G. W. and Mrs. Ross, Mr. and Mrs. Duncan C. Ross, Hon. W. S. and Mrs. Fielding, Hon. A. G. Blair, Mrs. and the Misses Blair, Hon. Lieut.-Col. J. M. Gibson and Mrs. Gibson, the Misses Gibson, Hon. R. Harcourt and Mrs. Harcourt, Hon. E. J. and Mrs. Davis, Hon. John and Mrs. Dryden, Hon. J. R. and Mrs. Stratton, Hon. F. R. and Mrs. Latchford. In the special seats were Mrs. Howland, Mrs. Merritt, Mr. and Mrs. Stewart Houston, Miss Houston the Postmaster-General and Mrs. Mulock, Hon. Dr. and Mrs. Borden, General and Mrs. O'Grady-Haly. Among the city's representatives were his Worship Mayor Howland, Ald. E. S. and Mrs. Cox, Miss Evelyn Cox, Ald. and Mrs. Oliver, Hon. Senator, Mrs. and Miss Lyman Melvin Jones occupied seats in the centre of the front. Prominent visitors from outside places were Sir Mackenzie Bowell, E. S. Clouston, Montreal; Mr. and Mrs. Frank B. Walker, Detroit; Mr. and Mrs. Harry Corby and the Misses Corby, Belleville; Mr. and Mrs. F. B. Robins, Buffalo; Capt. and Mrs. Eaton, Mr. and Mrs. Albert E. Jones, Buffalo; Professor and Mrs. H. J. Dawson, Kingston; Captain and Mrs. W. A. Grant, Kingston; Col. and Mrs. H. A. Ward, Port Hope; Mr. and Mrs. J. G. Seagram, Waterloo; Col. and Mrs. Macdonald, Ottawa, who were with Col. and Mrs. Mason.

AO

Mail and Empire, Oct. 11, 1901

Mail and Empire, Oct. 11, 1901 — AO

Mail and Empire, Oct. 11, 1901 — AO

MTLB

DAME NELLIE MELBA, eminent Australian soprano, first sang with her own Concert Company at Massey Hall in 1895 and returned frequently during her lengthy singing career.

GOS

EMMA JUCH, American soprano, was one of the participating artists in Toronto's second Music Festival which opened Massey Music Hall on June 14, 1894.

SYBIL SANDERSON (Juliette) American soprano for whom Massenet composed *Esclarmonde* and *Thais*.

French baritone CHARLES GILIBERT (Capulet). He died on Oct. 10, 1910, exactly two months before he was due to create the role of Jack Rance in *The Girl of the Golden West*.

MATTHILDE BAUERMEISTER (Gertrude) made her second appearance with the Metropolitan Opera in Toronto in the Royal Musical Festival.

Famous American soprano LOUISE HOMER (Ortrud) appeared with the Metropolitan Opera at Massey Hall in 1901 and, on later occasions, in concert.

Polish soprano, MARCELLA SEMBRICH (Elsa) sang with the Metropolitan Opera for the second time in Toronto in 1901.

MASSEY HALL

PROGRAMME — Continued

SATURDAY EVENING, OCTOBER TWELFTH
AT EIGHT O'CLOCK

BIZET'S OPERA, "CARMEN"
(IN FRENCH)

Carmen	-	Mme. Emma Calve
Frasquita	-	Miss Bauermeister
Mercedes	-	Miss Van Cauteren
Micaela	-	Miss Fritzi Scheff
Don Jose	-	Mr. Salignac
Zuniga	-	Mr. Dufriche
Morales	-	Mr. Vanni
Dancairo	-	Mr. Gilibert
Remendado	-	Mr. Reiss
and		
Escamillo	-	Mr. Journet

Conductor, Mr. Seppilli

SYNOPSIS
ACT I.—A public square in Sevilla. ACT II.—Lillas Pastia's Tavern.
ACT III.—A wild mountain pass. ACT IV.—A public square in Sevilla at the entrance of the circus.

—— WEBER PIANOS USED ——

NORDHEIMER PIANOS "Are productions of the highest grade."

PERRIN'S GLOVES
ARE THE BEST   ASK FOR THEM

THE TORONTO VIAVI CO.
GOVERNING
—— ONTARIO PROVINCE ——
LOCAL OFFICE:
Suite L, Confederation Life Building

Office Hours, 9-5   MRS. L. A. SULLIVAN, Manager

One of the Most famous Carmens, French soprano EMMA CALVE (Carmen), created the role of Suzel in Mascagni's *L'Amico Fritz*, and is seen here as Santuzza in *Cavallezia Rusticana*

Austrian soprano FRITZI SCHEFF (Micaela) was popular in both opera and operetta.

MARCEL JOURNET, French baritone (Escamillo) spent most of his career at LaScala, Milan.

THE DIVINE PATTI

It seems almost certain that the appearance of Mme. Patti at Massey Hall on December 3 will be "positively" her farewell to Toronto. She was first heard here as a child in November, exactly fifty years ago. It is a marvel that with sixty-one years to her credit she should be touring the United States and Canada and receive a fee per concert that is greater than any of the other great singers of the world can command. According to all accounts Patti does not look any older than when she sang in this country nine years ago, and all the critics are agreed that her voice is in a phenomenal state of preservation. It may be expected that Massey Hall will be crowded on December 3 by an audience curious to see and hear the world-renowned diva, but having among them a fair proportion of her old admirers who cherish delightful recollections of her beautiful voice in its best days, and who entertain for her in consequence a feeling of grateful regard and esteem.

Speaking of Patti the other day, her manager, Mr. Grau, said:

"Patti is a marvel in more ways than one. It is not merely that she is a wonderful singer; she is a wonderful woman as well. Many times in her career she has faced danger—that most horrible danger of a panic-stricken mob in a great theatre—faced it down by her own self-control, imposing self-control in others and saving hundreds of lives. Twice during her Russian tours she has been in danger from fire. Once in her own dressing-room, when she overturned a candle and set fire to the voluminous filmy draperies which were the fashion of the day; and once on the stage when the curtain caught fire, and a panic was imminent. Realising the terrible calamity that would ensue if everyone rushed for the door, she stood still and made a speech which held the audience for the critical quarter of a minute. Once down in New Orleans there was a terrible crowd to hear her, and it overcrowded a balcony so that it began to sag and was in danger of immediate collapse. Every one was scared out of his wits, the orchestra stopped playing and a terrible disaster seemed unavoidable. Patti began to sing 'Home, Sweet Home,' and the audience paused a moment, face to face with death, to listen. The panic passed and the building was safely emptied.

"Probably the most melodramatic incident of her forty-three years of stage life was the bomb incident out in San Francisco, when some anarchist threw a bomb on the stage which he had meant to throw in the box of a prominent banker. In the hubbub that ensued somebody shrieked 'You might have killed Mme. Patti!' as if that were a calamity so terrible and worldwide that he could have meant to bring it about; to which the man heartlessly replied, 'I shouldn't have cared if I had. She makes too much money.' Another of the most exciting incidents of the diva's career also happened in San Francisco, where in some unexplained way every seat on the main floor was

sold twice over. The result was something like a riot, and the curtain was not rung up until 9 o'clock, when a very nervous Patti sang to a packed and excited house."

Of her voice and its preservation Herman Klein in a recent Century writes:—

"Patti says that she never studied the art of producing or emitting the voice. Nature, alone and unaided, accomplished that marvel. To keep her voice in perfect condition it suffices for her to run over the scales ten minutes every morning. Her vocalization is one of those miracles that cannot be explained. Its wondrous certainty and finish are assuredly not arrived at without some labor, but in the end the miracle seems to have accomplished itself. Her 'ear' is phenomenal. She never forgets a tune, and will instantly name the opera or composition in which it occurs. Another mystery is the perennial freshness of her voice, which, after half a century of constant use, retains well-nigh unimpaired the delicious sweetness and bell-like timbre of early womanhood. No other such example of perfect preservation stands on record in the annals of the lyric art. To analyze its secret one can only say, Here is surely a singer of marvellous constitution, heavenly gifted with a faultless method, who has sedulously nursed her physical resources, and has never, under any circumstances, imposed the smallest undue strain upon the exquisitely proportioned mechanism of her vocal organs."

Globe, Nov. 28, 1903

Globe, Nov. 14, 1903 — AO

Globe, Nov. 26, 1903 — AO

Mme. Adelina Patti is sure of a magnificent reception in Massey Hall next Thursday, when she sings for the last time in Canada. In Buffalo (where she sings to-night) the immense Convention Hall was nearly all sold out on Saturday. There are still some good seats for the Toronto concert, to be had at Nordheimer's, where the plan is now open.

Globe, Nov. 30, 1903 — AO

OUR ADELINA.

Adelina Patti is an institution. Irreverent persons may say that she is a venerable institution, but the scoffer we have always with us, and he is incurable. It is he who becomes jocose about the finally final farewell, but the rest of us who are neither irreverent nor jocose would vainly hope that there would never be a final farewell to something so altogether admirable, so little changed, so full of glorious reminiscence, unparalleled triumphs, and sustained eminence.

Who could help reflecting on the millions of hearts whom that golden voice has transported in the last half-century—heard from manhood to old age, or till hearing is no more, or till it awakens again to the music of choirs immortal? What it has lost of the lark or the nightingale it has gained from association and real affection. The mighty audience as she appears just takes the little woman to its bosom and sets her down on the stage again and submits itself to her beguiling. The advantages of years are difficult to realize, but some of the elders were conscious last night that they were admitted to keener emotions than were possible to the young men and maidens who saw the incomparable diva for the first time. They refuse to accept a farewell. They were touched by the vocal leave-taking, but they were unshaken in the conviction that once again they would see the confident little woman quickly stepping to the footlights, with her humorous and intimate coquetries and blandishments, her frankly delighted acknowledgments of the plaudits of her adorers, and, in fact, all the little characteristics and even eccentricities that proclaim our undying goddess of song. Will there ever be another Patti? There are greater vocalists, but they are not Patti. And with that incontrovertible proposition we say farewell—for a while.

Globe, Dec. 4, 1903 — AO

MUSIC AND THE DRAMA.

The magic of Patti's name drew an audience of four thousand people to the Massey Hall last night on the occasion of her farewell here. Not only was the regular auditorium crowded, but the platform usually occupied at oratorio concerts was packed to its utmost capacity. The average reign of an opera or concert queen is about twenty-five years, but Mme. Patti seems to have extended that period to half a century, so far as this city is concerned, seeing that she made her first appearance here at the Ole Bull concert on November 23, 1853. It will be interesting to note that her programme numbers at the Ole Bull concert were "Brilliant Cavatina," from Verdi's "Ernani; "Home, Sweet Home," celebrated ballad by Sir Henry Bishop, and Jenny Lind's "Echo" song, and that the price of admission was $1, with seats reserved without extra charge. Mme. Patti may be truly said to be a physiological marvel. She sang last night with undeniable beauty of voice and neatness of technique, while in everything she did the artist was conspicuous. But it goes without saying that her voice is not what it was thirty years ago, and the inevitable was shown in a constant clipping of the value of notes, the curtailment of phrases, and in a comparatively poor quality of tone in the lower and upper registers. Mme. Patti, however, made a complete conquest of her audience, whose enthusiasm increased till it reached a climax on her final number. In her opening number the "Vol che Sapete," from Mozart's "Nozze di Figaro," she revealed her command of the pure singing style, which, free from artifice, was yet an achievement of art. As an encore she gave "Robin Adair" with much expressive charm. Her second programme number, the "Jewel" song from "Faust," was, in the circumstances, an astonishing vocal feat. The intonation in this excerpt, so naive in its brilliancy, was remarkably true, and probably few cared if the trill was but an excuse for the real thing. To the intense delight of the audience she gave as an encore "Home Sweet Home," and as a second recall number "Coming Through the Rye." The latter was rendered with a juvenile archness of expression that apparently charmed her hearers. Her second encore number after her first programme song was "The Last Farewell," a weak, sentimental composition by Charles K. Harris of New York, which, so far as the words are concerned, reminded one of the conventional speech which is made by popular actors when they are called several times before the curtain, and the musical setting of which, besides being reminiscent, is of a milk-and-water order. Mme. Patti was assisted by a much better company than is usually engaged to accompany a star on tour. Mr. Wilfrid Virgo, the tenor, it may be remembered, was one of the soloists of the Mackenzie festival early in the year. He made a greater impression than he did on his first introduction, and in the well-known "Songs of Araby," and the love song of Don Jose in "Carmen," he was at his best. The baritone, Mr. Claude A. Cunningham, who has a pleasing voice, sang the somewhat hackneyed prologue from "I Pagliacci," with smoothness and earnest expression. Mrs. Roza Zameis, solo violinist, made her first appearance before a Toronto audience, and, both in her solos and in the trio by Widor, with 'cello and piano, proved herself to be an accomplished player with warm temperament, a good technique, and an elastic velvety tone. Had the hall not been so crowded, her violin would have been heard to greater advantage in regard to resonance and power. The solo violoncellist, Mr. Anton Hegner, apparently produced a sweet and small tone, but his instrument is one that suffers more than the violin from a loss of brilliancy and volume in crowded halls. He showed he was at least a master of technique in Popper's difficult staccato study, "Dance of the Fairies." Miss Vera Margolies was the solo pianist, and contributed Liszt's "Hungarian Rhapsody, No. 12," in which she displayed flexible execution and much play of fancy in interpretation. The accompanist was Signor Sapio, whose restraint of power in his support of the soloists was exceptionally judicious.

Globe, Dec. 4, 1903 — AO

MME. PATTI ARRIVES.

TO BID A LAST FAREWELL TO TORONTO.

To be Heard To-morrow Night in Several of Her Old Favorites— Large Advance Sale.

Mme. Patti, with her husband, Baron Cederstrom, arrived in the city yesterday from Buffalo, and the party are staying at the King Edward. Madame Patti's professional career will come to a conclusion to-morrow evening, so far as Toronto is concerned, when she will sing in Massey Hall for the last time. The appreciation of this fact is evident in the large advance sale. At Buffalo the advance sale was the largest ever known in the history of that city. The concert went off splendidly, and Madame Patti proved never to have been in better voice.

It was made evident at Mme. Patti's last concert in New York, where she sang Wagner's selections, that the general public would much prefer to hear her in those airs which have become so identified with her career, and Toronto will hear her to-morrow in six or seven of her most popular and charming melodies, notably the "Voi-Che-Sapete," from Mozart's "Marriage of Figaro"; the "Jewel Song," from "Faust," and, for encores, such selections as "Comin' Through the Rye," "Robin Adair," and "Home, Sweet Home." With this last song will terminate Madame Patti's professional acquaintance with Toronto.

Globe, Dec. 2, 1903   AO

Patti to Steinway.

Chicago, Ill.
Messrs. Steinway & Sons,
   New York:
Dear Sirs,—Allow me to express to you the great satisfaction and pleasure that I have experienced from the use of your famous Pianos, which you have placed at my disposal during my concert tour now in course of progress in the United States.

During my artistic career in the art centres of the world, I have used the pianos of nearly all celebrated manufacturers, but none of them can be compared to yours—none possess to such a marvelous degree that sympathetic, poetic and singing tone quality which distinguishes the Steinway as peerless among them all. Before returning to Europe, I shall select and purchase one of your Grand Pianos for Craig-y-nos Castle, my residence in South Wales.

Respectfully yours,
ADELINA PATTI.

The Nordheimer Co., Limited, are sole agents for the world-renowned Steinway & Sons' Pianos.

Madam Patti will appear in Grand Concert in Massey Hall this evening. Miss Margolies, the famous pianiste, will use the Steinway Piano.

Globe, Dec. 3, 1903   AO

Postcard
Museo alla Scala Milan
ADELINA PATTI

MM
PATTI as Lady Harriet in Flotow's *Martha*.

BEWARE OF TICKET SPECULATORS.

PATTI

TO-NIGHT MASSEY HALL.

Following seats are still available:
250 Good Reserved Seats at $2.00 Each
310 Better   "   " $3.00 "
95 Choice   "   " $4.00 "
106 Best   "   " $5.00 "

Letters and telegrams for above to-day will receive the prompt attention of I. E. SUCKLING, Manager Patti Concert.
SPECIAL—250 Rush Seats at $1.00 each (on stage behind the artists) will be placed on sale at the stage entrance on Victoria St. at 7 o'clock. Plan until 5 o'clock at "House of Nordheimer." Main doors open at 7.20. Steinway piano used.

Globe, Dec. 3, 1903   AO

MTLB
LILLIAN NORDICA, versatile American soprano, sang both the Wagnerian and Italian repertoire. She was the first American artist to appear at Bayreuth.

GOS
ALICE NIELSEN, American soprano, who appeared in Toronto on several momentous occasions.

THE GREAT OPERATIC FESTIVAL.

San Carlo

Grand Opera Company—Director Mr. Henry Russell.

**MADAME LILLIAN NORDICA
MISS ALICE NIELSEN
SIGNOR CONSTANTINO**

| MASSEY HALL | Fri. and Sat. Evgs. Sat. Matinee | APRIL 26 & 27 |

Fri. Evg. at 8—"La Bohême"—Miss Nielsen, Mlle. Dereyne, Signor Constantino.
Sat. Mat at 2—"Don Pasquale"—Miss Nielsen, Signors Sacchetti, Fornari, Boracchi. "Cavalleria Rusticana"—Mlle. Tarquini, Signor Allamani.
Sat. Evg. at 8—"Il Trovatore"—Mme. Nordica, Signor Seguroh.
Prices $1, $1.50, $2, $2.50; first rows balcony $3.

Globe, Apr. 25, 1907   NLC

MASSEY HALL

The Metropolitan Musical Bureau
of New York
(Local Management - I. E. Suckling)
presents

ENRICO CARUSO
IN CONCERT

Assisting Artists:
ALICE MIRIAM   ALBERT STOESSEL
Soprano   Violinist

At the Piano:
For Mr. Caruso - Mr. Salvatore Fucito
For Miss Miriam and Mr. Stoessel - Mr. Louis Grunberg

Thursday Evening,
September 30th, 1920
at 8-15

MASSEY MUSIC HALL
(Norman M. Withrow - Manager)

LG

GOS

ENRICO CARUSO, the touchstone by which succeeding tenors are still judged.

...Programme...

1. Prelude and Allegro — *Pugnani-Kreisler*
   ALBERT STOESSEL
2. Aria—"Depuis Le Jour" from "Louise" — *Charpentier*
   ALICE MIRIAM
3. Aria—"Che gelida manina" from "La Boheme" — *Puccini*
   ENRICO CARUSO
4. (a) Spanish Serenade "La Media Noche" — *Aviles-Stoessel*
   (b) Humoresque — *Albert Stoessel*
   ALBERT STOESSEL
5. (a) Values — *Frederick W. Vanderpool*
   (b) A Song in the Night — *Marshall Bartholomew*
   (c) Ecstasy — *Walter Morse Rummel*
   ALICE MIRIAM
6. Aria—"Una Furtiva Lagrima" from "L'Elisir d'Amore" — *Donizetti*
   ENRICO CARUSO

INTERMISSION

7. (a) Berceuse — *Faure*
   (b) La Clochette — *Paganini*
   ALBERT STOESSEL
8. Aria—"Un bel di" from "Madame Butterfly" — *Puccini*
   ALICE MIRIAM
9. Aria—"Vesti La Giubba" from "Pagliacci" — *Leoncavallo*
   ENRICO CARUSO

GOD SAVE THE KING

"Ye Olde Firme" Heintsman & Co. Piano Used

MTLB

ALMA GLUCK, American soprano of the opera and concert stage.

OPERATIC STARS IN CONCERT

Globe, Feb. 8, 1913   NLC

MTLB

Italian soprano Amelita Galli-Curci, popular Metropolitan Opera artist during the 1920's.

MTLB

Austrian tenor LEO SLEZAK, leading dramatic tenor of the Vienna State Opera 1901-1926, father of film actor Walter Slezak.

Recital
by
AMELITA GALLI-CURCI
Soprano

Assisting Artists:
Manuel Berenguer   Homer Samuels
Flutist   Pianist

MONDAY EVENING
JUNE 3rd
at 8-15

MASSEY HALL

Toronto is the only city in Canada that has had the advantage of hearing MME. GALLI-CURCI

EMB

Violinist Efrem Zimbalist and Alma Gluck were husband and wife.

MONDAY, May 13th—CONCERT DE LUXE
Great Singers from the Metropolitan Opera House
FRANCES ALDA, Soprano   CAROLINA LAZZARI, Contralto
GIOVANNI MARTINELLI, Tenor   GIUSEPPE DE LUCA, Baritone
Mme. Alda and Messrs Martinelli and De Luca are
EXCLUSIVE VICTOR ARTISTS

JOINT CONCERT by
Mme. ALMA GLUCK & EFREM ZIMBALIST
Soprano   Violinist

Programme

I.
Concerto, D minor .... Spohr
   Allegro
   Adagio
   Rondo
MR. ZIMBALIST.

II.
a. With Verdure Clad .... Haydn
b. Come, Beloved .... Handel
c. Hey! for a Fiddler .... Ott
MME. GLUCK.

III.
a. Nocturne .... Chopin-Sarasate
b. Waltz .... Chopin-Powell
c. L'Alouette (The Lark) .... Glinka-Auer
d. Orientale .... Cui
e. Caprice Chinois .... Kreisler
MR. ZIMBALIST.

IV.
a. Starlet, Where Art Thou .... Moussorgsky
b. Spring Song .... Rubinstein
c. Little Russia Folksongs .... Zimbalist
d. Green .... Debussy
e. Fantoches .... Debussy
f. Eili, Eili .... Arr. by Schindler
MME. GLUCK.

V.
a. Sing Me to Sleep .... Green
b. Elegie .... Massenet
c. God Be With You .... Giebel
MME. GLUCK AND MR. ZIMBALIST.

God Save the King

MISS ELEANOR SCHEIB .... Accompanist for Mme. Gluck
MR. SAMUEL CHOTZINOFF .... " for Mr. Zimbalist

Management: WOLFSOHN MUSICAL BUREAU
The Piano is a KNABE

The Executive of the National Chorus desires to announce that it has secured the services of EFREM ZIMBALIST, violinist, for its Sixteenth Annual Concert in Massey Hall, Jan. 23rd, 1919.

April 9, 1918   EMB

MASSEY HALL

FRANCES ALDA, New Zealand soprano, wife of the fabulous Giulio Gatti-Cassaza, director of the Metropolitan Opera from 1908 to 1935.

GIUSEPPE DE LUCA, Italian baritone.

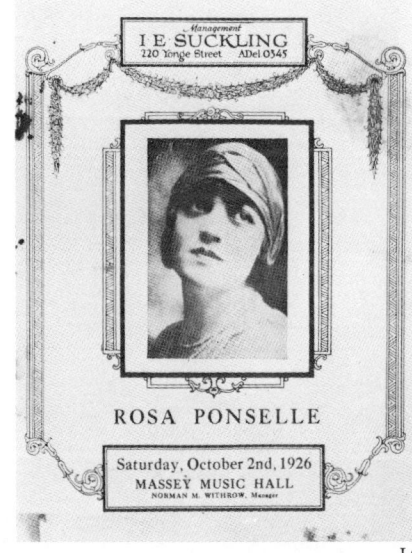

American soprano, ROSA PONSELLE, considered one of the greatest singers of the 20th century.

Russian bass, FEODOR CHALIAPIN.

OPERATIC STARS IN CONCERT

Italian tenor, GIOVANNI MARTINELLI.

EDWARD JOHNSON, Canada's first internationally-acclaimed tenor, General Manager of the Metropolitan Opera 1935-50.

American baritone LAWRENCE TIBBETT.

Italian baritone ANTONIO SCOTTI, brought the Scotti Grand Opera Company to Massey Hall in 1921 with performances of *Tosca*, *Il Barbiere di Siviglia*, *La Boheme*, *La Navarraisse* and *L'Oracolo*.

```
Annual Festival of Grand Opera
Nine Days, Beginning Thursday, September 24th

MASSEY HALL
43rd SEASON

FORTUNE GALLO
Presents the
San Carlo Opera Co.
Twenty-Seventh Transcontinental Tour

LA BOHEME ............... Saturday Matinee, Oct. 3
IL TROVATORE ........... Saturday Evening, Oct. 3
```

```
Programme
THE BARBER OF SEVILLE
OPERA IN THREE ACTS
BOOK BY CESARE STERBINI
(In Italian)
MUSIC by GIOACHINO ROSSINI

The Count of Amaviva .......... JOSEPH BOBROVICH
Dr. Bartolo ........................ GUISEPPE LA PUMA
Rosina ............................. ELVIRA DE HIDALGO
Figaro .............................. GIORGIO DURANDO
Don Basilio, Village organist & music teacher..FEODOR CHALIAPIN
Fiorello ............................. GIACOMO LUCCHINI
Berta ............................... ANNA LISSETSKAYA
An Official
          Musicians, Soldiers, Citizens
Conductor ........................ EUGENE PLOTNIKOFF

Act I.   A Square in Seville.
Act II.  A Room in the House of Dr. Bartolo.
Act III. Same as Act II.

Scenery Designed and Painted by Konstantin Korovine
Costumes Designed by Konstantin Korovine and Executed by
                William Kogan.

HEINTZMAN & CO. PIANO USED

Tuesday, November 9th
JOSEF HOFMANN
"The Master Pianist"
```

SAN CARLO OPERA CO.

Two great operas are being given by the San Carlo Opera Company in Massey Hall today. The matinee performance affords Toronto opera lovers the opportunity of enjoying "Lucia di Lammermoor." Much to Toronto's loss, Donizetti's famous opera is seldom done here, though it is one of the most popular in the repertoire of the world's leading music temples. As sung by Lucille Meusel (as Lucia), Kenneth Sakos (as Ravenswood), Mario Valle (as Ashton) and Harold Kravitt (as Raymond), the performance this afternoon should be a memorable one. Tonight the San Carlo offers Verdi's celebrated "Aida," with Bianca Sarota. Another great artist to be heard in tonight's opera will be Coe Glade, of the Chicago Opera in the role of Amneris. Aroldo Lindi, Mostyn Thomas and Harold Kravitt sing the leading male parts. Next week's repertoire introduces several more distinguished stars.

Globe, Sept. 26, 1936

SAKOS SHINES IN "LUCIA."

Local Tenor Wins Ovation in Tuneful Opera at Saturday Matinee.

It was a genuine delight to hear good old "Lucia" again, after a fifteen-year interval for this reviewer, and to hear it so agreeably given as it was by the San Carlo Company at Massey Hall last Saturday afternoon. In particular it was a pleasure to see Kenneth Sakos, Greenk-Canadian tenor from Kitchener, win a deserved ovation in the hero's role, when his friendly fellow-artists left him to take a dozen enthusiastic curtain-calls single-handed at the end of the performance.

The sombre overture strikes only too accurately the keynote of this gloomy opera, which condenses in brief compass all the painful happenings in Sir Walter Scott's tragic story, "The Bride of Lammermoor," without utilizing any of his relieving comedy as provided chiefly by the immortal Caleb Balderstone. The last scene is cheerily laid in a cemetery! However, Donizetti was a lyrical rather than a dramatic genius, so that we are more struck by the tunefulness of his characters than by their sufferings. It is easy to make fun of this type of opera, but it is far from easy to match the almost continuously beautiful melodiuiness of its score, and this flowing cantabile was well handled by the principals in the San Carlo production.

To mention all the musical high-spots would be to list almost all the solos, duets and ensembles in the score; but this listener especially enjoyed and admired Lucille Meusel's pensive solo, "Silence O'er All" and her beautiful duet with Edgar, "My Sighs," in Act I; the chorus, "Hope Brightly," and the ever-marvelous sextet, in Act II; the world-famous Mad Song in Act III, very delicately rendered by Miss Meusel; and the two fine solos by Mr. Sakos as Edgar in Act IV, where his impassioned singing and acting brought the opera to a stirringly climactic conclusion.

Since Toronto is Mr. Sako's "home town," so far as the San Carlo itinerary is concerned, and he has a large and loyal following here, one wonders why the usually astute Fortune Gallo uses him so sparingly in this Massey Hall season. Many Canadians would like to hear Mr. Sakos in "Butterfly," "Pagliacco," or "Trovatore," as well as in "Lucia" and "Boheme," and his presence in the cast would make an appreciable difference at the box-office.

Another point needs comment. Mr. Sakos may fairly be said to be a "natural" for grand opera, just born to make the classic tenor roles live and thrill on the stage; so, knowing what that gifted artist can do if given a chance, this reviewer wonders if he is being wisely handled in his present engagement. Forcefully despotic directing is undoubtedly necessary to whip en amateur production into shape at short notice, but with professional artists does it not tend to give a mechanical and stereotyped character to the performances?"—L. M.

Globe, Sept. 28, 1936

MASSEY HALL

THE CANADIAN GRAND OPERA ASSOCIATION

BRAHEEN A. URBAN — *General Director*

GENERAL MUSICAL DIRECTOR — RICHARD HAGEMAN

PREMIERE SEASON
1936

MASSEY HALL - TORONTO

REPERTOIRE

Saturday, February 1st		AIDA (Verdi)
Saturday, February 8th		CARMEN (Bizet)
Saturday, February 15th		RIGOLETTO (Verdi)
Saturday, February 22nd		FAUST (Gounod)
Wednesday, February 26th		IL TROVATORE (Verdi)
Saturday, March 7th		LA TOSCA (Puccini)

Assistant Conductors — ANGELO CANARUTTO (Chicago City Opera), FRANK A. MICELI, Toronto
Stage Manager — CHARLES DRUMHELLER (Chicago City Opera)
Assistant Stage Manager — J. N. C. ANDERSON
Ballet Mistress — LOUISE BURNS
Executive Assistant to Mr. Urban — FRANCIS LONGWORTH
Orchestra Manager — ERNEST JOHNSTON
Staff Accompanist — ROBERT HODGSON
Scenic Artists — WILLIAM DRAKE, VICTOR DELL' ANGELA
Press Representatives — WELLS RITCHIE (Central News Bureau)

Costumes by MARTIN
Cosmetics and Make-up for Principals only by ELIZABETH ARDEN

COCA

BRAHEEN A. URBAN, Founder and General Director, Canadian Grand Opera Asociation.
COCA

JEANNE PENGELLY as Tosca.
COCA

Globe, Mar. 5, 1938   MTLB

Week of Grand Opera

The Columbia Grand Opera Company has been in existence for the past twelve years. It paid its first visit to Canada last season when it fulfilled engagements at Montreal and Quebec. Both were financial, as well as artistic, successes, and this season the Canadian Artists' Bureau arranged with Armand Bagarozy, the general director of the Columbia Opera, to play a return engagement and to include Toronto in the itinerary.

Mr. Bagarozy, in addition to bringing the same company of principals that has appeared with his company at Montreal, Washington, Baltimore, Rochester and other cities, has engaged two guest artists from the Metropolitan Opera Company. On Friday evening Sydney Rayner, leading tenor of the Metropolitan, will be heard as Don Jose in "Carmen," and on Saturday evening Anna Leskaya, Russian soprano of the Met., will sing the Leonora role in "Il Trovatore."

In order to give this city first-class productions throughout, Director Bagarozy has added twenty local musicians to his roster, thus bringing his orchestra to around forty. With chorus, ballet, principals, musicians and technicians, approximately one hundred people will be participating in the Massey Hall offerings.

Globe, Mar. 5, 1938   NLC

Tannhauser by the Opera Guild of Toronto, 1937

The Opera Guild of Toronto

CÉSAR BORRÉ, Conductor

TUESDAY EVENING, APRIL 13, 1937, at 8 o'clock
WEDNESDAY EVENING, APRIL 14, 1937, at 8.30 o'clock

As various members of the orchestra are engaged in radio programmes which do not finish until 8 o'clock, the Wednesday evening curtain is being held until 8.30 o'clock.

"TANNHAUSER"

Opera in Three Acts (Four Scenes)
(In English)

BOOK and MUSIC by RICHARD WAGNER

Hermann, Landgrave of Thuringia	Norman Lucas
Tannhauser	Paul Althouse
Wolfram von Eschenbach	Robert Hately
Walter von der Vogelweide	Reginald Heal
Biterolf	Gordon McLaren
Heinrich der Schreiber	Murray Bosley
Reinmar von Zweter	Irvine Levine
Elizabeth, Niece of the Landgrave	Doris Godson Gilmour
Venus, Goddess of Love	Jeanne Pengelly
A Young Shepherd	Dorothy Allan Park
Four Noble Pages	Margaret Bowden, Molly Hately, Margaret Grant, Dorothy Cox

Chorus of Thuringian Nobles and Knights, Ladies, Pilgrims, Pages, Nymphs, Bacchantes and Satyrs.

ACT I. "Bacchanale", by Group of Dancers from the Boris Volkoff School of the Dance. Directed by BORIS VOLKOFF.

PRODUCED UNDER THE DIRECTION OF
CÉSAR BORRÉ

GC

MASSEY HALL OPERAS SEEN VIVID CONTRAST

"Lucia" Scottish Italian, Has Small Crowd — "Faust", German-French Packed

MELI CHIEF STAR

By AUGUSTUS BRIDLE

Two operas at Massey Hall yesterday were a violent contrast. "Lucia" in matinee drew about 700 people. "Faust" at night just about packed the hall for the Columbia troupe.

"Lucia" was sung by San Carlo last year to about as many. It will soon be dead here where it never really lived. The composer, a Scot, Izzett, changed his name in Italy to Donizetti. He had read Scott's novels. The sombre, sadistic tragedy of "Lammermoor" entranced him. He got an Italian to write a libretto for his music. And yesterday it was done as well as could be expected by a light-opera troupe who have a grand time with comedies, but rather go to pieces on parts of grand opera. The story is love and death. The lovers are all sad souls. The heroine, Lucia, was well sung by the enchanting lyric soprano Coronina, who caught the spirit of tragedy remarkably well for one who was so much' more at home as Rosina in "The Barber". "Attanasia" was the true lover Edgar, whose duets with Lucia were all better than his solos. Polande did a better job vocally as Bucklaw, the rival lover whom Lucia marries at the castle after a song-seance with the villain, Lord Henry (A. Meli), who has stolen the lands of Edgar whose arrival begins the famous sextet in which Meli is the baritone, Whitfield as the parson the bass, Polande and Attanasia the tenors, Coronina the soprano and Rose d'Amato contralto. This was splendidly sung. Honors for solo art were about equal between Coronina and Meli, with odds on the lady in the mad scene song.

"Faust" used three of the "Lucia" artists, with four others. Polande had the title role; good in climaxes with full orchestra or chorus, tonally rather sewn-up in straight middle-voice solo. Lloyd Harris, former wrestler, basso, clever actor, was the most athletic comedian-Mephisto ever seen here. He sang all the middle and low voice passages with rolling basso splendor—especially in comic episodes—but he went a bit flabby on all the tragic high notes where Mephisto is supposed to be solemnly impressive and devilish. His laughs were devastating; his comedy, pure opera bouffe; his gait, decidedly athletic. Continuously he jazzed what was meant by Goethe — and sometimes Gounod—to be an enormous tragi-comedy role. His "Calf of Gold" solo was excellent. He made love to old Martha as flippantly as any Don Juan. In the most solemnly religious scenes he was decidedly comic opera. His Mephisto was about one-tenth as good as his Bartolo on Monday, which was a comedy knockout.

Ina de Martino sang Marguerite; soprano voice of lovely quality, flexible, at times of quite thrilling intensity; her acting was better than her vocalism, except in the Jewel song; in the prison scene she was decidedly good.

Meli was consistently the best performer as Valentine. His "Even Bravest Heart", the soldier's adoration of his sister, was the finest thing in the opera—except his death scene. Georgia Standing was effectively comic as Martha. Rose d' Amato was a charming Siebel. Raoul Carrere was excellent as Wagner.

The chorus was sometimes rather collegiate—particularly the men in the soldiers' chorus, the scene of which was a very effective tableau, in the same set as was used in "The Barker"—which is rather reminiscent of Mantell's Sheakespeare scenics. The orchestra was excellent; the finale a rousing climax. Bagorzy conducted with virile authority.

Star, Mar. 10, 1938

1939 PRESENTING LOHENGRIN

OPERA GUILD OF TORONTO

THIRD SEASON OF GRAND OPERA
THE PERFORMANCES WILL COMMENCE AT 8.15 P.M. SHARP
At Massey Hall, Toronto ... February 28th and March 2nd.

Under the distinguished patronage and in the presence of His Honour the Lieutenant-Governor of Ontario

The Opera Guild of Toronto
presents
RICHARD WAGNER'S OPERA
"LOHENGRIN"

Conductors
SIR ERNEST MacMILLAN — Tuesday, Feb. 28
ETTORE MAZZOLENI — Thursday, March 2

Stage Director
PHILIP FEIN, Stage Director, Chicago City Opera

MASSEY HALL
Tuesday, February 28th, and Thursday, March 2nd, 1939

CAST

LOHENGRIN, Knight of the Holy Grail .... Myron Taylor
HENRY I, King of Germany .... Norman Lucas
FREDERICK TELRAMUND, a noble of Brabant ... Norman Roland (Randolph Crowe)
THE ROYAL HERALD .... Eric Tredwell
GOTTFRIED, Elsa's brother .... Beatrice Fair
ELSA OF BRABANT .... Doris Gilmour
ORTRUD, wife of Telramund .... Eileen Law

Saxon and Thuringian Counts and Nobles, Brabant Counts and Nobles
Ladies of Honour, Pages, Retainers, Lady Attendants

The Scene passes in Brabant. Period: The first half of the Tenth Century.

SERVICE ON CANADIAN SECURITIES

Orders Executed on All Exchanges

Our statistical department invites your inquiry.

H. B. HOUSSER & CO.
Members
The Toronto Stock Exchange

ROYAL BANK BUILDING, TORONTO
ELgin 7193

Opera Guild of Toronto's *Lohengrin* 1939

MASSEY HALL

JEANETTE MACDONALD, popular co-star of Nelson Eddy in numerous operettas.

Globe and Mail, May 19, 1943

WILFRID PELLETIER, eminent Canadian conductor, pianist and administrator, for whom Montreal named its Opera House in the Place des Arts.

Italian bass, EZIO PINZA, charismatic star of opera and films.

Globe and Mail, May 21, 1943

Telegram (?) 1938

FORTUNE GALLO was born in 1878 and died in 1963. The San Carlo Opera Company's last Toronto appearance was at the Odeon Carlton Theatre in March, 1950.

LILY PONS AS LUCIA OPERATIC SENSATION

By AUGUSTUS BRIDLE

Opera "as is" returned to Massey Hall last night with "Lucia" by Donizetti—said by some to be a Scot, though he wrote 63 operas in Italy where he was born, only two of which are famous; which is no way for a thrifty Scot. Last night, Lucia was Lily Pons; which explains why a man who turned in one ticket at the box-office was nearly mobbed by Ponsites.

After the mystic musicality of "Pelleas," this reversion to glittering grand opera was like going from a siesta to a carnival. The choral opening was a robustious jangle of kilties with halberds— the sort of Hielanders pictured in Scott's novel, from which the opera was concocted. A Don Cossacks drive in this lusty prelude to Lily Pons, who, as Lucia, could have been more sensational only if she had sung with a Scotch burr instead of limpid Italian.

Storm of Applause

Her entry into the Ravenswood forest scene was a storm of applause, which after she had sung three decorative arabesques of arias—one of them a duet with her tenor lover Edgar—rendered to a gale of hailstorms. Such prima donna acclamation has not been heard here since Tetrazzini's last recital. Less than 100 of the audience had ever heard Lily in a real opera. Her vocal art, and her white-gowned singing personality were a sensation. After years as queen of all decorative singers, she is still on the throne as a coloratura artist who has the rare lyric gift of merging her precarious top-note finesse into the melody of an operatic scene. Her role was obvious melodramatic romance; but she flung herself into the mood of the operatorial melodrama. Vocal art and thematic voice gave her entry arias a glorious tang of imaginative realism.

Supreme in Mad Scene

In the mad scene song she was supreme. We have seen Ophellias more exquisitely mad; but the rather flamboyant mad music of this double aria has never been quite equalled here.

Peerce as Edgar was exceptionally good in the love-duet with Lucia; but he reached his audience climax in the two arias of his death scene, which for dramatic verve of vibrant tenor singing he has never equalled here on the concert stage. His ovation was second only to that of Lily Pons, who was curtain-called six times for her mad song.

Moscona as Raimondo was exceptionally impressive. John Dudley, tenor, as Arturo was a dramatic extra in a brief double role. Votepka as Lucia's maid was an effective contralto.

The famous Sextet was a grand ensemble sonority, to a tremendous brass crescendo from the orchestra. The flautist for the mad song was marvellously adept; so was the harpist in Act I. The ballet was cramped by just room enough to turn around. Pelletier effectively conducted.

Star, Sept. 22, 1944   JPB

French soprano LILY PONS, famous coloratura soprano from 1931-59 at the Metropolitan Opera.

Brazilian soprano, BIDU SAYAO, one of the Metropolitan Opera's most enchanting artists during the Edward Johnson regime.

THIS THURS. at 8:30 p.m.
INTERNATIONAL ARTISTS presents
An evening of operatic arias and duets with
Maria Callas AND Giuseppe di Stefano
Tickets available at Box Office
MAIL ORDERS NO LONGER ACCEPTED
$17.50, $25.00.
MASSEY HALL

Globe, Feb. 19, 1974   MTLB

LA DIVINA

27th CONCERT SEASON

International Artists

presents

LUCIANO PAVAROTTI
TENOR

EUGENE KOHN
PIANIST

MASSEY HALL, TORONTO
SUNDAY EVENING, DECEMBER 9, 1973

COCA

The Toronto Symphony   58th Season
Andrew Davis, Music Director

Tuesday, Wednesday and Friday,
January 22, 23 and 25, 1980 at 8:00 p.m.

Conductor:	ANDREW DAVIS
Guest Artists:	MARIA EWING, Mezzo-soprano (Margaret) ROBERT TEAR, Tenor (Faust) °JOSE VAN DAM, Bass-baritone (Mephistopheles) CHRISTOPHER CAMERON, Bass (Brander) THE TORONTO MENDELSSOHN CHOIR (Dr. Elmer Iseler, Conductor) ST. MICHAEL'S CHOIR SCHOOL (Mr. Brian Rae, Acting Choral Director and Conductor)
Programme	
BERLIOZ	LA DAMNATION DE FAUST, *LEGENDE DRAMATIQUE*, OP. 24 PART I PART II
Intermission	
	PART III PART IV

°Toronto Symphony Debut

Tuesday/Wednesday performances sponsored by GULF OIL CANADA LIMITED

The Toronto Symphony records for CBS Records

LUCIANO PAVAROTTI, Italian tenor. "King of the High C's"

JOSE VAN DAM, Belgian bass-baritone.

MARIA EWING, American soprano.

MASSEY HALL

NICOLAI GEDDA, Swedish tenor.

ELISABETH SODERSTROM, Swedish soprano.

DON GARRARD, Canadian bass.

SELECTED APPEARANCES

CONCERTS

1894	Toronto Music Festival – Inc. Lillian Blauvelt and Emma Juch
1903	Adelina Patti – Farewell Concert
1908	Enrico Caruso Concert
1910	Emilio di Gorgoza Concert
1910	Toronto Symphony Orchestra – Two Grand Concerts
1912	Alice Nielsen – Operatic Concert
1913	Nellie Melba and Edmund Burke Concert
1914	Clara Butt Concert
1914	Alma Gluck Concert
1915	Nellie Melba Concert
1915	Canadian Music Festival with Pauline Donalda
1918	Louise Homer Concert
1918	Alma Gluck Concert
1918	Amelita Galli-Curci Concerts
1918	Frances Alda, Carolina Lazzari, Giovanni Martinelli, Giuseppe de Luca Concert
1919	Amelita Galli-Curci Concert
1919	Frances Alda, Carolina Lazzari, Giovanni Martinelli, Giuseppe de Luca Concert
1919	Giovanni Martinelli Concert
1920	Enrico Caruso Concert
1921	Rosa Ponselle Concert
1923	Ernestine Schumann-Heink Concert
1923	Edward Johnson Concert
1926	Rosa Ponselle Concert
1928	Mary Garden Concert
1928	Tito Schipa Concert
1928	Edward Johnson Concert
1931	Lily Pons Concert
1935	Toronto Symphony Orchestra – Wagner programme
1935	Feodor Chaliapin Concert
1935	Lawrence Tibbett Concert
1944	Bidu Sayao Concert
1945	Bidu Sayao Concert
1945	Toronto Symphony Orchestra – *Carmen* (concert version)
1953	Toronto Symphony Orchestra and CBC – *Gianni Schicchi* (concert version)
1961	Toronto Symphony Orchestra – *Bluebeard's Castle* (concert version)
1964	Toronto Symphony Orchestra – *Salome* (concert version)
1973	Luciano Pavarotti Concert
1974	Maria Callas, Giuseppe di Stefano Concert
1976	Maralin Niska, Cesare Siepi Concert
1979	Luciano Pavarotti Concert
1980	Toronto Symphony – Wagner evening
1980	Toronto Symphony – *Damnation of Faust*
1980	Toronto Symphony – *Eugene Onegin* (concert version)
1982	Luciano Pavarotti Concert

PRODUCERS

1895	Melba Operatic Concert Company
1901	Sembrich Opera Company 1901 Metropolitan Opera Company
1902	Mascagni & Co.
1906	Leoncavallo & Co.
1907	San Carlo Opera Company – Director – Mr. Henry Russell
1912	Majestic Grand Opera Company
1922	Scotti Grand Opera Company
1923	San Carlo Opera Company
1926	I.E. Suckling presents *The Barber of Seville*
1934	San Carlo Opera Company
1935	San Carlo Opera Company
1936	Canadian Grand Opera Assoc. 1936 San Carlo Opera Company
1937	Opera Guild of Toronto
1938	Columbia Opera Company 1938 San Carlo Opera Company
1939	Opera Guild of Toronto 1939 San Carlo Opera Company
1941	Columbia Opera Company
1943	Charles Wagner presents *Romeo et Juliette*
1944	France-Film Company presents singers of the Metropolitan Opera Company
1944	San Carlo Opera Company
1945	France-Film Company presents singers of the Metropolitan Opera Company

PRINCESS THEATRE

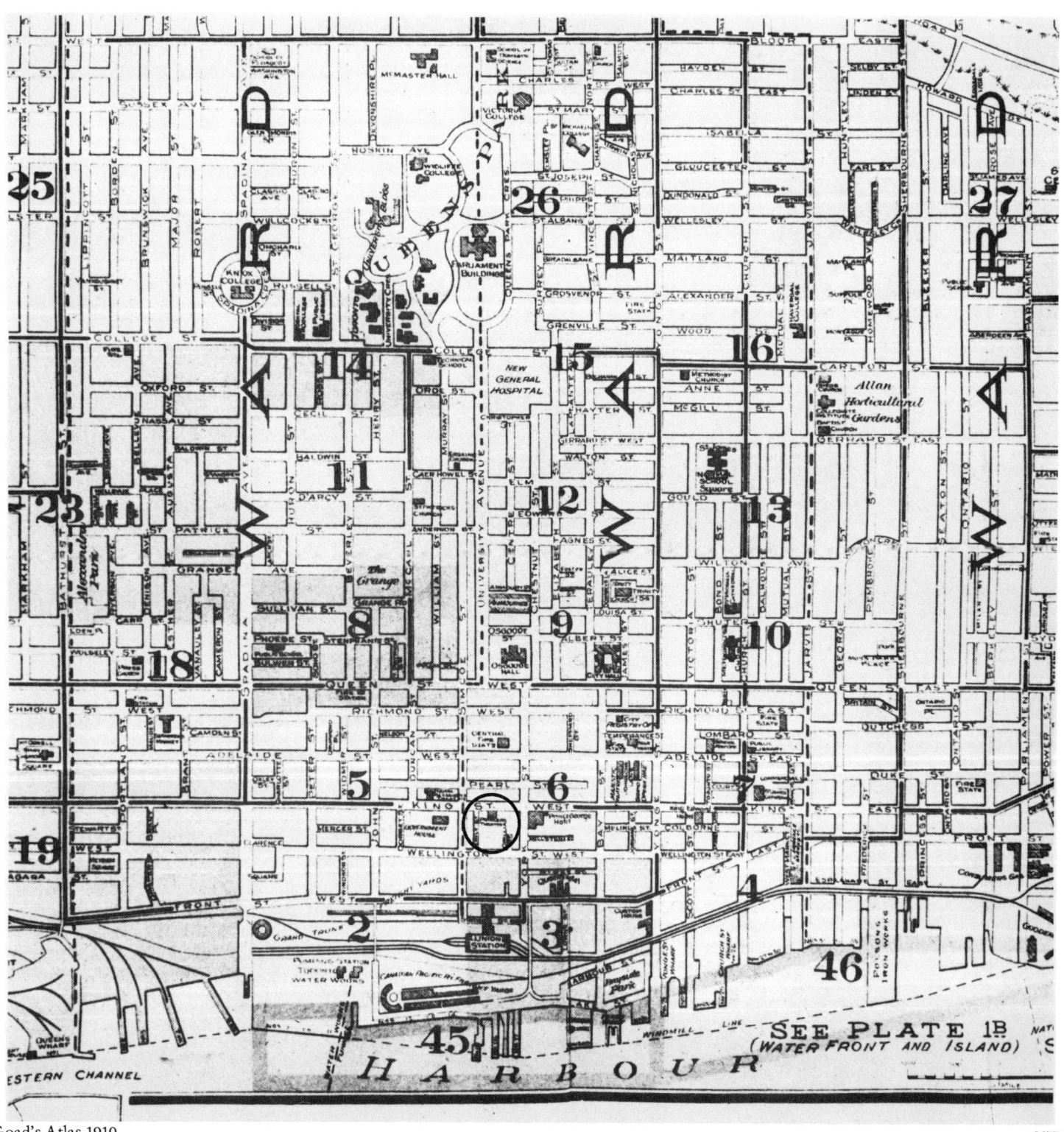

Goad's Atlas 1910

MTLB

1896
PRINCESS THEATRE

A complete renovation of the Academy of Music.

THE PRINCESS during the 1920's

PRINCESS THEATRE

During the interval between the theatre seasons in 1895 the Academy of Music on King Street West was almost entirely rebuilt. The name was changed to the Princess Theatre and, on 31 August 1895, the new facility opened with a musical programme by the house orchestra and two vocalists. There was doubt in many minds as to whether Toronto could accommodate a second theatre like the Grand Opera House (the Toronto Opera House was apparently not considered in the same class) but both houses continued to offer lyric theatre – increasingly, as time went by, of the "operetta" variety. The versatile Henry W. Savage, dealer in light and grand opera, brought to the Princess in 1905 the first performance in Canada of Wagner's *Parsifal* and in 1907 of Puccini's *Madama Butterfly*, 3 years after the latter's premiere in Milan. On 7th May, 1915 at 2 a.m. fire broke out and destroyed the auditorium. After renovation the theatre continued to operate until 1930 when it was expropriated by the city at a cost of $550,000 in order to make way for the University Avenue extension.

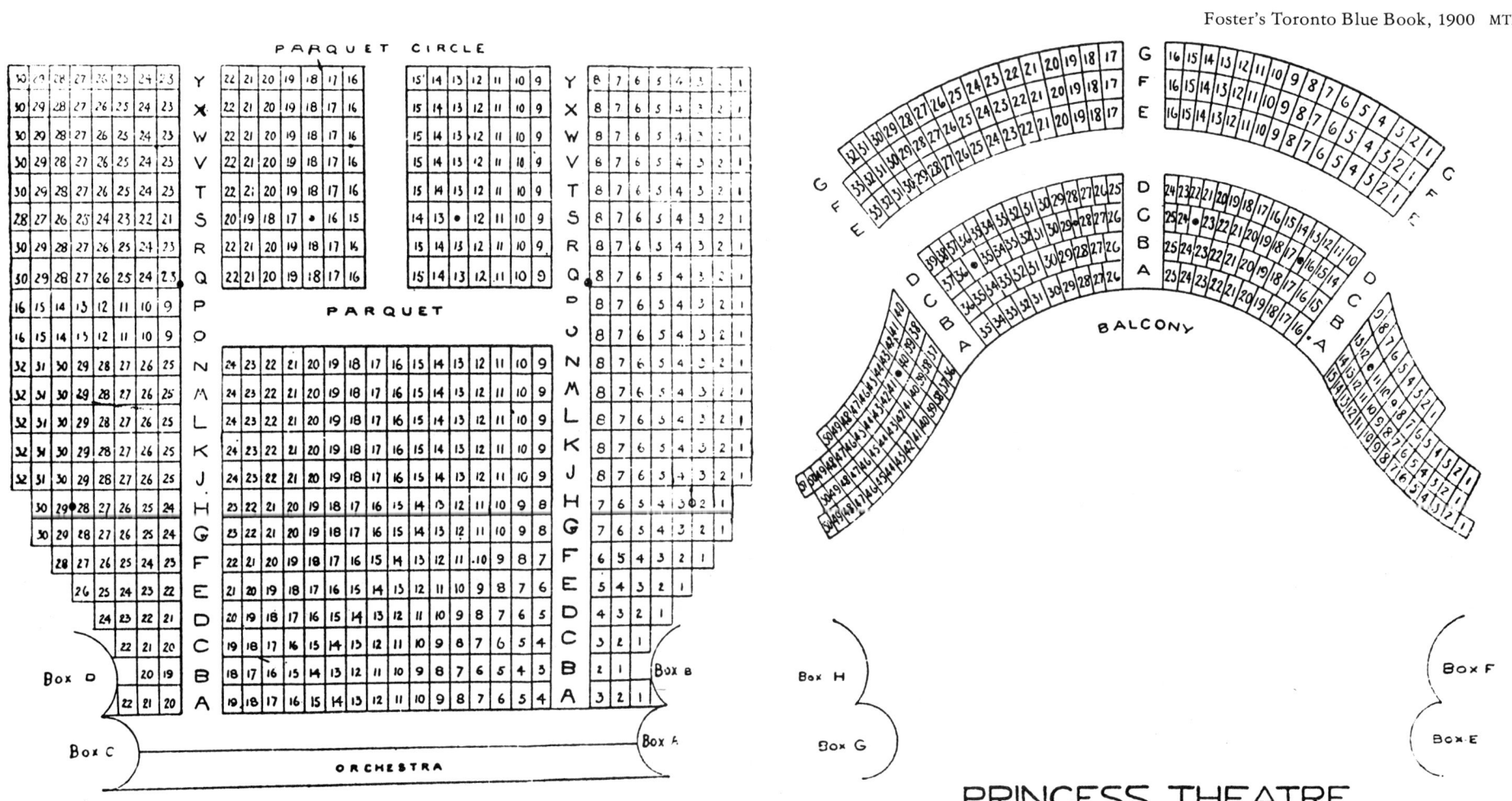

Foster's Toronto Blue Book, 1900 MTLB

PRINCESS THEATRE—GROUND FLOOR.

PRINCESS THEATRE

THE PRINCESS THEATRE.

A large number of ladies and gentlemen assembled at the Princess theatre on Saturday evening by special invitation of Mr. Frank Conolly to assist at the informal opening of the new theatre. By eight o'clock the whole of the auditorium and the first balcony was more than crowded, and a good many of the guests had to find their way into the top gallery. The picture presented by the new theatre was a very pretty one, and commendation was general all round at the use made of the short interval from the close of the last theatrical season in having completed what is practically a new building in so brief a time, with such practical and artistic results. There is no need to specify what has been done, as there will doubtless be a large audience of expectant sightseers this evening (Monday); and in addition to the attraction of Mr. Frederic Warde in "Runnymede," the curiosity to see what has been accomplished in the way of reconstruction will be dominant, and the gratification of this feeling would be to a certain extent spoiled by any kind of description. It is sufficient to say that the Princess theatre is one of the most handsome buildings devoted to the drama that can be found in Canada to-day. On Saturday evening a musical programme was given by the orchestra of the house under the able direction of Mr. Faeder, assisted by Mlle. Strauss and Signor Pierre Delasco, as vocalists. Mlle. Strauss was enthusiastically recalled each time she sang; the same compliment was also paid when Mlle. Strauss and Signor Delasco sang a duet; and the "Good Night! Farewell," by Signor Delasco, was the occasion of hearty applause. The various numbers were well executed by the orchestra, and very flatteringly received by the audience. The public went away extremely well pleased with what they had seen and heard, and later on, at about 9.30 p.m., Mr. Conolly entertained a party of personal friends and others connected more or less directly with the theatre at a little social soiree, when many cigars were smoked, various compliments paid, and several bottles of apollinaris were opened.

Among the large audience were the following ladies and gentlemen:—Mr. and Mrs. E. W. Cox, Mr. and Mrs. Widmer Hawke and Mrs. Watson, Mr. and Mrs. Walter S. Lee and Miss Lee, Misses Ferguson, Mr. C. A. B. Brown, Mr. Alfred Beardmore, Mr. Fred. Beardmore, Mrs. James Carruthers and Miss Gooderham, Mrs. Alfred Cameron, Mr. H. S. Crews, Mrs. E. W. Gardner and Miss Keefer, Dr. and Mrs. Moorehouse, Mr. C. R. Palmer, Capt. Irving and Miss Riche, Dr. Riordan, Mr. J. Bryson and Miss Gardner, Mr. and Mrs. Samuel May and Miss May, Misses Strachan, Dr. O'Reilly, Dr. Lehmann, Mr. and Mrs. Harry Wright, Mr. H. P. Blackey, Mr. and Mrs. Bicknell, Mr. and Mrs. Cappell, Mr. and Mrs. Malone, Mr. Fellows, Mr. Kenneth Cameron, Mrs. Ketchem, Miss Benton and Miss Bessie Benton, Mr. and Mrs. J. D. Matheson, Mr. Harry Drummond, Mr. Roden Kingsmill, Miss Eckert and Miss Mary Eckert, Misses Bailey, Mr. George Carruthers, Mrs. and Miss Williams, Mrs. Campbell and Mr. Bedford Campbell, Mr. E. Youngheart, and many other well-known citizens.

Mail and Empire, Sept. 2, 1895   NLC

PRINCESS THEATRE

To the disappointment of a very large number who had purchased tickets ahead, the Gordon-Shay Grand Opera Company, which was to have opened at the Princess Theatre last night with "Carmen" as the first presentation did not give a performance. The fault was not due to the company at all, which had been in the city during Holy Week, but, unfortunately, their musical director, Max Wynne, who had gone to New York on a visit was, owing to a train accident in New York State, unable to make connections so as to reach Toronto in time for the opening performance. In his absence Mr. J. Saunders Gordon considered it better to cancel the first performance. The company will, however, carry out their engagement here, and to-night will present "Cavalleria Rusticana" and "Il Pagliacci," with Miss Rose Cecilia Shay as Santuzza in the former opera. "Carmen" will be presented on Wednesday night and Saturday matinee, and the rest of the programme will be carried out as previously announced.

Globe, Apr. 14, 1903 — NLC

Amusements.

PRINCESS | TO-NIGHT and Balance of Week.

JULES MURRY presents

SADIE MARTINOT

IN

"THE SECOND MRS. TANQUERAY"

Regular Matinee Saturday.

SEATS on sale TO-DAY FOR NEXT WEEK

JOHN C. FISHER'S stupendous production

THE **SILVER SLIPPER**

By the authors of "Florodora."

Globe, Dec. 31, 1903 — AO

"The Silver Slipper," the great spectacular piece which has been produced by the firm which brought "Florodora" to this country, will be given its premiere at the Princess the week after next. Many Toronto people heard the English opera during its long runs in London and New York.

Globe, Nov. 28, 1903 — AO

To-night at the Princess Theatre the Walter Jones Comic Opera Company will produce for the first time in this city Mr. George V. Hobart's latest and greatest success, "The Sleeping King." The company is headed by Mr. Walter Jones, who is recognized as one of the cleverest comedians of the present time. There will be only four performances, including a Wednesday matinee.

Globe, Nov. 30, 1903 — AO

Toronto has been distinguished by being selected as the locale for the first production in Canada of Wagner's sacred music drama, "Parsifal," which is announced for performance at the Princess Theatre by the Henry W. Savage Company in Easter week. It is worthy of note that Toronto people will hear the work in advance of its production in the British metropolis. The representations, it is certain, will arouse profound interest among the musical community. The first production of the work outside of Bayreuth was given at the Metropolitan Opera House, New York, in December, 1903, and attracted an audience that represented $20,000 in box office receipts. The version used was the German original, which, it is safe to say, the large majority of the audience did not understand. It occurred to Mr. Savage that a production with an English version would be welcomed by the general public of the large cities of the United States and Canada, and with characteristic daring he organized a special company for the purpose, and sent them on an extended tour. This company, who have met with a series of brilliant successes in the United States, will give four performances of "Parsifal" here, opening on Monday evening, the 24th inst. They bring with them a double cast of principals, a large chorus and an orchestra of fifty-seven members. There seems to be a conflict of critical opinion as to the exact status of "Parsifal," but the master's enthusiastic admirers acclaim it as the greatest inspiration of his genius, and as the one in which he has most perfectly blended poetry, music and scenic illusion. The music is less complex than that of "Der Ring des Niebelungen," and its comparative simplicity appeals more directly to the average listener than that of any of the composer's most elaborate dramas. It is expected that the Princess Theatre will be crowded at every representation, as many parties from outside towns will attend.

Globe, Apr. 15, 1905 — NLC

When "The Prince of Pilsen" comes to the Princess Theatre next Monday evening, it is a fair presumption that the handsome costumes provided by Henry W. Savage for both the feminine members of the cast and the chorus will be a revelation to Toronto playgoers. All of the costumes were designed by Will R. Barnes, an Australian, who, since his arrival in America five years ago, has earned the name of being the best designer in America. Polly Guzman, the brilliant comedienne, who possesses a cultivated coloratura soprano, wears some strikingly handsome gowns, among which may be mentioned one of yellow Pongee silk, richly embroidered in Russian effect round the square-cut neck and down the stole fronts. The skirt, which is a close-fitting habit back, is of sheath-like form till it reaches the knee, where it flares in full knife pleating, the hem embedded in the rich embroidery to correspond with the bodice. With this stunning costume is worn a large Gainsborough hat and the tout ensemble is certainly a creation upon which the feminine portion of the audience at least feast their eyes with delight. Another charming costume is a heliotrope gown made decollete. The theme of beautifully variegated butterflies makes this dress one of the daintiest creations imaginable. A large glittering butterfly forms the central figure of the waist, while a smaller one serves as the left sleeve, the right arm being outlined by a network of heliotrope velvet criss-crossed. A spray of the same dainty design of butterflies embellishes the network of the skirt, which is made over a drop skirt of taffeta silk, also of the heliotrope shade. The hosiery and lingerie worn with this costume are in keeping, being of the same tone and prettily spangled with the glittering wings of the tiniest of these creatures. Miss Guzman carries with this creation a dainty muff of chiffon and old lace, which, with the large picture hat laden with ostrich plumes, makes a charming finish to this beautiful gown. Probably one of the handsomest of Miss Guzman's many handsome gowns is known as the poppy gown, which is, as its name indicates, composed almost entirely of this flower, the sleeves being formed of two large flowers, their stems pendant, crossing over the bodice, which is handsomely embellished with gold sequins. The skirt, in the present tight-fitting mode, is draped with sprays of the same flower and appliqued around the hem, the edge being outlined in gold. The whole glittering robe is surmounted by a poppy hat of tricorn shape, and with this costume is carried a poppy muff and parasol. Probably nothing half so dashing has been seen on the modern stage.

Globe, Nov 14, 1903 — AO

The Walter Jones Comic Opera Company, with a dozen or more "top liners" in the cast, is to appear at the Princess for four performances next week in a presentation of the musical comedy, "The Sleepy King." From a musical standpoint, this piece probably surpasses all its predecessors by the same author. The book was written by George V. Hobart, whose success in literary fields is well known. Giovanni Conterno, the well-known New York bandmaster and musician, is responsible for the music. The music is described as tuneful, catchy and bright, yet it is said to be not trashy or lacking in the elements which good music must have. The plot is sufficient to sustain the interest, but with no more intricacy than is usual with comic operas. King Ozo, ruler of Ruralania, is a monarch, whose one desire on earth is to sleep—to get "two hours' sleep in fifteen minutes"—and he does not care much who runs his kingdom, so long as he can get his naps. To aid this desire, he makes his prime minister change places with him and attend to the cares of state. A number of interesting and humorous complications grow out of this. The sentimental interest in the story comes through the suing for the hand of the beautiful daughter of the King by a number of foreign Princes, and the final triumph of true love, the fair Princess being won by the King of Arcadia, disguised as one of his own subjects. Mr. Walter Jones is making a distinct hit as King Ozo, but everyone is prepared for this, his clever work of past seasons having established him as a clever comedian. His vehicle this year is by long odds superior to anything he has hitherto had an opportunity to appear in before the public. Little Ed. Redway, who will be remembered in connection with "The Chaperones," is a host in himself. He has a German character part, Picklesauer, of Pittsburg, with four charming daughters, "by a frendt who vas my vife," and in it he can give play to all of the drollery and cleverness of feet of which he is master. George Henrey, playing the prime minister, is an elongated individual, whose every appearance is funny, and he, too, is making the most of the multitude of possibilities in the part. Miss Catherine Linyard, prima donna, is pretty, engaging in manner, has a good figure, and has a voice that is said to delight all from the first note. Nellie O'Neill, the contralto, is engaging and magnetic. Among other members of the cast who are favorites in most American cities, might be mentioned Geo. Fiske, James Stevens, David Abrahams, Frank Farrington, Harriet Packard, Kathryn Pearl Redway, Louise Skillman, Laura Witt, Gertrude Stillman and Amy and Edith Stuart.

Globe, Nov. 28, 1903 — AO

PRINCESS THEATRE

Wagner's Masterpiece "Parsifal"
AT THE PRINCESS

Toronto has at last had the opportunity of hearing "Parsifal"—the masterpiece of the master worker, Wagner—for itself, thanks to Henry W. Savage and his excellent company, which is presenting that opera at the Princess Theater for the first three days of this week. Torontonians will now be able to judge for themselves this much discussed music-drama.

In writing his sacred festival play, Wagner assuredly had in mind much more favorable conditions of production than could possibly be obtained in this city, and with a traveling company. But Mr. Savage and his assistants have done their work well, and a performance such as given last night will enable all who see it to form an adequate idea of the opera when given under perfect conditions. In itself, Mr. Savage's production is wonderfully impressive, and to either the lover of drama or the music-lover a thing for which he may well be grateful. The scenic arrangements are excellent, the principal artists of high merit, the chorus well trained and competent, and all with the support of a good orchestra.

NOT HARD TO COMPREHEND.

From the many disquisitions upon "Parsifal" one might have thought that the ability to comprehend it was bound up with the ability to remember and recognize multitudinous motifs. To the musician Wagner's dramatic music has its peculiar charm, but to anyone with a fair knowledge of the story and its allegorical intent, with any love of music, the opera was wholly comprehensible and enjoyable. Last night the title role was sung by a brilliant young Canadian, Mr. Francis Maclennan. He was most successful. Possessed of a fine voice, which he uses with great skill, and histrionic power of no mean order, he filled the difficult role admirably. As the foolish boy of the first act, in the awakening scene in the second act, and as the victor, assuming his kingly office, he sang and acted with a sustained power and unwavering consistency which was most praiseworthy.

Mme. Hanna Mara, as the weird woman, Kundry, was also most successful. As Kundry, the beautiful, in her attempt to overcome Parsifal in the second act, she was especially successful. The trying part of Amfortas was essayed by Mr. Franz Egenieff, who depicted in strong fashion the sufferings of the unfortunate King. Mr. Putnam Griswold, as the aged knight, Gurnemanz, sustained one of the heaviest parts in the opera with unflagging vigor. Mr. Homer Lind, as Klingsor, also achieved a considerable success.

AS A SCENIC PRODUCTION.

The scenic setting and stage ensembles were most effective. The scene between Parsifal and the flower maidens was most excellently arranged and most beautiful. The sudden destruction of the enchanted castle and the transformation of the scenery from the woodland to the castle interior were two instances of very clever scenic arrangements, although the slight mishap last night served to indicate the difficulty of setting the production on such a small stage as that at the Princess Theater.

The impressive scenes reach a climax in the final one, where in the castle of the holy order Parsifal stands, transfigured by the light from heaven, the dove descending from heaven upon him, and he holding aloft the Holy Grail as the knights kneel in adoration before it.

NO HUMAN PASSION.

The interest of the drama lies in its religious character. There is no human passion. The music is sublime, but austere, but simple and easily followed. The motifs of the Love Feast, of the Grail, and the faith motif are the principal constituents of the musical texture. The setting of choruses on different heights, the youths' choir at mid-height, and the boys' voices in the dome gave a unique effect. The orchestra, under the direction of Mr. Walter H. Rothwell, gave a faithful and sympathetic rendering of the dramatic music, Mr. Rothwell apparently being deeply imbued with the true spirit of the work. The work does not afford any opportunity for pure vocal work, the parts being altogether declamatory, but the voices of all the principals were of excellent quality, and when any opportunity was given they showed themselves masters of their art.

The audience last night was one which had studied the proper conduct at a "Parsifal" performance. Few were late, and there was no applause. The majority wore their evening clothes to the afternoon portion of the opera.

Star, Apr. 25, 1905   NLC

During the performance of Parsifal *which began at 5 P.M. an intermission of an hour and a quarter between Acts I and II gave the audience an opportunity to have dinner.*

Globe, Apr. 15, 1905   NLC

ALOIS PENNARINI who sings the role of Parsifal

PRINCESS | MATINEE TO-DAY.
HENRY W. SAVAGE OFFERS HIS
ENGLISH GRAND OPERA COMPANY in
MADAM BUTTERFLY

All Next Week— Matinees Wed. and Sat.

CHARLES FROHMAN will present

Otis Skinner

In the Parisian Success

THE DUEL   SEAT SALE NOW OPEN.

MASSEY HALL | **APRIL 18, 19, 20 SAT. MAT.**

Gilbert and Sullivan's Comic Opera,

THE PIRATES OF PENZANCE
95—PERFOMERS—95
SEAT SALE NOW OPEN.

Globe, Apr. 15, 1907   NLC

Puccini's "Madam Butterfly" is specially interesting to the experienced musician as illustrating the effort of the younger school of Italian composers to treat dramatic action logically without making use of the voice as a mere instrument or confining the expression of the storm and stress of passion and emotion to the medium of the orchestra. Puccini's orchestration as exemplified in "Madam Butterfly" is delightful to listen to. It is always graceful, always well restrained, and is more suggestive than expressive. The general public perhaps may not be impressed with his music, for their craving is for the square-cut tune, for something that, if they cannot carry away with them on first hearing and whistle, must at least be something that they would like to whistle. The main consideration of the old Italian school of opera composers was to write music in which the melody was supreme. If the melody was inappropriate to the action of the play as a whole or incongruous with the sentiment of the words, so much the worse for the action or the words. Puccini's opera, "Madam Butterfly," is in every way interesting and instructive for the cultured lover of music to follow and analyze. The opera-going public of Toronto should really feel indebted to Mr. Savage for giving them opportunities of hearing new operas satisfactorily interpreted. And it is specially a testimony to Mr. Savage's ambition to produce opera in English in a worthy manner that he should go to the expense of bringing here so large and efficient an orchestra. The average manager is of opinion that the engagement of five or six extra strings or of oboes, bassoons or other instruments that the score may call for will not bring him an extra dollar in receipts at the box office. And consequently he does not attempt to meet the requirements of the composer, confident in the belief that the public care only to hear the singers. Mr. Savage could probably make more money if he carried with his company on tour an orchestra of one-half its present strength, but it is to his credit that he is more anxious to produce an artistic effect, to create the musical atmosphere that the composer intended, than to save a few dollars. The musician can, therefore, fervently wish him a continued career of success in his undertaking to supply the public with well-balanced productions of opera in English.

Globe, Apr. 13, 1907   NLC

Saturday night brought the successful engagement at the Princess Theatre of Henry Savage's opera company in "Madam Butterfly" to a close. The auditorium was once more well filled, and the opera was followed with close attention. The title role was taken by Rene Vivienne, a young American soprano, who sang the part for Puccini in Milan. Her first appearance here was a delightful surprise, for greater expectations had not been entertained of an artiste who had been selected to close the engagement. Miss Vivienne has a pure fresh voice, of excellent carrying power, and one with depth of color in the lower register. She acts with intelligence and earnestness, and her Toronto debut was altogether a genuine triumph. Owing to the indisposition of Mr. Sheehan, his place was taken by Henry Taylor as Pinkerton. He has a light lyric tenor. His dramatic power has yet to be developed, but he made a pleasing impression on the whole. The performance as a whole was much appreciated, the applause being enthusiastic on the close of the first and second acts.

Globe, Apr. 15, 1907   NLC

Globe, Jan. 25, 1913 NLC

PRINCESS THEATRE,
Oct. 21, 1912 MTLB

Conductor HEALEY WILLAN COCA

MUSIC and the DRAMA

CONDUCTED BY E. R. PARKHURST.

"Il Trovatore," the 1853 opera of Verdi, has still power to attract large audiences, evidence of which was given last night at the Princess Theatre on the occasion of its presentation by the Sheehan English Opera Company. "Il Trovatore" retains its hold upon the music-loving public of the present day simply by virtue of its continuous charm of melody, a quality for which grand operas of the present day are rarely distinguished. The Sheehan Company offer grand opera at popular prices, and it goes without saying that they cannot give productions with star artists at such low rates. But as was shown last night they can produce opera in a manner that illustrates the beauty of the music—simply considered as music. Mr. Joseph F. Sheehan sang the role of Manrico with the vitality and attraction of voice that distinguished him when he was here with the Savage Grand Opera Co. Louis Lavalle as the Comte de Luna revealed a baritone voice of excellent quality and power, the effect of which was however often marred by a wavering or oscillation of the tone on sustained notes that caused impure intonation. Miss Gladys Caldwell, a youthful soprano of much talent, as Leonora sang with a bright, fresh voice, which it may be supposed will gain in dramatic power as also in flexibility in the course of a few years. Alma Stetzler, the Azucena, a mezzosoprano of sympathetic quality, won a special demonstration of approval for her scene in the second act. The "Miserere" act, with its thrilling duet for Manrico and Leonora, did not fall of its time-honored effect. One cannot even in these days of cynical analysis in regard to the dramatic situation in relation to its musical exposition of this act, be insensible to the enthralling and poignant power of the music. The chorus was meritorious in many respects, and the addition of French horn, harp and bassoon to the ordinary theatre orchestra was very welcome. The opera for this evening will be "The Tales of Hoffman."

Globe, Jan. 28, 1913 NLC

Interior of the PRINCESS THEATRE, May 10, 1915 CTA

"Beggar's Opera" Revived

THE revival of Gay's "The Beggar's Opera," during the week of January 8th at the Princess Theatre, was a notable achievement for the producers as well as individual soloists taking part. Dr. Willan's settings of the familiar tunes were distinctive and yet held the original charm.

Mr. Alfred Heather, who was stage director as well as principal tenor with the production sent out from London four years ago, brought to the performance a masterly knowledge of deportment, costuming, etc., and deserves great credit for the splendid success of this production. The cast included a number of the finest artists in Toronto, and in the chorus were many young students from the Conservatory.

"In Toronto this week we have the privilege of hearing yet another arrangement by Dr. Healey Willan, whose knowledge of all the early forms of music, as well as of Bach, is internationally famous.

"The new score of Dr. Willan is less theatrical in character than earlier versions. It is remarkably atmospheric in the chronological sense and its delicacy approximates to the style of chamber music. His aim seems to have been to treat the airs after the manner of the comic cantatas of Bach; and he introduces a merry Bach air as an interlude.

"The work of Alfred Heather, who was stage director of the production sent out from London four years ago, proved masterly. Such an achievement in training inexperienced performers to a rococo style of expression and to decorative singing of a very difficult order has not been witnessed in local annals. It is so efficient from a theatrical standpoint that the sense of amateurishness entirely disappears. From the standpoint of vocal artistry, despite orchestral difficulties, this presentation of Gay's opera, excels any local production yet done in Canada."—HECTOR CHARLESWORTH in *Saturday Night*.

"'The Beggar's Opera' was well performed in eighteenth century style before a crowded and appreciative house at the Princess last night. The technical stage management was especially good, to begin with that phase of a very carefully thought out and artistic production. The conventional architectural set, with locality indicated by back-drop between draperies, the consequent elimination of waits between scenes; the steps, the use of the main stage as an apron, for direct address to the audience; the pointing of songs, tableaux and witticisms straight out at the house—all these things were very satisfying and enjoyable evidences of competent stage direction. Furthermore, the handsome costumes, the gracious manners and spacious stateliness brought back the ampler atmosphere of an elder day, even while the villainous seamy side of it all furnished a continual contrast."—LAWRENCE MASON in *The Globe*.

UTFM

Toronto University Royal Conservatory of Music Quarterly Review, Feb. 1925

"The Beggar's Opera of 1925—lacking three years of being 200 years old—was worth waiting for. There perhaps never was quite so good a presentation of it in many of its most sparkling and engaging particularities, as that of this week at the Princess, by Mr. Alfred Heather and his company, including so much of the best stage and singing talent of the city.

"Much has been said about it; all worth while. The production is remarkably fine. It bears the marks of many hands. Besides the technique of Mr. Heather in direction, there is the exquisite orchestration by Dr. Healey Willan, who conducted the work, from the original Gay-Pepusch edition used by Austin for his Hammersmith version, and a much more seductive orchestration than Austin's, betraying the rare aesthetic craft of one who understands the value of colour and subdued suggestion and half lights in an orchestra necessarily so small, select and piquant.

"Such a company never could be got together for any road show of this opera. Toronto has the distinction of the finest Beggar's Opera presentation ever known since the days of old, and musically better than that. The house was deservedly packed."—AUGUSTUS BRIDLE in *The Daily Star*.

UTFM

Toronto University Royal Conservatory of Music Quarterly Review, February 1925

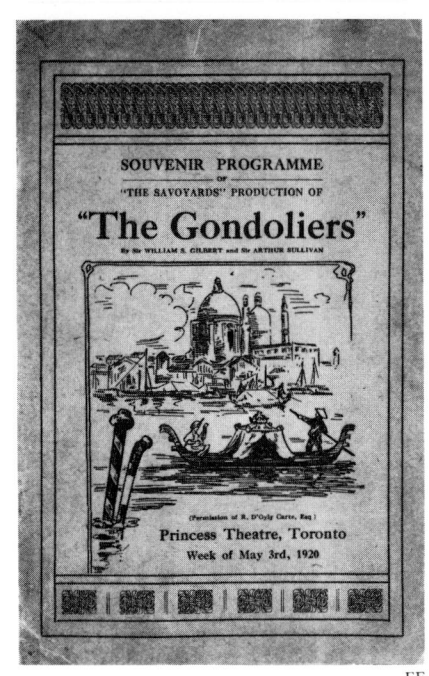

KENNETH ANGUS as Marco
RUTH CROSS as Tessa
THOMAS FIELDER as Giuseppe
LEE WOODLAND as Gianetta

Star, Nov. 18, 1929   MTLB

SELECTED APPEARANCES

PERFORMANCES		PRODUCERS	
1904	*The Red Feather* (De Koven)	1896	Italian Grand Opera Group
1904	*Erminie*	1896	De Koven & Smith
1905	*Babes in Toyland*	1902	John C. Fisher & Thos. W. Ryley
1906	*H.M.S. Pinafore*	1903	Gordon Shay Grand Opera Company
1906	*The Red Feather*	1903	Walter Jones Comic Opera Company
1906	*Captain Careless*	1903	Henry W. Savage's Company
1912	*The Spring Maid*	1905	Henry W. Savage's English Grand Opera Company
1913	*The Quaker Girl*	1905	English Grand Opera Company
1913	*The Chocolate Soldier*	1907	Henry W. Savage's English Grand Opera Company
1913	*The Count of Luxembourg*	1911	Montreal Musical Society
1925	*The Beggar's Opera*	1913	Sheehan English Opera Company
1929	*The Silver Swan*	1920	The Savoyards
		1923	Gilbert and Sullivan Opera Company

Extending University Avenue 1931
Printing of an etching on paper by
Henry Draper Wallace. In the City of
Toronto's Market Galleries.

Photo: Gary Beechey

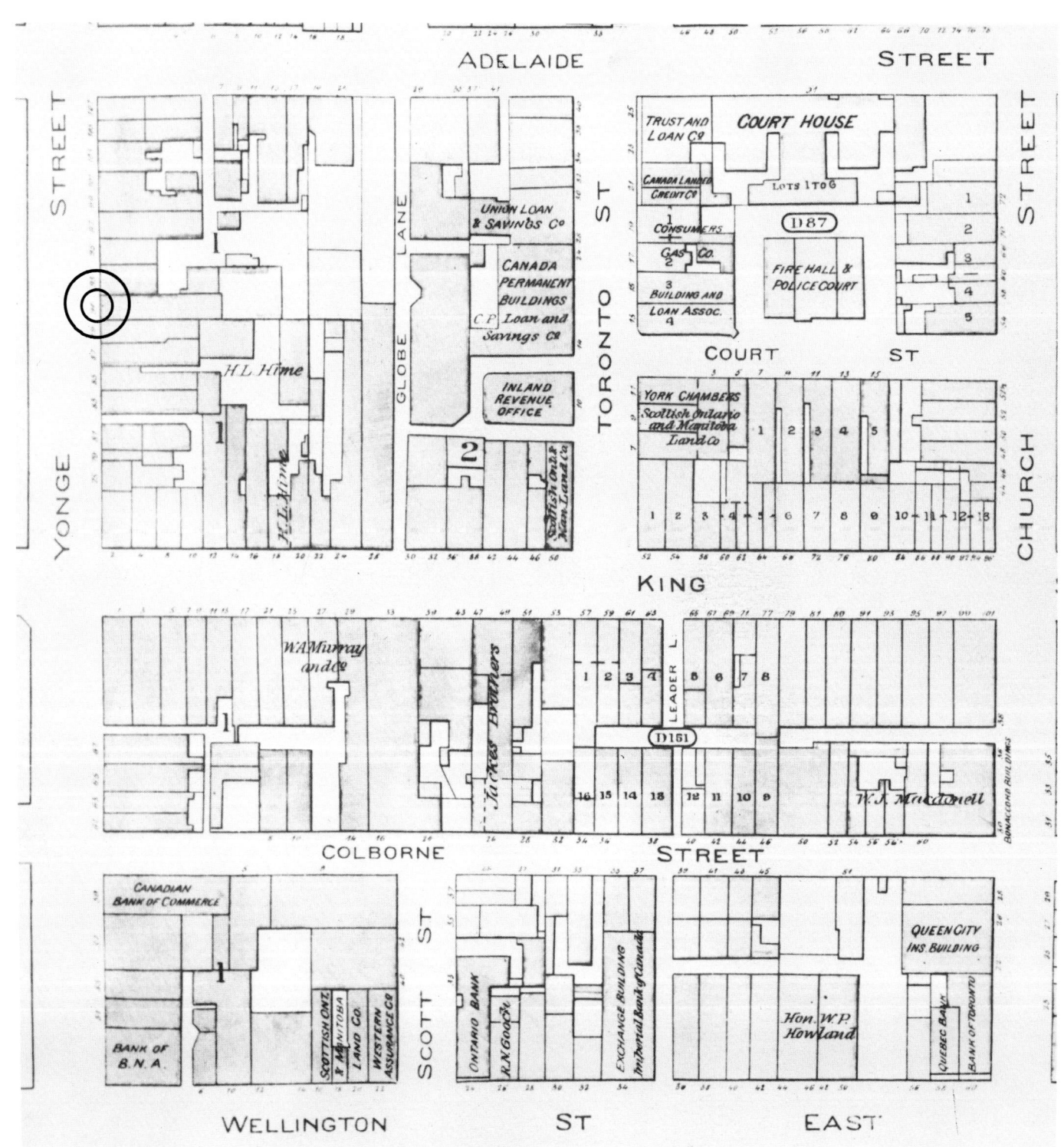

Goad's Atlas, 1894

1903
SHEA'S THEATRE

In the course of a varied career as a showcase, during a brief spell as a theatre, even Shea's was used by a visiting opera company.

In 1983 #91 Yonge Street displays an
oxidized sign indicating THE STRAND (formerly Shea's new theatre).

SHEA'S THEATRE

#91 Yonge Street, midway between King and Adelaide Streets, opened in 1891 as Wonderland Museum. Between 1892 and 1897, when it was gutted by fire, it was known successively as Moore's Musee Theatre, Crystal Theatre and Eden Museum, and finally Bijou Musee Theatre. The whole structure was rebuilt and in 1899 opened as Shea's Theatre with a lease until 1911. In December 1905 it was again destroyed by fire which was supposedly caused by defective wiring in the kinetograph machine. After this the Shea Amusement Company of Buffalo acquired land at the southeast corner of Richmond and Victoria Streets in order to replace the theatre on Yonge Street. The latter was the Strand Theatre by 1912.

Globe, Apr. 22, 1893   MTLB

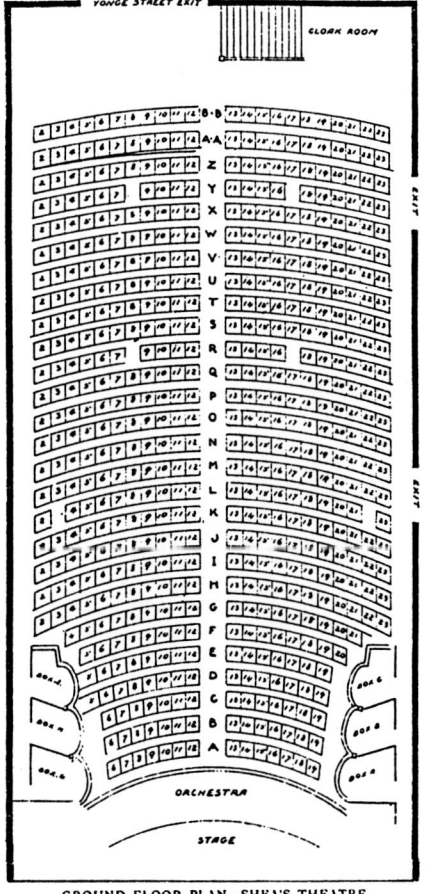

GROUND FLOOR PLAN—SHEA'S THEATRE.

Balcony Plan—Shea's Theatre.

MTLB 792.097135-T59

Theatre Toronto, The 1904-5 Theatre Season.

THEATRE IMPROVEMENTS.

Permits have been granted to the Musee for alterations $1,200, and to the Academy of Music, alterations and additions, $8,000.

Mail and Empire, July 10, 1895   NLC

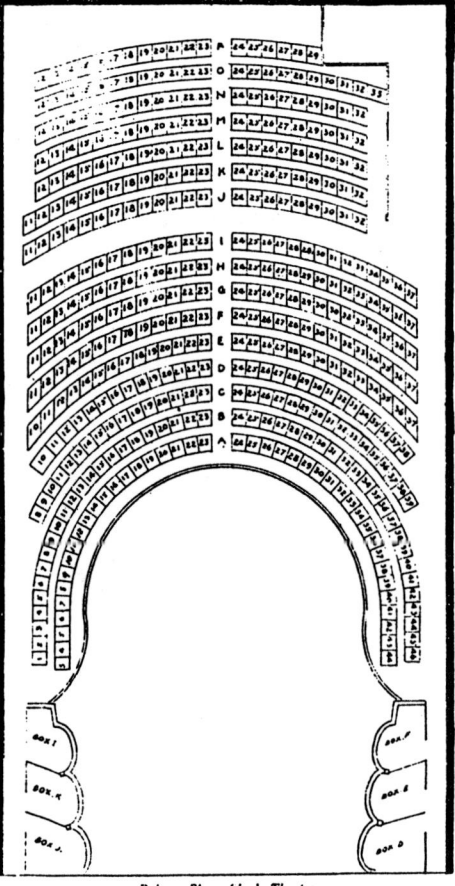

Globe, Sept. 2, 1899   MTLB

Shea's new theatre on Yonge street was opened for the first time last night to the public with an excellent vaudeville entertainment. The manager had every reason to be satisfied with the encouragement he received for his initial performance, as the curtain rose in front of an audience of about 1,700 people, and a few minutes after the first act had begun only standing room could be obtained. The auditorium has been very conveniently constructed for the comfort of the audience. The seats are so arranged that the occupants, whether on the ground floor or the galleries, can see perfectly what takes place on the stage. In the brilliant illumination of the hundreds of electric lights the auditorium presented a very attractive appearance and was generally admired. The music of the evening was supplied by an effective little orchestra, under the direction of Mr. Willie Anderson, the well-known young Toronto violinist. It is perfectly clean. There were many good and amusing acts on the programme, but perhaps the most clever exhibition was that given by Professor Leonida and his trained dogs and cats. The most astonishing tricks were performed by the dogs, both individually and in combination. One of these had been taught to act as the comedian of the company, and his humorous mischief-making provoked roars of laughter. Other acts specially worthy of praise were the comedy juggling and trick bicycling of Henry French, who is remarkably clever in his line, and executed some unique feats; and the performance of Charles R. Sweet, "the musical tramp." Some skilful grotesque dancing was done by Montgomery and Stone, and altogether the evening's bill proved very satisfactory. Commencing to-day there will be a matinee every afternoon at this theatre.

Globe, Sept. 5, 1899   MTLB

SHEA'S THEATRE

MUSIC AND THE DRAMA.

An enormous audience attended the opening performance yesterday afternoon of the Aborn Comic Opera Co. at Shea's Theatre. In the first gallery the side aisles were blocked up by people who were allowed to stand there, and had there been a panic the consequence would have been serious. The opera was Victor Herbert's "Serenade," first given in Toronto by the Bostonians. It has never gained a great success here, although the music is light and tuneful. The company gave a fair presentation with an augmented orchestra, a fair-sized chorus, and a cast of principals who pleased in their respective roles. The supply of programmes ran short, so that a large proportion of the audience were in the dark as to the names of the principals. The opera is billed for the week.

Globe, Apr. 14, 1903   NLC

For this week's show at Shea's Theatre has been secured an attractive number of vaudeville feature acts, including Edmund Day & Co. in the sketch called "Shipmates"; Adolph Zing, "little man, big comedian"; Gallagher and Barrett; Charlotte Guyer George, contralto ; Billy S. Clifford, Robertus and Wilfredo, A. D. Robbins and the kinetograph with new pictures.

Globe, Nov. 30, 1903   AO

APPEARANCES

1903   Aborn Comic Opera Company

SHEA'S THEATRE BADLY BURNED.

Stage Saved But Auditorium Ruined.

DUE TO DEFECTIVE WIRING.

For the second time in eight years the building occupied by Shea's Theatre was destroyed by fire last night. The interior of the theatre is a total wreck and the loss will exceed $25,000. The origin of the fire is not exactly known, but, as it had started in the upper gallery, it was probably caused by defective wiring at the kinetograph machine, which was moved from the first to the second gallery about a month ago.

At 11.20 last night the last of the performers had left the theatre, and five minutes afterwards "Bob" Newman, the stage manager, locked up and left the building. Everything was all right at that time. While Mr. Newman was on the street car going home, less than 10 minutes after leaving the theatre, he saw the fire reels going down town, but did not know the theatre was on fire until he reached his home.

Patrol Sergeant "Andy" Levine was standing at the corner of King and Church Streets when he saw the smoke and flames from the fire, and, thinking it was from the Rice, Lewis Co.'s premises, he pulled the alarm at the corner of King and Church. An alarm at the Market was rung in at the same time. The fire reels responded to the alarm and went to the corner of King and Church Streets, but saw no fire. They could see the reflection and at once hurried back to Yonge Street and commenced work.

The sprinklers on the ceiling threw tons of water into the galleries and the floor of the theatre. As the firemen did not know where the pipes were turned on and off, it was impossible to shut off the flow of water. Chief Thompson and Deputy Chief Noble directed operations and tarpaulins were placed in the boxes to protect the upholstering.

Precisely at 12 o'clock the roof fell in with a crash, and carried with it part of the upper gallery. The seats in the lower part of the orchestra were all destroyed. The walls were completely soaked with water, and plaster fell in many places.

The firemen did all in their power to fight the fire, which was in one of the worst possible places to reach with the hose. Ladders were raised from Yonge and Adelaide Sts., from which streams were sent into the building. A general alarm was turned in, and all the men in the city were on hand.

House Badly Wrecked.

At 12.30 a.m. the fire was under control, but by that time the interior of the theatre was badly wrecked. The roof burned through and the dome fell into the pit, ruining about half the seats on the bottom floor. The floors, ceiling, and walls were all drenched with the water, which was poured on from a dozen lines of hose, and the whole interior will require to be replastered and decorated.

A two-foot fire wall and the asbestos curtain prevented the fire from gaining a hold back of the footlights, and no damage was done to the stage or scenery with the exception of a sprinkle of water. Mr. Robert Newman, chief stage carpenter, who hurried to the theatre on being apprised of the fire, busied himself in seeing that the trunks and other effects of the employes and performers were out of danger. The Military Octette, the headliner of the week, got all their scenery, properties and instruments out in good order, and will open a New York engagement on Monday. The Grand Opera House stage staff came over and assisted in getting out the instruments and music of the theatre orchestra.

Mr. Jerry Shea, the local manager of the theatre, was summoned from his residence by telephone. On his arrival he gave instructions for saving the contents of the box office, and then hastened to call up the principal lessee, Mr. Michael Shea, of the Park Theatre, Buffalo, to apprise him of the fire. The latter replied that he would come over by the first morning train, bringing with him his partners, Messrs. Kreitner and Schelling, for the purpose of arranging with the owners of the theatre for immediate repairs.

The theatre is owned by the McGee estate, managed by Messrs. John A. and Alex. McGee, and is assessed at $76,000. It has been used for years as a theatre, having been first known as Moore's Musee, and later as Robinson's Musee. In September of 1897 it was gutted by a fire, which was attended by a fatal accident, a team of horses attached to a heavy engine running through a crowd on Victoria Street, killing a boy and injuring a dozen persons. The whole interior was rebuilt after the fire, and in September of 1899 it was opened as Shea's Theatre, under a lease which will terminate in 1911. The McGee estate own the building and all its contents except the scenery, which is valued at about $15,000, and is practically uninjured. As the lease has six years to run, it is probable that the McGee estate will at once refit the theatre, a work which will take about two months.

Shea's theatre is one of the best-paying theatrical properties in the city, capacity audiences being the rule, and by having it out, of commission during the holiday season, Mr. Shea will incur considerable loss.

Joseph Rose, the caretaker of the theatre, who lives in the front part of the upper flat, was in the cellar when the fire started. He smelled smoke, and, on running into the lane, he saw the reflection in the sky, but by that time the reels began to arrive. Mr. Sol Solman, manager of the Majestic Theatre, turned in an alarm from the corner of Yonge and Adelaide Streets.

Mr. Geo. Moran, assistant treasurer of the theatre, superintended the work of getting the cash and books out of the office.

The last day car traffic and the Yonge night car service were demoralized, and cars had to be sent round by York or Church Streets. The firemen in raising their ladders were obliged to break a number of wires, and, as some were live ones, the policemen were kept busy seeing that unwary firemen or others within the lines did not walk into them.

The insurance on the building amounts to about $60,000, distributed among the Northern, Commercial Union, Royal, Liverpool, and London and Globe, and Guardian companies. Mr. McGee, one of the owners, accompanied by Mr. Shea, made an inspection of the building shortly before two o'clock, and stated that repairs would be commenced as soon as an adjustment of the losses could be secured.

One of the incidents of the fire was a lively scrap between a fireman and a policeman, at Yonge and Adelaide Streets. The fireman had been off duty, and tried to pass the lines by showing his button. The patrolman refused to recognize it, and the fireman gave the policeman a good trouncing.

Mail and Empire, Dec. 2, 1905   MTLB

TO RUSH REPAIR WORK ON SHEA'S.

Theatre Will be Reopened by Christmas Week.

FIRE ORIGINATED ON ROOF.

Insurance Appraisers Will Report on Monday, and Workmen Will be Busy on Tuesday.

If the present intentions of the owners and lessees are fulfilled Shea's Theatre, which was badly damaged by fire on Thursday night, will be again open to the public by Christmas week. Mr. John Kreitner, of the Shea Amusement Company, Buffalo, came over yesterday morning and conferred with Messrs. John A. and Alexander McGee, the owners, and the latter gave the assurance that as soon as the insurance is adjusted the work of repairing the building will be begun and pushed to completion, and it is expected that the theatre will be ready for reopening inside of three weeks.

Insurance appraisers were appointed yesterday afternoon, Mr. John Hanrahan representing the owners and Mr. J. Munro the interested companies. These gentlemen will probably present their report on Monday, and by Tuesday the workmen will be clearing out the debris and building a new roof.

The origin of the fire is still a mystery, but an inspection of the premises indicates that the fire did not originate in the gallery or dome of the theatre, but on the outside of the roof, the fire thence working downward. This is shown by the fact that the transverse stringers which supported the roof are badly charred, while the stringers eight feet below, to which the dome was attached, were not even scorched. Large sections of the dome, carried down by the falling roof, also show no marks of fire. The only rebuilding necessary will be the roof, as the galleries and walls of the theatre were not touched by the flames. While only a few of the seats were injured by the blazing debris which fell upon them, nearly all were wet by the floods of water, and will therefore have to be renewed, as the soaking will cause the veneered surface to warp. The electric wiring will also probably require to be done again.

The Shea company's loss is not covered by insurance, but fortunately it is light, consisting principally of the upholstery of the boxes and the floor and stair carpets. Nothing on the stage was damaged, and Stage Manager Robt. Newman stated yesterday, with pride, that the performers lost nothing, "not even a shoe-lace."

Mr. John A. McGee stated last night that the present intention of the owners is to put on a permanent roof, but make only temporary repairs to the interior of the house, as new plaster would not dry quickly enough. During the Summer vacation the whole interior will be plastered and decorated anew, reopening in September with what will be practically a new theatre.

The box office will be open at 10 a.m. to-day for the redemption of tickets. There was a large advance sale for yesterday, to-day, and next week.

Mail and Empire, Dec. 1, 1905   MTLB

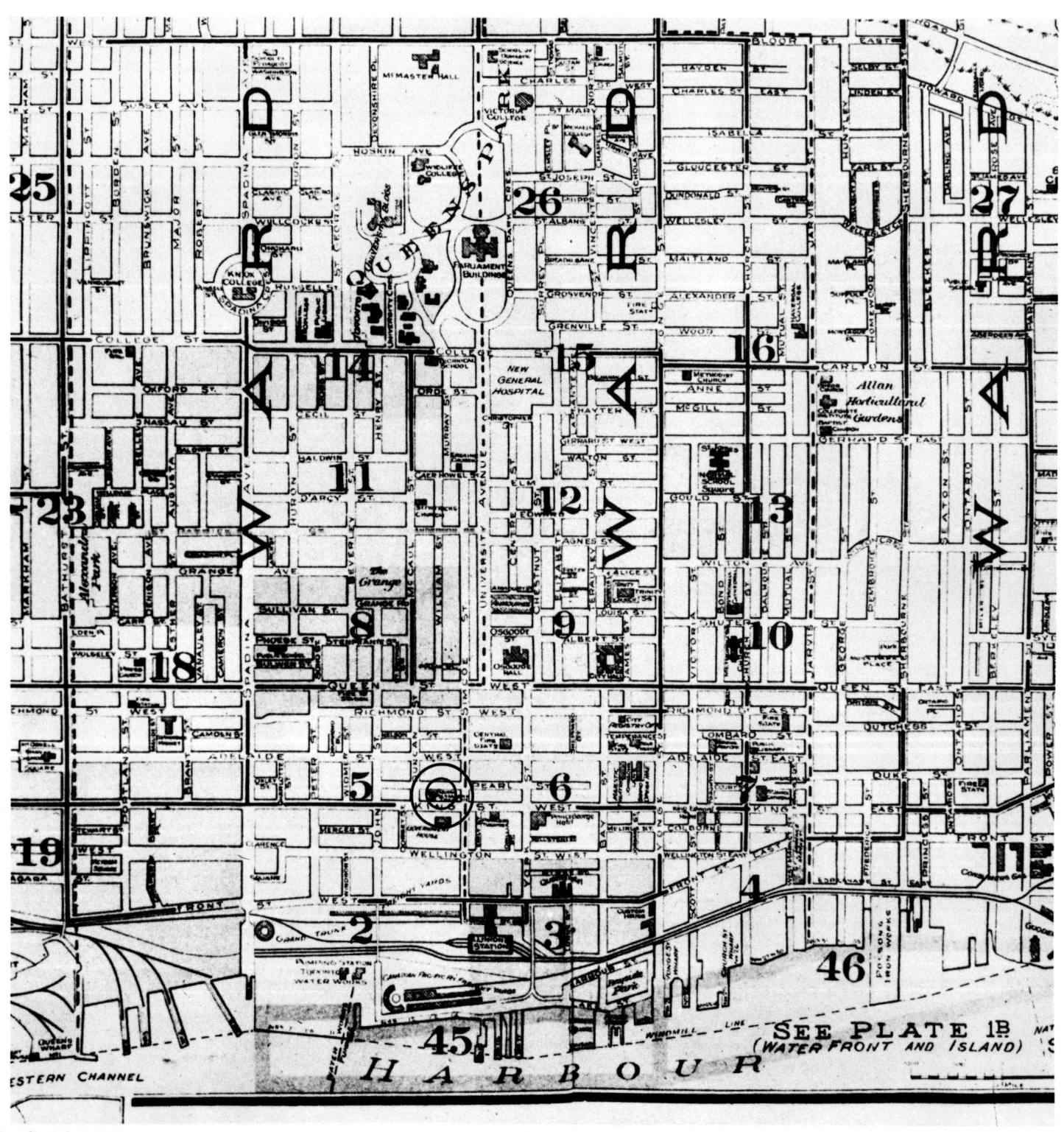

Goad's Atlas, 1910

1910
ROYAL ALEXANDRA THEATRE

This beautiful structure offered more for opera than had any previous facility.

Postcard   RAT

ROYAL ALEXANDRA

In 1907 Cawthra Mulock, son of Sir William Mulock, distinguished Canadian statesman, jurist and postmaster-general, requested from the architect Peter Lyle 'the finest theatre on the continent'. The result was the beautiful Royal Alexandra Theatre, named after King Edward VII's beautiful consort, and called variously, The Royal, The Alexandra, and the Royal Alex. The magnificent mural on the proscenium was painted by Toronto artist Frederick Challener whose wife, then 24 years old, served as the model for the figures.

The trend toward musical comedies (forerunners of the Broadway musical) by composers such as Franz Lehar, Rudolf Friml, Sigmund Romberg and Victor Herbert, was very pronounced at the beginning of the 20th century and they appeared at the Royal Alex in a steady stream. At the same time opera companies brought noteworthy productions.

The advantages and facilities of the theatre encouraged and attracted several Canadian opera companies:-

- The Montreal Opera Company which brought, among its artists, renowned Canadian soprano Louise Edvina.
- The Savoyards who specialized in light operas.
- Dr. Ernest MacMillan's Conservatory Opera Company which presented *Hugh, the Drover* and *Hansel and Gretel* but which succumbed to the blight of the great depression of the 1930's.
- The Opera Guild of Toronto which, in its turn, suffered from the austerity of World War II.
- The Royal Conservatory Opera Company which, after a successful 2-week run of Johann Strauss's *Rosalinda* in 1948, ventured a 1-week opera festival with full productions of *La Boheme, Rigoletto* and *Don Giovanni* in 1950. In 1951 the newly-formed Opera Festival Association of Toronto presented the Royal Conservatory Opera Company's second festival which was an annual event thereafter. In 1955 the performing company became the Opera Festival Company and in 1959 the Canadian Opera Company.

In 1963 Toronto businessman Ed Mirvish purchased the theatre and proceeded to restore its original charm and elegance. The ambiance of the area surrounding the theatre was enhanced by this restoration which has led to the conversion of once-ugly buildings into attractive restaurants.

Photo: Paul Forsyth — TOTS
THE MURAL ON THE PROSCENIUM ARCH

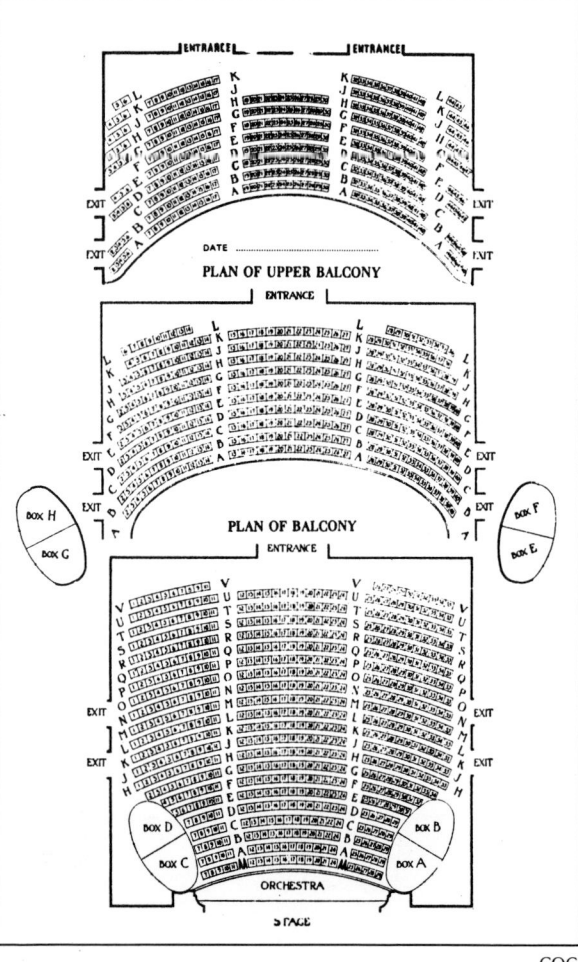

COCA

Photo: Paul Forsyth — TOTS
THE STAGE FROM THE FIRST BALCONY.

Toronto World Nov. 19, 1910   NLC

At the Royal Alexandra

"The Merry Widow."

To commend "The Merry Widow," an adaptation of the Viennese operetta, set to music by Franz Lehar, to a Toronto audience, is hardly necessary. It is almost enough to say that the presentation now offered at the Royal Alexandra is as full of charm as was its original production. The music is as luscious, the setting as superb and the vocal accessories just as delightful as when it charmed its first hearers. Certainly there was no lack of appreciation and enthusiasm last night, and the popular numbers could not have been more responsively received.

All Savage offerings have the reputation of being thoroly well filled, and yesterday's did nothing to decrease that belief. From beginning to end the presentation was wholly satisfactory and its completeness of detail was shown in every role. The connection of the plot with the Near East of Europe, as it was when the operetta was written, has not been impaired by the dramatic changes that have taken place, but these have rather lent additional interest to the theme. Certainly they did not interfere with the fascination of "The Merry Widow."

Miss Mabel Wilber invested the role of Sonia, the young widow, with all the charm of song and dance which it needs to bring it into proper prominence, and her offerings were received with full appreciation by the large audience. Miss Ivy Scott, as Natalie, equally filled her part. Charles Meakins, as Prince Danillo, was seen to much advantage, as was R. E. Graham, as Popoff, the Marsovian ambassador. Harold Blake, as Camille de Jolidon, and Fred Frear, as Nist, were also noteworthy. The piece is finely staged.

Toronto World, Nov. 22, 1910   NLC

Toronto World, Nov. 19, 1910   NLC

MABEL WILBER as the Merry Widow

Globe, Jan. 25, 1913,   NLC

Yet another name for *Die Fledermaus*.

"THE MERRY COUNTESS."

An eager, anticipating crowd at the Royal Alexanda Theatre last night witnessed the first production of "The Merry Countess," a transposition of popular European opera from the pen of Johann Strauss. There was no disappointment at the score; the music is bright and sparkling, with an abundance of color. While the sensuous characteristics of Strauss' composition have been preserved, the libretto, on the other hand, lacks vivacity and coherence. The action drags somewhat in the first two acts. Most of the comedy is provided by Mr. Tom A. Shale as Governor Hochheimer of the New Age Prison, and Mr. A. W. Baskomb in the role of the new Warder, Mattoni. Hochheimer himself is arrested at a raid of the Arum Lily Club, where Prince Orloffsky is providing his guests with entertainment in the form of a Hungarian dance. His protests against his incarceration upset the new tenets of penology and temporarily suspend the discipline of the New Age Prison, where "no violence is used." Mattoni is the unfortunate Warder who is the victim of all these strenuous protests, and finally leaves to get a "soft" job as guard in an insane asylum. The musical ensemble is strong. Miss Jose Collins as Countess Rosalindi Cliquot possesses a soprano voice of vibrant quality and splendid compass. Mr. Claude Fleming as Dr. Bernsastler has a robust baritone of fine texture. Mr. Forest Huff as Count Max Cliquot is recalled as the popular tenor who won fame as the "Chocolate Soldier" several years ago, and Miss Fritzie Von Busing as Ilka is piquant and delightful. Mr. Maurice Farkoa in the role of the impetuous Hungarian deserved every credit for his characteristic wooing. The play is embellished by a splendid ballet in the second act. The costuming is elegant and rich in color effects, while the scenic investiture is on a lavish scale. Of the song gems, "Just That You Are You," sung to the tune of the "Beautiful Blue Danube," and "Must We Say Goodbye," received rounds of appreciative applause.

Globe, Jan. 28, 1913   NLC

Austrian soprano FRITZI SCHEFF in *Night Birds (Die Fledermaus)* in 1912 and in *Mademoiselle Modiste* in 1930.

Globe, Jan. 27, 1912   NLC

Globe, Feb. 8, 1913   NLC

Globe, Feb. 8, 1913 NLC

Photo: Jack Branker
Saturday Night, Dec. 2, 1916, UTL

Hector Charlesworth first wrote for *Saturday Night* anonymously under the pseudonym Touchstone. He eventually became Managing Director of the publication. He was also first head of the Canadian Broadcasting Commission.

Photo: Elliott & Fry MTLB

Noted Canadian soprano LOUISE EDVINA sang *Tosca* and *Louise* with the Montreal Opera Company in 1913.

Outstanding Russian ballerina, ANNA PAVLOVA whose Ballet Russe Company joined the Boston Grand Opera Company to present two evenings and a matinee of Opera *and* Ballet in January, 1916.

CPI

GOS

Dame MAGGIE TEYTE, English soprano who excelled in the French repertoire, especially in the role of Melisande.

ROYAL ALEXANDRA
Week Commencing Monday, Jan. 24th, 1927.
MATINEES WEDNESDAY AND SATURDAY

THE D'OYLY CARTE OPERA COMPANY

Direct from the Prince's Theatre, London.

in

"THE GONDOLIERS"
or
The King of Barataria

Written by W. S. GILBERT
Composed by ARTHUR SULLIVAN

The Duke of Plaza-Toro		Henry A. Lytton
Luiz (his Attendant)		David Hutchison
Don Alhambra del Bolero (the Grand Inquisitor)		Leo Sheffield
Marco Palmieri		Charles Goulding
Giuseppe Palmieri		Martyn Green
Antonio	Venetian Gondoliers	Richard Eaton
Francesco		Herbert Aitken
Giorgio		Ronald Stear
Annibale		T. Penry-Hughes
The Duchess of Plazo-Toro		Bertha Lewis
Casilda (her Daughter)		Irene Hill
Gianetta		Winifred Lawson
Tessa		Aileen Davies
Fiametta	Contadine	Louise Wittock
Vittoria		Beatrice Elburn
Giulia		Hilary Davies
Inez (the King's Foster-Mother)		Mollie Mennie

Chorus of Gondoliers, Contadine, Men-at-Arms, Heralds and Pages.

Act 1 . . . . . . Venice
(Designed and Painted by Philip Howden)
Act 2 . . Pavilion in the Palace of Barataria
(Designed by W. Bridges Adams and Painted by Juan Sackman)
An interval of three months is supposed to elapse between Acts 1 and 2. Date 1750.

Costumes designed by Percy Anderson, and made by B. J. Simmons & Co., and Mary Fisher, Ltd.
Shoes by Gamba.
Wigs by Clarkson and Gustave.

General Manager	Richard Collet
Stage Manager	Frederick Hobbs
Musical Director	Harry Norris
Chorus Master and Asst. Musical Director	Isidore Godfrey
Assistant Stage Managers	T. Penry-Hughes / Harry Haste
Press and Canadian Representative	B. E. Lang

LG

Globe, Nov. 10, 1927

American tenor ALLAN JONES (Hugh) and Canadian soprano NELLYE GILL (Mary).

DR. ERNEST MACMILLAN conducted the Conservatory Opera Company's productions of *Hugh, the Drover* and *Hansel and Gretel* in 1930.

Canadians BEATRICE MORSON (Aunt Jane) and NELLYE GILL (Mary)

Telegram, Nov. 18, 1929

CANADIAN OPERA WEEK SET NEW PRECEDENT

Display of Native Talent Inspired Faith in Big Projects.

Last year the National Council of Education shot an arrow in the air. It was not a wild shot so far as artistic direction was concerned, for they knew the worth of the enterprise they sponsored, but only faith in growing musical appreciation in Toronto could guarantee its landing on the tricky mark of success. But it did, thus setting a precedent for other large ventures in Canadian music.

Their project was the week of Canadian opera which, with entirely local cast except for one singer, opened with Vaughan Williams' "Hugh the Drover," at the Royal Alexandra Theatre on March 24, Dr. Ernest MacMillan conducting.

The success of the week has significant features. While the first two houses were comprised for the most part of ticket-holders whose interest had been inspired by the energetic committee, the public took over the matter by the middle of the week. Friday night was a full house and Saturday a case of "all sold out." At the end of the week not only had the project proven that good native ability abounded, but the business sheets about balanced despite the short run.

It is the interest of the National Council of Education to watch in each of its centres to advance enterprises which give to individuals opportunity to spend their leisure hours profitably. Following the festival at the Royal York the previous Autumn, the local executive of the National Council of Education approached Dr. Ernest MacMillan and F. R. MacKelcan with the suggestion that the opera be produced so as to give wider opportunity to hear it. Dr. MacMillan and Mr. MacKelcan offered readily to do what they could, but ways and means had to be considered.

In Toronto were found Canadians with confidence enough to back the project, and, with the help of Sir Joseph Flavelle, an amount of about $12,000 was guaranteed by the following group: Sir John Aird, C. S. Blackwell, Dr. H. A. Bruce, C. L. Burton, C. M. Candee, Lady Eaton, R. Y. Eaton, Sir Joseph Flavelle, B. A. Gould, Col. A. E. Gooderham, Col. Walter Gow, G. H. Gundy, Edward Johnson (the noted tenor was the only guarantor outside Toronto), Lady Kemp, J. S. McLean, Denton Massey, Col. J. F. Michie, G. A. Morrow, N. L. Nathanson, Mrs. John W. Nesbitt, Allan Ross, W. E. Rundle, Dr. F. N. G. Starr, Dr. Harold Tovell, W. R. Wadsworth, Miss Wallberg, A. F. White, E. R. Wood, Frank P. Wood, T. H. Wood. When the box office was closed, the guarantors had only to be called on for a very small amount, for the enterprise had about broken even.

The women's committee was headed by Mrs. Horace Hunter, who was assisted by Miss Ethel Shepherd and others, and who enlisted the interest of many organizations.

A cast of about 150 artists, with an orchestra of symphony proportions under the direction of Dr. Ernest MacMillan, gave a performance which critical listeners found it easy to praise and which the public were glad to attend.

The week of Canadian opera left many speculating on what might be done if the Toronto Conservatory had the facilities to offer such outlet for the talent which is to be found in the bounds of its membership. It enlarged ideals of what Canada might reasonably accomplish. Native opera was not unthinkable after the performance had shown art, the public had shown itself interested and the faithful guarantors had come off so easily.

"There is no need to limit our ambitions," said one leader when the adventurous week had ended.

Mail and Empire, Nov. 14, 1930

ROYAL ALEXANDRA

Program   The Opera Guild of Toronto

TUESDAY EVENING, MAY 12th, 1936, at 8.20 p.m., and
SATURDAY AFTERNOON, MAY 16th, 1936, at 2.20 p.m.

DOUBLE BILL
CAVALLERIA RUSTICANA
Book by Targioni-Toggetti and Menasci. Story by Giovanni Verga.
Music by PIETRO MASCAGNI.

Opera in One Act
(In English)

Santuzza	Doris Godson Gilmour
Lola	Gwendolen Hale
Turiddu	Lawrence Power (guest)
Alfio	Irvine Levine
Lucia	Evaleen Kilby
Conductor	Reginald Stewart
Stage Director	Angelo Canarutto
Stage Manager	Charles H. Drumheller

Chorus of Villagers, etc.
SCENE—A Public Square in a Sicilian Village.
(for short story of opera, etc., see page 7)

Followed by
PAGLIACCI
Book and Music by RUGGIERO LEONCAVALLO.

Opera in Two Acts
(In English)

Nedda	Alice Strong
Canio	Kenneth Sakos
Tonio	Robert Hately
Beppe	Leslie Mardall
Silvio	Albert Kennedy
Conductor	Reginald Stewart
Stage Director	Angelo Canarutto
Stage Manager	Charles H. Drumheller

SYNOPSIS OF SCENES
ACT I. Outskirts of a Village in Calabria. Afternoon.
ACT II. Same scene. Evening.
(for short story of opera, etc., see page 6)

Scenery designed by G. K. Pokorny and painted by William Drake.

—9—

DORIS GILMOUR as Santuzza and EVALEEN KILBY as Mama Lucia.

KENNETH SAKOS as Canio, ROBERT HATELY as Tonio.

Program   The Opera Guild of Toronto

THURSDAY EVENING, MAY 14th, 1936, at 8.20 p.m. and
SATURDAY EVENING, MAY 16th, 1936, at 8.20 p.m.

TOSCA
Book by Victorien Sardou, Luigi Illica and Giuseppe Giacosa.
MUSIC by — GIACOMO PUCCINI.

Opera in Three Acts
(In English)

Floria Tosca	Doris Godson Gilmour
Mario Cavaradossi	Lawrence Power (guest)
Baron Scarpia	Poul Bai
Cesare Angelotti	A. Campbell Munro
The Sacristan	W. Shelden
Spoletta	Frank Starr
Sciarrone	John Burt
A Jailer	Robert C. Kowin
A Shepherd	Gwendolen Hale
Conductor	Reginald Stewart
Stage Director	Angelo Canarutto
Stage Manager	Charles H. Drumheller

SYNOPSIS OF SCENES
ACT I. Interior of the Church of St. Andrea della Valle, Rome.
ACT II. Scarpia's Room in the Palazzo Farnese, Rome.
ACT III. Platform of the Castle of St. Angelo, Rome.

Scenery designed by G. K. Pokorny and painted by William Drake.

—11—

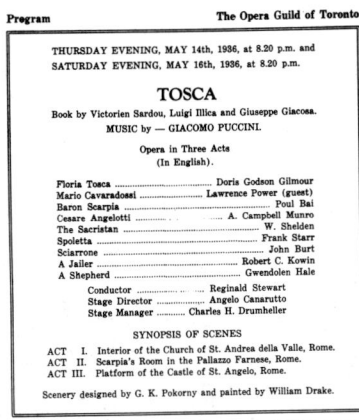

Announcing the opening of the
SUMMER ROOF GARDEN
JUNE FIFTH
KING EDWARD HOTEL
TORONTO   P KIRBY HUNT, MANAGER   CANADA

LAWRENCE POWER as Cavaradossi, DORIS GILMOUR as Tosca

Stage Director FELIX BRENTANO, Music Director NICHOLAS GOLDSCHMIDT, Royal Conservatory of Music Principal ETTORE MAZZOLENI plan the Conservatory Opera's production of *Rosalinda* with JEANNE MERRILL who will sing the title role.

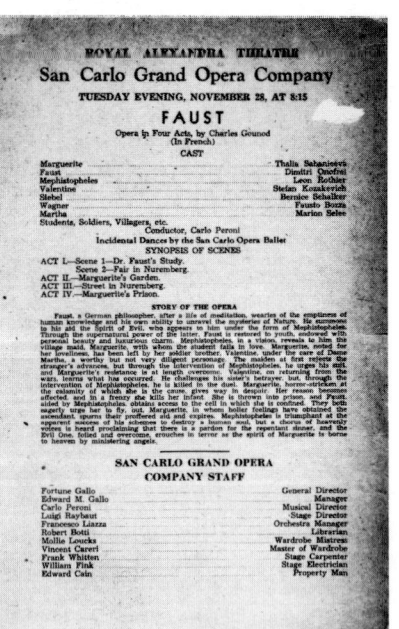

1933

ROYAL ALEXANDRA

Stage Director, HERMAN GEIGER-TOREL.

GILLES LAMONTAGNE (Rigoletto) and JUNE KOWALCHUK (Gilda) 1950.

1950

Opera Festival Returns to Toronto As $18,000 Subscribed in 48 Hours

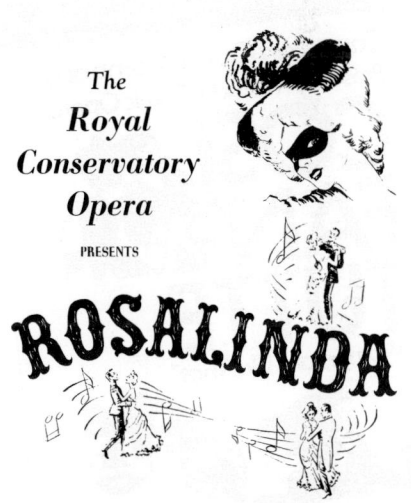

Toronto will have an operatic season, with Toronto or Toronto-trained talent—and all because of a new organization which worked so hard to keep musical talent in this country that it raised $18,000 within the short space of 48 hours.

The announcement that last year's Opera Festival at the Royal Alexandra Theatre will be put on again this year at the same theatre, but under different management and administration, was made last night at the home of Dr. David W. Pratt, 2 Lynwood Ave.

Last year's Opera Festival was staged by the Royal Conservatory Opera Company, but the conservatory felt that it was impossible for its staff to undertake the heavy burden of administration and financial responsibility again.

A group of private citizens took up the burden and had just 48 hours to raise $18,000, select a board of directors, arrange for a theatre, choose a general manager and perform any number of other seemingly impossible feats.

Dr. Edward Johnson, former general manager of the Metropolitan Opera, agreed to be honorary chairman. The chairman of the citizens' group is R. H. Lorimer Massie. Others on the board are Donald C. Carlisle, Robert B. Dale-Harris, John M. Godfrey, Anthony M. Marston, Dr. Ettore Mazzoleni, Dr. David Pratt, Ernest M. Rawley, Donald M. Springer, Richard S. Van Valkenburg, Mr. Justice Welles and J. D. Woods Jr.

This year's Opera Festival will be held from Thursday, Feb. 8, until Saturday, Feb. 17. It will include Mozart's Marriage of Figaro, Puccini's Madame Butterfly and Gounod's Faust.

The complete program is: Thursday, Feb. 8, Marriage of Figaro; Feb. 9, Madame Butterfly; Feb. 10, Marriage of Figaro; Monday, Feb. 12, Madame Butterfly; Feb. 13, Faust; Wednesday matinee, Feb. 14, Madame Butterfly; Wednesday evening, Marriage of Figaro; Feb. 15, Faust; Feb. 16, Marriage of Figaro; Saturday matinee, Faust; Saturday evening, Madame Butterfly.

Dr. Mazzoleni, principal of the Royal Conservatory of Music, said the new association had the enthusiastic backing of the conservatory and of the board of governors of the University of Toronto.

He told of the start of the opera school at the conservatory, of the first performance five years ago when operatic excerpts were staged. The school is not equipped to stage operas, but to train young Canadian artists who show operatic talent, he said.

The Opera Festival in February will be conducted by Nicholas Goldschmidt. Herman Geiger-Torel will be stage director. Assistants will be John Coveart, George Crum and Andrew MacMillan.

One of the prime purposes behind the new organization is to erect a framework for an eventual National Opera of Canada. So enthusiastic are the backers that their success seems assured.

ROYAL ALEXANDRA

JAN RUBES and SUZETTE NADON in *The Consul* 1953.

The first "name" guest singer – REGINA RESNIK as Carmen 1955

JON VICKERS as the Duke of Mantua in *Rigoletto* 1954

ANDREW MacMILLAN, JAN RUBES, JOHN McCOLLUM, TERESA STRATAS, NORMAN MITTELMAN, PATRICIA SNELL – *La Boheme* 1958.

The end of an era – the last annual season in the Royal Alexandra.

RETURN VISITS IN 1973, 1978 and 1979.

ROYAL ALEXANDRA

ALDO BERTOCCI (Otello), PHIL STARK (Cassio) and CORNELIS OPTHOF (Montano) in *Otello* 1960.

Photo: Andrew Oxenham — COCA
Mezzo-soprano JUDITH FORST as Cinderella 1979

SELECTED APPEARANCES
PERFORMANCES

1910	*The Merry Widow*
1910	*The Bohemian Girl*
1910	*The Chimes of Normandy*
1911	*The Chocolate Soldier*
1912	*Night Birds (Die Fledermaus)*
1913	*The Merry Countess (Die Fledermaus)*
1914	*Girl of the Golden West (Belasco's Play)*
1914	*Adele*
1915	*Madame Sherry*
1915	*The Peasant Girl*
1915	*The Mikado*
1916	*Two is Company*
1919	*Maytime*
1919	*Chu Chin Chow*
1920	*Chu Chin Chow*
1922	*Chu Chin Chow*
1923	*Maid of the Mountains*
1923	*Blossom Time*
1930	*Mademoiselle Modiste*
1930	*The Merry Widow*
1931	*Naughty Mariette*
1932	*The Merry Widow*
1945	*The Vagabond King*
1945	*The Merry Widow*
1947	*The Merry Widow*

PRODUCERS

Year	Producer
1911	Aborn English Grand Opera Company
1912	Montreal Opera Company
1913	Gilbert and Sullivan Festival Company
1913	Montreal Opera Company
1913	Henry W. Savage Company
1914	San Carlo Opera Company
1914	New York Hippodrome
1915	San Carlo Grand Opera Company
1916	Boston Grand Opera Company and Pavlova Ballet Russe
1916	San Carlo Grand Opera Company
1916	Boston National Grand Opera Company
1916	New York Hippodrome
1917	Aborn Grand Opera Company
1917	Boston Grand Opera Company
1918	San Carlo Opera Company
1919	Gallo English Opera Company
1923	The Savoyards
1923	Henry W. Savage Company
1923	Russian Grand Opera Company
1927	D'Oyly Carte
1927	New York Grand Opera Company
1929	American Opera Company
1930	Conservatory Opera Company
1931	English Light Opera Company
1933	San Carlo Opera Company
1936	The Opera Guild of Toronto
1940	San Carlo Opera Company
1941	San Carlo Opera Company
1943	San Carlo Opera Company
1944	Gilbert and Sullivan Opera Company
1948	Royal Conservatory Opera
1950-54	Royal Conservatory Opera Company Festival
1955-57	Opera Festival Company Seasons (Spring)
1957-58	Opera Festival Company Seasons (Fall)
1959-60	Canadian Opera Company Seasons (Fall)
1973	Canadian Opera Company
1978	Canadian Opera Company Season (Spring)
1979	Canadian Opera Company Season (Spring)

MUTUAL STREET ARENA

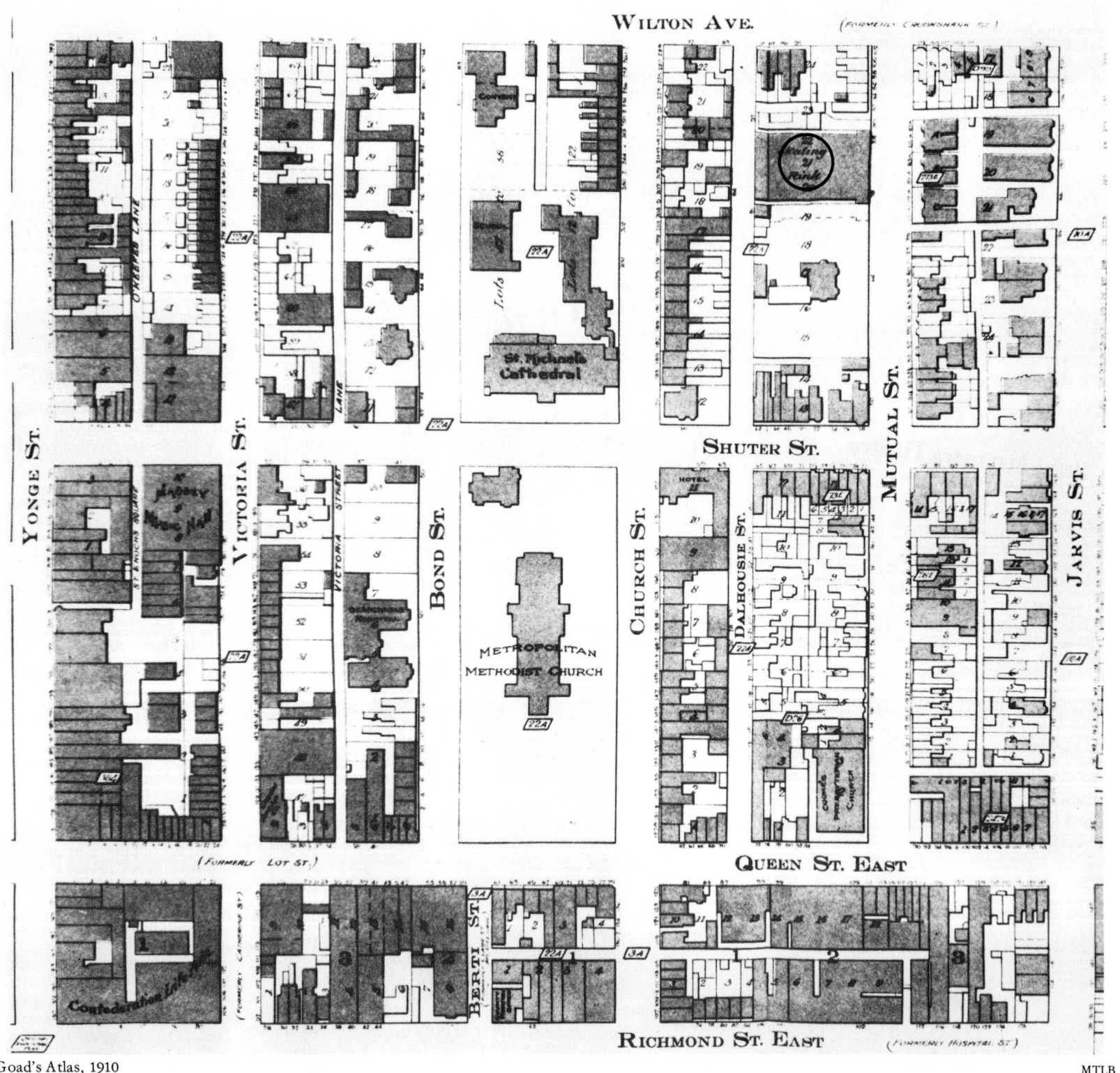

Goad's Atlas, 1910

1912
MUTUAL ARENA

Festivals demand great capacity.

Artist's rendering of the ARENA – 1912

MUTUAL STREET ARENA

Toronto historian Mike Filey has provided the delightful information that Mutual Street was so named because it was originally a mutual drive between the estates of Messrs. Jarvis and McGill. The first rink on Mutual Street, the Caledonia, opened in 1873 and was chosen as the location for Toronto's first Musical Festival on June 15, 16, 17, 1886. The event was organized and conducted by Dr. F. H. Torrington, eminent Toronto conductor, and featured, among others, the celebrated soprano Lilli Lehmann. In 1911 the Caledonia Rink was demolished to make room for the much larger present rink, the first artificial ice rink in Ontario. The latter opened with a week long Music Festival which presented such international artists as Marcella Sembrich, ("the most glorious voice in the world"), Johanna Gadski, Olive Fremstad and Alice Nielsen. It remained the only facility suitable for mammoth musical events until the construction of Maple Leaf Gardens. In 1954 Melody Fair gave its first performances which included young Canadian baritone Robert Goulet.

The promised versatility of the building has been demonstrated by the variety of events which it has accommodated. It was home to the St. Pats Hockey team (forerunner of the Leafs) and the Toronto Maple Leafs as well. Musical events have included name bands during the "big band era" and single acts of the calibre of Frank Sinatra.

LILLI LEHMANN, German soprano, who sang Woglinde, Helmwige and Waldvogel in the first Bayreuth *Ring* in 1876. She sang 170 roles during her long career.

MUTUAL-STREET RINK!

THE BAND WILL BE IN ATTENDANCE
THIS EVENING.

NO EXTRA CHARGE FOR ADMITTANCE.

Globe, Feb. 14, 1879 — NLC

TORONTO MUSICAL FESTIVAL.

CHORUS ENROLMENT.

Students residing west of Simcoe and south of Queen's Park intending to join the Festival Chorus will meet for organization

THIS (MONDAY) EVENING, FEB. 1ST

at eight o'clock, at St. Andrew's Hall.
By order. E. L. ROBERTS, Sec.

Telegram, Feb. 1, 1886 — NLC

The First Music Festival on the Site of the Arena

THE first Music Festival held in Toronto took place on the very site now occupied by the Arena, in the Mutual Street Rink. The expenses were guaranteed by the citizens to the extent of $25,000, but this fund was never drawn upon, the receipts giving a small surplus of $500. The Festival, which consisted of four concerts on June 15th, 16th, 17th, 1886, was conducted by Dr. F. H. Torrington, the present dean of our conductors, and enlisted the services of an adult chorus of one thousand, a children's chorus of twelve hundred, an orchestra of one hundred, and the following soloists: Lilli Lehmann, E. Aline Osgood, Gertrude Luther, sopranos; Agnes Huntington, contralto; Albert L. King, tenor; Max Heinrich, baritone; D. M. Babcock, bass; Frederick Archer, organ; Otto Bendix, piano; Josephine Chatterton, harp; Henri Jacobsen, violin. Mr. E. R. Parkhurst, the editor of the official programme, in his introduction, said: "The projectors of the first musical festival may fairly claim that the undertaking is one which will mark a new epoch in the musical history of the city, and that in years to come it will be looked back to as a conspicuous landmark on the road of progress." The numerous periodic festivals of music held in England, the United States and Germany, sufficiently attest the importance attached to these gatherings as a powerful means of stimulating interest in music, and of promoting a more general cultivation of the art.

MF

TORONTO MUSICAL FESTIVAL,
Mutual St. Rink Building.

SEATING CAPACITY, 3,000.

15th, 16th and 17th June, 1886.

Order of Concerts :—Tuesday Evening, June 15th, Gounod's Sacred Trilogy, "Mors et Vita." Wednesday Afternoon, June 16th, Festival Matinee, consisting of vocal and instrumental selections. Wednesday Evening, June 16th, Handel's Sublime Oratorio, "Israel in Egypt." Thursday Evening, June 17th, Children's Festival, Jubilee and Miscellaneous Concert. Artists :—Fraulein Lilli Lehmann, Berlin, Germany ; Mrs. E. Aline Osgoode, Philadelphia ; Miss Agnes Huntington, New York ; Mrs. Gertrude Luther, Buffalo ; Mr. Albert L. King, New York ; Mr. Max Heinrich, New York ; Mr. D. M. Babcock, Boston ; Mr. Otto Bendix (pianist), Boston ; Madame Josephine Chatterton (harpiste), New York ; Frederick Archer (organist) New York ; H. Jacobsen (solo violinist) Toronto, and a

Grand Festival Adult Chorus of 1,000.
  Children's Festival Chorus of 1,400.
    Magnificent Orchestra of 100.

F. H. Torrington, Musical Director.

PUBLIC REHEARSALS, ADMISSION 50c

The public will be admitted to the rehearsals on the evenings of Saturday, the 12th, and Monday, 14th inst.
Members of SCHOOL CHORUS will be admitted free on presentation of their tickets at Saturday evening rehearsal.
Tickets for sale at Messrs. A. & S. Nordheimers', Mason & Risch's and I. Suckling & Sons'.
Doors open at 7 p.m.
Entrance for the public from Dalhousie street; chorus and orchestra from Mutual street. 56

Telegram June 12, 1886 — NLC

Excerpt from the programme of the Musical Festival which opened the new Arena in 1912.

MUSICAL FESTIVAL:

Gentlemen who are not supplied with an evening hat or cap should not fail to call and purchase one before attending the Musical Festival. We have a large and well-assorted stock of Soft Felt Hats, Tweed Hats and Creedmore Caps. These goods will be found indispensable to those attending the Festival.

JAS. H. ROGERS,

Cor. King and Church sts.

☞ The oldest established Hatter and Furrier in the Dominion. y

Telegram, June 15, 1886 — NLC

TORONTO MUSICAL FESTIVAL, RINK MUSIC HALL.

PERFORMANCES :—
TO-NIGHT,
  Gounod's "Mors Et Vita."
Wednesday Afternoon, 2 p.m.
  Grand Festival Matinee.
Wednesday Evening,
  Handel's "Israel in Egypt."
Thursday Morning, 9 a.m.
  Full rehearsal of Children's Chorus and Orchestra.
Thursday Evening,
  Children's Jubilee Concert.
See programmes.

ADMISSION { TO REHEARSAL 50c.
           { EACH CONCERT, - $1.

Reserved seats to each concert, on ground floor, $1.50, in gallery, $2. Tickets for rehearsals and concerts to be had from Messrs. A. & S. Nordheimer, Mason & Risch, and I. Suckling & Sons.

SECURE YOUR SEATS.

Telegram, June 15, 1886 — NLC

MUTUAL STREET ARENA

Globe, Oct. 5, 1912

THE OPENING NIGHT.

"Mors et Vita" Grandly Rendered—The Musical Festival Opened with Great Eclat.

The immense auditorium of the Caledonian rink, on Mutual street, was filled in all parts last night when Conductor Torrington and the soloists stepped upon the platform. Fourteen electric lights made the rink as light as day, and banks of flowers served to render the building attractive, while the choruses with their tiers of white-robed ladies and gentlemen in sombre black, combined to make up an effective ensemble. In the west gallery was the box of honour, and the centre seat was occupied by President Nordheimer.

Before the singing began the audience occupied themselves in admiring the platform, with its perfect arrangements and interesting occupants. The level part of the structure was about five feet above the floor and on this were Conductor Torrington, the soloists and the orchestra. Behind were the choruses beautifully dressed and arranged. The grand organ was back of all the chorus, being backed by a beautiful festooning of flags. After letting the audience gaze for a few moments, Mr. Torrington sounded the warning with his ivory baton and the sopranos sang the first verse of the national anthem, accompanied by the organ. The altos sang the second verse and the last verse was rendered by the full chorus and orchestra. The oratorio was then begun and for over two hours the audience was held spell-bound by the grand and soul-inspiring music. The four divisions of the chorus had about the same amount of work to do, and all showed that the training received during the last few months had not been given in vain. The light and shade effects produced in some parts of the trilogy were simply perfect, the exquisite modulation and perfect enunciation bringing forth rounds of applause. In the very difficult intervals which occur throughout the work Mr. Torrington's practised hand was clearly visible.

The soloists did grand work although the solos do not admit of great display. The quartettes were listened to with rapt attention. The orchestra on the whole performed very acceptably, the apparent faults being of a nature easily remedied. The demand for places at the miscellaneous concert this afternoon, in which the famous vocalist, Fraulein Lilli Lehmann, will be the bright particular star, has been brisk, and the prospect of a big attendance is good.

Telegram, June 16, 1886

ALICE NIELSEN,
American soprano.

The History of the Arena

THE present Musical Festival was organized as a fitting inaugural for the largest auditorium in the Dominion of Canada, which is to be known from now onward as the Arena. For some years past the growth of the City of Toronto in wealth and population has made it apparent that an institution of vast seating capacity and comprehensive scope was necessary, not only for musical festivals of large dimensions, but for sporting events, such as horse shows, hockey matches, bicycle meets, and for pageants, balls, banquets and conventions. Already well equipped with concert halls and theatres, the city has lacked any vast building that could be used for so great a variety of purposes. It was their confidence in the future of the City of Toronto that induced the Montreal and Toronto capitalists to undertake the building of such a costly modern structure. The cash outlay involved has been more than $500,000 and the building replaces a once famous edifice, known as the Mutual Street Rink, which, of course, did not have the modern equipment that this structure possesses. The building of closed auditoriums of this character is purely a development of modern civic conditions, though it will be noted that in general form the interior is modelled on the old Roman amphitheatres. The circular system of seating on gradually ascending tiers, and the use of the space beneath these tiers for the accommodation of performers and for other services, was characteristic of all auditoriums designed for the entertainment of vast audiences in the classical epochs of Western civilization. It has remained for the ingenuity of the modern architect and builder to perfect the same system under a roof and inside four walls. One great feature of the ancient hippodromes was that they gave every spectator an unobstructed view of the entire amphitheatre, but until modern steel construction was brought into being this was impossible in an enclosed edifice. The spectator in the Arena is afforded the same facilities for seeing everything as was the visitor to the Coliseum at Rome, two thousand years ago. This desirable result has been obtained by the use of immense steel roof trusses, which span the entire width of the auditorium, doing away with all pillars and supports. This feature is said to be possessed by the Arena alone of all structures of its type on this continent. Special attention has also been paid to the matter of exits and entrances, which are so commodious as to enable an audience of several thousand people to assemble and retire in a comparatively short space of time without inconvenience. There are in all fourteen public exits from the building. In this structure, moreover, panics are impossible, inasmuch as it is absolutely fireproof. The arrangement of boxes, it will be noted, is one that, while it gives special privileges to no one in the matter of seeing and hearing, brings into a prominent position those public figures whom the audience at large is desirous of seeing. The attention of the audiences at these concerts is directed to the manner of lighting. In the daytime the auditorium is amply lighted by a huge skylight in the roof and as well by numerous windows in sidewalls; while at night a blaze of light is concentrated on the Arena proper from the innumerable electric light bulbs that outline the roof trusses.

Some statistics regarding the structure will no doubt be of interest to the public. In the construction of the building, no less than two million pounds of steel, over one million bricks and over one million feet of lumber were used. If all the seats on the raised tiers, exclusive of those in the Arena proper, were placed side by side they would extend for a distance of over two miles. The circumference of the building itself is about a fifth of a mile, and the apex of the roof is one hundred feet from the centre of the ground floor.

The all-round utility of the building has already been demonstrated by the fact that recently it was the scene of an immense banquet to the Prime Minister of Canada, the largest ever held in the history of Canada. The present festival shows what an immense boon it is to music-lovers in offering them the privilege of hearing the very greatest singers in the world at prices within the reach of everyone, and it is hoped that this autumn festival will become an annual event. In the winter time the Arena proper will become an ice rink and will afford the greatest facilities available on this continent for contests in Canada's greatest of winter sports—hockey. In fact, it would be difficult to set a limit on the possibilities and uses of such a structure for the whole community.

From the programme of the Musical Festival which opened the new Arena in 1912.

The Toronto Musical Festival

NAHAN FRANKO

AND HIS ORCHESTRA OF SIXTY-TWO SOLOISTS
From the Metropolitan Opera and Philharmonic Orchestras, New York City

AT EVERY PERFORMANCE

THE FOLLOWING NOTED ARTISTS WILL APPEAR

JOHANNA GADSKI *Soprano*	RODOLFO FORNARI *Baritone*	FELICE LYNE *Coloratura Soprano*
MARCELLA SEMBRICH *Coloratura Soprano*	ROSA OLITZKA *Contralto*	GUISEPPE CAMPANARI *Baritone*
ALICE NEILSEN *Lyric Soprano*	YVONNE DE TREVILLE *Soprano*	JOSE MARDONNES *Basso*
ALFREDO ROMELLA *Tenor*	OLIVE FREMSTAD *Soprano*	LUIGI TAVECCHIA *Basso-Buffo*
CHARLOTTE MACONDA *Soprano*	JESKA SWARTZ *Contralto*	DAN BEDDOE *Welsh Tenor*
ORVILLE HARROLD *Tenor*	FERY LULEK *Baritone*	ARTURO TIBALDI *Violinist*
	HERBERT SACHS-HIRSCH *Pianist*	
ALBERT SPALDING *American Violinist*	PAUL MORENZO *Tenor*	MARIE DRESSLER *Operatic Comedienne*
	CHARLES GILBERT SPROSS *Official Accompanist*	

From the programme of the Musical Festival which opened the new Arena in 1912.

Toronto World, Oct. 3, 1912

NO CONFUSION OVER ARENA TICKETS

Red and Blue Lights Will Be Arranged to Show Ticket-Holders Which Doors to Use—Millions of Yards of Bunting and Hundreds of Flags for Decorations.

Tonight the Arena will be the scene of the most distinguished and the largest audience that has ever been assembled in the history of Canada. The occasion is the opening concert of the Toronto Musical Festival, and everything conceivable to make the event a success has been done by the sponsors of the festival, Mr. Lawrence Solman of Toronto and Mr. J. H. Dalton of New York. For several days past a bevy of decorators have been busy, so that the vast vistas of the auditorium present a scene of color that will delight the eye. In the Arena proper, which, when the cold weather comes, will be a hockey rink, chairs as comfortable as those in any concert hall in this city, have been placed. Hitherto it has been the custom in improvised concerts to bring in ordinary wooden chairs, but genuine orchestra seats have been provided for those who have bought tickets on the ground floor. In addition, mattings have been laid, in order to deaden the sound and to add to the general comfort of all who attend the concerts. Some idea of the extent of the Arena may be gained from the fact that measured yard by yard this matting represents a length of upwards of a mile. The perfect lighting of the auditorium will appeal to everyone, because it will in no way hurt the eye and the number of electric bulbs of various percentages of candle power is practically countless. In the decorations upwards of one million square yards of red, white and blue bunting have been used, and the number of Union Jacks, which form a prominent feature in the general scheme, runs into many hundreds. A novel idea never before presented to the Canadian public, is that of colored lights for the various entrances. The holders of blue tickets will go in at the entrance where the blue light hangs, and the holder of red and white tickets will be similarly guided. The unobstructed view, which the architects who built this remarkable edifice, have provided, makes one seat almost as good as another, a boon which is further enhanced by the perfect acoustics of the Arena. The two chief singers tonight will be Alice Nielsen and Orville Harrold, together with the wonderful orchestra that Mr. Nahan Franko has assembled from among the very finest instrumentalists of the country.

Toronto World, Oct. 7, 1912

Photo: Dupont, N.Y.

JOHANNA GADSKI, German soprano, made her North American debut as Elsa in *Lohengrin*, 1895.

SOCIETY AT ARENA

The Arena was in gala attire last night for the opening of Toronto's greatest musical event. Every box and most of the seats were filled, and the beautiful toilettes and jewels made an unforgettable picture. Miss Alice Neilsen looked lovely in her gown of clinging white brocade, partly veiled with white ninon and girdled with pearls and crystal, a little cap of the same covering her pretty hair. A very few noticed in the wonderful audience were: Those in the government house box—Sir James and Lady Whitney, the Misses Gibson, Major Clyde Caldwell and Mr. Sydney Fellowes, Gen. and Mrs. Cotton, Mrs. H. D. Warren, Miss Archie Armour, Miss Nevitt, Col. and Mrs. A. E. Gooderham, Sir Edmund Osler, Mr. and Mrs. Jack Osler, Mr. and Mrs. Willmott Matthews, Mr. and Mrs. Victor Cawthra, Sir Lyman and Lady Melvin Jones, Rev. T. and Mrs. Crawford Brown, Mr. Kelly Evans, Dr. Lang, Mr. Alfred Beardmore, Misses Warren, Mr. and Mrs. James Suydam, Mr. and Mrs. J. J. Main, Mr. and Mrs. T. J. Clark, Mr. and Mrs. D. Ross, Capt. Larking, Mr. and Mrs. Watt, Prof. and Mrs. Mackenzie, Mrs. Edward V. Renyolds, Mrs. E. F. B. Johnston, Mrs. Barwick, Col. Stimson, Col. Carpenter, Mr. J. K. Osborne, Mr. H. H. Suydam, Mrs. Wright, Miss Mollie Plummer, Mrs. Williams, Mrs. Moore, Mr. and Mrs. C. C. James, Miss Maud Arthurs Weir, Mr. Justice and Mrs. Riddell, Mr. and Mrs. Harry Paterson, Mr. and Mrs. Duncan, Mr. and Mrs. Jack Drynan, Mr. and Mrs. Alfred Hawes, Mr. Finucane, Mrs. and the Misses Hagarty, Mr. and Mrs. C. S. Macdonald, Mrs. Edmund Bristol, Miss Mona Murray, Mr. and Mrs. D. B. Hanna, Miss Mary Hanna, Mr. and Mrs. Bruce Macdonald, Mrs. John Foy, Miss Foy, Lady Thompson, Mr. and Mrs. Irving, Lady Mann and her son, Mr. D. Mann, Mrs. Cassels, Mr. and Mrs. A. P. Burritt, Mrs. George Hagarty, Mrs. Casey Wood, Mrs. B. Morton Jones, Mr. and Mrs. Gerhard Heintzman, Mr. and Mrs. Bascom, Mr. and Mrs. Palm, Miss Cornelia Heintzman, Dr. and Mrs. Primrose, Mr. and Mrs. J. A. M. Alley, Mr. and Mrs. H. C. Tomlin, Miss Tomlin, Mr. and Miss Brouse, Mr. and Mrs. G. H. Hees, Mr. and Mrs. Frank Arnoldi, Mr. Errol Arnoldi, Miss Nanno Hughes, Sir Edmund and Lady Walker, Sir Henry and Lady Pellatt, Mr. George Broughall, Dr. Augusta Stowe-Gullen, Mrs. W. J. Wilkinson, Mr. and Mrs. W. B. MacLean, Misses Plummer, Mr. and Mrs. de Singh Wilson, Mr. Bob Davidson, Mr. Eric Armour, Mr. and Mrs. Harry Martin, Col. and Mrs. Sterling Ryerson, Miss Laura Ryerson, Mr. and Mrs. Gordon Osler, Mr. Stuart Strathy, Mr. George Alexander, Mr. Edmund Phillips, Mr. and Mrs. G. Plunkett Magann, Mr. and Mrs. A. H. C. Proctor, Mr. Alexander Laird, Miss Margaret Laird, Mr. and Mrs. Dwight Turner, Mr. and Mrs. Lawrence Harris, Mr. and Mrs. Frank Baillie, Mr. and Mrs. George Gooderham, Mr. and Mrs. R. S. Wilson, Mrs. Bruce, Lady Moss, Mr. and Mrs. Louis MacMurray, Mr. and Mrs. Frank Brentnall, Mr. and Mrs. Stephen Haas, Mr. and Mrs. George Evans, Mr. and Mrs. Archibald Huestis, Lady Mackenzie, Misses Mackenzie, Mr. and Mrs. Williams Beardmore, Mr. George W. Beardmore, Mr. J. H. Plummer, Mr. and Mrs. Grace, Mr. Frank McCarthy, Mr. and Miss Wigmore, Mrs. Phippen, Miss Mary Campbell, Mr. Norman Perry, Mr. Albert Dyment, Mrs. J. J. Palmer, Mr. A. M. Stewart, Mr. J. S. Willison, Mr. Willison, Mrs. F. Smith, Miss Florence Smith, Miss Catharine Welland Merritt (St. Catharines), Mrs. Reginald Pellatt, Mr. Winnett, Mrs. G. H. Thompson, Mrs. Clyde Caldwell, Miss Lucy McLean Howard, Misses Davidson, Mr. J. H. Dalton, Mr. Ernest H. Ball, Mrs. J. C. Eaton, Mrs. C. B. Powell, Mr. F. H. Herbert, Mme. Johannna Gadski, Mme. Olive Fremstad, Mme. Yvonne de Treville, Mme. Charlotte Maconda, Miss Marie Dressler, Mr. and Mrs. Angus Sinclair, Mr. Rea, Mr. and Mrs. Wm. Laidlaw, Miss Laidlaw, Mr. and Mrs. Frederick Mercer, Dr. and Mrs. Aikins, Mr. and Mrs. Capon, Mr. H. S. Mara, Mrs. Timothy Eaton, Mrs. Scott Raff, Miss O'Connor (New York), Miss Shanley, Mr. and Mrs. Wyly Greer, Mrs. Geo. Dickson, Mrs. Jackson, Mrs. J. D. A. Tripp (Vancouver), Miss Rianelli, Miss Meredith, Miss Maud Arthurs Weir, Chevalier and Mme. Albertine, Prof. and Miss Hambourg, Mr. and Mrs. Ryrie, Misses Morgan, Mr. and Mrs. Wm. Davidson, Major and Miss McColl, Mrs. Harry Beatty, Miss Lily Lee, Mrs. Dyce Saunders, Miss Isobel Saunders, Mr. and Mrs. Trees.

Toronto World, Oct. 8, 1912

Toronto World, Oct. 8, 1912

Seven Thousand People Heard Gadski at Arena

Famous Singer Was Given an Ovation and Nahan Franko Orchestra Received Still Greater Applause—Madame Olitzka and Mr. Tibaldi Shared Honors.

Seven thousand persons at a political meeting makes the party leaders talk about the swing of victory. Seven thousand persons at a musical performance indicates something still more hopeful in the development of humanity. In fact, the attendance at the Arena list night is something phenomenal for Canada, and the spectacle of the great structure entirely filled, with the exception of a small space behind the orchestra, was something to ponder and remember. No more brilliant audience could have been assembled in Ontario, and it is only in the great capitals of the world that the sight could be paralleled or surpassed. The spectacle outside on Mutual st., with rows of motor cars and carriages extended to Shuter and east and west on that street and south to Queen, evoked many a tribute to the police and traffic arrangements.

Nothing but a superlative attraction could have drawn such an audience and last night's Festival program had every element of musical charm both in composition and performance. There is no doubt that Nahan Franko has assembled in his 62 men an orchestra of very distinguished quality. It is almost incredible that such results could be attained by such a large body of men without long-continued practice. But every man is in the first rank and the result is practically an all-star orchestra whose virtuosity procured such a rendering for Grieg's "Peer Gynt" suite and Lassen's "Festival Overture," as was absolutely ravishing. Nor were the Wagner numbers in any degree lacking. Few realize the tenderness of a chorale, but tenderness on the highest plane is devotion, is religion, and Bach conveys the profoundest tenderness in the majestic measures of the chorale, so adequately rendered last night. Then came the fugue, opening on the first violins, and given with the crisp incisiveness of a mathematical equation. The severity of form and feeling in this number was immediately contrasted with the Wagner item following, the overture from "Die Meistersinger." The wealth and fulness of Wagner's orchestration was presented with glorious power and color. The double bass section was wonderfully effective, giving a diapason-like foundation to the whole structure, and the brass, without a hint of blare, was beyond praise. The trombones were a triumph. In the Lassen overture special attention was given to an exquisite passage on the English horn, but the reeds thruout are superb. Music is the architecture of precious tones, and such a rendering as was given the Grieg suite approaches the dreams of Orpheus and Pythagoras.

Madam Gadski was the favorite among the soloists, and she added largely to her constituency last night both by her fine singing and her good nature. She gave "Elsa's Dream" in the first part with faultless intonation and unaffected feeling, tho she seemed at time to feel the strain of the huge hall. A bouquet and most insistent applause secured "The Erl King" as an encore, and this met with still greater applause. The singular sweetness with which she sang "Annie Laurie" as a second encore, placed the ballad high among the classics, and nothing was more appreciated during the evening. With Madam Olitzka she sang the duet from "Aida," and that from "The Magic Flute," with Mr. Campanari. Their voices blended most effectively. Her last number was Weber's "Ocean du Ungeheuer," and in response to a rapturous encore she sang "The

Continued on Page 7, Column 6

Call of the Valkyrie," and sang it so that the audience insisted on its repetition. Madam Gadski was strikingly gowned in a magenta watered silk half sheath on each side over white, and she wore a diamond tiara.

Madam Olitzka has a powerful virile contralto, very clear and pure in the higher range, and she was highly applauded for the air "Ah, Mon Fils" from Meyerbeer's "Le Prophete." Mr. Campanari sang the buffo patter song from "The Barber of Seville," and the Toreador song as an encore.

Mr. Tibaldi's violin solos were again highly appreciated, and in the Swedish melody especially his lovely tone and the delicacy of his harmonics were notable.

Toronto World, Oct. 9, 1912 — NLC

MME. BLAUVELT SINGS TONIGHT

Miss Felice Lyne Too Ill to Appear and Another Noted Prima Donna Was Secured.

Messrs. Solman and Dalton, who are the sponsors of the Toronto Musical Festival, last evening made the announcement that it has been necessary to substitute for Miss Felice Lyne, who was to have made her first appearance here tonight, the noted prima donna, Madame Lillian Blauvelt. This news will, no doubt, be welcome to many music lovers, for she has long been one of the most popular singers in the world.

To illustrate the celerity with which these gentlemen work, it may be said that the news that Miss Lyne was so ill that she would possibly be unable to get to Toronto only reached them by wire on Sunday night. For hours the wires were kept hot sending telegrams to replace her, and it was learned that Madame Blauvelt was expected to arrive from Europe on a steamer due on Monday afternoon. A wireless message was sent to her on board, requesting that she arrange to leave for Toronto as soon as she arrived in New York.

She accepted the handsome terms offered and will be on hand for rehearsal this morning. There will be no change in the numbers of the program, since, as many Torontonians are aware, every number in Miss Lyne's repertoire is well within the range of Madame Blauvelt. As a mere child she sang in the last Toronto Musical Festival, held on the occasion of the opening of Massey Hall in 1894, and has since won noted successes in many parts of the world, particularly in Russia, France and Belgium.

Toronto World, Oct. 9, 1912 — NLC

Polish soprano, MARCELLA SEMBRICH

ARENA — TORONTO MUSICAL FESTIVAL

WEDNESDAY MATINEE
NAHAN FRANKO and his wonderful orchestra.
SOLOISTS—
ORVILLE HARROLD—The greatest of them all. His last appearance.
YVONNE DE TREVILLE—First appearance since her great triumph of all Europe.
ALBERT SPALDING—The greatest living American violinist.

WEDNESDAY EVENING
NAHAN FRANKO and his wonderful orchestra.
SOLOISTS—
LILLIAN BLAUVELT, Soprano.   DAY BEDDOE, Tenor.
ROSA OLITZKA, Contralto.   ARTHUR TIBALDI, Violinist.
G. CAMPANARI, Baritone.   and a Great Musical Program.

Tickets at Bell's, 146 Yonge St. and Arena. Good seats to be had before every performance at the Arena.
Orchestra, $1.50.   Circle, 50c and $1.00.   4000 seats to be at 50c.

Toronto World, Oct. 9, 1912 — NLC

TO MAKE DEBUT IN GRAND OPERA

Madame Yvonne de Treville's Appearance at Arena Matinee Today Is Her First as Grand Opera Star.

A genuine surprise awaits the musical public of Toronto and the visitors from other cities who have come to the city in shoals for festival week, when Madame Yvonne de Treville makes her first appearance in Canada at the matinee performance today.

Her appearance at the Toronto musical festival is her debut in America as a grand opera artist. She is ranked by European critics with the five greatest living coloratura singers, the others being Marcella Sembrich, Emma Tetrazzini, Selma Kurz, and Frieda Kempel. She is admitted to have highest range of them all. She sings the Mozart "Magic Flute" aria in the original key, and in the cadenza of the "Bell Song" from "Lakme," reaches the high F's (F in alt.) with perfect ease. This is an unparalleled achievement in the present generation.

An attractive feature of Madame Treville's appearances is that she is an accomplished harpist and in encore numbers usually accompanies herself on that instrument.

Toronto World, Oct. 9, 1912 — NLC

ARENA — TONIGHT

NAHAN FRANKO and His Wonderful Orchestra.
SOLOISTS—
Mme. Olive Fremstad .... Prima Donna Soprano
Mme. Rosa Olitzka .... Contralto
Mr. Dan Beddoe .... Tenor
Dr. Fery Lulek .... Baritone
Mr. Arturo Tibaldi .... Violinist

Tickets at Bell's, 146 Yonge; Massey Orchestra, $1.50, Circle, 50c and $1.00. Reserved seats before each performance at the Arena. All Reserved.

FRIDAY SPECIAL POP MATINEE
The Management of the Musical Festival have decided to give a Special Pop Matinee on Friday Afternoon at 2.30.
POPULAR PRICES: Entire Orchestra, 50c; Entire Circle, 25c; Box Seats, $1.00. NAHAN FRANKO and His Wonderful Orchestra of thirty-two Men, All Soloists, and the following artists will appear:
Yvonne de Treville, Coloratura Soprano.   Dr. Fery Lulek, Baritone.
Mme. Lillian Blauvelt, Soprano.   Mr. Arturo Tibaldi, Violinist.
Mme. Rosa Olitzka, Contralto.   Mr. Herbert Sachs-Hirsch, Pianist.
All seats for this Special Pop Concert will be on sale at the Arena, Friday Morning at 8.30 o'clock.

DOORS OPEN AT 2 P.M.
POP CONCERT COMMENCES AT 2.30 P.M.

Toronto World, Oct. 10, 1912 — NLC

MME. BLAUVELT IN FINE VOICE

Won Immediate Favor by Her Selections on First Appearance, While Madame Olitzka Scored Again.

If the audience at the Arena last night did not equal that of Tuesday evening in numbers, it was no less representative and enthusiastic. All the boxes were tenanted by the elite of the city and an atmosphere of virtuosity pervaded every section of the vast building, bright with decorations and with its arched vault of roof spanned with blazing electric lamps. Each day that has passed of this wonderful musical week has added its quota of evidence to the great boon conferred on the Toronto public by the enterprise of Mr. Lawrence Solman and those who have aided him. Now, indeed, the Ontario capital has an auditorium which, notwithstanding its vast capacity, is perfect acoustically.

The principal artiste, Madame Blauvelt, requisitioned by wireless to take the place of Miss Felice Lyne, incapacitated from regrettable illness, showed no trace of the worry of her hurried travel. Her superb voice and exquisite vocalization carried her into immediate favor. Her first selection was the well-known jewel song of Margaret from Gounod's "Faust," rendered with a charm and brilliancy that held the audience captive. In the second part Madame Blauvelt sang the Bolero from Verdi's "Sicilian Vespers," and again exhibited incomparable flexibility and purity of tone. During the evening several beautiful floral tributes were presented to this queen of song.

Madame Olitzka deepened the impression made at the earlier performances. Her rich contralto and cultured style was heard to great advantage in the Adriana Aria from Wagner's "Rienzi," and the aria, "My Heart at Thy Dear Voice," from "Samson and Delilah" by Saint Saens. Mr. Beddoe scored a triumph in "Lend Me Your Aid" from Gounod's "Queen of Sheba." Mr. Campanari was warmly acclaimed as an established favorite and gave a fine rendering of the aria "Non Piu Andrai" from "The Marriage of Figaro" by Mozart.

The orchestra, under Mr. Franko, again revealed itself as of exceptional quality. It is specially remarkable for precision of attack, immediate response to the baton of the conductor, and mastery of tone. Particularly noticeable for these merits was Weber's "Invitation to the Waltz," with instrumentation by Dr. Felix Weingartner. In response to a vociferous encore, the conductor very appropriately responded with the old but never surpassed "Blue Danube" waltz of Strauss, he himself emphasizing the seductive themes on the violin. This most expressive of instruments had also a revealing touch in the three numbers contributed by Signor Tibaldi, who again displayed his fine technic and responsive interpretation.

Toronto World, Oct. 10, 1912   NLC

MARIE DRESSLER APPEARS TONIGHT

Funniest Woman on English-Speaking Stage Will Be Headliner at Last Arena Concert.

The great festival at the Arena which has delighted thousands this week, will be wound up tonight with a unique feature, in the form of comedy recitations and a series of imitations of most of the noted artists of the week by the operatic comedienne, Miss Marie Dressler, who is admittedly the funniest woman on the English-speaking stage, is a capital one. It is the aim of Miss Dressler to give the public something of a higher order than mere broad burlesque. Those who saw her imitation of Tetrazzini last season will remember how excruciatingly funny it was, but her imitations of the singers to be heard here during the festival will be marked by more artistic finesse; for, while she is primarily a purveyor of mirth, she has also serious ambitions, and tho it is not generally known, a most thoroly trained musician, familiar with every detail of her art. This training began with early childhood, for she is a daughter of Professor Koerber, at one time one of the best-known musicians in Ontario. It is this musical training that enables her to so skilfully satirize the prima donnas of the day. Born in 1871, she has been on the stage since the age of fifteen, and all her early training was musical and operatic. Burlesque came later when she had fully developed all the technique of her art. At the age of sixteen she sang the fine contralto role of Katisha in the Mikado, and for ten years with the Bennet Moulton Opera Company, the Lillian Russell Opera Company and similar organizations she appeared in the entire repertoire of classic light opera. In truth, it may be said that if the essentially unctuous and humorous qualities of her personality had not marked a career for her in comic roles, she would have won distinguished success as a vocalist. Her contribution to the festival will, therefore, be of immense interest to the critics and the public.

Toronto World, Oct. 12, 1912   NLC

At the Opera

A wealth of color and song filled the Arena last night, when Madame Pavlowa came back to Toronto and Miss Felice Lyne, the long-expected and long-wished for, came at last. Pavlowa is still the creature of fire and air and mysterious movement which appeal to all the subtler senses, and Felice Lyne has all the sweet clearness which advance notices have credited her with, and underneath is a depth of feeling which charms heart, as well as ear. Her costumes, the white and silver brocade of the bride, the gold and blue of the later scene, were beautiful, their richness but accentuating the girlishness of the little songstress who has such a human personality.

His Honor the Lieutenant-Governor of Ontario and Lady Hendrie occupied a flag-draped box, and with them were Miss Enid Hendrie, Col. Clyde Caldwell being in attendance.

Globe, Oct. 22, 1915   NLC

Boston Grand Opera Co.
—AND—
Pavlowa Ballet Russe

BENEFIT OF
Red Cross (Trafalgar Day) and
Field Comforts for Fighting Canadians.

4 Performances
October 21-22-23

The Dumb Girl of Portici.... .... Thursday
Carmen .... Friday
Madame Butterfly, Saturday Mat.
The Love of Three Kings, Saturday

Seat Sale at Mason & Risch 230 Yonge Street.

Prices—$1.00, $1.50, $2.00, $2.50, $3.00, $3.50, $5.00.

Globe, Oct. 21, 1915   NLC

SELECTED APPEARANCES			
1886	Toronto Musical Festival	1949	Frankie Laine
1912	Toronto Musical Festival	1949	Patti Page
1915	Boston Grand Opera	1952	Don Messer
	Company and Anna Pavlova	1952	Grand Ole Opry
	and her Ballet Russe	1953	Red Foley
		1954	Melody Fair
1949	Peggy Lee	1960	Brenda Lee
1949	Frank Sinatra	1961	Wilf Carter

ANNA PAVLOVA. Legendary Russian ballerina who toured extensively with her own company, appearing at Mutual Street Arena in 1915.

Canadian comedienne MARIE DRESSLER, famous for her portrayal of the title role in the film *Tugboat Annie* with Wallace Beery.

IN PERSON!
ONE NIGHT ONLY

CARL SMITH
with his entire
GRAND OLE OPRY
SHOW

Singing all his COLUMBIA RECORD Hits!
"Don't Just Stand There"
"Little Girl in My Home Town"
"Old Mother Nature"
"Let's Live a Little"
and many others

MONDAY, MAY 26
8.30 P.M.

GET YOUR ADVANCE TICKETS NOW!
ADULTS $1.50, CHILDREN 50c (Tax Included)

FRED RODEN'S RECORD CORRAL
144 QUEEN ST. E.   WA. 4493

AND MUTUAL ARENA — WA. 1554

MUTUAL ARENA

Globe and Mail, May 24, 1952   NLC

1922
THE COLISEUM – CNE

When completed it was described as the largest single building under one roof in the world.

THE COLISEUM circa 1925

COLISEUM, CNE

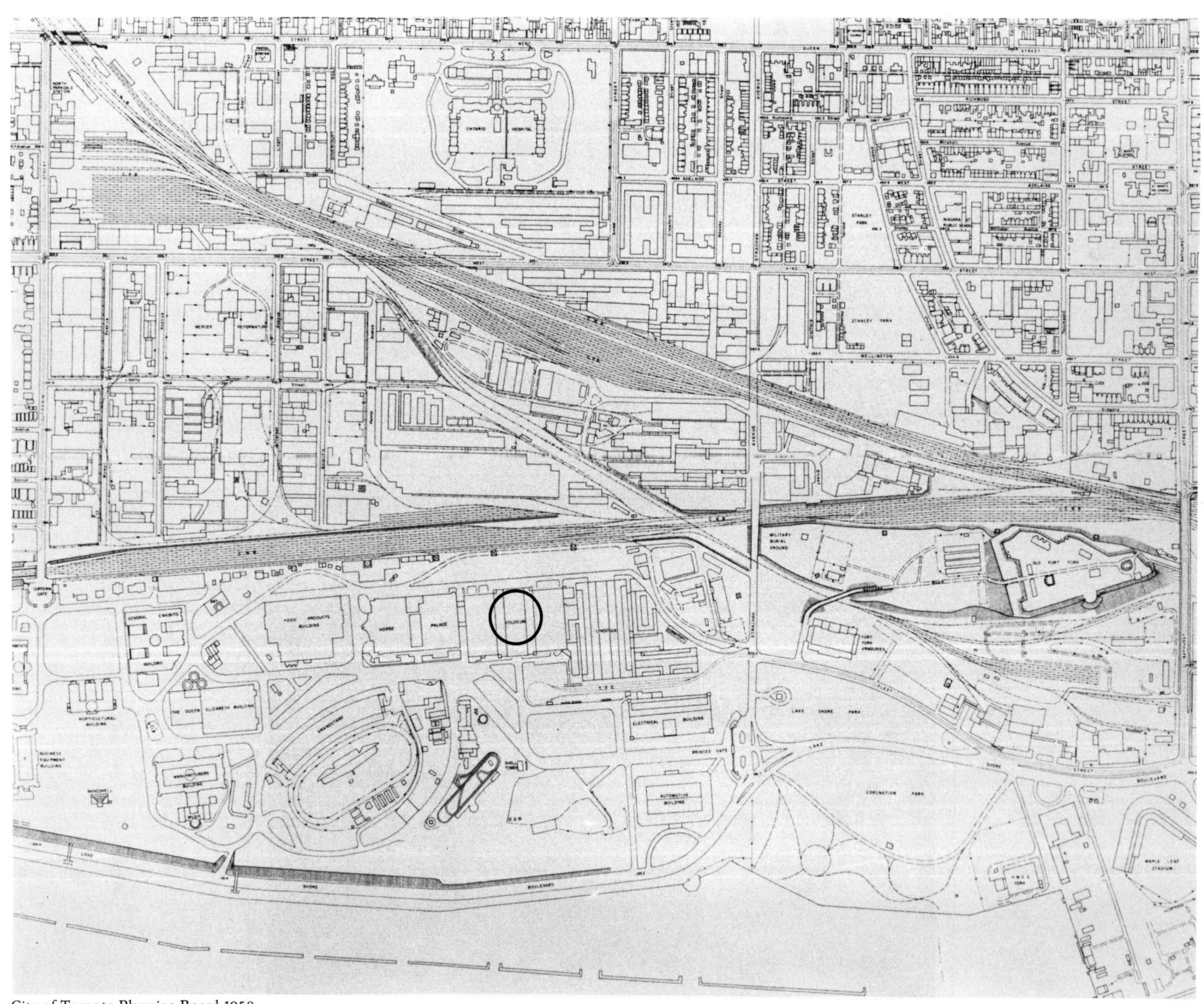

City of Toronto Planning Board 1958

COLISEUM, CNE

In 1879 the rivalry among the towns of Ontario to play host to the Provincial Exhibition led to the incorporation of the Industrial Exhibition Association of Toronto. For the first exhibition of the new association 23 buildings were on the grounds of the present Canadian National Exhibition. Music Day was established in 1921 since music had always had its place, with international bands and choruses in concerts at the Bandshell and the Transportation Building. The Coliseum was built in 1922 and was, at that time, the largest building under one roof in the world. In 1922 and 1923 Giorgio De Feo, described by the Official Catalogue Canadian National Exhibition as "long connected with Covent Garden and a close personal friend of Signor Gatti-Casazza of the Metropolitan Opera", brought to the Coliseum a company which performed operas from the popular repertoire. During World War II the Eaton Operatic Society presented Gilbert and Sullivan operas for the men stationed at Manning Pool.

The Coliseum is most familiar as the site of livestock judging, dog and cat shows, and the Royal Agricultural Winter Fair with its Horse Show which was once one of Toronto's most glamorous annual events.

THE COLISEUM – The Parade of Champions.

COLISEUM
Canadian National Exhibition.

ENTIRE WEEK OF SEPTEMBER 4, Evenings Only.

De Feo Grand Opera Co.

In Six Superb Performances at Popular Prices.

Monday and Friday— "AIDA"
Tuesday and Thursday— "MADAME BUTTERFLY"
Wednesday and Saturday— "CARMEN"

Complete Scenic Productions under cover on fully equipped stage.

30 Famous Principals—Organisation of 120—Auxiliary Corps, 200.

Six thousand seats. General admission 50 cents. Reserved seats 75 cents and $1. Plan at Moodey's, 33 King Street West.

Globe, Aug. 29, 1922 NLC

EXHIBITION COLISEUM
(IMMEDIATELY OPPOSITE EASTERN ENTRANCE)

TONIGHT AND EVERY NIGHT THIS WEEK

Hear the World's Immortal Melodies In Their Proper Dramatic Settings

THE DE FEO GRAND OPERA COMPANY
(Giorgio De Feo, late of Covent Garden, Director-General)

Famous Singers From the Great Opera Houses of Europe and America—Symphonic Orchestra and Splendid Chorus—Beautiful Costumes and Scenery

Principals—Mesdames Lavinia Darve, Dreda Aves, Genia Zielinska, Luisa Hunter, Grace Ann Yeager, Lavinia Puglioli, Vera Burdette and others. Messieurs Leonardo del Credo, Ralph Errolle, A. Palermo, Charles Mihlon, A. Gandolfi, A. Velenti, G. Cehanovsky, E. Canti, G. Interante, Amedee Baldi, S. Canova and others. Conductors, Ugo Barducci and G. Coroshansky.

Repertoire—Monday, "IL TROVATORE"; Tuesday, "CAVALLERIA RUSTICANA" and "PAGLIACCI"; Wednesday, "RIGOLETTO"; Thursday, "CARMEN"; Friday, "MARTHA" (in English); Saturday Night, "IL TROVATORE."

Children's Matinee Saturday—A superb spectacular production of the greatest of all fairy operas, "HANSEL AND GRETEL" (Babes in the Wood).

Seat sale at Moodey's, 33 King St. West, and Coliseum Box Office. Unparalleled scale of prices: General admission, 50 cents, tier seats; reserved seats, boxes, $1.25; ground floor, $1.

Globe, Sept. 3, 1923 NLC

MUSIC AND THE DRAMA
Conducted by E. R. PARKHURST

OPERA AT THE "EX."

De Feo Company Gives "Trovatore" Before Immense Audience.

The De Feo Grand Opera Company, reorganized since its appearance here last year, last night opened a week of repertory in the Coliseum at the Exhibition. It was greeted by a vast audience of several thousand people, although the capacity of the auditorium was not exhausted.

The opera selected for the occasion was Verdi's ever-popular "Il Trovatore," which, although in its 70th year, can still be depended upon as a popular offering. The cast was as follows: "Lenora," Lavinia Darve; "Azucena," Dreda Aves; "Manrico," L. Del Credo; "Conte di Luna," Alfreda Gandolfi; "Ferrando," Alfredo Valenti; "Ruiz," Amedee Baldi; "Inex," Lavinia Puglioli. The conductor was Signor Ugo Barducci, and there was a compact and capable orchestra and a good-sized chorus.

The production was a meritorious one in regard to most of the essentials, and evidently, judging from the nature of its reception, afforded much pleasure to those present. In the opinion of the writer the performance was superior to any of the efforts of the company last year. The leading singers were enthusiastically recalled before the curtain after the principal acts, the plaudits being marked by gratifying unanimity.

Lavinia Darve, who proved herself the possessor of a clear soprano voice, telling in the upper register, made a very favorable impression in the role of the ill-fated Leonora. She sang her principal arias with good judgment and with well-governed dramatic expression. She was given many grateful recognitions of appreciation.

Dreda Aves in the role of Azucena revealed a warm-colored mezzo voice with uncommon carrying power in emotional climaxes. She won special triumphs in the agitated "Strida la Vampa," with its sinister narrative, and also in the delightful melody which dies away as she falls asleep, known best by its English title, "Home to our Mountains."

Signor Del Credo made an excellent showing as Manrico. His voice is of good timbre, and particularly showed to advantage in his solo in the "Miserere" scene, in which the ensemble did not fail in its traditional effect. His work throughout was conscientious, and his interpretation was free from any forced or exaggerated expression.

Alfredo Gandolfi, who has a resonant, powerful baritone, sang the music of the Conte di Luna with considerable fervor. In the suave "Il Balen" his singing was distinguished by smooth vocalization and symmetrical phrasing and he fairly divided the honors throughout the opera with his associate solo singers.

ticularly strong in dynamic effects, they sang very creditably as a rule, especially in the "Anvil" chorus and the "Miserere."

Signor Barducci in his conducting proved that he had his score well studied, and that he had a method of direction that left no doubt as to his intention.

The bill for this evening will consist of "Cavalleria Rusticana" and "I Pagliacci." The other selections will be as follows: Wednesday, "Rigoletto;" Thursday, "Carmen;" Friday, "Martha," in English; Saturday matinee, "Hansel and Gretel," and Saturday evening, a repeat of "Trovatore." One may note here that the scale of prices for seats is exceptionally moderate.

Globe, Sept. 4, 1923 NLC

THE COLISEUM in Wartime. During World War II the HORSE PALACE, as it was known to visitors to the Ex, served as Manning Pool for service men – an estimated 12,000 were billetted between 1939 and 1945.

APPEARANCES

1922	De Feo Grand Opera Company
1923	De Feo Grand Opera Company
1940	Eaton Operatic Society
1942	Eaton Operatic Society
1943	Eaton Operatic Society
1944	Eaton Operatic Society

1923
HART HOUSE

Again the Massey family provided for the cultural needs of the community.

HART HOUSE from Queen's Park

HART HOUSE

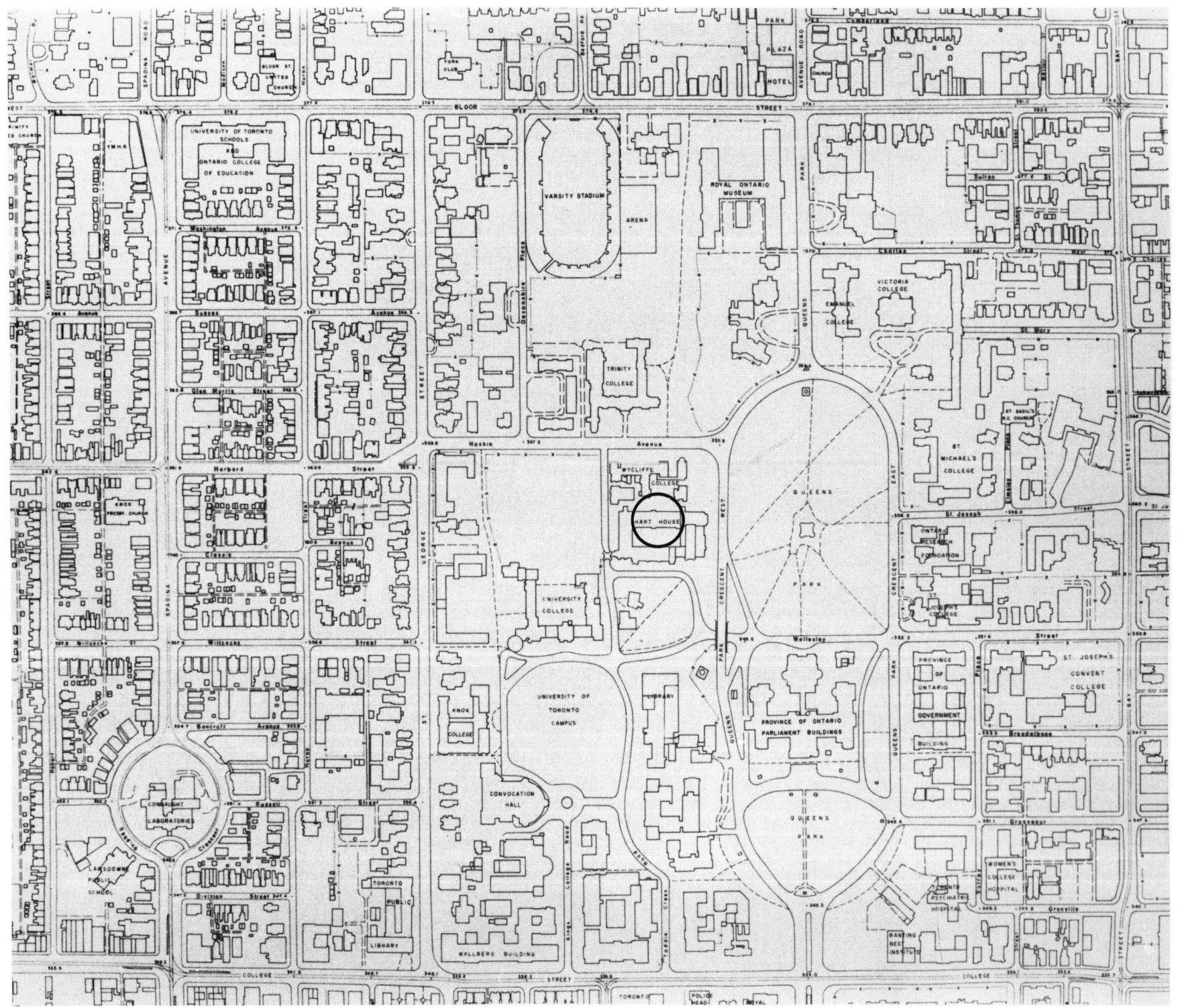

City of Toronto Planning Board 1957

HART HOUSE

Built by the Massey Foundation under the directorship of Vincent Massey, HART HOUSE, in the words of a University of Toronto publication, *Hart House Theatre Toronto. A Description of the Theatre and the Record of its First Nine Seasons 1919-1928,* 'seeks to provide for all the activities of the undergraduates' life which lie outside of the actual lecture room'. An experimental theatre for the use of the University and 'the wider community which it serves' was opened in the sub-basement in 1919. The first opera performance, Gluck's *Orpheus and Euridice*, was given in 1923. Here, in 1929, Dr. Ernest MacMillan's Conservatory Opera Company presented Purcell's *Dido and Aeneas,* Von Suppe's *Boccaccio* and Bach's *Peasant Cantata*. In the late 1940's the fledgling Opera School of the Royal Conservatory of Music presented opera excerpts, progressing in the course of time to full productions. Since 1972 the Gilbert and Sullivan Society of Toronto has given productions annually.

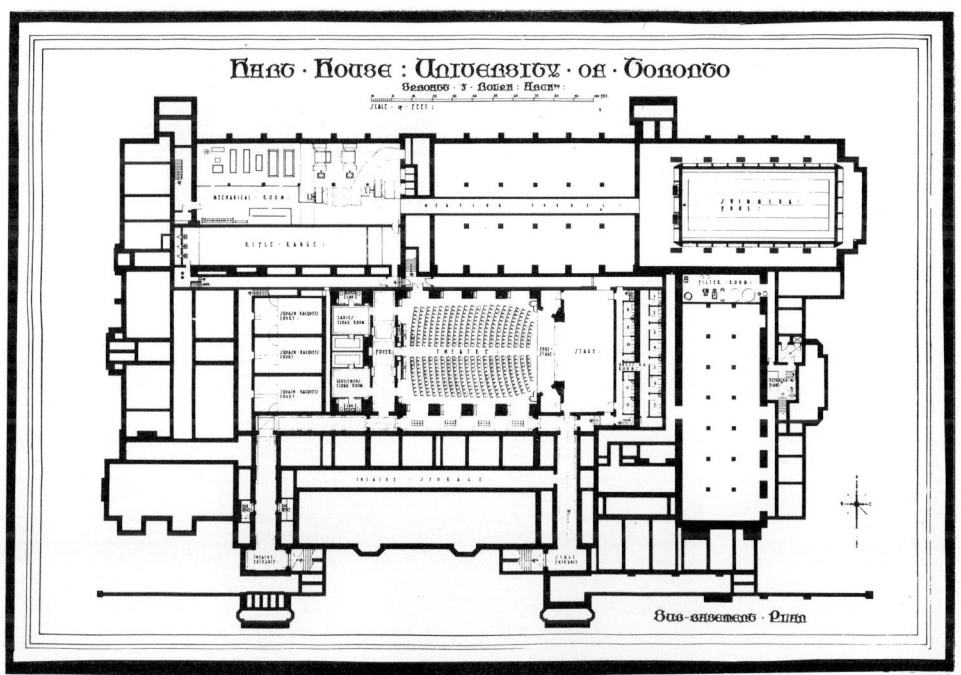

SUB-BASEMENT PLAN

THE FOYER

Photos: Vincent Massey 1919

THE AUDITORIUM

The first Opera to be given at Hart House was naturally of much interest to musicians. It is a curious coincidence too that it should come at a time when the Royal Academy of London is making an appeal for £35,000 for the erection of an auditorium and stage suitable for the training of students for this hitherto neglected branch of music in England. Whether the English or Canadian temperaments will ever make opera a national plank in their musical life is still much open to differences of opinion. So far there has been very little English opera excepting of the kind that runs to riotous humour, and it will be interesting to see if any marked degree of change has come over English character to permit of its taking a hold on their affection. Of the Hart House affair it was possible I think to divide the audience into three classes. There were a few who had seen a fine production of the same work (Gluck's "Orfeo") which had been given here many years ago, and there were likewise some who had seen finely staged productions in Europe. Then there were two other classes: those to whom the opera was new; and, those who while never having heard the music yet knew of its historical import. It was to the last named that the production made its most successful appeal. A splendid Orpheus and some delightful dancing were to my mind the outstanding features, and we can offer, therefore, congratulations to Mrs. Pearl Whitehead, Miss Lorna Maclean, and to Mr. Campbell McInness who undertook the training of the soloists and chorus. The resources of the stage hardly permitted the best scenic effects, and the absence of a proper place for the orchestra naturally affected the instrumental work rather adversely. But in spite of this one is indebted to Mr. Bertram Forsyth for the opportunity of hearing one of the most talked of and epoch-making works in the realm of Operatic history.

Of the Opera itself I think Mr. Newman's criticism, written some years ago in his book on "Gluck and the Opera", is very penetrating and judicial. For, despite its greatness the opera suffers from too many anti-climaxes. One can see so well how Gluck, despite his theories, was yet restricted by the conventions of his day. For instance, his remark, "that when I am composing I try to forget I am a musician," seems very contradictory when Orpheus begins singing roulades at the end of the first act. And it seems a pity that the final fall of the curtain should not take place after the beautiful *Che Faro*, sung by Orpheus at the close of the second act.

* * *

Conservatory of Music,
Quarterly Review, Aug. 1923

DR. ERNEST MacMILLAN, Conductor of *The Peasant Cantata* and *Dido and Aeneas*.

1929

RANDOLPH CROWE, Fritz in *The Peasant Cantata*.

LAURA DE TURCZYNOWICZ, Producer and Director of *Dido and Aeneas*.

ORFEO – Gluck 1923

HART HOUSE

DIDO AND AENEAS 1929

BOCCACCIO 1929

HART HOUSE THEATRE
(by permission of the Syndics)

The
Conservatory Opera Company

PRESENTS

"DIDO and AENEAS"
(Purcell)

preceded by

"THE PEASANT CANTATA"
(Bach)

IN AN ORIGINAL STAGE VERSION

Monday, Wednesday, Friday Evenings
Saturday Matinee

AND

"BOCCACCIO"
(Von Suppé)

Tuesday, Thursday, Saturday Evenings
Wednesday Matinee

EVENINGS 8.15 MATINEES 2.30

DURING THE WEEK COMMENCING

APRIL 1st, 1929

Programme cover

PROGRAMME

Preceding each performance of "Dido and Aeneas" there will be presented

"The Peasant Cantata"
(J. S. BACH)

in an original stage version translated and arranged by Ernest MacMillan.

The "Peasant Cantata" was written in 1742 and performed in honour of Carl Heinrich von Dieskau on the occasion of his becoming "Lord of the Manor". It includes a number of folk-songs and country dances.

CAST OF CHARACTERS

FRITZ .... Randolph Crowe
GRETEL .... Marjorie Vincent
Chorus of peasants:
Misses Ruth Bell, Dorothy Campbell, Laura Hetherington, Grace Holtby, Eleanor Hughes, Margaret McCague, Kathleen McKee, Maude McQuillan, Doris Pettitt, Winnifred Polkinghorn, Jean Ratcliffe, Willa Robb, Bessie Welch, Emily Wilkinson, Camela Young. Messrs. Arthur Bartlett, P. E. Clayton, Lumsden Cummings, Llewellyn DeFoe, George Gibson, Bert Green, Frank Green, Victor Hutchison, Charles Jacques, Ronald Johnston, A. J. Udall, Harry Welch.
(Members of the Bloor Street United Church Choir)

DANCERS: Wanda de Turczynowicz, Betty Byers, Marguerite Lasserre, Philippa Chapman.

VON DIESKAU .... Weldon Kilburn
FRAU VON DIESKAU .... Ethel Tamblyn Cooper
SCHÖSSER (Tax Collector) ... Gordon McLaren
PFARRER SCHMIERKÄSE ...... Sydney Beaney

Flute obligato played by E. Sellen.

"DIDO and AENEAS"
(Henry Purcell)

CONDUCTOR—Dr. Ernest MacMillan.
PRODUCER AND DIRECTOR—Madame Laura de Turczynowicz.

CAST

DIDO (or Eliasa, Queen of Carthage) ... Dorothy Allan Park
Belinda, a Lady in Waiting .... Betty Priestman
Ladies in Waiting .... Elfrida Boulton, Wanda de Turczynowicz
Sorceress .... Jean Davidson
First Witch .... Enid Grey
Second Witch .... Jane Mason
Mercury .... Alex Montgomery
A Sailor .... Aylmer Macdonald
A Slave .... Randolph Crowe
AENEAS .... Reginald Heal

Chorus of courtiers, people, witches, sailors:
Misses Ruth Bell, Dorothy Campbell, Laura Hetherington, Grace Holtby, Eleanor Hughes, Margaret McCague, Kathleen McKee, Maude McQuillan, Doris Pettitt, Winnifred Polkinghorn, Jean Ratcliffe, Willa Robb, Bessie Welch, Emily Wilkinson, Camela Young. Messrs. Arthur Bartlett, P. E. Clayton, Lumsden Cummings, Llewellyn DeFoe, George Gibson, Bert Green, Frank Green, Victor Hutchison, Charles Jacques, Ronald Johnston, A. J. Udall, Harry Welch.

"Dido and Aeneas"—Continued

THE PLOT as outlined in Mr. Dennis Arundell's book on Purcell is as follows:

THE STORY:—Dido, filled with a melancholy love for her guest, the Prince Aeneas, escorts him to hunt in the hills near the town. Suddenly a storm brewed by some anarchistic witches springs up and the court is frightened back to Carthage, leaving Aeneas to be accosted by a sorceress, who, in the guise of Mercury, orders him to set sail at once for the shores of Italy. The pious prince bids farewell to Dido, his ships put out, and the forsaken queen dies in the arms of her maidens.

Concert Master .... Harold Sumberg
Chorus Master .... Harvey Robb
Co-repetitor .... Weldon Kilburn
Assistant Co-repetitor .. Reginald Godden

"BOCCACCIO"
(Franz Von Suppé)

Conductor .... Thomas J. Crawford
Producer and Director ... Madame Laura de Turczynowicz

ALTERNATE CAST

BOCCACCIO, a novelist and poet .... Aylmer Macdonald
                                       Reginald Heal
LEONETTO, his friend, a student ...... Randolph Crowe
PIETRO, Prince of Palermo .... Alex Montgomery
LOTTERINGHI, a cooper .... Howard Heritage
LAMBERTUCCIO, a grocer .... Hugh Snell
SCALZA, a barber .... Edward Holbrook
FIAMETTA, Lambertuccio's adopted daughter ... Betty Priestman
                                       Alice Strong
BEATRICE, Scalza's daughter .... Ida Munro
ISABELLA, Lotteringhi's wife .... Elfrida Boulton
                                       Enid Grey
PERONELLA, Lambertuccio's sister ..... Ethel Tamblyn-Cooper
                                       Elizabeth Lumenfeld
CHECCO, a beggar .... Sydney Beaney
FRATELLI, a bookseller .... Jack Wainberg
FRESCO, the cooper's apprentice ...... Betty Byers
THE UNKNOWN .... Weldon Kilburn
LO CASCIO, Major-domo of the Duke .... Sydney Beaney
Lotteringhi's journeymen:
  ALBERTO .... Weldon Kilburn
  RICCIARDO .... Sydney Beaney
  GERBINO .... Roderick Gordon
  FEODORO .... Albert Punter
  GUIDOTTO .... Jack Wainberg
Florentine Students:
  TOFANO .... Arthur Bartlett
  CHICHIBIO .... Keith Barber
  GUIDO .... Ralph Wales
  GIOTTO .... Llewellyn Defoe
  RINIERI .... Ivy Bass
  LANTO .... Barbara George
Padre .... Llewellyn Defoe
Pages .... Betty Byers Wanda de Turczynowicz
Beggars:
  CHIACOMETTO .... Weldon Kilburn
  ANSELMO .... Roderick Gordon
  TITO .... Albert Punter

(Continued Overleaf)

Lambertuccio's servants:
  FILIPPA .... Marjorie Beaney
  ORETTA .... Dorothy Manchester
  VIOLANTA .... Gladys Jay
DONNA MARIA .... Edna Baggs
DONNA JANCOFIERE .... Lillian Frappe
ELIZA, Donna Jancofiere's daughter ... Eleanor Young
MARIETTA, a citizen's daughter .... Mollie Hamilton
DONNA PULCI .... Madeline Watt
Donna Pulci's daughters:
  AUGUSTINA .... Amelia Hanna
  ELENA .... Marion Wibby
  ANGELICA .... Ruby Bass
DONNA JULIA .... Doreen Wood
MARGARITA .... Helen Fisher
JULIETTE .... Wanda de Turczynowicz
LUCIA .... Annie Torgis
NINA .... Sylvia MacNab
TERESA .... Yvette Gillier
EMILIA .... Jean Irwin
CAROLINA .... Elsa Damm
CHECCO'S DOG .... "Bob"

TIME: The XIVth Century
PLACE: Florence

ACT I—Public Square in Florence, the 24th of June, St. John's Day, when all Italy rejoiced, and many joined the procession to the church of Santa Maria Novella.

ACT II—The adjoining gardens of Lotteringhi and Lambertuccio.

ACT III—Sunset Fete in the gardens of the Ducal Palace.

PIETRO, the Prince of Palermo, goes to Florence, in accordance with the wishes of his father, to marry FIAMETTA, the daughter of the DUKE OF TUSCANY. FIAMETTA, when a child, had been adopted by LAMBERTUCCIO, a Grocer, who was not aware of her noble birth. The DUKE had caused her to be reared in this humble manner, for reasons of his own, intending to wed her to PIETRO, to whom she had been in infancy betrothed. Upon PIETRO's arrival in Florence, before presenting himself to the DUKE and FIAMETTA, he joins in several adventures with the Students. BOCCACCIO, the novelist and poet, who is hated by the men of Florence for having ridiculed them in his novels, is deeply in love with FIAMETTA. PIETRO is mistaken for BOCCACCIO, and is severely beaten by the indignant Florentines. As PIETRO is about to be solemnly betrothed to FIAMETTA, for considerations of state (although he does not love her and she dislikes him), BOCCACCIO, knowing that his affection for her is reciprocated, arranges a play which illustrates the follies of PIETRO so strongly, that the latter surrenders the hand of FIAMETTA to BOCCACCIO.

Concert Master .... Frank Blachford
Co-repetitor .... Weldon Kilburn

STAGE SETTINGS AND COSTUMES .... Arthur Lismer
SETTINGS EXECUTED BY .... John Byers
Some of the Costumes in "Dido and Aeneas" executed by:
                                       Mrs. Herbert H. Stansfeld

Costumes in "Boccaccio" by Hart House Costume Department.—
                                       Melville Keay, Manager

LIGHTING, AND STAGE MANAGEMENT .... Colin Tait

We are indebted to Hart House for supplying Stage Properties.

187

HART HOUSE

The Senior School
Toronto Conservatory of Music

presents

An Evening of

Operatic Excerpts

in Hart House Theatre
on Monday, December 16th
at 8.15 o'clock

1946

COSMOPOLITAN STAGE DIRECTOR OF OPERA HERE

Native of Germany, Herman Geiger-Torel Became Citizen of Argentine and Works in Canada or Brazil

Telegram Headline & Photo, Mar. 30, 1948
HERMAN GEIGER-TOREL

MUSIC IN TORONTO
By JOHN KRAGLUND

Few annual events can as readily be counted upon to give an evening of real enjoyment as the program of one-act operas presented by the Royal Conservatory of Music. That promise was again fulfilled last night when the Collegium Musicum and the Opera School of the Conservatory performed the second act of Monteverdi's The Coronation of Poppea (in place of a one-act opera) and Puccini's Gianni Schicchi at Hart House Theatre.

Apparently there are few opera lovers in Toronto who have been as impressed as we have by previous performances. The small theatre was no more than half full. Others will have an opportunity to see the works this evening when they will be repeated.

It is more than 300 years since Monteverdi wrote The Coronation of Poppea, yet there is a contemporary quality in the psychological insight of this forerunner of Italian opera and German music drama. The setting is Rome in the time of Nero. The complex struggle involves Ottone, his wife Poppea (choice of Nero as a new empress), Nero's wife Ottavia, Drusilla (in love with Ottone) and Seneca, Nero's adviser, who has been asked by the emperor to commit suicide because he disapproves of Nero's actions.

Ernesto Barbini conducted the small orchestra that provided a suitably rich, intense accompaniment which rarely interfered with the singers. We did not entirely approve of the maestro's snapping-finger cues to his singers, but at least they were effective.

The singing, not all of it of professional standard, was generally competent and in some cases outstanding. We liked the performance of Victor Braun as Ottone. His voice was rich, round and well controlled. Teresa Stratas as Drusilla reached passionate heights in her big aria when Ottone persuaded her to help him murder Poppea.

Ossyp Hoshulak was a most thoughtful and vocally impressive Seneca, providing some truly moving moments in his acceptance of the order to commit suicide. And Maire Gauley, while missing the desired vocal clarity, gave a good interpretation of the role of Poppea. There was excellent singing also by Constance Fisher as the vindictive Ottavia and a fair measure of charm in the light-hearted intermezzo, in which Damigella (Anne Stephenson) teaches Valletto (Ann Marie Clark) the joy of a kiss.

Neither Margaret Briggs as Arnalta nor Lillian Petrie as Amore was quite secure enough to make the most of the lovely arias allotted to them at the end of the act.

The acting, particularly of Mr. Braun, left much to be desired. Herman Geiger-Torel had not quite succeeded in removing the stilted actions of the several singers unfamiliar with the stage.

Ginni Schicci, using two pianos instead of an orchestra, was conducted by Nicholas Goldschmidt. The story of deathbed intrigue suffered more from over-acting than too little of it. However, its comic element lent itself quite well to this treatment, providing enjoyment for both audience and singers.

There is less opportunity for vocal display in the Puccini opera. We felt that a little less raucous enthusiasm might have provided more charming, and no less amusing ensembles. Miss Stephenson sang the role of Lauretta, giving a commendable performance of the familiar aria, My Beloved Daddy. And Bernard Turgeon was a happy choice as the bluff, scheming and good-natured Schicci—in good voice too.

The cast was entirely acceptable and too numerous to allow individual mention. However, we were favorably impressed with the work of Donald Bartle as Rinuccio, once he had overcome a rather strident opening.

The two pianos provided a reasonable adaptation of the score, at the hands of Mario Bernardi and Paul Timan.

Our only real regret is that it is not possible for more frequent performances of similar works to be seen and heard during the regular music season.

Globe and Mail, Apr. 25, 1957

THE CORONATION OF POPPEA by students of the Opera School, Royal Conservatory of Music.

NICHOLAS GOLDSCHMIDT, Musical Director, and, behind him, HERMAN GEIGER-TOREL, Stage Director, rehearse *Gianni Schicchi* 1949.

HART HOUSE

UNIVERSITY OF TORONTO
ROYAL CONSERVATORY OF MUSIC

THE OPERA SCHOOL

presents

"AMELIA GOES TO THE BALL"
by GIAN-CARLO MENOTTI

"PRIMA DONNA"
by ARTHUR BENJAMIN

HART HOUSE THEATRE

April 16, 17 and 18, 1959, at 8:30 p.m.

By Permission of The Board of Syndics

Programme cover   COCA

1959

UNIVERSITY OF TORONTO
ROYAL CONSERVATORY OF MUSIC

THE OPERA SCHOOL

presents

"THE MARRIAGE CONTRACT"
by GIOACCHINO ROSSINI

"GALLANTRY"
by DOUGLAS MOORE

"RIDERS TO THE SEA"
by RALPH VAUGHAN WILLIAMS

HART HOUSE THEATRE

April 20 (2:30 p.m.), 21, 22, 23 (8:30 p.m.), 1960

By Permission of The Board of Syndics

The performances on April 20, 21 are being sponsored by the Ontario Education Association.

Programme cover   COCA

1960

GILBERT & SULLIVAN SOCIETY OF TORONTO

proudly presents

Iolanthe

written by
W.S. Gilbert

composed by
Arthur Sullivan

HART HOUSE THEATRE
by permission of the Drama Centre

Wednesday to Saturday
APRIL 19, 20, 21, 22

Tuesday to Saturday
APRIL 25, 26, 27, 28, 29, 1978

Producer and Director
WARREN HUGHES

Conductor
MICHAEL EVANS

Programme cover   COCA

1978

GILBERT & SULLIVAN
SOCIETY
OF TORONTO

The Gondoliers

written by
W.S. Gilbert

composed by
Arthur Sullivan

HART HOUSE THEATRE
by permission of the Drama Centre

Thursday to Saturday
APRIL 24, 25, 26

Tuesday to Saturday
APRIL 29, 30, MAY 1, 2, 3, 1980

Musical Director, Derek Bate
Stage Director, Michael Albano*
Producers, John Guy and Joan Woodland

Programme cover   COCA

1980

ROYAL CONSERVATORY OPERA SCHOOL
at HART HOUSE THEATRE

APR. 23 — Saturday EVE. at 8:30

THE MARRIAGE CONTRACT,
GALLANTRY AND RIDERS
TO THE SEA

$2.00 RESERVED

RETAIN STUB GOOD ONLY EVE., SATURDAY APRIL 23
J. KERR & SON, GALT

RESERVED   Left   T 13

Ticket   COCA

1960

Opera bravely tries to tell sprawling tale

By Ronald Hambleton

What a weekend it must have been for 66-year-old Graham George, a professor emeritus of Queen's University and a figure in the music department for over a generation.

After brooding for 30 years on the idea of an opera based on the adventurous life of Theodore von Neuhoff, and after more than seven years of research and writing, the finished work, a three-act opera in the grand manner called A King For Corsica, was finally given two concert performances, one on Friday in Kingston and the second in Toronto's Hart House on Saturday afternoon.

It was a great moment for Graham George.

Von Neuhoff, born in 1686, was a military adventurer under many flags who conned the Corsicans into making him their king, to save them from Genoa. Crowned at age 50, he blew his chances and fled to London, where he died a 70-year-old deadbeat.

Excitable music

George's libretto bravely tries to tell most of this history, through sung narrative, spoken dialogue and readings and chorus, all within the frame of declamatory, even excitable music, played by a 17-member ensemble under William Shookhoff.

The libretto tries to do too much, and the drama is not concentrated. It sprawls across more than 20 years, and far too much of the literary material testifies to a writer infatuated with his research.

It is heavy with superfluous scenes, text obscured by a belligerent score, and a clouded view of what the dramatic line really is. However, even with such flaws, in a concert performance the event was impressive. And the effect is almost nobler than the subject.

Huge cast

The opera has a huge cast. In fact, two actors doubled in 16 parts between them. The four main characters were Theodore (John Keane); the King's Chancellor Costa (James Anderson); a Corsican chief Luccioni; Theodore's adversary (Rod Campbell); and his niece Saveria (Joanne Dorenfeld).

Without their stalwart and vigorously dramatic performances, the work as a whole would have been far less immediate in its effects, if only because they succeeded most of the time in rising above the orchestra.

Call the work an opera, as Graham George does, and its theatrical imperfections take centre stage. But call it a cantata, and its strengths are obvious.

There is the sense of history passing in review, the detail of one man's ambition and inglorious end, and many rich musical canvases depicting desperate figures struggling for survival.

☐ **Ronald Hambleton writes frequently on music for The Star.**

Star, Jan. 26, 1981   COCA

Baritone ROD CAMPBELL

Photo: Robert C. Ragsdale
Soprano JOANNE DORENFELD

Bass-baritone JAMES ANDERSON

Tenor JOHN KEANE

APPEARANCES

1923	*Orfeo*
1929	Conservatory Opera Company
1946	Toronto Conservatory of Music – Senior School
1948	Royal Conservatory Opera
1949	Royal Conservatory Opera
1952	Royal Conservatory Opera
1953	Royal Conservatory Opera
1954	Royal Conservatory Opera
1955	Royal Conservatory Opera
1956	Royal Conservatory Opera
1957	Royal Conservatory Opera
1958	Royal Conservatory Opera
1959	Royal Conservatory Opera
1960	Night Blooming Cereus
1960	Royal Conservatory Opera
1961	Royal Conservatory Opera
1962	Royal Conservatory Opera
1963	Royal Conservatory Opera
1972-83	Gilbert and Sullivan Society
1981	*A King for Corsica*

1928
REGENT THEATRE

Times change – movie houses were taking over.

Postcard　　　　　　　　　　　　　　　　　　　　　　　　　　　　MTLB

REGENT THEATRE

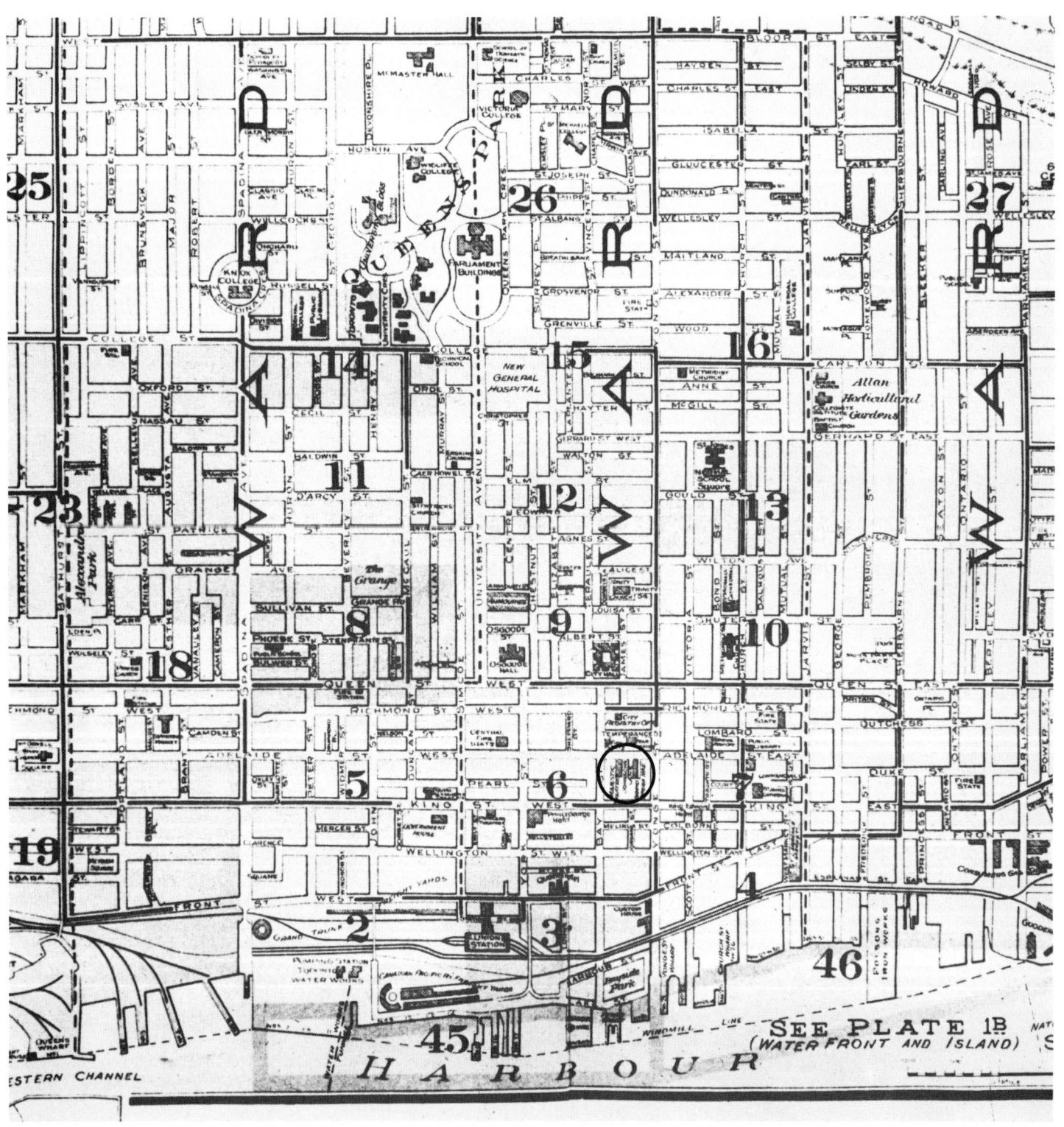

Goad's Atlas 1910

MTLB

REGENT THEATRE

On May 27, 1903, after the destruction by fire of the Toronto Opera House, a permit was issued for the erection of a new theatre on the same site. On October 26 the Mail and Empire reported that the Majestic Theatre had arisen from the ashes of the Toronto Opera House and on November 3 the same paper praised "Toronto's newest and most handsome theatre" which had opened the previous evening. It was under the proprietorship of A.J. Small who had been manager of the Toronto Opera House. In 1910 it was known as the Majestic Music Hall under new management. However, according to contemporary reports, it deteriorated sadly over the years and became an exceedingly disreputable place of entertainment. In 1916 it was renovated and the name changed to the REGENT THEATRE. It was here that, for the week of April 16, 1928, the Conservatory Opera Company under Dr. Ernest MacMillan, gave performances of *The Sorcerer* and *Hansel and Gretel*. The building was demolished in the late 1930's.

Emergency Exit, Majestic Theatre   CTA

Globe, Dec. 3, 1903   AO

REGENT THEATRE

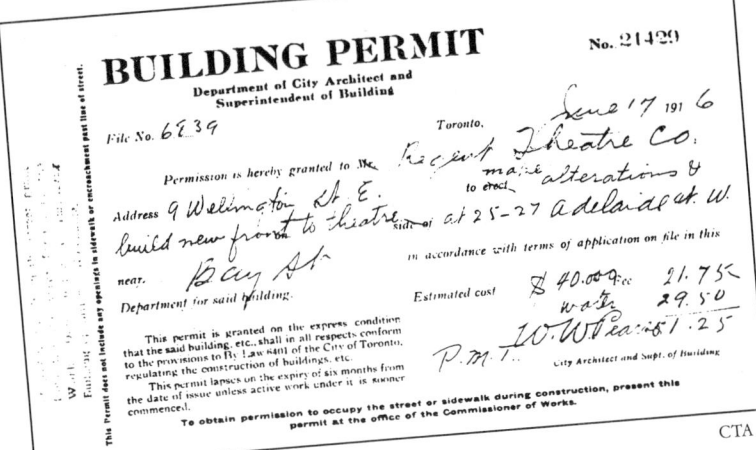
CTA

MTLB

REGENT THEATRE in the 1920's

DR. ERNEST MacMILLAN, Conductor and creator of the Conservatory Opera Company.

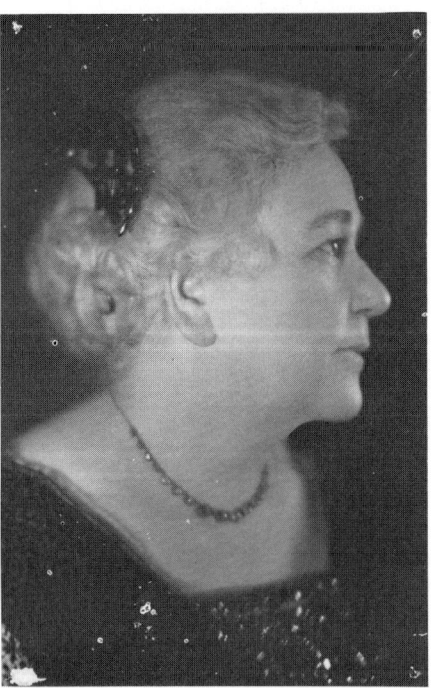
COCA

LAURA DE TURCZYNOWICZ, Stage Director of the Conservatory Opera Company.

The production of the newly-organized Conservatory Opera Company, given in the Regent Theatre, was "The Sorcerer." It must be admitted that the shortcomings of the performance were due in no small part to the authors, Gilbert and Sullivan, for they achieved something in "The Sorcerer" that they never did again; they wrote an exceedingly dull act. Of course, it will be remembered that the operetta was first produced in 1877, and during the year that followed the composer and the librettist found themselves. True, they had done "Trial by Jury" earlier than that date, and it has much to commend it, but with "Pinafore" in 1878, the great partnership started their immortal series of comic operas. There are a few real Gilbertian touches in "The Sorcerer," like the remark of the lovelorn vicar who wished to bury his grief in the "congenial gloom of a colonial bishopric." How Gilbert loved to bait the clergy. He did it to his heart's content in "The Bab Ballads," and even as late as the writing of "Patience," he wanted to do an operetta about the rival curates. But even the plot of "The Sorcerer" lacks the humorous ingenuity that Gilbert developed later, and Sullivan's score showed signs of immaturity in the operatic form. It had its delightful melodies, but they were hardly as irresistible as they became later.

However, the young people from the Conservatory did everything possible with the story of how John Wellington Wells' love potion worked havoc in the village. The best singing last night was done by Mr. Lawrence DeFoe as Alexis. He started well with his aria in the slow paced first act, and made a real success of his waltz song in the second, Miss Madeline Bell sang prettily as Aline, and vocally her duet with Mr. DeFoe was most attractive. Mr. Frederic Manning, who gave a vigorous performance in the title rôle, was easily the most at home on the stage of all the performers. His experience in broad comedy was evident in his impersonation. There was inclined to be an edge, not altogether pleasant, on the concerted numbers done by the chorus, and they showed a tendency to collide in their stage movements, but that will, of course, be smoothed out of their future performances. The large orchestra, under the baton of Mr. Donald Heins, was a pleasing addition to the quality of the presentation.—FRED JACOB in *The Mail and Empire*.

Hänsel and Gretel at the Regent reassembled some of the opera talent of Toronto with a fresh idea—to make opera a legitimate extension of Toronto Conservatory work. The first experiment, it was in most respects brilliantly successful. And the house was packed. Dr. MacMillan conducted.

The two chief characters are in the title. This Hänsel and Gretel are a delightful pair. Miss Marjorie Vincent as Gretel is almost better than her Polly was in Beggar's Opera. She makes up for the part like a second Mary Pickford; her singing is quaintly beautiful. Miss Elfrida Boulton makes a jolly little scamp of a Hänsel and sings the part with lovely tone and freedom of expression.

Miss Hilda Calvin, as the mother, was much better in action than in voice. Randolph Crowe did the father rôle splendidly, both as to singing and impersonation. Miss Dorothy Ranger made up into a perfectly devastating old witch and one of her voices was delightfully ugly. Miss Myrtle Hare sang the Sandman song exquisitely. Bessie Priestman, as the chief Dew Fairy, did a nice bit of singing.

The finale to Act II was one of the finest bits of "mise en scene" ever shown on any stage in Toronto. The handling of the scenics was done with great skill, except for one mishap and too much spotlight for the drop of the screen curtain in Act II. The costumes were a gorgeous riot of harmony in colour. The band was remarkably good. Dr. MacMillan conducted with absolute mastery.—AUGUSTUS BRIDLE in *The Daily Star*.
UTA

Conservatory Quarterly Review, Vol. X #40, 1928, Summer term.

COCA

RANDOLPH CROWE, The father in *Hansel and Gretel*.

APPEARANCES

1928	Conservatory Opera Company

1928 view of the Toronto skyline showing the Royal York Hotel and Toronto Star building under construction and the City Hall clock tower, one of the few skyscrapers.

Photo: Gordon Jarrett

NOGC

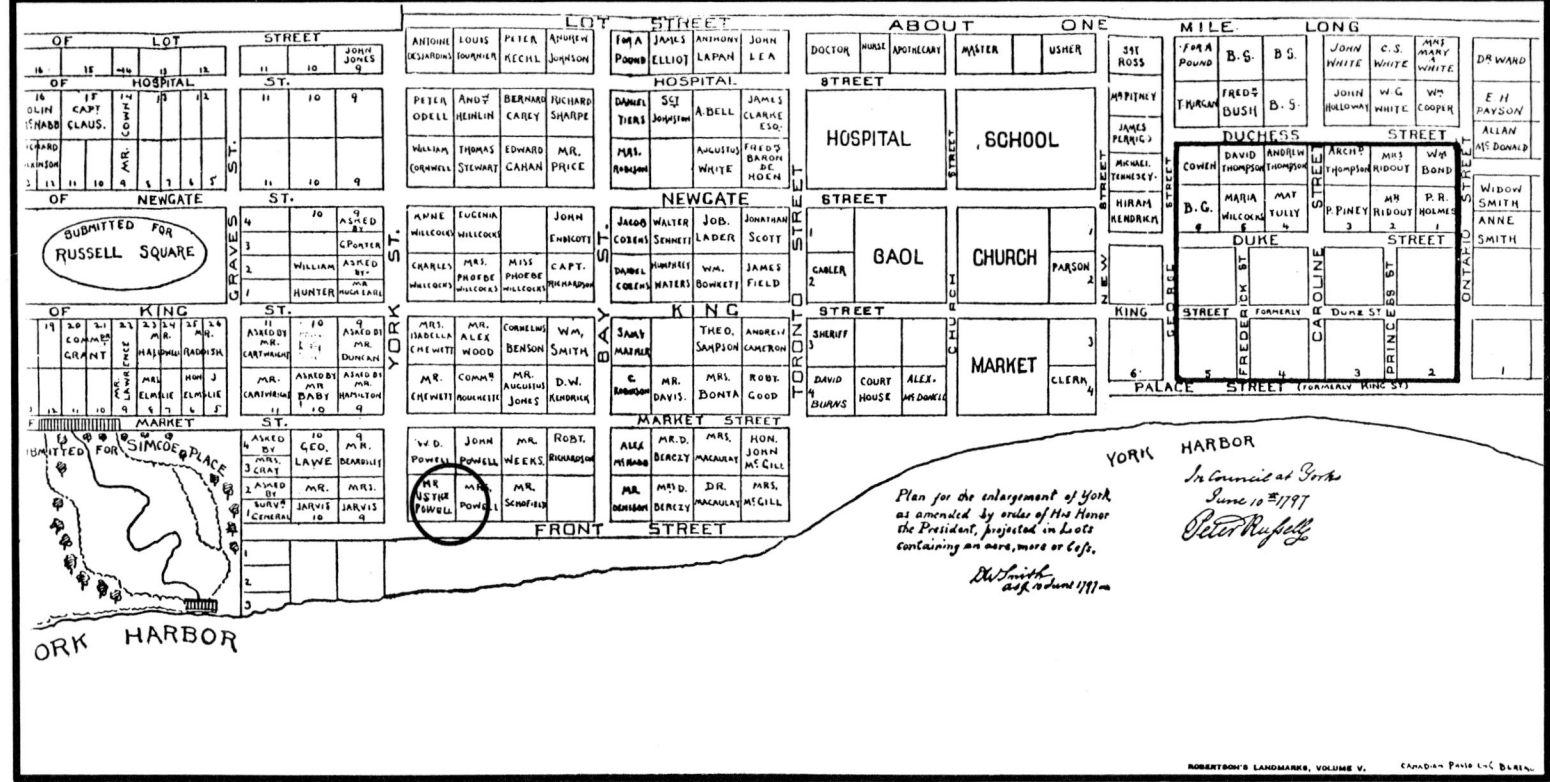
Royal York Hotel Booklet, 1929

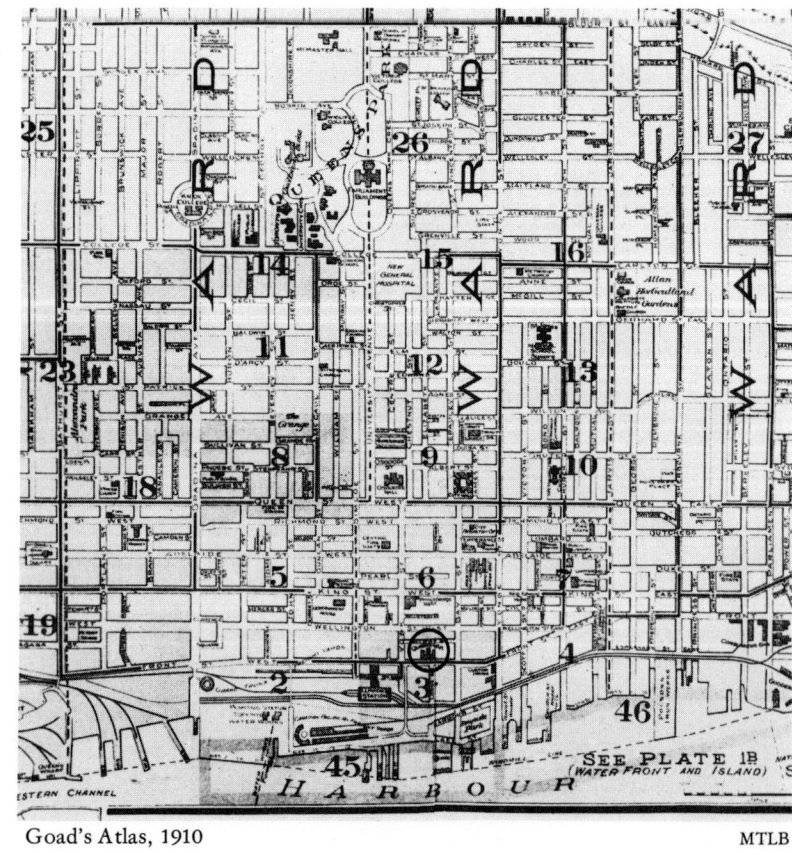
Goad's Atlas, 1910

1929
ROYAL YORK HOTEL

Shades of Franks' Assembly Rooms!

ROYAL YORK HOTEL,
nearing completion in 1929.

MTLB T11077

ROYAL YORK HOTEL

In June 1929 the Royal York Hotel, "the largest hotel in the British Empire", opened its doors with considerable eclat. Situated on Front Street West, it covered the sites of the earlier Queen's Hotel and the Zoological Gardens. In November, as part of the festivities to mark the opening, the Canadian Pacific Railway, which was sponsoring a series of festivals across the country, presented in its new hotel the English Music Festival. The programme included two performances of Ralph Vaughan Williams' opera *Hugh the Drover*, conducted by Dr. Ernest MacMillan, designed by Arthur Lismer of the Group of Seven and starring the young American tenor Allan Jones (later to gain fame for his performances in *Showboat* and *The Firefly*) as Hugh. One voice connected with the production was to become extremely familiar, bringing the immortal words "He shoots! He scores!" into millions of Canadian homes every Saturday night. Foster Hewitt recalls that, in an early instance of opera promotion by radio, he recorded a blow-by-blow account of the prizefight which is a feature of the opera. He remembers hearing himself later, "probably on CFCA".

Queen's Hotel 1927
MTLB 971-26 71

About 1843 Captain Thomas Dick built, to the east of Chief Justice Powell's house at York and Front Streets, (northeast corner) a row of dwelling houses called Ontario Terrace. A few years later these were occupied by Knox College until the latter moved to Government House. From 1853 to 1862 the building housed Sword's Hotel and from then until its demolition in 1927, the Queen's Hotel.

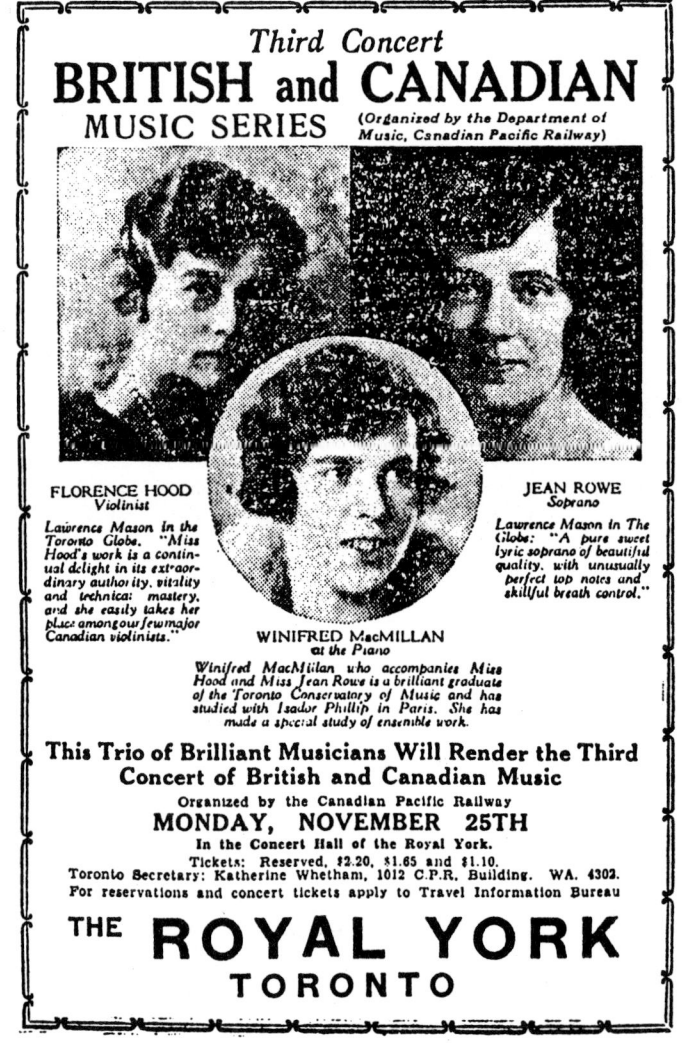

Star, Nov. 16, 1929 © Toronto Star Newspapers Ltd.   MTLB

Winifred MacMillan was a sister of Ernest

ROYAL YORK HOTEL

CONCERT HALL 1981. The orchestra pit has been removed.

Forthcoming Programmes

THURSDAY, NOV. 14
TALK ON ENGLISH MUSIC BY J. CAMPBELL McINNES
In the Concert Hall at 3 p.m.
FOLK MUSIC TEA
English Folk Dancers   The Festival Quartette
In the Ballroom at 4.30 p.m.
EVENING CONCERT
Felix Salmond, England's Great 'Cellist   Norman Wilks, Brilliant Pianist
Edgar March, Boy Soprano
Dancers from the Margaret Eaton School in COURT DANCES
Port Arthur Ladies' Choir, in Madrigals and Part Songs
Folkdancers from the English Folkdance Society

FRIDAY, NOV. 15
TALK ON ENGLISH MUSIC BY J. CAMPBELL McINNES
In the Concert Hall at 3 p.m.
FOLK MUSIC TEA
English Folk Dancers   The Festival Quartette
In the Ballroom at 4.30 p.m.
EVENING CONCERT
R. Vaughan Williams' Opera, "HUGH THE DROVER," produced by Alfred Heather, conducted by Ernest MacMillan.

SATURDAY, NOV. 16
TALK ON ENGLISH MUSIC BY J. CAMPBELL McINNES
In the Concert Hall at 3 p.m.
FOLK MUSIC TEA
Court Dances by students of the Margaret Eaton School
The Festival Quartette
In the Banquet Hall at 4.30 p.m.
EVENING CONCERT
Herbert Heyner, England's Great Baritone
Jeanne Dusseau, Canada's Supreme Soprano
Hart House String Quartette, Canada's Pride
Sea-Chantey Play, "BOUND FOR THE RIO GRANDE," by Frederick William Wallace.
Ottawa Temple Choir, in English Choruses, Ancient and Modern

SUNDAY, NOV. 17
EVENING CONCERT (By Invitation Only)
Jeanne Dusseau, Soprano   Herbert Heyner, Baritone
Hart House String Quartette   The Festival Quartette
Harvey Robb, Organist, on the great Casavant Organ

MONDAY, NOV. 18
EVENING CONCERT
Repeat Performance of "HUGH THE DROVER"

The talks on music by J. Campbell McInnes are free to the public.
Folk Music Teas—Tickets $1.00 each.
EVENING CONCERTS—Reserved Seats $2.75; $2.20 and $1.65 (tax included)
Unreserved Seats $1.10 (tax included)
For Reservations and Tickets apply to the Travel Information Bureau
THE ROYAL YORK

CPR's English Music Festival

ERNEST MacMILLAN

HUGH THE DROVER

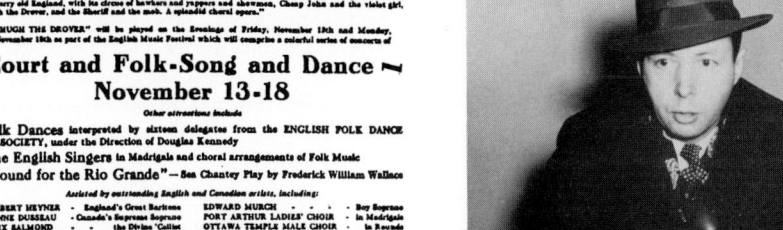

Globe, Nov. 9, 1929

FOSTER HEWITT

ALLAN JONES as Hugh the Drover, RANDOLPH CROWE John the Butcher.

NEW ENGLISH OPERA IS A REAL KNOCKOUT

"Hugh the Drover" Has Canadian Cast, Fine Music and Stages Realistic Fight

By AUGUSTUS BRIDLE

New York may have its jazz opera, "Jonny," its Skyscrapers ballet and its "King's Henchman"; but since last night Toronto has "Hugh the Drover," by Vaughan Williams, the first performance in America except one little known production of it in Washington last year. Dr. MacMillan conducted. The production was what sporting men call a knockout. It created a sensation. It was the peak point, not only of this English festival, but, according to those who have seen all the other C.P.R. festivals—of all of them.

It was the best of all English operas conducted, produced, scene-painted, played in orchestra, costumed and sung by Canadians—all but the one principal, Allan Jones, in the title role. As presented last night it would have been a sensation even in the repertory of the American Opera. No apology for its Canadianism is needed. These people—mainly amateurs—made "Hugh the Drover" a real creation in spite of handicaps such as no opera of its calibre ever encountered on this continent. The stage had to be doubled in size, completely covering the orchestra pit; that put the orchestra on the floor level, partly masking the stage and effectively barraging a few of the solo parts and one or two choruses. A new fabric proscenium had to be built, that put a soft pedal on the tone. All the lighting had to be forwarded. The stage was twice too small for the production. There was only one stage entrance, which kept all the action starting and ending on one side. To cap the climax of handicap, the conductor's full orchestra score failed to arrive from Curwen in London, and Dr. MacMillan had to cue all the orchestra parts in from every separate player's score and use a vocal score for conducting.

Yet I doubt if there was ever any opera in America where so little change had to be made after a premiere. This is due to management, direction and talent engaged. Alfred Heather studied this opera inside out even more than he did the "Beggar," which he directed here on three occasions. He almost slept with this one. Upon occasion almost any principal at rehearsal was called to do the work of some other unavoidably absent. Randolph Crowe did four or five roles in succession.

Even the choristers knew most of the solo roles. Ever since Harvey Robb, chorus master, began to take up the score months ago, these singers began to master it in the spirit of the work. Allan Jones came here weeks ago to

199

rehearse continuously with chorus and cast; and, unlike some New York stars, he had learned his part before he came. Other members of the company got individual coaching from experts in Toronto. Arthur Lismer, who designed and painted the sets, did them in the spirit of Michael Angelo; and the second scene was as brilliant in design as the music itself. The women's costumes were designed, the colors selected and even fabrics dyed under the supervision of Mrs. Dr. MacMillan. By no means least, Dr. MacMillan, whose own idea it was to produce this opera at all in the festival, made it a work of absolute intensive mastery, so that his beat in the performance contained the whole vivid life of the opera. And he had an orchestra of many of the very best players in Toronto, with Frank Blachford as concert-master.

No wonder Murray Gibbon looked like a papal benediction and Eustace Key beamed like a rising sun when it was finished. The actual performance must be judged largely by what the opera is—a great piece of modern music skilfully woven into old English folk melodies, as the text was written from characters so realistic in old English life. The complex is difficult. Vaughan Williams has a Wagnerian respect for orchestra, and an Elgarian regard for chorus. He made every choral entry as baffling as it might be. He kept the chorus on stage more than half the time, and gave them something to do worth the doing.

The choruses alone are fine works: intensively modern and enharmonic, with an old-fashioned melodic rhythm throughout. The orchestration is rich and luxurious without being overwhelming. As opera, the thing is as big for English life as Tannhauser is for Germany. It is the life of England compressed into opera; the life of a nation that for centuries has been supposed to be incapable of opera.

Nothing more English has ever been done anywhere. Nothing more musical in any genre has ever been done in England. The choral and orchestral scoring of "Hugh the Drover" will stand up to Elgar's best. As a solo writer Williams far excels Elgar. And as an interpreter of English folk-song, characters and idioms, no English composer has ever quite equalled him.

All this put a big load on the company. And the load was well carried. One of the most exhilarating things was the rhythm and the movement of the chorus, on a stage only half big enough.

The solo roles are too numerous for detailed comment. The title role was superbly done by Allan Jones, who, as a daring rustic lover in a vagabond poetic role, was everything he should have been except for a slight lack of thrilling resonance in top notes. He is a splendid, eager young artist who fitted into every mood of the opera. Two of his airs were poetic masterpieces. Nellye Gill, as Mary, was always a fascination, and in climaxes her voice was thrilling against the ensemble.

Randolph Crowe was amazingly fine in action, character, acting and voice. He had never a moment without a mastery of what was wanted. The first fight of the drover and the butcher was a real one in two rounds, ending in a knockout; both men in bare pelts to the waist—and the whole fight set to music and conducted from the orchestra. After the fight the drover sings. How does he? Donald McLaren made a splendid constable; big, bluffing, sonorous in voice and comic in character. Fred Manning did brilliant work as the nimble showman. George Oldcroft had one fine song and business as sergeant and did it to the king's taste. Alfred Heather supplied pungent comedy as the Turnkey, and Henry Batton as the Fool was briefly a close second. Beatrice Morson as Aunt Jane was real in character and vocally equal to everything in the role.

The opera will be repeated next Monday evening to close the festival.

Star, Nov. 16, 1929
© Toronto Star Newspapers Ltd.   MTLB

WITH PICK AND SHOVEL

SLAMS AND SALVE — KNOCKS AND BOOSTS

By LOU E. MARSH

Flame is fleeting.

☆ ☆ ☆

Last year "Ace" Bailey and Andy Blair were the darlings of the gods—and the reserved sections, too—but in just two games "Sniper" Conacher has chased them out of the local hockey limelight.

☆ ☆ ☆

In fact the little brother of "Big Train" has grabbed all the Kleig sunshine and has already been elected to a mighty descriptive nickname—"Sniper."

☆ ☆ ☆

When he draws a bead the goalies just duck and pray.

☆ ☆ ☆

Three goals in two games is like learning to swim in a bathtub in July and then winning the Wrigley in August.

☆ ☆ ☆

And "Sniper's" head still fits his hat.

☆ ☆ ☆

And another youngster who will be right in there and make himself just as popular is young Gordie Brydson. All he needs is more chance. He isn't a five minute flash. Let him warm up and get rid of his smile, and then watch him go in and battle.

☆ ☆ ☆

If Playfair Brown wants a real headline attraction for his red-blooded "Six-Six" card on the Arena ice heap Friday night all he has to do is to step down to the Royal York and sign on Hugh the Drover and John the Butcher, a couple of light heavies.

☆ ☆ ☆

I saw them fight it out over the sheriff's daughter down there last night with bare knuckles—and what a pip of a battle it was!

☆ ☆ ☆

Hugh the Tremolo Tenor, was outweighed a full stone and had to give away a couple of octaves, but he wasn't a bit of scairt.

☆ ☆ ☆

In fact he was a hero and he had to win the blonde dame so he took on the Bauling Baritone at catch-weights, and no holds barred.

☆ ☆ ☆

In the first round he was knocked cuckoo and continued to fight from memory.

☆ ☆ ☆

In the second the Butcher slipped the knee into Hugh's ale department and little Hughie hit the floor in a bow knot with the ale coming out of his ears.

☆ ☆ ☆

The referee was a game little cuss outfitted with high baritone trimmings. He gave Hugh the bout on a foul and then ducked out of the ring before the Butcher could step on his ears.

☆ ☆ ☆

Hugh was still a hero despite the fact that he was still trying to pry his appendix loose from his eye teeth so he pipes up from the floor, "No, Mister Referee, let the fight go on. I'll lick the big slob or die."

☆ ☆ ☆

And he did. In the third round he hits the big bum under the chin and the Butcher boy takes a Koloff right clean out over the ropes.

☆ ☆ ☆

But the big sheep-sticker is game—I gotta give him that one. He comes back. His legs are full of gin but his fists are full of punch. He lets go a right. Hugh forgot to duck and the battle pretty near ended with the Battling Baritone a winner. That wasn't according to the book.

☆ ☆ ☆

But Highie is still game—and still the hero—and still groggy. He brought another right up from China and landed on the chop-cutter's chin. John went over the ropes so fast that he skinned his elbows, and he hit the floor so hard he finished out the piece as a soprano. He knocked him for a full flat.

☆ ☆ ☆

Anyway Hugh the Drover got the frill, but John the Butcher declares that he won on a luck punch and offers to fight him a return bout for charity.

☆ ☆ ☆

Here is your chance, Brown. Sign 'em up, and you'll have the best heavyweight scrap Toronto ever saw.

☆ ☆ ☆

Brown has a smart looking card of real battlers for Friday night but a return bout between Hugh and John would pack in a new crowd, especially if he also signed up Doc MacMillan as special master of ceremonies for this one bout.

☆ ☆ ☆

Roy Chisholm of the Soo, a former O.H.A. hockey player and referee, has started a hockey team.

☆ ☆ ☆

It's a girl.

☆ ☆ ☆

Belleville hockey fans are all excited over the new $115,000 artificial ice rink now nearing completion there. The new rink has an ice surface of 190 by 85 and will seat 3,500 with room for a thousand pairs of extra feet. William J. Hume is the man who made the rink possible. He tossed $50,000 into the pot. The opening game will be an N.H.L. tiff between Ottawa and Chicago Christmas night. That should pack them in.

☆ ☆ ☆

Did you ever hear the one about the Scotsman who smoked his cigar so short that a newsboy halted him to tell him that his chewing tobacco was on fire? This is one of Cliff Armstrong's specials.

☆ ☆ ☆

Keith Balfour tells one about a Scotsman and an Irishman who had an argument over which had the most brains, the Scots or the Irish. Sandy offered to prove his contention with a real experience. He said that his brother had had an accident and as a result his brains had all been removed. He escaped from the hospital and they found him years later teaching school over in Ireland.

Star, Nov. 19, 1929
© Toronto Star Newspapers Ltd.   MTLB

APPEARANCES

1929   *Hugh the Drover*

1931
EATON AUDITORIUM

Imagine Toronto without the auditorium for those forty-six years!

EATON'S COLLEGE STREET STORE
opened on October 30, 1930.

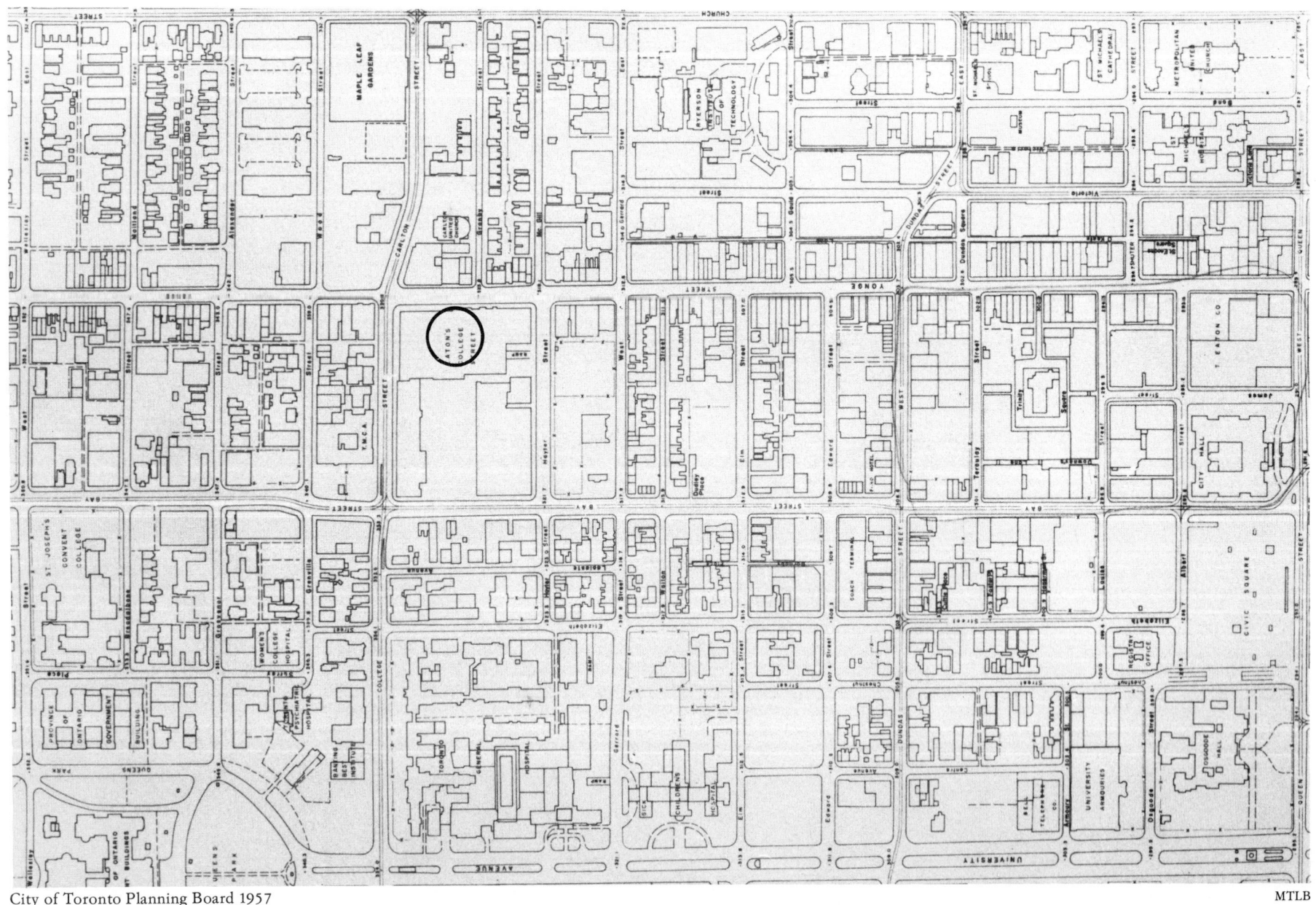

City of Toronto Planning Board 1957

MTLB

EATON AUDITORIUM

When the Eaton family opened its beautiful new store at Yonge and College Streets on October 30, 1930, the auditorium and restaurant, which were to be the showplaces of the building, were not yet completed. French interior designer Jacques Carlu, one of the outstanding exponents of the new "Art Deco" was chosen to design the seventh floor. On March 26, 1931, the 1014-seat auditorium with walls of pale gold fabricoid, bird's eye maple panelling and lighting set between bands of ebonized wood, was officially opened. The acoustics proven as excellent as those of Massey Hall. The opening event was a recital by soprano Florence Austral and, at the organ, young Torontonian Ernest MacMillan.

The occasion was sponsored by St. Dunstan's Chapter IODE and the season's debutantes served as ushers. For nearly 50 years events at the audtorium maintained an aura of elegance and dignity.

The contribution to the musical and operatic life of Toronto is inestimable. The Variety Series, the Concert Series, the Artists Series and the Musical Arts Series brought the great contemporary artists in concerts. When the famous stars became too expensive their places were taken by travelogues, opera performances by the Royal Conservatory Opera School and by the Salzburg Marionettes, and concerts sponsored by groups such as the Women's Musical Club which presented promising artists. The last concert to be given under the aegis of the Women's Musical Club featured I Soloisti di Zagreb on March 10, 1977.

The Auditorium, combined with the huge foyer and the Round Room Restaurant, was admirably suited to activities other than concerts, e.g. balls, festivals and exhibitions. For many years St. Clement's School held its Annual Closing here and, before permanent seating was installed, the Constance Waugh Chapter IODE presented the Frosty Frolic for secondary school students at Christmas time.

The last public event was the appearance of the *Farband Jewish Review* on March 26, 1977. Since then much has been said for and against retaining the theatre – the Toronto Historical Board has designated the building a historical landmark – and its fate is still undecided.

THE AUDITORIUM

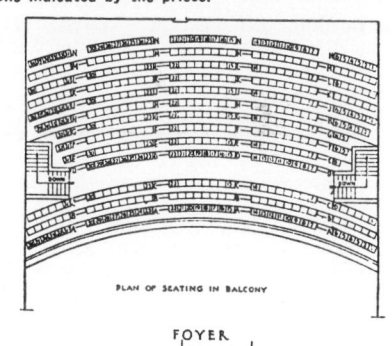

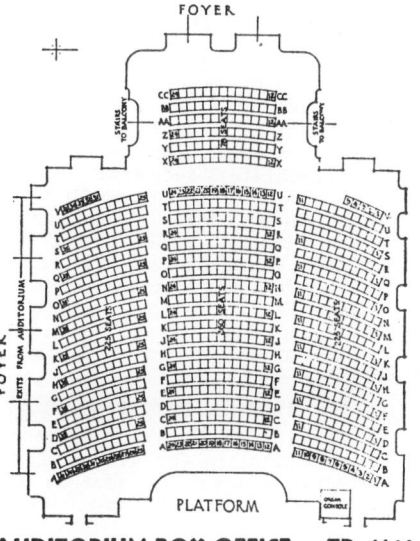

EATON AUDITORIUM

EATON'S NEW AUDITORIUM TO BE OPENED BY I.O.D.E.

St. Dunstan's Chapter Plans Large Entertainment Under Patronage of Lieutenant-Governor and Mrs. Ross—Ward One Conservatives to Hold Huge Party at Royal York

The most striking thing about next week's social program is the great activity of Toronto's I.O.D.E. chapters, who are engineering a series of entertainments in aid of their philanthropic work. One of these, the reception and concert under the auspices of the St. Dunstan's Chapter, will be one of the largest and most interesting affairs of the whole Lenten season. The date is Thursday night, and the setting is Eaton's College St. Auditorium, which will be opened in this spectacular fashion under the distinguished patronage of his honor the lieutenant-governor and Mrs. William D. Ross.

The other patrons and patronesses include the Hon. George S. Henry and Mrs. Henry, Sir Joseph and Lady Flavelle, Col. and Mrs. A. E. Gooderham, Lady Eaton, Col. and Mrs. R. Y. Eaton, Col. and Mrs. Harry McGee, Mrs. Josephine S. Burnside, Sir Thomas and Lady White, Mrs. C. E. Burden, Mr. L. M. Wood, Mrs. Lionel H. Clarke, Lady Baillie, Lady Kemp, Mrs. George Dickson and his worship the mayor.

The new auditorium will seat 1,200 guests, and not a vacant seat will be left on the night of the opening. One of its most important features is the new organ, on which the opening selection will most fittingly be played by Dr. Ernest McMillan. The other artists will be Madame Florence Austral, soprano, and her husband, Amodeo Austral, flautist.

Mrs. Wallace Barrett, regent of the chapter, and Mrs. Bartlett Rogers, general convener, will be waiting in one of the private rooms on the seventh floor to receive the patrons and patronesses when they arrive on Thursday evening. On the other reception committees receiving upstairs will be Mrs. A. L. Ellsworth, Mrs. Horace Hunter, Mrs. Cecil Trotter and Mrs. Harry Love, and downstairs, Mrs. John Fraser, Mrs. Lawrence Harris, Mrs. Arthur Meighen and Mrs. W. J. Elliott. Assisting them will be Mrs. George Mitchell, Mrs. Fred Morrow, Mrs. D. A. MacKay and Mrs. Thomas Eakin.

Art Moderne Decorations

The beautiful hall, which is decorated throughout in the art moderne, in accordance with the rest of the seventh floor, will be enhanced that evening with palms and ferns, and a wealth of cut flowers. There will be a bevy of debutantes and other members of Toronto's younger set to assist in the seating of the guests, their names including the Misses Evelyn and Mary Booth, Miss Frances Wisner, Miss Betty Long, Miss Doris Long, Miss Kathleen Hobbs, Miss Dorothy Harding, Miss Ann Wright, Miss Peggy Harris, Miss Madeleine Wills, Miss Helen Eakin, Miss Joyce Lyon, Miss Isobel Pepall, Miss Helen McCrea, Misses Mary and Mabel Dunlop, Miss Mary Finlayson, Miss Elizabeth Hamilton, Miss Dorothy Campbell, Miss Mary Jarvis and Miss Ruth Vaughan. Mrs. H. G. Dingman is their convener, assisted by Mrs. Gordon Wills.

At the conclusion of the concert, the guests will have the opportunity of strolling around a bit, and inspecting the hall, while in the foyer, and in the attractive College St. restaurant, a buffet supper will be served, from long tables, beautifully arranged with flowers. Mrs. William Gale is in charge of all supper arrangements, assisted by a committee of twelve of the chapter members.

All the proceeds of the concert will be devoted to the excellent work carried on by the chapter in the service of the blind and along the lines of education. Mrs. J. J. Vaughan is in charge of all the tickets.

Star Weekly, March 21, 1931

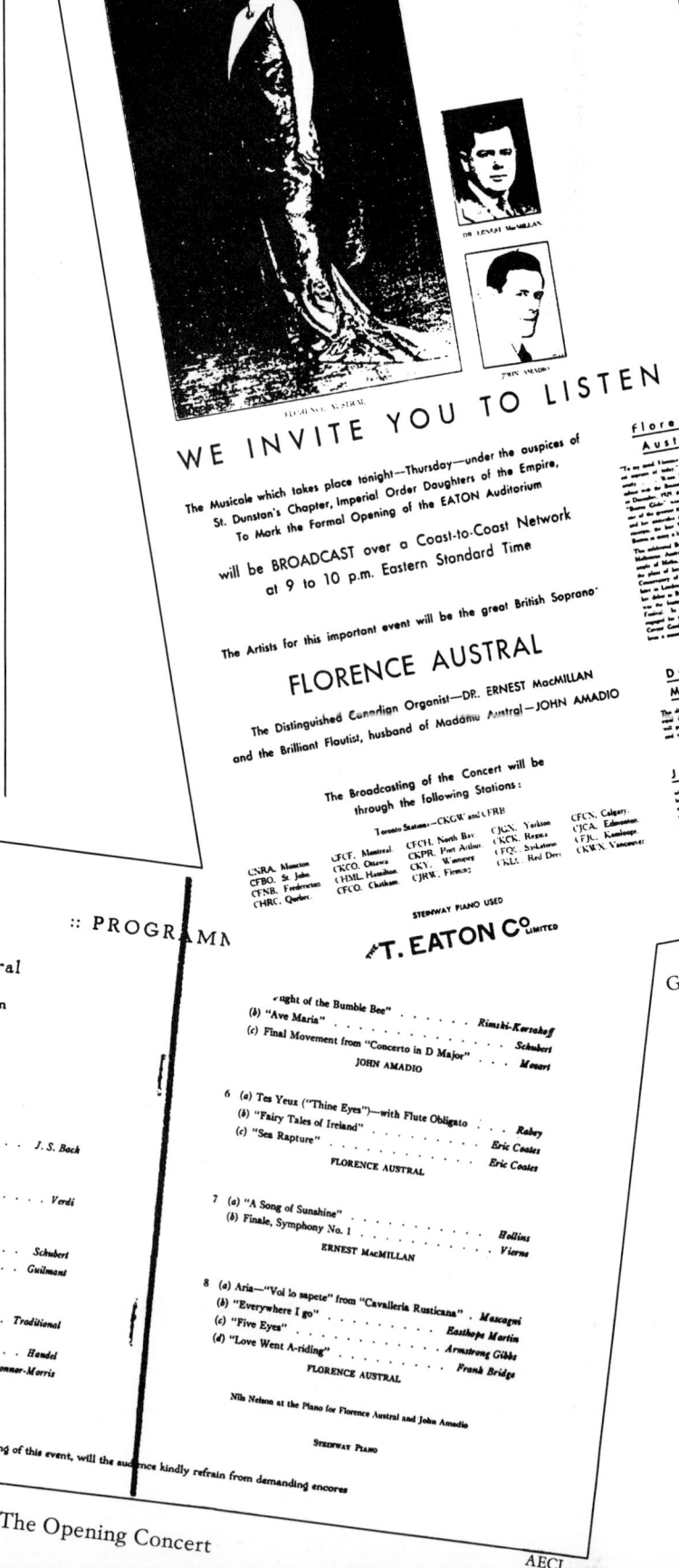

Globe, March 26, 1931

From the programme

The Opening Concert

EATON AUDITORIUM

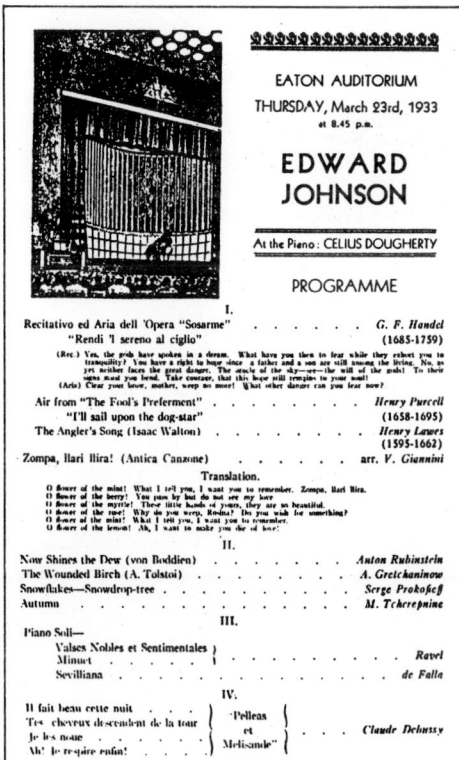

From the programme — AECL

Canadian tenor, EDWARD JOHNSON, 1933, 1934.

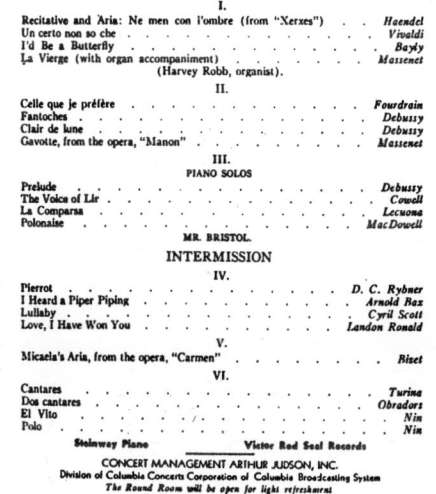

From the programme — AECL

Programme cover — AECL

Spanish soprano, LUCREZIA BORI, 1933.

Wimodausis Theatre Night, December 13, 1933. — AECL

EATON AUDITORIUM

American Tenor, RICHARD CROOKS
1934, 1938, 1940, 1941, 1944, 1945.

Norwegian soprano, KIRSTEN
FLAGSTAD, 1935, 1936, 1938, 1940.

French soprano, LILY PONS, 1936.

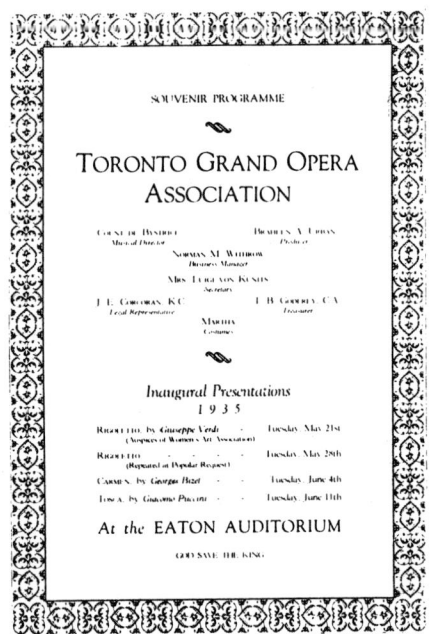

Programme cover — COCA

From the "Prom" programme, June 18, 1936.

American Tenor JAMES MELTON,
1936, 1945.

From the programme — AECL

EATON AUDITORIUM

Opera Guild Arrives: At left is Maria Merlo, Italian coloratura soprano, who sings the lead in Rossini's "The Matrimonial Market." Centre are, left to right: Von Thosvay, Hungarian contralto; Hedwig Treer, well known in all leading musical centres in Europe, and Aurora Dolci, dramatic soprano from Czechoslovakia. At the left is Ernst Krenek, who will conduct the Wednesday night premiere of the revival of "The Coronation of Poppea," by Monteverdi.—Staff Photos.

Globe and Mail, Nov. 1, 1937

Music & Drama DEPARTMENT
Conducted by LAWRENCE MASON

ONE OF OLDEST OPERAS.

Seventeenth Century Work Finely Given at Auditorium.

"The Coronation of Poppea," a little-known masterpiece by Claudio Monteverdi now nearly 300 years old, was revived at Eaton Auditorium last night by the Salzburg Opera Company in a carefully wrought modern recension by Ernst Krenek. The simple music of that elder day was rather overwhelmed by a modern orchestra, but the original shone through quite clearly in the closes, the clear melodic outlines, and the pensive recitatives, while the composer's genuinely dramatic power seemed to be not immeasurably far behind Gluck's. The opera was beautifully given, of course, with adroitly managed stagecraft, effective acting, admirable singing, and a most satisfying projection of the appropriately classical atmosphere. A high spot was the impressive sincerity and dignity of Seneca's death-scene.

Matinee Performance.

At the matinee yesterday afternoon Ibert's "Angelique" was repeated, and Rossini's charming little buffonada in one act, "The Matrimonial Market," was added. Sparkling music, handsome costumes, a highly ingenious scenic setting, and a much mirthful comedy in situation and by-play, made the latter a delightful little gem. An outstanding feature, of course, was "Slook of Canada," a wealthy merchant from the Dominion in A.D. 1810 who, alas, puts his feet on the table and kisses gentlemen on both cheeks, but who also most benevolently saves the day for the young lovers.—L. M.

Globe and Mail, Nov. 4, 1937

EATON AUDITORIUM

Monday, Tuesday and Wednesday
November 1st, 2nd and 3rd, at 8.30 o'clock
with Matinee, Wednesday, at 2.30 o'clock

Salzburg Opera Guild

PAUL CSONKA . . . . General Director
ALBERTO EREDE . . . . . . Musical Director
EUGENE SCHULZ-BREIDEN . . Stage Director

Programme Cover

Monday Evening, November 1st, at 8.30 o'clock
Under Patronage of The Women's Musical Club of Toronto

COSI FAN TUTTE
Opera Buffo in Two Acts

Music by Wolfgang Amadeus Mozart
Libretto by Lorenzo da Ponte

Conductor . . . . . . Alberto Erede
Stage Director . . . . Eugene Schulz-Breiden

CAST

Fiordiligi	Grete Menzel
Dorabella	Herta Glatz
Despina	Marisa Merlo
Ferrando	Franco Perulli
Guglielmo	Leo Weith
Alfonso	Desso Ernster

Soldiers, servants, musicians, boatmen, wedding guests, etc.
The action takes place in Naples

SYNOPSIS

ACT I

Ferrando and Guglielmo extol the constancy of their sweethearts to Alfonso, a skeptic. Alfonso insists that they are no more faithful in their affections, than any other woman, and wagers to demonstrate the fact. Ferrando and Guglielmo shall act as the tempters, and he will be the impressario of the comedy.

Alfonso arranges to have them summoned to war. There are tearful leave takings, vows of constancy, lamentations and grief.

They reappear in Oriental disguise, sponsored by Alfonso with the connivance of Despina, servant of the ladies. Each attaches himself to the other's betrothed, and protests violent love. The ladies are adamant, deaf to pleas and cajolery. The cavaliers vow that they will commit suicide, without impressing the two ladies, Dorabella and Fiordiligi. Finally they drain bottles labeled poison, and are revived by Despina in the guise of a doctor. Still the ladies remain disinterested, to the considerable delight of their lovers who flaunt their lack of success before Alfonso. He warns them, however, that the time agreed for the test has not yet elapsed.

ACT II

Ferrando and Guglielmo return to the attack. Under the taunts of Despina, the ladies consent to see them again. Finally Dorabella yields to the ardor of Guglielmo, and Ferrando, furious, assails Fiordiligi with more passionate avowals of love. At length she too wavers and succumbs.

The men meet again, each greatly distressed with the other's success. But Alfonso reappears to console them, rather more cynically than sympathetically. He arranges to have them appear again in their proper persons after assuring the lovers that the conduct of their fiancees is by no means exceptional—"Cosi fan tutte"—"So do they all"—Amid the proper contriteness, the opera ends with a double wedding.

Musical Assistant . . . . . . Walter Taussig
Stage Assistant . . . . . . Dr. Hans Neufeld
Scenery and Costumes . . . . Teo Otto

The Round Room will be open at the conclusion of the Evening Performance for Buffet Supper and Reception by the Executive of the Women's Musical Club and the Members of the Company. Tickets obtainable in the Foyer, 35c.

Tuesday Evening, November 2nd, at 8.30 o'clock
Under the Patronage of The Toronto Women's Press Club

LE PAUVRE MATELOT
(The Poor Sailor)
(In French)

Music by DARIUS MILHAUD
Libretto by Jean Cocteau

Conductor . . . . . . Alberto Erede
Stage Director . . . . Eugene Schulz-Breiden

CAST

The Sailor	Hans Joachim Heinz
His Wife	Herta Glatz
His Father-in-law	Ljubomir Pantscheff
The Friend	Leo Weith

SYNOPSIS

The sailor has been absent from his home and wife for fifteen years. It is supposed that he is drowned. His father-in-law advises the wife to remarry, but she is not convinced of her husband's death. His best friend urges her to forget and marry him, but she remains faithful to the missing man.

Suddenly, the sailor returns. He visits his friend to inquire after his wife. Torn by doubts of her fidelity, the sailor defers the reunion and calls upon her in disguise.

Posing as the sailor's friend, he tells her that her missing husband is alive, longs to return, but is ridden with debt. Surely a woman as attractive as she should have no difficulty in obtaining money for the husband she loves—he who had sacrificed so much to his marriage vows! Her husband had been offered fabulous treasure to renounce his wife, but had refused. In proof, the visitor produces a pearl necklace, gift of a mythical benefactor. Afraid to trust his jewels in the village, he asks to be allowed to sleep in her house. The wife consents, and the guest retires.

The pain of her misfortune besets her. Images of her ill-plighted husband, visions of the precious necklace dance on her brain. Suddenly she rises. With chilling deliberations, she murders her sleeping guest.

Musical Assistant . . . . . . Walter Taussig
Stage Assistant . . . . . . Dr. Hans Neufeld
Scenery and Costumes . . . . Eugene Schulz-Breiden

The Round Room will be open at the conclusion of the Evening Performance for Buffet Supper and Reception by the Toronto Women's Press Club and the Members of the Company. Tickets obtainable in the Foyer, 35c.

From the programme

EATON AUDITORIUM

German soprano, LOTTE LEHMANN, 1938, 1946, 1948, 1951.

American mezzo-soprano, RISE STEVENS, 1941, 1942.

American soprano, ELEANOR STEBER, 1941, 1956.

Brazilian soprano, BIDU SAYAO, 1938, "crystal voice, immaculate diction, impeccable musical sound". Columnist and connoisseur, Clyde Gilmour.

American contralto, MARIAN ANDERSON, 1938, 1939, 1940, 1942, 1944, 1948, 1950, 1951, 1953, 1955, 1960.

From the programme — Salzburg Opera Guild

From the programme — Salzburg Opera Guild

EATON AUDITORIUM

EATON AUDITORIUM

THE TORONTO CHILDREN'S OPERATIC SOCIETY

PRESENTS

"CINDERELLA"

SATURDAY EVENING, May 16th, 1942
at 8.30 o'clock

CORDA WARD BUCHNER, Musical Director
AMELIA ROBERTS, Dramatic Director

ACT I.—Drawing Room in Cinderella's Home.
ACT II.—Scene I.—Kitchen in Cinderella's Home.
  Scene II.—Ball-room in Prince's Palace.
  Scene III.—Kitchen in Cinderella's Home.
ACT III.—Prince's Palace.

CHARACTERS

(Note:—The small number denotes age of child).

"Cinderella" . . . . Marjorie Heaton (17)
"Fairy God-mother" . . . . Joyce Jennings (11)
"Priscilla" } Cinderella's Ugly Step-sisters . Peter Wakeling (17)
"Jane" } . . . . Kenneth Genge (13)
"Step-mother" . . . . . . Margaret Cunneyworth (13)
"Prince" . . . . Beth MacDonald (12)
"Baron Goodheart" (Cinderella's Father) . Ronald Grimes (15)
"Herald" . . . . Jim Mitchell (15)
"Lurline" } Fairy God-mother's Assistants { Margaret Sands (14)
"Symphony" } . . . . { Betty Smith (12)
"Chelseabun" . . . . "Jim" Scott (12)
"Marrowbone" . . . . . . Gordon Gregory (13)
 { "Gwen" Barker (7)
"Mice" . . . . { Janey Barton (4)
 { Dorothy Farmer (4)
 { Willa Simpson (8)

Chorus:—Guests, Fairies, Villagers, Soldiers, Pages.
Joan Bain (10), Barbara Barton (7), Muriel Barton (13), Joan Eastwood (11), Phyllis Genge (6), Velma Goldstone (9), Peggy-Ann Green (8), Sheila Hood (14), Betty Kelk (14), Margaret Lauder (10), Frances Leonard (10), Joyce McKay (13), Marion Norris (10), Betty Rickards (11), Marion Stephens (14), Kenneth Gregory (8), Arthur Scott (8), Albert Simpson (10).

REGISTRAR . . . . . WINIFRED TOMLINSON
COSTUMES . . . . EDITH WAKELING

For tickets and information, Telephone Auditorium Box Office, TRinity 1144.
RESERVED SEATS: $1.00, 75c AND 50c; TAX EXTRA

From the programme AECL

American tenor, JAN PEERCE, 1942, 1955. AECL

Baritone POUL BAI, Director of the Canadian Mastersingers in *Faust*, as Scarpia in the Toronto Grand Opera Association's Tosca, 1935. COCA

EATON AUDITORIUM — ARTISTS SERIES

Metropolitan Opera Artists Ensemble

JARMILA NOVOTNA, Soprano   HERTA GLAZ, Contralto
RAOUL JOBIN, Tenor   MARTIAL SINGHER, Baritone
LEO MULLER at the Piano

Fri. and Sat. Ev'gs, March 16 and 17, at 8.45 o'clock

1945 JPB

Under the Auspices of the Civic Theatre Association

The Canadian Mastersingers

Presents

"FAUST"

(In English)

Directed by Poul Bai
Orchestra conducted by Clarence Causton

THE EATON AUDITORIUM
TORONTO

Monday, November 19th, 1945
8.30 p.m.

Programme Cover AECL

The Philadelphia Opera Company's performance of Johann Strauss's *The Bat* in 1943.

AECL

Metropolitan Stars Superb in Concert

By HECTOR CHARLESWORTH

Four of the ablest artists of the Metropolitan Opera House appeared at Eaton Auditorium last night in an old-fashioned operatic concert, varied by the circumstance that all numbers were presented in costume. Tasteful costumes they were; and the plan had the advantage of permitting the artists to act the episodes as well as sing them. At least three of the group have high status in the field of dramatic interpretation.

The two women of the quartet, Jarmila Novotna, soprano, and Herta Glaz, contralto, are well known locally, through concert appearances—Miss Glaz especially. Raoul Jobyn, the distinguished Canadian tenor, and Marcel Singher, the superb French baritone, made their debuts here in the Metropolitan productions at Massey Hall last September, when Mr. Singher's Pelleas and Valentine were memorable.

Of the seven numbers on the program that which was most impressive was the renunciation scene from Act II of Verdi's "Traviata," when Violetta is persuaded by her lover's father to give up living with him. The pathos Novotna put into her tones was exquisitely touching, and Singher was equally beautiful in utterance.

The program contained a novelty which few in the audience, if any, had heard. Over a century ago the German composer, Otto Nicolai, wrote a comic opera based on "The Merry Wives of Windsor," of which only the overture has survived. Last night the scene in which Mistress Page and Mistress Ford compare Falstaff's letters was presented by Novotna and Glaz. The music is gay and sparkling, and the acting of the two women was enchanting.

The concert began with a most expressive declamation of the Prologue from "Pagliacci" by Marcel Singher. It was followed by the temptation scene from Act II of Massenet's "Manon," in which the prospective priest forgets his prayers when love calls. Novotna in her powdered wig and pompadour costume was a beautiful picture and put seduction into every tone she sang. Mr. Jobyn has a robust tenor voice of smooth and fervent quality, delightful to listen to even when his acting is wooden.

(Continued

EATON AUDITORIUM

It was the fate of Jobyn to be tempted several times last night. He appeared with Herta Glaz in a lengthy telescoped scene from Saint-Saens' "Sanson et Dalila," and looked rather hairy though his tones were admirable. Miss Glaz sang both Dalila's famous arias with passionate appeal, and a third figure was Singher, impressive as the High Priest.

The tenor and the contralto were heard again in a scene from Act II of "Carmen" when the gipsy lures Jose from duty. Jobyn sang the Rose song with beautiful warmth of utterance, and Miss Glaz was a real siren, expert with castenets. All four artists gave a beautiful rendering of the lovely "Good-Night" quartet from Flotow's "Martha."

Leo Miller, substituting for an orchestra on a grand piano, gave an able account of himself.

Globe and Mail, March 17, 1945   JPB

Incomparable and unforgettable Swedish tenor, JUSSI BJOERLING, 1946, 1950.   AECL

English soprano, MAGGIE TEYTE (DBE 1958), 1946.   AECL

Programme cover   COCA
1948

English Contralto KATHLEEN FERRIER, 1950.

Royal Conservatory of Music Diamond Jubilee Festival Programme, April 30, 1947.   AECL

Programme cover   PW
1947

Programme cover   AECL
1949

Programme cover   AECL
1949

EATON AUDITORIUM

AECL

Yugoslav Dramatic soprano, ZINKA MILANOV sang with Swedish tenor SET SVANHOLM in 1952.

AECL

American baritone, LEONARD WARREN, 1951, 1952, 1957.

1948

ROSSELINO OPERA COMPANY

PRESENTS

VON FLOTOW'S

MARTHA

AT
EATON AUDITORIUM
TORONTO
WEDNESDAY, MAY 19th, 1948
8.15 P.M.

Programme cover — AECL

"OPERA BACKSTAGE"

with stage director

Herman Geiger Torel

assisted by

Beth Corrigan — Soprano
Marguerite Gignac — Soprano
June Kowalchuk — Soprano
Mary Morrison — Soprano
Louise Roy — Soprano

Jimmy Shields — Tenor
Ernest Adams — Baritone
Gilles Lamontagnes — Baritone
Andrew MacMillan — Bass-Baritone

George Crum at the Piano

Eaton Auditorium, Toronto

Tuesday Evening, October 31st, 1950

PROGRAMME:

I. CURSE
(a) RIGOLETTO — G. Verdi
  Andrew MacMillan, Gilles Lamontagnes
(b) FAUST — Ch. Gounod
  Marguerite Gignac, Gilles Lamontagnes

II. MURDER
(a) DON GIOVANNI — W. A. Mozart
  Andrew MacMillan
(b) TOSCA — G. Puccini
  Andrew MacMillan

III. VENGEANCE
(a) MARRIAGE OF FIGARO — W. A. Mozart
  Ernest Adams
(b) RIGOLETTO — G. Verdi
  June Kowalchuk, Gilles Lamontagnes

INTERMISSION

IV. LOVE DEATH
(a) ORPHEUS AND EURIDICE — Ch. W. Gluck
  Louise Roy, Mary Morrison
(b) TRISTAN AND ISOLDE — R. Wagner
  Louise Roy

V. RENDEZVOUS
(a) PAGLIACCI — R. Leoncavallo
  Mary Morrison, Ernest Adams
(b) MARRIAGE OF FIGARO — W. A. Mozart
  Marguerite Gignac, Ernest Adams

VI. JEALOUSY
(a) MARRIAGE OF FIGARO — W. A. Mozart
  Andrew MacMillan
(b) PAGLIACCI — R. Leoncavallo
  James Shields
(c) LA BOHEME — G. Puccini
  Mary Morrison, Beth Corrigan, James Shields, Ernest Adams

Steinway Piano

HERMAN GEIGER TOREL

German born, Herman Geiger Torel, has, since 1928, directed opera in Germany, Austria, Czechoslovakia, and Switzerland. In 1938, he went to Argentina as stage director of the famous Teatro Colon in Buenos Aires. This was followed, in 1943, by appointment as stage director to the State Theatre in Montevideo, where he also directed the Opera School of the National Conservatory of Music and lectured in opera and the history of music at the University. In 1945, he became stage director of the Municipal Theatre in Rio de Janeiro and director of the Opera School of the Brazilian Conservatory.

He came to Canada in 1948 to become stage director to the Royal Conservatory Opera School in Toronto and later to the Royal Conservatory Opera Company. He is also artistic advisor of the CBC Opera Company. Since 1948, Mr. Geiger Torel divides his activities between Canada during the winter season and South America in the summer.

Mr. Geiger Torel was a pupil of the late Dr. Lothar Wallerstein, famous stage director of the Vienna Opera House, La Scala in Milan and the Metropolitan Opera. His original intention was to be a conductor and towards that end he conducted many concerts from the age of sixteen until he was twenty. But after completing his studies at the Frankfort University and at the Frankfort Conservatory of Music, he decided to dedicate himself almost exclusively to stage direction of opera and drama.

He has been a theatre and motion picture actor, and his musical background and wide theatrical experience have made him one of the best known opera stage directors on this continent.

From the programme — 1950 — AECL

EATON AUDITORIUM

CHARLES L. WAGNER

presents

ROMEO et JULIETTE

Grand Opera

★

Saturday, November 13th, 1948, at 8.30 p.m.

Programme cover

Charles L. Wagner presents

ROMEO et JULIETTE

OPERA IN FOUR ACTS
(in French)

BOOK BY JULES BARBER AND MICHEL CARRE
MUSIC BY CHARLES GOUNOD

• • •

Characters in Order of Appearance

Tybalt, nephew to Count Capulet ... Edward Nyborg
Count Capulet ... Livingston Smith
Juliette, his daughter ... Marguerite McClelland
Mercutio ... William Shriner
Gertrude, Juliette's nurse ... Lizabeth Pritchett
Romeo, a Montague ... Jon Crain
Gregorio, a Capulet retainer ... Denis Harbour
Friar Laurent ... William Wilderman
Stephano, page to Romeo ... Jean Rifino
Duke of Verona ... Reginald Nichols

Act I Divertissement by Mary Martinet, ballerina and Marc Beaudet, premier dancer

Musical Director, Walter Ducloux   Artistic Director, Desire Defrere
Concert Master, Diez Weismann

ENSEMBLE:—Alice Arnold, Olga Christie, Teresa Giuliano, Ann Kepic, Patricia King, Barbara Lewis, Charlotte Lyons, Alice Movitz, Louise Shriner, Sara Wilson, Jean Dubois, Edward Graham, Joseph Hancock, Frank Hart, Joseph Marchand, Harold Michener, Mathew Powers, James Vitale, Charles Williams, James Morrissey.

SYNOPSIS OF SCENES

PLACE: Verona
TIME: 14th century

ACT I. The Ballroom of the Capulets, at night
ACT II. Garden of the Capulet's Palace
ACT III. SCENE 1. Friar Laurent's Cell
     SCENE 2. A Street in Verona
ACT IV. SCENE 1. Juliette's Chamber
     SCENE 2. The Tomb of Juliette

STAFF FOR MESSRS. WAGNER AND SNOWDON

Company Manager ... Fred Cuneo
Wardrobe Mistress ... Elinor Alexander
Carpenter ... Ray Wilson
Electrician ... Edward Brennan
Property Man ... John McCarthy
Orchestral Contractor ... Joseph Fabbroni

Costumes by STIVANELLO-CULCASI, New York City
Scenery by CIRKER & ROBBINS, New York City
Lighting by COLUMBIA STAGE LIGHTING CO., New York City

For the season 1949-1950, Charles L. Wagner and Edward W. Snowdon will present the ever-popular double bill CAVALLERIA RUSTICANA and IL PAGLIACCI

From the programme — AECL

The New PLAY SOCIETY

"... to establish a living theatre in Canada on a professional but non-profit basis."

presents

"CINDERELLA"

(Or The Glass Slipper)

by

HERBERT AND ELEANOR FARJEON

WITH MUSIC BY CLIFTON PARKER

Stage Production adapted and directed

by

HERMAN GEIGER-TOREL

Musical Director: Mario Bernardi   Dance Director: Gweneth Lloyd

Saturday Matinee, December 26, to January 9

Matinees First Week—Monday, Tuesday, Wednesday, Thursday, Friday and Saturday at 2.30 p.m.
Matinees Second Week—Wednesday and Saturday at 2.30 p.m.
Evenings—8.00 p.m.

EATON AUDITORIUM

Programme cover — 1953 — AECL

EATON AUDITORIUM

Italian soprano, LICIA ALBANESE, 1953, 1958.

Flyer COCA
1956

Programme cover AECL

German soprano, ELISABETH SCHWARZKOPF, 1954, 1955, 1957, 1975.

SELECTED APPEARANCES
CONCERT

1931 Florence Austral and Ernest MacMillan
1933 Lucrezia Bori
1935-7 Variety Series
1933-60 Concert Series
1938-50 Artists Series
1944-50 Musical Arts Series
Some of the Operatic Artists Presented:- by the Eaton Auditorium Series.
Marian Anderson, Salvatore Baccaloni, Jussi Bjoerling, John Brownlee, Richard Crooks, Helen Jepson, Kirsten Flagstad, Claire Gagnier, Herta Glatz, Anna Kaskas, Alexander Kipnis, Charles Kullman, Marjorie Lawrence, Lotte Lehmann, Martha Lipton, Nino Martini, Lauritz Melchior, James Melton, Zinka Milanov, Lina Pagliughi, Lily Pons, Rosa Ponselle, Jan Pearce, Ezio Pinza, Elisabeth Rethberg, Erna Sack, Set Svanholm, Gladys Swarthout, Elisabeth Schwarzkopf, Ferruccio Tagliavini, Maggie Teyte, Blanche Thebom, John Charles Thomas, Thomas L. Thomas, Kerstin Thorborg, Lawrence Tibbett, Jennie Tourel, Helen Traubel, Richard Tucker, Ernesto Vinci, Leonard Warren, Portia White.
by the Women's Musical Club
Marian Anderson, Donald Bell, Dietrich Fischer-Dieskau, Maureen Forrester, Ernst Haefliger, Ingmar Korjus, Christa Ludwig, J. Campbell McInnis, Herman Prey, Leontyne Price, Ebe Stignani, Benita Valente.
by the York Concert Society – Dr. Heinz Unger
Elizabeth Benson Guy, Maureen Forrester, James Milligan, Jan Rubes.

OPERATIC

1931 An Evening of French Opera Comique
1932 Eaton Operatic Society
1933 Eaton Operatic Society
1934 Eaton Operatic Society
1935 Eaton Operatic Society
1936 Eaton Operatic Society
1937 Eaton Operatic Society
1938 Eaton Operatic Society
1932 Bohemian Light Opera Company
1933 Bride Ship
1933 Teatro Dei Piccoli
1935 Toronto Grand Opera Association
1937 Salzburg Opera Guild
1939 Eaton Operatic Society
1940 Eaton Operatic Society
1940 The Choral Group
1941 Eaton Operatic Society
1942 Eaton Operatic Society
1942 Toronto Children's Operatic Society
1943 Canada Packers Operatic Society
1943 Eaton Operatic Society
1943 Toronto Children's Operatic Society
1944 Canada Packers Operatic Society
1944 Eaton Operatic Society
1944 Toronto Children's Operatic Society
1944 Baccaloni Opera Company
1944 Rosselino Opera Company
1945 Rosselino Opera Company
1945 Eaton Operatic Society
1945 Canada Packers Operatic Society
1945 Metropolitan Opera Artists Ensemble
1945 Toronto Children's Operatic Society
1946 Canada Packers Operatic Society
1946 Eaton Operatic Society
1947 Canada Packers Operatic Society
1947 Eaton Operatic Society
1947 Royal Conservatory Opera School
1947 Rosselino Opera Company
1948 Royal Conservatory Opera School
1948 Canada Packers Operatic Society
1948 Rosselino Opera Company
1948 Charles Wagner – *Romeo and Juliette*
1949 Canada Packers Opera Society
1949 Eaton Operatic Society
1949 Royal Conservatory Opera School
1949 Rosselino Opera Company
1950 Eaton Operatic Society
1950 Royal Conservatory Opera School
1951 Eaton Operatic Society
1951 Opera with the Toronto Philharmonic Choir
1951 Philharmonic Choir *Bartered Bride*
1951 Opera with the Toronto Philharmonic Choir
1952 Eaton Operatic Society
1952 Salzburg Marionettes
1953 Canada Packers Operatic Society
1953 Eaton Operatic Society
1954 Canada Packers Operatic Society
1954 Eaton Operatic Society
1955 Canada Packers Operatic Society
1956 Eaton Operatic Society
1956 Canadian Music Association & Canadian League of Composers
1957 Eaton Operatic Society
1958 Eaton Operatic Society
1959 Eaton Operatic Society
1960 Eaton Operatic Society
1961 Eaton Operatic Society
1962 Eaton Operatic Society
1963 Eaton Operatic Society
1964 Eaton Operatic Society
1965 Eaton Operatic Society
1971 Salzburg Marionettes

1936
VARSITY ARENA

Remember the happy days of the Prom Concerts?

Completed 1924

VARSITY ARENA

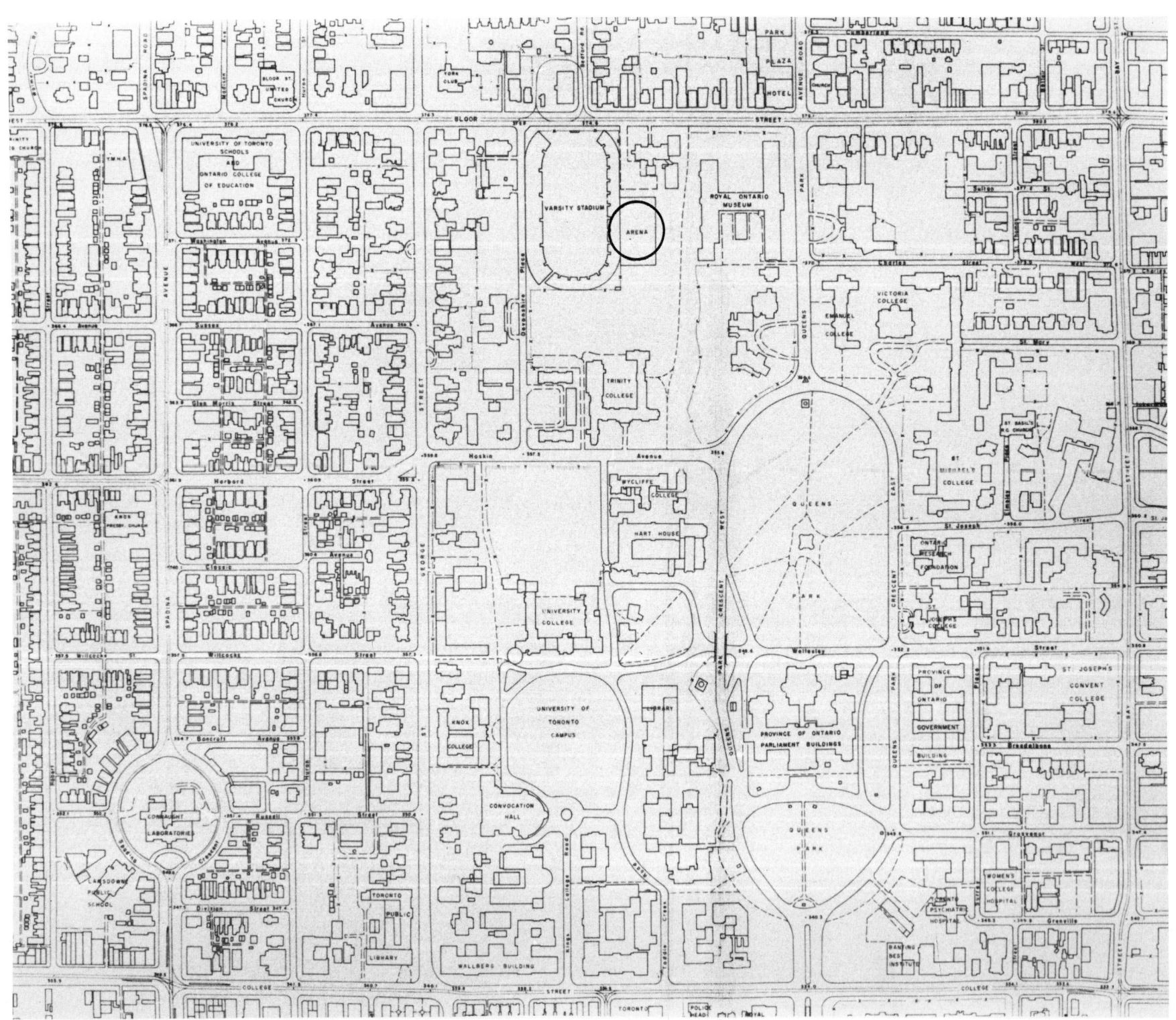

City of Toronto Planning Board, 1957

VARSITY ARENA

The present VARSITY ARENA was completed in 1924. In 1934 conductor Reginald Stewart formed an orchestra which was to give summer concerts ("The Prom Concerts") in the Arena. Many noted artists and conductors appeared between the years 1934 and 1956. The heat in the arena was intense on occasion but audiences were not discouraged – the habitues carried fans and the newcomers used their programmes – and during the intermissions a general promenade took place on the grass of Varsity Stadium. The Opera Guild of Toronto gave one act of *Tosca* in 1936 and a full production of *Cavalleria Rusticana* in 1941.

Football.

VARSITY ALREADY PREPARING.

The Varsity boys are called back for their first practice by the 12th of September. The majority of last year's three teams will be back again.

The university authorities have levelled and sodded the old Lorne grounds on Bloor street, where all the Varsity matches will be played this fall. A grand stand is to be erected immediately.

President Bayly, of the Canadian Rugby Union, is perfectly willing to admit the new College Union on even grounds with the other unions.

The Varsity management are after Killey, who played on the Ottawa city team last year.

The annual meeting of the Old Orchard Rugby Football Club will be held in the West-end Y. M. C. A. on Monday, 29th inst., at 8 p.m. The question of changing the club's present name to its original one, "Western," will be discussed at this meeting.

Mail & Empire, Aug. 24, 1898   NLC

Levelling the ground for the Arena. The Stadium is in the background.

Interior

VARSITY ARENA

DORIS GILMOUR in concert

Programme cover 1936

Programme 1936

DORIS GILMOUR

Conductor REGINALD STEWART

'PROMS' STAGE OPERA AS NEW EXCITEMENT

Greatest Opera Audience in Canada Sees Act II. of Heavy-Villain "Tosca"

DRAMATIC SINGING

By AUGUSTUS BRIDLE

To be exact, 5,496 people passed the turnstiles at the "Proms" grand-opera fest-carnival last night in Varsity arena. Much the largest crowd that ever heard opera in Canada. Cushions on the floor. Every seat taken except a few behind the stage. Control booth shifted to make room for a special stage; simple pillars and a red-curtained reredos for scenery; a few pieces of red plush furniture, a supper-table, tall flickering candelabra, and the whole scene cleverly lighted from a huge flood-light valance suspended from the rafters—which was Herman Voaden's part of the big novelty.

Thus about 4,000 of the 5,496 present on a serenely perfect June evening heard Act II of La Tosca, with about 50 of the entire orchestra in "the pit" of a hockey-arena concert-hall suddenly converted into a huge opera house. "The Met." never housed such a crowd. Few cities in America ever assembled so many for opera. With a Scotch-Canadian conductor, Danish baritone, Greek tenor, Canadian soprano, a German-Canadian electrical-drama expert and a fairly polyglot orchestra, this was one of the most cosmopolitan musical events ever known in Canada. Carboni, Von Kunits, Morando, Elliot Haslam, Ferrari-Fontana—all pioneers of the operatic idea here—yes, even Hageman and Edward [...], would have been [...]ratically thrilled by this ad[...] of the Proms orchestra and [...]to Opera Guild.

[...] a bold experiment. At least [...] of the audience had to see [...] across the stage, and about [...] saw the opera from the rear [...] in most opera houses is [...]ble. Scarpia the villain (Poul Bai) had a gloriously sinful time plotting the murder of Cavaradossi (Kenneth Sakos) and Angelotti, with the sweetheart of one and sister of the other (Doris Godson Gilmour) as his victim—till to the great satisfaction of a sporting operatic crowd, the villain himself got the knife, the candles and the crucifix. Doris Godson sang and acted superbly. The enormous crowd excited her to a high pitch of virtuosity. Bai was also roused by a vast mob of faces to make every syllable distinctly dramatic. His role had little music but a lot of acting and talk. Sakos as the tortured Cavaradossi was excellent. He crumpled down as picturesquely as a boxer taking a knockout. Bai staggered to his death as vividly as either Schmeling or Louis will go down in the big fight, and that was the end of part I.

While thousands strolled and smoked on acres of fresh grass, the stage was rearranged, the full orchestra assembled, a flashlight taken of orchestra and black and white stage chorus, and everything was set for Part II, which opened with the finale to "The Meistersinger"—exceptionally well played, apart for a lack of enough blare of brass. Sakos, togged as Canio, came on to do the clown's Lament, the tragic tenor aria of "Vesti la giubba" from "Pagliacci." He did it so well that he got seven recalls, he came back for an encore with the Cavaradossi's death aria in Act III of "Tosca," and repeated the encore. The chorus, weeks ago trained by D'Alton McLaughlin for the Toronto Opera Guild, sang the part-song of "Cavalleria," the orchestra played the Intermezzo, and the chorus did a finale with the Easter Alleluia—church harmonium played visibly on stage; and this was so thrilling it had to be repeated before the crowd rolled out to the miles of motors. It all was one splendidly exciting event as conducted by Stewart, one of the most sensational in three summers of "Proms."

Star, June 19, 1936

Opera Guild Performance Delights Large Audience

Singing of Mascagni Work Handsome Accomplishment — Orchestra Pleases

By ROSE MACDONALD

Off-hand it would be difficult to think of any opera better suited to the circumstances of a prom than Mascagni's "Cavalleria Rusticana," which was the magnet drawing a notably large audience to Varsity Arena last night. For one thing it is a one-act opera (as Mr. Leo Smith observes in his program notes, "perhaps the most played one-act opera ever written"). Being a one-acter the staging problems are less difficult than those of an opera more elaborate in design. Then it is not a work requiring any subtle handling. Principals and chorus get all their effects in a big tempestuous way. All very useful when the deficiencies—for opera purposes—of a sports arena are to be conjured with.

The critic, Krehbiel, by the way, once said of this opera of Mascagni's that its music was highly spiced, tasted "hot i' th' mouth." Which seems quite a good definition.

Last night's performance by the Opera Guild of Toronto, in conjunction with the Toronto Philharmonic Orchestra, was a handsome though scarcely unflawed accomplishment, giving pleasure generally to the audience.

Doris Gilmour sang the Santuzza role and in arrestingly fine voice, especially when the warming-up process had been got through with; measure taken of sound effect in the thronged arena. The reviewer cannot recall having heard Mrs. Gilmour sing in better voice.

SHOWED OPERATIC SKILL

Rather on the stately side for the role of the young peasant girl, and a bit formally dressed for a Sicilian village belle, she nevertheless sang with such conviction as to discount these matters. Vocal power and skillful operatic style marked her singing in highly satisfactory measure.

The Australian-born tenor, Lawrence Power, who came across the line to sing Turiddu in the presentation, gave a performance, often pleasing, but of uneven interest. For instance, he gave a beautiful full-toned performance in his first solo, and afterwards also was heard with pleasure, but there were times when his voice became rather faded; when the tones did not seem to project themselves as they should. Then in his acting he seemed rather unnecessarily fussy; we aren't referring, however, to the way he threw his wronged Santuzza around—that was a good, straight-smacking performance.

We expected a little more, frankly, from Lloyd Boleyn, who belayed with a fine swashbuckling air, but didn't seem to be letting that big voice of his out to its full capacity—he has a good bravura style—and this was a time where he could use it to advantage. But he did very acceptable work as Alfio notwithstanding, increasingly good with the progress of the performance.

CLEAR SOPRANO TONES

To Freda Fusco was assigned the part of the fickle Lola, who hadn't waited for her Turiddu, away on army service, but had married Alfio instead. This young singer displayed a clear, bright soprano, very well suited to the requirements of the part, gave, too, a clear, bright acting performance as the fickle, faithless quean Mascagni made her.

And finally but not least, when it comes to distribution of awards, there was Evaleen Kilby's performance as Lucia, the old mother. Miss Kilby's round-toned, warmly penetrating contralto made an excellent impression; was consistently distinctive; crooned with ease, and her make-up suggesting age was truly disguising.

The chorus developed a beautiful firm resonant body of tone and was a great enhancement to the production, once it had found its way about the boards and could put its mind to its singing. The stage choralists, it may be mentioned, came from Yonge Street United Church choir.

A scene which stands out, not only for its intrinsic beauty, but for the beautiful quality of the voices heard on this occasion, is the church scene in which Santuzza and Lucia lead the voices in the Easter music. This was impressively done.

Stage direction was in the hands of Glen Allen. Wilfred Powell was assistant music director.

ORCHESTRA EXCELS

Reginald Stewart, of course, conducted the public performance, keeping everything well in hand, and receiving unfailing co-operation from the orchestra. The reading given of the lovely Intermezzo, which briefly relieves the drama tension of the piece, was most felicitious.

The orchestra, too, had the first part of the program in charge, giving a charming reading of Weber's Oberon Overture and a skilfully vari-colored one of Rimsky-Korsakoff's Caprice on Spanish Themes.

Telegram, May 30, 1941 MTLB

CAVALLERIA RUSTICANA 1941

Programme 1941

APPEARANCES

1936	Opera Guild of Toronto
1941	Opera Guild of Toronto

MAPLE LEAF GARDENS

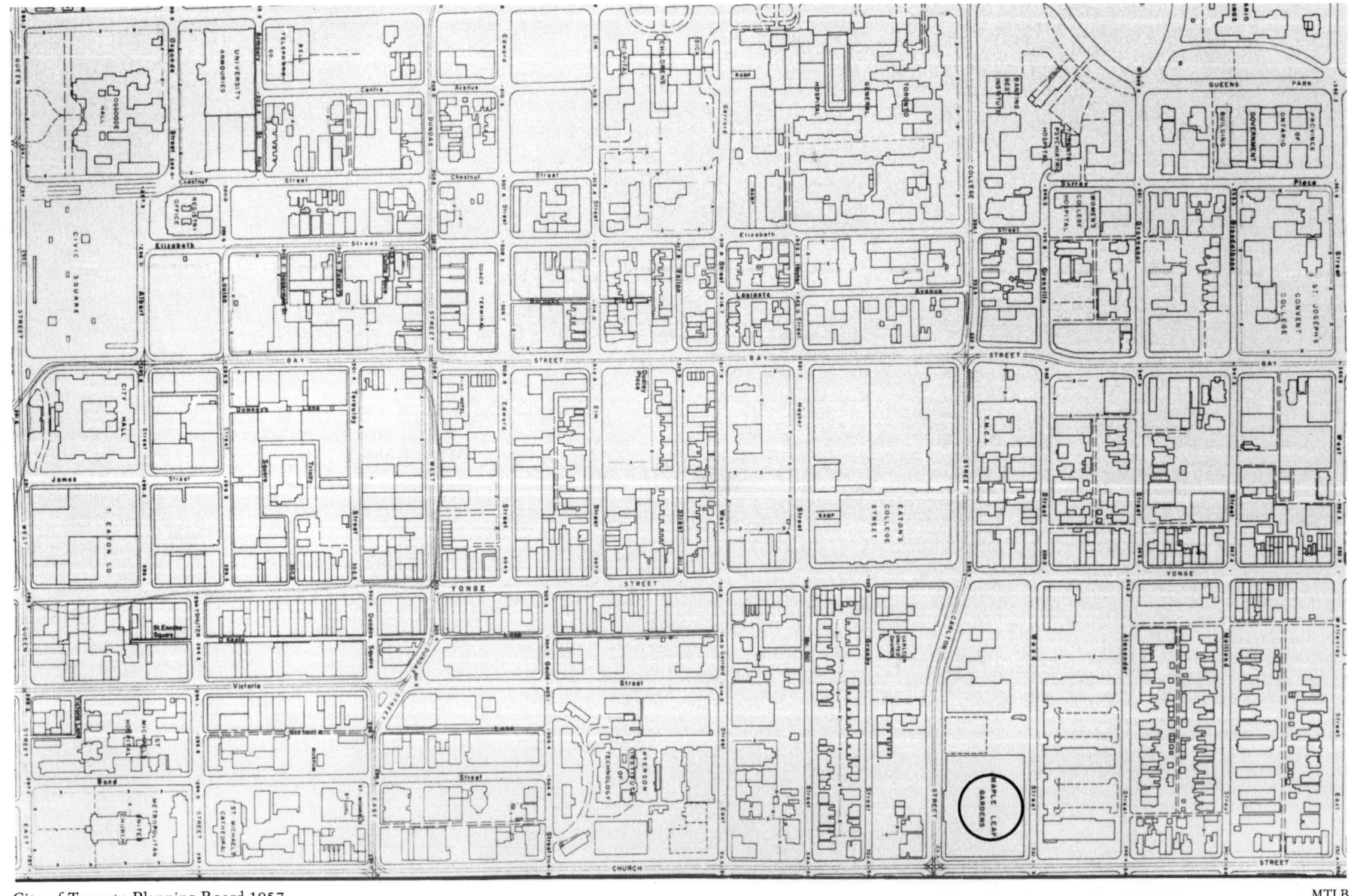

City of Toronto Planning Board 1957

MTLB

1936
MAPLE LEAF GARDENS

The most spectacular and varied use of all for a skating rink.

Photo: Roy Mitchell COCA

The largest audience in the Met's history, 11,352 saw *Carmen* at Maple Leaf Gardens.

MAPLE LEAF GARDENS

The late Director of Publicity for Maple Leaf Gardens, Stan Obodiac, in his book *Maple Leaf Gardens Fifty Years of History* (Van Nostrand Reinhold Ltd. Toronto 1981) presents a lucid and colourful account of this remarkable arena. He does not mention, however, that many conservative and cautious Torontonians in 1930 were convinced that Conn Smythe was mad and that the Gardens would prove to be a white elephant. From the beginning it was more than a hockey cushion. As well as a variety of sporting events (wrestling, boxing, lacrosse, badminton and tennis) it featured lecturers, pageants, rallies and dances. One of the earliest artistic events in the Gardens was the Toronto Skating Club Carnival, a pioneer in the art of spectacles on ice. Although with its structure and discipline, it was a far cry from the earlier carnivals (see Holman Opera House), it retained the same atmosphere of a social occasion. The championship skaters of the day, e.g. the world's darling Barbara Anne Scott, were featured. The Carnival sold out, including standing room, for most of the 5 nights of its annual run. In 1935 Radio City Ballet, with the Reginald Stewart Symphony Orchestra, gave the first ballet performances and in 1953 Sadler's Wells (later the Royal Ballet) made their first Toronto appearance presenting Margot Fonteyn who was to become the top ballerina of the day and would be honoured by the Queen. Opera was first presented by the Canadian Grand Opera Association in 1936 and, in what was undoubtedly a high point in the career of the Gardens, the Rotary Club brought in the Metropolitan Opera of New York from 1952 to 1960, attracting record audiences to hear the greatest singers of the day.

Globe, Oct. 13, 1936   MTLB

To Review Opera—Ettore Mazzoleni (left), principal of the Royal Conservatory of Music, and Robertson Davies, editor and playwright, who will review the performances of the Metropolitan Opera Company of New York at Maple Leaf Gardens next week for The Globe and Mail.

Globe & Mail, May 24, 1952   MTLB

Globe & Mail, May 26, 1952   MTLB

Two Years' Steady Work
Climaxed in the Met's Advent

Opening with Verdi's Aida on Monday night, the Metropolitan Opera Festival at the Maple Leaf Gardens brings 295 performers and technicians to take part. The event is sponsored by Toronto Rotary and will climax two years' steady work by Rotarians who have given their time to this civic enterprise. His Honor the Lieutenant-Governor will attend officially in the Royal box.

Because of special care taken to ensure even distribution of the 40,000 tickets available in total for the four performances, there are still best seats available. Net proceeds go to charities.

Thirty-odd baggage cars are required to transport the personal and stage effects required for this visit of the Metropolitan Opera. The whole enterprise has taken on something the proportions of moving a town. Stars, ballet, orchestra, conductors, stage directors, carpenters, acoustical technicians, scene shifters and administrative staffs make up a whole community of talents.

The Maple Leaf Gardens has been transformed into an opera house with red and gold decor.

Conductors will be: For Aida Monday night, Fausto Cleva; La Boheme Tuesday night and Rigoletto Thursday night, Alberto Frede; Carmen Wednesday night, Fritz Reiner.

Evidence that New York as well as Toronto looks upon the Metropolitan visit here as a highlight of operatic history is in the New York newspapers' preparation for coverage. Among critics coming to Toronto are Howard Taubman, music editor of The New York Times, and Paul Beckley of the New York Herald Tribune, as well as Miss Margaret Carson, press director of the Metropolitan.

Intrigue and Tragedy—That appealing opera, Rigoletto, is the last of the four being sung by the Metropolitan Opera Company at the Maple Leaf Gardens next week. The third act scene above shows the great depth of the proscenium. Patrice Munsel sings the tragic part of Gilda.

Globe & Mail, May 24, 1952   MTLB

MAPLE LEAF GARDENS

Photo: Gary Beechey

PROGRAMME COVER

From the programme 1952

From the programme 1952

From the programme 1952

MAPLE LEAF GARDENS

COC

1959 – MIGNON DUNN sang the Shepherd in *Tosca*, Mama Lucia in *Cavalleria Rusticana*, Giovanna in *Rigoletto*.

COC

1959 – CARLO BERGONZI sang Canio in *Pagliacci*, 1960 – Manrico in *Il Trovatore*.

COC

1960 – ELISABETH SODERSTROM sang Marguerite in *Faust*.

50th ANNIVERSARY BUTTON from the endpaper *Maple Leaf Gardens Fifty Years of History*.

Photo: Gary Beechey COCA

PROGRAMME COVER

APPEARANCES

1936   Canadian Grand Opera Association
1952-60 Metropolitan Opera of New York

1938
VICTORIA THEATRE

Here, according to hearsay, was the best house yet for operatic performances.

Toronto, Canada's Queen City BC
Shea's VICTORIA THEATRE c. 1912

VICTORIA THEATRE

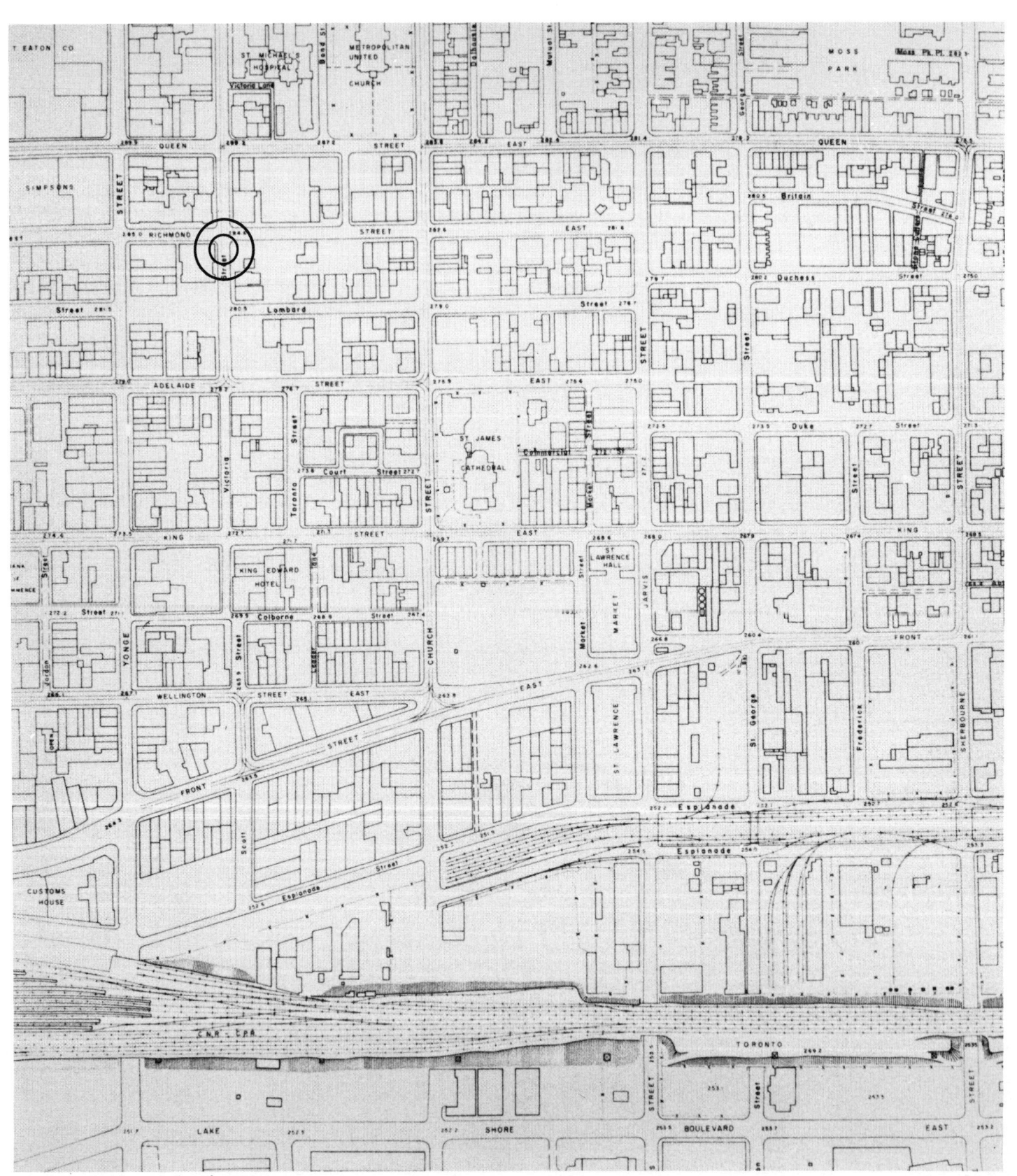

City of Toronto Planning Board, 1957

MTLB

VICTORIA THEATRE

Shea's Theatre at 91 Yonge was destroyed by fire in 1905 and the Shea Amusement Company of Buffalo built a new theatre in 1910 at the southeast corner of Richmond and Victoria Streets. The auditorium had two balconies and a seating capacity of 2,000 and the interior design was like that of an opera house. The Famous Players Company acquired it in 1927 as their head office and converted it to a movie house. From 1953 until its demolition in 1956 it served mainly as a facility for storage.

The VICTORIA THEATRE was on the southeast corner of Richmond and Victoria Streets, opposite the Tivoli Theatre.

Interior of the VICTORIA THEATRE – the stage.

Interior of the VICTORIA THEATRE – the auditorium.

VICTORIA THEATRE

Tenor JAMES MELTON sang with the National Opera Company at the Victoria Theatre in 1938.

AECL

BC

POUL BAI, who played Peter in the Toronto Opera Company's *Hansel and Gretel* in 1938 and the old Miser in *Chimes of Normandy* in 1939.

National Opera Company

Verdi heads the list of seven composers represented in the repertoire of the National Opera Company, which will present nine operas at the Victoria Theatre next week. Three of Verdi's most popular works will be sung, "Rigoletto" on Wednesday night, "La Traviata" on Thursday night, and "Aida" on Saturday night.

Monday night Puccini's "Mme. Butterfly" will be heard; Gounod's "Faust" will be sung Wednesday afternoon; Mascagni's "Cavalleria Rusticana" and Leoncavallo's "Pagliacci" on Tuesday night; Bizet's "Carmen" on Friday night, and Rossini's "Barber of Seville" on Saturday at the matinee. More than the usual interest is centred in the performances of "Mme. Butterfly" on Monday and "La Traviata" on Thursday, since the roles of Lt. Pinkerton and Alfredo will be taken by James Melton; and in the performance of "Cavalleria Rusticana" on Tuesday, and "Aida" on Saturday, since Viola Philo will be heard in the roles of Santuzza and Aida, respectively. Both these artists, well known to radio, stage and screen audiences, have been engaged as guest-artists by the company.

In some of the other performances artists will be heard who are already known to Toronto audiences because of their appearances here with the Columbia Opera Company of New York, which played at Massey Hall last season. Among them are Alfredo Chigi, Luisa Coronina, Phillip Whitfield, Lloyd Harris and Anthony Meli. The artistic roster of the company also lists Norma Nardi, Louise Bernhardt, John Chickering, Patrick Henry, Taissia Peters and Rocco Pandiscio, baritone of the Metropolitan Opera Company. The conductor is Otto Lehman.—Contributed.

Globe and Mail, Oct. 15, 1938   NLC

VICTORIA Richmond and Victoria Sts. Elgin 5808.

Pop. Prices: 50c, 75c, $1, $1.50

National Opera Co.
TONIGHT AT 8.30
MME. BUTTERFLY
with JAMES MELTON

Tomorrow Eve | CAVALLERIA
with Viola Philo. | & PAGLIACCI

Star, Oct. 17, 1938   MTLB

VICTORIA THEATRE
MARCH 23, 25, 27
TORONTO OPERA COMPANY
Presents the Romantic Opera
"THE BELLS OF CORNEVILLE"
CESAR BORRE Production
with the
VOLKOFF BALLET
Box Office - Elgin 5808
Tickets:
50c, 75c, $1, $1.50, $2, $2.50

Star, Mar. 23, 1939   MTLB

TORONTO OPERA COMPANY

Under the patronage of
THE HON. MITCHELL F. HEPBURN
Premier of Ontario

CÉSAR BORRÉ
General Director

Mrs. J. M. Burnett, Vice-President   Ruth Hanna, Treasurer

Robert Hodgson, Secretary

CHORUS OF SIXTY   ORCHESTRA OF FIFTY

BORIS VOLKOFF'S BALLET OF FORTY.

VICTORIA THEATRE—TORONTO

VICTORIA THEATRE
December 26th, 29th and 30th, 1938, at 8.30 p.m.

"HANSEL and GRETEL"
A FAIRY OPERA IN THREE ACTS
Music by Engelbert Humperdinck   Libretto by Adelheid Wette
Adapted from a fairy tale by Grimm
English translation by Constance Bache

Staged and directed by CÉSAR BORRÉ

PETER, a Broom Maker .... POUL BAI
GERTRUDE, His Wife .... IRENE MAHON
HANSEL ⎱ Their Children .... FREDA FUSCO
GRETEL ⎰ .... MARGARET RUPPEL
THE WITCH .... JEANNE PENGELLY
SANDMAN .... ROBERTA DUNN
DEWMAN (The Dew Fairy) .... EILEEN KELLY
CHILDREN .... Opera Chorus and Boys of the Schola
                     Cantorum of St. Michael's Cathedral
ANGELS .... VOLKOFF BALLET
MADONNA .... JANET BALDWIN

First Act—Home.   Second Act—The Forest.   Third Act—The Witch's House.

FOLLOWED BY
"Polovtsian Dances" from the Opera "Prince Igor"
Choral Ballet.   Music by Borodine.
POLOVTSIAN CHIEF .... BORIS VOLKOFF
POLOVTSIAN MAIDENS, SLAVES, and ARCHERS - VOLKOFF BALLET
Choreograph by BORIS VOLKOFF
CÉSAR BORRÉ, Conductor
Costumes by Field & Gilberthorpe and Patricia Card
Oriental Rugs with the Compliments of Babaian's Ltd., New Galleries, 56 Yonge St.

COCA

BORRE TO PRODUCE OPERA OF MYSTERY

Will Replace Low Comedy in "Chimes of Normandy" With Ballet

Cesar Borre's next opera before he produces "Samson and Delilah" will be "Chimes of Normandy" at Victoria theatre March 21, 23 and 25. This popular old opera by Planquette has been done very little in Toronto, except by amateur companies most of whom failed to get the real quality of its peculiar atmosphere of romance and mystery. The English text to be used by Borre is that of Farnie, which has crisp and powerful dialogue and calls for the use of all the music, much of which is entirely omitted from average productions. In England, as well as on this continent, much of the original beauty is sacrificed to incidental pantomime and low comedy. In restoring the original version, Borre cuts out the interpolated comedy. In place of it he introduces a ballet of three numbers in Act II to be danced by members of the Volkoff group who did the ballets for "Hansel and Gretel" Christmas week.

Star, Mar. 4, 1939   MTLB

CESAR BORRE LEADS NOTED LIGHT OPERA

"Chimes of Normandy" at Victoria Theatre Is Clever Production

By AUGUSTUS BRIDLE

Cesar Borre conducted "Chimes of Normandy" last night at the Victoria theatre; his first light opera in Toronto, and the most elaborate production of that opera ever done in Canada. It took more courage and experience to revive this hackneyed old parish-hall opera than to resurrect "Merry Widow." Borre knew he could make it snap with new interest. He had all the European traditions of this stupidly romantic old fairy-tale opera whose theme-song "Ding-Dong Bell" 40 years ago here people used to sing in parlors He brought it back with a chorus of 60, a splendid orchestra of 30, a buoyant cast of principals, scintillating costumes, three vivid scenics, and a ballet in three scenes for the last act.

Only a shirt-sleeve wizard of imagination, superb technique and patient hard work could have done this, mainly so well. But if II and III had not been ten times better than Act I this production would have been a flat tire. Nobody could have made Act I anything but amateur. The "hiring fair" scene was just a decorative muddle to music. Even the chorus was sleepy. The forest scene was rather better, but a much better picture than it was a performance. The best thing it did was to introduce the principals.

Act II was wonderfully good. The spooky fantasia of a haunted chateau, men in armor, flickering candles, choruses and songs, was climaxed in the old-miser acting of Poul Bai: whom nobody could have recognized from looks or voice, or in anything but his splendid comedy acting. We have seen Bai here as Scarpia in "Tosca" and as the father in "Hansel and Gretel"; never in anything so well characterized as this spooky old gold miser in the deserted chateau. As comedy-fantasia acting this ranks with anything of its kind seen here on the professional stage.

Freda Fusco is Serpoletto, the cocksure young village strut with a caustic tongue, posing as a marchioness in the finale. If her vocalism had been as good as her acting vivacity, she would have been a close second to Bai. Laura Barnett as the lost marchioness, discovered by the miser, was beautifully vibrant in her songs, especially one in Act II. James Flucker, who was Toreador in "Carmen" here two years ago, did the Marquis with considerable swagger and effective vocalism in songs of almost tenor range. His voice is exceptionally free in brilliant tone. Harold Tilbury sang the cockawhoop fisherman very clearly but with rather tight voice. G. Roch. de la Sabliere showed his usual instinct for atmospheric acting as the pomped-up bailiff.

In two numbers the chorus was the finest singing unit in the show. These young people lifted the whole scene in the two last acts; the Louis XIV Ballet to Gretry music in the garden scene was the most musically decorative scene in the opera; in three distinct rhythms an inspiring pattern of choreographic art invented by Volkoff, who also, with Janet Baldwin, led the classic comedy of elegant form and floating rhythm.

Star, Mar. 24, 1939   MTLB

VICTORIA THEATRE

TORONTO OPERA COMPANY

Owing to Illness Performance of

"Chimes of Normandy"

(The Bells of Corneville)

Postponed Tonight

Gala Performance Saturday Night

Monday's Tickets Honored

Star, Mar. 27, 1939   MTLB

RAMBLING with Roly
By ROLY YOUNG

The trouble with the Toronto amusement and cultural situation is that it needs somebody to get it organized so it can really function to advantage. This was brought home to me this week by a couple of letters I received from correspondents. One was a young lady from out of town, who suddenly decided to take a week of her holidays now and come to Toronto. I did some checking up for the young lady and found it was possible for her to take in the following attractions:

1. Paderewski in "Moonlight Sonata"—a picture version, yes, but certainly the next best thing to an actual concert by the great pianist.
2. "The Mikado"—again a picture version, but much more spectacular and beautiful than any stage production ever given, with most of the D'Oyly Carte Opera Company plus the London Symphony Orchestra.
3. "Pygmalion"—which even devotees of Bernard Shaw tell me they consider an improvement on the original play, with outstanding acting by Wendy Hiller and Leslie Howard.
4. The combination of the Toronto Symphony Orchestra and the Opera Guild of Toronto in a production of "Lohengrin" which has brought raves from everybody who saw it.
5. Nelson Eddy in person.
6. The Toronto Skating Club's spectacular annual carnival.
7. Mischa Elman.
8. The Conservatory Quartet.
9. "Angela is Twenty-Two," with Philip Merivale and Sinclair Lewis.

THE CURTAIN RISES—
Uptown — "Mikado" — 1, 3:15, 5:25, 7:30, 9:40.
Loew's — "Pygmalion" — 9:05, 12:10, 2:35, 5:05, 7:30, 10 p.m.
Shea's—Stage Show—1:33, 4, 6:27, 8:54.
"Fisherman's Wharf"—12:10, 2:37, 5:04, 7:31, 9:58.
Imperial—"The Little Princess" —10:40, 12:30, 3, 5:10, 7:15, 9:25.

Personally I think that's a very imposing list of attractions for a visitor to see in a week. Another correspondent brings to mind the fact that in a few weeks now there will be trainloads (literally) of Toronto folks going down to New York for the Easter weekend. It strikes me as being too bad that Toronto does not have a batch of such attractions as these around that Easter week-end and thus make itself a mecca for out-of-towners.

In southern cities there are annual fiestas and similar celebrations which not only advertise the cities all over the continent, but also bring in many thousands of visitors and their many more thousands of dollars.

There will be, of course, special Easter attractions here, but there certainly has never been, as yet, a really concerted and co-operative effort to make it a real gala festival. A program such as we have during the week (you'll have to stretch it over two week-ends) of March 4 to 13 is just a sample of what could be done along this line if the various organizations and companies would get together on the subject.

• • •

Speaking of getting together, may I again go into a lament over the fact that we are still sporting a number of operatic and musical factions, all doing very excellent work in their own way. But, think what could be done if these organizations would only get together. Instead of having spasmodic operatic presentations, we would be able to have a regular opera season each year, or possibly two shorter seasons, one in the late fall and another in the spring (Easter again). There are in Toronto productions (meaning scenery and costumes) and trained vocalists ready to produce a repertoire of about a dozen operas. Since each production is good for two or three presentations, without further effort we could have two "seasons" of local opera running for a month each. We have the Victoria Theatre, which is an ideal "opera house." If only our various operatic groups would forget their petty fights and jealousies and social differences, some one could surely band them together into one parent organization with the Toronto Symphony Orchestra and give us something in the line of a season that is really operatic, instead of being operatic as it is at present. If the groups would not work together, by which I mean become completely co-operative economically, any bookkeeper could easily arrange things so that each organization secured the funds it actually earned with its own effort.

Such a proposition would mean a great saving all the way round, because such outside talent and technicians as were required could be obtained much more cheaply for the period of a month than they can when they are brought here for individual appearances.

It might be argued that Toronto could not sustain grand opera for such a period, but I think there are two sides to that argument. Certainly it would require co-operation from outside sources as well as from the opera troupes. Opposition to such an effort would have to be kept to a minimum. It would be pointless, for example, to expect it to compete with a couple of big concert attractions or with a couple of symphony concerts which would call out most of the orchestra in addition to taking away prospective customers.

It's a fantastic idea, but I think it is worth a bit of consideration. Maybe some day somebody will do something about it . . . meanwhile it seems to me that we are letting a grand opportunity slip away from us.

Globe & Mail, Mar. 4, 1939   NLC

Demolition of Shea's VICTORIA THEATRE in 1956

MTLB SI-3524A

APPEARANCES

1938	National Opera Company	1939	Toronto Opera Company
1938	Toronto Opera Company	1945	National Opera Association

ART GALLERY OF ONTARIO

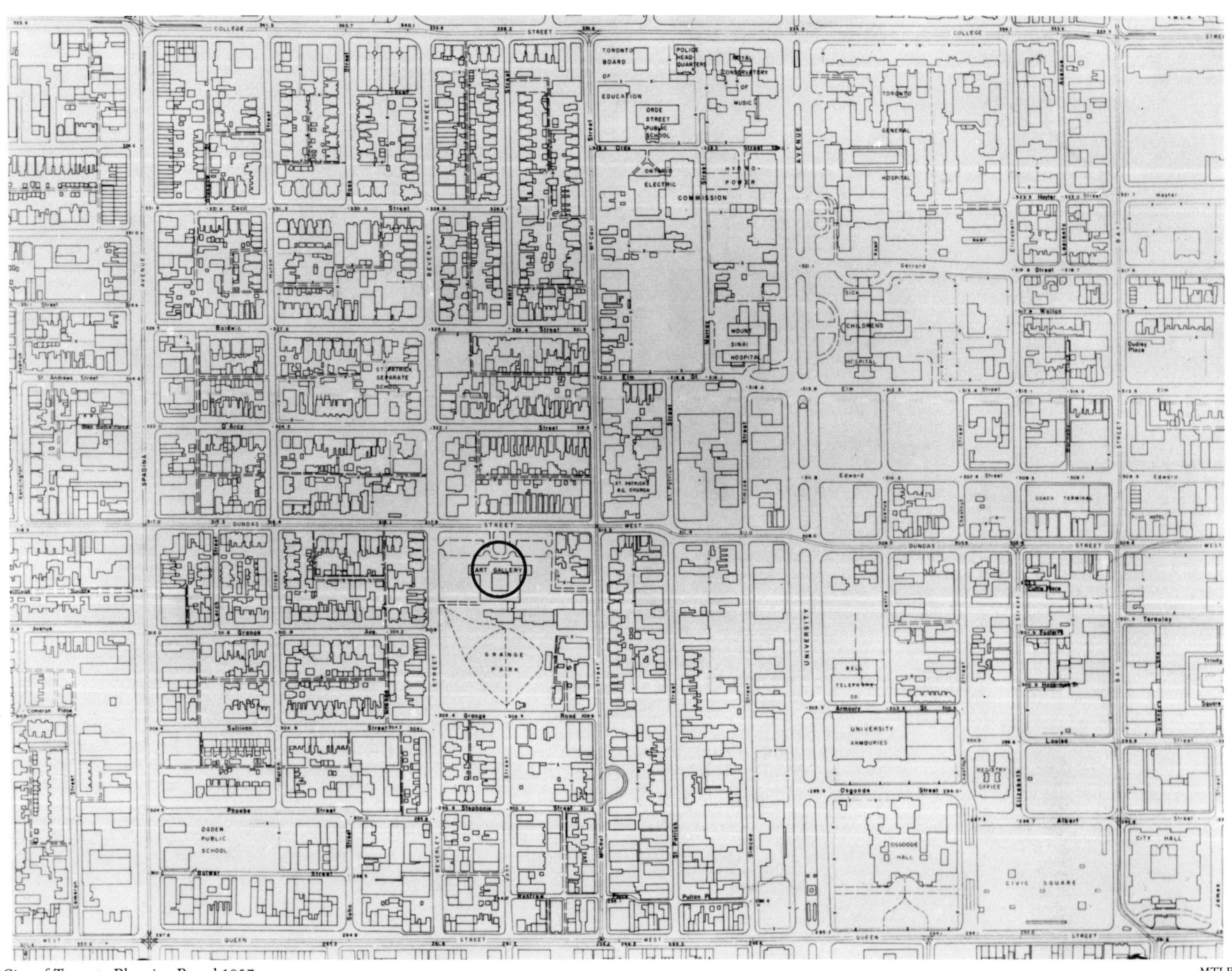

City of Toronto Planning Board 1957

1948
THE ART GALLERY OF TORONTO
(after 1966)
THE ART GALLERY OF ONTARIO

The surroundings lend themselves admirably to artistic presentations.

THE ART GALLERY OF TORONTO 1948

ART GALLERY OF ONTARIO

In 1900 the Provisional Committee of the Toronto Art Museum met several times and on July 4 the Museum was founded. It acquired its first permanent home in 1911 when Mrs. Goldwin Smith donated her historic house, The Grange, for a gallery. The surrounding parkland became a City Park. In 1918, when the name was changed to the Art Gallery of Toronto, three additional galleries were completed in time to provide the arena for the early battles over the Group of Seven. Eight years later further expansion created the Walker Sculpture Court (named after Sir Edmund Walker, for many years President and patron of the Gallery) and two sets of new galleries. It was in the Walker Court that the Opera School of the Royal Conservatory of Music gave a performance of Pergolesi's *La Serva Padrona* in 1948. 1966 brought another change of name when the institution became the Art Gallery of Ontario. Over the years musical events have continued to take place. In 1983 the Canadian Opera Company Ensemble presented, "Opera Highlights".

The most recent expansion, a major three-stage project, was completed in 1979.

Toronto Art Gallery.

The new Toronto Art Gallery will be opened on

Friday Evening, 22nd November, at 8 o'clock
WITH A
Magnificent Collection of PAINTINGS.

Miss LAURA McMANIS and the popular Orchestra of the Academy of Music will render a number of pieces. Admission 50 cents. Pictures received on Monday, 18th November.

Globe, Nov. 20, 1889   MTLB

Since the days of Toronto's first Art Gallery, the atmosphere of such an establishment has proved suitable for musical occasions. The Toronto Art Gallery was located at 165-173 King Street West. By 1896 the premises at 165 were listed in the name of the Ontario Society of Artists (see Ryerson Polytechnical Institute) and the Central Ontario School of Art.

Telegram, Jan. 29, 1926. By permission of the Toronto Sun   MTLB

ART GALLERY OF ONTARIO

4,000 LOVERS OF ART AT FORMAL OPENING OF NEW GALLERIES

His Honor the Lieutenant-Governor Declares New Wing Open, R. Y. Eaton Reads Dedication of the Sir Edmund Walker Memorial Court and Accepts Fudger Gallery and Cox Collection

TORONTO BECOMES GREAT ART CENTRE

Hon. Vincent Massey Looks Hopefully Toward the Future When Ambitions of the Building Committee Will Be Realized — Sir Joseph Flavelle Speaks for Mendelssohn Choir and Late Honorary President

Opens Art Gallery

HON. H. C. COCKSHUTT, Lieutenant-Governor of Ontario, who last night formally opened the new wing of the Toronto Art Gallery.

Four thousand people attended the opening of the new wing of the Art Gallery of Toronto last night. Against a background of pale grey stucco, under soaring arches, shadowed by pylons that rose, purposeful as truth, delicate as a lyric, the greatest picture yet to be witnessed by cultural Toronto was created. A moving picture it was—in which the men and women were not merely players, but spectators, too; a vast and splendid canvas, across which color marched in bold bravado, and which, in its easy lavishness, might have caused the Rembrandt and Tintoretto on the walls to shiver in amaze.

As it was, the masters of the past were supplanted in interest by the patrons of the present and the artists of tomorrow, who jostled good-naturedly as they sauntered in endless procession about the Sir Edmund Walker Memorial Court. Here, at the very heart of the building, the ceremony incident to the opening took place. For literally hours before his Honor the Lieutenant-Governor arrived to perform this duty, visitors poured through the new entrance doors on Dundas Street, securing strategic positions in the cloisters surrounding the court, or—in the case of the more fortunate guests—taking seats in the body of the court.

Lieutenant-Governor Arrives.

At 9.15 p.m., his Honor Lieutenant-Governor Cockshutt arrived, accompanied by Lord Willingdon, Mrs. Cockshutt, R. Y. Eaton, President of the Gallery; Hon. Vincent Massey, Chairman of the Building Committee; Mayor Foster; Hon. W. H. Price, Provincial Treasurer, and others. Behind the dais hung the portrait of the late Sir Edmund Walker, for years the President of the Gallery and its generous patron, while to the left of the Chairman sat the Mendelssohn Choir, still another organization which Sir Edmund had encouraged and supported.

Globe, Jan. 30, 1926

Telegram, Jan. 30, 1926, By permission of the Toronto Sun

The MENDELSSOHN CHOIR performed during the opening ceremonies for the Walker Sculpture Court.

The OPERA SCHOOL's first performance in the Walker Court.

ART GALLERY OF ONTARIO

Soprano SHARI SAUNDERS

Soprano IRENA WELHASCH

Mezzo soprano KATHARINA MEGLI

Music Director LESLIE UYEDA

Baritone THEODORE BAERG

Tenor BEN HEPPNER

The Canadian Opera Company ensemble in "Opera Highlights"

Bass CHRISTOPHER CAMERON

SELECTED APPEARANCES

1948	Opera School, Royal Conservatory of Music
1983	Canadian Opera Company Ensemble

1958
HEINTZMAN STREET HALL

Once again an eminent Toronto family was influential in making opera performances possible.

Wood engraving: Beale Bros. MTLB
HEINTZMAN & COMPANY 1874

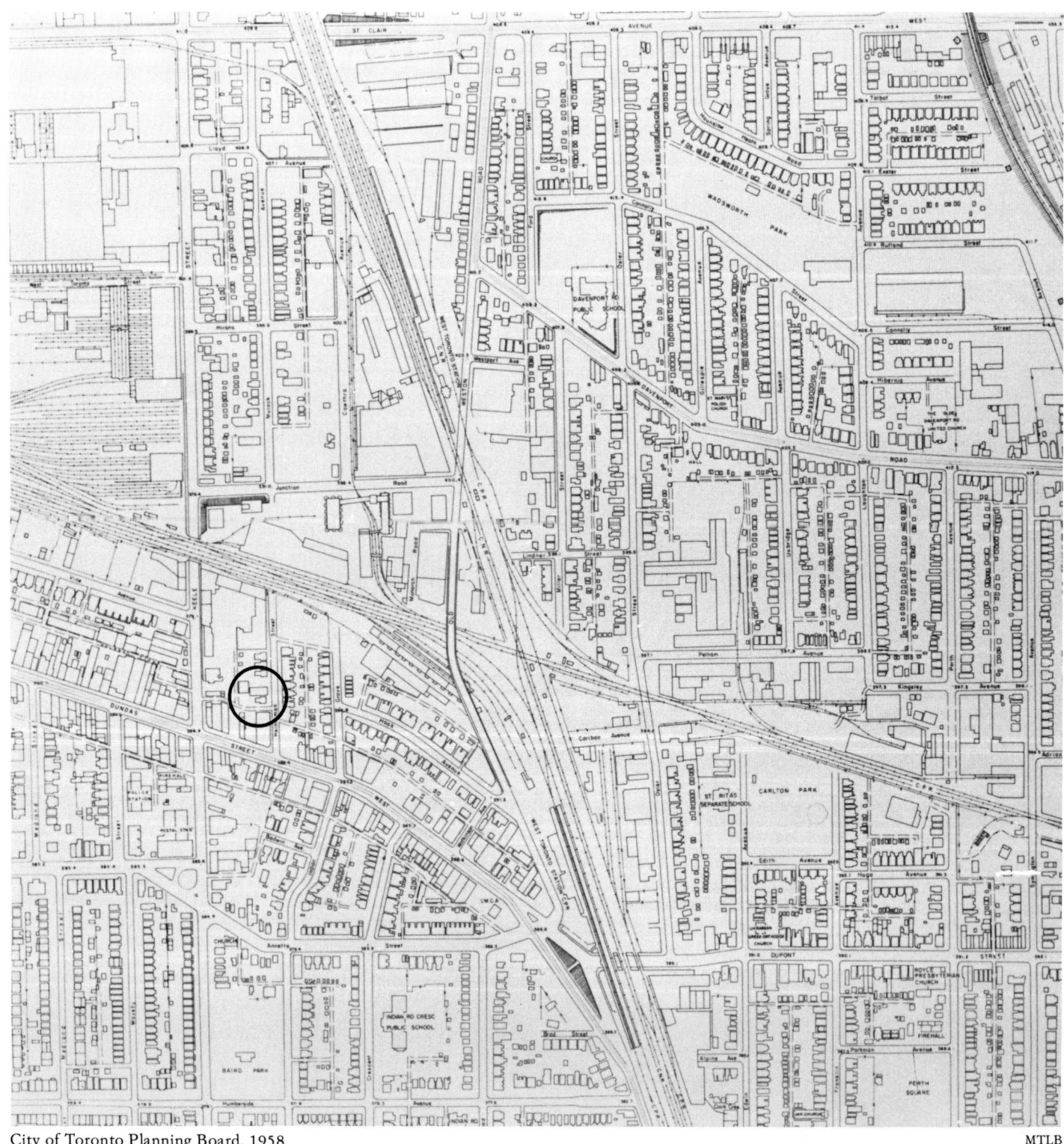

City of Toronto Planning Board, 1958

HEINTZMAN STREET HALL

Theodore Heintzman, piano maker and founder of Canada's most famous piano manufacturing company, moved from Buffalo to Toronto in 1860. His first factory was on Duke Street and from there he moved first to York Street north of King, next to 105 King Street West and thence to 117 King Street West, immediately east of the Rossin House. In 1887 the company acquired, from the CPR, lands in Toronto Junction. In 1911, 195 Yonge Street became the head office and here, on the fourth floor, a concert hall was established in which free concerts were given. Finally, in 1968 the factory was settled at Hanover, Ontario.

The street running north from Dundas, one east of Keele, in the old Junction, became Heintzman Street. Stories that the hall at #28 was built by the company for purposes of testing pianos cannot be verified. The first record of building on the site is in 1927 when a club house was erected by the Loyal Order of Moose. By 1940 the club had become the West Toronto Community Hall and is now the Polish Community Hall. In 1958 the Toronto Opera Society was organized by some of the singers who had been with the Rosselino Company. Harvey Cladman was the Society's first president and Leo Evason, formerly Treasurer and Publicity Director, became president and Managing Director in 1981. The Society presented operatic highlights and concerts at the Hall on Heintzman Street until 1967. In addition they have given summer concerts under the auspices of the Parks Department for 15 years.

Tenor LEO EVASON
Officer of Toronto Opera Society

POLISH COMMUNITY HALL 1983

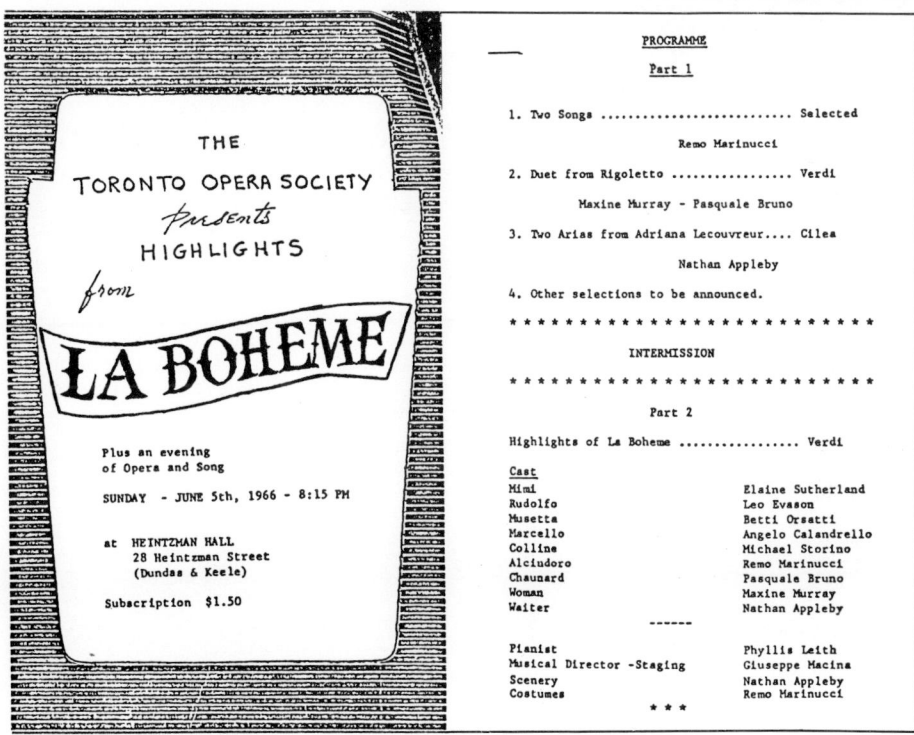

APPEARANCES
1958-67 Toronto Opera Society

O'KEEFE CENTRE

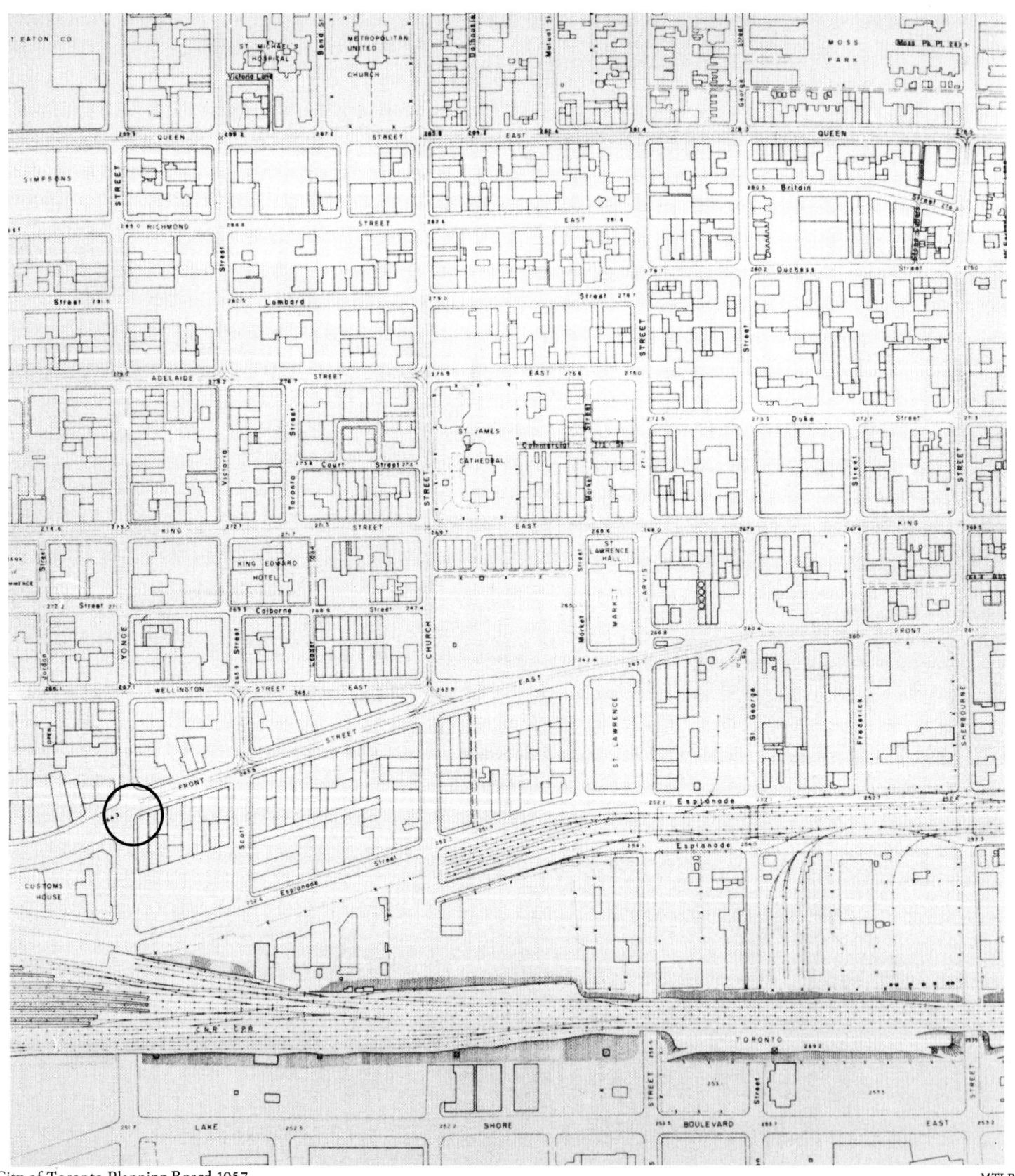

City of Toronto Planning Board 1957

1961
O'KEEFE CENTRE

The list of operas which could not have been produced without it is endless.

OKC

An advertisement in the York Gazette of May 23, 1811, informed the Public that "a gallant Display of various Performances" was to take place on "Monday Evening next, May 25, at Mr. O'Keefe's Assembly Room, which is fitted up on purpose, for the reception of the worthy Inhabitants of York and its vicinity". Eric Arthur, in *Toronto, No Mean City* (U. of T. Press, Toronto 1964), mentions the popularity of the tavern as a place for theatrical performances.

Unfortunately, neither the location of the Assembly Room nor the record of Mr. O'Keefe's decendants has been discovered.

Built by Canadian Breweries Limited (architect, Earl C. Morgan) the O'Keefe Centre has been called, derisively and/or affectionately, "the barn that beer built". Since its opening on October 1, 1960, with a pre-Broadway run of Lerner & Lowe's *Camelot* starring Richard Burton, its impact on Toronto's entertainment has been immense. In 1968 it was purchased by Metropolitan Toronto for $2.7 million. Over a period of 22 years it has been home to the Canadian Opera Company during the latter's growth from 17 to 38 performances in a year, and has accommodated performances and concerts by many of the most illustrious artists in the world of theatre and music.

O'KEEFE CENTRE *for the performing arts*

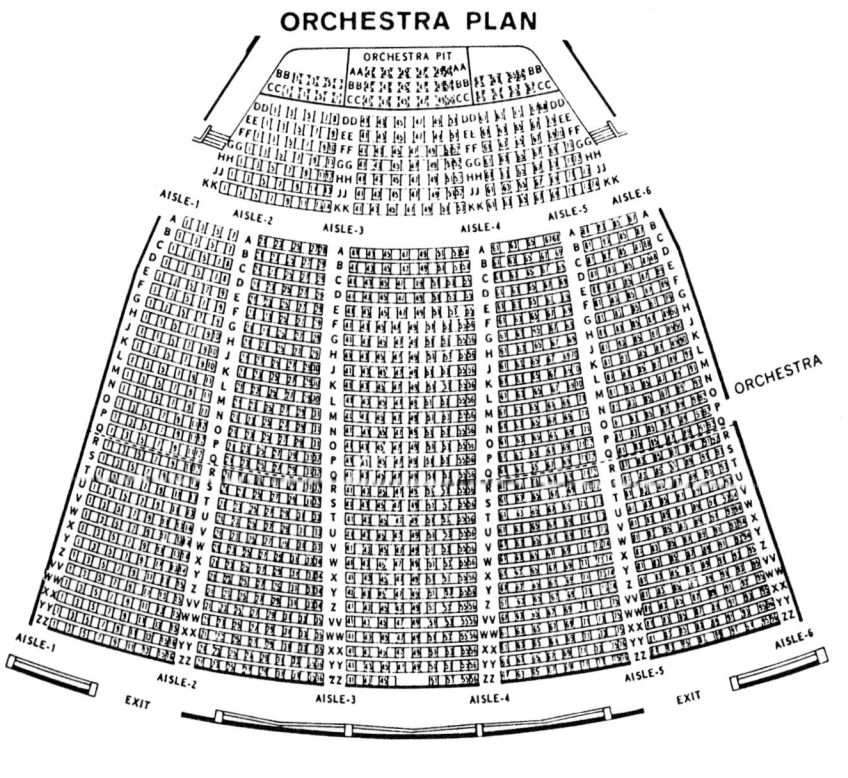

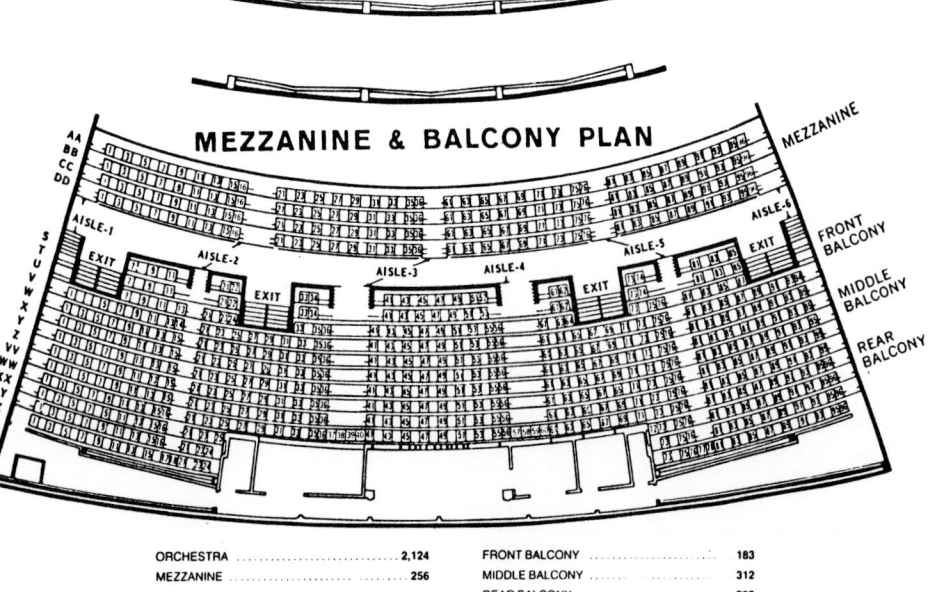

ORCHESTRA	2,124
MEZZANINE	256
FRONT BALCONY	183
MIDDLE BALCONY	312
REAR BALCONY	292
	787

TOTAL SEATS—3,167   EXTRA SEATS—56 (if orchestra pit not required)

LANDSCAPED COURTYARDS will be the setting for the new O'Keefe Centre on its two-and-a-half acre site in downtown Toronto. The $12 million auditorium opens on October 1 with the world premiere of the new Alan Jay Lerner-Frederick Loewe (author and composer respectively) musical CAMELOT which will be directed by Moss Hart.

The building will operate on a non-profit basis, and will seat 3,200 (with facilities for reducing that capacity to 1,200 for more intimate productions). It has a mechanically elevated orchestra pit, unique acoustical facilities, control rooms for production, radio and TV, kitchens for limited catering, eight "star" dressing rooms, plus accommodations for 100 chorus and cast. The 52-foot entrance is sheltered by an eight-foot canopy.

Acoustic control is built in: fire-resistant lattice-work conceals plywood sections, half of which will be perforated to absorb sound with the other half solid to reflect sound. By adjusting these movable sections the desired effect can be obtained by allowing the proper reverberation time for sounds originating on the stage.

The early subscription list has exceeded 10,000 members. In partnership with the Theater Guild-American Theatre Society and Council for the Living Theater in New York, patrons will be offered a package of ten top attractions from Broadway, Canada, and abroad, plus musicals, ballets, solo performances, dramas, and opera.

The most modern theatre in Canada—some say in the world—the O'Keefe Centre is another milestone in the cultural development of Canada's fastest-growing city.

Opera Canada, Sept.-Oct. 1960   COCA

O'KEEFE CENTRE

Globe & Mail, Oct. 3, 1960

Times Says Centre Enhances City

Following is The New York Times report of the O'Keefe Centre opening.

By LOUIS CALTA
© New York Times Service

Toronto, Oct. 2—The cultural milieu of this capital city of 1,500,000 persons was notably enhanced last night with the opening of a new, gleaming temple for the performing arts.

Constructed at a cost of $12,000,000 and the result of five years' planning, the O'Keefe Centre, as the multiple-purpose edifice is called, began its career with the world premiere of Camelot, the long awaited, Broadway-bound musical by the creators of My Fair Lady.

A modernistic structure of granite, glass and limestone, which successfully achieves grace and lightness of design, the theatre stands at the corner of Front and Yonge Sts., Toronto's main downtown arteries, within two blocks of the principal hotel, shopping and financial area.

Lieutenant-Governor Keiller Mackay, attending the gala opening-night ceremonies, hailed the new arts' centre as a real contribution to the Canadian art. "For our city it will always be a gem of continual beauty and delight," he said.

The funds for the theatre building, the Mayor said, were provided by the O'Keefe Brewing Co., which assumed financial responsibility for the annual expenses of depreciation and taxes.

The centre, named in honor of Eugene O'Keefe, founder of the company, is expected eventually to be able to pay its costs and to operate as a non-profit organization.

The 3,200-seat centre was filled to overflowing from its chartreuse-carpeted orchestra to its last balcony row. The formally attired first nighters, including some of Canada's distinguished names from the world of politics, society and the arts, paid $25 a seat for the benefit opening.

The premiere was sold out several weeks in advance. Only 71 single seats remain to be sold for the musical attraction's three-week stand. Camelot already has sold more than $2,000,000 worth of tickets in New York where it opens on Nov. 19.

A brass band, a group of the Queen's Own Rifles of Canada, forming an honor guard for the Lieutenant-Governor, television interviews, roving spotlights and fashionable display lent a note of general communal excitement to the event.

It could easily have been a scene from Hollywood or Broadway. It was estimated that about 1,100 vehicles, limousines, sports cars of varying shapes and color and taxis, delivered patrons at the theatre.

Mr. Hart, director and co-producer of the musical, strode to centre stage. In a brief speech, he explained that Camelot was woefully long; that theatre-goers who had left their children at home should be prepared to see them at college; and please bear with us.

Globe & Mail, Oct. 3, 1960

"MET" OPERA MUSINGS...

VICTORIA DE LOS ANGELES in the title role of Flotow's "MARTHA".

This season, the Metropolitan Opera is bringing to Toronto two new productions of operas long absent from its repertory—von Flotow's "Martha" and Puccini's "Turandot", which were last given by the company, respectively, in 1928-29 and 1929-30. Both heroines are ladies of royal lineage: "Martha" is, in reality, Lady Harriet Durham, a Maid of Honor to the Queen of England, while Princess Turandot is the legendary daughter of the Emperor Altoum of China. Each is wooed and won by a suitor whose identity, though at first in question, is finally proved to be worthy of the lady he seeks, and in both cases the endings are happy—a rarity in opera.

Musically, however, the two works are ages apart. A favorite for many years because of its melodious score and the opportunities it offers to singers, "Martha" has served such prima donnas and leading tenors as Patti, Sembrich, Hempel and Alda, Caruso, Campanini, Bonci and Gigli, to whom such arias as "The Last Rose of Summer" and "M'appari" were justifiably regarded as artistic plums. Whereas, the von Flotow work had its premiere in 1847, Puccini's "Turandot" was not performed until 1926—seventeen months after the death of the composer. Here the problem has been to find singers capable of dealing with the taxing soprano and tenor roles, which offer double challenges of range and endurance.

Fortunately, this season, the Metropolitan management has felt time and circumstance auspicious for the revival of both operas. The production of "Martha", conducted by Nino Verchi, staged by Carl Ebert, and provided with settings by Oliver Smith and costumes by Montley, has been sponsored by The Metropolitan Opera Guild. Sung in English, the charming story has helped acquaint a new generation of operagoers with an operatic "hit" of the past, too long out of the standard repertory.

As for "Turandot", the presence in the Metropolitan company of Birgit Nilsson and Franco Corelli for its leading roles made it a logical choice for revival. Through the generosity of John S. Newberry, a brilliant new production conceived by Yoshio Aoyama, directed by Nathaniel Merrill, and designed by Cecil Beaton, had its New York premiere last February, with Leopold Stokowski making his Metropolitan conducting debut. Once again, almost a generation of operagoers had the experience of becoming familiar with a twentieth century classic for the first time at the Opera House, and the final achievement of one of the most popular of operatic composers.

Thus Toronto will have a chance to confirm the judgment of music enthusiasts throughout the United States who have found that these two long-absent operas are deserving of permanent places on their operatic bill of fare.

RETURN OF TWO FAIR LADIES

BIRGIT NILSSON in the title role of Puccini's "Turandot"

RICHARD TUCKER as "Lionel".

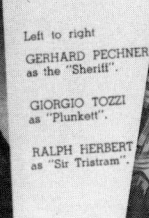
ROSALIND ELIAS as "Nancy".

Left to right
GERHARD PECHNER as the "Sheriff".
GIORGIO TOZZI as "Plunkett".
RALPH HERBERT as "Sir Tristram".

From the Metropolitan Opera Programme

Photo: Gary Beechey

FRANCO CORELLI as "Calaf"
ALESSIO DE PAOLIS as "The Emperor".

Designer CECIL BEATON'S sketches for "Turandot"
Left to right
Act III—Scene 2
Act I—Scene 2
Calaf's costume
Turandot's costume

From the Metropolitan Opera Programme

1961 THE FIRST VISIT OF THE MET

O'KEEFE CENTRE

NO MORE REWRITING
Opera Promises to End 'Cheating' on Scores

After 12 years of self-confessed "cheating," the Canadian Opera Company will be able to present operas as they are written, for the first time this year.

General director Herman Geiger-Torel, explaining the opera's controversial shift from the Royal Alexandra theatre (1,500 seats) to the O'Keefe centre (3,200 seats) for the coming season, revealed yesterday that the lack of orchestra pit space in the Royal Alexandra had forced rewriting of the scores of every opera the COC had produced.

—Photo by Alex Gray
GEIGER-TOREL

"We have cheated for 12 years—in good faith," he told the first birthday luncheon of the Canadian Opera guild. "Many companies have to do it. But now we can stop."

The 1961 season will include five operas, two more than ever before, he said. Key to the switch in theatres is the inclusion of the opera on the Centre's subscription series. The operas will be the first Canadian productions at the Centre.

The 1961 productions, which Mr. Torel labelled "box office operas," will be "Carmen," "Tosca," "The Bartered Bride" and the double bill of "Cavelleria Rusticana," and "Pagliacci." The two-week season will open Sept. 30. Two student performances will be included in the run.

Mr. Torel hailed the Centre's acoustics as "among the best on the continent." Hugh Walker, manager of the theatre, added that the current show, the first to perform without microphones, is "clearly audible in every seat."

Vida Peene, chairman of the Opera guild, told the luncheon that in its first year the guild had enlisted 1,268 members and raised more than $10,000. The opera deficit for the year, however, is $120,000, of which $60,000 must come from individuals and corporations.

This year the Canadian Opera will play up to 90 performances in about 75 different Canadian towns and cities from coast to coast. The spring tour of "Orpheus in the Underworld," which starts late this month, will include 30 performances, two of them in Toronto on Feb. 20 and 21.

Star, Jan. 6, 1961   COCA

13th ANNUAL SEASON SEPT. 30-OCT. 14

CANADIAN OPERA COMPANY

CARMEN SAT., SEPT. 30, 8.30 P.M. GALA OPERA
GUILD OPENING—GOOD SEATS AVAILABLE

CARMEN Sept. 30, Oct. 3, Oct. 5, Mat. Oct. 7, Oct. 13	CAVALLERIA Oct. 2, 4, 10 PAGLIACCI 12, 14
With: • SANDERS • CASSILLY • RUHL • TESSIER • BRAUN • RUBES • SUSSKIND, CROSS	With: • SIMMONS • GRANT • JOANISSE • CRAIN • RUHL • CASSILLY • RAYSON BARBINI, BERNARDI, CROSS MAJOR
THE BARTERED BRIDE Fri., Oct. 6, (Sold Out) With: • RUBES • PIERCEY • McCOLLUM • CROFOOT MAZZOLENI, MOORE	**TOSCA** Oct. 7, 9, 11 Sat., Mat. Oct. 14 With: • KOMARINK • VERREAU • RAYSON BARBINI, GEIGER-TOREL

EVENINGS 8 P.M., EXCEPT SEPT. 30—SATURDAY MAT. 2 P.M.

	Mon.-Thurs.	Fri. & Sat.	Sat. Mat.
Front Orchestra and Mezzanine	$3.50	$4.00	$4.50
Rear Orchestra and Balcony	4.25	4.50	3.50
Middle Balcony	3.25	3.50	2.75
Rear Balcony	2.50	2.75	2.00

BOX OFFICE OPEN 11-10, PHONE ORDERS EM. 3-6633

Globe & Mail, Sept. 25, 1961   MTLB

Mrs. Geza Por (left) and Mrs. George Mulligan, active supporters of the opera, were first-nighters.

Globe & Mail, Oct. 2, 1961   MTLB

Jean Sanders as Carmen

CANADIAN OPERA COMPANY'S LUCKY 13

Royal York Magazine, October 1961

CELEBRATING its lucky 13th annual Toronto season, the Canadian Opera Company is presenting its most extensive opera program from September 30 through October 14 at the O'Keefe Centre.

A spectacular new staging of Bizet's "Carmen" sung in English opens this season at a special performance sponsored by the Canadian Opera Guild. Puccini's "Tosca", Mascagni's "Cavalleria Rusticana" and Leoncavallo's "I Pagliacci" is being performed in Italian. For one night only, Friday October 6, the company sings, in English, "The Bartered Bride", a comic folk opera written by Czech composer, Smetana.

Jean Sanders of the New York City and Philadelphia Grand Opera Companies is making her Toronto debut as Carmen. Alternating as Don Jose are Richard Cassilly, tenor of the Chicago Lyric Theatre and Eddy Ruhl, renowned tenor of the Maggio Musicale in Florence, Italy, who also makes his Toronto debut.

Singing the famous title role of "Tosca" which won her such acclaim four years ago, is Ilona Kombrink. The celebrated French Canadian tenor, Richard Verreau (Royal Opera House, Covent Garden) makes his Toronto debut as Cavaradossi.

The leading role of Santuzza in "Cavalleria Rusticana" is being performed by the distinguished soprano, Mary Simmons, also making her debut with the Company. Alternating as Canio are Richard Cassilly and Eddy Ruhl, while the American baritone of the San Francisco and New Orleans Opera Companies, Benjamin Rayson, is Tonio.

Popular Jan Rubes, Sheila Piercey and American tenor John McCollum are the protagonists in "The Bartered Bride".

Staging "Carmen" and "Cavalleria Rusticana" is one of England's most distinguished artists, Joan Cross of London's Royal Opera House and Covent Garden. "Mr. Opera", Herman Geiger-Torel, general director of the Canadian Opera Company, is staging "Tosca" while brilliant young director Leon Major will do "I Pagliacci". Mavor Moore is responsible for "The Bartered Bride".

Conducting this star-studded 13th season for the Canadian Opera Company is Walter Susskind, Ernesto Barbini, Dr. Ettore Mazzoleni and young Canadian Mario Bernardi.

Ernest Adams was twice the winner of the nation-wide competition, CBC's "Singing Stars of Tomorrow". Having built up a highly successful career in Western Canada, Mr. Adams, a baritone, travelled eastwards in 1948 to become one of the original members of the Canadian Opera Company. He is the touring manager of the company.

THE ROYAL YORK MAGAZINE   COCA

Buffet Dinner Precedes Opera Season Opening

Well before six o'clock on Saturday evening handsomely dressed guests were pouring into O'Keefe Centre for the opening of the thirteenth annual season of the Canadian Opera Company was preceded by a reception and buffet supper arranged by the Canadian Opera Guild.

It was a country-wide gathering for the board of the Dominion Drama Festival was meeting in town and all were invited. In addition number of opera-goers had come in from other cities to see the season open with Carmen.

Receiving in the large foyer were Miss Vida Peene, chairman of the Opera Guild, Lt.-Col. Frank F. McEachren, president of the Canadian Opera Association, Mrs. Geza Por, Dr. Herman Geiger-Torell and Mr. Hugh Walker. Miss Peene wore a short dinner dress of red print with the pattern picked up by beading and Mrs. Por was in pale beige with re-embroidered lace top.

It was a black tie affair and short dresses predominated but Mrs. Henry Krug, down with her husband from Kitchener, wore a superbly cut black crepe sheath with fringe trimming. Mrs. Nathan Phillips' off-shoulder brocade was floor length and Mrs. Samuel Hersenhoren was in embroidered emerald satin, the half overskirt faced with gold lame.

Mrs. Hugh Walker had also chosen emerald satin and the whole audience was brightened by satin ensembles in varied shades of red. Mrs. O. D. Vaughan's theatre coat was just redder than coral. Mrs. R. W. Finlayson's closer to ruby as was Lady Butler's short draped dinner dress.

Mrs. Russell Payton, chairman of the Canadian Opera Women's Committee, wore a lovely white beaded sheath with a pattern or roses picked up by a rose cummerbund.

Judging by the opening it will be a season of soft satins and brocades. Mrs. Ralph Salter was in cafe au lait satin with pleats, Mrs. Floyd Chalmers in soft blue satin, Mrs. A. G. Volpe, also in blue and Mrs. Hugh Allward in off-white. Mrs. Walter Lind's pale beige dress had a fitted bodice, closely embroidered. Mrs. George McCullagh was in an ensemble of pale beige brocade.

Mrs. M. K. Rudd wore a theatre suit of light blue brocade, Mrs. C. H. E. Stewart had chosen a slightly darker blue, Mrs. Fletcher Sharp's draped dress was in an interesting copper and gold pattern and Mrs J. R. W. Wilby's was a dark flower pattern in multi-color. Mrs. Samuel Zacks wore silver lame with pleated skirt and faintly bloused top.

Mrs. Donald McGibbon, busy with Drama Festival guests, wore a grey-violet taffeta and Mrs. Fergus Mutrie, come from Ottawa for the occasion, had a dull purple chiffon.

Mrs. Charles Tisdall and Mrs. Frank McEachren were both in navy lace and Mrs. N. F. Kelly wore black lace, fashioned in tiers. Smart, short black dinner dresses were worn by Mrs. Robert Winters and Mrs. Ettore Mazzoleni, the latter's with a black panel falling into a train.

MTLB

Mrs. Yves Bourassa of Montreal (middle), in Toronto for the meeting of the Dominion Drama Festival board, was a guest at dinner and opera of Mr. and Mrs. Donald McGibbon. Mrs. Bourassa wore red, Mrs. McGibbon grey-violet.

Globe & Mail, Oct. 2, 1961

O'KEEFE CENTRE

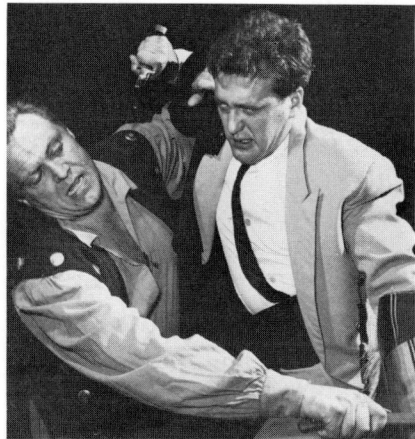

Photo: Alex Gray   COCA
RICHARD CASSILLY AND VICTOR BRAUN in *Carmen*

Conductor MARIO BERNARDI, *Pagliacci*.   COC

Bass JAN RUBES, *The Bartered Bride*.   COC

Photo: David Wulkan   COC
Mezzo-soprano PATRICIA RIDEOUT, *Cavalleria Rusticana*.

Conductor ERNESTO BARBINI, *Cavalleria Rusticana, Tosca*.   COC

Tenor PHIL STARK, *Carmen, Tosca, The Bartered Bride*.   COC

Costume Designer SUZANNE MESS, *Carmen, Tosca*.   COC

Designer WILLIAM LORD, *Cavalleria Rusticana* (sets & costumes) *The Bartered Bride* (costumes).   COC

Director LEON MAJOR, *Pagliacci*.   COC

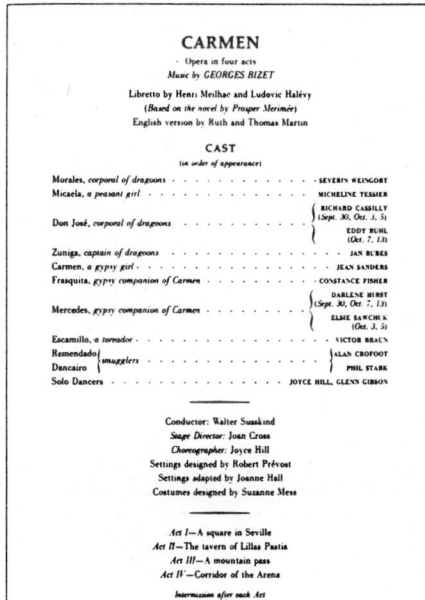

Programme   COCA

Tenor ALAN CROFOOT *The Bartered Bride, Carmen, Pagliacci*.   OC

Set Designer MURRAY LAUFER, *The Bartered Bride*.   COC

SELECTED FIRSTS . . . 1961

O'KEEFE CENTRE

SELECTED FIRSTS

1961

ILONA KOMBRINK, BENJAMIN RAYSON
Sheer theatrical oomph!
—Star Photo by Mario Geo

1962

The COC's first Wagner, *Die Walkure*, Wotan – Paul Schoeffler, Die Walkure – Constance Fisher, Elizabeth Elliott, Irene Loosberg, Sylvia Grant, Marguerite Desjardins, June Grant, Mona Kelly.

Photo: Alex Gray   COCA

MUSIC / with John Beckwith

Canadian Opera's 'Tosca' Full-Blooded, Polished

There aren't too many good reasons for reviving Puccini's "Tosca" today, unless sheer theatrical oomph seems to you a good reason.

The score is more pretentious but less genuine than "La Boheme;" it's motivically more tight-knit but melodically considerably less beautiful than that earlier success. In fact what hangs over all the Puccini operas after "La Boheme" may well be what Tennessee Williams has called "the catastrophe of success." Certainly a rehearing of "Tosca" confirms it has practically no integrity, only great skill.

"Tosca" is receiving a full-blooded, polished and well-sung production by the Canadian Opera company in its current O'Keefe centre run. The first of four presentations took place Saturday. Herman Geiger-Torel is the stage director, Ernesto Barbini the conductor; and there are three excellent performances in the leading parts of Tosca, Cavaradossi, and Scarpia—the singers being Ilona Kombrink, Richard Verreau, and Benjamin Rayson.

The best of the three acts, the second, comes vividly to life right from the splendid barking aria of Scarpia through to Tosca's desperate and furtive execution of the murder and her escape. A new device, a book-shelf concealing the torture-chamber door, is rather overworked, but this is the act's only serious weakness.

On the other hand the church scene (act one) is visually confused, since in Hans Berends' pleasing-enough setting we're left wondering whether the unseen nave of the church is offstage to the left or out in the auditorium.

The lighting of it, moreover, is far brighter than any European church-interior I was ever in, and Mr. Torel's staging of the procession at the end, though reasonably impressive, makes liturgically little sense.

(The same could be said for Puccini's indiscriminately-harmonized chants and bell-motives. It's not really aboveboard that he and his librettists should make such dramatic hay out of the fact that their fugitive's hiding place is a church, any more than out of Tosca's supposed piety, which they seem able to remember or forget as the theatrical moment requires.)

Mr. Rayson's gift for exuding authority through both voice and physical bearing was well displayed in his Tonio in "Pagliacci," and now receives further confirmation.

Mr. Verreau's tenor of romantic-pathetic cast is well suited to his role here. From his opening aria, onward, he makes an outstanding impression in a season of unusually high-standard tenor performances. There isn't much he can do about his slightness of build, nor about the overdone torture-wails, offstage, which Puccini hands him in act two; but he is handsome, moves with agility, and assumes the torture-victim's appearance believably.

Miss Kombrink's Tosca was the first big success of many she has had with the COC. I missed that 1957 production, so can't say how much she's matured in her handling of the role, only that she's obviously well at home in it, and looks and moves graciously in Suzanne Mess' well-conceived gowns.

Few of the subtleties of act two escape her attention. Surprisingly, though, her "Non posso piu!" and "Assassino!" ejaculations are more varied and better projected than the stillness of the central musical piece, the aria "Vissi d'arte." Perhaps this is partly because the director here has Scarpia distract us with unneeded bits of business, when the attention should be Tosca's alone.

But the fault lies also partly with Miss Kombrink's vocal delivery. The sounds she makes are large and sympathetically colored, but tend to lose interest in middle and low range at the softer levels.

I was disturbed again on Saturday, as at times in earlier performances of hers, by that jerkiness and wobbly jawed forcefulness she assumes in difficult stretches: such stretches always come off well, but with so little energy to spare you feel a bit nervous for her.

Vaclovas Verikaitis is rich-voiced and impassioned as Angelotti, the political fugitive in act one, and Phil Stark is suitably oily as Scarpia's henchman. Ernest Adams as the Sacristan, complete with exaggerated makeup and gross belly, performs in the hammy old opera-comedy style of which I was hoping the Met's Gerhard Pechner was the last living representative.

Star, Oct. 10, 1961   COCA

Instead of a dreaded sepulchre awaiting the remains of the Canadian Opera Company, the O'Keefe Centre turned out to be almost ideal.

Audience and singers were inspired by new opera home

BY CRITICUS

WE FEEL it can be truthfully said that the recent opera season in Toronto was a triumph for all concerned. The all-round advance in standards on previous seasons was quite incredible. Many factors seem to have contributed toward this, with one topping them all.

The hero of the piece was, undoubtedly, the O'Keefe Centre itself. Far from being the dreaded sepulchre awaiting the remains of the Opera Company (according to many Jeremiahs prophesying for months beforehand), it turned out to be an almost ideal theatre for opera.

The secret, of course, was that the theatre was at last allowed to speak for itself. For once, it was not festooned with microphones and loud-speakers, and everything was heard naturally and clearly for the first time.

While the Metropolitan Opera Company had removed the acoustic-destroying microphones, it did not have time to assess the theatre for projection of both voices and instruments. The Canadian Opera Company had a week in which to try it out, and the results were quite amazing. It is a joy to know that Toronto at last possesses one of the world's most magnificent opera houses.

As to the performances, it was generally agreed that only perhaps twice during the Metropolitan's week-long stay did that Company surpass our own native group. Our mostly-young singers seemed inspired by their surroundings and the excellent visiting team seemed to catch enthusiasm from their fellow artists. The orchestral

Large stage enabled the COC to mount dramatic sets. Design for scene one of Carmen shows the depth and perspective achieved.

playing throughout the two weeks retained a very high standard and the sounds from the correctly adjusted pit floor were quite uncannily clear, every strand of the orchestral texture being heard in every part of the house.

The only serious criticism that could be found was that the season was limited to two weeks, which meant that only one evening performance of *The Bartered Bride* was possible. As this was the opera that most people wanted to see, there was much disappointment. It is hoped that future seasons will become more and more interesting, as they are bound to do. The aim of the company should be to get many of the Canadian singers now working abroad to come back and swell the ranks. If all these artists could be gathered up from the world's opera houses, a company second to none could be formed. We hope that it is only a matter of time.

Another factor which contributed so much to the success of the season was the way it caught on with the public. There is no doubt that musical people in Toronto are much more discerning than had been realized. These lovers of opera know full well that any attempt at operatic performances in the Royal Alexandra was doomed to half failure before it was even put on the stage, owing to the theatre itself, which is utterly unsuitable in every way for opera.

It is true to say that Toronto had never really heard an opera properly before this year. The opera-loving public had obviously stayed away from the Royal Alexandra performances in large numbers. The move to O'Keefe's (which is three times as large) immediately produced a 90% house. Some of this was undoubtedly due to the subscription arrangements at O'Keefe's, but not by any means all of it, as simple arithmetic will show.

Opera in Toronto has certainly had the biggest shot in the arm it has ever had. Next year, the superb opera theatre in the new Faculty of Music building at the University of Toronto will be in use by the Opera School, so that the city will have become, in a short space of time, one of the main operatic centres of the continent.

Opera Canada, Sept.-Oct. 1961   COCA

O'KEEFE CENTRE

SELECTED FIRSTS

1962

Photo: Alex Gray — COCA

LOUIS QUILICO'S first *Rigoletto* with the Canadian Opera Company with ENRICO DI GIUSEPPE as the Duke and VICTOR BRAUN as Monterone.

1962

COC

Canadian Baritone LOUIS QUILICO

1963

Photo: Alex Gray — COCA

The COC's first *Aida* GLORIA LANE as Amneris OSYP HOSHULIAK as the King.

1964

Photo: Alex Gray — COCA

MARILYN HORNE as Amneris in *Aida*.

1965

COCA

Turandot – GIUSEPPE CAMPORA and JEANNINE CRADER

1965

COCA

SALOME – PHIL STARK, MARGARET TYNES, ARLENE MEADOWS.

O'KEEFE CENTRE

Photo: Alex Gray COCA
The Luck of Ginger Coffey, HARRY THEYARD as Coffey.

COC
Composer RAYMOND PANNELL
The Luck of Ginger Coffey.

COC
Librettist RONALD HAMBLETON, *The Luck of Ginger Coffey.*

Photo: Alex Gray COCA
BERNARD TURGEON as Louis Riel.

SELECTED FIRSTS...
1967 Centennial
Two World premieres
of Canadian Operas.

COC
Composer, HARRY SOMERS, *Louis Riel.*

COC
Librettist MAVOR MOORE, *Louis Riel.*

1969
Photo: Ludvik Dittrik COCA
ASTRID VARNAY – the title role in *Elektra.*

1967

COC
Young Canadian tenor ERMANNO MAURO sang his first lead role with the COC when he replaced the tenor who was singing the role of Manrico in *Il Trovatore.*

Photo: Studio Claessens OC
Co-librettist JACQUES LANGUIRAND, *Louis Riel.*

O'KEEFE CENTRE

1974

Photo: Robert C. Ragsdale — COCA
Boris Godunov – DON GARRARD in the title role.

1970

Photo: Robert C. Ragsdale — COCA
CHESTER LUDGIN, DON McMANUS, ANJA SILJA, GLADE PETERSON, in *Fidelio*.

1971

Photo: Robert C. Ragsdale — COCA
LYNNE CANTLON as the Merry Widow

1975

Photo: Robert C. Ragsdale — COCA
Manon Lescaut – HEATHER THOMSON and ERMANNO MAURO.

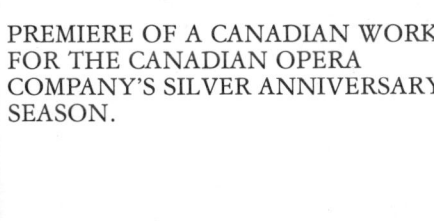
PREMIERE OF A CANADIAN WORK FOR THE CANADIAN OPERA COMPANY'S SILVER ANNIVERSARY SEASON.

1973

COCA

ALLAN MONK and HEATHER THOMSON in *Heloise and Abelard*.

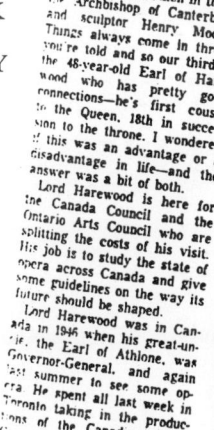
Excerpt from the Globe and Mail, Oct. 19, 1971

MTLB

The Earl of Harewood is the founder of the distinguished British magazine *Opera*.

SELECTED FIRSTS

COC
Librettist EUGENE BENSON, *Heloise and Abelard*.

Globe & Mail Sept. 1, 1973 — MTLB
Composer CHARLES WILSON and sculpture of the ill-fated Heloise.

245

O'KEEFE CENTRE

European stage director named head of Canadian Opera Company

Globe & Mail Headline Aug. 19, 1975

Photo: Walter Curtin

First season for the Canadian Opera Company's new General Director LOTFI MANSOURI. 1977

DON CARLOS, CLARICE CARSON as Elisabeth, PAUL PLISHKA as Philip II, VICTOR BRAUN as Rodriguez.

Photo: Robert C. Ragsdale

1977

Photo: Robert C. Ragsdale

Canadian Premiere of *Wozzeck* ALLAN MONK in the title role JOHN KEANE as the Fool.

1978

Photo: Robert C. Ragsdale

LYN VERNON as Tchaikowsky's Joan of Arc.

SELECTED FIRSTS

PROGRAMME COVER

Simon Boccanegra, Father and son – LOUIS QUILICO as Simone, GINO QUILICO as Paolo.

1979

Photo: Robert C. Ragsdale

1979

Photo: Robert C. Ragsdale

Tristan und Isolde – JOHANNA MEIER and SPAS WENKOFF.

1980

Photo: Robert C. Ragsdale

Peter Grimes – WILLIAM NEILL as Peter and THOMAS STEWART as Balstrode.

O'KEEFE CENTRE

1980

Photo: Robert C. Ragsdale — COCA
Lulu – CAROLE FARLEY in the title role and EVELYN LEAR as the Countess Geschwitz.

1981

Photo: Robert C. Ragsdale — COCA
Swedish soprano ELISABETH SODERSTROM as Anna Glawari in *The Merry Widow*.

1981

Photo: Robert C. Ragsdale — COCA
Norma – JOAN SUTHERLAND as Norma, TATIANA TROYANOS as Adalgisa.

1982

Photo: Robert C. Ragsdale — COCA
Jenufa – PATRICIA WELLS in the title role.

1981

Ensemble members THEODORE BAERG as Enrico and CARALYN TOMLIN as Lucia in *Lucia di Lammermoor*.

Photo: Robert C. Ragsdale — COCA

SELECTED FIRSTS

1981

PROGRAMME

1981

Photo: Ken Batiuk — COC
DEREK BATE, Conductor of the Canadian Opera Company Ensemble's *Lucia di Lammermoor*.

1983

The Coronation of Poppea CARMEN BALTHROP as Poppea and MICHAEL MEYERS as Nero.

Photo: Robert C. Ragsdale

SELECTED APPEARANCES	
1961	Metropolitan Opera Company
1961 et seq	Canadian Opera Company Seasons
1965	Metropolitan Opera National Company
1966	Metropolitan Opera National Company
1974	Marilyn Horne and the Canadian Brass
1979	Canadian Ukrainian Opera Association
1981	Canadian Opera Company Ensemble
1982	Canadian Opera Company Ensemble

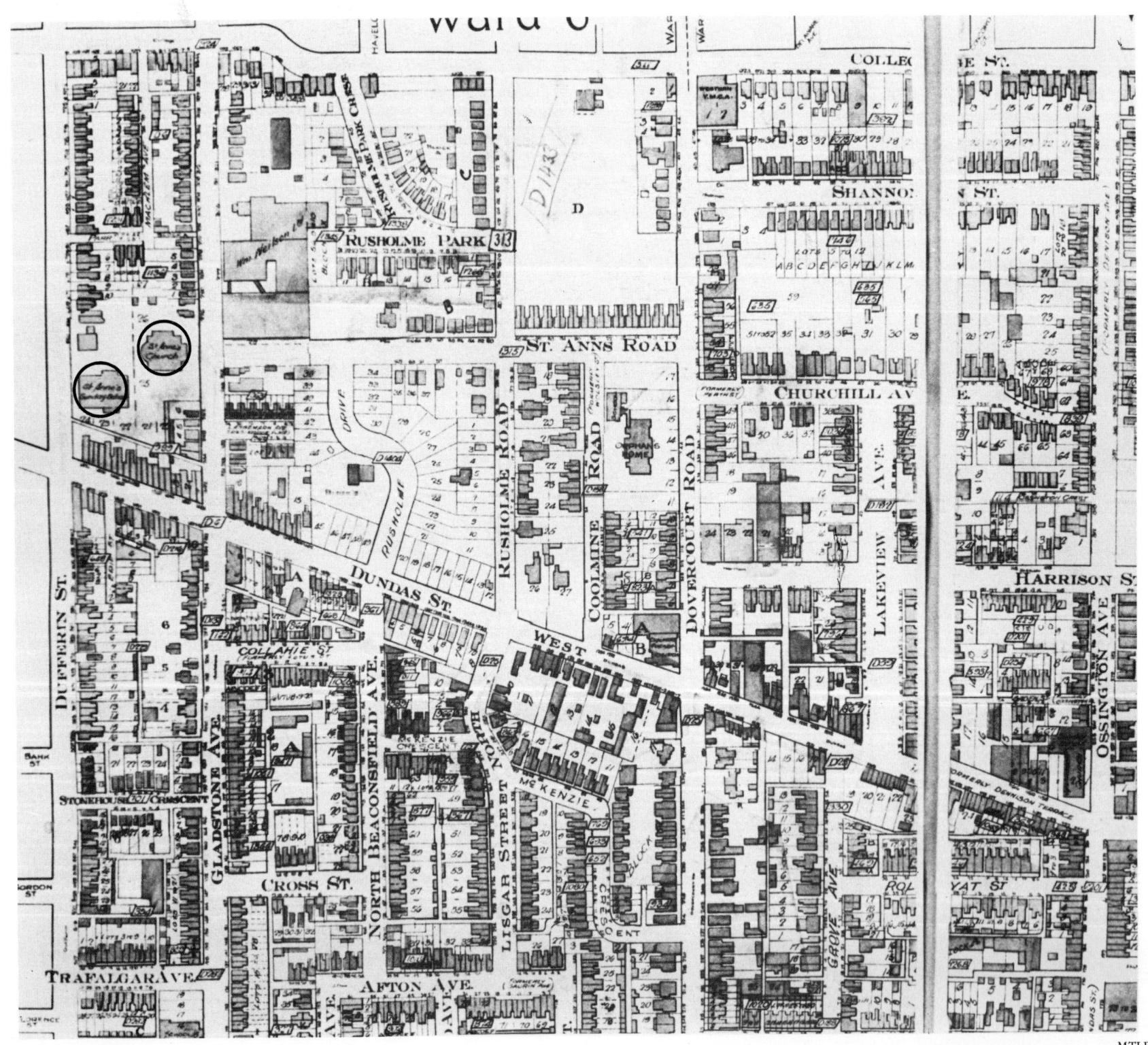

Goad's Atlas 1910

1964
ST. ANNE'S CHURCH

A uniquely beautiful church and a parish hall which is a boon to Gilbert and Sullivan devotees.

Postcard SAC

ST. ANNE'S CHURCH

The parish of St. Anne's was established in 1862 and the first church faced onto Dufferin Street. The present church on Gladstone Avenue is the only example in Canada of pure Byzantine architecture and was erected in 1907 under the leadership of the Rector, Lawrence Skey. It was closed for renovations during 1923, re-opening in December of that year. The improvements included, in the sancturary, oil paintings by the Group of Seven. Since 1964 St. Anne's Music and Drama Society has given annual productions of Gilbert and Sullivan operas in the parish hall, under Stage Direction of Roy Schatz and the Musical Direction of Clifford Poole and Lloyd Bradshaw.

1980   COCA

APPEARANCES
1964-83 St. Anne's Music and Drama Society
1975 *The Messiah* – Burnetta Day, Margaret Ann Richards, Robert Heard, Louis Quilico
1983 *Amahl and the Night Visitors*

1964
MacMILLAN THEATRE

The ideal auditorium for opera-lovers.

THE EDWARD JOHNSON BUILDING

MACMILLAN THEATRE

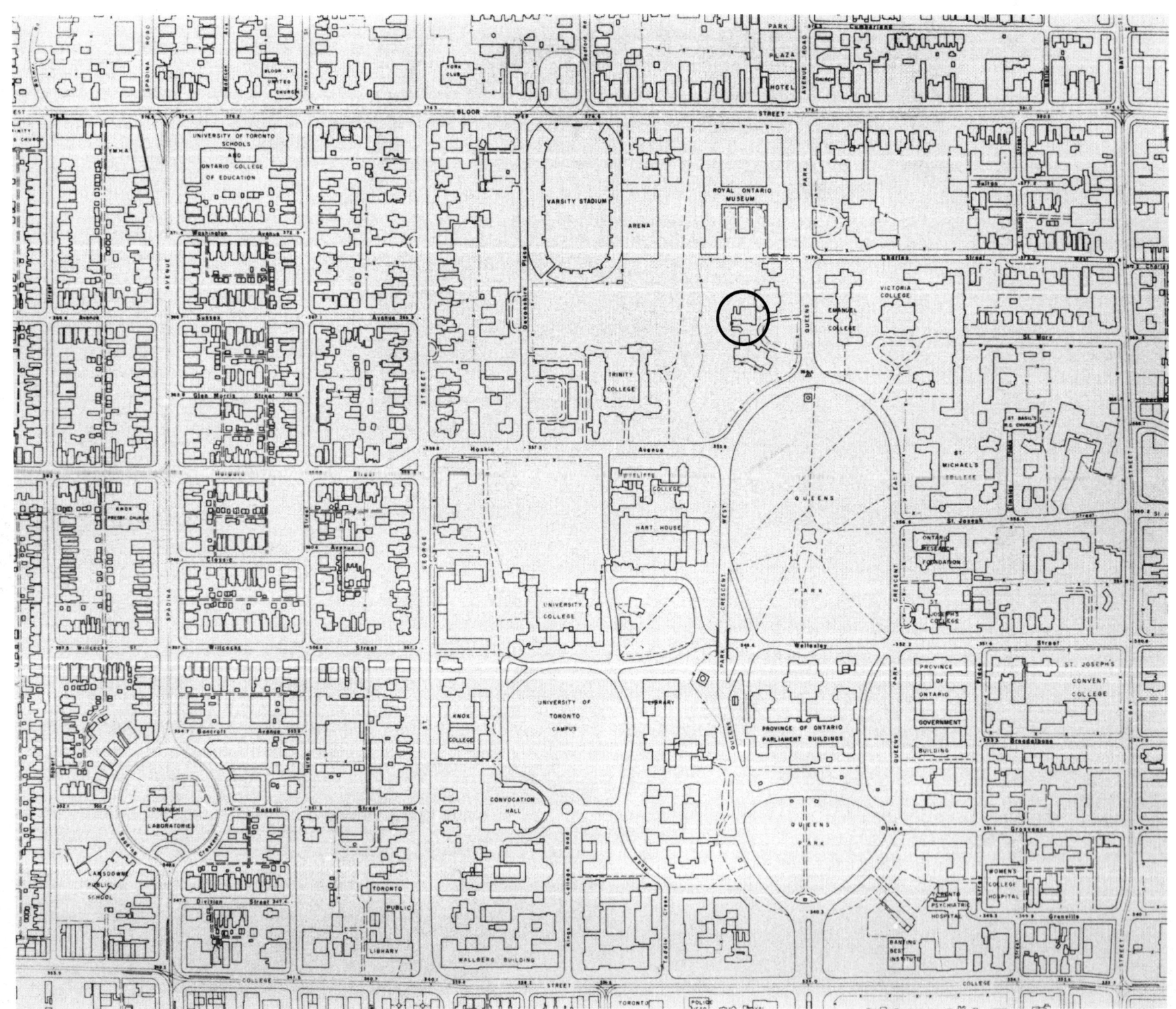

City of Toronto Planning Board 1957

MACMILLAN THEATRE

At the time of the National Council of Education's sponsorship of a week of opera in 1930 (see Royal Alexandra Theatre) the Chairman of the Council was Dr. Harold M. Tovell, a son-in-law of Hart Massey's son Walter. In a letter to his friend Henry Button, Dr. Tovell expressed his satisfaction with the venture and his conviction that "a truly magnificent operative centre can be formed by the utilization of the staff of the Conservatory in all its departments". What was needed to bring this about was suitable accommodation. He proposed the sale of Massey Hall and the Conservatory (south-west corner of College and University) and the construction of a "truly worthy building". After writing this letter he visited opera houses in Europe and garnered much useful information. The depression of the 1930's and World War II in the 1940's forced the shelving of such dreams. After the war the expansion of the Conservatory's activities, e.g. the establishment of the Opera School in 1946 by Arnold Walter, Director of the Toronto Conservatory of Music, demonstrated very clearly the inadequacies of the old building. In 1953 Boyd Neel was appointed Dean of the (by then) Royal Conservatory of Music and the Faculty of Music of the University of Toronto. With men such as Arnold Walter, Ettore Mazzoleni, Herman Geiger-Torel and Edward Johson (the Canadian tenor whose term as General Manager of the Metropolitan Opera was noted for the encouragement of native talent and who had been a guarantor for the week of opera in 1930), Neel brought Dr. Tovell's dreams to reality – if not for the city, at least for the Conservatory and the University.

On April 20, 1961, Fiorenza Drew, daughter of Edward Johnson and wife of Canada's High Commissioner to London, laid the cornerstone of the Edward Johnson Building which was to contain an opera theatre named for Sir Ernest MacMillan. The theatre, with a seating capacity of 815, has a stage 134 feet wide, 50 feet deep and 85 feet high. The orchestra pit holds an orchestra of 80.

THE EDWARD JOHNSON BUILDING is located on a rising slope on the North Campus where the towering profile of the opera house has already become an outstanding feature of the skyline.

The new building offers facilities which are second to none on the continent. The building is sound-proofed and air-conditioned. It includes forty-one individual practice rooms; classrooms equipped for the use of tape and disc recording, along with the most modern visual aids; individual lockers for full-time students; common rooms; recording control rooms; special sections for instrument storage and repair. The department of Electronic Music has laboratories and studios in the building.

The entire third floor is devoted to the Edward Johnson Memorial Music Library, the nucleus of which is Dr. Johnson's own priceless collection of scores and books, contributed during his lifetime. The shelves can accommodate over 75,000 books, scores and records; and the Library, in addition to an extensive reading room, has individual listening cubicles and sound-proof booths for both monaural and stereophonic listening; workshops, and a seminar room.

Most striking features of the building are the two auditoria. The larger, the MacMillan Theatre, seats 815 and is designed specifically for opera, but will also be used for orchestral, band and chorus concerts. This auditorium provides opera students with an opportunity to perform on one of the largest and best equipped stages on the continent. The smaller auditorium, a Concert Hall, seats 500 and is used for recitals, primarily by and for students.

COCA

From the programme, Opening Ceremonies, Mar. 2-8, 1964.

New building in Toronto will house opera house and recital hall

DR. BOYD NEEL   UTA

Photo: Cavouk   UTFM
DR. ARNOLD WALTER

Opera School will get 'perfect' home
by DR. BOYD NEEL, *Dean of the Royal Conservatory of Music*

IN THE FALL of 1961, the Faculty of Music of the Royal Conservatory will move into its new building in Toronto. It will find there an opera house of the most modern design, constructed especially for the training of students in stagecraft.

This will end a sorry state of affairs. Founded some fourteen years ago, the Opera School of the faculty has become, in effect, a National School of Opera. There is nothing else like it in Canada. It has trained a great number of Canadian singing actors now before the public on stage, television and film. But all this has been achieved under conditions which would never have been tolerated in any other profession.

Would the Medical Faculty of the University dream of training a student without a laboratory or hospital? Would the Faculty of Law undertake the training of a student without an adequate library? Would the Engineering Department train students without workshops or laboratories? Of course they would not.

Yet we musicians have had to try and do this very thing with our opera students, since we have had no theatre or even adequate space in which to work.

Stagecraft is a comprehensive term which includes not only acting and singing, but everything to do with the theatre, from the designing and construction of scenery to the running of the business side of the house.

In fact, students will be able to come to the University and study operatic production in all its facets, and we hope that this school will become a magnet which will draw students from all over the world, as it should be unique of its kind.

The theatre will seat 850 people and should be acoustically perfect, since we are able to design an auditorium which is not too large. Size has hitherto always been the bugbear of acoustic design because enough seats have had to be provided to make the theatre a going concern commercially. We are in the happy position of not having to bother about this side of the matter and we feel that our auditorium will be of ideal cubic capacity.

The stage and lighting systems will be of the most modern design and the orchestra pit capable of seating the largest symphony orchestra.

Besides the Opera House, the building will contain a Recital Hall seating 500 people, which can be used for student recitals and also for visiting chamber music ensembles. The platform of this hall will be large enough for a small chamber orchestra.

Added to this will be the Electronic Music Department and many lecture-recital halls, lecture rooms, and practice rooms. It is hoped that it will be the most comprehensive and up-to-date music school in the world today.

September-October 1960

Opera in Canada

COCA

MacMILLAN THEATRE

For 20 years this facility has been used by the Canadian Opera Company for rehearsals.

The opening of a new University building is usually an affair of ritual and ceremony, since the substance of what goes on in the building cannot be easily displayed.

But the opening of a music building is not so circumscribed: to ritual and ceremony we can add what actually emerges from the work of student and teacher. We celebrate the opening of the Edward Johnson Building with a festival of music, created by the composer and recreated by the performer. In this way we proclaim the double purpose of this magnificent building—a centre for musical studies and an addition to the cultural resources of the community and the country.

Claude Bissell, PRESIDENT.

COCA

From the programme, Opening Ceremonies, Mar. 2-8, 1964.

THE MacMILLAN THEATRE.

The MacMillan Theatre, in the Edward Johnson Building, new home for the University of Toronto's Faculty of Music is named after Sir Ernest MacMillan, Varsity graduate, Dean of the Faculty from 1927 to 1952, for many years principal of the Royal Conservatory of Music and for twenty-five years conductor of the Toronto Symphony Orchestra.

Sir Ernest was the first musician resident in the British Dominions to be knighted; the first Canadian to be elected a Fellow of the Royal College of Music. He holds a Doctor of Music degree of the University of Oxford and honorary degrees of the universities of British Columbia, Queens, Laval, McMaster, Toronto, Rochester, Mount Allison and Ottawa. As President of CAPAC, honorary President of Les Jeunesses Musicales de Canada, President of the Canadian Music Centre and Canadian Music Council, Sir Ernest is certainly the most distinguished musician in the Dominion, equally famous as composer, conductor and educator.

COCA

SIR ERNEST MACMILLAN

EDWARD JOHNSON

The Edward Johnson Building bears the name and honours the memory of a man without whose leadership and guidance it might never have been built. Edward Johnson had three careers in music, each as brilliant as the other two—as a singer, famous in all quarters of the globe; as an administrator, managing the Metropolitan Opera Company in New York for fifteen years; and as an educator, serving as Chairman of the Board of the Royal Conservatory of Music from 1947 to 1959. His conviction that music in North America can flourish only if sheltered by universities lead to the re-organisation of the Royal Conservatory and ultimately to the decision to provide the Faculty of Music with a building of its own.

COCA

From the programme, Opening Ceremonies, Mar. 2-8, 1964.

MACMILLAN THEATRE

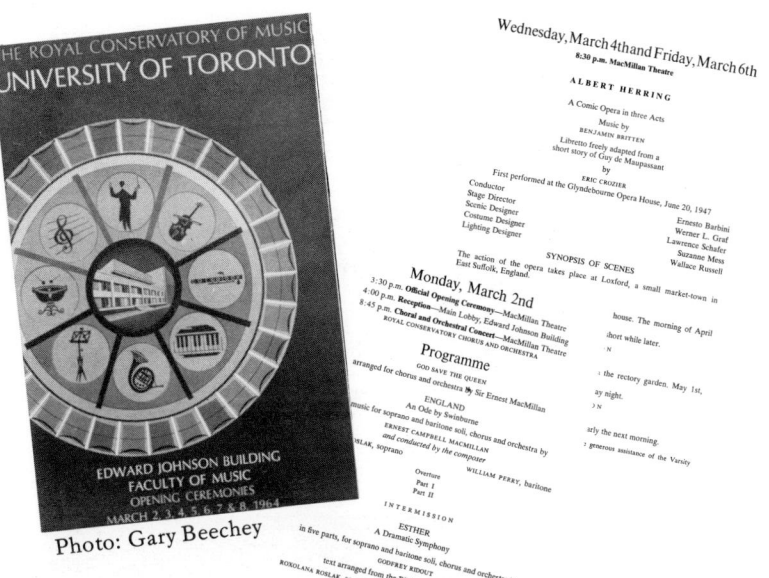

Photo: Gary Beechey

From the programme, Opening Ceremonies, Mar. 2-8, 1964.

Set Designer LAWRENCE SCHAEFER, RCM Principal ETTORE MAZZOLENI, Librettist JOHN COULTER, Composer HEALEY WILLAN, Stage Director, HERMAN GEIGER-TOREL.

ALBERT HERRING, 1964
GARNET BROOKS, NAOMI ALEXANDROFF, RICHARD BRAUN.

DIALOGUES OF THE CARMELITES (Poulenc) 1967
JEANNETTE ZAROU, NANCY GREENWOOD.

DEIRDRE 1965,
LILLIAN SUKIS, as Deirdre,
a role she shared with Jeannette Zarou.

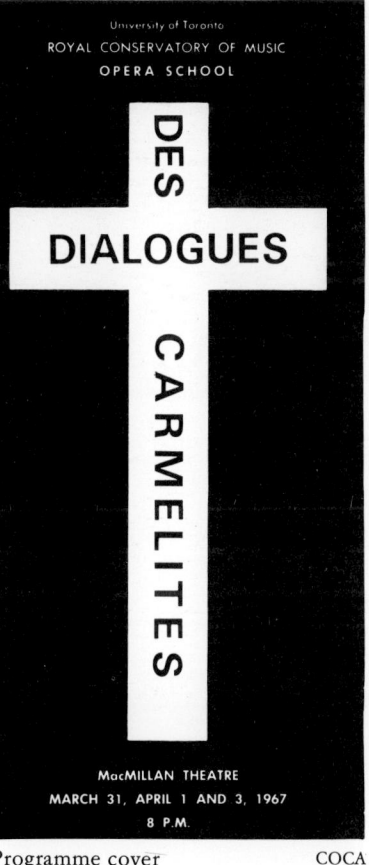

Programme cover

Programme cover

255

MACMILLAN THEATRE

Programme cover, 1968   COCA

PELLEAS AND MELISANDE, 1968 DANIELLE PILON, PAUL TREPANIER.

UTFM

Programme cover, 1971   COCA

HAMLET 1969, STEVEN HENRIKSON, TED WALKER, DONALD RUTHERFORD (Hamlet) ROLPH OOSTWOOD, THEODORE GENTRY.

Photo: Robert Lansdale   UTFM

THE RAKE'S PROGRESS 1971 JILL PERT as Baba the Turk.

Photo: Arnold Matthews   UTFM

Programme cover 1969   COCA

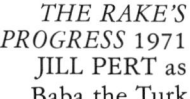

The Opera School
Royal Conservatory of Music
General Director, Anthony Besch

presents

The North American Premier
of

HAMLET

by Humphrey Searle

Produced and Directed by: Anthony Besch
Conductor: Victor Feldbrill
Designer: John Stoddart

Lighting Designer: William Severin
Chorus Master: Lloyd Bradshaw
Repetiteurs: George Brough, Bruce Grant, Alfred Strombergs
Assistant Director: Danny Jellis
Assistant Chorus Master: Kenneth Jones
Assistant to the Designer: Donald McLeod
Duel arranged by: Patrick Crean

February 12, 13, 15 and 16, 1969
at 8:00 p.m.

MacMillan Theatre
Edward Johnson Building
University of Toronto

Programme 1969   COCA

Programme cover 1973   COCA

L'Ormindo MARION HARVEY and BRUCE KELLY

Photo: Robert C. Ragsdale   UTFM

MACMILLAN THEATRE

Programme cover, 1976   COCA

Photo: Robert C. Ragsdale   UTFM

THE CRUCIBLE (Ward) 1976, RICHARD BRUNNER, NANCY HERMISTON, JOHN NIEBOER.

Flyer 1978   EJMF

Photo: Gerard Macdonald   EJMF

NICHOLAS GOLDSCHMIDT, O.C.
First Music Director: Royal Conservatory Opera School 1946-57. First Music Director: Opera Festival Association of Toronto 1950-7. Artistic Director: Edward Johnson Music Foundation 1967 ... Artistic Director: Algoma Fall Festival 1975 ... Conductor: *Seabird Island*.

Photo: Andrew Oxenham   UTFM

KATYA KABANOVA, 1977, KATHERINE TERRELL, JOHN KEANE.

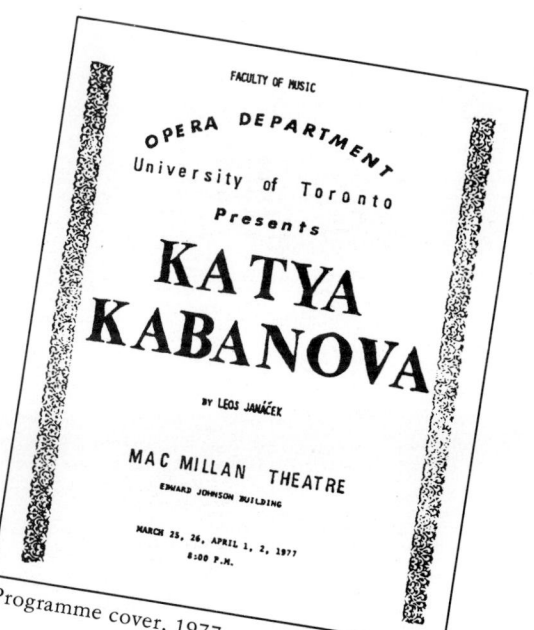

Programme cover, 1977   COCA

DEREK HEALEY, Composer: *Seabird Island*.

Photo: V. Tony Hauser

257

MACMILLAN THEATRE

Programme cover, 1979

ROXOLANA ROSLAK Odarka in *Kupalo*.

CORNELIS OPTHOF, Omar in *Kupalo*.

Photo: Andrew Oxenham

LA PERICHOLE 1981, DONNA HURST, MARK MANGUS, MARY JO MASTERSON, LEE RYAN, JAMES LEATCH.

Programme cover 1981

APPEARANCES
1964-69 Royal Conservatory Opera
1970   University of Toronto, Faculty of Music
1978   Guelph Spring Festival
1979   Canadian Ukrainian Opera Association
1980   Cosmopolitan Opera Association
1981   Cosmopolitan Opera Association
1981   Toronto Lyric Theatre

1967
CENTRAL TECHNICAL SCHOOL

Negative: J. Salmon
TORONTO ATHLETIC CLUB
MTLB S1-3861A

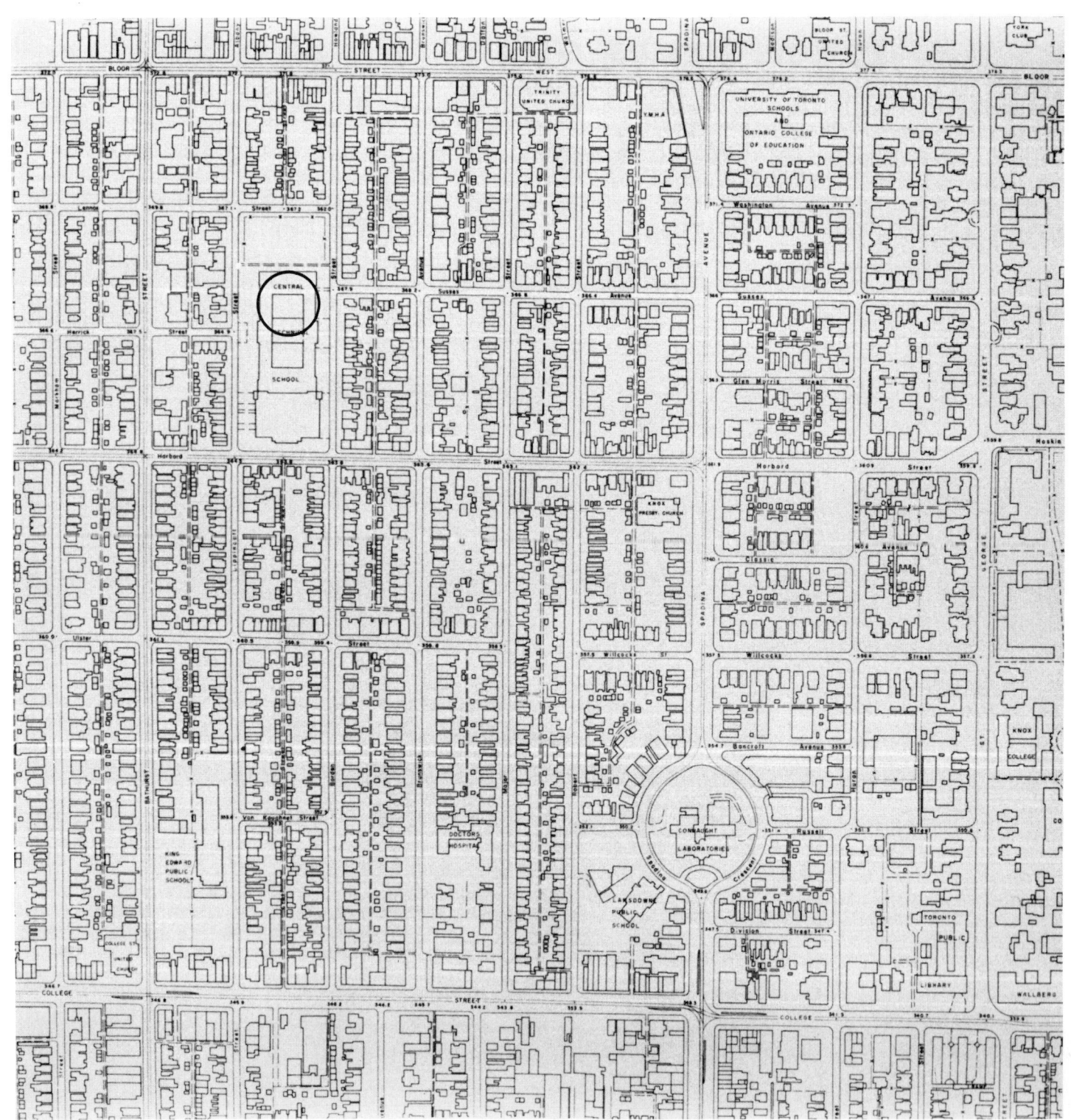

City of Toronto Planning Board 1957

CENTRAL TECHNICAL SCHOOL

Toronto Technical School (later Central Technical School) occupied the Toronto Athletic Club on College Street circa 1910-15. The school opened its new quarters at Bathurst and Harbord in 1915 and in 1946 an opera workshop was established by James Rosselino who was succeeded in the 1950's by Dr. Ernesto Vinci and Andrew MacMillan. In 1967 Giuseppe Macina organized the programme under the auspices of the Toronto Board of Education. Mr. Macina initiated programmes of excerpts, expanding in 1969 into full productions, and two years later Central Tech Opera Workshop became Toronto Opera Repertoire. In 1980 the Toronto City Opera was incorporated to sponsor the productions.

Toronto's 100 Years – Middleton

CENTRAL TECHNICAL SCHOOL, 1913 CTA

JAMES ROSSELINO who established the first Opera Workshop at Central Tech in 1946.

SEVEN ACRES OF FLOORS: A MILE OF BLACKBOARDS

Wonders of the New Technical School

CITY MUST BE IN EARNEST

Prosperity Does Not Hinge on Real Estate Man, but on Intelligent Industry—Impressive Inspection of Fine New Building Now Going Up.

"A unique and prophetic dinner," were the apt terms in which Mr. J. H. Cherrard of Montreal described the gathering of educationists last evening at the National Club. The occasion was the climax of a unique, prophetic and profitable two and a half hours spent by the Advisory and Industrial Committee of the Board of Education and other members and officials of the board inspecting the new Central Technical School on Harbord street, which is rapidly nearing completion.

The party was personally conducted by Principal Dr. McKay, who seemed to know every nook and corner of the building, from the "infernal regions," forty feet below the ground floor, up to the spacious roof, where the party walked under the ample blue of heaven.

A Remarkable Underworld.

Perhaps one of the greatest wonders among the many that the genii-like Principal revealed to the party was the underworld, upon which the school is based. The heating, ventilating, electrical and power-generating plants, which are being installed in the deep and extensive basements of the new school, are in themselves truly magnificent examples of technical ingenuity and skill. The boiler and engine rooms are like the interior of an ocean liner. The heating and air-purifying plants are the latest of their kind. The air supplied to the rooms is washed, and then passed through great ventors, and by means of a mighty fan is driven to all parts of the building. The bunkers will hold nearly two thousand tons of coal, which is automatically weighed as it goes in, and comes out in ash at the other end of the furnace.

On the first basement is a 25 x 60 foot swimming pool, which will be finished in white tile, and will be the most modern bath in existence, the water being in continual circulation.

Will Build Houses There.

The construction room is the largest in the building, and is intended for the erection of at least two full-sized houses, to teach the various branches of the building trade. When each house is built it will be torn down, and the pupils will begin again. Even the brick and tiles for the construction of these houses are to be made in the kilns of the school.

The plumbing room is to be equipped by the Plumbers' Association, and scholarships are to be established for this trade. Trustee Ellis said there were to be no more plumbers, only "sanitary engineers." The machine shop is the brightest room in the building, being at the base of the light well, and is light enough even for watch-making.

The ladies' department contains rooms for the teaching of everything a woman can do, from millinery to housekeeping. Model apartments are being prepared where every household duty can be actually gone through, to teach girls how best to take care of a home.

There are seven lecture rooms and no end of class rooms where art, chemistry, printing, photography, electroplating and all the trades are to be taught.

Seven Acres of Floors.

There are in all seven acres of floor space, and not an inch of it is wasted. Some of the party became detached and got lost in the interminable rooms and corridors. There is over a mile of blackboards throughout the building. The school will accommodate 7,500 pupils.

The exterior is of beautiful Credit Valley piebald stone, quarried, dressed and trimmed in Canada. The style of architecture is Gothic in its main features and feeling.

Must be in Earnest.

Speaking at the dinner which followed the inspection, Principal McKay said he believed Toronto should be desperately in earnest about technical education in the days of stress. "We are just realizing," he said, "that the things done in the past were not the essential things. The prosperity of Toronto does not depend upon the activities of the real estate man, but ultimately upon the industrial life of the community. Toronto is a great manufacturing city to-day, and it is to be greater to-morrow. Four-fifths of the people are engaged in industrial work. This is a scheme to assist these people. The strongest recuperative force in these times of stringency is the technical school."

Must Train the Young.

Trustee Fairbairn said we must train men as quickly as possible and not worry about the expense. To get a fair wage it was necessary to train men so that they can earn it.

Trustee Chairman Ellis, Inspector Cowley, Secretary Wilkinson and other board officers and members of the committee spoke. Messrs. Clark, Brigden, Mason and Fairbairn provided the dinner.

Globe, Oct. 14, 1914 NLC

COCA

ANDREW MacMILLAN, Bass-baritone and stage director.

OC

DR. ERNESTO VINCI, Teacher and singer

CENTRAL TECHNICAL SCHOOL

Photo: Susan porter — TOR

GIUSEPPE MACINA, Teacher, Founder/Director, Toronto Opera Repertoire.
In 1977 he was made an honorary (since he comes from Bari in southern Italy) Alpino because of his work with the Chorus of Santa Cecilia and he was awarded Queen Elizabeth's Silver Jubilee Medal for his contribution to the teaching of Italian art in Canada.

TORONTO OPERA REPERTOIRE
(Board of Education Night School)
presents

MADAMA BUTTERFLY
by GIACOMO PUCCINI

DIRECTED BY · GIUSEPPE MACINA
CONDUCTED BY · JOSÉ HERNANDES
ACCOMPANISTS · MARGOT RUTGERS-KRYGER
· DEREK BATE

8:00 pm
CENTRAL TECH THEATRE
(725 Bathurst Street — Harbord Street Entrance)

Programme cover — COCA
1973

Photo: Eugene Federenko — TOR
UN BALLO IN MASCHERA 1971

Photo: Eugene Federenko — TOR
NORMA 1973
MARIA DYMEK in the title role,
DIANE LOEB as Adalgisa

1982-83 SEASON
TORONTO OPERA REPERTOIRE
sponsored by Toronto City Opera
Director: Giuseppe Macina

Programme cover — COCA

ELISIR D'AMORE by Donizetti in Italian
Toronto Opera Repertoire
Sponsored by
Toronto City Opera
at
Central Tech Theatre
Harbord & Bathurst Streets
(Harbord St. Entrance)
Nº 2661
Saturday, February 19, 1983
8 p.m.

Ticket — COCA

Photo: Andre Pierre & Associate — TOR
MEDEA 1983
RAISA SADOWA as Medea, ROBERT KUNZLI as Creonte.

APPEARANCES
1967-71 Central Tech Opera Workshop
1971 Toronto Opera Repertoire

1970
VAUGHAN ROAD COLLEGIATE INSTITUTE

Representing

Northern Secondary School
George Harvey Secondary School
Earl Haig Collegiate Institute
Cedarbrae Collegiate Institute
Castle Frank High School

Auditoria which have made opera accessible to all.

VAUGHAN ROAD COLLEGIATE INSTITUTE 1983

VAUGHAN ROAD COLLEGIATE INSTITUTE

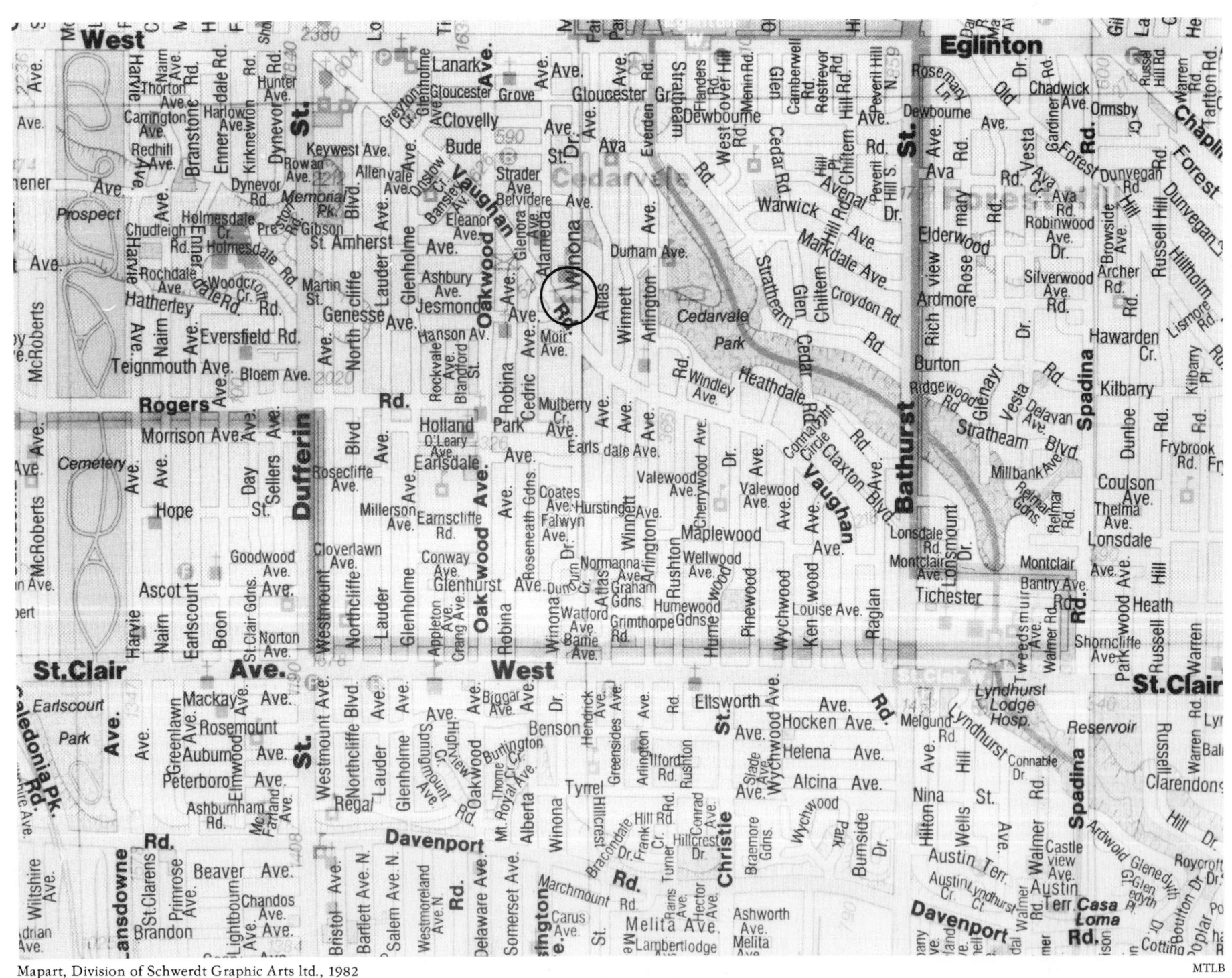

Mapart, Division of Schwerdt Graphic Arts ltd., 1982

VAUGHAN ROAD COLLEGIATE INSTITUTE

VAUGHAN ROAD COLLEGIATE INSTITUTE began as Vaughan Road High School in 1928. The Toronto Opera Society (see Heintzman Street Hall) first gave operatic evenings in the auditorium in 1970. In 1982, The Board of Education for the City of York established York Community Opera – a night course for opera, similar to Central Tech's programme and, like it, under the Artistic Directorship of Giuseppe Macina.

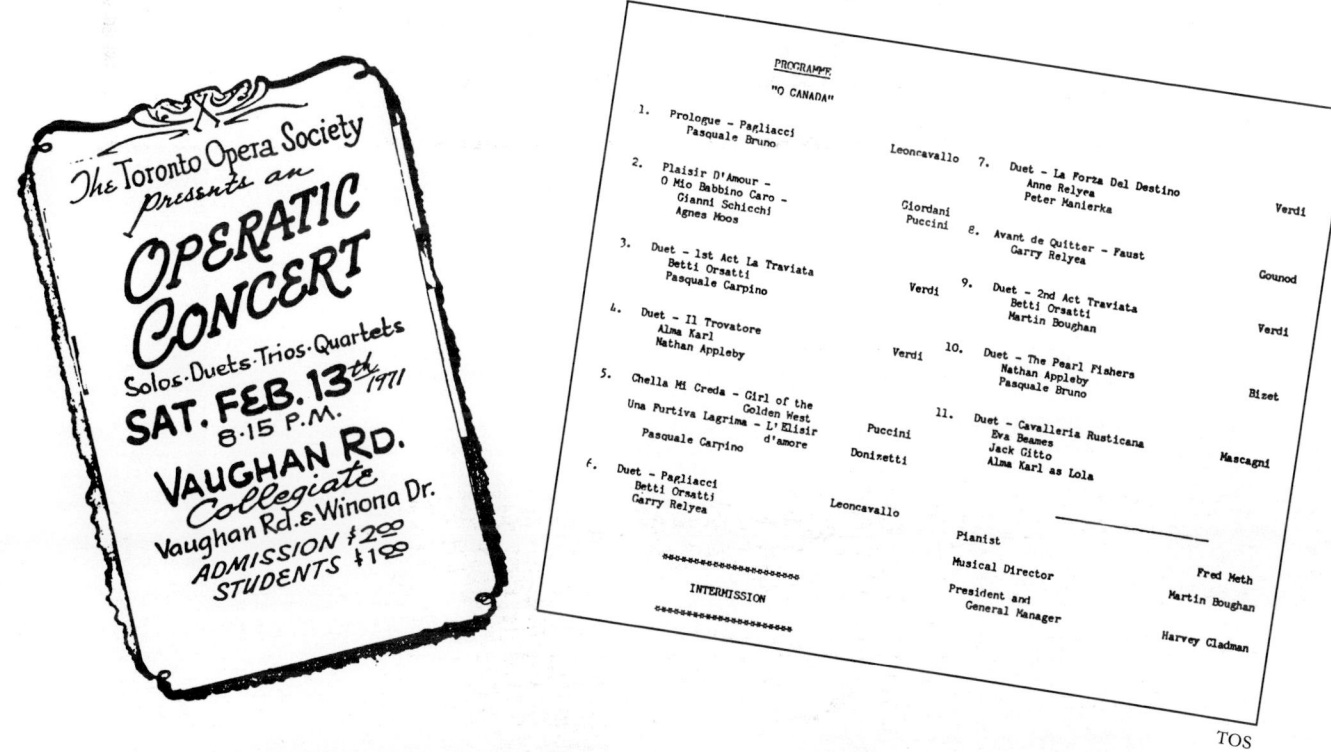

Baritone GARY RELYEA sang with the Toronto Opera Society at Vaughan Road, C.I.

Bass DAVID MILLS sang with the National Opera Company at Northern Secondary School.

VAUGHAN ROAD COLLEGIATE INSTITUTE

Vaughan Road Collegiate Institute is representative of other schools which have provided facilities for performances of lyric theatre: NORTHERN SECONDARY SCHOOL – The National Opera Company in the early 1950's; GEORGE HARVEY SECONDARY SCHOOL – Toronto Opera Society; EARL HAIG COLLEGIATE INSTITUTE – The Yorkminstrels; CEDARBRAE COLLEGIATE INSTITUTE – Scarborough Choral Society; CASTLE FRANK HIGH SCHOOL – Metropolitan Music Theatre and Zarzuela.

Photo: TTSU By permission of the Toronto Sun

GIUSEPPE MACINA, Artistic Director, York Community Opera.

Programme cover, 1969   TOS
George Harvey Secondary School

Programme cover, 1983   JPB
Cedarbrae Collegiate Institute

The Metropolitan Music Theatre
margaret alderton/guillermo silva-marin, directors

PRESENTS
Gilbert & Sullivan's

IOLANTHE
or The Peer and the Peri

30th ANNIVERSARY PRODUCTION

METROPOLITAN MUSIC THEATRE, 35 Commons Dr., Agincourt, Ontario.

Programme cover, 1981   JPB
Castle Frank High School

THE YORKMINSTRELS present

My Fair Lady

Book and Lyrics by
Alan Jay Lerner

Music by
Frederick Loewe

Adapted from George Bernard Shaw's Play and Gabrial Pascal's motion picture 'PYGMALION'

EARL HAIG THEATRE AUDITORIUM
WILLOWDALE, ONTARIO

APRIL 20, 21, 22, 26, 27, 28, 29, 1978

CURTAIN
8:00 P.M.

by arrangement with Tams-Witmark Music Library Inc.
757 Third Avenue, New York, N.Y. 10017, U.S.A.

Programme cover, 1978   JPB
Earl Haig Collegiate Institute

Photo: Andre Pierre & Associates   YCO

ROBERT KUNZLI (Enrico) CATHERINE BOLGER (Lucia) in York Community Opera's *Lucia di Lammermoon* 1982.

Photo: Andre Pierre & Associates   YCO

FERGUSON MacKENZIE (Pinkerton), RAISA SADOWA (Cio-Cio-San) in York Community Opera's *Madama Butterfly* 1982.

CATHERINE BOLGER (Lucia), JOHN NIEBOER (Raimondo) in York Community Opera's *Lucia di Lammermoor* 1982.

Photo: Andre Pierre & Associates's   YCO

1973
ST. LAWRENCE CENTRE

Despite the exclusion of an Opera House, opera has appeared frequently at Toronto's Centennial project.

THE ST. LAWRENCE CENTRE

ST. LAWRENCE CENTRE

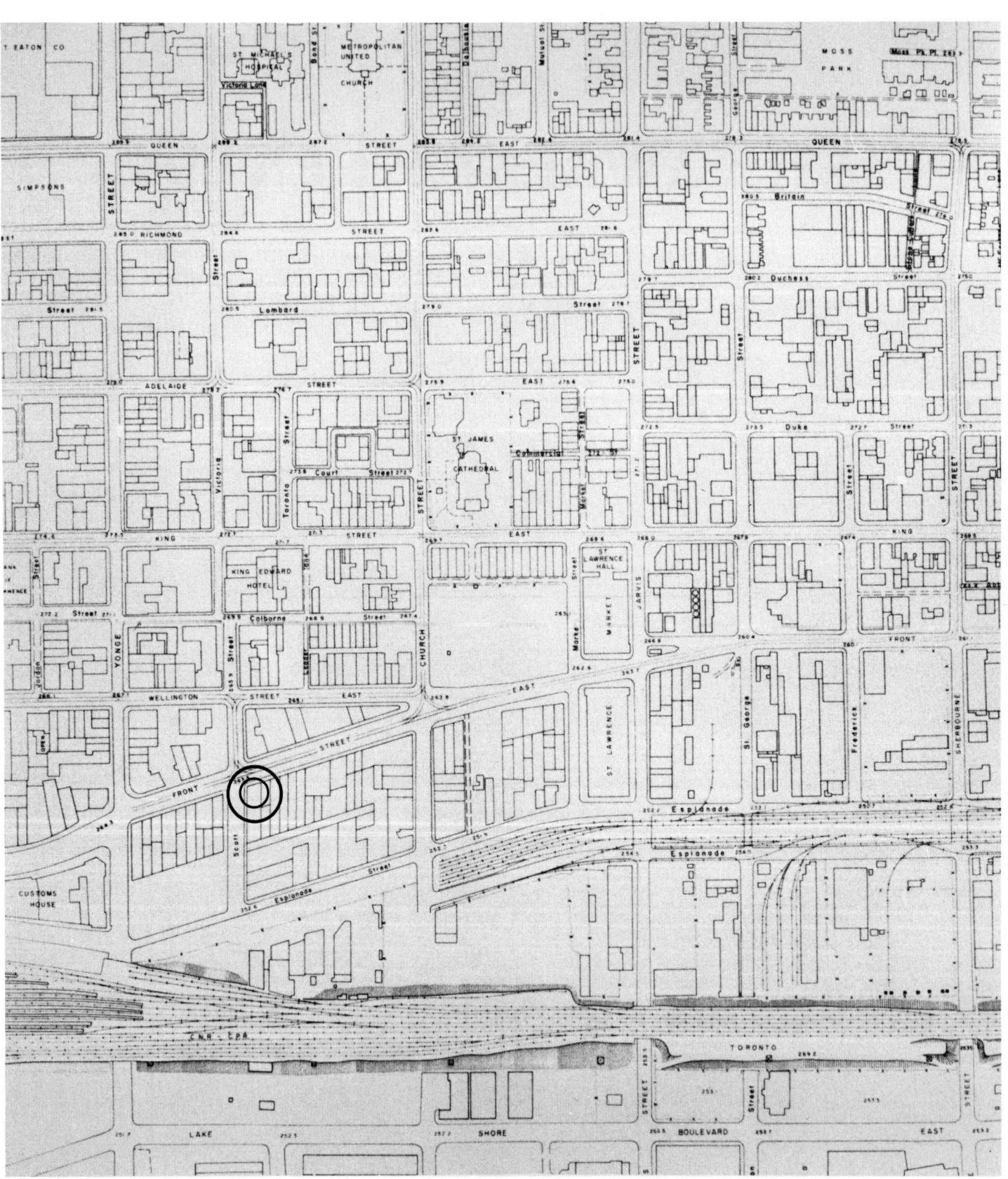

City of Toronto Planning Board 1957

MTLB

Toronto, in common with other major Canadian cities, chose as its Centennial project, a Performing Arts Centre. Plans for an Opera House were abandoned in the early stages but, in established Toronto tradition, opera was performed within four years of the opening on December 31, 1969, in the smaller of the two theatres – the 481-seat Town Hall. Between 1981 and 1983 the Centre, with the exception of the Town Hall, underwent extensive renovations. The larger auditorium was re-named The Bluma Appel Theatre.

THE TOWN HALL

THEATRE
Cast lacks style but St. Lawrence is a hit

By HERBERT WHITTAKER

The performances may have only been adequate and definitely lacking in style but the opening of the St. Lawrence Centre for the Arts was obviously a hit with the audience which had fought its way through the snow to see Mayor William Dennison turn over the city's double auditoria to the Toronto Arts Foundation, a citizens' committee created to raise and run it.

It was an audience, of course, made up entirely of planners, plumbers, pushers, campaigners, contributors, politicians and a few late-comers to its bandwagon. It was an 'in' crowd or, to be more exact a 'finally-in' crowd which fitted easily, and comfortably, into the 483-seat Town Hall.

In the leading role of the opening spectacle, Mayor Dennison gave a familiar characterization, although his material was only fair and he had to be prompted. Milking applause for the members of the council provided a weak and somewhat tasteless finale, considering the opposition which the project has met.

"For safekeeping and direction," the Mayor read well, as he performed his major scene, but he went on to complain that the city's delayed Centennial Project had received what he termed "more than its share of publicity," which also seemed tactless to the people who had worked for it.

Tributes were paid to ex-Mayors Summerville and Givens for their part in supporting the project, and Mayor Nathan Phillips took a bow, presumably for his contribution in launching the centre's next-door neighbor, the O'Keefe.

Donald MacDonald made a better impression, playing straight man to the Mayor's comedy act. His reference to the centre's history so far as an old-fashioned melodrama, in which it looked as if the train would really run over the heroine, was well taken. He described its final appearance (in the Rosedale ward) as "a national triumph," which pleased all.

The romantic lead of the performance was ably impersonated by James Auld, although his role was somewhat thankless, especially when he had to explain that his chief Premier John Robarts, was too busy to get to the theatre often.

But for sincerity, nobody in the small cast could match John Lockwood, playing a farewell scene as retiring chairman and president of the Toronto Arts Council, that body of knights which defeated the Lamport-dragon and raised up this precious Camelot.

Lockwood was also remarkable for his restraint. He recounted the history of the effort from 1963 without a trace of bitterness.

Finally, a word of praise must go to the occasion's stage-manager, Mayor Moore, even though his grand march finale was wrecked by the Mayor. Moore evoked Macbeth in his promise to "put out more flags on the outward walls" when the centre opens for the regular public of Toronto and got in a quick thrust about still needing more space, preparatory to a campaign to build the still-missing facilities building.

However, when Moore, ever the Pied Piper of the project, led the smiling audience off on a tour of the building the real impact of the performance was made.

This was provided by the view of the 830-seat theatre, a unique structure capable of thrust, proscenium and triptych productions. In proportion, coloring and size it has a nobility missing in the cut-down Town Hall, and held promise of theatrical experiences unmatched in other Toronto theatres.

One glimpse of this, even though the tricky thrust stage is still unfinished and a borrowed black front curtain masks the arch, made the long, painful whole effort seem worth while. It made up for that opening performance, the tawdry floral arrangements and even the City Hall sound-track.

Globe and Mail Jan. 1, 1970

ST. LAWRENCE CENTRE

Photo: V. Tony Hauser   COC
CHARLES WILSON composer of *The Selfish Giant*.

COC
LOUIS QUILICO who sang the role of the Selfish Giant

COC
STUART HAMILTON, O.C., Creator and director of OPERA IN CONCERT.

Pianist-accompanist-teacher STUART HAMILTON was concerned over the plight of many Canadian singers of proven excellence and with many years of training to their credit, who were forced to find employment in fields unrelated to singing. During its first ten seasons in the St. Lawrence Centre his Opera in Concert series gave close to 150 singers an opportunity to display their talents and enlarge their repertoires.

> OPERA in CONCERT
> presents
> HAMLET
> by
> AMBROISE THOMAS
> Monday, October 21, 1974 8:30 p.m.
>
> ✩ ✩ ✩ ✩ ✩ ✩
>
> BEATRICE ET BENEDICT
> by
> Hector Berlioz
> Monday, January 6, 1975 8:30 p.m.
>
> ✩ ✩ ✩ ✩ ✩ ✩
>
> THAÏS
> by
> JULES MASSENET
> Monday March 3, 1975 8:30 p.m.
>
> ✩ ✩ ✩ ✩ ✩ ✩
>
> Musical Director and Pianist
> STUART HAMILTON
>
> TOWN HALL,
> ST. LAWRENCE CENTRE
> FOR THE PERFORMING ARTS

1975   OIC

Canadian composer Charles Wilson rounded out his operatic year with *The Selfish Giant* presented in the St. Lawrence Centre's Town Hall. The brief children's opera, based on Oscar Wilde's story, is more a staged oratorio than an opera. It was commissioned and performed by the Canadian Children's Opera Chorus, with the assistance of grants from the Ontario Arts Council and the Canada Council. Despite the weather, it was one of the Young Canadian Performers series most successful events, with the house embarrassingly oversold until the snow forced enough cancellations to leave no more than a capacity audience.

Wilson's work was successful in more than box office terms. Although the idiom was of the restrained contemporary variety favored by the composer, the general treatment had a simplicity wholly appropriate to the tale and the transparent instrumental score that supported the performers instead of threatening to take over the action. In fact, the orchestra consisted of pianist Stuart Hamilton and percussionist Allen Beard, plus a sort of Orff ensemble—delicate percussion instruments and a recorder, played by members of the chorus.

But then, if there was any chance for success, this production had it, with Wilson conducting and baritone Louis Quilico as the Selfish Giant—looking more like the Jolly Green variety. Moreover, designer William Lord has had enough experience with budget opera to provide colorful and workable sets to underline the mood of the story. Director John Leberg made generally good use of them, with unobtrusive costume changes and seasonal changes of the trees fitting well into the action.

If the music conveyed much of the Giant's selfishness, I missed it in the resonant warmth of Quilico's performance, but then it is difficult for an actor to sing both the narration and his own lines and to separate the two aspects of his role. His music was rarely memorable, except in the duet with the Linnet, expressively sung by Tracey Atin.

Although there were a number of solo parts for members of the chorus, including that of the Little Boy, sung in a very white voice by Kent Magee and touchingly acted by him in the final scene, the work relies more on choral singing. This was quite marvellous in its precision and security, but sometimes short on intelligible enunciation.

Words fared better in the second half of the program, also conducted by Wilson, which included Vaughan Williams' delightful settings of four Christmas folk songs, a cheerful *Christmas Cantata* by Vincent Luebeck, a witty *Madrigal* by Robert Fleming, Willan's gentle *Christmas Lullaby* with Quilico and a wordless chorus, and Harry Freedman's rhythmic *Ookpik*.
—John Kraglund

Reprinted from the Globe and Mail, Toronto.

Opera Canada, Spring 1974   OC

COC
CARROL ANNE CURRY, soprano, later mezzo-soprano. Performances with Opera in Concert in 1974, 1975, 1977, 1980, 1981.

COC
GUILLERMO SILVA-MARIN, baritone, later tenor. Performances with Opera in Concert in 1975, 1976, 1977, 1978, 1979, 1981, 1982, 1983.

ST. LAWRENCE CENTRE

JANET STUBBS, mezzo-soprano. Performances with Opera in Concert in 1976, 1981.

MARY LOU FALLIS, soprano. Performance with Opera in Concert in 1976.

Thomas'
MIGNON

Monday, March 1, 1976, 8:30 p.m.

Cast in order of Appearance

Lothario	RONALD BERMINGHAM
Philine	MARY LOU FALLIS
Laerte	FERGUSON MacKENZIE
Jarno	JOEL KATZ
Mignon	JANET STUBBS
Wilhelm Meister	HENRY INGRAM
Frederic	CATHERINE ROBBIN
PIANIST	STUART HAMILTON

INTERMISSION BETWEEN EACH ACT

1976

OPERA IN CONCERT

STUART HAMILTON — PRODUCER
presents

L'AMORE DEI TRE RE
by
Italo Montemezzi

Sunday, October 24, 1976 — 3:00 p.m.

CAST IN ORDER OF APPEARANCE

Archibaldo	—	Giulio Kukurugya
Flaminio	—	Mark DuBois
Avito	—	Paul Frey
Fiora	—	Roxolana Roslak
Manfredo	—	Jonas Vaskevicius
Handmaiden	—	Patricia Griffin
PIANIST	—	STUART HAMILTON
Understudy for Archibaldo	—	Joel Katz

INTERMISSIONS BETWEEN ACTS
ST. LAWRENCE CENTRE, TOWN HALL

1976

PAUL FREY, tenor. Performances with Opera in Concert in 1975, 1976, 1977, 1978.

ROXOLANA ROSLAK, soprano. Performances with Opera in Concert in 1975, 1976, 1977, 1980, 1981 and 1982.

DEBORAH MILSOM, mezzo-soprano. Performances with Opera in Concert in 1978, 1979, 1980, 1981.

1976

Photo: Gerard Macdonald

NICHOLAS GOLDSCHMIDT, O.C. Artistic Director, Guelph, Spring Festival Conductor: *The Beggar's Opera.*

OPERA IN CONCERT

STUART HAMILTON — PRODUCER
presents

FRANZ SCHMIDT'S

NOTRE DAME

adapted from the novel by Victor Hugo

DEREK BAMPTON — MUSIC DIRECTOR

SUNDAY, NOVEMBER 19, 1978 — 2 P.M.
MONDAY, NOVEMBER 20, 1978 — 8 P.M.

centre
27 Front Street East

1978

Photo: V. Tony Hauser

JOHN DODINGTON, bass. Performances with Opera in Concert in 1977, 1978, 1983.

ST. LAWRENCE CENTRE

GLYN EVANS, tenor. Performances with Opera in Concert in 1975, 1976, 1977, 1978, 1979, 1981.

PETER BARCZA, baritone. Performances with Opera in Concert in 1976, 1978, 1981, 1982, 1983.

OPERA IN CONCERT

Stuart Hamilton, Producer
presents

Jules Massenet's
MANON

Saturday, December 6, 1980 - 8p.m.
Sunday, December 7, 1980 - 2p.m.

centre
27 Front Street East

1980

OPERA IN CONCERT

STUART HAMILTON — PRODUCER
presents

GEORGES BIZET'S
LES PÊCHEURS DE PERLES

SUNDAY, JANUARY 28, 1979 — 2 P.M.
MONDAY, JANUARY 29, 1979 — 8 P.M.

centre
27 Front Street East

1979

ROSEMARIE LANDRY, soprano. Performances with Opera in Concert in 1978, 1980, 1983.

MARK DUBOIS, tenor. Performances with Opera in Concert in 1976, 1978, 1979, 1980, 1983.

CARALYN TOMLIN, soprano, Daisy in *The Shivaree*.

JAMES McLEAN, tenor, Jonathon in *The Shivaree*

AVO KITTASK, baritone. Quartz in *The Shivaree*

Toronto: Comus Music Theater

Canadian/poet/librettist John Reaney and composer John Beckwith, who are frequent collaborators, saw the world premiere of their second opera together, *The Shivaree*, in Toronto's St. Lawrence Centre, April 3. It was a Comus Music Theatre production, designed by Geofrey Dinwiddie, conducted by Howard Cable, staged by Paula Sperdakos, and featuring a large cast of young Canadian artists.

The set that greeted the audience as they entered the St. Lawrence Hall was colorful, amusing, provocative and eye-catching, with a cleverly designed horse and buggy, centre stage. After a promising opening, with the newly-married couple in the buggy, the horse was wheeled off by a groom—to the appreciative amusement of the audience.

The story was inspired by the early Ontario custom of the young men of a village collecting all available home-and-kitchen instruments with which they would serenade a newly-married couple. In this case, a somewhat stuffy and miserly keeper of the local store, has married Daisy, whose only reason for the wedding was to arouse the jealousy of her true love, Jonathan. She succeeds so well that in the end she forsakes her groom and goes off with Jonathan, while the local schoolteacher gets the object of her heart's delight, the storekeeper, and all ends happily.

Thirteen years elapsed between the composition of the first act of the work and the second, a fact that is reflected in the music. For the first act, in spite of some laudable moments, was slow and the orchestration less sympathetic insofar as the voices were concerned. But things came alive in the second act, beginning with the Shivaree itself—a hilariously noisy sequence which everyone on both sides of the footlights thoroughly enjoyed—which was musically inventive tightly-knit and rewarding. While the score is definitely of our time, it also boasts much melodic material, in solo numbers, duets, and a rousing "horse-and-buggy" ensemble.

The uniformly good cast was headed by baritone Avo Kittask as Quartz, the storekeeper; soprano Caralyn Tomlin as the bride, Daisy; tenor James McLean as the hero, Jonathan, and soprano Kathy Terrell as the schoolteacher, Miss Beech. But each role in the cast of 12 was so written that each stood out as a definite character, particularly as well as they were sung and acted by Patricia Rideout, Susan Gudgeon, Henry Ingram, John Keane, Paul Massel, Peter Barcza, Tom Goerz and Gregory Cross. Paula Sperdakos, directing her first opera, was able to apply most effectively her experience in musicals and legitimate theatre productions.

My feeling was that with some changes in Act I, *The Shivaree* could be a winner. Meanwhile, one must applaud the enterprise and commitment of Comus Music Theatre in making it possible for such works to be seen and heard.

—*Ruby Mercer*

Opera Canada, Summer 1982

ST. LAWRENCE CENTRE

Photo: Robert C. Ragsdale   OC

JOHN BECKWITH, Dean of the Faculty of Music, University of Toronto 1970-77. Composer: *The Shivaree*.

COC

GARY RELYEA, baritone. Performances with Opera in Concert in 1975, 1983.

OPERA IN CONCERT
Stuart Hamilton, Producer presents

Tenth season!

Jules Massenet's
Grisélidis

Saturday, October 22, 1983 - 8:00 p.m.
Sunday, October 23, 1983 - 2:00 p.m.

27 Front Street East Toronto
St. Lawrence Centre for the Arts

1983   COCA

COC

JOANNE KOLOMYJEC, soprano. Performance with Opera in Concert in 1983.

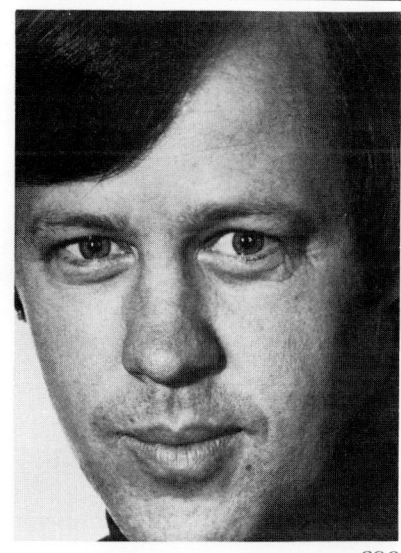

COC

BARRY STILWELL, tenor
Performances with Opera in Concert in 1977, 1982, 1983.

Il Giuramento
by Saverio Mercadante
Libretto by Lauro Rossi

CAST
(in order of appearance)

Viscardo (a spanish nobleman) .... Barry Stilwell (Sat.)
(Tenor)   Guillermo Silva-Marin (Sun.)
Manfredo (Governor of Syracuse) .... Paul Massel (Sat.)
(Baritone)   Rudolf Neufeld (Sun.)
Elaisa (a northern Italian noblewoman) .... Lynn Blaser (Sat.)
(Soprano)   • Marion Harvey (Sun.)
Brunoro (Manfredo's secretary & spy) .... James Leatch
(Tenor)
Bianca (Manfredo's wife) .... Deborah Milsom (Sat.)
(Mezzo soprano)   Eleanor James (Sun.)
Isaura (Bianca's handmaiden) .... Avalee Beckman
(Soprano)
Chorus Director .... Robert Cooper
Pianist .... Stuart Hamilton
• Debut with Opera in Concert

HISTORICAL NOTE
MERCADANTE (1795-1870) was from about 1835 to 1850, considered the most important composer in Italy. He wrote nearly 60 operas, of which *Il Giuramento* (1837) is the most widely performed. His operas were performed all over Europe during the nineteenth century until they were overtaken and submerged by the works of Verdi. Recent performances of *Il Giuramento* in Vienna and New York have led to a resurgence of interest in Mercadante. The libretto is based on a play by Victor Hugo — *Angelo* or the *Tyrant of Padua* which also served Boito for his libretto to Ponchielli's *La Gioconda*. This is the work's first performance in Canada.

COCA

OPERA IN CONCERT Dec. 3 & 4, 1983

COC

LYNN BLASER, soprano. Performances with Opera in Concert 1982, 1983.

COC

KATHERINE TERRELL, soprano. Miss Beech in *The Shivaree*

APPEARANCES	
1973	Canadian Children's Opera Chorus
1974-83	Opera in Concert
1976	Guelph Spring Festival
1981	Canadian Opera Company Ensemble
1981	Canadian Opera Piccola
1982	Comus Music Theatre

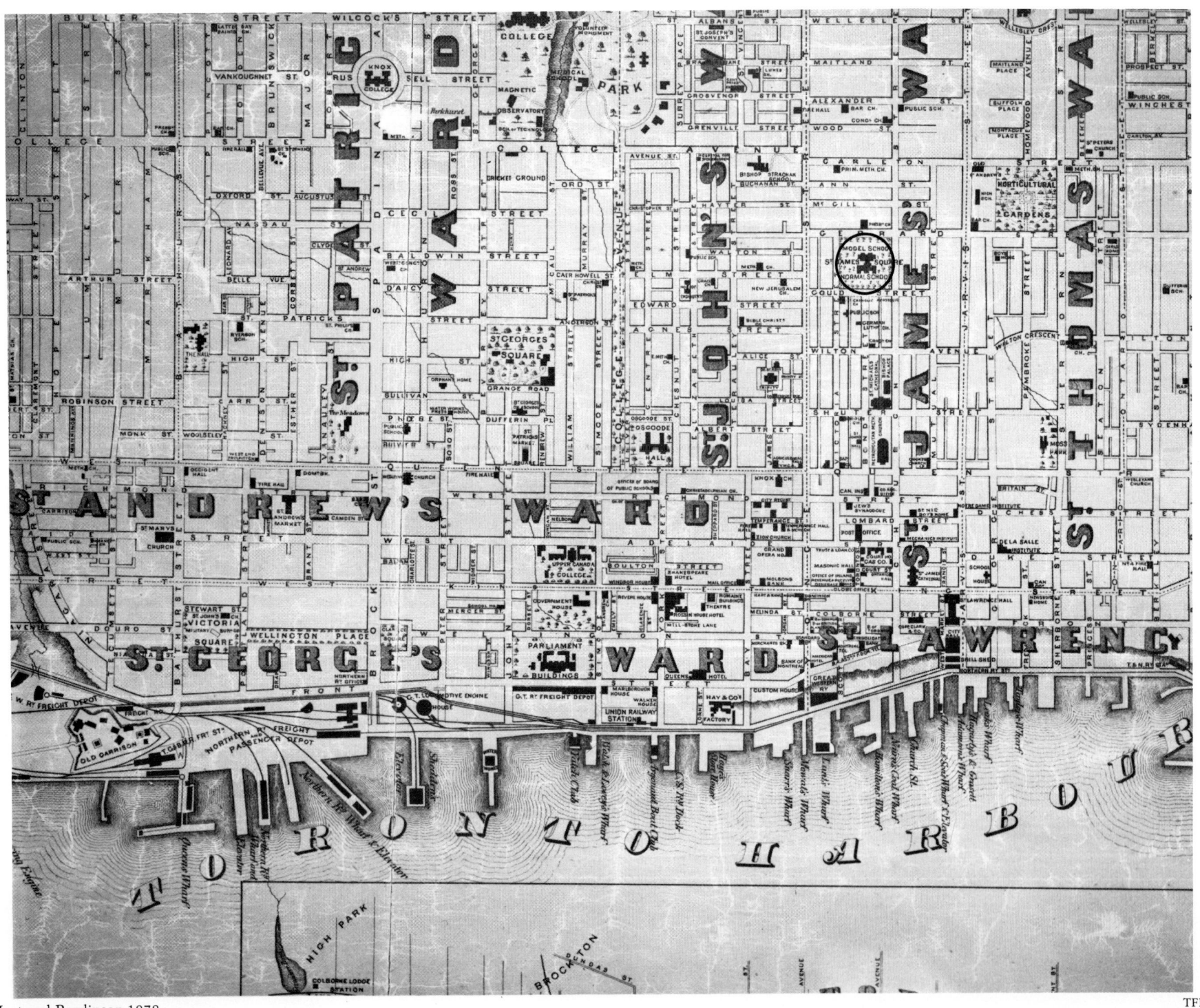

Hart and Rawlinson 1878

1979
RYERSON POLYTECHNICAL INSTITUTE

Probably the ghost of Egerton Ryerson attends performances in this theatre – it is so very much in keeping with his philosophies.

RYERSON HALL

RYERSON POLYTECHNICAL INSTITUTE

As an operatic stage, Ryerson's story compares with the convolutions of any operatic plot. Its origins rest in the politics and development of the country. With the Act of Union of 1841 (following the rebellions of Upper and Lower Canada) the Parliament of the new province of Canada met for three years in Kingston and later, prior to Confederation, the seat of Parliament alternated between Montreal and Toronto. For periods of time, as a result, Government House in Toronto (see Open Air) was unoccupied. The Upper Canada Normal School, established by the School Act of 1846, opened its door in Government House in 1847. Under the leadership of Egerton Ryerson, founder of the Ontario school system, teachers were taught to teach at the Normal School. A Model School for the accommodation of pupils on whom the teachers would practise was set up in refitted stables. On Parliament's return to Toronto in 1849 the school was dispossessed and was re-located in Temperance Hall (see Temperance Hall) until a new building on Gould Street was erected. In addition to his interest in public education, Ryerson was also concerned with textbook publishing and with the community's demand for performing and visual arts. As a result, in 1853 the first publicly-supported Museum, forerunner of the Royal Ontario Museum, was housed in the school and in 1872 a group of artists founded the Ontario Society of Artists, later the Ontario College of Art. During World War II No. 6 Initial Training Centre for RCAF pilots occupied the buildings and after the war the Training and Re-establishment Institute took over. On Sept. 16, 1948, The Ryerson Institute of Technology was established and the construction of Kerr Hall, a quadrangle around the old Normal School (and named after the Institute's first principal Howard Hillen Kerr) was begun. Kerr Hall has become the focus for a number of opera and opera related productions.

In 1963 the name became Ryerson Polytechnical Institute and the Ryerson Theatre School was created in 1971-2 for the teaching of acting, technical knowledge and dance. The Institute was first empowered to grant University degrees in 1971.

EGERTON RYERSON, creator of
Ontario's educational system.

Stereo: William Notman

NORMAL SCHOOL, Gould Street ca 1859.

RYERSON POLYTECHNICAL INSTITUTE

Photo   MTLB T12241
NORMAL SCHOOL, North side 1860.

Photo   RPIA
Demolition of RYERSON HALL/
Construction of KERR HALL 1963.

Photo: Chris Bell   RPIA
KERR HALL 1979. Reinforced reverse side of facade of original Ryerson Hall shown against south section.

Photo   RPIA
KERR HALL AUDITORIUM

NICHOLAS GOLDSCHMIDT, Artistic Director of the Guelph Spring Festival RUBY MERCER, Editor of Opera Canada and founder of the Canadian Children's Opera Chorus and GIAN-CARLO MENOTTI, composer of *Chip and His Dog*.

World Première of Chip and His Dog by GIAN CARLO MENOTTI commissioned and performed by the Canadian Children's Opera Chorus

From the Guelph Spring Festival Programme 1979.

Commissioned for the International Year of the Child.
Premiered at the Guelph Spring Festival, May 4, 1979.
Performed in Toronto at Ryerson Theatre in December 1979.

Photo: Colin M. Clarke

CHIP AND HIS DOG
Members of the Canadian Children's Opera Chorus.

Three singers formed the COSMOPOLITAN OPERA ASSOCIATION to provide opportunity for Canadian artists.

LORNA CASTANEDA, soprano

AVO KITTASK, baritone

MICHELE STRANO, tenor

Photo: Gary Beechey 1979

APPEARANCES
1979 Cosmopolitan Opera Association
1979 Canadian Children's Opera Chorus
1980 Cosmopolitan Opera Association

1980
HARBOURFRONT

A two-purpose location to suit Torontonians.

FIRST CANADIAN OPERA COMPANY ENSEMBLE, JULY 1, 1980.

Photo: Steve Behal COCA
LtoR: Michael Shust, Caralyn Tomlin, Roxolana Roslak, Barry Stilwell, Shawna Farrell, Eleanor James, Mark Pedrotti, Stuart Hamilton, Janet Stubbs, Theodore Baerg, Guillermo Silva-Marin, Deborah Milsom,

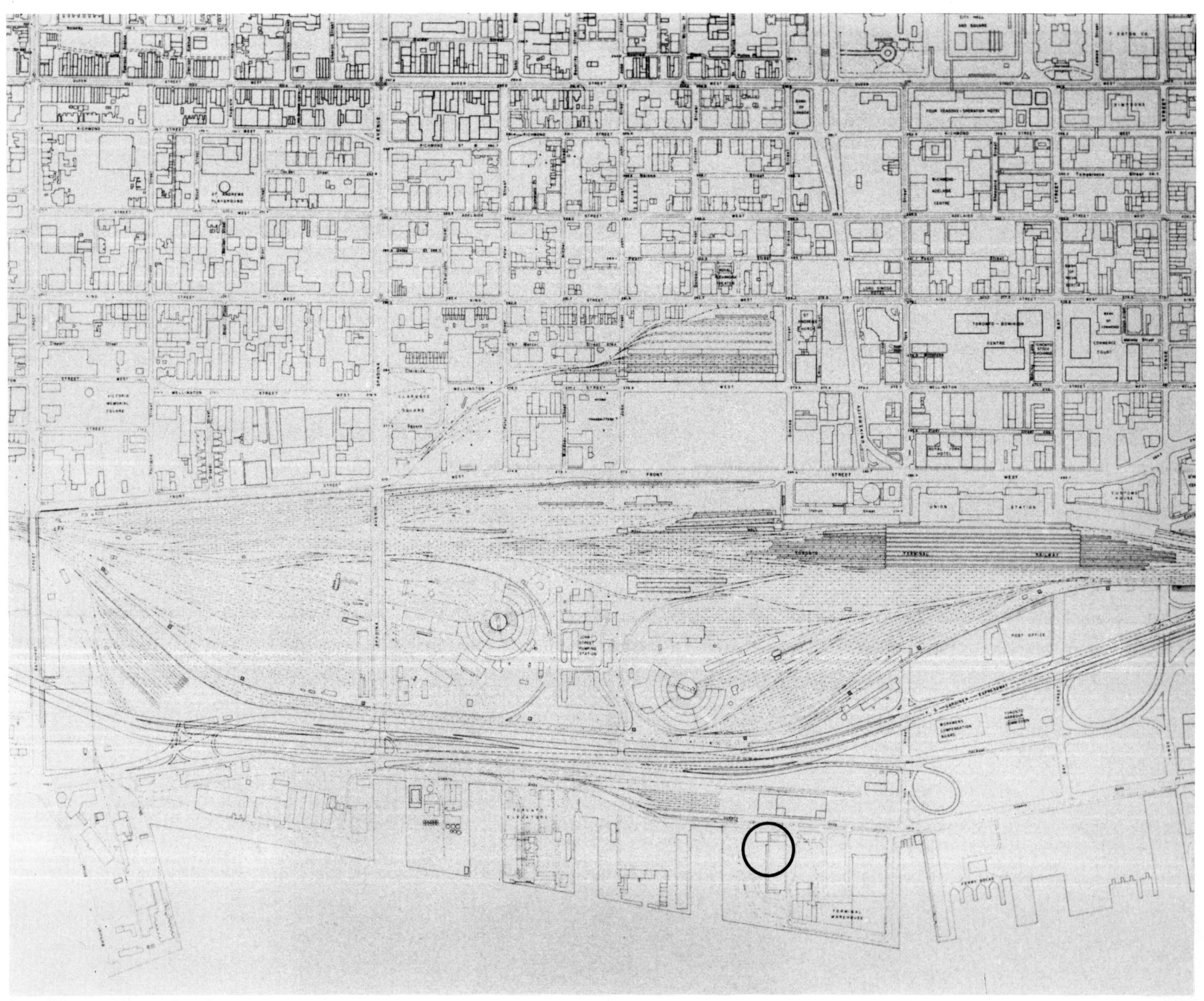

City of Toronto Planning Board 1957

HARBOURFRONT

The Toronto characteristic of enjoying opera and concerts in the parks has remained constant regardless of the changing racial backgrounds of the population. In 1972 the Crown acquired lands along Toronto's waterfront with the expressed intention of converting them into a park for the enhancement of the city and the pleasure of its inhabitants. As soon as the various levels of government reached agreement on the administrative structure and the implementation of the scheme began, the public took it to its heart. During the year 1979-80, 3,000 events took place and 1.3 million people visited the site. In June of 1980 the Federal Government approved the expenditure of $25.53 million for the development of Harbourfront over 7 years and later that summer the Canadian Opera Company Ensemble, Canada's first company to provide year-round employment for young singers, performed "capsule" operas in the Tent during the Canadian Opera Company's Summer Festival. At Christmas time the same group gave the first operatic performance in the Studio Theatre.

THE TENT

Photo: Steve Behal   1980   COCA

HANSEL AND GRETEL, Janet Stubbs, Shawna Farrell.

Photo: Gary Beechey   1981   COCA

MADAMA BUTTERFLY, Roxolana Roslak, Roger Jones, 1983.

Photo: Gary Beechey   1982   COCA

LA BOHEME
Susan Austin, Ben Heppner

Photo: Gary Beechey   1983   COCA

THE MERRY WIDOW
Irene Welhasch

APPEARANCES	
1980	Canadian Opera Company Ensemble
1981	Canadian Opera Company Ensemble
1982	Canadian Opera Company Ensemble
1983	Canadian Opera Company Ensemble

HARBOURFRONT

THE STUDIO THEATRE

INTERNATIONAL CHILDREN'S FESTIVAL

Photo: Robert C. Ragsdale   1980   COCA

AMAHL AND THE NIGHT VISITORS
Canadian Opera Company Ensemble
Canadian Children's Opera Chorus
Christopher Cameron, Ben Heppner,
Viorel Dihel, Roxolana Roslak,
Benjamin Carlson.

Photo: Milan Chvostek   1982   CCOC

DR. CANNON'S CURE
John Dodington, Canadian Children's
Opera Chorus, James McLean, Laurie
Bassett.

Photo: Milan Chvostek   CCOC

DR. DAVIES WITH MEMBERS OF
THE CANADIAN CHILDREN'S
OPERA CHORUS.

Photo: Milan Chvostek   CCOC

Librettist ROBERTSON DAVIES,
Composer DEREK HOLMAN

PERFORMANCES
1980 Canadian Children's Opera Chorus
1980 Canadian Opera Company Ensemble
1981 Canadian Opera Company Ensemble
1981 Canadian Children's Opera Chorus
1981 Equity Showcase Theatre
1981 Canadian Opera Company Ensemble and Canadian Children's Opera Chorus
1982 International Children's Festival – Canadian Children's Opera Chorus
1983 Canadian Children's Opera Chorus

1982
ROY THOMSON HALL

It was predictable – opera appeared during the week-long gala opening.

ROY THOMSON HALL beside the equally distinctive CN TOWER.

ROY THOMSON HALL

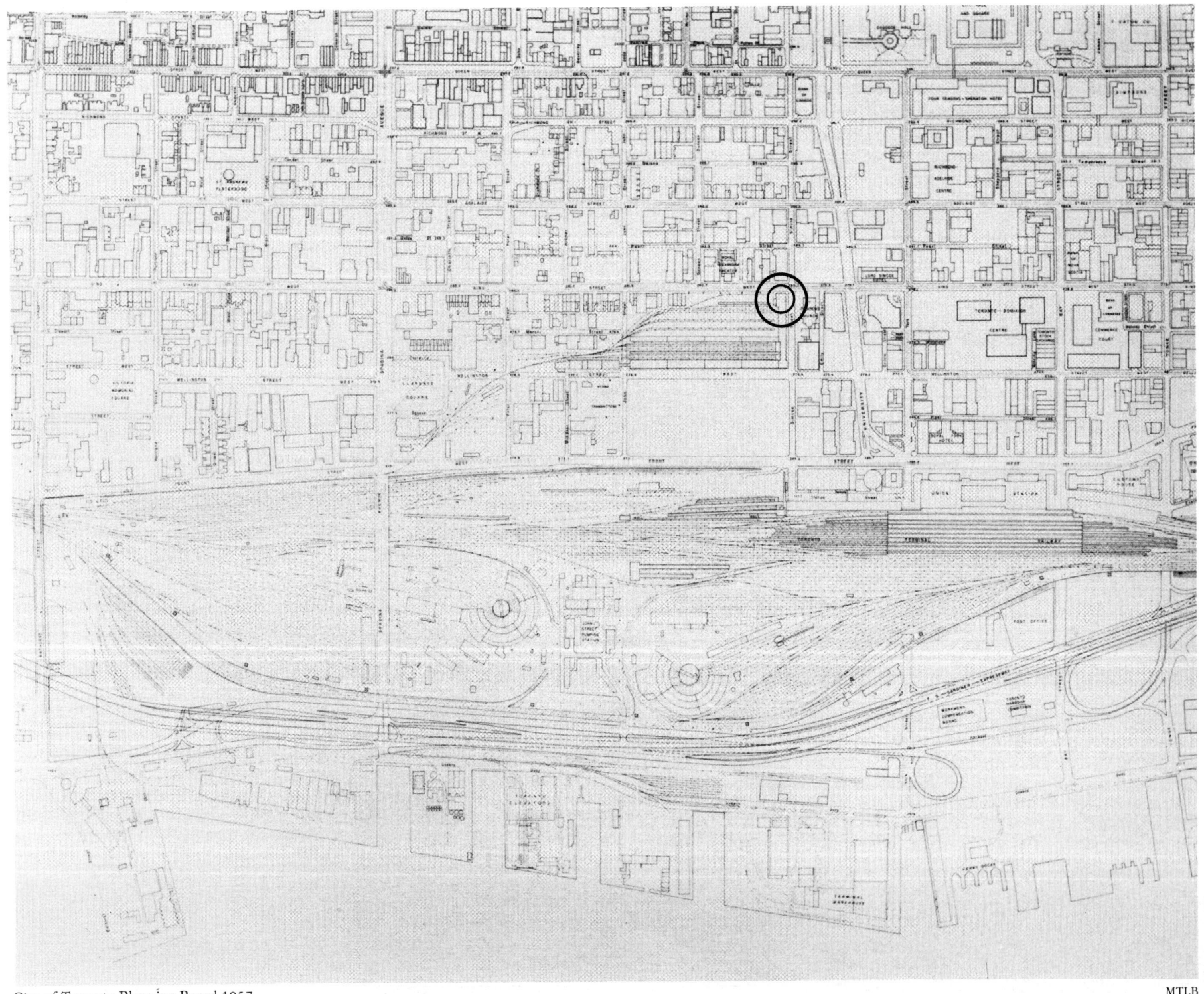

City of Toronto Planning Board 1957

MTLB

ROY THOMSON HALL

Massey Hall in its turn became inadequate for the demands that were made on it and in 1972 plans for a "new Massey Hall" began to take shape. Kenneth Thomson of the great newspaper family was searching for a project to honour his father Roy, Lord Thomson of Fleet. He contributed $4 ½ million to the funds for the new facility which was to arise on the site of the former Government House at King and Simcoe Streets and to be the new home of the Toronto Symphony and the Mendelssohn Choir. September 13, 1982 was the first night of a week of gala performances.

ROY THOMSON HALL

Photo: Barry Gray   1982, COCA

CAPRICCIO
Soprano JOHANNA MEIER as the Countess, mezzo-soprano SHEILA M. SMITH as Clairon.

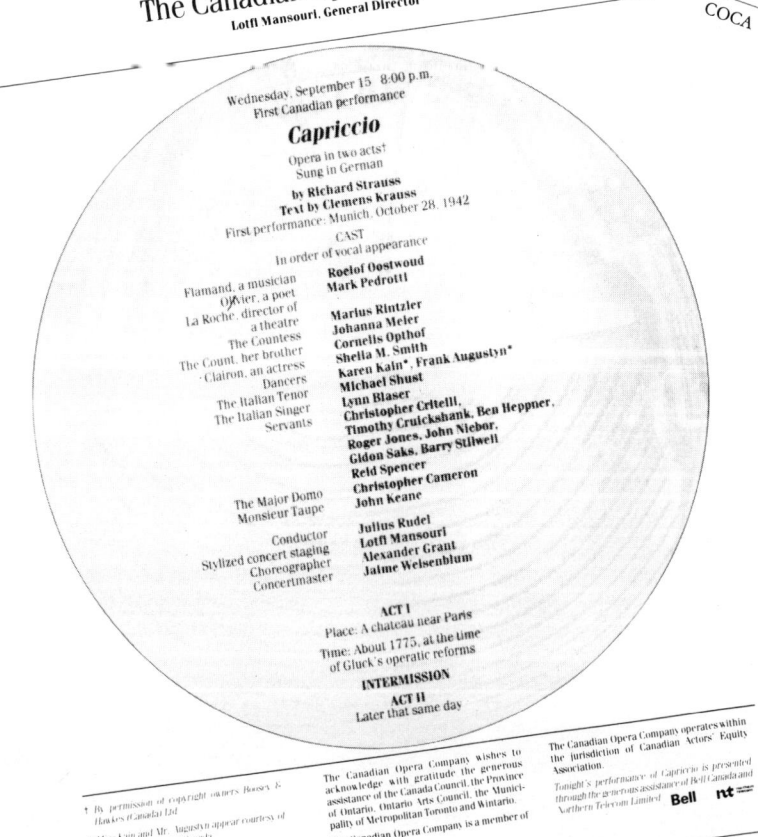

ROY THOMSON HALL

Welsh mezzo-soprano PATRICIA KERN

THE TORONTO SYMPHONY
62ND SEASON

Programme

Thursday and Saturday
November 17 and 19, 1983 at 8:00 pm
Special Concerts

CONDUCTOR
Andrew Davis

GUEST ARTISTS
*Mechthild Gessendorf, Soprano
  The Marschallin
*Barbara Hendricks, Soprano
  Sophie
†Cynthia Clarey, Mezzo-soprano
  Octavian
†Derek Hammond-Stroud, Baritone
  Faninal
†Richard Best, Bass-baritone
  Baron Ochs
Vinson Cole, Tenor
  Italian Singer
Roxolana Roslak, Soprano
  Marianne
Patricia Kern, Mezzo-soprano
  Annina
†Barry Stilwell, Tenor
  Valzacchi
The Elmer Iseler Singers
  Dr. Elmer Iseler, Music Director
OFF-STAGE CONDUCTOR
Errol Gay

RICHARD STRAUSS
• Der Rosenkavalier, Op. 59
  Act I

Intermission

Act II

Intermission

Act III

Thursday performance sponsored by GLENFIDDICH PURE MALT SCOTCH WHISKEY

*Canadian Debut
†Toronto Symphony Debut
• First Toronto Symphony Performance

Due to illness Arthur Korn originally scheduled to sing the part of Baron Ochs in these performances is unable to appear. We are grateful to Richard Best for agreeing to perform on such short notice.

November/December 1983

COCA

THE TORONTO SYMPHONY
PRESENTS
RICHARD STRAUSS' BEST-LOVED OPERA
DER ROSENKAVALIER
TWO CONCERT PERFORMANCES ONLY!
Thurs. November 17 and Sat. November 19 8:00p.m.
ROY THOMSON HALL
with The Toronto Symphony
Andrew Davis, conductor
Mechthild Gessendorf, soprano (The Marschallin)
Barbara Hendricks, soprano (Sophie)
Cynthia Clarey, mezzo-soprano (Octavian)
Artur Korn, baritone (Baron Ochs)
Derek Hammond-Stroud, baritone (Faninal)
Vinson Cole, tenor (Italian Singer)
Roxolana Roslak, soprano (Marianne)
Patricia Kern, mezzo-soprano (Annina)
Barry Stilwell, tenor (Valzacchi)
The Elmer Iseler Singers
TICKETS: $10.00, $26.50, $21.50, $13.00
ON SALE NOW!
Thurs. sponsored by: Glenfiddich Pure Malt Scotch Whiskey

TICKETS ON SALE NOW — Toronto Symphony Box Office, Roy Thomson Hall, lower level, and all Ticketron outlets

PHONE TELETRON **766-3271**
Visa and Mastercard

Globe & Mail, Oct. 28, 1983   COCA

Photo: Christian Steiner   COC
Contralto MAUREEN FORRESTER

GREAT CHORAL WORKS WITH
ORCHESTRA SERIES

TENTH ANNIVERSARY GALA CONCERT

ROY THOMSON HALL
Sunday, May 29, 1983, 8:00 P.M.

GIUSEPPE VERDI
REQUIEM MASS

GUILDA CRUZ-ROMO, Soprano
MAUREEN FORRESTER, Contralto
LANDO BARTOLINI, Tenor
PAUL PLISHKA, Bass

MUSICA SACRA CHORUS OF TORONTO
CHOIR OF ST. GEORGE'S UNITED CHURCH
KITCHENER-WATERLOO SYMPHONY ORCHESTRA

T. WOOLARD HARRIS
Conductor

COCA

APPEARANCES

1982	Canadian Opera Company – *Capriccio*
1982	Canadian Children's Opera Chorus
1982	Maureen Forrester – vocal concert
1983	Leontyne Price – vocal concert
1983	Elly Ameling – vocal concert
1983	Toronto Symphony – Wagner concert
1983	Toronto Symphony – *Oedipus Rex; The Soldier's Tale*
1983	Canadian Children's Opera Chorus & Toronto Symphony – *Noye's Fludde*
1983	Nicolai Gedda – vocal concert
1983	Music at St. George's – Verdi *Requiem*
1983	Jon Vickers – vocal concert
1983	*Der Rosenkavalier*
1983	Grace Bumbry – vocal concert
1983	Kiri te Kanawa – vocal concert

EPILOGUE

Each of us has our fantasy. Mine is to see the shades of Sig. Jacopo Peri, Giulio Caccini (composers), Ottavio Rinuccini (poet), Claudio Monteverdi and Pier Francesco Cavalli (composers) in the house seats at the O'Keefe Centre for operatic performances by the Canadian Opera Company – preferably in extremes of style such as *The Coronation of Poppea*, *Lucia di Lammermoor* and *Lulu*. Would they be appalled or ecstatic at the issue of their brainchild?

The first three gentlemen were Florentines (members of a group of poets and musicians known as Camerata) and the other two, Venetians. At the close of the 16th century they agreed that music needed a new direction – toward something simpler than the complex and massive oratorios, chorales and masses of the day. With true Renaissance minds they turned to classical Greece for inspiration – to what they believed was ancient Greece's pure theatre, with its sung narrative. Scholars and historians agree that their knowledge of ancient Greek music was insufficient to enable them to re-create the original. Instead they conceived *lyric* theatre – spoken dialogue and narrative with the added potency and emotionalism of music. What they had not anticipated was the immeasurable impact, on audiences, of the solo human voice, a phenomenon which has remained constant in its control over the destiny of this "unreal" entertainment.

It is hard to believe that any art form has been subjected to as much ridicule, condemnation, satirizing, burlesque and caricature, as opera. Few people are dispassionate about it – protagonists and antagonists are inconvertible. And yet, or perhaps therefore, it has survived. It has altered with the times and styles and with the countries to which it has spread and which have given it their own touch. But the basic concept of emotions expressed in music remains unchanged. Most of us, at one time or another, would give much to scream at the frustrations and setbacks of living. We are restrained by the horror of making ourselves ridiculous or of being diagnosed as mannic, schizoid or psychotic. The emotions expressed so unmistakably on the operatic stage are comprehensible and familiar to all.

Toronto had a population of 10,000 when it was incorporated as a city in 1834. But even before that there had been citizens who recognized the intangible benefits which only this happy combination of words and music can convey, and who were prepared to do something to make it available – even if it meant the Assembly Rooms of Franks' Hotel. This determination has continued to manifest itself for nearly one hundred and sixty years and is apparently as strong in 1984 as it was in 1884 and 1834.

There is a very strong temptation to conjecture about the reasons for the intermittent drops in the incidence of performances (see Figure 1) but that will have to wait, since it could take years. The period 1890-1910 is particularly intriguing. Was there an economic recession? Were there changes in the social strata in Toronto? Did theatre managers bow to or govern the tastes of the public? Did the opening of the Metropolitan Opera in 1883 kill off the smaller companies? Is there any significance in the fact that of the great impresarios of the day Maurice Grau became one of the Met's three permanent directors in 1891, Max Strakosch died in 1892 and Henry Mapleson in 1901? What caused the decrease in the number of prima donnas who toured with their own companies? Was it part of the feeling throughout the operatic world that the end of the Verdi/Wagner era meant the death of opera?

It is not possible to record here all the sites which have served as opera stages. Hundreds of presentations of Gilbert and Sullivan's works have been given in schools and church auditoria. The educational programme *Prologue to the Performing Arts* and the Canadian Opera Company Ensemble have taken capsulized versions to countless public schools. Puppet operas have been given at birthday parties. Because lyric theatre is a multi-media art form, limitations on the style and format of its presentation are set only by the imagination of the producer.

The foregoing account ends with the close of 1983. In the first five months of 1984, even before the International Festival with performances at the O'Keefe Centre, by Metropolitan Opera of New York and the Canadian Opera Company, Toronto saw performances at the OKeefe Centre, and St. Anne's Church, the Central Technical School, the MacMillan Theatre, Earl Haig Collegiate, Cedarbrae Collegiate and Hart House Theatre.

As in the past, lyric theatre continues to attract audiences.

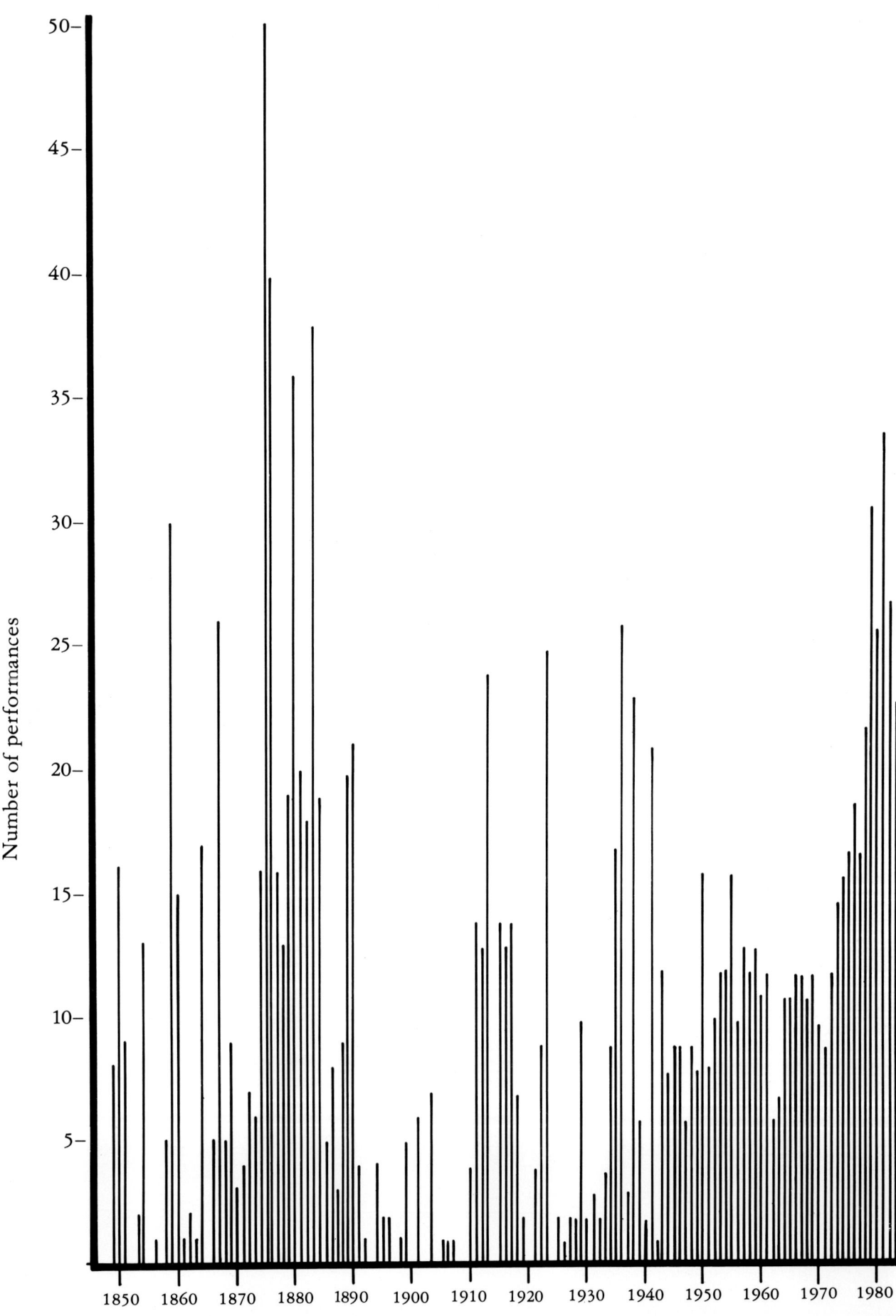

FIGURE 2   LYRIC THEATRES IN TORONTO: 1825-1984

Theatre	Timeline
FRANKS' HOTEL	1825 **
THEATRE ROYAL	1840s * *
OLD CITY HALL	1850s * **
DEERING'S THEATRE	1850s *
OPEN AIR	1850–1984 **
NEW CITY HALL	1850s * *
TEMPERANCE HALL	1850s–1860s * * **
ROYAL LYCEUM	1850s–1870s *** ********* * *******
MASONIC HALL	1850s *
ST. LAWRENCE HALL	1860s *********
CRYSTAL PALACE	1870s * *
HORTICULTURAL GARDENS	1870s–1890s * ** * *********** * **
YORKVILLE TOWN HALL	1870s * ** *
MUSIC HALL	1870s * ********* *
GRAND OPERA HOUSE	1880s–1930s **** ***** ****** * *** *
ROYAL OPERA HOUSE	1880s ** ****
ALBERT HALL	1880s * *
SHAFTESBURY HALL	1880s *
ST. ANDREW'S HALL	1880s *
ZOOLOGICAL GARDENS	1880s **
HOLMAN OPERA HOUSE	1880s *
THEATRE ROYAL	1880s *
SUMMER PAVILION	1880s *
HANLAN'S POINT	1880s * ... 1940s **
TORONTO OPERA HOUSE	1890s *** *
ACADEMY OF MUSIC	1890s *
MASSEY HALL	1890s–1980s ** **** ** **** ****** * * ****** * *** * * ** **
PRINCESS THEATRE	1890s–1920s * ***** *** * * *
SHEA'S THEATRE	1900s *
ROYAL ALEXANDRA THEATRE	1910s–1970s * ** * ***** ** *** ** *********** **
MUTUAL STREET ARENA	1910s * *
COLISEUM, CNE	1920s **
HART HOUSE THEATRE	1920s–1970s * * ** *********** ************
REGENT THEATRE	1920s *
ROYAL YORK HOTEL	1930s *
EATON AUDITORIUM	1930s–1960s ****************************** *
MAPLE LEAF GARDENS	1930s * ... 1950s *********
VARSITY ARENA	1930s–1940s ** *
VICTORIA THEATRE	1940s ** *
ART GALLERY OF ONTARIO	1950s * ... 1980s *
HEINTZMAN STREET HALL	1950s **********
O'KEEFE CENTRE	1960s–1980s *******************
ST. ANNE'S CHURCH	1960s–1980s *****************
MacMILLAN THEATRE	1960s–1980s *******************
CENTRAL TECHNICAL SCHOOL	1960s–1980s ***************
VAUGHAN ROAD C.I.	1960s ** ... 1980s **
ST. LAWRENCE CENTRE	1960s–1980s ************
RYERSON POLYTECHNICAL INSTITUTE	1980s **
HARBOURFRONT	1980s ***
ROY THOMSON HALL	1980s **

*based on a minimum of three full or part performances

Chart: Trevor Baillie

FIGURE 3 OPERAS PRESENTED IN TORONTO: 1825-1984*

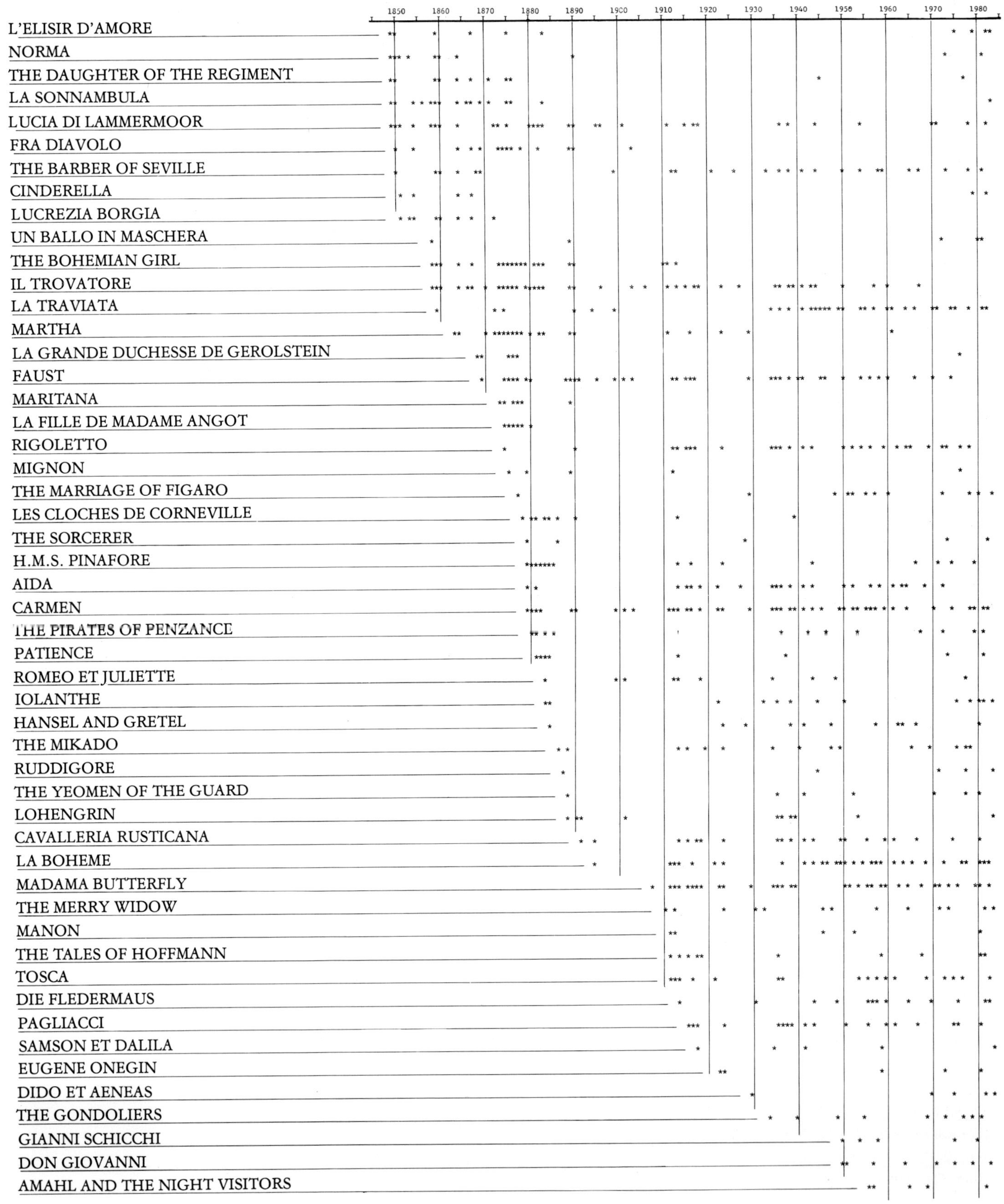
1850
1860
1870
1880
1890
1900
1910
1920
1930
1940
1950
1960
1970
1980
L'ELISIR D'AMORE
NORMA
THE DAUGHTER OF THE REGIMENT
LA SONNAMBULA
LUCIA DI LAMMERMOOR
FRA DIAVOLO
THE BARBER OF SEVILLE
CINDERELLA
LUCREZIA BORGIA
UN BALLO IN MASCHERA
THE BOHEMIAN GIRL
IL TROVATORE
LA TRAVIATA
MARTHA
LA GRANDE DUCHESSE DE GEROLSTEIN
FAUST
MARITANA
LA FILLE DE MADAME ANGOT
RIGOLETTO
MIGNON
THE MARRIAGE OF FIGARO
LES CLOCHES DE CORNEVILLE
THE SORCERER
H.M.S. PINAFORE
AIDA
CARMEN
THE PIRATES OF PENZANCE
PATIENCE
ROMEO ET JULIETTE
IOLANTHE
HANSEL AND GRETEL
THE MIKADO
RUDDIGORE
THE YEOMEN OF THE GUARD
LOHENGRIN
CAVALLERIA RUSTICANA
LA BOHEME
MADAMA BUTTERFLY
THE MERRY WIDOW
MANON
THE TALES OF HOFFMANN
TOSCA
DIE FLEDERMAUS
PAGLIACCI
SAMSON ET DALILA
EUGENE ONEGIN
DIDO ET AENEAS
THE GONDOLIERS
GIANNI SCHICCHI
DON GIOVANNI
AMAHL AND THE NIGHT VISITORS

*based on a minimum of five full or part performances

Chart: Trevor Baillie

FIGURE 4 COMPOSERS OF WORKS PRESENTED IN TORONTO 1825-1984*

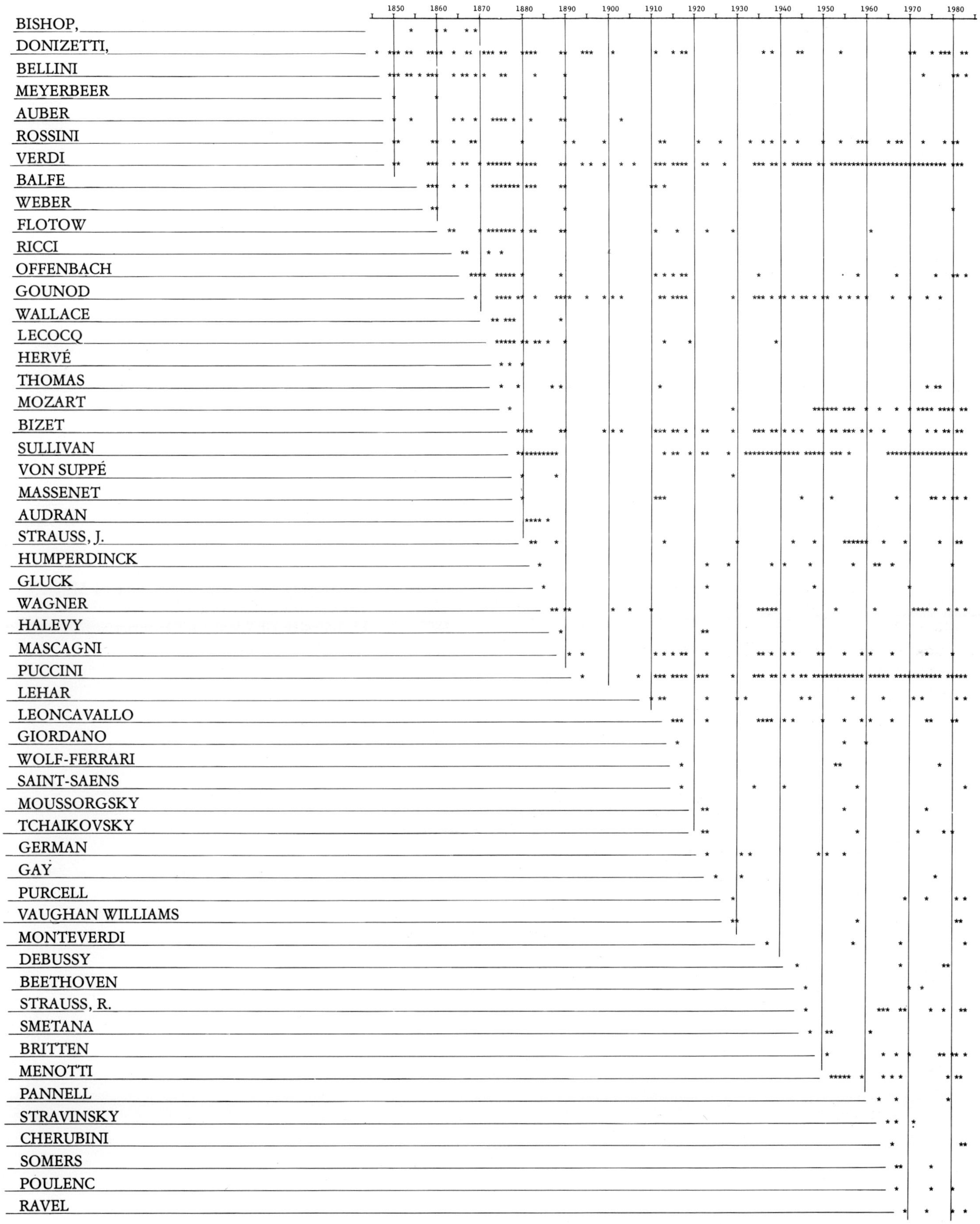

*based on a minimum of three full or part performances

Chart: Trevor Baillie

CREDIT/SOURCE ABBREVIATIONS

AECL	Archives, Eaton's of Canada Limited		MTLB	Metropolitan Toronto Library Board
AGOA	Art Gallery of Ontario Archives		NGC	National Gallery of Canada
ALCA	Arts and Letters Club Archives		NGI	National Gallery of Ireland
AO	Archives of Ontario		NLC	National Library of Canada
BC	Bill Cousintine, Winter Garden Theatre		NOGC	Northway-Gestalt Corporation
CCOC	Canadian Children's Opera Chorus		NPGL	National Portrait Gallery, London
CCT	Corporation of the City of Toronto		NYPL	New York Public Library
CNEA	Canadian National Exhibition Archives		O	Opera
COC	Canadian Opera Company		OC	Opera (in) Canada
COCA	Canadian Opera Company Archives		OIC	Opera in Concert
CPD	City Property Department		OKC	O'Keefe Centre
CPI	Culver Pictures Inc.		ON	Opera News
CSC	CentreStage Company		PW	Pat Wardrop
CTA (-JC)	City of Toronto Archives (-James Collection)		RTH	Roy Thomson Hall
CW	Clarke Walker		RAT	Royal Alexandra Theatre
DBT	David Boyd-Thomas		RYH	Royal York Hotel
EJMF	Edward Johnson Music Foundation		RPIA	Ryerson Polytechnical Institute Archives
EMB	Edith M. Baillie		SAC	St. Anne's Church
FF	Freda Fusco		SL	Simpson's Limited
FH	Foster Hewitt		TFRB	Thomas Fisher Rare Book Library
GC	Gilmour Collection, COC Archives		TOR	Toronto Opera Repertoire
GM	Guelph Mercury		TOS	Toronto Opera Society
GOS	*Great Opera Stars in Historic Photographs*, by James Camner 1978 Dover Publications, New York		TOTS	*Turn Out the Stars Before Leaving*, by John Lindsay Boston Mills Press, Toronto 1984
ILN	Illustrated London News		TS	Toronto Symphony
JPB	Joan Parkhill Baillie		TTER	The Terrace
JRG	Jessie Reade Greenaway		TTSU	The Toronto Sun
LG	Louise Goldring		UTA	University of Toronto Archives
MOA	Metropolitan Opera Archives		UTFM	University of Toronto, Faculty of Music
MCNY	Museum of the City of New York		UTL	University of Toronto Library
MF	Mike Filey		UWO	University of Western Ontario
MM	*The Mapleson Memoirs*, Edited by Harold Rosenthal 1966 Putnam, London		YCO	York Community Opera
MTCV	Metro Toronto Convention and Visitors Association			

Items from publications –
    from The Toronto Globe, The Mail, The Mail and Empire and The Globe and Mail by permission of The Globe and Mail
    from The Toronto Star and The Toronto Star Weekly by permission of The Toronto Star Syndicate
    from The Evening Telegram and The Toronto Sun by permission of The Toronto Sun
    from Opera in Canada and Opera Canada by permission of Opera Canada
    from Saturday Night by permission of Saturday Night.

INDEX

Abbott, Emma, 76
Aborn Comic Opera Company, 161
Aborn English GrandOpera Company, 171
Academy of Music, 151
Adelaide Street Skating Rink, 104 105
Adele, 171
Agricultural Fair, 57
Aimee, 73
Aird, Sir John, 167
Albanese, Licia, 212
Albani, Emma, 61, 78
Albano, Michael, 189
Albert Herring, 255
Alda, Frances, 143, 149
Alexandroff, Naomi, 255
Alfred Street, 37
Alice Nielsen Opera Company, 83
Alice Oates and Her Superior English Opera Company, 83
Alice Oates nd Oates' English Comic Opera Company, 89
Allan, G. W., 65
Allan, William, 60
Allomand, Pauline, 80, 126
Althouse, Paul, 145
Amateur Juvenile Company (Toronto), 62
Amateur Operatic Society of Toronto, 62
Ambrose, Small, 40
Ameling, Elly, 287
American Opera Company, 167, 171
Amore dei tre re, 271
Anderson, James, 190
Anderson, Marian, 208
Angelique, 208
Arab, John, 31
Arditi, Luigi, 41, 61, 62, 78
Artists' Association Italian Opera Company, 44
Artists' Association Italian Opera, 41
Attila, 57
Austin, Susan, 281
Austral, Florence, 203, 204
Babes In Toyland, 156
Baccaloni Opera Company, 212
Baerg, Theodore, 232, 247, 279
Bagarozy, Armand, 145
Bagnani, Stewart, 231
Bai, Poul, 206, 209, 226, 227
Baillie, Robert L.T., 8, 31
Baines, C., 65
Baines, Thomas, 8
Baines, W.J., 73
Baldwin, Janet, 227
Balthrop, Carmen, 247
Barbini, Ernesto, 9, 241
Barcza, Peter, 31, 272
Barili, Ettore, 54
Barnett, W.E., 54
Bartered Bride, 212, 241
Bartolini, Lando, 287
Bassett, Laurie, 282
Bate, Derek, 247
Bauermeister, Matthilde, 80, 81, 138
Bayreuth, 141
Beatrice et Benedict, 270
Beckwith, John, 273
Beggar's Opera, 155, 156, 271
Bengough, J.W., 117
Benson, Eugene, 245
Bergonzi, Carlo, 222
Bernardi, Mario, 241
Bertocci, 171
Bijou Theatre, 95
Billie Taylor, 104
Bishop, Anna, 24, 37, 43, 50, 54, 57, 60, 62, 68, 69
Bishop, Sir Henry Rowley, 17, 19, 21, 25, 27
Bjoerling, Jussi, 210
Black Swan, 42, 44, 47, 54, 69

Blackwell, C.S., 167
Blaser, Lynn, 273, 286
Blauvelt, Lillian, 135, 149, 177, 178
Blossom Time, 171
Bluebeard'sCastle, 149
Bluma Appel Theatre, 269
Boccaccio, 185, 187
Bochsa, Mr., 50
Bogle, Stephanie, 31
Bohemian Light Opera Company, 212
Bolger, Catherine, 266
Bori, Lucrezia, 205
Boris Godunov, 245
Borre, Cesar, 145, 226, 227
Bosley, Murray, 145
Boston Grand Opera Company, 171, 178
Boston Ideal Opera Company, 83, 130, 131
Boston Ideals, 79, 80
Boston National Grand Opera Company, 171
Boston Opera Company, 79, 83
Bostonians, The, 79
Botanical Garden, 60
Boutet, Pierre, 149
Bradshaw, Lloyd, 250
Brady, Matthew, 60
Braham, John, 24
Braham, John, 27
Braun, Richard, 255
Braun, Victor, 241, 243, 246, 286
Brentano, Felix, 168
Bride Ship, 212
Brienti, Eliza, 41
Brignoli Italian Opera Company, 44, 62
Brignoli Opera & Concert Society, 62
Brignoli's Opera Company, 69
Brignoli, Pasquale, 43, 52, 54, 60, 61, 69, 75
Brooks, Garnet, 255
Bruce, Dr. H.A., 167
Brunner, Richard, 257
Bubbles, 114
Bumbry, Grace, 287
Bunthorne Abroad, 117
Burke, Edmund, 149
Burton, C.L., 167
Butt, Clara, 149
Button, Henry, 253
Cadet Girl, 83
Callas, Maria, 148, 149
Calve, Emma, 80, 81, 136, 139
Cameron, Christopher, 148, 149, 232, 282, 286
Campbell, Rod, 190
Campora, Giuseppe, 243
Canada Council, 9
Canada Packers Operatic Society, 210, 212
Canadian Children's Opera Chorus, 273, 278, 282, 286, 287
Canadian Grand Opera Association, 120, 121, 145, 149, 220, 222
Canadian League of Composer, 212
Canadian Mastersingers, 209
Canadian Music Association, 212
Canadian National Exhibition, 57
Canadian Opera Association, 12
Canadian Opera Company Ensemble, 230, 232, 247, 273, 279, 281, 282
Canadian Opera Company Seasons, 247
Canadian Opera Company, 9, 164, 170, 171, 240, 286, 287, 289
Canadian Opera Piccola, 273
Canadian Ukrainian Opera Association, 247, 258
Cantlon, Lynne, 245
Capoul, Victor, 88
Capriccio, 286, 287
Captain Careless, 156
Carleton Comic Opera Company, 83
Carlson, Benjamin, 282

Carmen, 153
Carre Lyceum Company, 65, 92
Carson, Clarice, 246
Carte, Richard D'Oyly, 79, 88
Carter, John, 54, 57, 65
Caruso, Ernico, 142, 149
Cary, Annie Louise, 69, 75
Cassilly, Richard, 241
Castaneda, Lorna, 278
Castle Frank High School, 263, 266
Cedarbrae Collegiate Institute, 263, 266, 289
Cehanovsky, George, 181, 221
Central Tech Opera Workshop, 261, 262
Central Technical School, 289
Chaliapin, Feodor, 143, 144, 149
Challener, Frederick, 164
Charlesworth, Hector, 155
Child Of The Regiment, 44
Children's Crusade (Pierne), 210
Chip And His Dog, 278
Chocolate Soldier, 156, 171
Choral Group, 212
Chu Chin Chow, 171
Clarke, J.P., 65, 68
Cockshutt, Hon. H.C., 231
Colborne, Sir John, 11
Collier & Rice's Comic Opera Company, 62
Columbia Grand Opera, 145
Columbia Opera Company, 149
Comley and Barton's Company, 83
Comus Music Theatre, 273
Conner, Nadine, 221
Conservatory Opera Company, 12, 164, 171, 185 187, 190, 193, 194
Consul, 170
Cooper English Opera Troupe, 42
Corelli, Franco, 239
Coronation of Poppea, 188, 207, 208, 247
Corwing Hen, 125
Cosi Fan Tutte, 170, 207
Cosmopolitan Opera Association, 258, 278
Coulter, John, 255
Count of Luxembourg, 156
Crader, Jeannine, 243
Crane, Drew and Davidge Operatic Combination, 69
Craven's Minstrels and Burlesque Opera Troupe, 54
Crofoot, Alan, 241
Crowe, Randolph, 146, 186, 187, 194, 199, 200, 220
Crucible, 257
Cruz-Romo, Guilda, 287
Crystal Palace, 30, 57
Curran's Ethiopian Opera Troupe, 54
Curry, Carrol Anne, 270
D'Oyly Carte Opera Company, 62, 79, 83, 166, 171
Dale-Haris, Robert B., 169
Damnation De Faust, 148, 149
Davies, Robertson, 220, 282
Davis, Andrew, 148, 149, 287
De Feo Grand Opera Company, 181
De Koven & Smith, 156
De Los Angeles, Victoria, 239
De Luca, Giuseppe, 143, 149
De Paolo, Alesso, 239
De Reszke, Edouard, 80, 81
De Treville, Yvonne, 175, 177
De Turczynowicz, Laura, 186, 194
De Wolf Hopper & His Gilbert & Sullivan Comic Opera Co., 83
Dean and Forrest's Company, 27
Del Monaco, Mario, 221
Del Puente, Giuseppe, 61, 62, 80
Desjardins, Marguerite, 242
Devil's Bridge, 18
Devries, Rosa, 37, 41, 52, 54

Di Giuseppe, Enrico, 243
Di Gorgoza, Emilio, 149
Di Stefano, Giuseppe, 148, 149
Dialogues of the Carmelites, 255
Dido and Aeneas, 186, 187
Dihel, Viorel, 282
Dodington, John, 271, 282
Don Caesar, 124, 125, 246
Don Pasquale, 141
Donalda, Pauline, 149
Dorenfeld, Joanne, 190
Dr. Cannon's Cure, 282
Draper, Mrs., 30
Draper, C.B., Chief Justice, 65
Dressler, Marie, 178
DuBois, Mark, 272
Dunn, Mignon, 222
E. A. McDowell's Company, 76, 83
Earl Haig Collegiate Institute, 263, 266
Earl haig Collegiate, 289
Earl of Harewood, 245
Eaton Operatic Society, 181, 182, 205, 212
Eaton's College Street Store, 201
Eaton's, 95
Eaton, Lady, 167
Eaton, R.Y., 167, 231
Edvina, Louise, 164, 166
Edward Johnson Building, 253
Edward VII, 60
Elektra, 244
Elias, Rosalind, 239
Elixir of Love, 41
Elliott, Elizabeth, 242
Elmsley Villa, 30
Emily Soldene & Her Most Complete English Comique Opera, 83
Emma Abbott Grand English Opera Company, 83
Emma Albani Opera Company, 83
Emma Juch English Opera Festival, 83
Emma Juch Festival, 130
Emma Juch Grand English Opera Company, 131
Empire Theatre, 37
English Comic Opera, 44
English Grand Opera Company, 154, 156
English Light Opera Company, 171
English Music Festival, 199
English Opera Company, 77
Equity Showcase Theatre, 282
Erede, Alberto, 207, 208
Erminie, 156
Ernani, 54
Evans, Glyn, 272
Evans, Michael, 189
Evason, Leo, 235
Ewing, Maria, 148
Exhibition Park, 101
Exhibition, 30
Fabris, Amanda, 126
Faculty of Music of the University of Toronto, 253
Fallis, Mary Lou, 271
Farrell, Shawna, 279, 281
Fauvette, 130
Fay Templeton And Her Star Opera Company, 62
Fay Templeton's Opera Company, 62
Ferrier, Kathleen, 210
Fidelio, 245
Fifth Avenue Opera Company, 62
Fille De Madama Angot, 73
Fisher, Constance, 242
Fisher, John C., 156
Flave le, Sir Joseph, 167, 231
Flying Dutchman, 124, 126
Fonteyn, Margot, 220
Fool, 212
Ford Comic Opera Company, 83

Forrester, Maureen, 287
Forst, Judith, 171
Fortune Gallo, 144
Fortune Teller, 83
Foy, J.J., 73
Fra Diavolo, 57, 77
France-Film Company, 147, 149
Franko, Nahan, 175, 177
Franks' Hotel, 7, 11, 289
Free Library By-Law, 68
Fremstad, Olive, 174, 175
French Opera Troupe of New Orleans, 37
French Operatic Concert Troupe, 44, 54
Frey, Paul, 271
Fulton, A.T., 72, 73
Fusco, Freda, 227
Gadski, Johanna, 174, 175, 176, 177
Galassi, Antonio, 78
Gallantry, 189
Galli-Curci, Amelita, 142, 149
Gallo English Opera Company, 171
Gallo, Fortune, 9, 147
Garden, Mary, 149
Garrard, Don, 149, 245
Garrison Reserve, 57
Gatti-Cassaza, Giulio, 143
Gedda, Nicolai, 149, 287
Geiger-Torel, Herman, 9, 12, 31, 169, 188, 211, 231, 240, 253, 255
Gentry, Theodore, 256
George Christy's Minstrels, 54
George Harvey Secondary School, 263, 266
Ghioni, 53, 54
Gianni Schicchi, 149, 188
Gilbert and Sullivan Festival Company, 171
Gilbert and Sullivan Opera Company, 156, 171
Gilbert and Sullivan Society of Toronto, 185, 189 190
Gilbert, W. S., 79, 87, 88, 104, 117, 250
Gilibert, Charles, 138
Gill, Nellye, 167, 200
Gilmour, Clyde, 208
Gilmour, Doris Godson, 145
Gilmour, Doris, 146, 168, 216
Gilmour, Harrison, 12
Girard, Jacques, 147
Glade, Coe, 144
Glaz, Herta, 207, 208, 209, 221
Globe, 50, 140
Gluck, Alma, 142, 149
Godfrey, John M, 169
Golden Vanity, 286
Goldschmidt, Nicholas, 168, 188, 231, 257, 271, 278
Goldschmidt, 9
Gooderham Jr., William, 73
Gooderham, A.E., 167
Gooderham, Gen., 73
Gooderham, William, 72, 73
Gordon-Shay Grand Opera Company, 153, 156
Gottschalk, L.G., 76
Gottschalk, L. M. and Troupe, 69
Goulet, Robert, 174
Government House, 28, 29, 30, 57, 276, 285
Gow, Col. Walter, 167
Grand English & Italian Opera Combination, 62
Grand English Opera Co., 83
Grand English Opera Combination, 62
Grand Italian Opera Company, 9
Grand Italian Troupe of Associate Artists, 44
Grand Opera House, 9, 40, 50, 76, 87, 152
Grand Opera Lane, 9, 83
Grant, June, 242
Grant, Sylvia, 242
Grau Opera Company, 62, 101

Grau, Maurice, 61, 80, 81, 101, 136, 289
Great Exhibition of 1851, 55, 57
Greenwood, Nancy, 31, 255
Grip, 117
Griselidis, 273
Guelph Spring Festival, 258, 273, 278
Guy, Elizabeth Benson, 54
Guy Mannering, 27
Gundy, G.H., 167
Gzowski, Lieut.-Col., Casimir, 73, 74
H.C. Cooper's English Opera Troupe, 44
H.L. Bateman's French Opera Bouffe, 69
H.M.S. Parliament, 76
H.R.H. The Duchess of Cornwall and York, 136
H.R.H. The Duke of Cornwall and York, 136
H.R.H. The Prince of Wales, 57
Hambleton, Ronald, 244
Hamilton Amateur Opera Company, 83
Hamilton Musical Union, 83
Hamlet, 256, 270
Hanlan, Edward, 120
Harmony Club, 83
Harrison, Robert, 72, 73
Hart House, 289
Harvey, Marion, 256
Hately, Robert, 145, 168
Hauk, Minnie, 77
Hauser, Miska, 54
Haverly Comic Opera Company, 62
Haverly's Church Choir Company, 83
Haverly's Juvenile Pinafore Company, 83
Haverly's Minstrels, 83, 89
Haverly's Opera Company, 83
Hayes, Catherine, 51, 54
Heal, Reginald, 145, 187
Healey, Derek, 257
Heather, Alfred, 155, 199, 200
Heinrichs, Gustav, 80
Heintzman and Company, 85
Heloise and Abelard, 245
Henrikson, Steven, 256
Henry W. Savage's Company, 156, 171
Henry W. Savage's English Grand Opera Company, 156
Heppner, Ben, 232, 281, 282, 286
Her Majesty's Opera Company, 83
Her Majesty's Theatre, 77, 78
Hermiston, Nancy, 257
Hewitt, Foster, 199
Hines, Jerome, 221
Holman Company, 87
Holman English Opera Company, 89
Holman English Opera Troupe, 62, 89, 108
Holman George, 104
Holman Opera Company, 87, 101, 114
Holman Opera Troupe, 69, 104, 105
Holman Parlor Operas, 54
Holman Troupe, 40
Holman's Juvenile Opera Troupe, 54
Holman's Opera Troupe, 44
Holman, Derek, 282
Holman, George, 9, 40, 43, 101, 114
Holman, Sallie, 43, 114
Homer, Louise, 136, 138, 139
Horne, Marilyn, 243, 247
Horticultural Gardens, 30
Hoshuliak, Osyp, 243
Howland, W.H., 95
Hugh The Drover, 199, 164, 167, 200
Hughes, Warren, 189
Hurst, Donna, 258
I.O.D.E., 204
Il Giuramento, 273
International Children's Festival, 282
International Festival, 289
Italian Grand Opera Group, 156
Italian Opera Company, Academy of Music

of New York, 37, 44, 53, 54
Italian Opera Company, 44, 69
J. C. Duff Comic Opera Company, 83
J. C. Duff English Opera Company, 83
Jacobs and Sparrow's Opera House, 124
James, Eleanor, 279
Jarvis, Lieut. Colonel, 65
Jarvis, S.P., 18
Jefferys, C.W., 33
Jenufa, 247
Jerusalem, 37
Joan of Arc, 246
Jobin, Raoul, 209
Johnson, Dr. Edward, 143, 149, 167, 169, 205, 253, 254
Jones, Allan, 167, 199, 200
Jones, Roger, 281, 286
Journet, Marcel, 136, 139
Juch, Emma, 62, 79, 126, 130, 131, 135, 137, 149
Julia Matthews English Opera Bouffe & Burlesque Troupe, 89
Juvenile Opera Company (Toronto), 83
Juvenile Pinafore Company, 98
Katya Kabanova, 257
Keane, John, 190, 246, 257
Kellogg English Opera Company, 83
Kellogg, Clara Louise, 75
Kelly, Bruce, 256
Kelly, Mona, 242
Kemp, Lady, 167
Kern, Patricia, 287
Kero, Mr., 88
Kerr Hall, 277
Kerr, Howard Hillen, 276
Ketchum, Jesse, 37
Kilburn, Weldon, 187
Kilby, Evaleen, 168
Kimball Opera Company, 127
King For Corsica, 190
Kirke La Shelle Company, 81
Kittask, Avo, 272, 278
Kolomyjec, Joanne, 273
Kombrink, Ilona, 242
Kowalchuk, June, 169
Kullmann, Charles, 206
Kunzli, Robert, 266
Kupalo, 258
Lakes of Killarney, 104
Lady Eaton, 167
Lady Kemp, 167
Lakme, 126
Lamont, Helen, 79
Lamontagne, Gilles, 169
Land of Smiles, 212
Landry, Rosemarie, 272
Lane, Gloria, 243
Languirand, Jacques, 244
Laufer, Murray, 241
Laurier, Sir Wilfred, 136
Lazzari, Carolina, 149
Le Pauvre Matelot, 207
Le Prophete, 37
Lear, Evelyn, 247
Leatch, James, 258
Leavitt's Grand English opera Burlesque Company, 89
Lehmann, Lilli, 174
Leoncavallo & Co., 149
Les Pecheurs de Perles, 272
Leskaya, Anna, 145, 220
Lilliputian Opera Company, 83, 87
Lind, Jenny, 50, 51, 54
Lismer, Arthur, 187, 200
Lodge-Wilcocks, Georgina, 8
Lodge-Wilcocks, John, 11
Lodge-Wilcocks, Maria, 11
Lohengrin, 124
London's Crystal Palace, 55

Loosberg, Irene, 242
Lord, William, 241
Lorini, 53, 54
Louis Riel, 244
Luck of Ginger Coffey, 244
Ludgin, Chester, 245
Lulu, 247
Lurline, 44
MacDonald, Jeanette, 147
Macina, Giuseppe, 12, 261, 262
MacKenzie, Ferguson, 266
MacMillan Theatre, 289
MacMillan, Andrew, 170, 231, 261
MacMillan, Dr. Ernest, 167, 185, 186, 193, 194, 199, 203, 204
MacMillan, Sir Ernest, 9, 12, 253, 254
Madame Sherry, 171
Mademoiselle Modiste, 165, 171
Maggiorotti, 53, 54
Maid of Cashmere, 21
Maid of the Mountains, 171
Maitland, Sir Peregrine, 11
Majestic Grand Opera Company, 149
Majestic Theatre, 193
Major, Leon, 241
Malinowska, Julia, 149
Mancinelli, Signor, 80
Mangus, Mark, 258
Manning Pool, 182
Manning, Alexander, 76, 80
Manon Lescaut, 245
Manon, 147, 272
Mansouri, Lotfi, 9, 12, 246, 286
Mantelli Opera Company, 83
Manvers, Mr., 41, 47
Maple Leaf Gardens Fifty Years of History, 220, 222
Maple Leaf Gardens, 9
Mapleson, Henry, 289
Mapleson, 'Colonel' J.H., 78
Maria Padilla, 54
Marquis of Lorne, 61
Marriage Contract, 189
Marshall, Lois, 149
Marston, Anthony, M., 169
Martha, 141
Martinelli, Giovanni, 143, 149
Masaniello, 57
Mascagni & Co., 149
Massey Hall, 9, 154
Massey, Denton, 167
Massey, Hon. Vincent, 185, 231
Massie, R. H. Lorimer, 169
Masterson, Mary Jo, 258
Matrimonial Market, 208
Matthiessen, Ed., 31
Maurice Grau's Great French Opera Company, 88, 89
Mauro, Ermanno, 244, 245
Max Strakosch and Troupe, 69
Maytime, 171
Mazzoleni, Dr. Ettore, 9, 12, 168, 169, 220, 253, 255
McCaull Opera Comique Company, 125, 127
McCollum, John, 170
McGibbon, Donald and Mrs., 240
McLean, J.S., 167
McLean, James, 272, 282
McManus, Don, 245

Meadows, Arlene, 243
Mechanics' Institute, 67, 68
Medea, 262
Meek, David, 31
Megli, Katharina, 232
Meier, Johanna, 246, 286
Melba Operatic Concert Company, 149
Melba, Dame Nellie, 37, 149
Melis, Carmen, 166

Melton, James, 206, 226
Mendelssohn Choir, 231, 285
Menotti, Gian-Carlo, 278
Mercer, Ruby, 240, 278
Merrill, Jeanne, 168
Merrill, Robert, 221
Merry Countess, 165, 171
Mess, Suzanne, 241
Lord Minto, 136
Metropolitan Music Theatre, 266
Metropolitan Opera Artists Ensemble, 209, 212
Metropolitan Opera Company, 9, 62, 69, 80, 81, 83, 143, 149, 221, 222, 239, 247, 289
Metropolitan Opera House, New York, 80
Metropolitan Opera National Company, 247
Meyers, Michael, 247
Michener, Roland, 54
Michie, Col. James, F., 72, 73, 167
Milanov, Zinka, 211, 221
Miller and His Men, 18
Mills, David, 265
Milne, Peter, 31
Milsom, Deborah, 271, 279
Mirvish, Ed, 164
Mittelman, Norman, 170
Model School, 28, 276
Mohalbi Grand Italian Opera, 83
Monk, Allan, 245, 246
Montreal Arts, 147
Montreal Musical Society, 156
Montreal Opera Company, 164, 165, 171
Montreal, 87
Moore, Mavor, 244
Morrison, Mrs. Charlotte, 40, 72, 73
Morson, Beatrice, 167, 200
Moscona, Nicola, 147
Mountaineers, 17, 18
Mowat, Sir Oliver, 136
Mrs. Henry Drayton's Opera Company, 89
Mrs. W.J Obernier's Company, 83
Mulock, Cawthra, 164
Munsel, Patrice, 221
Music at St. George's, 287
Music Hall, 42
Nadon, Suzette, 170
National ballet, 54
National Centennial Act, 54
National Council of Education, 253
National opera Association, 227
National Opera Company, 126, 127, 131, 226, 227, 265, 266
Naughty, Marietta, 171
Neel, Boyd, 9, 253
Neill, William, 246
Neuendorff, Adolph, 130
Nevada, Emma, 61
New American Opera Company, 83
New Bijou Theatre, 95
New French Opera Bouffe Company, 73
New French Opera Bouffe, 83
New Play Society, 211
New Royal Lyceum, 40
New York Grand Opera Company, 167, 171
New York Hippodrome, 171
Nicolini, Ernest, 44
Nieboer, John, 266, 286
Nielsen, Alice, 141, 149, 175
Night Birds, 165, 171
Night Blooming Ceruis, 190
Nilsson, Birgit, 239
Nilsson, Christine, 69, 78
Niska, Maralin, 149
No Song, No Supper, 17, 18
Norcross Comic Opera Company of Boston, 62
Nordheimer, A & M, 34
Nordheimer, Mr., 37, 41, 50, 87, 98, 101
Nordheimer, S., 73

Nordheimers' Music Store, 95, 125
Nordica, Lillian, 141
Normal School, 277
Northern Secondary School, 263, 266
Notman and Fraser, 69, 84
Notre Dame, 271
Novotna, Jarmila, 209
Noye's Fludde, 287
O'Keefe Centre, 289
Oddie, Donald, 31
Odeon Carlton Theatre, 9
Oedipus Rex, 287
Old City Hall, 30
Old St. Andrews Market, 97
Olivette, 104, 117
Oliviero, Lodovico, 147
Ontario Arts Council, 8
Ontario Association of Architects, 54
Ontario Place, 30, 31
Oostwood, Rolph, 256
Oostwoud, Roelof, 286
Opera Backstage, 211
Opera Canada, 7
Opera Division, Faculty of Music, U. of T., 12
Opera Festival Association of Toronto, 12, 164
Opera Guild of Toronto, 12, 145, 146, 149, 164, 171, 215, 217, 227
Opera In Concert, 273
Opera School, Royal Conservatory of Music, 188, 189, 210, 230, 231, 232, 253
Opthof, Cornelis, 171, 258, 286
Oracolo, 144, 256
Orfeo, 186, 190
Orpheus and Euridice, 185
Orpheus in Hades, 43
Orpheus, 210
Osgoode Hall, 115
Othello, 37, 170, 171
Pannell, Raymond, 244
Parepa-Rosa, Euphrosyne, 69
Park, Dorothy Allan, 187
Parkhurst, E.R., 155, 182
Parodi's Opera (Italian) Company, 44
Parodi, Teresa, 34, 50, 54
Parsifal, 152, 153, 154
Patterson's New York Opera Company, 83
Patti, Adelina, 9, 44, 51, 52, 53, 54, 60, 61, 62, 78, 139, 140, 141, 149
Patti, Amalia, 34, 50, 51, 53, 54
Patti, Carlotta, 37, 54, 69
Patti-Strakosch, Amalia, 34, 54, 68
Paunova, Mariana, 149
Pavarotti, Luciano, 148, 149
Pavlova, Anna, 178
Pavlowa Ballet Russe, 178
Peasant Cantata, 185, 186
Peasant Girl, 171
Pechner, Gerhard, 239
Pedrotti, Mark, 279, 286
Peerce, Jan, 209
Pellatt & Pellatt, 108
Pelleas and Melisande, 256
Pelletier, Wilfrid, 147
Pengelly, Jeanne, 120, 145
Pennarini, Alois, 154
People's Theatre, 114
Perichole, 73, 258
Pert, Jill, 256
Peter Grimes, 246
Philadelphia Opera Company, 209
Piccoli, The, 205
Piccolomini, Marietta, 52, 54
Pierce's Ethiopian Opera Troupe, 54
Pierson, Bertha, 126
Pilon, Danielle, 256
Pinza, Ezio, 147
Pitou, Ambrose Augustus, 72

Place Des Arts, 147
Plishka, Paul, 246, 287
Polish Community Hall, 235
Pons, Lily, 148, 149, 206
Ponselle, Rosa, 143, 149
Poole, Clifford, 250
Por, Geza, 240
Postillion of Longjumeau, 41, 44
Power, Lawrence, 168
Pratt, Dr. David, 169
Prima Donna, 189
Prince of Pilsen, 153
Prince of Wales, 40, 60
Prince of Wales Theatre, 40, 44
Princess Chic, 81
Princess Louise, 61
Princess Theatre, 76, 130
Princesse de Trebizonde, 73
Prologue to the Performing Arts, 289
Prom Concerts, 215
Promenade Symphony Concerts, 216
Provincial Exhibition Buildings, 55
Public Library, 68
Pyne-Harrison English Opera Company, 54
Quaker Girl, 156
Queen of Sheba, 124, 126
Queen's Hotel, 87, 198
Queen's Own Rifles, 30
Queen's Park, 30
Quilico, Gino, 246
Quilico, Louis, 243, 246, 250, 270
Rake's Progress, 256
Ravelli, Luigi, 78, 80
Rawley, Ernest M., 169
Rayner, Sydney, 145
Rayson, Benjamin, 242
Red Feather, 156
Reginald Stewart Symphony Orchestra, 220
Relyea, Gary, 265, 273
Rentz-Santley Novelty and Burlesque Company, 83
Rentz-Stantley Novelty Company, 89
Report of the Commission on Canadian Studies 1975, 7
Requiem, 287
Resnik, Regina, 170
Rice and Dixey, 83
Rice's Opera Comique Company, 83
Rideout, Patricia, 241
Riders to the Sea, 189
Ritchey, John, 40
Roberto Devreux, 54
Robinson, J. Beverly, 65, 73, 78
Robinson, Mrs., 78
Rombouts, Herman, 31
Rosalinda, 164, 168, 169
Rose of Castile, 95
Rosedale Pleasure Grounds, 30
Roslak, Roxolana, 258, 271, 279, 281, 282, 287
Ross, Lieutenant-Governor and Mrs., 204
Rosselino Opera Company, 210, 211, 212
Rosselino, James, 261
Rossin House, 85, 87, 115
Rotary Club of Toronto, 220, 221, 222
Rotenberg, David, 31
Rowland, W.H., 73
Roy Thomson Hall, 30, 135
Royal Alexandra, 9
Royal Ballet, 220
Royal Conservatory of Music of Toronto, 210, 231
Royal Conservatory of Music, 12, 185, 188, 189, 230, 253
Royal Conservatory Opera Company, 9, 164, 169
Royal Conservatory Opera School, 12, 212
Royal Conservatory Opera, 190, 258
Royal Lyceum, 9

Rubes, Jan, 170, 241
Rudel, Julius, 286
Rudolph Aron-On Comic Opera Company, 79 83
Russell's Hotel, 45, 47
Russell, Henry, Dir. San Carlo Opera Co., 141, 149
Russian Grand Opera Company, 171
Rutherford, Donald, 256
Ryan, Lee, 258
Ryerson Hall, 275, 277
Ryerson, Egerton, 275, 276
Ryley, Thos. W., 156
Sadler's Wells, 220
Sadowa, Raisa, 266
Saint Anne's Music and Drama Society, 250
Sakos, Kenneth, 144, 168
Salzburg Marionettes, 212
Salzburg Opera Guild, 207
San Carlo Company, 8, 9
San Carlo Grand Opera Company, 141, 168
San Carlo Opera Company, 144, 149, 171
Sanders, Jean, 240
Sanderson, Sybil, 138
Sanford's New Orleans World-Renowned Opera Troupe, 44
Sanford's Opera Troupe, 44
Saunders, Shari, 232
Savage, Henry W, 152, 153, 154
Saville English Opera Company, 83
Savoyards, 156, 164, 171
Sayao, Bidu, 9, 147, 149, 208
Scadding, Rev. Henry, 17, 108
Scarborough Choral Society, 266
Schaefer, Lawrence, 255
Schalchi, Sofia, 78
Schatz, Roy, 250
Scheff, Fritzi, 136, 139, 165
Schipa, Tito, 149
Schoeffler, Paul, 242
Schumann-Heink, Ernestine, 149
Schwarzkope, Elisabeth, 212
Scott, Sr., Thomas H., 82
Scotti Grand Opera Company, 144, 149
Scotti, Antonio, 144
Seabird Island, 257
Seguins Operatic Troupe, 37
Seidl, Anton, 62 & Co., 83
Selfish Giant, The, 270
Sembrich Opera Company, 149
Sembrich, Marcella, 80, 81, 138, 174, 175,177
Semiramide, 37, 54
Serva Padrona, 230, 231
Shea's Theatre, 95
Shehhan English Opera Company, 155, 156
Sheehan English Opera Company, 156
Sheehan, Joseph F., 155
Sheppard, O.B., 61, 62, 72, 76, 79
Shivaree, 272, 273
Showgirl, 83
Shust, Michael, 279, 286
Shuttleworth, Edythe, 206
Siepi, Cesare, 149
Silja, Anja, 245
Silva-Marin, Giullermo, 270, 279
Silver Slipper, 153
Silver Swan, 156
Simon Boccanegra, 246
Singher, Martial, 147, 209
Sir Edmund Walker Memorial Court, 231
Sir Oliver Mowat, 136
Sleeping King, 153
Slezak, Leo, 142
Small, Ambrose, 72, 81, 193
Smith, Sheila, M., 286
Snell, Patricia, 170
Soderstrom, Elisabeth, 149, 222, 247
Soldene Opera Comique Company, 83
Soldier's Tale, 287

Somers, Harry, 244
Sontag, Henrietta, 52, 54
Spalding, Albert, 175
Spring Maid, 156
Springer, Donald M., 169
St. Anne's Church, 289
St. Michael's Choir School, 148
St. Quinten Opera Company, 117, 120, 121
St. Quinten, 101, 117
Stark, Phil, 171, 241, 243
Steber, Eleanor, 208
Stetson Opera Company, 83
Stevens, Rise, 208, 221
Stewart, George, 156
Stewart, Reginald, 156, 215, 216, 220
Stewart, Thomas, 246
Stilwell, Barry, 273, 279, 286, 287
Stilwell, Richard, 149
Strakosch and Hess Grand Opera Company, 83
Strakosch English Opera Company, 83
Strakosch Grand Italian Opera Company, 76, 83
Strakosch Grand Italian Opera, 76
Strakosch, Max, 74, 75, 289
Strakosch, 75, 77
Strand, 159
Stran, Michele, 278
Stratas, Teresa, 170
Stubbs, Janet, 271, 279, 281
Studio Theatre, 282
Sutherland, Joan, 247
Svanholm, Set, 211
Swarthout, Gladys, 206
Tagliapietra's Grand Italian Opera Company, 89
Tannhauser, 131, 145
Te Kanawa, Kiri, 287
Tear, Robert, 148
Teatro Dei Piccoli, 212
Temperance Hall, 276
Tent, The, 281
Terrell, Katherine, 257, 273
Teyte, Maggie, 166, 210
Thais, 165
Theatre Royal, 108
Thebor, Blanche, 221
The Yard, Harry, 244
Thomson, Heather, 245
Tibbett, Lawrence, 143, 149
Tokatyan, Armand, 147
Tom Jones, 210
Tomlin, Caralyn, 247, 272, 279
Toronto Athletic Club, 259
Toronto Children's Operatic Society, 209, 212
Toronto Church Choir Opera Company, 83
Toronto Conservatory of Music, 188, 253
Toronto Conservatory Orchestra, 135
Toronto Curling & Skating Rink, 105
Toronto Grand Opera Association, 206, 212
Toronto Historical Board, 203
Toronto Lyric Theatre, 258
Toronto Mendelssohn Choir, 135, 148, 149, 286
Toronto Music Festival, 149
Toronto Musical Festival, 98, 174, 175, 176, 177, 178
Toronto Opera Company, 89, 226, 227
Toronto Opera House, 152
Toronto Opera Repertoire, 261, 262
Toronto Opera Society, 235, 265, 266
Toronto Philharmonic Choir, 212
Toronto Philharmonic Society, 74, 108
Toronto Symphony Orchestra, 149, 227
Toronto Symphony, 135, 285, 286, 287
Toronto Zoological and Acclimatization Society, 101
Toronto's Harmony Club, 83
Torrington, Dr. F. H., 108, 135, 174
Tovell, Dr. Harold, 167, 253
Town Hall, 269
Tozi, Giorgio, 239
Trepanier, Paul, 256
Tristan Und Isolde, 246
Troyanos, Tatiana, 247
Tucker, Richard, 221, 239
Turgeon, Bernard, 244
Two Is Company, 171
Tynes, Margaret, 243
Une Mesure De Silence, 212
University of Toronto Royal Conservatory of Music, 255
University of Toronto, Faculty of Music, 258
University of Toronto, 189
Urban, Braheen, A., 145
Uyeda, Leslie, 232
Vagabond King, 171
Valerga, M'lle, 78
Van Dam, Jose, 148
Van Valkenburg, Richard S., 169
Varnay, Astrid, 244
Vernon, Lyn, 246
Vickers, Jon, 170, 287
Vinay, Ramon, 221
Vinci, Dr. Ernesto, 261
Voaden, Herman, 216
Volkoff, Boris, 227
Wagner, Charles L., 147, 149, 211, 212
Walker, Sir Edmund, 230
Walker, Ted, 256
Walkure, 242
Wallace, Zelda Seguin, 77
Walter Jones Comic Opera Company, 153, 156
Walter, Arnold M., 169, 253
Warren, Leonard, 211, 221
Welhasch, Irena, 232, 281
Welles, Justice, 169
Wells, Patricia, 247
Wenkoff, Spas, 246
Wilber, Mabel, 165
Wilbur Opera Company, 83
Willan, Healey, 255
William Hamilton's Opera Company, 95
William Tell, 76
Wilson, Charles, 245, 270
Woods, Jr., J.D., 169
Wozzeck, 246
YMCA, 95
York Community Opera, 265, 266
Yorkminstrels, 266
Zarou, Jeannette, 255
Zarzuela, 266
Zimbalist, Efrem, 142
Zion Congregational Church, 113
Zoological Gardens, 101